A series under the General Editorship of
Ia C. McIlwaine,
M.W. Hill and
Nancy J. Williamson

Other titles available include:

Information Sources for the Press and Broadcast Media
  edited by Sarah Adair
Information Sources in Architecture and Construction (Second edition)
  edited by Valerie J. Nurcombe
Information Sources in Art, Art History and Design
  edited by Simon Ford
Information Sources in Cartography
  edited by C.R. Perkins and R.B. Barry
Information Sources in Chemistry (Fourth edition)
  edited by R.T. Bottle and J.F.B. Rowland
Information Sources in Development Studies
  edited by Sheila Allcock
Information Sources in Engineering
  edited by Ken Mildren and Peter Hicks
Information Sources in Environmental Protection
  edited by Selwyn Eagle and Judith Deschamps
Information Sources in Finance and Banking
  by Ray Lester
Information Sources in Grey Literature (Third edition)
  by C.P. Auger
Information Sources in Information Technology
  edited by David Haynes
Information Sources in Law (Second edition)
  edited by Jules Winterton and Elizabeth M. Moys
Information Sources in Metallic Materials
  edited by M.N. Patten
Information Sources in Official Publications
  edited by Valerie J. Nurcombe
Information Sources in Patents
  edited by C.P. Auger
Information Sources in Physics (Third edition)
  edited by Dennis F. Shaw
Information Sources in Polymers and Plastics
  edited by R.T. Adkins
Information Sources in Sport and Leisure
  edited by Michele Shoebridge
Information Sources in the Earth Sciences (Second edition)
  edited by David N. Wood, Joan E. Hardy and Anthony P. Harvey
Information Sources in the Life Sciences (Fourth edition)
  edited by H.V. Wyatt
Information Sources in the Social Sciences
  edited by David Fisher, Sandra P. Price and Terry Hanstock
Information Sources in Women's Studies and Feminism
  edited by Hope A. Olson

Information Sources in
Music

Editor
Lewis Foreman

K · G · Saur   München 2003

Bibliographic Information published by Die Deutsche Bibliothek
Die Deutsche Bibliothek lists this publication in the Deutsche Nationalbibliografie;
detailed bibiography data is available in the internet at http://dnb.ddb.de

ISBN 3-598-24441-X

⊚
Printed on acid-free paper

© 2003 K. G. Saur Verlag GmbH, München

Cover design by Pollett and Cole

Typesetting by Florence Production Ltd., Stoodleigh, Devon

Printed and Bound in Great Britain by Antony Rowe Ltd., Chippenham, Wiltshire

ISBN 3-598-24441-X

Contents

Series Editor's Foreword

In the first years of the 21st century, there is a popular belief that the internet gives us easy worldwide access to all the information anyone can reasonably need. Experience, especially by those researching topics in depth, proves otherwise. It is ironic that, despite all the technical advances in information handling that have been made and the masses of information that assail us on every side, it remains as difficult as ever to ensure that one has what one wants when one needs it.

Of course the computer and the internet have made a huge difference to our information gathering habits, especially in the hands of those who, through experience have gained skill in their use, an ability to contain the amount of information within manageable limits and discrimination in assessing the reliability and adequacy of the resources accessed. No one nowadays would be without the internet but it is only one among several sources each of which has its values according to the searcher's needs. In all cases, the speed and effectiveness of a search can be greatly enhanced by the advice of those who are experts in the techniques and in the subject involved.

The aim of each volume of this K.G. Saur series of *Guides to Information Sources* is simple. It is to reduce the time, which needs to be spent on patient searching; to recommend the best starting point and sources most likely to yield the desired information. To do this we bring you the knowledge and experience of specialist practitioners in the field. Each author regularly uses the information sources and services described and any tricks of the trade that the author has learnt are passed on.

Like all subject and sector guides, the sources discussed have had to be selected. The criteria for selection will be given by the individual editors and will differ from subject to subject. However, the overall objective is constant: that of providing a way into a subject to those new to the field and to identify major new or possibly unexplored sources to those who already have some acquaintance with it.

Nowadays two major problems face those who are embarking upon research or who are in charge of wide-ranging collections of information. One is the increasingly specialised knowledge of the user and concomitant ignorance of other potentially useful disciplines. The second is the trend towards cross-disciplinary studies. This has led to a great mixing of academic programmes – and a number of imprecisely defined fields of study. The Editors are only too aware of the difficulties such hybrid subject fields raise for those requiring information and Guides for these sectors are being established as well as those for the traditional hard disciplines. In addition to commissioning new titles, constant attention is given to the production of updated editions for subject fields which are fast moving and subject to rapid development.

The internet now gives access to many new sources (and to some, but not all, of the old ones) and being discipline-free can be particularly attractive to those working in new fields. At the same time it gives access to an overwhelming mass of information, some of it well organized and easy to interrogate, much incoherent and ill-organized. On top of this there is the great output of new information from the media, advertising, meetings and conferences, regulatory bodies, letters, reports, office memoranda, magazines, junk mail, electronic mail, fax, bulletin boards and so on and so on. Inevitably it all tends to make one very reluctant to add to the load by seeking out books and journals. Yet they, and the other traditional types of printed material, remain for many purposes the most reliable sources of information. Quality encyclopaedias are excellent for an overview of a topic but there are also many other time saving reviews and digests of information. One still needs to look things up in databooks, to consult the full text of patent specifications, standards and reports, both official and commercial, and to study maps and atlases. Increasingly these are available on CD-ROM as well as in print and choice depends on one's circumstances. Some archives are becoming available electronically but the vast majority are still in paper form. Many institutions are making some at least of their expertise available on websites but contact with individuals there is often still necessary for in depth studies. It is also worth remembering that consulting a reference book frequently produces a more rapid result than consulting an online source.

Fortunately, in these times when the amount being published is increasingly rapidly, it is rarely necessary to consult everything that has been published on the topic of one's interest. Usually much proves to be irrelevant or repetitive. Some publications prove to be sadly lacking in important detail and present broad generalisations flimsily bridged with arches of waffle. Many publications contain errors. In such cases the need to check against other publications, first making sure that they are not simply derivative, adds greatly to the time of a search. In an academic field there is normally a "pecking order" of journals, the better ones generally having a "peer review" system, which self-published articles on the web do not (though there are moves to introduce a peer review process to some web-published journals). Research workers soon learn – it is part of their training – which sources in their field of study to use and rely on, which journals, co-workers and directories are trustworthy and to what extent. However, when searching outside their own field of expertise and for other people, lay researchers and information workers alike, serious problems have to be overcome. This makes the need for evaluative guides, such as those in this series, even more essential. The series attempts to achieve evaluation in two ways: first through a careful selection of sources, so that only those which are considered worthy are included, and second through the comments which are provided on those sources.

Guides to the literature and other sources of information have along and distinguished history. Some of them retain their value for many years as all or part of their content is still relevant but not repeated in later works. Where appropriate these are included in the sources referred to in this series along with the wealth of new sources, which make new Guides and new editions essential.

Preface

No book on this scale can be produced without the editor calling on a wide variety of expertise and assistance, and this, more than many, has needed much expert input in many fields. Many kind friends have helped and I would like to thank them here.

First a really big 'thank you' to my ever-patient contributors, who have responded to my many requests with good humour and resolution. The chapter on American government publications by Elizabeth Baur is reprinted from *Government Publications Review* (Vol 20, 1993) by kind permission of Pergamon Press. Beth Baur had started expanding this article to include more recent material but tragically she died from a brain tumour before she could finish it. I have therefore decided to reprint her very useful original article here, as its integrity is in no way constrained by it not being expanded. All involved truly regret the reason for not updating it here. I hope readers find it as useful as I have.

For the illustrations I have to thank: the Open Learning Unit at the University of Wales, Aberystwyth, for the diagram of types of music reference sources; the Mechanical Copyright Protection Society for their flowchart; Hyperion Records for a page from Bantock's symphonic poem *Thalaba the Destroyer*; the BBC and the BBC Written Archives Centre for a page from a BBC Archives file; and Elisabeth Agate for three illustrations from her own collection. The seven remaining illustrations are from the editor's personal collection.

Many libraries assisted with a multitude of reference queries and I am grateful to librarians at the British Library; Birmingham Central Library; Westminster Central Reference Library; Westminster Music Library; the London Library; the Royal College of Music Library; the Henry Watson Music Library, Manchester; Boston Public Library, Boston, Mass.; and the Arts Council of England Library. I am particularly indebted to Robert Tucker at the Barbican Music Library; Helen Glass and John Sweeney at the FCO Library; Felicitas Montgomery at the DCMS Library; Caroline

Underwood at Warner-Chappell and Alan Pawsey at HMSO. I must add my own to John Wagstaff's thanks to Peter Ward-Jones of the Bodleian Library for sharing his expertise on music publishing.

At the beginning the late John May and the late John Bishop were both very helpful, and I would like to remember them and their contributions here. John Wagstaff read the final draft and made innumerable helpful suggestions and I owe him much for his vast practical knowledge, his time and his patience. Richard Walshe copy edited a disparate first draft with sympathy and good humour. At an earlier stage Catherine Lain sympathetically managed the early editing and up-dating of the script. Chris Banks and the British Library were very helpful not only in providing information, but also in contributing the listing of the British Library's Novello Archive following Chapter 24, and for making available their working list of publishers' change of ownership referred to in compiling Appendix I, and giving permission for its use here.

Once in production, K. G. Saur's editors Geraldine Turpie in England and Andreas Brandmair in Munich were assiduous in getting the book into proof and the proofs processed. My wife Susan dealt with the formidable task of keyboarding the index into the Macrex software indexing programme in her customary style.

This book has been long in preparation, and in that time the internet as a generally available information source has become all-embracing. However, this is primarily a guide to printed and documentary sources. The internet has not yet totally effaced such sources, nor in my experience is it likely to, at least in the short term, but it becomes more and more valuable, and in addition to Melanie Groundsell's chapter on the internet every contributor refers to websites as appropriate. It therefore seemed a good idea to conclude this preface by mentioning my personal short list of practical web sources that I use every day.

As far as search engines are concerned I find that Google (Google.com) and especially its advanced searching option has an edge over the competition for musical sources and is an invaluable tool. One needs to keep an eye open for web search engines and internet scouts[1] that might be more specific for music enquiries, but for the moment Google seems to be very effective. Anyone not familiar with the internet, or first using such sources to seek material, say, on a composer, performer or specific work, will be amazed at the number of hits a search will generate.

Possibly my most-used source is Abebooks.com, for me the premier website for searching antiquarian booksellers worldwide, valuable not only for locating copies of books for purchase, but for pursuing bibliographical research, for making subject searches and for checking prices. Other similar sites are listed in Appendix 2 and are also helpful, but this has become my first port of call, and it has enabled me to find many of my most cherished wants. For bibliographical research, while the British Library catalogues (books and music: Blpc.bl.uk; manuscripts: molecat.bl.uk; recordings:

cadenza.bl.uk) are a huge resource, Copac (Copac.ac.uk) allows simultaneous searching of the 22 largest academic research libraries in the UK and Ireland and *includes* the British Library. It is therefore an invaluable short cut for printed material. Otherwise one is constantly seeking a way of being introduced to general or highly specific music research sources. There are many such doorways, but I would recommend the website of *Gramophone* magazine (gramophone.co.uk); the 'music internet resources' feature on the website for IAML(UK) which also gives convenient access to the *Encore!* database listing performance sets available from UK public and instuitutional libraries (<www.music.ox.ac.uk/IAML/>); and Royal Holloway College's 'Golden pages' (<www.sun.rhbnc.ac.uk/music/links/index.html>).

Perhaps as an occasional contributor I should also mention the MusicWeb – which covers an enormous number of CD reviews every month at a length and with a timeliness that no print journal can emulate (home page <www.musicweb.uk.net/index2.htm>). It claims to be the biggest CD review site on the internet, publishing between 250 and 300 classical CD reviews a month. The site also reviews concerts from around the World in a 'Seen and Heard' section and has specialist sections on British Light Music, a dictionary of composers, an encyclopaedia of popular music, and jazz and film music sections. The site hosts the majority of British composer Societies and the British Music Society.

Finally searches on the Public Record Office catalogue, PROCAT (PRO.gov.uk) and the National Register of Archives (NRO) websites are two quick ways of establishing initial archive sources for almost any query where British manuscript materials may be required.

This book is deliberately wide-ranging in its coverage. Chapters such as Nigel Simeone's on antiquarian dealers and auction houses, Sophie Fuller's on women in music, Diana Dixon's on newspapers and non-musical journals; Helen Faulkner's on that distinctive UK phenomenon Composer Trusts; Jacquie Kavanagh on the BBC's Written Archives and Elisabeth Agate on pictures and picture research are all areas that I am constantly asked about. By discussing them here I hope we have made a start towards guiding potential users to a wider appreciation of the sources appropriate for their particular musical interests and research.

LEWIS FOREMAN
Rickmansworth
August 2002

1   For web search engines and internet scouts see Barbara P. Semonche's chapter 'Good news, bad news: credibility of information and data gathered from the internet . . .' in Information Sources for the Press and Broadcast Media, 2nd edition edited by Sarah Adair (consultant editor Selwyn Eagle). London etc: Bowker Saur, 1999 pp. 115–126. Two useful specialised web indexes which can be accessed via the IAML(UK) website are MusicSearch (<www. MusicSearch.com>) and ClassicalSearch (<www.Classicalsearch.com>).

Figures and Illustrations

About the Contributors

Elisabeth Agate has worked as a picture researcher and editor since 1973, enjoying a long association with *The New Grove Dictionary of Music and Musicians* (1980 and 2/2001) and the many related reference works, including the *Man and Music* series. She has worked on a wide variety of projects, and since 1995 has been principal picture researcher on the sixty-book series the *Oxford History of Art*, also acting as picture consultant for the Glyndebourne Opera programmes. Elisabeth lives in Oxfordshire where she assists her husband, Brian Etheridge, in running a regular series of choral and chamber concerts, and the Burford Gallery, where she also designs jewellery.

Chris Banks studied music at Goldsmiths College, London. She worked for Travis and Emery and the English National Opera before joining the British Library in 1987. She is currently Curator of Manuscript Music and Deputy Head of Music Collections. She is or has been involved in several collaborative music documentation projects including *Cecilia*, *Encore!*, RILM and RISM. An elected member of the IAML(UK) Executive Committee, she is General Secretary of the New Berlioz Edition Trust, a member of the RILM Commission Mixte, a Trustee of the RISM(UK) Trust and a member of the Council of Central Music Library Ltd.

Elizabeth Baur was Government Documents Librarian at Memphis State University Libraries at Memphis, Tennessee, and Chair of the Government Documents Organisation of Tennessee, when she wrote her article. She previously worked at the William Ransom Hogan Jazz Archive at Tulane University and the library of Shenandoah Conservatory of Music. Sadly she died of a brain tumour in 1999.

Jeremy Dibble is Reader in Music at Durham University. Author of *Sir C Hubert H Parry – His Life and Music* (1992) he has written widely on

British and Irish music of the late nineteenth and early twentieth centuries including articles, essays and contributions for *New Grove*, the *New Dictionary of National Biography*, the *Revised Oxford Companion to Music, Musik* in Geschichte und Gegenwart and *Thoemmes Dictionary of Nineteenth-Century British Philosophers*. He has just completed a companion volume on Stanford for Oxford University Press and an edition of Parry's Violin Sonata for *Musica Britannica*.

Diana Dixon lectured at the College of Librarianship Wales and Loughborough University before taking early retirement. She has particular interests in the bibliography of the nineteenth century periodical press and in English provincial newspapers. She has been involved with two NEWS-PLAN projects and is currently working for a PhD at University College London on access to English provincial newspapers past and present.

Helen Faulkner started her career as a university music librarian and then became Manager of the BBC Music Library. She is currently Chief Executive of the Musicians Benevolent Fund which is the corporate Trustee of some 20 other Trusts. She is particularly involved with the Delius Trust and with the RVW Trust, of which she is the Secretary, and is a Trustee of the British Music Information Centre.

Lewis Foreman was a working librarian for 37 years ending with 11 years as Chief Librarian of the Foreign & Commonwealth Office, London. The author of many books, articles and broadcast talks on music, since taking early retirement he has worked as a freelance repertoire adviser and CD booklet annotator for some half dozen record companies, and writes musical obituaries for *The Independent* newspaper. Since 1998 he has been an Honorary Senior Research Fellow in the University of Birmingham, and is Chairman of the Council of Central Music Library Ltd.

Sophie Fuller is a lecturer in music at the University of Reading. Her publications include *The Pandora Guide to Women Composers – Britain and the United States* (Pandora, 1994), and (co-edited with Lloyd Whitesell) *Queer Episodes – Music and Modern Identity* (University of Illinois Press, 2002). Her research interests include many different aspects of music, gender and sexuality but focus in particular on the rôle that gender played in the musical life of late nineteenth and early twentieth century Britain, as well as the lives and work of Victorian and Edwardian women composers.

Matthew Greenall was born in London in 1960. After reading Music at Balliol College, Oxford, he studied at the Royal Academy of Music, winning a number of prestigious awards, before embarking on a career as a performing musician. In 1996 he founded the Elysian Singers of London, with whom he has made many festival appearances, radio and TV broadcasts and numerous commercial recordings. Since 1996 he had been the Director of the British Music Information Centre in London.

Melanie Groundsell is an information scientist, and an experienced adult educator, with a background in both academic and public libraries. She is currently working with Surrey Libraries as a Learning Centre Manager. A graduate of Colchester Institute School of Music she has maintained links with the fields of both musical performance and musicology. Her previous publications include abstracting for *RILM*, contributing to *New Grove II* and writing articles for several journals.

Jacqueline Kavanagh has been in charge of the BBC Written Archives Centre since 1974. After taking a degree in English, she qualified as an archivist at University College, London, and worked in local government archives at Worcester before joining the BBC. She has been involved in the development of the archives as a major resource both for the BBC and for academic research. She has been an Associate Editor for the *New Dictionary of National Biography* as well as the author of various chapters and articles on the BBC's archives.

Ian Ledsham is a professional musician and a qualified librarian. He was Librarian of the Barber Institute of Fine Arts and Music at the University of Birmingham, before deciding to pursue a freelance career. He now works as a choir trainer, organist and accompanist; runs The Music Information Consultancy, providing freelance research; and is a partner in Allegro Training, which provides information skills and management training. He is an Honorary Research Fellow in the Department of Music at The University of Birmingham, and also University Organist there.

Stephen Lloyd was for 17 years Editor of *The Delius Society Journal*, and his first book was a biography of Delius's great friend, H Balfour Gardiner (CUP, 1984). His other books have included a history of Dan Godfrey and the Bournemouth Municipal Orchestra (Thames, 1995), a comprehensive collection of Eric Fenby's writings on Delius (Thames, 1996), and more recently *William Walton: Muse of Fire* (Boydell & Brewer, 2001) in anticipation of the centenary of Walton's birth. He has also contributed to books on Elgar and Grainger as well as chapters on Delius, Walton and Bliss in Ashgate's 'Music and Literature' series.

Eve O'Kelly is Director of the Contemporary Music Centre in Dublin, Ireland's national archive and development centre for contemporary music. She is a specialist in the study and practice of the recorder as a modern instrument and has taught, lectured and written on this subject in the UK and USA. She is the author of *The Recorder Today* (Cambridge University Press 1990) and a former editor of *The Recorder Magazine*.

Jürgen Schaarwächter's special interest in bibliography started in the early 1990s, when he was awarded the MA at the University of Cologne, followed in 1995 by his Doctoral Thesis *Die britische Sinfonie 1914-1945*. He has worked as editor, bibliographer and author in a variety of projects, and, having contributed to *The New Grove Dictionary of Music and Musicians* (2/2001), is now a contributor to the second edition of *Die Musik in Geschichte und Gegenwart*. Since 1999 musicological assistant of the Max-Reger-Institut Karlsruhe, he is responsible for their libraries and extensive collection of musical manuscripts and illustrative material. Jürgen is a regular lecturer at Karlsruhe University and also edits the journals of the Robert Simpson Society and the Internationale Max Reger Gesellschaft.

Nigel Simeone is Senior Lecturer in Music at the University of Wales, Bangor. Before he became a teacher and academic he ran an antiquarian music business for ten years. His research is primarily on French music, Janácek, and the history of music publishing. Books include *Paris: a Musical Gazetteer* (Yale UP, 2000), *Janácek's Works* (with John Tyrrell and Alena Nemcova, OUP, 1997). He is currently working with Peter Hill on a new book, *Olivier Messiaen in Words and Pictures* for which the authors have been given access to Messiaen's diaries, correspondence and several hundred photographs from the Messiaens' collection.

Roderick Swanston is a Reader in Historical and Interdisciplinary Studies at the Royal College of Music. He is also a part-time lecturer at Imperial College of Science, Technology and Medicine, and a tutor for the Faculty for Continuing Education of Birkbeck College, and in 1995 and 1999 a Visiting Professor in Music at Dartmouth College, New Hampshire, USA. He is a writer, a frequent broadcaster and has lectured extensively in Europe, Asia and the United States.

John Wagstaff was born in Kidderminster, Worcestershire. After graduating in music from the universities of Reading and London, he was appointed Assistant Librarian in charge of music at King's College, London, in 1985. Since 1988 he has been Librarian of the Faculty of Music at Oxford University. He was editor of IAML(UK)'s journal, *Brio*, from 1990 to 1994, and also edited the second edition of the *British Union Catalogue of Music Periodicals* (1998). Since 2001 he has been editor of IAML's international journal, *Fontes artis musicae*.

David Whittle was awarded his doctorate by the University of Nottingham for work on the life of the composer Bruce Montgomery (1921-1978) who, as Edmund Crispin, is also known as a writer of detective fiction. His biography of Montgomery is due to appear in 2004. Amongst other publications, he has contributed to the *New Dictionary of National Biography* and *The Oxford Companion to Crime and Mystery Literature*. He is currently Director of Music at Leicester Grammar School.

Susi Woodhouse is a Senior Network Adviser within the People's Network Development Team, a part of the Libraries and Information Society Team at Resource. She leads on the New Opportunities Fund ICT training of public library staff and NOF-digitise programmes, and on the evaluation programme for the People's Network. Previously at EARL: the consortium for public library networking, where she was Development Manager, she had begun her career at the British Library, later becoming Music Librarian at the London Borough of Ealing. In 1992 she became Project Officer for IAML(UK)'s Music Library & Information Plan subsequently joining the Library Clientside Team at Westminster City Council developing their Quality Assurance programme. She is currently President of IAML(UK) and Project Director for the Cecilia project.

Simon Wright read music at University College, Cardiff, after which he undertook research on the life and music of the Brazilian composer Heitor Villa-Lobos for a book published in 1992. He began his career in music publishing with United Music Publishers, and in 1984 became Hire Library manager for Oxford University Press. He now administers Music Hire and copyright for Oxford University Press. He is Chairman of the Music Publishers Association Hire Librarians' Committee. Simon Wright has written, broadcast and lectured extensively, particularly on French and Latin American music of the twentieth century.

Introduction: music and its literature

Lewis Foreman

The literature of music may at first well be seen as somewhat forbidding to those not conversant with it, and even those experienced in one area may find another difficult. However, the great benefit of the bibliography of music is the extent to which it has been documented, and it quickly reveals its secrets to those who are interested.

The newcomer or infrequent user of musical literature is well advised to browse the shelves of their local library. Take down every book in your area of interest and flip through them. Quickly one finds cornerstones of familiar oft-used sources, and then builds onto them one's personal list of favourite sources, bibliographic knowledge growing and developing all the time. It cannot be too strongly emphasised that one can only learn the bibliography of a subject – any subject – by *using* the sources, and the more one uses them the more one will understand their strengths, idiosyncrasies and weaknesses. No matter what one's interest, every subject has its half-shelf of key sources, chosen according to individual needs. One also learns tricks and short-cuts, of which for me the first and still the most useful is Storm Bull's *Index to Biographies of Contemporary Composers* (1964–1987), which allows one to check for a less familiar name through a huge number of reference books without endless fruitless thumbing of many volumes. One needs to remember that in musical reference books there will be a common – internationally held – view of the core significant names, documented in all composer dictionaries or encyclopaedias, and a much larger sliding scale of leading figures whose fame may be more local.

▶ GENERAL REMARKS

Music itself is, of course, an international language, recognised throughout the world. Once it has been learned, materials from a wide range of sources are accessible to all musicians. Only in the literature about music does one encounter a language barrier. The present guide to information sources is largely addressed at an English-speaking audience. The size of that audience at the beginning of a new century is enormous, driven particularly by the dissemination of CD recordings of an ever-wider and still rapidly growing repertoire. Many non-academic as well as academic authors are involved in writing about and researching into music, and while we hope the scope of the present volume will make it of value to professional musicologists, teachers and performers, as well as many students at many levels, its intention is to pass on practical experience to the widest constituency.

However, those interested in music and the history of music do not necessarily have to read music nor to speak German or Italian or French fluently in order to find it an enormously rewarding area for research, with a massive literature in English. Undoubtedly, after a little time music's specialised vocabulary becomes more familiar to all working in it. The editor's personal experience is that even the foreign language sources can prove useful to one not conversant with the languages. The editor has thus proposed a chapter on dealing with foreign-language material, which it is hoped will prove useful and fill a very real gap for many less linguistically expert readers. Possibly those fluent linguists, particularly in German, may find this offensive, even laughable in its intention, but I am particularly grateful to Jürgen Schaarwächter for addressing himself (in CHAPTER 14) to this poisoned chalice, and making so useful a tool of a brief that many would have regarded as impossible.

Previous guides to the literature of music have concentrated on the documentary sources, the books and articles, and have much less dealt with the how and why, nor have they encompassed those more general areas which researchers with musical interests find so invaluable. So the scope of this handbook has arisen from the editor's personal experience of writing about music for over 30 years, and is conceived with the widest scope to take account of the fact that some of the most useful sources are the more general ones, such as newspapers and pictures. In all of these it is intended to provide the reader with first-hand advice arising from the practical experience of practitioners of many years' standing.

We need to appreciate that there is a clear difference between the literatures about music itself, about recordings of music, and about composers and the world of music. All of these are supported by a remarkable array of reference books, journals, organisations, indexing services, and increasingly the internet. Also, of course, there is a wide spread of libraries and institutions, though these tend to be concentrated in the great centres, and so for many users have to be accessed remotely.

▶ INTRODUCTIONS TO MUSIC

For those only just beginning to explore music, or wishing to develop their knowledge of the repertoire, perhaps moving onto modern music, or specialist genres, there have been various guides. First, general introductions to the rudiments of music. There have been many of these over the years, and you will find a selection in any library, though they can perhaps seem a little old fashioned in their language. Undoubtedly one of the most approachable self-help guides is the excellent course serialised in the *BBC Music Magazine* during 1998 and 1999, and supported by two compact discs to provide the essential aural element often lacking (details from the website: <http://www.bbcworldwide.com/musicmagazine>).

In building one's knowledge of repertoire there are several possible approaches. Generally, sympathetically written books of programme notes, or guides to the repertoire, can be very useful, one of the most approachable being the published texts of Antony Hopkins's celebrated BBC Radio talks (1977, 1979, 1982, 1983). Similarly, guides to record collecting are, in fact, a rewarding way for the beginner to make this kind of personal exploration; various titles are cited in CHAPTER 21. One of the best writers in this vein, though long out of print, and discographically outdated, was Martyn Goff, whose paperback guides (1957, 1974) can still be found cheaply second-hand. Very persuasively written, too, is Colin Wilson's *The Brandy of the Damned*, a personal exploration of music, taking his title from George Bernard Shaw's description of music (Wilson, 1964).[1]

▶ GUIDES TO REFERENCE BOOKS

The 'standard' guide to musical reference books is *Music Reference and Research Materials* (Duckles and Reed, 1997), often referred to as 'Duckles' after its founder. An annotated bibliography of (in its fifth edition) nearly 4000 entries, it is necessarily selective and in that sense critical. Arranged by topic and with extensive indexes, it is a book that is well worth browsing and the key to an enormous knowledge of sources.

At the time of writing the most recent reader's guide is that edited by Murray Steib (Steib, 1999). This consists of a series of essays, arranged alphabetically by topic, describing and evaluating the monographic literature in English on – mainly – western art music, but including articles on pop music, with extensive indexes. A formidable team of music librarians and academics have done a pretty good job: this is an impressive first edition. Generally sound in scope and judgement, reservations relate to its perceived American bias, particularly in the composer entries (e.g. it includes Norman Dello Joio and Amy Beach but not Gustav Holst, Percy Grainger or Michael Tippett), and to occasional lacunae in specific articles. A more general drawback is the sheer unwieldy bulk of a heavy large-format volume, which militates against its prime function as a handy narrative guide. Yet it is eminently readable and not purely a reference book. The range of entries is impressive, but the editor admits in his introduction that there is no Telemann entry because 'there is no monograph literature in English.' On the other hand, names such as Fanny Hensel (i.e. Fanny Mendelssohn) and Pauline Oliveros are given unexpectedly extensive coverage. The entries consist of a list of citations followed by a thumbnail sketch of each title. Among the best is that on Sibelius where the contributor is able to touch in much of Sibelius's background literature, without full citations – establishing a context not achieved by all the contributors.

Smaller and even more readable, if now beginning to be significantly out of date, are Bryant's *Music* (1965), whose easy narrative style reflects the authority of a leading music librarian of the 1960s, and *Musicalia* (Davies, 1969), a practical guide in which the then Music Librarian of the BBC distilled a lifetime's wide-ranging knowledge of sources, and still valuable for the breadth of its coverage.

▶ NON-MUSICAL SOURCES

Non-musical reference books will always be required by the writer on music, to help deal with all those contextual questions which constantly abound. What was the political situation when that work was performed? Who were the family circle of that composer's wife? Which date was the Thursday? Who was the addressee of this letter? Could he have travelled from Weimar to Warsaw by train at that time and how long would it have taken? When was St James' Hall demolished? Do we have a press cutting of that concert? When did war break out? Was the author of that text still alive? Did that house/road change its name in succeeding years? These are the sorts of question one constantly asks oneself and it is necessary to be familiar with a range of general reference books and library sources in order to answer them. Most of these can be seen at the local public/university library, but all writers will accumulate a personal quick reference shelf, these days coupled with favourite internet sites, to which reference is constantly made. For such general reference sources we need to note Keith Mixter's *General Bibliography* (1996). This is a unique guide to this requirement of music researchers, providing a guide to general *non-musical* reference books. Now in an enormously expanded and updated third edition after a quarter century gap from the second, its coverage includes 'Basic Guides to Research', 'Bibliography of Bibliographies', 'National and Trade Bibliographies', 'Dictionaries', 'Biography and Autobiography',

'Bibliographies', 'Indexes and Directories', 'Bibliographies and Indexes for Vocal Texts' (invaluable this), 'Union Lists' and 'Library Catalogues'.

▶ MUSIC RESEARCH

There have been various guides to music research, aimed at the under-graduate student, and Duckles discusses a range of them. Two examples are perhaps worth particular mention. First, John Druesedow's *Library Research Guide to Music* (1982), which guides the newcomer to using the music library and highlights some key sources. Secondly, although largely without annotations, Crabtree and Foster's *Sourcebook* (Crabtree and Foster, 1993) is also a practical guide for reading oneself into the litera-ture of music and the reference shelves of the music library, including a particularly useful feature 'Sources treating the History of Music'.[2]

▶ HISTORIOGRAPHY

The *New Grove* (1980) included an extended and thoughtful article on Historiography, and 'its study reveals the changing attitudes to music of the past as shown in writings about music' (Eggebrecht). This is further developed in Glenn Stanley's article in New Grove/2 (2001). Previous editions had contented themselves with an article on 'History' or 'Histories' with an extended bibliography of the main titles since 1600. This may most usefully be seen in the fifth edition ([Worsthorne, Simon Towneley]: 'Histories', *Grove's Dictionary of Music and Musicians* (5th edn.) 1954 vol. IV pp. 296–306). The first generally available book-length discussion of the changing perspectives of musical historians was by Warren D. Allen and appeared just before the Second World War. It is still a useful and stimulating read and has been widely disseminated as a Dover Books paper-back (Allen, 1962), while Sir Jack Westrup's *An Introduction to Musical History* (1973) provides a clear and concise statement of the problems of writing musical history in English. The implied interest in, and analysis of, aesthetics and criticism and its nineteenth-century roots is usefully discussed by Stephen Banfield in his article 'Aesthetics and Criticism' (1981).

A summary of the issues attendant on the development of the great dictionaries of music may be found in Ernest Livingstone's essay 'From Fétis to New Grove' (1989). Another useful personal discussion of the concerns and philosophies of music history by a distinguished musicologist is by Carl Dahlhaus (1983).

Particularly with today's enthusiasm for reception studies in mind, this soon touches on aesthetics, and for a wide-ranging consideration of all aspects see Roger Scruton's book of that title (1997).

► MUSICOLOGY

Musicology as we know it today originated particularly in Germany in the mid to late nineteenth century, and, as Denis Arnold has pointed out 'in the 1890s comes a regular stream of theses which continues to strengthen in the first decade of the present century. By 1914, the discipline is clearly well established . . . by the 1930s, some 70 to 80 theses were being presented each year in German universities' (Arnold, 1978). Musicology developed as a university discipline after the Second World War very much influenced by the big names of German scholarship who had left Germany largely for the USA before or after the war. At that stage the concerns of musicology were the composers and music up to the mid-nineteenth century. Ethnomusicology was an early additional facet to be considered respectable, but the study of twentieth-century British music and composers was certainly looked down on until the 1980s, and British Victorian music did not become a widely followed sub-discipline until the 1990s.[3]

The concerns of musicology are changing, however. Possibly the most accessible approach to the scope and definition of musicology today is Joseph Kerman's *Musicology*, widely disseminated in Fontana's paperback 'Masterguides' series (Kerman, 1985). Kerman describes the development of British and American musicology, summarising the agendas of the leading musicologists and their affiliations, and is forthright in his views, happily remarking on 'the unusually stodgy shelf of textbooks that guided their graduate study.'[4] In a review of a later study, Douglas Jarman noted that 'the publication of Joseph Kerman's *Musicology* in 1985 brought to public notice an issue that had been simmering in professional circles for some time, a disagreement about the nature and purpose of the discipline between musicologists who saw their concern as being the collecting and ordering of verifiable facts and those who felt that the subject should be more concerned with interpretation, criticism and evaluation' (Jarman, 1989).

Another widely disseminated guide which will often be found in general libraries is also a more severely practical one. This is by the conductor, violinist and pioneering recording musicologist Denis Stevens, who in his *Musicology – A Practical Guide* (1980) provides much practical advice on the 'how' of performing music of the eighteenth century and earlier. Kerman characterises Stevens's severely practical approach as a 'thoroughly blinkered view . . . one would never learn from Stevens that musicology is seriously implicated with the history of music, that history has merit in itself, or that history has anything to do with criticism.' Nevertheless, Stevens's is a practical manual that many may still find useful.

▶ NATIONAL HISTORIES

National or regional histories or reference books have been written about the music of most countries. Doing so in the case of a country where the musical tradition has only recently developed seems to be a recognised step in the acknowledgement of a country's musical maturity. This codifying and assessing a country's music is necessary before it can be fully explored or even performed. Thus the leading musical countries have long seen an extensive bibliography of histories and encyclopaedias about them. Of European countries, histories of music and composition in, say, Belgium (Bragard, 1946; Centre Belge de Documentation Musicale, 1964), Holland (Reeser, 1950), Norway (Grinde, 1991) and Spain (Livermore, 1972) help explore those countries' music in an age when the growth of repertoire of recorded music is exponential. Similarly for South America, and for the European tradition in the Far East.

When we consider countries such as Estonia or The Czech Republic we have the added problems of the Cold War period and socialist realism. There are doubtless those with the view that music produced under the communist system has passed its 'sell by' date. I do *not* subscribe to this view, preferring to assess individual works on their merits. However, what is true is that such music has ceased easily to be available either on disc or in printed score. In the antecedent countries of the Soviet empire a nationalist tradition continued to be in evidence despite political control, and Harry Olt on Estonian music (1980) or the Panton guide to the then Czechoslovakia (Gardavsky, 1965) can still provide useful information for those exploring the repertoire, but users need to be used aware of their background. Similar issues attend publications produced under fascist administrations in the 1930s.

In the case of South Africa, this construction of a national identity took the form of a four volume encyclopaedia (Malan, 1979–1986) largely devoted to the European tradition, though this will remain of considerable value for the number of British composers included who are not fully treated in British reference books. Similarly in the case of Canada (Kallmann, Helmut Gilles Potvin, Kenneth Winters, 1997), New Zealand (Thomson, 1991) and Australia (Bebbington, 1997). Certainly in these cases there is much work still to be done, and, for example, British music of the nineteenth century, which began to undergo a significant revaluation in the 1990s, despite several accounts,[5] still awaits an encyclopaedic first-hand treatment.

► WRITERS' GUIDES

Those who write infrequently are faced with the practical problems of 'how'; how to express their thoughts on paper. There are long-established and respected manuals which editors use every day. For an English writer probably the most useful is Judith Butcher's invaluable and practical handbook *Copy-editing* (1984). The American equivalents are *The Chicago Manual of Style* (1982) or *The New York Times Manual of Style & Usage* (Jordan, 1982). On the use of English, probably the most celebrated is Gowers' *Plain Words* (Gowers, 1973), and also of day-to-day practical interest is Partridge's *Usage & Abusage*, published in full and abridged editions (1954).

For students the standard guides to getting words on paper in essays and dissertations are the *MHRA Style Book* (latest edition 1996) and the *MLA Handbook* (1977). However, there are more specialised guides and in the field of music the journal *19th Century Music* has produced a guide (Holoman, 1988) which becomes the musical Bible of all who have discovered it. Its author, D Kern Holoman, disposes all his readers to read on with his opening sentence: 'Writing about music begins to be tricky, perhaps frustrating, the first time you try to reason out how to say Eroica Symphony in print . . .' This is an extended style sheet that was prepared from scratch in response to the practical problems that faced an inexperienced team running a new journal. As Holoman remarks in his introduction, they had two special audiences in mind, the university or college students trying to get their written assignments 'right', and performing musicians facing the need to produce programme notes for their performances. Although a slim volume, its scope is very wide, including terminology, names and titles, problems in narrative text, preparing the printed programme for a performance, electronic copy; there is even an appendix of problem words. One word of warning – this makes a splendid list of topics that need to be considered, but British writers may find they do not always feel comfortable with all the solutions offered, which reflect American practice. Indeed there is even a paragraph on 'Britishisms' advising students to 'enjoy *The New Grove*, which is a monument to English-speaking scholarship . . . but young writers should be especially careful not to absorb the Britishisms they will find there.' (This includes '-our' and '-ise' endings, and British terminology – not gramophone – not anglicised place names, etc.) Nevertheless this is a remarkable and readable guide, rooted in practical need, that many will find invaluable and enjoyable.

▶ **LIBRARIES**

In the United Kingdom the widespread network of public libraries has long supported music libraries and music librarians, and most large centres will have a collection of books and music. Barbara Penney's 'directory of resources' (1992) provides a basic guide to what is available where, soon to be updated on the internet by the Cecilia project (Linnitt and Andrews, 2001). From the 1950s onwards this was accompanied by a growing availability of recordings, at first of concert music (should we say 'serious' or 'classical'), later developing into the fields of jazz and popular music which later came to dominate many collections. Over the last 20 years sound (and video) collections have had a high priority in local authorities, not least because they have been a source of income (until the 1970s such collections were not charged for, but borrowed on the same basis as library books).

The outcome of all this in the UK has been a perceptible reduction in the availability of musical expertise through local authority libraries, accompanied by a regrettable disposal of some book stock. Nevertheless it should not be forgotten that interlending through libraries is especially valuable in the field of music, and particularly in the provision of sets of orchestral material for local and amateur orchestras. There remains an enthusiastic group of specialist music librarians who are focused in the UK by the International Association of Music Libraries, UK branch (IAML(UK)). This is a remarkably active and well organised group, with an excellent half yearly journal, *Brio*. Not the least of their achievements is the second edition of *BUCOMP*, the printed union catalogue of files of musical periodicals held in libraries in the UK and Ireland (Wagstaff, 1998).

▶ **CHRONOLOGIES AND DATING**

Another general tool that intending musicologists will find invaluable is an adequate chronology of music, together with a more general chronology of world events.

First one often finds that one has a day of the week but not an exact date (for example an otherwise undated cutting may say 'the symphony was first performed on Tuesday last' when the month and year are known. To calculate the day of the week or date from day of the week use the following formula:[6]

- Take the last 2 digits of the year and add a quarter of this number, discounting any remainder; add the date of the month; depending on the month add: Jan 1 (or in leap year 0); Feb 4 (3); March 4; April 0; May 2; June 5; July 0; August 3; September 6; October 1; November 4; December 6.

- Add for the eighteenth century 4; for the nineteenth 2; for the twentieth 0 and for the twenty-first century 6.
- Divide the resulting total by 7 and the remainder gives the day of the week from this key: 1 = Sunday; 2 = Monday; 3 = Tuesday; 4 = Wednesday; 5 = Thursday; 6 = Friday; 0 = Saturday.
- Before 17 September 1752 one needs to take account of the old style calendar.

For a simple chronology of world events any edition of *Pears Cyclopedia* (annual) or a similar annual compendium will be useful. For a comparative chronology of music and world events, at its simplest the chronologies that appear in every volume of the *Master Musicians* series[7] may well provide a useful source for everyday purposes. A more extended chronology appears in Harman and Mellers (Harman and Mellers, 1962). For an extended general chronology of music the appendix to *Grove V*[8] is as good as any, a shorter chronology appears in *The Hutchinson Encyclopedia of Music* (Cummings, 1995 15 pages unpaged). For composers and their works, *Greene's Biographical Encyclopedia* (Greene, 1985) is distinguished by the arrangement, which is by birthdate of the composers listed. For a chronology of twentieth-century music in exacting detail Nicolas Slonimsky's *Music Since 1900* (1971) is unrivalled, though Burbank's *Twentieth Century Music* (1984) is more up-to-date and provides a useful additional source if Slonimsky has not covered what one is looking for. Indeed, Slonimsky himself noted that it is 'immensely larger and more comprehensive in scope'.[9] A comparative chronology of the twentieth century comparing 'music and musicians' with 'politics, war and rulers'/ 'literature, philosophy, religion'/'science, technology, discovery'/'fine arts and architecture' is quite well done in the *Modern Times* volume of Macmillan's 'Music & Man' series (Morgan, 1993). For a more general calendar see Adele Manson's *Calendar of Music and Musicians* (1981). For pop music see Herb Hendler's *Year by Year in the Rock Era* (1983). For a chronology of the musical theatre, Gänzl's enormous two volume documentation is arranged in chronological order and *de facto* provides a chronology (1986).

▶ DICTIONARIES OF MUSICAL TERMS

The remaining tool that most inexperienced musicians will require is a multi-lingual dictionary summarising musical terms, tempo markings and the names of instruments in the main languages in which they will be encountered. The standard Italian musical terms will be quickly absorbed but German tempo markings can sometimes come as a shock when first encountered and those in other European languages even more so. Terms are defined in many standard musical dictionaries such as *The Oxford Dictionary of Music* (Kennedy, 1994) or the *Hutchinson Encyclopedia of Music* (Cummings, 1995) or its former incarnation as *Everyman's Dictionary of Music* (Blom, 1946).[10] Duckles lists more than 50 specialised dictionaries of musical terms. A useful parallel dictionary of terms in English/French/Italian/German was published by W.J. Smith (1961). Arranged by topics such as 'instruments of the orchestra', 'the conductor' or 'musical terms', it covers most requirements.

▶ MUSIC AND WORDS

Working in music, inevitably, sooner or later one will need a source for the words composers set. The texts or translations of songs for programmes; the source of words to know the context; details of writer for background; details of words to understand meaning and imagery. Basic requirements include a *King James Bible*, collected Shakespeare, and a substantial anthology of English literature.

For *The Bible*, James Laster's *Catalogue of Choral Music Arranged in Biblical Order* (1983) provides a valuable guide to the many passages set by composers.

There are many substantial anthologies of English literature. The most long-standing is *The Oxford Book of English* verse, often referred to as 'Q' after its compiler (Quiller-Couch, 1939). A more modern and elegantly produced anthology is *The Folio Golden Treasury* (Michie, 1997). But for its sheer massive size and scope, literally bulk buying of literature, and beloved of undergraduates hoping for an English degree from one book, *The Norton Anthology of English Literature* (Abrams, 2000) is unsurpassed, including prose as well as verse.

There have been many anthologies of sixteenth and seventeenth-century verse, which is still often set by composers. *England's Helicon* (MacDonald, 1949, 1962) is a handy source for Elizabethan and earlier poetry, while Doughtie's *Lyrics from English Airs 1596–1622* (1970), despite its short chronological compass, covers much familiar (and also unfamiliar) material. Boas's *Songs and Lyrics from the English Playbooks* (1955) is useful for the lyrics from plays often found as songs, and covers an enormous period from medieval to the nineteenth century.

Depending on one's specific area of interest, other anthologies or collected poems will be required. Walt Whitman's *Leaves of Grass*[11] would be well up my personal list of oft-used sources.

A more recent approach to words has seen anthologies compiled of all the words set by one specific composer, two excellent examples being Boris Ford on Benjamin Britten (Ford, 1996) and Margaret Cobb on Debussy, the latter translated into English (Cobb, 1982). To trace what settings exist of English poets one needs to consult the various reference books compiled by Bryan N.S. Gooch and David S. Thatcher (the series published by Garland Publishing, New York; the Shakespeare set by Oxford University Press):

- (1991) *A Shakespeare Music Catalogue* (5 vols).
- (1982) *Musical Settings of British Romantic Literature: a catalogue* (2 vols).
- (1979) *Musical Settings of Early and Mid-Victorian Literature: a catalogue.*
- (1976) *Musical Settings of Late -Victorian and modern British Literature: a catalogue.*

For the most popular poems by German writers set by composers see *The Fischer-Dieskau Book of Lieder* which provides the texts of over 750 poems (Fischer-Dieskau, 1976). Perhaps more practical but less elegantly presented, Lois Phillips's *Lieder Line by Line and Word for Word* (1996) provides both a literal and a poetic English text with the original, for well-known songs by Beethoven, Schubert, Schumann, Wagner, Brahms, Wolf, Mahler and Strauss. For Schubert, Richard Wigmore has provided the complete song texts both of German lieder and his Italian songs, in parallel texts with English translations, while John Reed's *The Schubert Song Companion* (1985) deals with each song, headed by an incipit and a brief account and history of each song, followed by the words in English or an English summary. For Schumann, Drinker's *Texts of the Vocal Works of Robert Schumann* is useful (1947).

For Italian repertoire, Schoep and Haim's word by word translations (1972), practically rather than elegantly produced, will be found useful. Emily Ezust's *The Lied and Song* website provides a vast archive of texts and translations of lieder and other art songs, which also lists composers who set each text. (<www.recmusik.org/lieder/>).

► REFERENCES

Abrams, M.H. (2000) (general ed.) *The Norton Anthology of English Literature* (2 vols) (7th edn.). New York: W W Norton & Co. [1962]

Allen, W.D. (1962) *Philosophies of Music History.* [New York: American Book Co., 1939] New York: Dover Books

Arnold, D. (1978) The profession of musical scholarship. In Olleson, E. (ed.) *Modern Musical Scholarship*, Stocksfield: Oriel Press p. 5.

Banfield, S. (1981) Aesthetics and Criticism. In: Temperley, N. (ed.) *The Athlone History of Music in Britain. Vol. 5: The Romantic Age 1800–1914*, pp. 455–73. London: The Athlone Press. Note that *The Athlone History* has since changed publishers and become the *Blackwells History*

Bebbington, W. (1997) *The Oxford Companion to Australian Music*. Melbourne: Oxford University Press

Blom, E. (1946) *Everyman's Dictionary of Music*. J.M. Dent/New York: E P Dutton

Boas, F.S. (1955) (ed.) *Songs and Lyrics from the English Playbooks*. London: The Cresset Press

Bragard, R. (1946) *Histoire de la musique belge*. Brussels: Office de Publicité

Bryant, E.T. (1965) *Music. (The Readers' Guide* series). London: Bingley

Bull, S. (1964–1987) *Index of Biographies of Contemporary Composers* (vol. 1: 1964; vol. 2: 1974; vol. 3: 1987). Metuchen, NJ: The Scarecrow Press

Burbank, R. (1984) *Twentieth Century Music*. New York: Facts on File Publications

Butcher, J. (1984) *Copy-editing* (2nd edn.). Cambridge: Cambridge University Press

Centre Belge de Documentation Musicale (1964) *Music in Belgium – contemporary Belgian composers*. Brussels: A Manteau Ltd.

The Chicago Manual of Style (13th edn.). (1982) Chicago: University of Chicago Press

Cobb, M.G. (1982) *The Poetic Debussy – a collection of his songs, texts and selected letters*. Boston: North Eastern University Press

Cook, C. (1984–85) (ed.) *Pears Cyclopedia* 93rd edition. London, Pelham (Current edition: London: Penguin)

Crabtree, P.D. and Donald, H.F. (1993) *Sourcebook for Research in Music*. Bloomington & Indianapolis: Indiana University Press

Cummings, D. (1995) (ed.) *The Hutchinson Encyclopedia of Music*. Oxford: Helicon Publishing

Dahlhaus, C. (1983) *Foundations of Music History*. Cambridge: Cambridge University Press

Davies, J.H. (1969) *Musicalia – sources of information in music* (2nd edn.). Oxford: Pergamon Press

Doughtie, E. (1970) *Lyrics from English Airs 1596–1622*. Cambridge, Mass.: Harvard University Press

Drinker, H. (1947) *Texts of the Vocal Works of Robert Schumann in English Translation*. New York: Association of American Colleges

Druesdow, J.E. (1982) *Library Research Guide to Music: illustrated search strategy and sources*. Ann Arbor: Pierian Press

Duckles, V.H. and Reed, I. (1997) *Music Reference and Research Materials – an annotated bibliography* (5th edn.). New York: Schirmer

Eggebrecht, H.H. (1980) 'Historiography' *New Grove vol. 8*, pp. 592–600

Fischer-Dieskau, D. (1976) *The Fischer-Dieskau Book of Lieder*, with English translations by George Bird and Richard Stokes. London: Gollancz

Ford, B. (1996) *Benjamin Britten's Poets – the poetry he set to music* (rev ed.). Manchester: Carcanet

Gänzl, K. (1986) *The British Musical Theatre* (vol. 1: 1865–1914; vol. 2: 1915–1984). London: Macmillan Press

Gardavsky, C. (1965) (ed.) *Contemporary Czechoslovak Composers*. Prague: Panton

Goff, M. (1957) *A Short Guide to Long Play – how to listen to music on and off the record*. London: Museum Press

Goff, M. (1974) *Record Choice, a guide to a basic collection*. London: Cassell

Gowers, Sir E. (1973) *The Complete Plain Words*, revised edition by Sir Bruce Fraser. London: HMSO

Greene, D.M. (1985) *Greene's Biographical Encyclopedia of Composers*. London: Collins

Grinde, N. (1991) *A History of Norwegian Music*. Lincoln, Nebraska; London: University of Nebraska Press

Harman, A. and Mellers, W. (1962) *Man and His Music – the story of musical experience in the west*. London: Barrie & Rockliff, pp. 1070–99 [This book first appeared in four volumes, but later appeared in one.]

Hendler, H. (1983) *Year by Year in the Rock Era*. Westport: Greenwood Press

Holoman, D.K. (1988) *Writing About Music: a style sheet from The Editors of 19th Century Music*. Berkeley: University of California Press

Hopkins, A. (1977) *Talking About Music: Symphonies, Concertos and Sonatas*. London: Dent

Hopkins, A. (1979) *Understanding Music*. London: Dent

Hopkins, A. (1982) *Sounds of Music*. London: Dent

Hopkins, A. (1983) *Pathway to Music*. London: Dent

IAML(UK) (1984) – *Annual Survey of Music Libraries*. London: IAML(UK)

Jarman, D. (1989) A Choice of Bias [review of Treitler, L. (1989) *Music and the Historical Imagination*. Cambridge, Mass.: Harvard University Press]. *TLS*, 29 September–5 October, 1068

Jordan, L. (1982) *The New York Times Manual of Style & Usage*. New York: Times Books

Kallmann, Helmut Gilles Potvin, Kenneth Winters (1997) (eds) *Encyclopedia of Music in Canada* (2nd edn.). Toronto, University of Toronto Press

Kennedy, M. (1994) *The Oxford Dictionary of Music* (2nd edn.). Oxford: Oxford University Press

Kerman, J. (1985) *Musicology*. London: Fontana Press/Collins

Laster, J. (1983) *Catalogue of Choral Music Arranged in Biblical Order*. Metuchen: Scarecrow Press

Linnitt, Peter and Paul Andrews (2001) 'The Metamorphosis of Mildred or Hail, Bright Cecilia' *Brio 38* no 2 Autumn/Winter pp. 10–14

Livermore, A. (1972) *A Short History of Spanish Music*. London: Duckworth

Livingstone, E. (1989) From Fétis to New Grove. In: Mann, A. (ed.) *Modern Music Librarianship: essays in honor of Ruth Wanatabe*. Stuyvesant New York: Pendragon Press, pp. 95–105

MacDonald, H. *Englands Helicon, edited from the edition of 1600 with additional poems from the edition of 1614*. London: Routledge and Kegan Paul (the Muses' Library), 1949, 1962

Malan, J.P. (1979–1986) (ed.) *South African Music Encyclopedia* (4 vols). Cape Town: Oxford University Press

Manson, A.P. (1981) *Calendar of Music and Musicians*. Metuchen: Scarecrow Press

MHRA Style Book: notes for authors, editors and writers of dissertations (1996). London: Modern Humanities Research Association

Michie, J. (1997) *The Folio Golden Treasury*. London: The Folio Society

Mixter, K.E. (1996) *General Bibliography for Music Research* (3rd edn.). Michigan: Harmonie Press

MLA Handbook for Writers of Research Papers, Theses and Dissertations. (1977) New York: Modern Language Association of America

Morgan, R.P. (1993) (ed.) *Modern Times from World War I to the present*. London: Macmillan Press Ltd. (Man & Music series vol. 8), pp. 412–35

Olt, H. (1980) *Estonian Music*. Tallinn: Perioodika

Partridge, E. (1954) *Usage & Abusage: a short guide to good English*. London: Hamish Hamilton

Penney, B. (1992) *Music in British Libraries: a directory of resources* (4th edn.). Library Association

Phillips, L. (1979) *Lieder Line by Line and Word for Word*. London: Duckworth; revised edn. Oxford: Clarendon Press, 1996

Quiller-Couch, Sir A., (1939) (ed.) *The Oxford Book of English Verse 1250–1918*. Oxford: Oxford University Press

Reed, J. (1985) *The Schubert Song Companion*. Manchester: Manchester University Press. [This book subsequently appeared in paperback from Faber (1993) and at the time of writing is available as a Mandolin paperback (1997) from Manchester University Press.]

Reeser, E. (1950) *Een eeuw Nederlandse muziek*. Amsterdam: Querido

Schoep, A. and Haim, D. (1972) *Word-by-Word Translations of Songs and Arias. Part II – Italian*. Metuchen: Scarecrow Press

Scruton, R. (1997) *The Aesthetics of Music*. Oxford: Clarendon Press

Slonimsky, N. (1971) *Music Since 1900* (4th edn.). New York: Charles Scribner's Sons (updated by *Supplement to Music Since 1900*. New York, Charles Scribner's Sons, 1986)

Smith, W.J. (1961) *A Dictionary of Musical Terms.in four languages.* London: Hutchinson

Stanley, G. (2001) 'Historiography' *New Grove* Vol II pp. 546–61.

Steib, M. (1999) (ed.) *Reader's Guide to Music – History, Theory, Criticism.* Chicago and London: Fitzroy Dearborn Publishers

Stevens, D. (1980) *Musicology – a practical guide.* London: Macdonald Futura (Yehudi Menhin Music Guides)

Thomson, J.M. (1991) *The Oxford History of New Zealand Music.* Auckland: Oxford University Press

Wagstaff, J. (1998) (ed.) *British Union Catalogue of Music Periodicals* (2nd edn.). Aldershot: Ashgate

Westrup, J.A. (1973) *An Introduction to Musical History* (2nd edn.). London: Hutchinson

Wilson, C. (1964) *Brandy of the Damned: discoveries of a musical eclectic.* London: John Baker

Zon, B. (1999) (ed.) *Music in Nineteenth-Century Britain; selected proceedings of the first conference.* Aldershot: Ashgate

▶ NOTES

1. Revised with a chapter on American music as *Chords and Discords* (1966) New York: Crown Publishers. The latter appeared in paperback in the UK as *Colin Wilson on Music* (1967) London: Pan Books.
2. Crabtree and Foster, 1993.
3. Papers from the first Conference of Music in Nineteenth-Century Britain were published as Music in *Nineteenth-Century Britain; selected proceedings of the first conference* (Zon, 1999).
4. Kerman (1985), p. 59.
5. The pioneering ground-breaking work is Temperley, N. (1981) *The Romantic Age 1800–1914*, vol. 5 of the Athlone History of Music in Britain, now the Blackwells History.
6. Thanks to Susan Bradbury for this formula.
7. Founded and for many years published by J M Dent, but now published by Oxford University Press.
8. Appendix I: Chronology of Composers and Contemporaneous Artists Grove V vol. ix pp. 435–569.
9. Slonimsky (1971), p. xxi.
10. There are several later editions. Probably the best edition is the third, of 1958.
11. There are many editions of Whitman. One needs to remember that *Leaves of Grass* is Whitman's collected poetry and was built up over a lifetime. Emory Holloway's edition for the Everyman Library is as useful as any [J.M. Dent, 1947, 1957].

2 Institutions, societies and broadcasting stations

Susi Woodhouse

▶ **INTRODUCTION**

This chapter deals with the many different kinds of specialist music societies and institutions there are in the United Kingdom and Republic of Ireland, and with broadcasting stations. The range and diversity of these societies is breathtaking, with every conceivable musical taste or special interest group catered for, from Black Music to Walton. Many of these are long-established and much-respected institutions such as the Royal Philharmonic Society or the Royal Musical Association, others are much younger in years but no less lacking in strength of purpose. The Contemporary Music Centre in Dublin is a case in point: established as recently as 1986, it has quickly built up a strong reputation in connection with the documentation and promotion of music in Ireland (see the section on Music Information Centres below). Over 300 of these specialist societies are listed in the *British Music Yearbook* (1973–), each of which almost deserves a chapter of its own. This is equally true in the broadcasting world. Here, the BBC, in true Shakespearean vein 'doth bestride the narrow world like a Colossus' (*Julius Caesar*), but there are also well over 100 thriving independent local radio stations, whose contribution to the diversity of musical life is considerable. This journey can be but an overview, a brief summary, pausing only occasionally along the way to examine random examples of the species in this family to give but a glimpse of the tip of the information iceberg that is available.

We are very fortunate to be so rich in specialised resources and expertise: at a time when economic and other pressures are mounting in the music library and information sector, such societies and institutions will become more and more important as sources of information and materials that are otherwise difficult to obtain. Indeed, one of the recommendations made in the *Library and Information Plan for Music: written statement* published in 1993 by the UK Branch of the International Association of

Music Libraries, Archives and Documentation Centres (Woodhouse, 1993) states 'The potential for co-operative links with music societies and institutions must be investigated, especially regarding documentation and access to collections of music and sound recordings they may hold.' There is no doubt that co-operative ventures of this kind, whether on an individual library/society basis or wider in scope, would benefit both sides. Societies and institutions working with libraries to improve access to information and materials would be able to publicise their services, reach potential new markets and sources of support and libraries would diversify their user base.

Broadly speaking, these specialist societies and institutions can be grouped as follows: umbrella organisations; educational organisations; Music Information Centres; composer societies; instrument societies; institutions covering a particular genre of music; and institutions providing services for particular sectors of the community. All the individual societies referred to in the text below are listed in the *British Music Yearbook* together with a contact address and telephone number in the 'organisations' section and there is a very useful list of the libraries of societies and institutions in the 'education' section. The Yearbook is annual and covers the whole of the UK, but we also need to note the *Scottish Music Handbook* issued by the Scottish Music Information Centre (Marshalsay, 1995).

The information and materials held by these bodies is as varied as the organisations themselves. The emphasis is usually on information (such as instrumental teachers, instrument makers, current awareness, lists of newly-published pieces, useful contacts, self-help advice and guidelines on particular topics) as many do not have the resources to acquire, much less maintain, collections of specialist material. Some institutions work with larger bodies where specialist expertise is available. For example, the financial administration of the Delius Trust is undertaken by the Musicians Benevolent Fund, as is the care of its considerable collection of research materials. All produce freely available publicity leaflets stating aims and objectives and services offered to members. Many publish more substantial documents such as annual reports, and a glance through some of these reveals an astonishing range of activities, in addition to information and advice in their specialist area, such as: lectures, workshops, catalogues, directories, discographies, bibliographies, instrument hire, performance set hire, events diaries, careers guides, music publishing, bursaries for study and other awards, and promotional events. This is evidence of the vibrant, highly active musical culture of which we can justly be proud.

▶ UMBRELLA ORGANISATIONS

These are typically societies with broadly-based aims and are often the UK branch of a larger international or EC body. They may also have more specialist bodies as members. The National Music Council of Great Britain is a good example. It states the following among its aims: 'to foster and increase the appreciation and understanding of the art of music in all its forms . . . to co-ordinate musical activity in the United Kingdom . . .' It is, itself, the UK representative on the International Music Council (a UNESCO body) and its members include societies covering every aspect of music, both professional and amateur, and each year it presents awards to those local authorities which have demonstrated an outstanding commitment to music.

One of the best-known umbrella bodies is Making Music previously known as the National Federation of Music Societies, which represents the interests of literally hundreds of thousands of amateur musicians in the UK. It has in excess of 1,900 amateur choirs, orchestras and music clubs in its membership and offers a wide range of services including its Music Exchange Scheme, enabling member societies to hire performance material to each other from their respective collections, complementing the comparable inter-library loan service. It also provides information leaflets and advice on topics such as charitable status, supports a loan fund for instruments and staging, and runs a programme note bank.

Other similar institutions include the Incorporated Society of Musicians, a professional association offering conferences, seminars and legal and financial advice, and the Worshipful Company of Musicians, a Livery Company of the City of London founded in 1500, which has a particular interest in assisting young musicians.

▶ EDUCATIONAL INSTITUTIONS

The most helpful directory to the music education world in the UK is the *Music Teachers' Yearbook*, a companion volume to the *British Music Yearbook*. In addition to listing schools and colleges of further and higher education, it also includes specialist societies and services in the field of music education. One such specialist umbrella body is the Music Education Council (formerly the UK Council for Music Education and Training). Its aims are 'to bring together and represent all organisations concerned with music education and training in the UK; to be a forum for all those involved in music education and training in the UK; to review and shape policies at all levels and to collate information and promote action.' It has over 100 corporate members (mostly educational institutions), produces a newsletter, organises regional forums, holds a biennial national conference and is the UK representative to the International Society of Music Education.

Other well-known educational organisations include the Benslow Music Trust, which runs over 100 short courses each year; the Ernest Read Music Association with its famous children's concerts, and Music for

Youth, which is a charity seeking to encourage music in schools (and organises the Schools' Prom as part of that). There are also a number of societies devoted to particular aspects of teaching such as the British Kodaly Academy, the British Suzuki Institute and the European String Teachers Association.

▶ INSTRUMENTAL SOCIETIES

Almost every instrument of the orchestra – and many that never appear anywhere near an orchestra – has a society devoted to it. Aims and activities of these institutions are very similar to those of the composer societies described above (i.e. to promote the teaching and playing of the particular instrument and its music) and again, a short list of examples illustrates the range in existence in the UK (there would be similar lists overseas): Bagpipe Society, British Double Reed Society, British Flute Society, British Horn Society, British Institute of Organ Studies, British Trombone Society, Clarsach Society, Handbell Ringers of Great Britain, International Viola Society (British Chapter), Lute Society, Northumbrian Pipers' Society and the Viola da Gamba Society. This last is a typical example and offers to its members a journal, membership list, newsletters, information and advice service, instrument hire, meetings and publications including a Thematic Index of Music for Viols. Similarly the British Institute of Organ Studies (BIOS) 'exists to encourage the study of the organ, its history and design, and to increase appreciation and understanding of its music by both organists and the general public. The Society also works for the preservation (and faithful restoration) of historic British organs.' These aims are pursued via meetings, journals and newsletters and through the compilation of registers of the country's pipe organs and redundant organs together with published Guidelines for Conservation and Restoration.

▶ ASSOCIATIONS COVERING DIFFERENT REPERTOIRES OF MUSIC

Many of the societies and institutions devoted to the interests of a particular genre of music act as the focal point of an entire industry, each with its own specialist organisations, products and support mechanisms. Jazz Services illustrates this very well: it is a registered charity funded by Arts Council of England money and its aim is 'to promote the growth and development of jazz within the United Kingdom by providing services in communications, touring, information and education.' It works in tandem with the National Network for Jazz (a regional network of jazz organisations) and organises tours and sponsorship for events. It has an extensive database of jazz-related information covering festivals, venues, promoters, agents, recording companies and the media. Jazz Services is also involved in educational projects and Jazz Newspapers publishes a quarterly regional newsletter. This is not the only jazz-related organisation; another is the National Jazz Foundation Archive (Loughton Library, Loughton, Essex IF10 1HD).

The Early Music Centre is very similar in structure to Jazz Studies in that it is an umbrella organisation funded in part with Arts Council money and responsible for the Early Music Network (a scheme offering perform-ance opportunities to early music ensembles), the Young Artists' Series and the International Young Artists' Competition, as well as providing work-shops, conferences and an information service. The National Early Music Association works alongside the Early Music Centre and the regional Early Music Forums as a co-ordinating organisation for all those concerned with early music. NEMA also publishes the *Early Music Yearbook*, a directory of services available in the early music field which incorporates the Register of Early Music (a directory of performers).

No account of such societies would be complete without a visit to the English Folk Dance and Song Society (EFDSS). The Society is at the heart of the English folk music world and its headquarters at Cecil Sharp House in London house the Vaughan Williams Memorial Library. The Library is open to members of the public upon payment of a very modest entrance fee. It has large collections of books and periodicals, audiovisual materials and microforms, plus most of the major twentieth-century manuscript collections of folk song and dance such as those of Cecil Sharp himself and George Butterworth. The Library also publishes a series of leaflets on aspects of folk culture. In addition to the library, EFDSS runs an educa-tion service organising workshops and multi-cultural events for children, schools and teachers, and provides an information service and educational project packs. There is also a shop selling books and audio materials.

The main centres for scholarship and research (and thus a valuable source of information) concerning the world of popular music are the Institute of Popular Music based at the University of Liverpool and the Popular Music Archive housed in the library of the Leeds College of Music. We should also note that the Popular Music Research Unit (PMRU) is based at University College, Salford. The Black Music Industry Association, founded in 1985, exists to promote the interests of black music and those working in that industry. It offers an information and advice service on aspects of the business and organises workshops, seminars and conferences for its members. Its magazine *Upfront!* focuses on education and the busi-ness. Other organisations covering specific genres of music include the Society for the Promotion of New Music (spnm), International Association for the Study of Popular Music, Light Music Society and the Plainsong and Medieval Music Society.

► SOCIETIES AND INSTITUTIONS OFFERING SERVICES TO PARTICULAR SECTORS OF THE COMMUNITY

People with disabilities

There has long been recognition of the crucial role of music in relation to people with disabilities (whether mental or physical) – either as a method of treatment or therapy, or as a career or an important and rewarding leisure activity. It is a matter of regret that the National Music and Disability Information Service (NMDIS), which provided a focal point for information on all aspects of this sector is no longer in existence. The service relied entirely on sponsorship and donations to support its work. Laura Crichton, who was Director of NMDIS, described the work of the service in an article in *Brio* as 'collecting information and disseminating this through various means. Sometimes the dissemination is purely reactive, as when answering . . . enquiries.

The Royal National Institute for the Blind (RNIB) is a large UK organisation actively involved in the provision of a support service to all visually impaired musicians. The services it offers are extensive, falling into three distinct sectors: the Enquiry and Transcription service, the Music Education Advisory service and the Music Leisure service. The Enquiry and Transcription service concentrates on fulfilling the needs of braille music users (of whom there are about 300 regulars), from the schoolchild learning to play an instrument to professional performers such as the harpsichordist John Henry. A full and informative article on the role of the RNIB and the work it does to provide access to music for visually-impaired people can be found in Page (1993).

Other organisations working on behalf of people with disabilities include: the Association of Professional Music Therapists, the British Society for Music Therapy, Artsline (which provides practical information on access to arts and entertainment), Music for Living and Sound Sense. There are many others, both national and local, listed in the *British Music Yearbook*, all of which offer access to information, advice and/or materials through various means. All draw together to form an invaluable group of associations whose work is of direct and tangible benefit to the community.

Other groups

Many other associations exist to represent the interests of specific sectors of the musical community, whether they be librarians (the International Association of Music Libraries, Archives and Documentation Centres), women (Women in Music, see also CHAPTER 8), choral directors (Association of British Choral Directors), composers (Association of Professional Composers, Composers Guild of Great Britain), religious groups (Baptist Music Network, Society of St. Gregory), retired musicians and those in financial need (the Musicians' Benevolent Fund, The Royal Society of Musicians of Great Britain) or young people (Youth and Music, Young Persons Concert Foundation).

▶ THE BBC

The BBC houses one of the richest range of collections of music and audio materials in the world. The Music and Gramophone Libraries comprise collections covering performance sets and scores of classical music (some three million items), music for television productions, popular music (including information on song histories, biographies of songwriters and librettists, reviews and obituaries), sound effects, mood music (about 5000 discs) and, in the main Gramophone Library, over 1,350,000 commercial recordings of all types of music (from current items on compact disc to cylinders dating back to 1888). There is a published catalogue of the printed classical music collection (*BBC Music Library Catalogue*, 1965–1982),[1] and a popular song index available – both invaluable reference tools. Access to the collections themselves is only for BBC production purposes, but loans of performance material are sometimes undertaken if no other source can be found and if copyright clearance has been granted to the borrower. BBC Sound Archive material can be accessed via the National Sound Archive at the British Library. The BBC Written Archives are discussed in CHAPTER 25.

▶ COMMERCIAL RADIO AND TELEVISION

Although the BBC dominates the broadcasting sector in terms of music materials and information, the many commercial radio and television stations which exist all have their own collections to support programme making. Local radio stations in particular are often set up with a specific audience in mind. One such example is Kiss FM. Aimed specifically at young people, it concentrates on broadcasting dance music such as soul, funk, rap and reggae and has built up its own library of sound recordings and is happy to respond to enquiries for information. The two well-known national independent radio stations are Classic FM and Virgin Radio.

In the television world the BBC again dominates, but all independent companies have their own collections. For example, Anglia Television, one of the ITV regional companies, has a library of sound recordings both commercial and otherwise, and some sheet music to support its programme-making activities. Once again, the *British Music Yearbook* is an excellent starting point, as in its 'broadcasting' section all radio and television companies are listed with addresses and telephone numbers. Further information on the world of the press and broadcast media can be found in a companion volume in this series: *Information Sources for the Press and Broadcast Media* (Eagle, 1999).

▶ CONCLUSION

This brief chapter provides only an overview of the many and varied sources of information that exist. If you are looking for specialist information on any musical topic then the most productive and efficient starting point can often be to contact the relevant special interest society, either personally or via your local music library. Now that many special interest societies have a website, increasingly the best starting point is to access the internet under the area of interest in a search engine such as AltaVista (<http://www.altavista.com>) or Google (<http://www.google.com>).

▶ REFERENCES

BBC Music Library Catalogue (1965–1982) (13 vols). London: British Broadcasting Corporation

British Music Yearbook (1973–) London: Rhinegold Publishing

Crichton, L. (1991) National Music and Disability Information Service. *Brio*, 28, No. 2, 71–4

Eagle, S. (1999) (ed.) *Information Sources for the Press and Broadcast media*. (Guide to Information Sources). [2nd edn. ed. by Sarah Adair] London: Bowker-Saur (Note the first edition of this book, published in 1991, was substantially different to this second edition, the changes reflecting the enormous developments in the press and newspaper industry during the 1990s.)

Early Music Yearbook. London: NEM

Faulkner, H. (1989) The Music Libraries of the BBC. *Fontes Artis Musicae* 36, 280–5

Marshalsay, K. (1995) (ed.) *Scottish Music Handbook, 1996*. Glasgow: Scottish Music Information Centre Ltd.

Music Teacher's Yearbook. London: Rhinegold Publishing [Formerly: British Music Education Yearbook]

Page, G. (1993) Music, Visually-impaired People and the Royal National Institute for the Blind. *Brio*, 30, No. 2, 71–82

Woodhouse, S. (1993) *Library and Information Plan for Music: written statement.* London: IAML(UK)

▶ NOTES

1.　For a history of the BBC Music Libraries, see Faulkner (1989).

3 Music information centres

Eve O'Kelly

The International Association of Music Information Centres (IAMIC) is a worldwide network of organisations promoting new music. Music information centres (or MICs, as they call themselves) are multi-purpose resource centres: 'working collections' where related material such as scores, recordings, programme notes, biographical material, newspaper reviews, magazine articles, books, photos, and so on are collected together, generally on open access.

MICs are active in some 40 countries internationally, documenting and promoting the music of that country or region, as well as co-operating internationally with the other centres on issues of common concern. Most MICs focus on contemporary art music, but this varies from country to country. Some also have responsibility for folk music; some for everything from rock and pop through jazz to so-called 'serious' music. In all countries, they serve as a focus of musical activity.

▶ FORMATION AND FUNCTIONS

The body which is now known as IAMIC was founded in 1958. The first meeting of 'National Music Centre Representatives', as they were then called, was organised by UNESCO's International Music Council in co-operation with the Donemus Foundation, Amsterdam, and the Dutch National Music Committee, with the aim of 'making available a wider knowledge of contemporary music.' Following the example shown by the work of Donemus, similar organisations were set up in other countries. In 1962, having decided that 'Music Information Centre' was a more apt description, it was decided to form the International Association of Music Information Centres as a constituent branch of the International Association of Music Libraries (IAML). This affiliation continued until 1991, when IAMIC, by then with some 40 member organisations, voted to become a fully-independent association under the aegis of the International Music Council. Close contact is still maintained with the International Association of Music Libraries, however, and the annual meetings of both organisations are sometimes run in parallel.

Music information centres differ from libraries in several important respects. Whereas a library aims to provide comprehensive materials and resources, and may have the care of many rare and valuable items, a music information centre is not generally dealing with irreplaceable materials and is more interested in seeing the collection well used than in conserving it for posterity.[1] A library will keep different types of material in different collections – books, CDs, scores, etc. – and there may be different conditions for access. In a music information centre, the focus is on enabling the user to have easy, integrated access to a wide variety of media relating to the particular composition or subject they are investigating. In an MIC the visitor should be able to sit with the score of a work and listen to the recording (or, preferably, a number of different recordings), while leafing through the composer's biography, a press clippings file, photos and magazine articles and with a list of relevant books, videos, CD-ROMs and, increasingly, internet addresses readily to hand. In this, MICs perhaps provide a bridge between the traditional library of the past and the fully interactive, multimedia library of the future. It is interesting to note, in passing, that the problem of how to unify and co-ordinate the differing computer catalogues of nearly 40 MICs, which was the subject of on-going debate within IAMIC for many years, has been made irrelevant by the arrival of the easy interfaces provided by the internet. In an area that changes as rapidly as contemporary music, the internet is proving to be a very important promotional tool, and the members of IAMIC now have their own sites on the internet, linking from the association's own website at <http://www.iamic.net>.

The other major difference between music information centres and libraries lies in the area of promotion. Composers, whether of jazz, concert music, rock, pop or any of the crossover genres, find it difficult to obtain representation by a publisher or record company until their name and their music is known. Even then, commercial considerations mean that only a few highly successful composers are taken up by the major publishers and record companies. This is where music information centres play a crucial role in promoting composers, and most centres are involved, to the extent that their budgets allow, in publishing and recording as well as acting as agent in obtaining live performances and broadcasts.

▶ FUNDING

The question of funding is an ever-present issue in all music information centres. Like all *pro bono* activities, it costs money to run an MIC and there are few areas of activity that can be made self-financing, let alone profit-generating. Local conditions dictate the funding for each MIC and, as might be expected, budgets are usually in fairly direct relation not only to the wealth of the country but to the respect in which its creative artists are held. Most music information centres are autonomous organisations with national status, and this give them access to funds from a range of sources including national, regional and local government, arts councils, major foundations and copyright organisations. Most MICs receive funding in some degree from the national copyright collection society and some, among them Finland and Sweden, are actually subsidiaries of the copyright society. Others (such as the American Music Center) receive no funding from this source and no state support and are constantly engaged in fundraising from private sponsors, foundations and members' subscriptions.

The music information centres of Sweden, Norway, the Netherlands and Canada are usually held up as the most fortunate in terms of annual budget, but even in these wealthy countries economic downturns and changes of government have, recently, had adverse effects. MICs in the countries of the former Eastern bloc are still struggling with the consequences of having the old, secure system of state funding withdrawn with no new system set up to replace it. Together with the technological gap still experienced in these countries, this makes it difficult for these MICs to promote and document their music effectively.

To illustrate the wide range of activities in music information centres in countries of different sizes and resources, four are used as examples: the MICs of Australia, Norway, Ireland and Britain.

▶ THE AUSTRALIAN MUSIC CENTRE

The Australian Music Centre was established in Sydney in 1973. Its mission is to collect and promote music by contemporary Australian composers, and it receives approximately 47% of its funding from government sources, primarily from the federal government via the Australia Council for the Arts. The balance of its funding is self-generated from retailing, membership subscriptions and donations. The AMC is also involved in several collaborative projects with Australian tertiary schools and copyright societies which provide in-kind staff and equipment support.

The Australian Music Centre (AMC) carries out a wide range of activities. The core activity is the library, which houses a collection of scores, recordings, videos and reference materials in many formats. All library materials are available for use on site and most items are available for loan. The library also provides a comprehensive information service accessible by telephone, mail, fax and e-mail. Since 1994 the library has provided electronic access to its catalogues, first through a bulletin board, then via its website, which was established in early 1996. The website allows access to considerable information by and about the AMC, including an on-going project to establish an internet presence for all composers represented by the centre.

The AMC operates a marketing service through its own retail shop in Sydney and by mail order (nationally and internationally). The marketing service collects and supplies all music materials pertaining to Australia, across all music genres, and includes an extensive facsimile production facility to make available the scores held in the library collection.

The centre carries out numerous publishing projects. The flagship publication is the *Sounds Australian* journal, a professional music journal which appears twice yearly, each issue dealing with a specific theme. Supplementing this is the bi-monthly *Sounds Australian Update*, which is issued six times a year and includes details of competitions, performances, commissions, recent library acquisitions, etc. which are of use to the professional membership. Also published six times a year, alternating with the *Update*, is the *Australian Music Calendar*, a diary in poster format of upcoming performances of Australian music throughout the country. Besides these regular magazines, the centre publishes educational kits for secondary schools, pamphlets, brochures for individual composers, music catalogues and directories.

As well as print publications the AMC produces CD recordings on its own label, *Vox Australis*. Two or three disks of contemporary Australian compositions are issued annually. It also awards the annual *Sounds Australian Awards*, which recognise significant contributions to Australian music by individuals and organisations.

▶ NORSK MUSIKKINFORMASJON

The brief of Norsk Musikkinformasjon, the Norwegian Music Information Centre, is 'to provide information on Norwegian music and music life.' The Centre was established in 1978 on the initiative of the Society of Norwegian Composers and with funds provided by the Norwegian Arts Council. Since 1982 the centre has been funded by the Ministry of Cultural Affairs

The centre's library has a collection of original manuscripts of some 190 living and 50 recently deceased composers. The library also contains most of the published works of contemporary Norwegian composers, and the orchestral depot can provide copies of scores and parts for performance. All the unpublished works in the library may be copied at low cost, and there is a unique collection of tapes, records and CDs available for study at the centre.

Information materials include 13 catalogues (listed by instrumentation) issued annually of published and unpublished Norwegian music available both from the MIC and from the major Norwegian publishing houses; the magazine *Listen to Norway*, which is distributed worldwide (three issues per year); an *Address Guide to Music in Norway* containing names and addresses of all major music institutions and organisations; and brochures on Norwegian composers, containing biography, work-lists and discography. The Centre also organises the copying of parts for works accepted for performance. Exhibitions are arranged in conjunction with concerts, festivals and other events, and there is co-operation with the other Nordic music information centres in Sweden, Denmark, Finland and Iceland. The MICs for these countries issue a joint quarterly publication, *Nordic Sounds*, under the auspices of the Nordic Music Council.

▶ THE CONTEMPORARY MUSIC CENTRE, IRELAND

The Contemporary Music Centre (CMC), Ireland's national archive and resource centre for contemporary music, is one of the smaller music information centres. Located in central Dublin and receiving its core funding from the Arts Council, its library contains the only major specialist collection of music by some 150 modern Irish composers, and its sound archive contains records, cassettes, CDs, DATs and videos, many of them rare recordings of live concerts and broadcasts. In addition, the centre has a collection of information materials of all kinds, from concert programmes and biographical data to specialist periodicals and books. *New Music News*, a free newsletter distributed internationally each February, May and September, contains articles on new developments in music in Ireland, interviews with composers, performers and other leading musicians, a 'News' section, listings of competitions and awards for composers, latest acquisitions in the library, a 'New Music Calendar' and a section of 'Composers News' which lists, for each composer, all premières, broadcasts, publications, recordings, and so on, since the last issue. Another regular publication is the directory, *Irish Composers*. Updated on an annual basis, this is a series of loose-leaf information sheets in a presentation folder, giving biographical details, a photo, a selected work-list and an introductory 'personal comment' for each of the most active Irish composers. CMC also issues a promotional CD series, *Contemporary Music from Ireland*, intended as a sort of musical 'calling card' to give an introduction to the music of Irish composers. The Contemporary Music Centre's site on the internet provides comprehensive information on all aspects of the work of the Centre, as well as enabling users to search the library catalogue, order music and give feedback (<http://www.cmc.ie>).

Project work includes running a nationwide series of talks and seminars under the heading 'Meet the Composer'; and issuing the

SoundWorks series of pedagogical publications, designed to involve students and teachers in the performance of contemporary Irish music.

▶ THE BRITISH MUSIC INFORMATION CENTRE

The British Music Information Centre (BMIC) is a promotion and documentation resource for contemporary British music. Full background and fully searchable catalogues can be found on the Web at <http://www.bmic. co.uk>. Resources and activities include:

- a major collection of scores, recordings and information on composers, accessible to the public;
- print, publicity and promotion schemes for composers;
- a live events programme, including The Cutting Edge, The Cutting Edge Tour and concert series at 10 Stratford Place, London WIN 9AE;
- publications;
- a general enquiry service.

The collection consists of scores, approximately 31,000 works by some 2,600 British composers. This makes it the largest of its kind in the UK. Starting with works written in 1900, it includes, in addition to published material, unpublished or out of print scores that are difficult or impossible to find elsewhere. Scores that are only available on hire from publishers may also be found in the catalogue. Much of this material is only available for reference but in most cases the centre can help enquirers to obtain copies of scores or recordings by putting them in touch with the relevant publishing house, composer or record company. Over 150 composers have made agreements with the BMIC, allowing photocopies of their scores to be made at BMIC for study purposes. In such cases only the cost of the photocopying will be charged.

Repertoire searches can be made: scores are easily tracked down as they are fully catalogued and immediately accessible on the computer database, also available on the centre's website. Lists can be printed out or users can search the database using visitor terminals at the BMIC. Searches can include (amongst others):

- complete list of a composer's works;
- the results of a specific search by instrumental combination (e.g. ensemble works for flute, clarinet, violin, cello and piano);
- a list by date (e.g. all symphonic works written in 1972);
- a list by duration;
- works suitable for children;

- a list by gender (e.g. all songs written by female composers);
- a list by author (e.g. all choral settings of A.E. Housman);
- a list by word in title.

Listings can be faxed or e-mailed to enquirers for no charge. Out of copyright scores from the early part of the century are kept in archive storage at the Royal College of Music, but can be made available on request.

The BMIC is also home to 15,000 recordings of British new music which are available for listening on the premises. In addition to commercial recordings, this collection includes rare examples of private and radio recordings that are not available elsewhere. As a registered sound archive, the BMIC is allowed to record from the radio for study purposes. BMIC also has a small collection of opera, music theatre and documentary film on video, including works by Britten, Tippett, Birtwistle, Nyman, Weir and Turnage. These items may be viewed by appointment. Since 1995, BMIC has housed a collection of over 200 recordings donated by the Place Dance Services of music written for contemporary dance groups and choreographers.

The centre also maintains extensive documentary files on the British composers. The BMIC composer files contain press cuttings, programme notes, articles, reviews, publisher's lists, photographs and biographies. BMIC cannot make copies of published material, but where BMIC has an agreement with a composer to copy unpublished material, then a study score can be made. They have these agreements with around 150 composers. Much of the information in the composer files may be photocopied on the premises.

Music information centres are open to the public and their extensive resources are at users' service in person, on the internet, or by telephone, fax, mail or e-mail. No matter what your query, the MIC of the country concerned will assist you, or put you in touch with a more appropriate organisation.

▶ LIST OF MUSIC INFORMATION CENTRES (ALL MEMBERS OF IAMIC)

Australia

Australian Music Centre
PO Box N 690
Grosvenor Place NSW 1200
Australia
Tel: +61-(0)2-9247 4677

Fax: +61-(0)2-9241 2873
Email: <info@amcoz.com.au>
URL: <http://www.amcoz.com.au/>
General Manager: John Davis
Liaison officer: Judith Foster

Austria

Music Information Center Austria
Stiftgasse 29
A-1070 Wien
Austria
Tel: +43-(0)1-521 040
Fax: +43-(0)1-521 0459
Email: <mica@mica.at>
URL: <http://www.mica.at>
*Managing Director: Peter
Rantasa*
*Liaison Officer: Katharina Gratzl-
Karnitschnig*

Belgium

*Centre Belge de Documentation
Musicale*
Belgisch Centrum voor
Muziekdocumentatie
Aarlenstraat 75–77
B-1040 Brussels
Belgium
Tel: +32-(0)2-230 94 30
Fax: +32-(0)2-230 94 37
Email: <music-centre@cebedem.be>
URL: <http://www.cebedem.be/>
Director: Alain van Kerckhoven

*Muziekcentrum Vlaanderen
(Flanders Music Centre)*
Steenstraat 25
1000 Brussels
Belgium
Tel: +32-(0)2-504 90 90
Fax: +32-(0)2-502 81 03
Email: <info@muziekcentrum.be>
URL: <http://www.muziek
centrum.be>
Managing Director: Stef Coninx

Brazil

CDMC-Brasil/UNICAMP
Centro de Documentacao de
Musica Contemporanea
Caixa Postal 6136 – CEP
13083-970 Campinas – SP
Brazil
Tel: +55-19-3788-6533
Fax: +55-19-3289-3965
Email: <cdmusica@obelix.
unicamp.br>
URL: <http://www.unicamp.
br/cdmc>
Director: José Augusto Mannis

Bulgaria

*Bulgarian Music Information
Center*
Soros Center for the Arts
10 Angel Kanchev Str.
1000 Sofia
Bulgaria
Tel: +359-(0)2-980 21 82
  or +359-(0)2-980 02 44
Fax: +359-(0)2-980 21 82
Fax: +359-(0)2-66 21 07
Email: <BulgMIC@yahoo.com>;
  <pvelichkova@yahoo.com>
Director: Pavlina Velichkova

Canada

Canadian Music Centre
Chalmers House
20 St Joseph Street
Toronto, Ontario M4Y 1J9
Canada
Tel: +1-416-961 6601
Fax: +1-416-961 7198
Email: <info@musiccentre.ca>
URL: <http://www.musiccentre.ca>
Executive Director: Elisabeth Bihl

Colombia

Centro de Documentación Musical
Calle 24, No. 5-60, 4 Piso
Santafé de Bogotá 1
Colombia
Tel: +57-1-342 20 97
Director: Jaime H. Quevedo

Croatia

Music Information Centre, Zagreb
Concert Management
Kneza Mislava 18
HR-10 000 Zagreb
Croatia
Tel: +385-(0)1-461 18 10
Fax: +385-(0)1-461 18 07
Email: <mic@zg.tel.hr>
URL: <http://www.mic.hr>
Director: Ivan Zivanovic
Editor and Database Manager:
    Jelena Vukovic

Czech Republic

Hudební Informacní Stredisko
Besední 3
11800 Praha 1
Czech Republic
Tel: +420-(0)2-57 31 24 22
Fax: +420-(0)2-57 31 74 24
Email: <his@vol.cz>
URL: <http://www.musica.cz>
Director: Miroslav Pudlák

Denmark

Dansk Musik Informations Center
Gråbrødre Torv 16
DK-1154 København K
Denmark
Tel: +45-33 11 20 66
Fax: +45-33 32 20 16

Email: <mic@mic.dk>
URL: <http://www.mic.dk>
Director: Birgit Bergholt
Export & Promotion: Bodil Hoegh

Estonia

Eesti Muusika Infokeskus
Lauteri 7
Tallinn 10145
Estonia
Tel: +372-(0)645 43 95
Fax: +372-(0)645 43 95
Email: <emik@zzz.ee>
URL: <http://www.kul.ee/emic/>

Finland

Finnish Music Information Centre
Lauttasaarentie 1
FIN-00200 Helsinki
Finland
Tel: +358-(0)9-68101 313
Fax: +358-(0)9-68207 70
Email: <info@mic.teosto.fi>
URL: <http://www.fimic.fi>
Executive Director: Kai Amberla
Chief Librarian: Meija Kangas

France

Centre de Documentation de la
Musique Contemporaine
Cité de la Musique
16, place de la Fontaine aux Lions
75019 Paris
France
Tel: +33-(0)1-47 15 49 85
Fax: +33-(0)1-47 15 49 89
Email: <cdmc@cdmc.asso.fr>
URL: <http://www.cdmc.asso.fr>
Director: Marianne Lyon
Documentation Department:
    Isabelle Gauchet

Georgia

Georgian Music Information
Centre
David Agmashenebeli Ave. 123
380064 Tbilisi
Republic of Georgia
Tel: +995-(8)32-960653
Fax: +995-(8)32-968678
Director: Natela Mamaladze

Germany

Deutsches Musikinformations-
zentrum
Weberstrasse 59
D-53113 Bonn
Tel: +49-(0)228-2091-180
Fax: +49-(0)228-2091-200
Email: <miz.dmr@t-online.de>
URL: <http://www.miz.org>
Managing Director: Margot
Wallscheid

Internationales Musikinstitut
Darmstadt
Nieder-Ramstädter Strasse 190
D-64285 Darmstadt
Germany
Tel: +49-(0)6151-132 416
     +49-(0)6151-132 417
Fax: +49-(0)6151-132 405
Email: <imd@stadt.darmstadt.de>
URL: <http://www.imd.darmstadt.
de>
Director: Solf Schaefer

Great Britain

British Music Information Centre
10 Stratford Place
London W1N 9AE
Great Britain
Tel: +44-(0)20-74 99 85 67
Fax: +44-(0)20-74 99 47 95
Email: <info@bmic.co.uk>
URL: <http://www.bmic.co.uk>
Director: Matthew Greenall
Information Manager: Daniel
Goren

Hungary

Magyar Zenei Információs
Központ (Hungarian Music
Information Centre)
Hungarian Music Council
H-1364 Budapest
P.O. Box 47
Hungary
Tel: +36-(0)1-317 95 98
Fax: +36-(0)1-317 82 67
Email: <hmic@mail.c3.hu>
URL: <http://www.c3.hu/~hmic>
Director: Eszter Vida

Iceland

Íslensk Tónverkamidstöd (Iceland
Music Information Centre)
Sídumúli 34
IS-108 Reykjavík
Iceland
Tel: +354-(0)568 31 22
Fax: +354-(0)568 31 24
Email: <itm@mic.is>
URL: <http://www.mic.is>
Director: Sigfridur Björnsdottir

Ireland

Contemporary Music Centre
19 Fishamble Street
Temple Bar
Dublin 8 Ireland
Tel: +353-(0)1-673 1922
Fax: +353-(0)1-648 9100
Email: <info@cmc.ie>
URL: <http://www.cmc.ie>
Director: Eve O'Kelly
Information Manager: Jonathan
Grimes

Israel

Israel Music Institute
24 Kibbutz Galuyot Rd
IL-68166 Tel Aviv
Israel
Tel: +972-(0)3-681 1010
Fax: +972-(0)3-681 6070
Email: <musicinst@bezeqint.net
<plandau@netvision.net.il>
URL: <http://acquanet.co.il/vip/imi>
Director: Paul Landau

Italy

AMIC – Archivi della Musica
Italiana Contemporanea
(CIDIM – Comitato Nazionale
Italiano Musica)
Largo di Torre Argentina 11
I-00186 Roma
Italy
Tel: +39-06-681 90650
Fax: +39-06-681 90651
Email: <amic@amic.it>
URL: <http://www.amic.it>
President: Francesco Agnello
Liaison Officer: Caterina Santi

Japan

Nippon Kindai Ongakukan
(Documentation Center of
Modern Japanese Music)
8-14, Azabudai 1-chôme
Minato-ku, Tokyo
106 Japan
Tel: +81-(0)3-3224 1584
Fax: +81-(0)3-3224 1654
Director: Kazuyuki Toyama

Lithuania

Lithuanian Music Information and
Publishing Centre
Lithuanian Composers' Union
Mickeviciaus 29
2600 Vilnius
Lithuania
Tel: +370-(8)2-72 69 86
Fax: +370-(8)5-212 0939
Email: <info@mic.lt>
URL: <http://www.mic.lt>
Director: Daiva Parulskiene

Luxembourg

Luxemburger Gesellschaft für
Neue Musik
Luxembourg Music Information
Centre
B.P. 828
L-2018 Luxembourg
Tel: +352-22-5821
Fax: +352-22-5823
Email: <lgmn@lgmn.lu>
URL: <http://www.lgmn.lu>
Director: Marcel Wengler
Liaison Officer: Luc Rollinger

Mexico

Centro Nacional de Investigación,
Documentación e
Información Musical
(CENIDIM)
Centro Nacional de las Artes
Torre de Investigacion 7° Piso
Calz. Tlalpan y Río Churubusco
Col Country Club, 04220
Mexico D.F.
Mexico
Tel: +52-(01)5-420 44 15
Fax: +52-(01)5-420 44 54
Director: José Antonio Robles
Cahero

Netherlands

Muziek Groep Nederland,
vestiging Amsterdam
(Donemus)
Paulus Potterstraat 16
1017 CZ Amsterdam
Netherlands
Tel: +31-(0)20-305 89 00
Fax: +31-(0)20-673 35 88
Email: <info@muziekgroep.nl>
URL: <http://www.muziekgroep.nl>
Managing Director: Drs Jan
Willem Ten Broeke
Information and Repertoire:
Els van Swol

Gaudeamus Foundation
Swammerdamstraat 38
1091 RV Amsterdam
Netherlands
Tel: +31-(0)20-694 7349
Fax: +31-(0)20-694 7258
Email: <info@gaudeamus.nl>
URL: <http://www.gaudeamus.nl>
Director: Henk Heuvelmans
Liaison Officer: Fons Willemsen

New Zealand

Centre for New Zealand Music
(SOUNZ)
Level 1
39 Cambridge Tce
PO Box 10 042
Wellington
New Zealand
Tel: +64-(0)4-801 86 02
Fax: +64-(0)4-801 86 04
Email: <info@sounz.org.nz>
URL: <http://www.sounz.org.nz>
Executive Director: Scilla Askew

Norway

Norsk Musikkinformasjon
Tollbugata 28
N-0157 Oslo
Norway
Tel: +47-22 42 90 90
Fax: +47-22 42 90 95
Email: <info@mic.no>
URL: <http://www.mic.no>
Director: Morten Walderhaug
Liaison Officer: Lisbeth Risnes

Poland

Library of the Polish Composers'
Union
Polish Contemporary Music
Documentation Centre
27 Rynek Starego Miasta
PL-00-272 Warsaw
Tel: +48-(0)22-831 16 34
Fax: +48-(0)22-831 06 07
Email: <bifo@nuta.pl>
URL: <http://www.bifo.nuta.pl>
Director: Mieczyslaw Kominek
Assistant Director and Liaison
Officer: Izabela Zymer

Portugal

Fundação Calouste Gulbenkian
Carlos de Pontes Leca
Avenida de Berna 45
P-1093 Lisboa
Portugal
Tel: +351-21-782 3000
Fax: +352-21-782 3041
Email: <cbarbosa@gulbenkian.pt>
URL: <http://www.musica.
    gulbenkian.pt>
Director: Luis Pereira Leal

Scotland

Scottish Music Information Centre
1 Bowmont Gardens
Glasgow G12 9LR
Scotland
Tel: +44-(0)141-334 63 93
Fax: +44-(0)141-337 11 61
Email: <info@smic.org.uk>
URL: <http://www.smic.org.uk>
Director: Andrew Logan
*Information Officer: Alasdair
    Pettinger*

Slovak Republic

Music Centre Slovakia
Michalská 10
SK-81536 Bratislava
Slovakia
Tel: +421-(0)7-54 43 13 - 80
Fax: +421-(0)7-54 43 03 - 79
Email: <hc@hc.sk>
URL: <http://www.hc.sk>
Director: Ol'ga Smetanová
*Documentation, Databases,
    Information: Alena Volna*

South Africa

MCCOSA
Music Communication Centre of
    Southern Africa
P.O. Box 1010 Auckland Park
ZA 2006 Johannesburg
South Africa
Tel: +27-(0)11-642 2995
Fax: +27-(0)11-642 1408
Email: <mccosa@ibi.co.za>
Director: Herman van Niekerk

Spain

Centro de Documentación Musical
Torregalindo 10
E-28016 Madrid
Spain
Tel: +34-(0)91-353 1370
Fax: +34-(0)91-345 1761
Email: <cdmyd@inaem.mcu.es>
*Director: Antonio Alvarez
    Canibano*

Sweden

STIM/Svensk Musik
Swedish Music Information Centre
P.O. Box 27327
S-102 54 Stockholm
Sweden
Tel: +46-(0)8-783 8800
Fax: +46-(0)8-783 9510
Email: <swedmic@stim.se>
URL: <http://www.mic.stim.se>
*Executive Director: Roland
    Sandberg*

Switzerland

Fondation SUISA pour la musique
Rue de l'Hôpital 22
CH-2001 Neuchâtel
Switzerland
Tel: +41-(0)32-725 25 36
Fax: +41-(0)32-724 04 72
Director: Claude Delley

Ukraine

Music Information Centre of the
*   Ukraine Composers Union*
ul. Sofiuska 16/16
252001 Kiev 1
Ukraine
Tel: +380-(8)44-228 33 04
Fax: +380-(8)44-229 69 40
Director: Olga Golynski

United States of America

American Music Center
30 West 26th Street, Suite 1001
New York, NY 10010-2011
USA
Tel: +1-212-366 52 60
Fax: +1-212-366 52 65
Email: <center@amc.net>
URL: <http://www.amc.net>
<http://www.newmusicbox.org>

Executive Director: Richard Kessler
New Music Information Specialist:
*   Lyn Liston*

Wales

Ty Cerdd – Welsh Music
*   Information Centre*
15 Mt. Stuart Square
Cardiff CF10 5DP
WALES, UK
Tel: +44-(0)2920-462 855
    or +44-(0)2920-465 700
Fax: +44-2920-462 733
Email: <wmic@tycerdd.org>
URL: <http://www.tycerdd.org>
Director: Keith Griffin
Information Officer: Sarah Hill

Yugoslavia

SOKOJ-MIC (Yugoslav Music
*   Information Centre)*
c/o Misarska 12-14
11000 Belgrade
Yugoslavia
Tel: +381-(0)11-324 51 92
Fax: +381-(0)11-324 51 92
Email: <sokojmic@eunet.yu>
Director: Mrs. Marija Cvijanovic
Liaison Officer: Natasa Danilovic

NOTES

1. The conservation function is generally fulfilled by the national library or national archives of the country concerned. Some 50 centres operate a 'cut-off date' whereby material older than, say, 50 years, is sent for permanent archiving in another more appropriate national institution. This also solves the problem of defining what is 'contemporary music'.

4 The second-hand trade: dealers and auctions

Nigel Simeone

The antiquarian trade in music and books on music has a long tradition in Britain and remains very well established. It also does so in Germany, Switzerland, France, The Netherlands and Italy. By contrast, in the United States and Australasia there are really very few second-hand and anti-quarian dealers specialising entirely in music. Increasingly dealers – and interesting musical material – can be found by a world audience on the internet.

Second-hand and antiquarian material is disseminated principally through two mechanisms. First through auctions, some of them very well publicised, and second through dealers' catalogues, where a large amount of interesting and often inexpensive music and music literature is to be found. Catalogues, both of auctions and of second-hand dealers, which may be illustrated, sometimes become quite important documents in their own right, particularly when the original material disappears into private owner-ship and the catalogues remain the only accessible scholarly source for it.

One particularly useful function of dealers arises from the rather ephemeral nature of much printed music. It often has a very short shelf-life, and it goes out of print quickly. This is nothing new: a lot of material by important composers became remarkably elusive early on. The early works of Anton Bruckner or Gustav Holst, for example, were published by tiny firms, and although pieces were sometimes reprinted following a take-over by a larger firm, this was more often not the case. The same, to a lesser extent, is also true of composers like Elgar and Vaughan Williams, where there are, even now, published pieces from long ago that are hard to track down in any edition. If these are going to be found at all, it is likely only be through a second-hand dealer's catalogue.

Recently, such sources of supply have become particularly useful, with the increasing streamlining of music publishers and the consequent slim-ming-down of their catalogues. This has been a consequence of some large publishing houses concentrating on the commercial value of a relatively small number of important musical copyrights, leaving less significant earners go out of print. Without dealer's lists such material would be at risk of disappearing altogether.

The distinction between a 'second-hand' dealer and an 'antiquarian' one is as much a matter of presentation as it is a matter of content. People who need to acquire music should use all the means at their disposal, and there is almost a kind of one-upmanship in being called 'antiquarian'. It does not necessarily mean expensive, and it is through the catalogues these dealers have produced that one can find very important material that would otherwise, very possibly, be lost altogether simply because it had not been properly described.

As well as printed music, that is to say scores, and books about music, there is also a growing interest among scholars in the peripheral documentation of music. People have always been fascinated by things like the little tokens that were sold to attend concerts at the Vauxhall Gardens in the eighteenth century, or some of the printed tickets that were issued for Haydn's concerts in London which are little engraved works of art in their own right.

More recent material, some which is of much greater importance in terms of its documentary value, comes in the increased interest in things like handbills, posters and programmes. These not only help document concert life as it happened, they allow us to form a picture of what actually was going on in concert rooms and concert halls. Also, if it is late enough, in other words if it is from or after the time of John Ella's Musical Union concerts in the 1840s, these things also have programme notes, which of themselves tell us a great deal about how commentators viewed the music. This is fascinating in the case of, for example, Debussy and Schoenberg's visits to conduct at the Queens Hall for Henry Wood, in Debussy's case on 27 February 1909, where the programme book is blankly incomprehending about the *Trois nocturnes* for Orchestra and *Prélude à l'après-midi d'un faune*. And how exciting to hold a programme with the conductor listed as Debussy! Later, in the twenties, we find exactly the same problem with, for instance, a Bruckner symphony.

So these documents are of considerable interest to those looking at the reception of music in this country, an area of increasing academic study, and as Stephen Lloyd recounts in CHAPTER 26, not always easily found in libraries. It is as well that dealers actually notice these things. They are often inexpensive but that does not lessen their value as documents of often great occasions, important additions to the literature of the artists concerned, and evidence of interesting contemporary viewpoints on works that perhaps we now take for granted. Even the advertisements, perhaps of other concerts, can be of considerable interest. Also, as Elizabeth Agate makes clear in CHAPTER 27 programmes and handbills often provide a convenient source for (often out of copyright) photographs and portraits, particularly of less well-known artists, which may be in themselves unique.

Other kinds of ephemeral material that can be of great interest are things like contracts between composers and publishers, which give us a real insight into the day-to-day business of being a composer or being a publisher. Publishers' catalogues which, of course, tell us what was actually published and when, can be very valuable. A particularly interesting example to lovers of British music is Goodwin & Tabb's hire library catalogue, particularly the edition which appeared immediately before the Second World War, including as it does much music of the inter-war period which was never printed but merely hired out in manuscript copies, and in some cases is now hard to find. There are many such examples. Novello, for instance, issued an enormous hard bound catalogue around the turn of the century, a catalogue of their complete output. Later, Novello took over Goodwin & Tabb.

Almost all major continental publishers had British agents, who very often put out catalogues. In many cases, the import catalogues that were issued in this country are often of great importance because the records of the publishers in, say, Germany or France were destroyed as a result of war.

These various categories tend to get mixed in dealers' catalogues, often with valuable historical or bibliographical commentary supplied by the dealer. The very act of browsing in a rigorously written scholarly catalogue like those of the late John May (May & May) is of itself a significant educational activity, and can be more informative than browsing a great library collection. For this reason runs of such dealer's catalogues have a research value entirely their own.

This sort of activity tends to be one focused on dealers' catalogues. Auction houses, for obvious reasons, tend to like lots where there is a larger unit, a single value as it were, because it is not worth their while cataloguing such small items.

► AUCTION HOUSES

Auctions of music in London are a phenomenon that goes back a long way. James Coover's book (Coover, 1988) about the Puttick and Simpson sales is a fascinating source of information as to how these worked, particularly in the nineteenth century. (Coover is also valuable for his note 'A Word About Sources'.) Most of the business that was conducted then by auction houses was in fact sales of publishers' stocks and the sales of the printing plates, which could very often be fantastically valuable. A single song often went for a fortune: these were hot commercial properties.

The interest in collecting antiquarian music developed during the second half of the nineteenth music. Some collectors were inclined to be omnivorous, acquiring large and extremely varied collections of interesting or unusual material. One such was the remarkable George Powell, a friend of Swinburne and an acquaintance of Wagner, who lived some of the time in Mornington Crescent, London, and some of the time in North Wales. He was, for example, a voracious collector of Italian manuscript material from the mid-eighteenth century and as a result acquired some quite important source material. He also collected letters by composers he admired, including a substantial batch of Mendelssohn.[1]

Alec Hyatt King's study of such collections (King, 1963) makes clear that Powell was by no means alone. Widely cultured people with collecting instincts from the 1850s onwards, would often amass quite large libraries for a relatively small financial outlay. In many cases this material was then regarded as 'old' rather than of any particular value. It is, however, interesting to note that manuscripts by some composers became highly prized shortly after their deaths, Mendelssohn being a noted example.

Stefan Zweig was another to assemble a major collection; he became more selective as he grew older, and he identified three collecting 'periods' in his life as a collector. His music collection is now in the British Library.

During the twentieth century, auction houses have moved away from their earlier function of acting as clearing houses for publishers' copyrights, developing instead as the most publicly prominent sources of important manuscript material, and significant printed editions. There have been many well-publicised examples of sales of musical manuscripts since World War II; in the last 20 years autograph manuscripts to have attracted major scholarly interest have included a volume containing a group of Mozart symphonies, Mahler's Symphony No. 1, Stravinsky's *Le sacre du printemps*, Schumann's Piano Concerto and the Brahms Clarinet Sonatas. This last example is interesting, as the manuscripts had remained in the hands of the family of the works' dedicatee, the clarinettist Richard Mühlfeld, until their sale at Sotheby's in 1997, 90 years after his death. The emergence of a manuscript of this importance is a useful reminder of what treasures often remain in the hands of families of performers and composers who are long dead.

Of the many interesting manuscripts to emerge from publishers or other sources, the various fragments of Elgar's *The Fringes of the Fleet* (which seemed to appear biannually for several years in the early 1980s) were an intriguing and largely unknown curiosity. More spectacular was the sale of the fabulous manuscript relating to Stravinsky's *Les noces*, which came from the archives of the work's publisher, J & W Chester.

Auction houses have also offered important, but perhaps less glamorous, lots of letters from composers. Insofar as they are not anything like as valuable commercially, such lots offer the scholar and private collector the opportunity to bid for interesting material themselves. Examples from the last two decades have included personal correspondence from Verdi, Poulenc and Shostakovich, material which had hitherto been unknown. Sotheby's catalogue entries for their sales of Shostakovich letters, notably the correspondence with Tanya Glivenko[2] and Elena Konstantinovskaya[3] with their English translations, make them valuable as sources in their own right.

The sales of material relating to Diaghilev and the Ballets Russes have included original costumes, drop curtains and set designs, carefully described and extensively illustrated in a series of catalogues for Sotheby's sales in London,[4] Monte Carlo and New York. Ballets Russes items continue to emerge and as recently as 1999 Sotheby's offered a substantial quantity of documentary material, including several contracts, much of it originally owned by Diaghilev's *régisseur*, Serge Grigoriev.

The sale of musical manuscripts is not only a British phenomenon: it has flourished in Europe and in the United States. At an auction in Paris in 1979, the earliest autograph manuscript of Debussy's *Pelléas et Mélisande* was offered for sale. This emergence of what is one of the most important sources for a major musical masterpiece was a notable event. The same sale contained completely unknown works by composers such as Chausson and Fauré, as well as some early Debussy four-hand piano pieces which remain unpublished even today. Such sales take place regularly in Paris. In Germany, the huge sales by Stargardt have yielded some very important music manuscripts, many of them, unsurprisingly, by Austro-German composers, but by no means all.

Auction catalogues thus constitute an important source of documentary information. They provide evidence that an item has been seen in public and often a useful description of that item. Of course, many private collectors choose to let scholars know of their holdings, but others wish to keep that information to themselves. In these latter cases a manuscript may disappear from view altogether, perhaps until the death of its owner, with the only record being the original sale catalogue.

It is important to point out, however, that auction catalogues are less useful where large mixed lots are concerned. For example, when some of the printed music belonging to Edward Clark was offered for sale at Sotheby's, it was offered as a large single lot in a number of cardboard cartons. It consisted almost entirely of twentieth-century scores by major composers. Clark, the husband of Elisabeth Lutyens, was the BBC's main contact with the musical avant-garde of the 1930s and he had a great enthusiasm for this repertoire. He had arranged the British premières of many such works and music offered at Sotheby's included first editions of Debussy, Schoenberg, Berg, Stravinsky and others. The catalogue mentioned all this, but failed to point out that the copy of the score of *La mer* was a particularly important one: it was one of only two copies owned by the composer, containing extensive revisions in his own hand. He gave one of these copies to the composer Edgard Varèse, and the other found its way into Clark's library. Clark's copy is now in the British Library,[5] has been consulted for the new edition in the Debussy *Oeuvres complètes*, and is readily available to scholars. But it was only through the vigilance of an antiquarian dealer that this source was recognised for what it was. In short, auction catalogues do not always tell the whole story.

Conversely, they sometimes tell the story in considerable detail and over the last few decades auction houses have taken increasing trouble to describe manuscripts with real care. It is not only the high-profile sales of musical manuscripts that provide useful material: sometimes sales of musical instruments have interesting manuscript and printed ephemera relating to a particular maker, and some music appears in general book sales. It is not only at the major houses, especially Sotheby's and Christie's, that music is to be found. Smaller auction houses, including provincial ones, sometimes offer musical items and it is still possible to find real bargains and, more importantly, to make exciting discoveries.

Auction catalogues themselves are readily found in large research libraries, and in the Copyright Deposit libraries. In the British Library there are also some auction records on index cards (compiled by the late A Hyatt King) which can provide an index to when an item was sold. Marked-up copies of sale catalogues, recording the destination of the material sold, are harder to find, though dealers often have these in their own reference collections. Sotheby's and Christie's publish price lists shortly after sales (these are now available on the internet), But they can be misleading, or provide incomplete information. On the printed price list, names are sometimes misspelt and sometimes do not appear at all. Material which has been bought in (i.e. has not sold), having failed to reach its reserve price, is seldom identified as such. It is here that the records of dealers who were present can be useful; in some cases a dealer's collection of catalogues, marked up by someone who was actually present at the sale, are to be found in libraries, but there are few if any major collections of such material in the public domain.

So the hardest thing to ascertain about material at auction, particularly one long ago, is the identity of the buyer (much less the vendor) and its current whereabouts. Catalogues serve as a marker for where something was on a particular day, but unless it was bought by a public collection, any extra information can be difficult to find. In one notorious case it was not difficult but distressing: the autograph manuscript of a Mozart Divertimento was bought by an American manuscript dealer and sold off one page at a time. Happily, such instances are rare.

Auction catalogues are of use to scholars not only for their descriptions of manuscripts but also because also because they may print some of the text of otherwise unknown letters, or be a useful source of illustrations. It should be remembered, however, that such illustrations are the copyright of the auction houses, who will almost certainly charge a reproduction fee to use them.

▶ DEALERS AND THEIR CATALOGUES

Second-hand and antiquarian dealers' catalogues can also be of considerable value, though the material itself is often not as glamorous as that
offered at auction. The alert dealer is often careful to describe, for instance
small musical differences between different editions of a work, drawing
attention to discrepancies and variants that might otherwise remain
unknown. One small but important example springs to mind: a dealer's
catalogue from the early 1990s which offered two ostensibly identical
copies of the Stravinsky piano sonata, both apparently the first edition.
These two copies contained substantial musical differences which would
not have been apparent from even the closest scrutiny of the title page, the
wrappers, or the printing details. It takes a dealer with a wide experience
and a flair for such bibliographical curiosities to discover and describe such
interesting differences in editions. In this case it was Richard Macnutt, an
immensely respected bibliographer in his own right as well as a distinguished dealer, in his last catalogue before his retirement, who had these
Stravinsky items, and it took a dealer with that sort of knowledge and
interest to notice that there were these differences. This is one example of
many that could be cited: dealers, unlike auction houses, hold stock and
live with the material, acquiring a detailed first-hand knowledge, and thus
the ability to identify important or interesting copies.

Another valuable aspect of the imaginative dealer is the building of a
collection or a catalogue on a particular type of music or theme. A fine
example was the enormous collection of music by women composers
offered by Richard Macnutt in his Catalogue 110 in 1980. Similarly, his
two or three catalogues devoted to opera offered important material in a
clearly focused way. In my own years as an antiquarian dealer, my firm of
Burnett & Simeone Ltd issued two catalogues devoted to a single publisher
– Universal Edition – which included several hundred items. In Germany,
Hans Schneider, of Tutzing, (who celebrated 50 years as an antiquarian
music dealer in 1999) has made a speciality of this kind of catalogue, having
issued several devoted to a single composer such as Brahms, or a single
publisher such as Schott. This was a particularly impressive catalogue,
ranging from some of Schott's very earliest publications in the eighteenth
century to Hindemith, Hans Werner Henze and beyond. Lisa Cox's catalogue of keyboard music (summer 1997) included many items signed by
the composers concerned, while May & May's catalogue of Full Scores of
British composers (No. 232, June/July 1997) included much material
(acquired from a job lot of Novello's file copies) that is otherwise very difficult to find.

Some non-specialist antiquarian dealers have issued music catalogues
in the past. Among the most consistent and impressive of these are those
issued by Maggs Bros., a firm whose first important music catalogue was

an immense publication from the 1920s. Later Maggs catalogues included their *Catalogue 1012: English Composers of the Twentieth Century* (February 1981), which contains some particularly useful descriptions of Elgar material.

More than auction houses, dealers have particular specialities. The late Hermann Baron (whose business still thrives under the direction of Christel Wallbaum), was always strong on rare music literature and unusual opera vocal scores, as well as having a fine general stock. These pockets of specialisms, often the result of personal enthusiasms, are true of many dealers now. Valérie Emery, whose business, Travis & Emery, has continued since her death, was often strong in British music, including important seventeenth and eighteen-century material. Travis & Emery is now the only remaining British antiquarian music dealer with retail premises in central London.

There are in England some dozen active specialist music dealers. Unlike auction houses, they come and go: Richard Macnutt has retired, firms like Cecil Hopkinson's First Edition Bookshop have become distant and cherished memories, and my own firm of Burnett & Simeone Ltd issued its last catalogue in the early 1990s. May & May, who issued their first catalogue in April 1964, was active until John May's death in December 1998.[6] Others remain: the doyen of these is, without doubt, Albi Rosenthal, whose firm, Otto Haas, has been responsible for some of the most spectacular manuscript sales of the last last-century. He is a magnificent scholar as well as someone with a real passion for music and he is perhaps the most distinguished and respected of all music dealers of modern times. A much more recent entrant to the field is Lisa Cox of Exeter, whose distinctive and elegantly produced catalogues have included some very important material in the last few years: magnificent set designs for opera and ballet, as well as portraits, manuscripts, printed music and some intriguing ephemera. Items such as early librettos – unlikely to appear at auction – are important but relatively inexpensive sources, and significant examples have regularly appeared in Cox's catalogues.

May & May's catalogues, the last of which was No. 250, broke into two types: those for music literature in which John May was a leading specialist, and a less frequent series devoted to printed music, notably an impressive multi-issue series devoted to piano music, divided into alphabetical segments. The firm's interests were very wide-ranging, including unusual material from Eastern Europe, and careful description of ostensibly ephemeral material such as concert programmes. Since John May's death his stock has been acquired by another distinguished specialist in musical literature, Rosemary Dooley of Grange-over-Sands. May & May's catalogues and business records are now at the British Library. Travis & Emery's catalogues divided into those for music literature, and two typed for printed music: 'London' catalogues containing second-hand material and 'Sarum' catalogues with some distinguished antiquarian items, particularly of British music.

It is often through dealers rather than auction houses that musicologists, composers and others dispose of their music libraries. John May had through his hands material from the collections of Christopher Palmer, Anna Instone, Julian Herbage and Trevor Harvey. My own firm offered books and music from the library of Humphrey Searle, the Harrison sisters, Basil Lam and others. Such collections are the life-blood of any dealer and often contain important and interesting material.

Many composers, conductors, critics and others have given their music to, or has been bought by, libraries. Examples include the library of Sir Thomas Beecham, now acquired by the University of Sheffield, and that of Sir Adrian Boult, which was given to the Royal College of Music. Many of Sir John Barbirolli's scores are now to be found in the Royal Northern College of Music.

Another conductor with a large library, but a much older one, was Sir George Henschel, friend of Brahms and one of the most important musicians active in late nineteenth-century London. Some of his music and books were still available from dealers in the 1980s, especially among the vast stock of Kenneth Mummery, whose business was wound up after his death. His stock also included a large quantity of early twentieth-century British music from the library of Gordon Bryan. As well as music, Mummery had a passion for cars: nobody who visited him will forget the sight of his magnificent Bentley with its registration number KM 15.

Each issue of the quarterly journal *Notes* includes a listing of recent catalogues received. This is always worth checking to see which dealers are the most active and what specialist catalogues may have appeared.

▶ REFERENCES

Coover, J. (1988) *Music at Auction – Puttick and Simpson of London, 1794–1971*. Warren, MI: Harmonie Park Press (Detroit Studies in Music Bibliography No. 60)

King, A.H. (1963) *Some British Collectors of Music, c 1600–1960*. Cambridge: Cambridge University Press

Searle, A. (1999) preface to the *Catalogue of the Music Manuscripts in the British Library Stefan Zweig Collection*. London: British Library

▶ NOTES

1. See the article by David Evans and Larry Todd promised for *Current Musicology*, but not published as this book closes for press.
2. Sotheby's sale on 6 December 1991, lot 184.

3.   Sotheby's sale on 26 May 1994, lot 457.
4.   The first of these in London were: [Ballet] Books, Drawings, prints and Music relating to the Ballet and Dancing. (Sotheby's 16 July 1968); Ballet, Theatre & Opera Decor & Costume Designs, Portraits and Posters (Sotheby's 3 June 1971); and Sale of Ballet & Theatre Designs (Sotheby's 15–16 December 1969). Even the prospectus is worth having for its many illustrations.
5.   Shelfmark K.5.d.16.
6.   See Lewis Foreman's obituary in *Brio*, Spring/Summer 1999 36, No. 1, 2–5.

5 Copyright

Ian Ledsham

> 'Copyright is a political and economic, not a moral, issue.'
>
> (Frith, 1988)

▶ THE HISTORICAL PERSPECTIVE

These trenchant words, written in the late twentieth century, would have been well understood by the eighteenth-century exponents of copyright. Then, the idea of copyright as a property right was initially dismissed. Its aim was to provide protection for the economic investment made by a publisher. It is interesting that, in the late twentieth century, the concept of copyright as a property right is now fully accepted.

Copyright is a child of the age of printing. Before the (comparatively) easy reproduction of a written text the printing process offers, the control of written material could be exercised in simple ways: chaining up the books (as in the medieval library), or restricting access to them (so vividly described in Umberto Eco's classic, *Il Nome della Rosa*). The threat posed by mass reproduction was both political – creating a more literate and knowledgeable proletariat – and economic – in that the printer-publishers and authors had created a market, and once having placed their product in the market-place, made it available to rivals who could use the same system of mass reproduction to exploit their competitors' material.

The earliest copyright act in the UK worthy of the name is generally accepted to have been the Statute of Anne, 1709, and was designed to protect against this exploitation. The protection was granted to the publisher, not the author. It was to be another 65 years before the separate but intertwined concepts of 'the proprietary author and the literary work' (Rose, 1993, p. 91) finally emerged. Many of the arguments which went on in the eighteenth century were about establishing such 'moral' rights. The opposition to these ideas was strong:

> *'All the plaintiffs can claim is, the ideas which the books commu-nicate. These, when published, the world is fully in possession of as the author was before. From the moment of publication, the author could never confine them to his own enjoyment ... The act of publication has thrown down all distinction, and made the work common to every body; like land thrown into the highway, his become a gift to the public.'*
>
> Sir Joseph Yates, defending in the case of *Tonson v Collins* [1760], quoted in Rose, 1993, p. 77

The opponents to this argument continued the estate metaphor, as, for example, William Blackstone, who replied to Yates that publishing a book was 'more like making a way through a man's own private grounds, which he may stop at pleasure; he may give out a number of keys, by publishing a number of copies; but no man who receives a key, has thereby the right to forge others, and sell them to other people (Rose, 1993, p. 91).

Finally, in 1774, the House of Lords ruled that there was no perpetual property right under Common Law, and re-affirmed the supremacy of the statute law, which granted a limited term of copyright.

The third constituent in this explosive mixture, the information consumer, did not become a powerful force until the means of mass repro-duction became widely available at an affordable price. The development of film and broadcasting, the tape recorder, the photocopier, and more recently the personal computer, the digital sampler and the World Wide Web, has created economic pressures which in their own way are no less disruptive than the pirate publishing of the seventeenth and eighteenth centuries.

The relentless technological development has widened the concept of author and publisher. If one regards 'author' as originator and 'publisher' as facilitator, then in the former category must come not only author (for which read 'composer' in the context of music) but performer, producer and photographer; and in the latter group, not only publisher, but recording company, film company, broadcasting organisation. In the arguments that have raged over the last 20 years and are still raging, it is easy to take extreme positions. On the one side, the developers of electronic equipment and soft-ware are cast as parasitic cowboys intent on depriving authors and publish-ers of their just rewards, whilst on the other side, rights owners are portrayed as latter-day Canutes, striving to hold back the tide of technological pro-gress. In the middle is the bemused user, uncertain what is permissible and, depending on one's viewpoint, either exploiting this uncertainty for personal gain or wandering heedless in the minefield that is intellectual property law.

Rose (1993) gives a very readable account of the development of copy-right – at least from the general standpoint. Music, as ever, lagged behind in the development of copyright, and it was not until 1777 that music was granted a copyright. Hunter (1986) gives an excellent account of the development of music copyright in the UK in the eighteenth century. Coover (1985) looks at the problem a century later, using articles from the trade press of the period.

▶ THE PRESENT SITUATION

Copyright in the UK is currently governed by the provisions of the Copyright, Designs and Patents Act 1988, and by various pieces of amending regulation issued since the Act came into force. The most significant of these are:

- Copyright (Librarians and Archivists) (Copying of copyright material) Regulations 1989
- Computer Copyright (Computer Programs) Regulations 1992
- Duration of Copyright and Rights in Performance Regulations 1995
- Copyright Rights in Performance: the Copyright and Related Rights Regulations 1996.
- Copyright and Rights in Databases Regulations 1997 [SI 1997 No. 3032]

At the time of going to press, the Copyright (Visually Impaired Persons) Bill is almost at the point of enactment. Its aim is to remove some of the difficulties facing visually-impaired people who need conversions of copyright materials into alternative formats while balancing any solution with the rights of copyrights owners.

Recent acts stem in part from the harmonisation of legislation within the European Union, as outlined in the EEC Council Directive 93/98.

Successive copyright acts this century have expanded in length exponentially.

'The [UK] Act of 1911 was a timid little creature. It contained a mere 37 sections. Some believe it was the best Copyright Act we ever had. The 1956 Act was a formidable affair. It contained 57 sections. It held sway during a period in which copyright legislation burgeoned. But the 1988 Act puts all of this to shame. It contains over 300 sections, about 280 of which relate to copyright and its new offspring, design right. The increase in size cannot be attributed merely to a trend toward verbosity in modern legislation, although there certainly is some of that present in the 1988 Act. To a large extent, it reflects the spread and creation of new copyright-type rights . . .'

Laddie, 1996, p. 253

The amount written on the subject has similarly exploded. Far from being a legal backwater, intellectual property law is now seen as an exciting, and presumably profitable, area of the profession.

Much that has been written is for the lawyer. The standard English legal text on intellectual property law is Laddie *et al.* (1995). One or two good general guides have been written – again, covering the whole topic. Dworkin and Taylor (1990) provides useful explanations and examples to illustrate the individual sections of the act, the complete text of which is printed as an appendix.

Performers' rights and recording right are covered exhaustively by Arnold (1990) – but this too is a lawyer's text. The 1996 regulations have rendered this somewhat obsolete.

An early series of articles on the 1988 Act, designed for the legal profession but eminently readable, appeared in the *Solicitors Journal* in 1989 (Walton and De Freitas, 1989). These look at the act chapter by chapter and discuss the likely effects. Despite their age – written before any case law had arisen from the act – they usefully bridge the gap between lawyer and non-specialist.

For the lay reader, two very useful guides have emanated from the information professionals' bodies, the Library Association (LA) (since January 2002 the Chartered Institute of Library and Information Professionals (cilip)) and Aslib. Wall (1993) – Aslib's contribution – and Cornish (2001) (from the LA) in many ways adopt similar styles. The main provisions of the act are outlined clearly, and their effects on different types of material are examined. Wall writes at rather more length; Cornish's revised edition has been able to take account of EU harmonisation. In addition to these full-length books, the LA has produced a series of short booklets (LA, 1999a–f) aimed at specific library sectors.

All of these, however, are general books. Despite the fact that music lagged behind the book world in establishing copyright, music and the music industry are, in many respects, at the leading edge of copyright development. The value of rights – as opposed to simple publishing – has been recognised by music publishers for many years. And it is certainly true that many music publishers make their living not from printing and selling music or records, but from owning and exploiting the various rights subsumed under the term 'copyright'. The spawning of these so-called related rights – performing, recording and now rental rights – has been driven to a considerable extent by the powerful interests of the music world, now allied with the wider media industry.

There have been a number of articles on music copyright, and occasional monographs. Frith (1993), for example, gives radical – some might say polemical – coverage of the political and economic aspects of copyright. His is not – nor does it set out to be – a guide to music copyright. De Freitas (1989) examines the music aspects of the 1988 Act – but again, almost *ante factum*. A similar review of the 1976 US Act will be found in Lichtenwanger (1979).

A search of the World Wide Web for material on music copyright will reveal a vast number of items. Many are ephemeral in nature and of limited value. The Music Library Association in the USA produces a website guide, *Copyright for Music Librarians* (<http://www.lib.jmu/org/mla>), though this is, naturally, geared to the US situation. In the UK, the British Educational Communications and Technology Agency produces a useful information sheet on copyright involving electronic materials on its website (<http://www.becta.org.uk/technology/infosheets/ntml/copyright.html>). Though aimed at schools this contains useful information. Quite a number of law firms also maintain websites.

For this reason, it seemed sensible to devote a good part of the remainder of this chapter to an analysis of the 1988 Act (and successive regulations) in the context of music.

The 1988 Act lays down principles in five main areas:

- what is protected;
- who owns the copyright;
- what rights the owner may exercise;
- how long the rights in a particular work last; and
- exceptions and permitted use.

WHAT IS PROTECTED?

- *Literary works*: not only books, but any written work, including letters, memos, computer programs, etc.
- *Dramatic works*: including choreography and mime. There must be some spoken words or dramatic actions. Lack of dialogue is no disqualification.
- *Artistic works*: Graphic works, photographs, sculptures, etc. regardless of merit. Works of architecture require artistic merit to qualify.
- *Musical works*: Musical score, including any annotations or directions, but not the words of vocal works.
- *Sound recordings*: Every type and medium of recording.
- *Films*: Any medium from which moving images can be reproduced.
- *Broadcasts*: Transmission by 'wireless telegraphy', including cable services.
- *Published edition*: The right in the layout and typography of literary, musical and dramatic works.
- *Publication right*: The right in the first publication after the expiry of copyright protection of a previously unpublished work.

The following sections, sometimes accompanied by tabular or other representations, attempt to summarise the main provisions in these areas. They cannot, in the space allotted, cover every contingency, but attempt to provide a summary of the basic principles.

Literary works

The inclusion of computer programs as literary works was a valuable recognition of the fact that copyright extends to the digital medium. The act was formulated before the rapid expansion of the 'information superhighway', and the instant transmission of data across national boundaries and legal jurisdictions. This provision is restricted to the content of the actual programs which manipulate the data. The intellectual content of individual files – e.g. the text of this chapter – is covered as literary work, or as a musical work or artistic work, as appropriate. The question of copyright in the digital context is currently under discussion world wide.

Dramatic works

The actions of a dramatic work – such as choreography – are now covered by copyright. Rightly so, since they are creative works. The musical content of a dramatic work – the songs in a musical, for example, would be covered by musical copyright.

Artistic works

The important provision here is that artistic merit is not a criterion in deciding whether something is a work of art. This is a quite reasonable provision: the determination of artistic worth is generally a matter of some contention! In the case of architectural works, however, artistic merit is taken into consideration. From the musicians' viewpoint, this is not a major consideration. What is important is that most photographs and drawings are covered by copyright – subject to the time limits noted later.

Musical works

The notes, expressions marks and other annotations – but not the words or editorial preface, commentary, etc. – are covered by the musical copyright. The words and editorial material may, of course, be covered by literary copyright. This means that in the case of most musico-dramatic and vocal works there will be at least two copyrights. In fact, many musico-dramatic works could have several copyrights. A musical based on a novel would have copyrights covering the novel, the libretto and the music. If translated into another language, then an additional copyright comes into existence! And that is just in the printed version.

Sound recordings, films (and videos) and broadcasts

The wording of the act attempts to cover all existing and likely future types of recording and broadcasting in its definition of what constitutes these formats. The copyright here is in the actual format.

Published edition

This is a confusing term for this right. It covers the typographical layout, and is effectively an additional protection for a publisher. It does not refer to the intellectual content of an edition.

Publication right

This is a new right introduced in Copyright Rights in Performance: the Copyright and Related Rights Regulations 1996 and applies to literary, dramatic, musical and artistic works and films.

WHO OWNS THE RIGHT?

- *Literary, dramatic and musical works*: The author
- *Artistic works*: The artist
- *Sound recordings and films*: The person making the arrangements for the recording or filming
- *Broadcasts and cable*: The person making the broadcast
- *Published editions (i.e. typography, etc.)*: The publisher
- *Publication right*: The publisher

Notes

'Author' here means composer, playwright, librettist, translator, choreographer, etc. 'Artist' includes photographer, engraver, sculptor, etc.

Where a work has been created by an employee wholly as a part of his or her employment, the rights belong not to the individual creator but to the employer. The employee may, however, have a moral right (SEE p. 65) in the work.

The original owner may assign the copyright to another person or body. For example, a composer may assign his or her rights to a publisher. Moral rights, however, cannot be assigned.

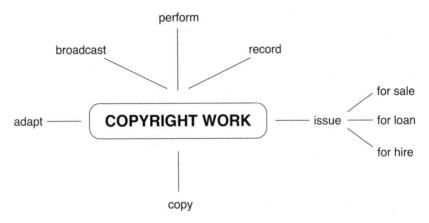

Fig. 5.1: The copyright holder's rights.

It should be clear by now, that music – especially dramatic music – can have a complex range of copyrights. The broadcast of a video of a Britten opera will have copyrights covering: the broadcast, the video, the soundtrack (should that be issued as a sound recording), the choreography of dance routines, the musical score, the libretto and the book on which it is based. The problem is often ascertaining who owns which right (see 'Who owns the right?').

Copying

The right to copy is the one that affects most people. Copying in any form without the right holders permission is, in theory, prohibited. The impracticality of this prohibition, and its potentially detrimental effect, have led the law-makers to allow certain exceptions to this prohibition. These are discussed in more detail in the section on 'Fair dealing'.

Issuing

This means issuing copies to the public. To most book publishers, this is the straightforward act of issuing copies for sale. In the music world, however, issuing copies for hire (rental) only is increasingly common. This has the dual benefit for the rights owner of controlling other rights – such as performing – and of increasing return through repeat fees. It is also significant that such hire rights are generally exercised through contracts – and therefore subject to contract law.

In 1979, the Public Lending Right Act (PLR) established the principle of remuneration to authors for the loan of their books by public libraries.

The 1988 Act created a rental right for sound recordings, and encouraged the creation of a licensing scheme to administer this right. The 1996 regulations have extended lending and rental right to all literary, musical and dramatic works, and to most artistic works. A new performer's property right has also been created, which not only makes it an offence to record a live performance, but also grants rental and lending rights to performers. The specified permitted exceptions are discussed in the section on 'Fair dealing'. Existing licensing schemes – which might provide the model for future schemes under these extended provisions – are discussed in the section on 'Licensing schemes'.

Performing/Broadcasting/Recording

The exercise of certain of these rights may lead to a new work with its own copyrights. For example, once the copyright holder has given permission for the public performance of a work, that performance is also subject to copyright – the rights holder in the performance being the performer. If the performance is recorded, a new set of copyrights for the producer of the recording is created. If that recording is then broadcast, a fourth layer of

---

HOW LONG DOES COPYRIGHT LAST?

Literary, dramatic and musical works:

- *Single author:* Author's life + 70 years
- *Joint authors:* 70 years after death of last author to die
- *Anonymous works:* 70 years from first publication
- *Artistic works:* Artist's life + 70 years

Sound recordings:

- *Published:* 50 years from date of publication
- *Unpublished:* 50 years from date of 'fixation'
- *Broadcasts & cable programmes:* 50 years from first broadcast
- *Films:* 70 years from death of last surviving of: principal director, author of screenplay, author of dialogue and composer of music specially composed for the film.
- *Computer-generated works:* 50 years from date of creation
- *Published edition:* 25 years from date of publication
- *Publication right:* 25 years from date of publication.

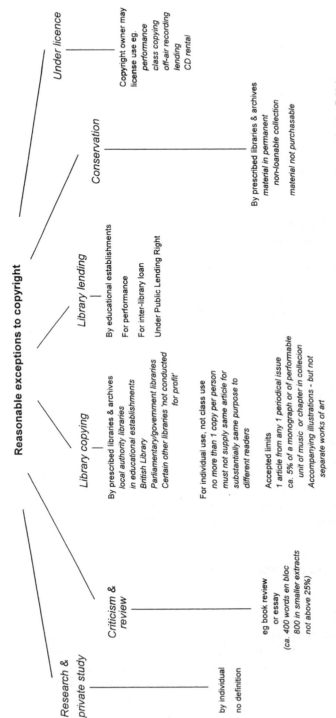

Reasonable exceptions to copyright

Research & private study

by individual
no definition

Criticism & review

eg book review
or essay
(ca. 400 words en bloc
800 in smaller extracts
not above 25%)

Library copying

By prescribed libraries & archives
local authority libraries
in educational establishments
British Library
Parliamentary/government libraries
Certain other libraries 'not conducted
for profit'

For individual use, not class use
no more than 1 copy per person
must not supply same article for
substantially same purpose to
different readers

Accepted limits
1 article from any 1 periodical issue
ca. 5% of a monograph or of performable
unit of music or chapter in collecion
Accompanying illustrations - but not
separate works of art

Library lending

By educational establishments
For performance
For inter-library loan
Under Public Lending Right

Conservation

By prescribed libraries & archives
material in permanent
non-loanable collection
material not purchasable

Under licence

Copyright owner may
license use eg.
performance
class copying
off-air recording
lending
CD rental

NB. The Act does not lay down specificlimits to fair dealing. The above suggestions are taken from guidelines drawn up by the British
Copyright Council and similar bodies.

Fig. 5.2: Reasonable exceptions to copyright.

rights is added – those of the broadcaster. Each of these sets of rights will overlap – and will be the source of financial reward for the rights owner. It is little wonder that the world of multimedia is seen as a minefield for the unwary and a pot of gold for the rights owners.

The complexity of administering these rights led to the creation of collecting agencies, of which the Performing Right Society was one of the earliest. These agencies are licensed by the rights owners to collect fees on their behalf. The concept of licensing – subject as it is to contract law – is being extended to more and more areas of copyright. It is in this area that most conflict and development will be seen in coming years. For more details see the section on 'Licensing schemes'.

► FAIR DEALING

The Act lays down certain circumstances in which a copyright work may reasonably be copied without the express permission of the copyright holder. These exceptions – outlined in Table 5.2 – are referred to under the general heading of 'Fair dealing'. In the US, such exceptions are referred to as 'Fair use'. The difference is more than merely semantic. Fair use implies a presumption in favour of the user of the material. It protects the right of the user to make reasonable use of copyright material. Certain criteria have been laid down which must be used in assessing whether or not contested use may be described as 'fair use'.[1] Fair dealing, on the other hand, is concerned with protecting the copyright holder, and is allowed only in limited circumstances.

In recent years the term 'permitted exceptions' has been used instead. This implies an even closer restriction and a stronger emphasis on protecting holder's rights. It should be noted, also, that the exceptions apply principally to literary and musical material. There is no fair dealing provision for artistic work or recordings – with the specific exception of the home videoing of material for the sole purpose of 'time-shifting'.

Research and private study

No guidelines are offered as to what may be copied under this heading. What is clear, is that *private* study means that. It is clearly indicated that, for example, instructing the individual members of a class to go and make copies of the same article for study is not private study but class use, even though each individual will make only one copy of the relevant article. How much may be reasonably copied is not specified either. The generally available advice is to follow the guidelines laid down for library copying.

Library copying

Prescribed libraries may copy material on behalf of a library user or another library provided that only one copy of a work is being supplied and that the librarian has no reason to believe that other users are copying substantially the same material at substantially the same time – in other words, that class use is not suspected. As many librarians would agree, this puts an almost impossible responsibility on library staff – who may be held personally liable for any illegal copying. Guidelines as to what proportion of an item may be copied have been drawn up by various organisations representing copyright holders. The guidelines for literary material are listed in Table 5.2. Music is dealt with in the section on 'Fair copying for music'. Artistic works included in a literary work – for example the plates in a book – may not be copied. Incidental copying – where, for example a small illustration is embedded in text which is being legally copied – is not usually regarded as infringement.

Library lending and rental

Copyright and performer's property right are not infringed by the lending for non-commercial rental of material by educational establishments or prescribed libraries and archives *except* public libraries. Nor is copyright infringed by the lending by public libraries of books included in the PLR scheme.

The definition of lending and rental does not include making available material:

- for public performance, or playing or showing in public;
- for public exhibition;
- for 'on-the-spot' reference; or
- for lending between libraries.

These are not matters of fair dealing: these acts are not considered lending or rental and there is no lending or rental right to be exercised in these cases.

In the context of music, the loan or non-commercial rental of sets of orchestral parts and vocal scores is clearly designed for 'public performance', and so such materials would seem to be excluded from lending right. The lending of a study score or piece of piano music for home use is clearly not public performance. It remains unclear exactly how this new right – which could affect not just music, but the loan of pictures from picture libraries, of videos and films, and, presumably, of talking books – will operate. The legislators clearly hope that some agreement similar to the BPI/LA licence will emerge (see the section on 'Licensing schemes').

Criticism and review

Criticism – even bad criticism – is rarely economically damaging. Most copyright holders are only too glad of the free advertising that criticism constitutes.

Conservation

It is interesting, and encouraging, that the Act should consider the question of preserving material. Such copying is limited to certain prescribed libraries and under certain stringent conditions. It is, however, a welcome step in the right direction.

Licensing

Though covered by the Act under the heading of exceptions, licensing is a special type of fair dealing, involving, as it does, the establishment of a contract between copyright holder and user. It is dealt with in a separate section on 'Licensing schemes'.

▶ FAIR COPYING FOR MUSIC

In the 1980s, the Music Publishers' Association (MPA) produced a booklet outlining guidelines for what it considered to be reasonable copying of copyright material. A revised version was issued in 1992. These guidelines are only agreed by members of the (UK) Music Publishers' Association and only apply to those publishers. In the absence of other guidelines, however, they provide a useful framework. Amongst the provisions are:

- Private study and research: Up to 5% of a performable unit (i.e. a of a single song or a movement from a symphony).
- Out-of-print material: With the permission of the copyright holder. If the copyright holder cannot be traced or does not reply within a reasonable period of time (e.g. six weeks), copying might be done on issuance of notice to the copyright holder – though it is not clear how you issue notice to an untraced copyright holder.

It should be mentioned at this stage that, compared with the 1970s and early 1980s, most publishers now offer excellent reprint-on-demand services. These will usually produce far better copies than the average public photocopier. This service also extends to obtaining copies (including sets) of works only published in an anthology. In many cases, payment will be required in advance because the set is being made to order, and a reasonable lead time is required.

- Page turning: A performer may make a copy of a page to avoid an awkward turn.
- Additional parts: Additional parts may be copied for a hired orchestral set (in an emergency) provided that the number of such parts does not exceed 25% of the total and that all such parts are returned to the publisher.
- Bowed parts: A society may make a single copy of hired string parts containing its bowings before erasing such markings and returning the hired material.

▶ LICENSING SCHEMES AND COLLECTING AGENCIES

Licensing schemes are a means by which copyright holders can authorise the use of their works on a large scale whilst retaining control of their rights without excessive administrative cost to themselves. Collecting agencies are bodies authorised by the rights holders to collect fees on their behalf – usually through some sort of licensing scheme. There is much to be said for licensing schemes from the viewpoint of both user and rights holders. For example, most performers and composers would not individually have the political or legal clout to insist on reasonable remuneration for the use of their work. The Performing Rights Society, on the other hand, can bring significant influence to bear, and, at the same time, simplify the process of gaining permission for performances for the user.

On the other hand, there is a growing feeling that the extension of licensing schemes to areas previously covered by fair dealing is eroding the limited rights of the users of copyright material.

Collecting agencies

Performing Right Society

Formed in 1914, the PRS licenses venues and charges on a sliding scale for performances. Monies collected are distributed to performers and composers.

PRS only licenses the performance of non-dramatic musical works (chamber music, pop songs, etc.) The fee charged is usually based on a sampling system. The responsibility for licensing lies with the venue.

The performing right in dramatic musical works (usually referred to as grand rights) is retained by the publisher. Permission to perform must be sought on each occasion, and the fee charged will be related to the type of performing group, the number of performances, etc. To protect this (economically) valuable right, publishers usually control the use of the parts by the simple expedient of not publishing them.

The licence to perform non-musical dramatic works must be sought from the publisher. For *amateur* dramatic performance, many plays are licensed by two of the main script publishers, Samuel French and Warner Chappell.

Mechanical Copyright Protection Society, Phonographic Performance Ltd.

Equivalent of the PRS for recorded music, acting as collection agencies.

Licensing schemes

Copyright Licensing Agency

Licenses educational establishments, commercial copy shops and so on, to make copies over and above 'fair dealing' limits. This is particularly in the area of 'class sets'. This usually involves having designated 'multiple-copying' machines and paying a levy on such copies. The scheme may also relieve libraries of the tedious business of obtaining declaration forms.

Educational Recording Agency

Issues licences allowing educational establishments to record 'off-air' for educational purposes and to retain such copies. Recording 'off-air' at home, for private use, is legal in the UK 'to enable a programme to be viewed or listened to at a more convenient time. This time-shifting exception does not cover the making of recordings for placing in a collection for repeated viewing or listening' (DTI).

Licensing agencies only act on behalf of their members – usually the copyright owners. It is important to remember this. The CLA does not represent most UK music publishers, since the MPA has specifically opted not to be part of a licensing scheme. This means that class sets of music materials cannot be made under a CLA licence. The CLA publishes a list of exceptions to its licences. In a similar way, the ERA licence does not include permission to record Open University programmes – permission must be sought directly from the Open University.

BPI/LA

This agreement was drawn up between the British Phonographic Industry (representing the recordings manufacturers) and the Library Association (representing UK public libraries). It took several years to reach an agreed conclusion that allowed libraries to continue lending recordings and convince the rights holders that their commercial position was not under threat. The agreement allows public libraries to lend sound recordings (vinyl, CD and cassette) on the following conditions:

- only four copies of any recording per service point;
- no more than two of these should be in the same format;
- these two requirements may be applied on an authority-wide basis;
- new releases may not be issued for a period of three months after their release;
- this holdback may be waived by individual BPI members; and
- recordings may be issued for private domestic or educational use only.

Design & Artists Copyright Society (DACS) scheme

The DACS scheme is aimed at licensing slide collections in libraries. There are two different licences: one legitimises existing collections, the other licenses new material.

Newspaper licensing scheme

This is intended mainly for cuttings agencies and other large-scale users of copyright newspaper material. Use of material within the 'fair dealing' guidelines is still possible – though it remains unclear what proportion of material would be considered 'reasonable'.

► MORAL RIGHTS

Whilst the concept of a moral right has been evident in much of the argument over copyright since the eighteenth century, and was defined as such in the nineteenth century, it was not until the 1988 Act that any such right was enshrined within UK copyright law. Such rights cannot be assigned, and are held by individuals, not by corporate bodies.

Four principal rights are defined under moral right, and these are described in Table 5.1. An author must assert his or her moral rights at the time of publication. This is usually done by incorporating a form of words into the copyright statement within the article in question.

Table 5.1: Moral right

Paternity	The right to be identified as the author (composer, etc.) of a work.
Integrity	The right to prevent or object to derogatory treatment of a work.
False attribution	The right not to have a work falsely attributed.
Disclosure	The right of the commissioner of the work to withhold certain photographs or films from publication, exhibition or broadcast.

▶ INTERNATIONAL QUESTIONS

This brief study of copyright has concentrated on the UK situation, whilst trying to enunciate broad principles which are increasingly being applied to intellectual property law in other areas. Harmonisation of aspects of European Union copyright is only one point in a long series of international actions on copyright.

In the late nineteenth century it became increasingly obvious, with the movement of literature across borders, that international agreements on copyright were needed. The first international agreement on literary and artistic copyright was the Berne Convention (properly called the International Convention for the Protection of Literary and Artistic Works) of 1886. Three broad principles were adopted to afford a degree of international protection to copyright works:

- foreign works are protected in each member country in the same way as national works;
- minimum standards of protection are set down by the convention;
- copyright is automatically granted – there is no need for the author to register a work in order for it to be protected.

The original convention has been revised several times. The most recent revision was completed in Geneva in December 1996.

Only 14 countries originally signed the convention. Within the Americas, only Canada and Brazil were signatories. There were several attempts to create a Pan-American agreement, of which the most notable were the 1910 Buenos Aires Convention and the 1946 Washington Convention. By the 1950s, the Washington and Berne Conventions were the two major agreements, with a third bloc of countries that were outside any international agreements.

An attempt was made to reconcile the difference between the two major conventions and to provide a framework which might also be acceptable to those countries outside any formal international agreements. This culminated in the Universal Copyright Convention of 1952.

These conventions, however, were concerned with literary and artistic works (including, *inter alia*, musical and dramatic works). In the years after the Second World War, attempts were made to provide similar agreements protecting performing, recording and broadcasting rights. The International Convention for Protection of Performers, Producers of Phonograms and Broadcasting organisations (the Rome Convention) came into force in 1964. Like the Berne Convention, it establishes protection on the basis of national laws.

In theory, the Rome Convention provides protection against the making and distribution of 'pirate' copies. But because the Convention was not widely accepted, a further international 'Convention for the Protection of Producers of Phonograms against Unauthorized Duplication of their Phonograms' (The Geneva Convention) came into force in 1973.

The need for a wider body to discuss international copyright problems was evident by the 1960s. At the conference of Berne Union members in Stockholm in 1967, it was agreed to reform the administrative structure. One result of this was the World Intellectual Property Organization (WIPO), which holds a General Assembly every three years, but also hosts a conference in which non-members may participate – thus encouraging broad, and genuinely international, discussion.

A very readable account of the development of international agreements is given in Ploman (1980).

▶ FUTURE DEVELOPMENTS

The example given above of the Rome and Geneva conventions – which so clearly overlap – shows the difficulty of policing intellectual property in a technological age. As the technological capability to transcend physical – and legal – boundaries expands, so the desire to control intellectual property ever more tightly increases. It is this constantly fluctuating, never static relationship between message and medium which will create the greatest challenge for future developments. The balancing act is almost impossible: like a high-wire act but on a flying trapeze!

The argument is between genuine protection of rights, and realistic economic exploitation of those rights, and the equally genuine development of ideas and re-creation which are at the root of human progress. Two recent international discussion documents have perhaps shifted the balance towards the rights holders. In a follow-up to the Green Paper on Copyright and related rights in the information society, the European Commission rightly comments that 'It is the environment in which works and other protected matter will be created and exploited which has changed – not the

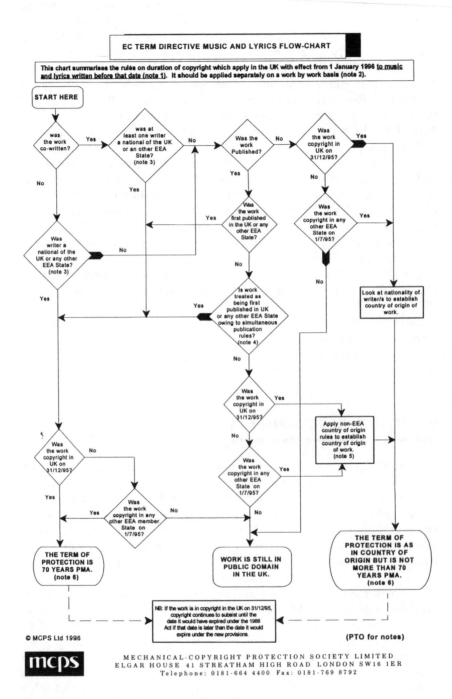

Fig. 5.3: EC term directive music and lyrics flow chart.

Notes for the Flow-Chart

1. Scope of the Flow-Chart

   The flow-chart cannot be used in the case of the following works :-

   1.1. Works of unknown authorship: please see the revised section **12** (3), (4), (5) and (8) of the Copyright Designs and Patents Act 1988 ("CDPA") for the rules applying here.
   1.2. Works generated by computer in circumstances such that there was no human author of the work: please see the revised section **12** (7) of CDPA for the rules applying here.
   1.3. Works written before 1 January 1996, but which have never been in copyright in the UK before that date: if these first qualify for copyright protection after 1 January 1996 they will be subject to the same rules as works written on or after 1 January 1996.

   It is emphasised that the flow-chart is a summary only of the relevant provisions of the Duration of Copyright and Rights in Performance Regulations 1995. On this basis, it does not cover all the peculiarities of the new rules and cannot be used as a substitute for legal advice.

2. Music and Words

   Please remember that words and music are separate copyrights in the UK and the flow-chart should therefore be applied to music and words separately.

3. EEA States

   The EEA Member States are: Austria, Belgium, Denmark, Finland, France, Germany, Greece, Holland, Iceland, Ireland, Italy, Liechtenstein, Luxembourg, Norway, Portugal, Spain, Sweden, UK.

4. Simultaneous Publication

   4.1. If published simultaneously in two or more countries only one of which was a Berne Convention country at the time of publication, and which is an EEA state, the work is treated as first published in the EEA.
   4.2. If published simultaneously in two or more countries two or more of which were Berne Convention countries at the time of publication, and at least one of which is an EEA state, the work is treated as first published in the EEA.
   4.3. Simultaneous publication means publication within 30 days of first publication.

   N.B. The drafting of the provisions relevant to 4.1 and 4.2 is not absolutely clear, and the above is MCPS's interpretation of the rules.

5. Non-EEA Country of Origin Rules

   5.1. If first published in a Berne Convention country which is a non-EEA state, and not simultaneously published elsewhere, the country of origin is that non-EEA state.
   5.2. If first published in a country which is neither a Berne Convention country nor an EEA state, and not simultaneously published elsewhere, the country of origin is the country of which the writer of the work is a national.
   5.3. If simultaneously published in two or more countries only one of which was a Berne Convention country at the time of publication, and none of which are EEA states, the country of origin is the Berne country.
   5.4. If simultaneously published in two or more countries two or more of which are Berne Convention countries, and none of which are EEA states, the country of origin is the Berne country with the shortest period of protection.
   5.5. Simultaneous publication means publication within 30 days of first publication.

6. 70 Years PMA

   This means 70 years after the end of the calendar year in which the author (or, in the case of a joint work, the last of the authors) dies.

Fig. 5.3: (continued)

basic copyright concepts.' (Commission of the European Communities, 1996, p. 8) In other words, the digital environment may be a new environment, but the principles of copyright are still applicable. However, it goes on to comment, in the context of reproduction rights, that:

> 'As regards reproductions for private purposes, the majority of parties consider that the issue should be tackled when harmonising the reproduction right, and this with respect to "digital" and "analogue" private copying. There is a substantial difference of opinion on the exact nature of "private copying." The majority of rightholders, editors[2] and parts of industry are against providing any kind of private copy exception (or any other limitation) [my emphasis] in the digital environment, arguing that such reproductions would conflict with the normal exploitation of the work. Such an unlimited exclusive right would in their view also be enforceable ... The need for an unlimited exclusive right is contested by other parties, most notably by user groups.'
>
> (Commission of the European Communities, 1996, p. 11)

In similar vein, Article 10 of the WIPO Copyright Treaty provides that:

> 'contracting parties may, in their national legislation, provide for limitations of or exceptions to the rights granted to authors of literary and artistic works ... in certain special cases that do not conflict with a normal exploitation of the work and do not unreasonably prejudice the legitimate interests of the author .. . [A]ny limitations of or exceptions to rights provided [shall be confined] to certain special cases that do not conflict with a normal exploitation of the work and do not unreasonably prejudice the legitimate interests of the author.'
>
> (WIPO, 1996a, p. 4)

The counter-argument is succinctly put by one of the leading authorities on UK intellectual property law, Mr Justice Laddie. In a lecture given in November 1995 he commented that 'modern copyright law provides, so some might say, an over-abundance of protection to the monopoly right owner.' (Laddie, 1996, p. 256) He points out – in the context of an exclusive licence to print government papers – the faintly ludicrous situation of 'the legislature seeking to make money out of the exploitation of the legislation which it passes and which should be available for all of us to see and consult' (p. 259). Frith (1993) compares the present situation, where rights holders seek to prevent not only the illegal exploitation of their material but also, seemingly, to control its use, with the eighteenth-century conditions which led to the establishment of copyright as we now know it.

'Copyright was designed to protect publishers not against authors and users but against other publishers, against piracy' (Frith, 1993, p. 19).

This has been what Law (1994) describes as 'but a stroll in the tangled fringes of copyright.' Though not written from the viewpoint of the legal specialist, it seems appropriate to leave the final word to a specialist. Mr Justice Laddie, concluding his 1995 lecture, comments:

> 'not all copying is bad ... sometimes, copying and developing are to the good ... I do not advocate an unprincipled free-for-all. But I suggest that the scales are at the moment weighted far too much in favour of would-be copyright owners.'
>
> (Laddie, 1996, p. 260)

▶ REFERENCES

Arnold, R. (1990) *Performers' rights and recording rights: UK law under the Performers' Protection Acts 1958–72 and Copyright Designs and Patents Act 1988.* Oxford: ESC Publishing (Intellectual Property Law Monographs)

Commission of the European Communities (1996) *Follow-up to the Green Paper on Copyright and related rights in the Information Society.* Brussels: The Commission [COM(96) 568 final]

Computer Copyright (Computer Programs) Regulations 1992. London: HMSO. [SI 1992/3233]

Copyright, Designs and Patents Act 1988. London: HMSO, 1988

Copyright (Librarians and Archivists) (Copying of Copyright Material) Regulations 1989. London: HMSO [SI 1989/1212]

Copyright Rights in Performance: the Copyright and Related Rights Regulations 1996. London: HMSO [SI 1996/2967]

Coover, J. (1985) *Music Publishing, Copyright and Piracy in Victorian England.* London: Mansell

Cornish, G. (2001) *Copyright: interpreting the law for libraries, archives and information services.* London: Library Association, Revised 3rd ed., 2001

De Freitas (1989) Copyright and music. *Journal of the Royal Musical Association,* 114, 69–79

Department of Trade and Industry. *Intellectual Property Portal*
<http://www.intellectual-property.gov.uk/index.htm>

Duration Of Copyright And Rights In Performance Regulations 1995. London: HMSO [SI 1995/3297]

Dworkin, G. and Taylor, R.D. (1990) *Blackstone's guide to the Copyright, Designs and Patents Act 1988.* London: Blackstone

Frith, S. (1988) Copyright and the music business. *Popular Music,* 7, 57–75

Frith, S. (ed.) (1993) *Music and copyright.* Edinburgh: Edinburgh University Press

Hudson, J. (1995) *UK copyright rules and regulations: help for the local church.* Croydon: Royal School of Church Music

Hunter, D. (1986) Music copyright in Britain to 1800. *Music and Letters,* 67, 269–82

Laddie, H., Prescott, P. and Vitoria, M. (1995) *The Modern Law of copyright and designs* (2nd edn.). London: Butterworth Law

Laddie, H. (1996) Copyright: over-strength, over-regulated, over-rated? *European Intellectual Property Review,* 18, 253–60

Law, S. and Lives, E. (1994) *Keep music legal: from the manuscript to mass production* (4th edn.). London: Sea Dream Music

Library Association (1996a) *Copyright in further & higher education libraries.* London: Library Association (4th ed., 1999)

Library Association (1996b) *Copyright in health libraries.* London: Library Association (3rd ed., 1999)

Library Association (1996c) *Copyright in industrial and commercial libraries* (3rd edn.). London: Library Association (4th ed., 1999)

Library Association (1996d) *Copyright in public libraries* (3rd edn.). London: Library Association (4th ed., 1999)

Library Association (1996e) *Copyright in school libraries* (3rd edn.). London: Library Association (4th ed., 1999)

Library Association (1996f) *Copyright in voluntary sector libraries* (2nd edn.). London: Library Association (3rd ed., 1999)

Lichtenwanger, W. (1979) 94–553 and all that: ruminations on copyright today, yesterday and tomorrow *Notes,* 35, 803–18 [Consideration of the 1978 US Copyright Act.]]

Ploman, E.W. and Hamilton, C. (1980) *Copyright: intellectual property in the information age.* London: Routledge & Kegan Paul

Wall, R.A. (1993) *Copyright made easier.* London: Aslib

Walton, A. and De Freitas, D. (1989) The Copyright, Designs and Patents Act 1988. *Solicitors Journal,* 133, 647–51; 670–75; 706–11; 734–36

WIPO (1996a) *WIPO Copyright Treaty: adopted by the Diplomatic Conference on December 20, 1996.* (as promulgated on the WIPO website at: <http://www.wipo.int/eng/diplconf/distrib/94dc.htm>)

WIPO (1996b) *WIPO Performances and Phonograms Treaty: adopted by the Diplomatic Conference on December 20, 1996.* (as promulgated on the WIPO website at: <http://www.wipo.int/eng/diplconf/distrib/94dc.htm>)

▶ USEFUL ADDRESSES

Authors' Licensing and Collecting Society
Marlborough Court
14–18 Holborn
LONDON EC1N 2LE
Email: <alcs@alcs.co.uk>
URL: <www.alcs.co.uk>

British Copyright Council
29–33 Berners Street
LONDON W1T 3AB
URL: <www.britishcopyright.
    org.uk>
    <copyright@bcc2.demon.
    co.uk>

British Phonographic Industry (BPI) Ltd
25 Savile Row
LONDON W1S 2ES
Email: <general@bpi.co.uk>
URL: <www.bpi.co.uk>

Copyright Licensing Agency
90 Tottenham Court Road
LONDON W1T 4LP
Email: <cla@cla.co.uk>
URL: <www.cla.co.uk>

Design & Artists Copyright Society
Parchment House
13 Northburgh Street
LONDON EC1V 0JP
Email: <info@dacs.org.uk>
URL: <www.dacs.org.uk>

Educational Recording Agency
New Premier House
150 Southampton Row
LONDON WC1B 5AL

Email: <era@era.org.uk>
URL: <www.era.org.uk>

Intellectual Property & Copyright Department
The Patent Office
Concept House
Cardiff Road
NEWPORT
Wales NP10 8QQ
Email: <enquiries@patent.gov.uk>
URL: <www.patent.gov.uk>
See also:<www.intellectual-
    property.gov.uk/index.htm>

Mechanical Copyright Protection Society
The MCPS-PRS Alliance
29–33 Berners Street
LONDON W1T 3AB
Email: Not available
URL: <www.mcps.co.uk>
See also: <www.mcps-prs-alliance.
    co.uk>

Music Publishers Association [UK]
3rd Floor
Strandgate
18/20 York Buildings
LONDON WC2N 6JU
Email: <info@mpaonline.org.uk>
URL: <www.mpaonline.org.uk>

Open University Worldwide Ltd.
Walton Hall
MILTON KEYNES MK7 6AA
Email: <ouwenq@open.ac.uk>
URL: <www.ouw.co.uk/home.
    shtm>

Phonographic Performance Ltd
1 Upper James Street
LONDON W1F 9DE
Email: Not available
URL: <www.ppluk.com>

Performing Right Society
29–33 Berners Street
LONDON WIT 3AB
Email: Not available
URL: <www.prs.co.uk>
See also: <www.mcps-prs-alliance.
   co.uk>

Samuel French
52 Fitzroy Street
LONDON W1P 6JR
Email: Not available
URL: <www.samuelfrench-
   london.co.uk>

Video Performance Ltd
Phonographic Performance Ltd
1 Upper James Street
LONDON W1F 9DE
*VPL shares offices with PPL and
does not have its own website. Its
trading division – Musicmall –
provides pre-licensed clips as well
as research and advice services at*
URL: <www.musicmall.co.uk>

Warner Chappell Music Group
161 Hammersmith Road
LONDON W6 8BS
Email: <webmaster.UK@
   warnerchappell.com>
URL: <www.arnerchappell.co.uk>

▶ NOTES

1. Those wishing to investigate the concept of fair use are referred to the Fair
    use website at Stanford University (<http://fairuse.stanford.edu>).
2. I take 'editor' here to mean 'publisher', in the sense of the French editeur,
    rather than the more usual English interpretation, equivalent to the French
    redacteur.

6 Computers and music – not forgetting CD-ROMs

Melanie Groundsell

Computers have played a growing role in musical research – and in musical composition – for some time now, a role given greater emphasis by the ever-increasing power and sophistication, and reducing costs, of personal computers and their peripherals including scanners, printers and specialised software. Those working in universities have access to the Joint Academic Network (JANET), and are privileged to enjoy effectively free provision of a range of services, including the internet. Those working independently may find that some of these services are more difficult to access, and at a personal cost that may inhibit access.

Many of the developments in music have been in multimedia. This seems to have been for a number of reasons. The development of compression techniques has made possible the use of video on CD-ROM, while sound cards are increasingly being used to facilitate musical excerpts and performances. Among the growing number of multimedia CDs are Voyager's Companion Series. These include Stravinsky's *The Rite of Spring*, and Schubert's *Trout* Quintet. These packages consist of a recording on CD and tutorial material. Similarly, Microsoft have produced Multimedia Strauss. Using this CD, users can view musical scores, learn about musical styles and learn about musical instruments. DVDs are yet another development in multimedia. Among the more notable ones are *Carols from King's* by Kings College Choir, directed by Stephen Cleobury, 2000. This includes external and internal shots of the chapel at King's College, Cambridge.

▶ CD-ROMs

Many of the resources now available on the internet are also available in CD-ROM format, allowing a choice of subscription options. Many of the CD-ROMs, such as the *International Index of Music Periodicals* (IIMP), are duplicates of their online equivalents. The *Répertoire International de Littérature Musicale* (RILM) is available in CD-ROM format as MUSE, which contains two databases, RILM (1969–) and the Music Catalogue of the US Library of Congress (1960–). In its combined format it includes citations for catalogues, journals, conferences, papers, books and sound recordings. Similarly, the magazine *Gramophone* hosts Gramofile, an online database of CD reviews on the internet (<http://www.gramofile.co.uk>). It also has an inexpensive CD-ROM format which offers the additional ability to bookmark, annotate and group particular recordings. This is a particularly useful feature for those who aim to build up their own catalogue of recordings. Software for this task is outlined under 'Record collectors' cataloguing systems' below. The CD-ROM also has the benefit of a fully updated listing of more than 30 000 non-reviewed items from the *Gramophone* database.

Many general reference works used by music researchers are also available in CD-ROM format. Among them is *CPM Plus*, which contains bibliographic records for printed music up to 1996 held in the British Library. Key general texts, such as The Bible, are also available in a searchable full text format on CD-ROM.[1]

▶ MUSIC SOFTWARE

Music software can be split into two categories: sequencer software and notation software. This chapter is concerned with notation software. Some of the sequencer packages, such as Personal Composer and Cubase, also have notation capabilities. However, music notation is complex, and producing scores for orchestras or choirs demands flexibility. Sequencing software rarely offers freedom over page layout, and the entry of special characters and types that is needed for publication. A listing of these packages can be found at several online sites, and in many printed resources. Printed listings include those in *Software and CD ROM Reviews on File*.[2] Produced monthly, this collection of software reviews goes back to 1985. There is also the more general *Software Encyclopedia*, which provides titles, publishers and brief descriptions of many software programmes.[3]

▶ NOTATION PACKAGES

Determining your needs is the key to obtaining a notation package. Some programmes will allow part extraction, change of page layout, multiple staves and transposition. Others will allow real time and step time MIDI input. There will be variations in the type of printer supported, and in the output of orchestral/instrumental parts. One of the main issues with any notation programme is how notes are entered on the screen. There are three different methods. The first is to use an alphanumeric code such as Digital Representation of Musical Score (DARMS). The second is to create notes on the screen by using either a mouse or a music keyboard. The third is to allow entry via a Musical Instrument Digital Interface (MIDI). Although entry of notes via MIDI in real time (i.e. the notes appear on the screen as played) sounds an ideal solution to an otherwise tedious process of inputting notes via a mouse or QWERTY keyboard, the result is often far from perfect. Here, the piano part must be input in two sessions, one for the right and left hand. It is often quicker to input via step entry. This allows the user to select pitches and rhythms from a MIDI keyboard, mouse or computer keyboard and enter the notes one step at a time.

One other way of inputting notation is to use music scanning software that will convert printed music into MIDI files. This can then be played back or edited. Photoscore works with Sibelius software, and can convert up to 32 staves of music per page into MIDI files. Midiscan can work with Finale or any other standard MIDI files, and can convert up to 24 staves of music per page. Both Photoscore and Midiscan recognise pitches, durations, chords, accidentals, ties, clefs, key signatures and staff size. Music Publisher has options to allow scanning of music, along with entry from the keyboard. Its window-based layout provides options from pick lists and toolbars, which are especially useful to those who are new to music. It will run under Windows 95 or higher, although higher specifications are recommended for faster printing and better quality display of music.

Coda Finale is just one of the notation programmes. It comes in several formats: Coda Finale and Finale Allegro; PrintMusic and Notepad. All are available on Mac and PC. Finale Notepad is free, and offers a first taste of music notation software. PrintMusic is entry level notation software giving access to basic functions. Allegro and Finale offer an expanded version of the program. All versions of Finale will allow real time input and step entry.

Encore, published by Gvox is again available for both Mac and PC. Encore caters for jazzy, free swinging tempos. Like Finale, it allows a variety of editing and page layout functions. One of the other major music notation software packages is Sibelius 2, written by the brothers Jonathan and Ben Finn, and available for Mac and Windows. Previously, Sibelius was only available for use on an Acorn computer as a package which cost several thousand pounds. Whilst many professional composers made the investment, it was not one which the amateur or student were able to make. However, its release in a Windows version during 1998 meant that, while still expensive, it attracted a far wider user base. The software is notable for its intuitive feel and user friendliness coupled with its superb professional appearance on the page when printed, even in the most complex scores.

Fig. 6.1: A full score prepared using Sibelius software. This example from the score specially made by Rodney Newton for a Hyperion recording session of Sir Granville Bantock's unpublished early tone poem *Thalaber the Destroyer*. The orchestral parts were subsequently output from the same computer file. (With thanks to Hyperion Records.)

SmartScore Pro Edition 2.0 – for the PC, like Finale – allows step input from MIDI. Templates are set up for page layout although the user always has some control over design. In addition to step input, score also allows entry by alphanumeric code from the keyboard. There is little that Score cannot do in terms of notation, once learned.

▶ BIBLIOGRAPHIC MANAGEMENT PACKAGES

There are a growing number of products that enable users to import references from online databases and CD-ROMs, and from them to generate footnotes and bibliographies. These are then exported into different styles, which often vary from one journal to another. The leading bibliographic managers are Reference Manager, Procite, Papyrus and EndNote.

Most managers will provide blank workforms in which users can fill in details of articles or books by hand. The workforms can usually be set up for different types of publications, i.e. Journals, book chapters, music, CDs. In many cases these workforms are already supplied within the manager.

Authority lists of journal abbreviations, authors' names or technical terms should also be provided. However, only some managers provide these. Once input into the database, the user can search the references, usually under title, journal, author names, and using Boolean operators.

These can then be added to an open word processed document. Managers differ as to which types of word processing programmes they recognise. Most seem to recognise Word for Windows or WordPerfect. It is worth checking with the supplier before ordering the product to see if a particular word processor is supported. Once the references are in the document, bibliographic managers should be able to construct a bibliography. This relies on the word processor being recognised and a system for identifying the bibliographic reference. Managers differ on how well this is achieved. Most managers will import records directly from online databases and CD-ROMs.

Again, the number and extent of sources supported by different managers varies. EndNote Plus 2 supports Dialog, ISI, Melvyl, OCLC and Silver Platter amongst others. It also supports MARC records, a particularly useful facility not available on all managers.

Of the four managers mentioned above, Reference Manager is designed for scientific publication. This affects the list of journal names and output formats. Procite has formats for music scores and CDs, and so may be of more use to musicians. A useful comparison of bibliographic management packages can be found at (<http://www.cse.bris.ac.uk/~ccmjs/rmeval99.htm>). With their ability to download references from external sources and to import them into standalone software, bibliographic management packages bring together both networked and non-networked sources. Although the two have been divided for the purposes of this book, they should be seen as complementary sources of information. Similarly, its is unlikely that printed sources of information will ever disappear. The expansion of electronic sources merely serve to provide other areas of research for scholars.

▶ COMPUTERS IN COMPOSITION AND ANALYSIS

Computers have for some time been used in the composition and analysis of music. Composers have been able to use sound synthesis techniques, algorithmic composition and computer analysis in new compositions. Some have even used analysis and pattern matching to create new pieces in the styles of various composers. David Cope's well-known experiments in the Musical Intelligence project allows just such creative applications, allowing music to be composed in the style of Bach and Mozart to Prokofiev and Scott Joplin.[4]

► RECORD COLLECTORS' CATALOGUING SYSTEMS

Although general computerised cataloguing systems such as Cardbox have been used to catalogue recordings, a variety of mainly specialist suppliers have marketed cataloguing systems for record collectors. Early versions of some of these have not been as user friendly as some might have wished, though they are generally inexpensive. However, with the move to Windows, these systems have become easy to use, a facility reinforced by the preloading of data for a substantial number of 'standard works' and composer details. Classic Collector 2000 is possibly the leading example of such software and can be viewed on the Web.[5] Comparative reviews of others have appeared in *BBC Music Magazine* and *Classic CD*.[6] Competitors and upgrades are advertised from time to time in the leading classical record collectors' magazines.

► BIBLIOGRAPHY

Bedell, J. (2001) Endnote 5.0 Biotech software & internet report. *The Computer Software Journal for Scientists*, 2, No. 6, 227–32

Biery, J. (1999) Sibelius Music notation software. *The American Organist*, 33, No. 11, 26

Cliff, T. (1996) The Path to Perfection. *Music Teacher*, 75, No. 1, 24

Coda Finale 2000 (Mac/Win) music-notation software. *Electronic Musician*, 16, No. 2 (2002), 202

Etter, S.C. (2000) Review of Reference Manager, Version 9. *Journal of Computing in Higher Education*, 11, No. 2, 136

Finale 2001: Music notation software. (2001) *Macworld: the Macintosh Magazine*, January, 91

Finale 2001: Music notation software (PC, Mac). (2000) *Keyboard*, 26, No. 11, 98

Hanson, T. (1995) *Bibliographic Software and the Electronic Library*. Hatfield: University of Hertfordshire Press

Herbert, T.L. (2002) Endnote 5 for Windows. *Journal of Chemical Information and Computer Sciences*, 42, No. 1, 134

Johnson, B. (1999) Credit Where Credit is Due – Research Information Systems Reference Manager 9.0 for Citation Management. *Scientist*, 13, No. 9, 17

Kuzmich, J. (1995) Music Scanning Software. *The Instrumentalist*, 50, No. 4, 70

Kuzmich, J. (1995) New Voyager Software Links Music CDs, CD Roms, Web. *Publishers Weekly*, 242, No. 31

Lefkowitz, D.S. (2001) Finale 2000: Music Notation Software. *Notes*, 57, No. 4, 975–81

McMahon, T.E. (1998) Endnote. *Journal of Academic Librarianship*, 24, No. 5, 430–1

New Wave Music. (2000) *PC World*, 18, No. 7, 125

Nordgren, L. (1994) Microsoft Musical Instruments: an interactive journey into the world of musical instruments. *CD Rom Professional*, 7, No. 6, 62

Procite Internet Enabler Helps Organize Web Resources Offline (1996). *Online*, 20, No. 4, 67

Rader, G. (1996) Creating Printed Music Automatically. *Computer*, 29, No. 7, 14

Reed, E.A. (1997) Computer Centers for Students: a survey of software programs for music students. *Clavier*, 36, No. 7, 14–18

Sandford, P. (2000) Off Theme: Evaluation of Endnote 4 Reference Management Software. *Vine*, No. 121, 55

Sandow, G. Notation Software Roundup. *Musician*, No. 239 (October 1998), 69

Satya-Murti, S. (2000) Endnote v.4 (CD-ROM); Reference Manager 9 (CD-ROM); Procite 5.0 (CD-ROM). *JAMA: the Journal of the American Medical Association*, 284, No. 12, 1579

Wilson, T. (1997) EndNote Plus 2.3 with Endlink 2.1. *International Journal of Information Management*, 17, No. 6, 470–2

▶ NOTES

1. The Bible in English (1996). Alexandria, VA: Chadwyck-Healey.
2. Software and CD ROM reviews on file. ISSN 1087-7367. (New York: Facts on File)

3.   Software Encylcopedia. Bowker 08352 43966 May 2001. (New Providence, NJ: Bowker, 2001)
4.   Cope, D. (1996) Experiments in Musical Intelligence. Madison, Wis.: Ar Editions.
5.   <http://ourworld.compuserve.com/homepages/lion elk>.
6.   Shop Window. Classic CD, May 1997, 86.

7 Internet and music

Melanie Groundsell

Over the last few years the internet has grown into an unprecedented medium of communication and resource on an international scale. The World Wide Web has made these resources accessible to a huge audience. The quantity of information is now so great that one of the problems of the internet is understanding where to access and locate the documents and data. The proliferation of search engines has sometimes confused rather than helped in the quest to index the 'Net'. Moreover, different service providers provide default search engines which many users doubtless accept. Each search engine makes claim and counterclaim that it has more sources than the others. The true picture is that only a small percentage of the internet is indexed by search engines (Lawrence and Lee, 1998). In addition to the traditional sites such as HotBot, AltaVista and Yahoo, there are specialist music search engines such as Music Search (<http://www.musicsearch.com>) which aim to target purely music resources.

This chapter will group internet resources into five categories :

1 libraries and their catalogues;
2 reference books and bibliographies also published in hard copy;
3 specialist databases and information not otherwise available, including radio stations, orchestras' and opera companies' websites, and composers' and artists' personal websites;
4 the record industry, magazines, record companies, retail organisations selling CDs and books, the second-hand trade;
5 the future development of the internet.

▶ LIBRARIES AND THEIR CATALOGUES

Many of the major university music departments and conservatoires of the UK now provide access to their catalogues via the World Wide Web. A full list of these is available from the Networked Information Services and Systems (NISS) home page (<http://www.niss.ac.uk>). Also available from the NISS listing are links to university music libraries and departments in France, Germany, Italy and the USA.

It is difficult to single out particular sites. However, LOCIS (<http://www.loc.gov>) the Library of Congress catalogue, is a useful site for musicians and librarians alike. The Harvard Online Library Information System (HOLLIS) (<http://hollisweb.harvard.edu>) also gives access to Harvard University Union Libraries Catalogues. Another catalogue worth an early visit is that of the Institut de Recherche et Coordination Acoustique/ Musique (IRCAM) (<http://www.ircam.fr>) in Paris. This gives much information on music and technology literature. Still in Europe, Gabriel, the information server for Europe's national libraries (<http://minos.bl.uk/ gabriel>), includes access to the OPACs of Die Deutsche Bibliothek and the Bibliotheque Nationale de France. The Norwegian Universities participate in a shared library system, called BIBSYS (<www.bibsys.no>).

The British Library Catalogue of Printed Music is another resource that has an enormous research value. It is available online through the British Library website. CPM plus, which combines data from the Catalogue of Printed Music and the 1981– catalogue (up to 1996) is also available on CD-ROM and is published by Bowker Saur. Many of the music manuscripts acquired by the British Library are now available as the Manuscripts Online Catalogue (<http://molcat.bl.uk/>). The National Sound Archive at the British Library has now launched its catalogue, CADENSA, which includes entries for almost two and a half million recordings, encompassing commercially issued material and off-air recordings from over 100 years of recorded sound. This is now accessible via the Web on <http://cadensa.bl.uk>. For those looking for sets of performance music, Encore, the UK catalogue of sets of performance music in libraries, is now available on the Web (<http://www.peri.nildram.co.uk/encore. htm>). This covers the catalogues of public, academic, national, private and special libraries. Compiled by the International Association of Music Libraries, Archive and Documentation Centres (IAML), it is a valuable resource for orchestras and choirs.

Many musical institutions have developed extensive links to other musical resources. Royal Holloway and Bedford New College is notable in this respect, providing a wealth of resources from its 'Golden pages' (<http://www2.rhbnc.ac.uk/Music/Links/index.html>). Another comprehensive listing is available from Music Resources on the internet, compiled by Indiana University School of Music (<http://www.music.indiana.edu/ music resources>). This latter site is worth visiting for individual musicians, popular groups, performance, composition, the commercial world of music, online journals and magazines, and is well worth bookmarking. More sites are listed on a page at King's College, London(<http://www.kcl. ac.uk/depsta/iss/schools/hlsp/humanities/music.html>). In talking about individual libraries and institutions, we should not leave out professional associations such as the [American] Music Library Association (MLA) (<http://www.musiclibraryassoc.org>) and the International Association of Music Libraries, Archives and Documentation Centres (IAML) (<http://www.cilea.it/music/iaml/iamlhome.htm>). The former is the main professional organisation for music librarians in the USA. Its site includes a clearing house which contains documents that are of interest to music librarians on different topics. These are archived in a searchable index. The latter organisation, IAML, assists in promoting activities within music libraries. There are 22 national branches in 45 member countries. Their website has information on their conferences, membership and the association's journal. The American Musicological Society (AMS) also has useful pages of internet sites of interest to musicologists, which are also published in printed format (Davis, 1999).

▶ ELECTRONIC VERSIONS OF HARD COPY REFERENCE BOOKS AND BIBLIOGRAPHIES

One of the most exciting developments in networked music sources has been the appearance of several hard copy publications in electronic format, the most recent being New Grove II, which is, accessible via the internet (<http://www.grovemusic.com>), though on a subscription basis. New Grove II now includes the full text of the *New Grove Dictionary of Music and Musicians*, and the *New Grove Dictionary of Opera*. It will soon be joined by the *New Grove Dictionary of Jazz*. As well as allowing a search of the complete dictionary, perhaps the most interesting feature is the announcement of a regular updating service, which will increase in value as the years pass from its initial publication in January 2001. It is possible to subscribe for both monthly, annual and a timed 'MetroPass' for limited hours.

RILM (*Répertoire International de Littérature Musicale*) (<http://www.rilm.org>) now provides access to its abstracting service via CD-ROM and the World Wide Web. However, both are available to subscribers only, either as an annual or as a 'pay per search' service.

Similarly, part of *RISM* (*Répertoire International des Sources Musicales*) can now be searched via the Web, but, unlike *RILM*, this is a free database. Another free database that is useful for musicologists is *Doctoral Dissertations in Musicology* (<http://www.music.indiana.edu/ddm>), available from Indiana University Music Department. This lists mainly American dissertations (but see CHAPTER 13). The *British and International Music Yearbook Directory* of websites also offers a useful search engine (<http://www.rhinegold.co.uk/musiconweb/bmyb.htm>).

There are an increasing number of electronic versions of paper-based music journals. A comprehensive listing is available from William and Gayle

Cook Music Library, Indiana University School of Music, (<http://www. music.indiana.edu/music resources/journals.html>). Some of these contain abstracts, whilst others are limited to tables of contents. There are also an increasing measure of full text from Chadwyck-Healey's indexing services, *International Index to Music Periodicals* (<http://iimpft.chadwyck.com>) and *International Index to the Performing Arts* (<http://iipaft.chadwyck. com>). One can imagine that, ten years on, this will become a significant source of such material. In addition to electronic journals available through subscription, there are some electronic journals such as *Music Analysis*, edited by Anthony Pople, which are available full text in electronic format free of charge if one has a print subscription. More listings of music journals available online can often be found by searching publishers' home pages (e.g. <http://www.blackwellpublishers.co.uk/jnl holding pg.asp>). Most journals available in this format require a subscription to be placed.

▶ SPECIALIST DATABASES

Many specialist databases are gathered together in The Performing Arts Data Service. This houses amongst other things, the Bach Bibliography Database, the Five Centuries of Scottish Music Multimedia Collection, the Scottish Music Information Centre Catalogue and the National Review of Live Art Reviews Database. They are also developing a Digital Archive of Medieval Music, the Bate Collection of Historic Musical Instruments Database and the Digital Performance Archive 1999–2000. They can be found at <http://www.pads.ahds.ac.uk>. Another hub, HUMBUL (<http:// www.humbul.ac.uk>), which is humanities-based and is maintained by Oxford University, is another excellent source of information. Many of these databases are listed on the Bulletin Board for Libraries (BUBL) page (<http://bubl.ac.uk/>). These subject lists include a whole host of other areas, such as dance, art and theatre.

Several other specialist databases are now available free of charge on the Web. These include CAIRSS (Computer-Assisted Information Retrieval Service System) at <http://imr.utsa.edu/CAIRSS.html>. This is a database of music research literature. It is a venture by faculty and staff at the University of Texas at San Antonio. It gives access to all articles that appear in 18 primary journals. The MuseData collection (<http://musedata. stanford.edu/>) is worth mentioning at this point, if only to highlight the important role that the Centre for Computer Assisted Research in the Humanities (CCARH) is playing in the development of new databases. MuseData is a database of musical information, including scores of Bach, Beethoven, Corelli, Handel and Haydn. Hundreds of works have been digitised since 1984.

For those whose interest is prior to Bach, the Fourteenth Century Music database, Scribe, (<http://www.lib.latrobe.edu.au/Audio-Visual/

Stinson/medmusic.htm>) contains information relating to all written musical works (except liturgical chant) of the fourteenth century. The database can be searched by text or melody and will return musical information in the form of a modern score. The site was set up by Latrobe University in Victoria, Australia, and is searchable free of charge. A database that covers the same area but with a slightly different angle is the Thesaurus Musicarum Latinarum (TML) (<http://www.music.indiana.edu/tml/>). This will eventually contain the entire corpus of Latin music theory written during the Middle Ages and the Renaissance. Thema (Theory of the Middle Ages) is a database of hypertext transcriptions of 18 manuscript copies of 14 Latin theoretical treatises related to *musica mensurabilis* of the thirteenth century (<http://www.uga.edu/~thema/>). For choral scholars, CANTUS, a database for Latin ecclesiastical chants, is yet another source of information (<http://publish.uwo.ca/~cantus/>). It is possible to search CANTUS for specific chants.

Progressing on in musical history, we find the Register of Music Data in London Newspapers. After many years' work this is now complete. Enquiries can be directed to Rosamund McGuinness at Royal Holloway and Bedford New College.[1] A minimal charge may be made for searches. The database contains notices about music, including information about concert life, music publishing and instrument manufacture from 1660–1800. A similar project based on concert life in nineteenth-century London will be covered by a database at Oxford Brookes University. This has been usefully introduced by Christina Bashford in an article in *Brio* (Bashford, 1999). In terms of specific composers of this era, the Beethoven Bibliography Database at San Jose State University (<http://www.sjsu.edu/depts/beethoven/database/database.html>) is well worth visiting.

Moving on in time, the Lester S Levy Sheet Music Collection (<http://levysheetmusic.mse.jhu.edu>) at Johns Hopkins University, Baltimore contains 29 000 pieces of popular American music spanning 1780–1960. All pieces of the collection are indexed on this site and a search will retrieve a catalogue description of the pieces. American sheet music 1870–85 also features in the Library of Congress's 'American memory' project (<http://memory.loc.gov/ammem/smhtml/smhome.html>). This consists of over 47 000 pieces of sheet music registered for copyright during the years 1870 to 1885. A project concerned with older music is the Bodleian Library's Broadside Ballad project (<http://www.bodley.ox.ac.uk/ballads/ballads.htm>). This makes digitised copies of over 30 000 ballads from the sixteenth to the twentieth century available online.

For those looking for orchestral information, the best starting point is OrchestraNet, which includes schedules for many of the major orchestras worldwide, along with links to their home pages and much other valuable information (<http://www.orchestranet.co.uk/orchests.html>). Opera companies have a 'Coordinated Opera Resource Page' (<http://operabase.com>) which has links to 50 000 opera performances since 1999.

Increasingly, composers and artists – and indeed a wide range of other musicians – are setting up their own personal pages. It is worth looking through one of the search engines that will enable one to narrow a search to personal pages (e.g. HotBot) for information about particular people. For example, the British composer John McCabe has an extensive web presence (<http://www.johnmccabe.com>), with lists of his works and a discography, as well as photographs of the composer. One interesting example is the page run by Christopher Yavelow (<http://www.xs4all.nl/~yavelow/>), from where one can access Countdown, the very first internet opera.

Pop music has an enormous web infrastructure, but is outside the scope of the present chapter. Readers should refer to one of the published directories such as Music and the internet revolution by Conrad Mewton (2001).[2]

Many of the sites mentioned have their own mailing lists and news-groups. These are too numerous to list here, but there are several indexes available over the Web. Mailbase (<http://www.mailbase.ac.uk/lists.html>), which provides electronic discussion lists for the UK higher education community, maintains a list of music-related groups. American lists can be searched via CATALIST (<http://www.lsoft.com/lists/listref.html>), the official catalogue of Listserv lists. Diane Kovacs's celebrated directory of scholarly electronic conferences (<http://www.kovacs.com/directory/>) is also a well established favourite. For US-based music lists, try Liszt Music (<http://www.liszt.com>).

► RECORD INDUSTRY

Record and CD reviews, previously only available in printed formats, have now become much more accessible with the introduction of *Gramophone* magazine on the internet. Once a registration form has been completed, it is possible to search by composer, title, artist, conductor, reviewer and other options. With the consolidation of MusicWeb as a major source of CD reviews, with its coverage of up to 300 reviews a month, it is already the largest single source of reviews of new classical CDs. (<www.MusicWeb.uk.net/index2.htm>).

Radio stations are also developing their own websites. For example, BBC Radio 3 covers diverse topics, including a 20 year run of 'Building a Library', record reviews and choices as the CD 'best buy', and this is now available as a fully searchable website to a world audience (<http://www.bbc.co.uk/radio3/building/>). Access to the *BBC Music Magazine* is available from <http://www.bbcmusicmagazine.com>.

Many retail organisations have also taken advantage of the internet to sell CDS. At BMG Classics site (<http://www.rcaredseal-rcavictor.com/index.jsp>) there is a search engine and the opportunity to download soundbites to sample the artist or composer before buying. Chandos Records (<http://www.chandos.net>) for example, have sought their contributor's permissions to mount their CD booklet notes on the Web, full text with the listings.

Moving Music (<http://www.movingmusic.co.uk>) is the place to go for low price videos and CDs. Many of the CDs are below £5.00, with cassettes and videos in the same range. The stock is not as extensive as other sites, but they do have some of the most popular CDs with comparatively low UK post and packing charges. In the US, probably the largest stock of remaindered and cheap classical CDs is the Berkshire Record Outlet (<http://www.broinc.com>), but many suppliers of new, remaindered and second-hand recordings can be found in the classified advertisements in Gramophone and Fanfare which these days almost always include a web address.

There is also a thriving second-hand trade in vinyl, 78s and CDs on the net. An example of the out of print labels featured on the net is Lyrita, the British label specialising in English music, of interest for repertoire, artist and audiophile reasons. If one keys 'Lyrita' into any of the general search engines such as AltaVista one will find various vendors of the LPs. One has the memorable name of Turnipseed (<http://www.turnipseed.com/lplyrita.html>). For those wanting lists of second-hand shops that can be visited in the high street, useful compendia are maintained by some on their personal homepages. For instance, <http://www.moremusic.co.uk/links/uk shops.htm> lists shops in the UK.

A brief mention was made above of magazines. To these can be added the journals or newsletters of composer societies, which are also becoming available in full text on the Web. Several magazines and journals are available only in electronic format, and recent years have also seen the development of web reviewing fora and discussion pages for those who disagree with printed opinion in the media. Contributions are often invited through an appropriate mailing list. The discussion list is also used as a means of communication and comment on various issues of the journal.

Music Theory Online (MTO) is one of the better known online journals. It is the product of the Society for Music Theory, which maintains a mailing list (subscribe via the SMT site at <http://societymusictheory.org/smt-list/>). It contains essays, work in progress, dissertation postings and employment opportunities. It also has automated database searching of its archival material via the World Wide Web. There are many more electronic journals in the field of general or popular music. A typical example is RPM or Review of Popular Music (<http://www.iaspm.net/rpm>), which contains music, news, reviews information and opinion. The Indiana site has a list of such titles (<http://www.music.indiana.edu/music resources/journals.html>). Many journals now run regular articles on new internet sites, and in the music field the most useful British journals in this respect are the 'Webwatch' feature in *Gramophone* and the *BBC Music Magazine*.

► THE FUTURE

The future for music on the internet will be firmly multimedia-based. Already the first online opera has been produced. Ultimately this could be developed for music students in a similar way to the PATRON (Performing Arts Teaching Resources Online) (<http://www.lib.surrey.ac.uk/Patron/Patron.htm>). Performers could record their own performance or practice sessions and obtain feedback via the internet. Masterclasses could be run in a similar way. For musicologists, there exists the facility to scan pictures, programme notes, memorabilia and photos as well as to publish electronic treatises. Music written in software such as Sibelius can be e-mailed to a performer and either played back as sound through the computer's speakers or the orchestral parts printed off for performance Other fields such as iconography and organology could use the multimedia capabilities of the internet to record pictures sound as well as scores, recordings and ideas. The appearance of the MP3 file format and the development of compression formats is making the dissemination of music via the internet ever easier to a larger and larger audience, and writing in the summer of 1999, George Cole estimated that at that time 'tens of thousands of MP3 sites and over 500 000 MP3 files' were available, adding that 'most of these files are illegally copied' (Cole, 1999).

► BIBLIOGRAPHY

Amrhein, R. (1995) Internet Resources for Music. *College & Research Libraries News*, 56, no. 11, 760

Gosain, S and Lee, Z (2001) The Internet and the Reshaping of the Music CD Market *Electronic Markets* 11 no. 2 140–5

Johnson, L. A. (2000) Downloading Zone *Opera News*, 65, no. 4, 48

Jones, S. (2000) Music and the Internet. *Popular Music*, 19, no. 2, 217–309

Lam, C.K.M. (2001) The Internet is Changing the Music Industry. *Communications of the ACM*, 44, no. 8, 62

Mason, R (2002) Music and the Internet: Friends or Foes? *Economic Review*, 19, no. 3, 30–3

Moloney, K. (1997) The Impact of the Internet on Musicological Research Methods. *Continuo*, 26, 1–16

MP3 Revolution (2000) *Science World*, 56, no. 8 (January), 8

Music on the Internet (1999) *PC Magazine*, 18, no. 4, 329

Music Educators National Conference (2001). Music at the Speed of Light: Sheet Music on the Internet. Teaching Music, 9, no. 3, 32–5

Music Educators National Conference (2001). Sharing Music programs through the Internet. *Teaching Music*, 9, no. 1, 30–4

Reid, J. (1995) Challenge of the Superhighway: information via the Internet and Superjanet. In Foreman, L. (ed.) *Who Needs Libraries: challenges for the nineties?* London: HMSO, pp. 64–72 [*State Librarian* 42 (2)]

Silverman, M. (1999) The Wonderful World of Websites. *American Music Teacher*, 48, no. 4, 21

Wandtke, A. and Schater, O. (2001) Music on Demand: a New Type of Use on the Internet? *IIC: International Review of Industrial Property and Copyright Law*, 32, no. 3, 285

▶ REFERENCES

American Musicological Society *WWW Sites of Interest to Musicologists*. <http:www.sas.upenn.edu/music/ams/musicology_www.html>

Bashford, C. (1999) Introducing the Concert Life in 19th Century London Database. *Brio*, 36, 111–16

Cole, G. (1999) Music via the Internet. *Gramophone*, Sept, 110–11

Lawrence, S. and Lee, G.C. (1998) Searching the World Wide Web. *Science*, 280, 5360 April 1998, 98–100

McGuiness, R. (1991) The Register of Musical Data in London Newspapers 1660–1800 *Brio* 28, 7–14

Mewton, C. (2001) *All You Need to Know About Music and the Internet Revolution*. London: Sanctuary

▶ NOTES

1. <R.Mcguinness@rhul.ac.uk>.
2. Mewton, Conrad. (2001) All You Need to Know About Music and the Internet Revolution. (London: Sanctuary).

8 Women in music: sources and literature

Sophie Fuller

Throughout the world and throughout history, women have played an important role in the musical life of their society, something that has not always been acknowledged by canonical musicological studies. But the exploration of women's different kinds of involvement with music – as composers, instrumentalists, singers, patrons, educators and critics in a wide variety of musics – has been a rapidly growing area of research since the 1970s.

A closely related and often intersecting field is that of gender studies or feminist criticism in music, which, together with other kinds of critical theory, is a central concern of what has come to be known as the 'new musicology', and which explores expressions of gender and sexuality in music and the musical world. Central texts of feminist criticism include Susan McClary's *Feminine Endings* (1991) and the collections of essays *Musicology and Difference* (Solie, 1993), *Queering the Pitch: The New Gay and Lesbian Musicology* (Brett *et al.*, 1994) and *Cecilia Reclaimed: Feminist Perspectives on Gender and Music* (Cook and Tsou, 1994). All these collections range widely in both subject matter and approach and contain much of relevance and importance for those investigating the lives and work of women musicians – the central concern of this chapter.

▶ WOMEN AS COMPOSERS OF WESTERN ART MUSIC

Dictionaries

Until recently women composers have been noticeably absent from the mainstream dictionaries and encyclopaedias of music. In *The New Grove Dictionary of Music and Musicians* (1980) (i.e. *Grove 6*), for example, the widely respected British composer Rebecca Clarke received an entry of just nine words, describing her as a violist, composer and wife of James Friskin, clearly an editorial afterthought.[1] Nearly 15 years later Clarke finally received the detailed coverage that she undoubtedly deserves from the prestigious Grove Dictionaries in *The New Grove Dictionary of Women Composers* (1994)[2], further expanded in the second edition of the *New Grove* (2001).[3] This most recent edition of the Grove Dictionary includes a lengthy entry (including a useful bibliography) on 'Women in Music' by Margaret Ericson, Ellen Koskoff and Judith Tick.

An awareness of women's work as composers is nothing new – in 1883, for example, the journalist Stephen Stratton produced a list of over 380 women composers for a paper he gave to the UK's Musical Association (now the Royal Musical Association). Specialist dictionaries were not long appearing. Otto Ebel's *Women Composers: A Biographical Handbook of Woman's Work in Music* was first published in 1902 and remains a useful guide to long forgotten nineteenth-century composers. Renewed interest in women's creativity since the 1970s has produced several different works. Aaron Cohen's second edition of his *International Encyclopaedia of Women Composers* (1987) has biographies and short work-lists for 3700 composers from nearly 70 countries, ranging from the twentieth-century Estonian composer Els Aarne to the nineteenth-century Frenchwoman Madame Zybine. Not always accurate, Cohen's information needs to be treated with caution and checked against more reliable sources, but even so the *International Encyclopedia* remains the most thorough starting place for basic facts about little-known composers and extremely useful for its careful listing of sources and its appendices of composers listed by country and instrumental or vocal genre.

The single volume *New Grove Dictionary of Women Composers* (Sadie and Samuel, 1994) is a much more scholarly, albeit less ambitious, enterprise, containing information on 875 composers. While many entries are frustratingly brief, most give the essential details of life and works as well as helpful bibliographies. Sophie Fuller's *The Pandora Guide to Women Composers* (1994) covers 102 women from Britain and the United States and is aimed at a more general readership, although also leaving the reader with guides to further investigation.

Introductions to a selection of contemporary women composers from the UK, Ireland, Australia, New Zealand and the United States, often in their own words, can be found in two recent volumes of the journal *Contemporary Music Review* (Fuller and LeFanu, 1994; Pendle, 1997).

General histories and textbooks

Women composers are rarely to be found in general musical textbooks. Those wishing to find out how women have played a part in the history of

Western music as composers will need to turn to specialist histories. *Women & Music: A History* (Pendle, 2nd ed. 2001) provides the most thorough coverage of the subject, including chapters on women in popular and non-western music, women as patrons and on feminist musical aesthetics, as well as a central chronological exploration of women composers and musicians working within the Western art music tradition. In its coverage of the twentieth century, *Women & Music* has a decidedly North American bias and therefore suffers from somewhat unsatisfactory coverage of European composers.

Carol Neuls-Bates's chronologically arranged anthology *Women In Music* (1996) has a similar bias but contains some fascinating source readings about composers as well as performers, educators and patrons. Those particularly interested in North American composers should also use Judith Tick's *American Women Composers Before 1870* (1983) and Christine Ammer's *Unsung: A History of Women in American Music* (2001), as well as consulting the monumental, although now somewhat out of date, *Women in American Music: A Bibliography of Music and Literature* (1979), compiled by Adrienne Fried Block and Carol Neuls-Bates. *Women Making Music* (1986), a pioneering collection of essays edited by Jane Bowers and Judith Tick, is arranged chronologically and so provides a historical perspective to its in-depth studies of individual women or groups of women, both composers and performers.

Monographs

Wide-ranging explorations of women's musical creativity can be found in Marcia Citron's *Gender and the Musical Canon* (1993) and Jill Halstead's *The Woman Composer* (1997). Nicola LeFanu's article 'Master Musician: An Impregnable Taboo?' (LeFanu, 1987) investigated the situation of contemporary women composers in the UK, pointing to the scarcity of performances of their music.

There are numerous biographies of various individual women composers, although full-length studies that include illuminating discussion of their music are much rarer. American composers seem to have fared best, with exemplary works such as Judith Tick's 1996 book on *Ruth Crawford Seeger* (a composer who is also well served by Joseph Straus's *The Music of Ruth Crawford Seeger* (1995)) and Adrienne Fried Block's study of Amy Beach (Block, 1998). Françoise Tillard's 1992 biography (English translation 1996) of Fanny Mendelssohn Hensel is not always entirely accurate but remains the only full-length work available in English and provides a detailed insight into the context in which Hensel lived and worked, particularly when read together with Marcia Citron's 1987 collection of Hensel's letters to her more famous brother (Citron, 1987). There are several studies of the remarkable twelfth-century composer, writer and mystic Hildegard of Bingen, although most, including the otherwise admirable works by Barbara Newmann (1987) and Sabina Flanagan (1989), pay only brief attention to her music. The bio-bibliography series from Greenwood Press (which gives a brief biography of a composer followed by an in-depth bibliography) often provides a good starting point for further research and includes volumes on Violet Archer (Hartig, 1991), Esther Williamson Ballou (Heintze, 1997), Radie Britain (Bailey and Bailet, 1990), Cecile Chaminade (Citron, 1988), Peggy Glanville-Hicks (Hayes, 1990), Thea Musgrave (Hickson, 1994), Germaine Tailleferre (Shapiro, 1994) and Eleanor Remick Warren (Bortin, 1990). Academic journals publish much pioneering work on women composers, such as Suzanne Cusick's exploration of what can be known about the life of Francesca Caccini (Cusick, 1993).

Autobiographies should not be overlooked as source material, although they often need to be treated with caution. Elisabeth Lutyens's memoirs, *A Goldfish Bowl* (1972), for example, make very good reading but are factually notoriously unreliable and should be read in conjunction with *A Pilgrim Soul: The Life and Works of Elisabeth Lutyens* by Meirion and Susie Harries (1989). Other recommended autobiographies include those by Liza Lehmann (1919), Clara Kathleen Rogers (1919, 1932), Ethel Smyth (1919, 1936, 1940) and Maude Valérie White (1914, 1932).

Musical scores

Finding the musical scores of women composers, even those that have been published, can be surprisingly difficult. Anthologies can provide a useful overview. James Briscoe's single volume *Historical Anthology of Music by Women* (1987) remains a useful introduction to works by 37 composers, from the ninth-century composer of medieval Byzantine chant, Kassia, to the contemporary American composer, Ellen Taaffe Zwilich, with the work of each composer introduced by an illuminating short essay from a relevant scholar. Briscoe has also edited a *Contemporary Anthology of Music by Women* (1997). A much more ambitious project is the chronological 12 volume series *Women Composers: Music Through The Ages*, edited by Martha Furman Schleifer and Sylvia Glickman, which started to appear in 1996. The chosen works have been carefully edited by the various contributors, who also write explanatory essays on the music and composers (Schleifer and Glickman, 1996–[volumes are still appearing]).

For the scholar looking for music by women of the Renaissance, Baroque and Classical periods, Barbara Garvey Jackson's *"Say Can You Deny Me"*: *A Guide to Surviving Music by Women from the 16th through the 18th Centuries* (1994) is a valuable guide to sources (both in manuscript and printed) in libraries and archives. More practical volumes, aimed at the performer, include the following: *Flute Music by Women Composers:*

An Annotated Catalog (Boenke, 1988); *The Women in Music Classical Repertoire Guide: Orchestral Music* (Fuller 1996); *Organ and Harpsichord Music by Women Composers: An Annotated Catalog* (Heinrich 1991); *Violin Music by Women Composers: A Bio-Bibliographical Guide* (Johnson 1989); *A Catalog of Compositions for Guitar by Women Composers* (MacAuslan 1984); *Keyboard Music by Women Composers: A Catalogue and Bibliography* (Meggett 1981); *Catalogue of Published Works for String Orchestra and Piano Trio by Twentieth-Century American Women Composers* (Schlegel 1993); *Women Composers: A Checklist of Works for the Solo Voice* (Stewart-Green 1980); *Piano Music by Black Women Composers: A Catalog of Solo and Ensemble Works* (Walker-Hill 1992).

In recent years there have been many new editions of works by women composers of the past. As demand and interest increase, mainstream publishers have started to reissue works by some of the better known women, such as Fanny Hensel or Clara Schumann. For many years, pioneering music publishers, such as Furore in Germany[4] or Vivace Press,[5] Hildegard Publishing Company[6] and ClarNan[7] editions in the United States, have focused, sometimes exclusively, on producing music by women, and their catalogues are an invaluable resource for finding easily obtainable performing scores. Da Capo Press[8] has issued many invaluable volumes of selected works including collections of songs by Amy Beach, Nadia Boulanger, Augusta Holmès, Josephine Lang and Louise Reichardt and of piano music by Agathe Backer-Grondhal and Cécile Chaminade. In the late 1970s and early 1980s several newly edited choral works by seventeenth-century composers appeared in the series 'Nine Centuries of Music by Women' published by Broude Brothers of New York.[9]

Music by many contemporary women composers is issued by main-stream publishers and details of their works can be obtained from the relevant Promotions Department. The Music Information Centres, found in over 30 countries world wide (see CHAPTER 3), are also very helpful in finding music by contemporary women.[10] Several have searchable databases of their holdings that can identify works by female composers. Archives, libraries and information centres concentrating on music by women include the International Institute for the Study of Music in California, which holds the materials collected by Aaron Cohen during his research for his Encyclopedia, and the International Female Composers' Library in Germany.[11] The organisation New York Women Composers produces a widely circulated catalogue of music by its members.[12]

Recordings

Given the current state of the recording industry, with CDs frequently disappearing from circulation soon after they first appear, compiling discographies is often a thankless task, but it is an essential one in documenting this music. Finding recordings is often a central task for those studying music. The broadest discography to date, representing the recorded work of 459 women composers on 775 CDs, is that produced by Barbara Harbach and published in the journal *Women of Note Quarterly* (Harbach, 1996). For those interested in early music, there is an extensive annotated discography of music by women composers born before 1765 on the 'Early Music by Women Composers' web page (<http://music.acu.edu/www/iawm/pages/>). The American distributors, Ladyslipper, can supply a wide range of music by women in many different genres and issue a highly informative Catalogue and Resource Guide of Recordings By Women.[13] In the UK a smaller range of recordings is available from the distributors WRPM.[14]

▶ WOMEN AS PERFORMING MUSICIANS

The Western art music tradition

Historically, the distinction between performer and composer is frequently unclear, if not meaningless, and indeed often remains so today. Nevertheless, studies of the contexts in which music is performed and of the people who performed it, although less numerous than studies of composers and their works, remain an important part of our wider understanding of music. Studies of the economic and social history of music have tended to be more inclusive of women than works focusing on composers and their music. A good example is Cyril Ehrlich's *The Music Profession in Britain since the Eighteenth Century* (1985) which includes invaluable information about the role of women. Richard Leppert's *Music and Image: Domesticity, Ideology and Sociocultural Formation in Eighteenth-Century England* (1988) provides a fascinating examination of women's involvement and roles within domestic music-making while Paula Gillett's *Musical Women in England, 1870–1914* (2000) explores the wider roles available to women of a later period.

There are few scholarly studies of individual women performers, although there are numerous biographies aimed at the general reader. Singers have been especially well covered, which is hardly surprising, since singing is the music profession in which women have had the longest and perhaps most successful history. Rupert Christiansen's *Prima Donna* (1995) is a useful history of female opera singers, while Susan Leonardi and Rebecca Pope's *The Diva's Mouth: Body, Voice, Prima Donna Politics* (1996) is a more broad-ranging exploration of the diva phenomenon. *Embodied Voices* (Dunn and Jones, 1994) presents a diverse exploration of 'female vocality', from the voices of early twentieth-century blues singers or the lamenting women of Finnish Karelia to an exploration of George Eliot's portrayal of a diva in her verse drama, *Armgart*. The place of the female within the world of opera, as performer, composer or listener, has intrigued many writers, including Catherine Clément, whose *L'Opéra, ou, La défaite des Femmes* (published in English as *Opera, or the Undoing of Women* (1988)) explores the doom-laden roles that the divas have sung, and the various contributors to *En Travesti: Women, Gender Subversion, Opera* (Blackmer and Smith, 1995). Jacqueline Letzter and Robert Adelson's authorative *Women Writing Opera* (2001) explores the role of women as opera composers and librettists in late eighteenth- and early nineteenth-century France.

Biographies of female instrumentalists are less common than those of singers. Some of the most thorough studies include Karen Shaffer and Neva Greenwood's *Maud Powell, Pioneer American Violinist* (1988) and Nancy Reich's *Clara Schumann: The Artist and the Woman* (1989). *The Marriage Diaries of Robert and Clara Schumann* (Nauhaus, 1994) makes fascinating reading for one period in this remarkable woman's life. There is also considerable material on Schumann available only in German, such as Eva Weissweiler's *Clara Schumann, eine Biographie* (see CHAPTER 14). Kathryn Talalay's biography of the now little-known twentieth-century pianist and composer Philippa Schuyler, *Composition in Black and White* (1995), demonstrates the painstaking research that such undertakings involve.

Studies of groups of female musicians often provide a particularly clear insight into the ways in which women have played their part in various musical worlds. Notable contributions covering earlier periods of history include: *The Voice of the Trobairitz: Perspectives on the Women Troubadours* (Paden, 1989); *Disembodied Voices: Music and Culture in an Early Modern Italian Convent* (Monson, 1995); *Celestial Sirens: Nuns and Their Music in Early Modern Milan* (Kendrick, 1996); and *Women Musicians of Venice: Musical Foundations 1525–1855* (Baldauf-Berdes, 1996). There are several helpful books on the late nineteenth- and early twentieth-century phenomenon of women's orchestras: *Blowing Her Own Trumpet. European Ladies' Orchestras and Other Women Musicians 1870–1950 in Sweden* (Myers, 1993); *Evening the Score: Women in Music and the Legacy of Frédérique Petrides* (Groh, 1991), which reproduces the newsletters produced by this pioneering conductor of the Orchestrette Classique; and *A View From the Bandstand* (Kent, 1983), an enthralling collection of photographs of female musicians in various turn-of-the-century British women's orchestras and bands.

Ethnomusicology

Needless to say, women have not only made music within the Western art music tradition. This is firmly acknowledged by the collection of essays *Rediscovering the Muses* (Marshall, 1993) which examines women musicians from that tradition (in fifteenth-century Scotland or Renaissance Italy) as well as from cultures as diverse as Aboriginal Australia or Pharaonic

Egypt. Other ethnomusicological collections include *Women and Music in Cross-Cultural Perspective* (Koskoff, 1987), with essays discussing women's participation in musical traditions from Afghanistan, the Balkans, Brazil, Moroccan Jewish Canada, Greece, India, Japan, Java, Malaysia, Tunisia and the United States, and *Music, Gender and Culture* (Hernden and Ziegler, 1990), which looks at musical traditions in Algeria, China, Karelia, Liberia, Sweden, Thailand, Tonga, Turkey, the United States and Yugoslavia.

Popular music

Many of the issues surrounding women working in the various different genres of popular music are much the same as those that have faced women working within the Western art music tradition. Similar too, is the disappearance of these women, with the exception of those who worked as singers, from the mainstream histories and encyclopaedias. Two books from the 1980s redressed the balance as far as jazz was concerned: Sally Placksin's *American Women in Jazz: 1900 to the Present* (1982) and Linda Dahl's *Stormy Weather: The Music and Lives of a Century of Jazzwomen* (1984). Leslie Gourse's more recent study of jazz performers *Madame Jazz: Contemporary Women Instrumentalists* (1995) is also recommended. A more in-depth look at three key figures from the world of jazz is provided by Angela Davis in *Blues Legacies and Black Feminism: Gertrude 'Ma' Rainey, Bessie Smith, and Billie Holiday* (1998) while Sherrie Tucker's *Swing Shift* (2000) explores the "all-gin" bands of the 1940s.

The more truly 'popular' genres, such as rock, soul, pop, R'n'B and rap, are covered by two general histories: American writer Gillian Garr's *She's a Rebel: The History of Women in Rock and Roll* (1992) and British journalist Lucy O'Brien's enjoyable *She Bop II: The Definitive History of Women in Rock, Pop and Soul* (2nd ed., 2002), which includes discussion of jazz musicians such as the celebrated bandleader Ivy Benson. The British experience is also reflected in the collection of essays *Girls! Girls! Girls!: Essays on Women and Music* (Cooper, 1995), which also contains two essays on music in the classical tradition.[15] Three perceptive collections of interviews with women musicians ranging from Tori Amos, Björk and Courtney Love to Angelique Kidjo, Monie Love and Yoko Ono were put together in the mid-1990s by Liz Evans (1994), Karen O'Brien (1995) and Amy Raphael (1995). A more academic approach to the subject can be found in Mavis Bayton's *Frock Rock: Women Performing Popular Music* (1998) and the collection *Sexing the Groove: Popular Music and Gender* (Whiteley, 1997), which looks at both masculinities and femininities in popular music and contains a very useful guide to further reading and resources. The thoughtful exploration by journalists Simon Reynolds and Joy Press, *The Sex Revolts: Gender, Rebellion, and Rock 'n' roll* (1995), is also recommended as is Sheila Whiteley's *Women and Popular Music: Sexuality, Identity and Subjectivity* (2000).

Women as patrons

Women's important role as patrons and enablers of music has begun to receive particular attention in recent years. Most material is only available in doctoral theses or journal articles, although a notable exception is the fascinating collection *Cultivating Music in America: Women Patrons and Activists since 1860* (Locke and Barr, 1997). European patrons, especially of the nineteenth and twentieth centuries, remain neglected. Michael De Cossart, for example, in his 1978 biography of Winnie Singer, the Princesse de Polignac, fails to take his subject entirely seriously or to explore fully her remarkable influence on the music of the early twentieth century (De Cossart, 1978). Jeanice Brooks's article 'Nadia Boulanger and the salon of the Princess de Polignac' (1993) redresses the balance somewhat. This article is an example of the substantial scholarly sources that are to be found in the periodical literature. Another useful study is that by Stephen Banfield's on the wealthy American patron of chamber music composition and performance, Mrs Elizabeth Sprague Coolidge (Banfield, 1986).

Women, music and education

Women teachers and educators have also received scant attention, with the notable exception of the French composition teacher and conductor, Nadia Boulanger. Leonie Rosenstiel has written biographies of both the Boulanger sisters – Nadia's sister Lili was a successful composer who died in her early twenties (Rosenstiel, 1978, 1982). Bruno Monsaingeon's *Mademoiselle: Conversations with Nadia Boulanger* (1985) is also useful. Lucy Green's *Music, Gender, Education* (1997) is the best introduction to more general issues surrounding women and gender in connection with musical education. Several papers from the 1993 Music, Gender and Education Conference held at Bristol University were published in the November 1993 issue of the *British Journal of Music Education*, including articles by leading researchers in the field of gender and music education such as Lucy Green and Roberta Lamb, as well as an investigation into the sex-stereotyping in children's choices of instruments by Rosemary Bruce and Anthony Kemp.[16]

Further resources

One of the most useful resources concerning women and music is the website of the International Alliance of Women in Music (<http://music.acu.edu/www/iawm/home.html>). This contains a wealth of information and further links, including articles from the *IAWM Journal* (published three times a year); lists of women world wide in music organisations, archive, libraries and projects; contact details for publishers and distributors of women's music (both scores and recordings); discographies and bibliographies; and audio clips of music by women. The site provides a link to possibly the most detailed and up-to-date bibliography of work on gender and music, that maintained by the Society of Music Theory's Committee on the Status of Women (<http://home1.gte.net/esayrs68/CSWBibIndex.html>). The most useful printed bibliography, although already limited by its end date, is Margaret Ericson's *Women and Music: A Selective Bibliography on Women and Gender Issues in Music 1987–1992* (1995). The three volumes of *The Musical Woman: An International Perspective* (Zaimont, Overhauser and Gottlieb, 1984, 1987, 1991) provide a collection of reports, interviews and features that reflect on women's position within many different aspects of the musical world, from publishers and critics to conductors and teachers, as well as important scholarly articles and repertoire lists.

Journals

Several academic journals have devoted whole or partial issues to studies of women in music. The Spring 1992 issue of *Women: A Cultural Review*, for example, published several papers from the Music and Gender Conference held at King's College, London in 1991. Individual articles on issues surrounding women in music are increasingly found in a wide range of academic journals from the *Journal of the Royal Musical Association* to *Popular Music*. *Women of Note Quarterly*, published by Vivace Press, is one of a small handful of journals devoted to the subject of women and music. A recent arrival is *Women and Music: A Journal of Gender and Culture*, a scholarly journal published by the IAWM which contains academic articles and reviews in contrast to the more news-oriented *IAWM Journal*. Online 'webzines' include *Rockrgrl* (<http://www.rockrgrl.com>) and *Womanrock* (<http://www.womanrock.com/index.html>).

Organisations

The IAWM is the largest of the women in music organisations, but other groups which have documentation centres able to supply information about women and music in their own countries include Frau und Musik in Germany,[17] Fondazione Adkins Chiti: Donne in Musica in Italy[18] and Stichting Vrouw en Muziek in the Netherlands[19]. The British organisation Women in Music publishes an informative newsletter *Women in Music Now* as well as campaigning for equal access to opportunities for all women.[20] There are also organisations in Austria, Canada, Finland, Japan, Spain and the UK, as well as several local organisations in the United States.

► REFERENCES

Ammer, C. (2001) *Unsung: A History of Women in American Music* (2nd edn.). Portland, Oregon: Amadeus Press

Bailey, W.B. and Bailey, N.G. (1990) *Radie Britain: A Bio-Bibliography*. Westport, CT: Greenwood Press

Baldauf-Berdes, Jane L. (1996) *Women Musicians of Venice: Musical Foundations 1525–1855*. Oxford: Clarendon Press

Banfield, Stephen (1986) "Too Much of Albion?" Mrs Coolidge and Her British Connections. *American Music*, Spring, 59–87

Bayton, M. (1998) *Frock Rock: Women Performing Popular Music*. Oxford: Oxford University Press

Blackmer, C.E. and Smith, P.J. (1995) (eds) *En Travesti: Women, Gender Subversion, Opera*. New York: Columbia University Press

Block, A.F. (1998): *Amy Beach, Passionate Victorian: the life and work of an American composer, 1867–1944*. New York: Oxford University Press

Block, A.F. and Neuls-Bates, C. (1979) (eds) *Women in American Music: A Bibliography of Music and Literature*. Westport: Greenwood Press

Boenke, H.M. (1988) *Flute Music by Women Composers: An Annotated Catalog*. Westport CT: Greenwood Press

Bortin, V. (1990) *Elinor Remick Warren: A Bio-Bibliography*. Westport, CT: Greenwood Press

Bowers, J. and Tick, J. (1986) (eds) *Women Making Music: The Western Art Tradition, 1150–1950*. London: Macmillan

Brett, P., Wood, E. and Thomas, G.C. (1994) (eds) *Queering the Pitch: The New Gay and Lesbian Musicology*. London: Routledge

Briscoe, J. (1987) (ed.) *Historical Anthology of Music by Women*. Bloomington: Indiana University Press

Briscoe, J. (1997) (ed.) *Contemporary Anthology of Music by Women*. Bloomington: Indiana University Press

British Journal of Music Education 10, 3 (November 1993)

Brooks, J. (1993) Nadia Boulanger and the salon of the Princess de Polignac. *Journal of the American Musicological Society*, 46, 415–68

Christiansen, R. (1995) *Prima Donna: A History* (2nd edn.). London: The Bodley Head/Pimlico

Citron, M. (1988) *Cecile Chaminade: A Bio-Bibliography*. Westport, CT: Greenwood Press

Citron, M. (1987) *The Letters of Fanny Hensel to Felix Mendelssohn*. Stuyvesant, NY: Pendragon

Citron, M. (1993) *Gender and the Musical Canon*. Cambridge: Cambridge University Press

Clément, C. (1988) *Opera, or the Undoing of Women*, trans. Betsy Wing. London: Virago (originally published in French as *L'Opéra, ou, La défaite des femmes*)

Cohen, A.I. (1987) (ed.) *International Encyclopedia of Women Composers* (2nd edn.). New York: Books and Music

Cook, S.C. and Tsou, J.S. (1994) (eds) *Cecilia Reclaimed: Feminist Perspectives on Gender and Music*. Urbana and Chicago: University of Illinois Press

Cooper, S. (1995) (ed.) *Girls! Girls! Girls!: Essays on Women and Music*. London: Cassell

Cossart, M. De (1978) *The Food of Love: Princesse Edmond de Polignac (1865–1943) and her Salon*. London: Hamish Hamilton

Cusick, Suzanne G. (1993) "Thinking from Women's Lives": Francesca Caccini after 1627. *Musical Quarterly*, 77, 281–304

Dahl, L. (1984) *Stormy Weather: The Music and Lives of a Century of Jazzwomen*. New York: Pantheon Books

Davis, A. (1998) *Blues Legacies and Black Feminism: Gertrude 'Ma' Rainey, Bessie Smith, and Billie Holiday*. New York: Pantheon

De Cossart, M. (1978) *The Food of Love: Princesse Edmond de Polignac (1865–1943) and her Salon*. London: Hamish Hamilton

Dunn, L.C. and Jones, N.A. (1994) (eds) *Embodied Voices: Representing Female Vocality in Western Culture*. Cambridge: Cambridge University Press

Ebel, O. (1902) *Women Composers: A Biographical Handbook of Woman's Work in Music*. New York: F.H. Chandler

Ehrlich, C. (1985) *The Music Profession in Britain since the Eighteenth Century*. Oxford: Clarendon

Ericson, M. (1995). *Women and Music: A Selective Bibliography on Women and Gender Issues in Music 1987–1992*. Boston: G.K. Hall, 1995

Evans, L. (1994) *Women, Sex and Rock'n'Roll: In Their Own Words*. London: Pandora

Flanagan, S. (1989) *Hildegard of Bingen: A Visionary Life*. London and New York: Routledge

Foreman, L. (1995) Women Composers. In *Fairest Isle: BBC Radio 3 Book of British Music*. London: BBC Radio 3 in association with BBC Books, 95 (see also p. 73)

Fuller, S. (1994) *The Pandora Guide to Women Composers: Britain and the United States, 1629-present*. London: Pandora

Fuller, S. and LeFanu, N. (1994) (eds) Reclaiming the Muse. *Contemporary Music Review* 11

Fuller, S. (1996) *The Women in Music Classical Repertoire Guide: Orchestral Music*. London: Women in Music

Gaar, G. (1992) *She's a Rebel: The History of Women in Rock and Roll*. Seattle, WA: Seal Press

Gillett, P. (2000) *Musical Women in England, 1870–1914*. London: Macmillan

Gourse, L. (1995) *Madame Jazz: Contemporary Women Instrumentalists*. Oxford: Oxford University Press

Green, L. (1997) *Music, Gender, Education*. Cambridge: Cambridge University Press

Groh, J.B. (1991) *Evening the Score: Women in Music and the Legacy of Frédérique Petrides*. Fayetteville: University of Arkansas Press

Halstead, J. (1997). *The Woman Composer: Creativity and the Gendered Politics of Musical Composition*. Aldershot: Ashgate

Harbach, B. (1996). A Compact Discography Women Composers on CD. *Women of Note Quarterly*, 4, No. 4, 3–34

Harries, M. and Harries, S. (1989) *A Pilgrim Soul: the life and work of Elisabeth Lutyens* London: Michael Joseph

Hartig, L. B (1991) *Violet Archer: A Bio-Bibliography*. Westport, CT: Greenwood Press

Hayes, D. (1990) *Peggy Glanville-Hick: A Bio-Bibliography*. Westport, CT: Greenwood Press

Heinrich, A. (1991) *Organ and Harpsichord Music by Women Composers: An Annotated Catalog*. Westport, CT: Greenwood Press

Heintza, J.R. (1987) *Esther Williamson Ballou: A Bio-Bibliography*. Westport, CT: Greenwood Press

Hernden, M. and Ziegler, S. (1990) (eds) *Music, Gender and Culture*. Wilhelmshaven: Florian Noetzel Verlag

Hixon, D.L. (1984) *Thea Musgrave: A Bio-Bibliography*. Westport, CT: Greenwood Press

Jackson, B.G. (1994) *"Say Can You Deny Me": A Guide to Surviving Music by Women from the 16th through the 18th Centuries*. Fayetteville, AR: The University of Arkansas Press

Johnson, R-M. (1989) *Violin Music by Women Composers: A Bio-Bibliographical Guide*. Westport, CT: Greenwood Press

Kendrick, R.L. (1996) *Celestial Sirens: Nuns and Their Music in Early Modern Milan*. Oxford: Clarendon Press

Kent, G. (1983) *A View From the Bandstand*. London: Sheba Feminist Publishers

Koskoff, E. (1987) (ed) *Women and Music in Cross-Cultural Perspective*. Westport, CT: Greenwood Press

LeFanu, N. (1987) Master Musician: An Impregnable Taboo? *Contact*, 31, Autumn, 4–8

Lehmann, L. (1919) *The Life of Liza Lehmann*. London: T. Fisher Unwin) repr. (1980) New York: Da Capo Press

Letzter, J. and Adelson R. (2001) *Women Writing Opera: Creativity and Controversy in the Age of the French Revolution*. Berkeley, CA: University of California Press

Leonardi, S.J. and Pope, R.A. (1996) *The Diva's Mouth: Body, Voice, Prima Donna Politics*. New Brunswick: Rutgers University Press

Leppert, R. (1988) *Music and Image: Domesticity, Ideology and Sociocultural Formation in Eighteenth Century England*. Cambridge: Cambridge University Press

Locke, R. and Barr, C. (1997) (eds) *Cultivating Music in America: Women Patrons and Activists since 1860*. Berkeley: University of California Press

MacAuslan, J. and Aspen, K. (1997) *Guitar Music by Women Composers: An Annotated Catalog*. Westport, CT: Greenwood Press

Marshall, K. (1993) (ed) *Rediscovering the Muses*. Boston: Northeastern University Press

Meggett, J.M. (1981) *Keyboard Music by Women Composers: A Catalogue and Bibliography*. Westport, CT: Greenwood Press

McClary, S. (1991) *Feminine Endings: Music, Gender, and Sexuality*. Minneapolis: University of Minnesota Press

Monsaignon, B. (1985) *Mademoiselle: Conversations with Nadia Boulanger*, trans. Robyn Marsack. Manchester: Carcanet Press

Monson, C. (1995) *Disembodied Voices: Music and Culture in an Early Modern Italian Convent*. Berkeley, University of California Press

Myers, M. (1993) *Blowing her own trumpet. European Ladies' Orchestras and other women musicians 1870–1950 in Sweden*. Göteborg: Göteborg University

Nauhaus, G. (1994) *The Marriage Diaries of Robert and Clara Schumann*, trans. Peter Ostwald. London: Robson Books

Neuls-Bates, C. (1996) (ed.) *Women in Music: An Anthology of Source Readings from the Middle Ages to the Present* (2nd edn.). Boston: Northeastern University Press

Newmann, B. (1987) *Sister of Wisdom: St Hildegard's Theology of the Feminine* Berkeley: University of California Press

O'Brien, Karen (1995) *Hymn to Her: Women Musicians Talk*. London: Virago

O'Brien, Lucy (2002) *She Bop II: The Definitive History of Women in Rock, Pop and Soul*. (2nd edn.). Harmondsworth: Penguin Books

Paden, W.D. (1989) (ed.) *The Voice of the Trobairitz: Perspectives on the Women Troubadours*. Philadelphia: University of Pennsylvania Press

Pendle, K. (2001) (ed.) *Women & Music: A History* (2nd edn.). Bloomington: Indiana University Press

Pendle, K. (1997) (ed.) American Women Composers. *Contemporary Music Review*, 16

Placksin, S. (1982) *American Women in Jazz: 1900 to the Present*. New York: Wideview. Published in the UK (1985) as *Jazzwomen: 1900 to the Present. Their Words, Lives, and Music*. London: Pluto Press

Raphael, A. (1995) *Never Mind The Bollocks: Women Rewrite Rock*. London: Virago

Reich, N. (1989) *Clara Schumann: The Artist and the Woman*. Oxford: Oxford University Press

Reynolds, S. and Press, J. (1995) *The Sex Revolts: Gender, Rebellion, and Rock 'n' roll*. London: Serpent's Tail

Rogers, C.K. (1919) *Memories of a Musical Career*. Norwood, MA: Plimpton Press

Rogers, C.K. (1932) *The Story of Two Lives: Home, Friends and Travel*. Norwood, MA: Plimpton Press

Rosenstiel, L. (1978) *The Life and Works of Lili Boulanger*. Rutherford, NJ: Farleigh Dickinson University Press

Rosenstiel, L. (1982) *Nadia Boulanger*. New York: Norton

Sadie, J.A. and Samuel, R. (1994) (eds) *The New Grove Dictionary of Women Composers*. London: Macmillan

Schlegel, E.G. (1993) *Catalogue of Published Works for String Orchestra and Piano Trio by Twentieth-Century American Women Composers*. Alabama: Colonial Press

Schleifer, M.F. and Glickman, S. (1996–) (eds) *Women Composers: Music Through The Ages*. Boston: G.K. Hall

Shaffer, K.A. and Greenwood, N.G. (1988) *Maud Powell, Pioneer American Violinist*. Arlington, VA: The Maud Powell Foundation

Shapiro, R. (1994) *Germaine Tailleferre: A Bio-Bibliography*. Westport, CT: Greenwood Press

Smyth, E. (1919) *Impressions That Remained*. London: Longmans

Smyth, E. (1936) *As Time Went On . . .* London: Longmans

Smyth, E. (1940) *What Happened Next* London: Longmans

Solie, R. (1993) (ed.) *Musicology and Difference: Gender and Sexuality in Music Scholarship*. Berkeley and Los Angeles: University of California Press

Stewart-Green, M. (1980) *Women Composers: A Checklist of Works for the Solo Voice*. Boston: G.K. Hall

Straus, J.N. (1995) *The Music of Ruth Crawford Seeger*. Cambridge: Cambridge University Press

Talalay, K. (1995) *Composition in Black and White: The Life of Philippa Schuyler*. Oxford: Oxford University Press

Tick, J. (1983) *American Women Composers Before 1870*. Ann Arbor: UMI Research Press

Tick, J. (1996) *Ruth Crawford Seeger: A Composer's Search for American Music*. New York and Oxford: Oxford University Press

Tillard, F. (1996) *Fanny Mendelssohn*, trans. Camille Naish. Portland, Oregon: Amadeus Press

Tucker, S. *Swing Shift: "All-Gin" Bands of the 1940s* Durham: Duke University Press

Walker-Hill, H. (1992) *Piano Music by Black Women Composers: A Catalog of Solo and Ensemble Works.* New York: Greenwood Press

Weissweiler, E. (1990): *Clara Schumann: eine Biographie.* Hamburg: Hoffmann und Campe (In German)

White, M.V. (1914) *Friends and Memories.* London: Edward Arnold

White, M.V. (1932) *My Indian Summer.* London: Grayson and Grayson

Whiteley, S. (1997) (ed.) *Sexing the Groove: Popular Music and Gender* London and New York: Routledge

Whiteley, S. (2000) *Women and Popular Music: Sexuality, Identity and Subjectivity* London: Routledge

Women: A Cultural Review, 3, No. 1, Spring 1992

Zaimont, J.L., Overhauser, C. and Gottlieb, J. (1984) (eds) *The Musical Woman: An International Perspective 1983.* Westport, CT: Greenwood Press

Zaimont, J.L., Overhauser, C. and Gottlieb, J. (1987) (eds) *The Musical Woman: An International Perspective. Vol. 2, 1984–1985.* Westport, CT: Greenwood Press

Zaimont, J.L., Overhauser, C. and Gottlieb, J. (1991) (eds) *The Musical Woman: An International Perspective. Vol. 3, 1986–1990.* Westport, CT: Greenwood Press

▶ NOTES

1. Unsigned article, 'Clarke, Rebecca' *The New Grove Dictionary of Music and Musician*s vol. 4 (London: Macmillan, 1980), 448.
2. Stephen Banfield, 'Rebecca Clarke' (Sadie and Samuel, 1994), 119–220.
3. Liane Curtis: 'Clarke [Friskin], Rebecca (Thacher)' *The New Grove Dictionary of Music and Musicians* Second edition. vol. 5 Grove/Macmillan Publishers, 2001 919–21.
4. Furore Verlag, Naumburger Strasse 40, D-34127 Kassel, Germany. Tel. 0561 897352. Fax 0561 83472.
5. Vivace Press, PO Box 157, Readfield, WI 54969, USA. Tel. 920 667 5280. Fax 920 667 5237. <http://www.vivacepress.com>.
6. Hildegard Publishing Company, Box 332, Bryn Mawr, PA 19010. Tel. 610 649 8649. Fax 610 649 8677 <http://www.hildegard.com>.
7. ClarNan Editions, 235 Baxter Lane, Fayetteville, Arkansas 72701, USA. Tel. 501 442 7414 E-mail: <clarnan@ipa.net> <http://music.acu.edu/www/iawm/clarnan/>
8. Da Capo Press, 233 Spring Street, New York, NY 10013, USA.
9. The series includes the following works: Raffaella Aleotti, *Ascendens Christus in Altum* (edited by Ann Carruthers-Clement, 1983), Francesca Caccini, *Aure*

Volanti (edited by Carolyn Raney, 1977), Isabella Leonarda, *Ave Regina Caelorum* (edited by Stewart Carter, 1980) and Barbara Strozzi, *Con Le Belle Non Ci Vuol Fretta* (edited by Carolyn Raney, 1978).

10. For contact details see CHAPTER 3. The website of the International Association of Music Information Centres is <http://www.iamic.ie>.

11. International Institute for the Study of Women in Music, California State University, Northridge, CA 91330, USA; International Female Composers' Library (Europäisches Frauenmusikarchiv und Internationale Komponistinnen-Bibliothek), Nicolaistrasse 2, D-4750 Unna, Westfallen, Germany. Tel. 02303 23111 Fax 02303 103475.

12. New York Women Composers, 114 Kelburne Ave., North Tarrytown, NY 10591, USA. Tel 914 631 4361. E-mail: <nywomencomposers@hotmail.com> <http://www.ibiblio.org/nywc/>

13. Ladyslipper, 3205 Hillsborough Road, Durham, North Carolina, USA. Tel. 919 383 8773. Fax 919 383 3525. <http://www.ladyslipper.org>.

14. WRPM, 7 Thornbridge Avenue, Chorlton, Manchester M21 9DN. Tel. 0161 861 8727. E-mail: <music@wrpm.net> <http://www.wrpm.net/>

15. Jennifer Barnes, 'Where are the mothers in opera?' and Sophie Fuller, '"Dead White Men in Wigs": Women and Classical Music'.

16. Lucy Green, 'Music, Gender and Education: A Report on Some Exploratory Research', Roberta Lamb, 'The Possibilities of/for Feminist Music Criticism in Music Education', Rosemary Bruce and Anthony Kemp, 'Sex-stereotyping in Children's Preferences for Musical Instruments', *British Journal of Music Education* 10, 3 (November 1993).

17. Frau und Musik, Internationaler Arbeitskreis e. V., Geschäftsstelle, Naumburger Strasse 40, D-34127, Kassell, Germany. Tel. 0561 890 0061. E-mail: <ArchivFrauMusik.kassel@t-online.de>

18. Fondazione Adkins Chiti: Donne in Musica, Teatro Comunale, Piazza Trento e Trieste, 03014 Fiuggi Citta, Italia. Tel/Fax 0039 775 549071. <http://www. donneinmusica.org/index.htm>.

19. Stichting Vrouw en Muziek Swammerdamstraat 38, 1091 RV Amsterdam, Netherlands. Tel. 020 6947 317. <http://music.acu.edu/www/iawm/ wimusic/stichting.htm>l.

20. Women in Music, 7 Tavern Street, Stowmarket, IP14 1PJ Tel. 01449 673990 E-mail: <info@womeninmusic.org.uk>

9 The early music revival: sources and literature

Roderick Swanston and Lewis Foreman

► **INTRODUCTION**

The early music revival, by which until fairly recently we have meant the revival of music composed before 1750, is something that was slowly growing during the nineteenth century, perhaps seen as starting with Mendelssohn's performance of Bach's *St Matthew Passion* in 1829. To us it tends to refer to that period since the mid-1950s when, driven by a boom in recordings of music newly rediscovered in archives, and possibly as a reaction to a musical avant-garde rejected by most music lovers, baroque music fulfilled many concert-goers' need for new works. This was reinforced by the authentic instrument movement, again largely driven by recordings, and such charismatic performers as the late David Munrow (1942–76), and later the requirements of CD recordings.

Today this movement has encompassed more and more of the nineteenth-century repertoire, perhaps better described as an 'authentic instrument' revival of romantic and early modern scores, characterised by violins strung with gut strings, and wind and brass players using instruments made at the time of the music they are used to perform. Perhaps the most celebrated example of this work is found in the recordings of Sir Roger Norrington and Sir John Eliot Gardiner, and the re-establishment of the New Queen's Hall Orchestra as a recording orchestra for such now celebrated recordings as Holst's suite *The Planets*.[1]

► **HISTORY**

There's an understandable tendency these days to regard the revival of early music as a modern phenomenon. But in Britain, at any rate, there's been an on-going love affair with the music of the past for a very long time.

In the 1730s Dr John Pepusch, most famous as the arranger of the music for *The Beggar's Opera*, re-formed a 25-year-old Academy of Ancient Music, to show the excellencies of early music, such as Purcell, Palestrina, Byrd, Morley and others. And on his death Pepusch bequeathed to the Academy the manuscript of the Fitzwilliam Virginal Book, amongst many other musical relics.

Nor was Pepusch alone in his interest in 'early music'. His contemporary John Immyns founded the Madrigal Society, which still exists, no doubt in part due to the fact that meetings have always taken place in pubs. Between 1785 and 1848 the *Concerts of Ancient Music* flourished, whose original purpose was to preserve through regular performance great works of earlier composers, the most modern music allowed being no less than 20 years old. Behind all this eighteenth- and nineteenth-century music-making in Britain lay the figure of Handel, who after his demise in 1759 was not so much buried as immortalised.

By the end of the eighteenth century Handel was subjected to performances of elephantine proportions. Choruses and orchestras of hundreds were formed to lollop their way through *Messiah* and other oratorios. Haydn wept at a performance in Westminster Abbey which boasted the best part of three hundred performers. But that was nothing compared with the Crystal Palace Handel extravaganzas in the nineteenth century, which at their largest in 1859, the centenary of the composer's death, mustered a choir of between 2500 and 3000 singers and an orchestra of 450.[2] To suit contemporary taste, however, it was performed with, as they put it, 'additional musical accompaniments'. That is to say, the score performed had less and less to do with Handel's original – a point to which we shall return.

What this example of the concert life of the last 250 years shows, is that music of earlier times formed a significant part of the musical diet of this country, and that performers and audiences have always been aware of, if not over-familiar with, early music, albeit only a very small sample of it. But though there has always been a knowledge, even an interest, in early music, the early music revival is essentially a twentieth-century phenomenon; or to stretch a point just, a late nineteenth-century one, as the bicentenary of Purcell's death in 1895 is a landmark in present-day developments.

▶ THE TWENTIETH CENTURY

At the beginning of the twentieth century, a variety of issues concerning early music began to surface. First, did a few works of Handel or Bach and a handful of sixteenth-century vocal pieces constitute all there was of early music? Secondly, what about the musical texts? How reliable were the ones used? Thirdly, what did the music originally sound like? What instruments was it written for and how did they sound? And would their sound affect the perception of the music? Fourthly, how much did the present age impose its aesthetic on the music of former times? During the twentieth century these concerns have formed the basic issues addressed by the revival of early music.

Perhaps the modern movement can be traced back to a kind of anti-Darwinian philosophy that held that music was not subject to the same laws of the survival of the fittest in the animal kingdom. New did not necessarily mean best. The Irish composer, organist and teacher Sir Charles Stanford, surveying the service lists of English cathedrals at the beginning of this century complained: 'Purcell's Evening Service in G minor, one of the very finest works we possess, appears only in eight lists, on the other hand, a modern service of wonderful vapidity, which shall be nameless, appears in thirty-four. Gibbons's magnificent anthem, *O Thou the central orb* appears only in three. Of foreign composers, . . . Palestrina receives but thirty-four performances of seventeen works, and is recognised only in eighteen cathedrals; Sebastian Bach, the greatest of all, received ninety-nine performances in twenty-six cathedrals . . . While a modern foreign composer, alien to our style, and representing all that is most showy and superficial in religious music gets two hundred and thirty-one performances of thirty-three anthems in no less than forty-four of our cathedrals.'

Behind Stanford's outraged harangue hides the assumption that earlier is better; and this, despite 70 years of Darwinian evolutionary theories. Indeed the gradual unearthing of the past music led to an increasing respect for it as *the* repository of excellence and value. Stanford himself had been a vital part of the Purcell bicentenary celebrations in the 1890s, staging performances and editing texts for the Purcell Society. At the same time, Sir John Stainer published two collections of early music: *Dufay and his Contemporaries* and *Early Bodleian Music*.

A little later, the Reverend Edmund Horace Fellowes, in the wake of the great complete editions of earlier composers published in Germany, began to edit and publish a monumental collection of English Tudor and Stuart sacred and secular music. This included the Collected Works of William Byrd, the English madrigalists and something of almost every other English musician living between about 1560 and 1640. (While Fellowes's autobiography *Memoirs of an Amateur Musician* (1946) is written in a notably unpretentious style, it conveys a vivid picture of the period. For a comparison of Fellowes with Philip Heseltine, see Turbet (1999).)

What is important about these first moves is that they were concerned with publishing texts, which, it seemed to some, could only be of interest to scholars and antiquarians. Some even believed that much of the music unearthed could never be the concern of the average concert-goer. In 1843 the antiquarian, Edward Rimbault, had written of Gibbons's viol fantasies that they showed 'the infantine state of instrumental music at the period at which they were composed, and the limited powers of the instruments upon which they were performed.' And J.A. Fuller-Maitland remembered that the lectures on early music he had heard in Cambridge 'nearly always took it for granted that there was no beauty such as could appeal to modern ears.'

► THE AUDIENCE

The next battle in the revival of early music that had to be won was persuading musicians and their public that early music was not only important historically, but could be enjoyable to listen to, and to achieve this the music had to be heard. Two great pioneers emerged at the beginning of this century.

In choral music, Richard Terry[3] not only performed at Westminster Cathedral much of the music that was flowing from the editing pen of Fellowes, but also interested a host of composers in the music his choir was singing. Holst took Byrd's masses to Salonica, and Vaughan Williams performed madrigals at Leith Hill and incorporated a melody by Tallis into his best-known instrumental work. A kind of Elizabethan fever spread across the country, at any rate for vocal music.

Instrumental music, on the other hand, and the revival of old instruments was a tougher battle to win. To hear early instrumental music required old instruments, but though these had been lovingly exhibited and preserved by some nineteenth-century enthusiasts, no co-ordinated movement for their practical revival got under way till the arrival in England in 1885 of a 25-year-old Belgian emigré, Arnold Dolmestch.

Dolmetsch was a strange man, who sometimes appeared in velvet knee britches and was immortalised in George Moore's *Evelyn Innes*. He was befriended by Bernard Shaw and William Morris, with whose Arts and Crafts movement his revival of old instruments had much in common. Dolmetsch began by restoring and copying old string instruments and then keyboard instruments. He was so keen to promote their use for the performance of early music that he sometimes built instruments at a loss. But his enthusiasm was prophetic, since he showed that the instruments for which music was written were as vital a part of its being known and understood as the printed notes. Until his death in 1940 Dolmetsch was an influential teacher and propagandist, asking many stylistic questions that are still the concern of modern musicians.[4]

Between them, Terry and Dolmetsch helped scotch the idea that early music was of purely antiquarian interest, an attitude reinforced for a wider constituency by the harpsichordist Wanda Landowska (see Restout, 1965; Sabin, 1959) and in the UK by Violet Gordon-Woodhouse (see Douglas-Home, 1997). Even so, none of these could really claim to have inaugurated a mass market. For the first half of this century, interest in early music and its performance remained something of a byway.

▶ **AFTER 1945**

After the Second World War, however, the revival of early music gathered momentum. Once again, on the crest of the growing swell of interest one or two prominent figures stand out. One was the scholar and keyboard player Thurston Dart. Dart was a charismatic and mercurial figure whose scholarship was unfailingly imaginative and often risk-taking. He carried the torch of Dolmetsch into the enemy camp – the halls of academe at Cambridge and London, where, perhaps more than anyone, he helped bridge the harmful gap between scholarship and performance. Dolmetsch, once rejected by the scholarly establishment, scorned its stuffiness all his life, and later the counter-tenor Alfred Deller felt performance and scholarship should always be separate. But Dart, in his early recordings, his solo performances and his collaborations with the Academy of St Martin-in-the-Fields, the Boyd Neel Orchestra, the Philomusica of London and other groups, made his brilliant scholarship meet his instinctive music-making, and in so doing set a new set of criteria for the next generation of early music revivalists.

Dart's vocal counterpart was the counter-tenor Alfred Deller, who, despite his antipathy to scholarship, nonetheless in his performances helped heal the divide between academe and the concert platform. His natural gift, a beautiful counter-tenor voice, coupled with a special sensitivity for English music of the sixteenth and seventeenth centuries, opened many people's ears to the power and beauty of the music, and encouraged a new awareness of what had seemed to some the lost world of Purcell and Dowland.[5]

Tempting as it is to think of great men leading the way, neither Dart nor Deller were alone. In the post-war years there was a surge of interest in early music, perhaps focused in the UK by the activities of the composer Michael Tippett. Conductors like Arnold Goldsborough and Walter Goehr and scholars such as Dr Ernest Meyer vigorously promoted early music on the BBC, and the publishing house L'Oiseau Lyre acquired a recording company to bring to life the music it published. Conductors such as Anthony Lewis emerged, and composers like Britten and Tippett took an active interest in both performing and absorbing into their music the early music they had heard.

But the post-war years have not just continued and expanded the past; they have witnessed three significant major developments. First, the revival of early music has become led by the increased interest, and professionalism, in playing period instruments. Secondly, the enormous expansion in the range of what now comes under the heading of 'early music'. Thirdly, the active revival, indeed reconstruction, of a huge repertoire of scores from opera's inception to Handel and beyond. And all developments have gone hand in hand with the recording industry. Before the war very few professional musicians argued with what seemed self-evident, that the modern piano was superior to the harpsichord, that present-day strings sounded better than old, and that modern woodwind and brass played much better in tune. All that has changed. Nowadays modern orchestras are often expected by prominent international conductors to be able to vary string phrasing according the period of the music being played; and many woodwind and brass players are as adept on period as on modern instruments. The sound of old instruments has revolutionised our understanding of music from Machaut to Mozart and, more recently, beyond. And this interest in old instruments is no longer just antiquarian. The old instruments have rescued whole repertoires, and these repertoires have proved enduringly popular with musicians and audiences. Your modern early music revivalist no longer travels to work by pony and chaise, but by Porsche and plane.

How has all this come about? Partly by early musicians and early music following the way of all other classical music. Personalities and stars have emerged, as have virtuosi and maestri. David Munrow, for instance, playing every conceivable woodwind instrument, showed that not only that the most esoteric early music could be highly popular and immediately accessible, but that its performers could hold massed audiences. Landini's *Ecco la Primavera*, for instance, from fourteenth-century Florence, was highly unexpectedly encored several times when it was performed at a Promenade Concert by David Munrow and the Early Music Consort.

Gone now also are the days of the high-minded amateur, for many epitomised by the strengths and weaknesses of Arnold Dolmetsch. In England, performance on period instruments is a lucrative career, making the same demands on performers as any other part of the performing world. The revival of early music in England has spawned a generation of brilliant performers, the equals of any in the world. Early music is no longer a sideline, and part of what has made this development possible has been the recording industry. In the 1960s and 1970s recording companies began eagerly to promote performances of early music on period instruments, beginning with what had been the heartland of the early repertoire, Renaissance and Baroque music; but they soon moved from the low road to the high road into the musical mainstream by tackling Mozart, Haydn, Beethoven and more lately Brahms and Wagner. Christopher Hogwood and the Academy of Ancient Music, Roger Norrington with the London Classical Players and John Eliot Gardiner with both the Monteverdi Choir and Orchestra and the Orchestre Romantique et Revolutionnaire have all applied the same mixture of scholarship, period instruments and performance attitudes to this repertoire.

► RECORDING

And where did this start? Principally with recording companies and some enlightened record producers anxious to record experiments that would

have been too expensive in the 1960s and 1970s to risk as live performances. Much the same story can be told of vocal music. Groups such as
Peter Phillips's Tallis Scholars and Christopher Page's Gothic Voices have
each pioneered apparently esoteric repertoire and made it popular.

The whole concept of an early music revival, in England at any rate,
has changed. Nowadays the concepts and aims that underlay the rediscovery performance of early music have found their way into the
performance of Beethoven and Wagner, and the performances on period
instruments are finding their place amongst the best interpretations. Gone
are words like 'authentic', since no such thing was ever available. But questions have been asked by the early music revival that now have to be asked
by all performers. And perhaps that's the most pervasive influence. Even
the most die-hard concert pianist now worries about the edition he uses,
and some about the instrument they play on. How long before the ideas
of such as Anthony Rooley and Philip Pickett about steeping oneself in the
general culture and ideas of the works they perform to gain insights into
such technical aspects as speed and mood become the norm for all
performers. Who knows? One wouldn't dare predict, though we do see
signs; and if the revival of early music becomes as influential over the next
50 years as it has over the last, then *nothing* would surprise us.

▶ HISTORIES

There are two source histories of the early music revival, which all interested should start by reading: Harry Haskell's excellent overview *The Early
Music Revival: a history* (1988), and Joe Cohen and Herb Snitzer's *Reprise:
the extraordinary revival of early music* (1985). Haskell is particularly valuable for his excellent narrative bibliography, which provides an ideal
starting point for wider reading. Cohen and Snitzer complement this with
a less closely argued discussion from an American perspective, characterised
by over 100 pages of photographs of those engaged in the revival.

There is a third essential source for all interested in the early music
revival, and one that has the advantage of being more recently published.
This is Bernard D Sherman's *Inside Early Music: conversations with
performers* (1997). This valuable source book is a model of how such
volumes should be compiled, for the editor engages closely with his subjects
and the issues, in a wide-spanning, vivid account that includes extensive
reference to the sources and the issues. This is particularly useful for the
way he quotes a variety of views on any given topic rather than adopt a
fixed position himself. As such it becomes a valuable introduction to the
various views and issues in a notably disputatious and opinionated field. It
is also valuable for the 18 thumbnail narrative bibliographies and discographies that close each chapter.

During the Second World War, interest in 'early music' transferred to the UK, and particularly owing to the circle round Michael Tippett at Morley College in London, revivals of Purcell and Monteverdi attracted a considerable following in the post-war years. Apart from Tippett's own performances,[6] there were the activities of Walter Bergmann as a harpsichordist and accompanist to Carl Dolmetsch on the recorder, Bergmann producing many editions of eighteenth-century works for recorders for the publisher Schott, music which soon found a wide constituency of amateur players. However, among the Tippett circle the two principal forces that drove the early days of the revival were the counter-tenor Alfred Deller, in his day a remarkable phenomenon, and the conductor Walter Goehr, who during the war had been a champion of Tippett in particular and modern music in general, but who also made some of the earliest recordings of Monteverdi, in the 1950s.[7]

These various growing centres of enthusiasm and expertise were given new focus in the 1950s by the appearance of the long-playing record, which broke the long-standing monopoly of a few major record companies (in the UK really only EMI (HMV, Columbia and Parlophone) and Decca). Now, with the emergence of new small companies with access to pioneering new performers, the general availability of halls and churches capable of being used as recording studios, and the availability of professional quality tape recorders at affordable prices, together with independent engineers, pressing plants and all the infrastructure of the recording industry, the independent companies interested in unexplored repertoire were free to 'do their thing', and were so successful at it that they were soon emulated by the major companies.

▶ PERIODICALS

While there have long been a number of specialist journals interested in early music – notably *The Consort* (the journal of the Dolmetsch Foundation) and, for instruments, the *Galpin Society Journal* – they were a very specialist interest, and the exploration of this repertoire in performance was consolidated by the foundation of a number of more widely read and influential journals, in the UK particularly *Early Music*. Indeed anyone reading themselves into the field would find it useful to scan a file of back issues of *Early Music*, which effectively constitutes a history of the revival as it happened.

Most countries have their early music journals, which are increasingly glossy in presentation. Many of these are listed in the *International Directory of Current Early-music Periodicals* (1994), but the principal examples in English are:

- *Goldberg: Early Music Magazine/Magazine de Musique Ancienne et Baroque* (in English and French);
- *Concerto;*
- *Continuo;*
- *Early Music America;*
- *Early Music Today;* and
- *Flute a Bec.*
- *Journal of Seventeenth Century Music:* <www.sscm.harvard.edu>

The specialist societies have all been influenced by this growth of the literature and their journals have been revamped and made to appeal to a growing audience, in addition to the two long-standing titles mentioned, examples being:

- *Bach: Journal of the Riemenschneider Bach Institute;*
- *Chelys: the Journal of the Viola da Gamba Society;*
- *The Lute: Journal of the Lute Society of Great Britain;* <www.ds.dial.pipex.com/silvius/lute/>
- *Plainsong and Medieval Music* (successor to the *Journal of the Plainsong and Mediaeval Music Society*).

▶ REFERENCE BOOKS

A range of reference books have appeared to service the requirements of what is now a very active sector. *The Early Music Yearbook* provides a range of general reference information including lists of societies periodicals, publishers, record companies, artists and their agents, instrument collections and fairs and exhibitions. The instrument buyer's guide contains lists of manufacturers and retailers, restoration, conservation and repair. This yearbook is published by the National Early Music Association, an organisation that has tended to change its address, making the *Yearbook* difficult to keep track of. At the time of writing the current edition is believed to be that for 1998.

Other yearbooks are issued by specialist composer societies, though there is a tendency for them to be in German. The most notable examples are:

- *Bach-Jahrbuch* (Leipzig: Evangelische Verlagsanstalt);
- *Händel-Jahrbuch;* and
- *Schütz-Jahrbuch* (Kassel: Bärenreiter) (mainly in German, occasional article in English).

The full range of scholarly texts relating to the various periods now regarded as 'early music' may be traced through Duckles' *Music Reference and Research Materials* (Duckles and Reed, 1997). This is a notably swiftly-moving area.

► PERFORMERS' GUIDES AND PERFORMANCE PRACTICE

With the interest in the recorder as a schools instrument after the Second World War, many performers' introduction to performance practice issues was simply at the very basic level of when and how to ornament authentically, with trills, turns, etc. Here Robert Donington's books filled a real need and were for many years the standard source and still worth having (Donington, 1973, 1974). One of the most valuable spin-offs from the *New Grove*, New Grove Handbooks in Music is Howard Mayer Brown and Stanley Sadie's *Performance Practice* (1989). As the field of early music being explored in performance widened and deepened, increasingly such guides become more and more specialised, an example being Timothy J. McGee's *Medieval and Renaissance Music: a Performer's Guide* (1985) The extent of such material may be consulted in Roland Jackson's *Performance Practice, Medieval to Contemporary: a Bibliographic Guide* (1988), which is updated in the journal *Performance Practice Review* to 1995. *Performance Practice Review* ceased hard copy publication in 1997 and is now available free on the internet (<http://www.performancepractice. com>) and in a very attractively presented and up-to-date source as *Performance Practice Encyclopedia*.

The field of performance practice is now subject to developing heavyweight academic series from the leading academic presses. Perhaps the leader in this development is the Cambridge University Press with their series *Cambridge Handbooks to the Historical Performance of Music*, and the journals *Early Music* and the clothbound annual volumes of *Early Music History*, edited by Iain Fenlon, whose most recent volume at the time of writing (vol. 19) included articles on: Ritual and Ceremony in the Spanish Royal Chapel, c.1559–Dc.1561; Urban Minstrels in Late Medieval Southern France; Mapping the Soundscapes: Church Music in English Towns 1450-D1550; A New Look at Old-Roman Chant. (CUP November 2000).

► DISCOGRAPHIES AND CD REVIEWS

The early music revival has essentially been a movement that has been established and financed by recordings. For a beginner's introduction to the earlier period, keyed to recordings, Derrick Henry's *The Listener's Guide to Medieval & Renaissance Music* (1983) is very readable and an excellent introduction to the whole field for the layman, though preceding the CD era and thus already significantly out of date. However, there has not been a revision or a later guide in similar style. Also pre-dating CD, the whole period is exhaustively documented by Trevor Croucher's *Early Music Discography* (Library Association, 1981). As the compiler notes in his introduction: 'faced with the problem of arranging some three thousand records (over half of which are anthologies) into a convenient and logical order, I have opted for a chronological layout based on the six periods generally referred to by music historians [Early Medieval; Ars Nova; Early Renaissance; Late Renaissance; Early Baroque; Late Baroque].' The whole compilation is made to work by indexes of Composer, Plainsong, Anonymous Work and Performer Indexes.

Music issued on CD has tended to be documented in reference books to specific composers or general guides to current recordings where such material is now treated as mainstream. Trace these through Gray and Gibson's *Bibliography of Discographies* (see pp. 281–2). The change from vinyl to compact discs in the 1980s saw an enormous expansion of the early music discography, and widespread reviewing of such material. For specialised coverage of these recordings see *Early Music Review* (ten issues per year). *Early Music Quarterly* (1999), started by *Gramophone* in 1999, appears to have only lasted three issues owing to the sale of its parent magazine, though it briefly signalled the vigour and extent of activity in the recording field. Its editor Meredith McFarlane, in introducing her first issue, highlighted the rapid development and growth of the movement her magazine had been created to espouse:

> '*Roughly 30 years ago, a movement seeking to recreate lost sounds gathered extraordinary momentum, ultimately forcing a dramatic transformation of the way we perceive and listen to music of the past. It rapidly moved on from its turbulent early days when zealous claims for 'authenticity' were pitted against accusations of 'iconoclasm'. Now termed 'historically informed,' the self-assured stance which has emerged carries with it an alluring sense of discovery, risk-taking and imagination. Early music not only continues to challenge our musical habits but also the once-entrenched conventions of classical music ... controversies abound as period performers continue to combine two essential ingredients: historical principles and personal expression.*'

Specialist record shops also issue their own lists and catalogues.

▶ FAIRS AND CONFERENCES

A notable activity which has helped to define the sector and its infrastructure is the regular exhibitions or fairs devoted to early music. Here can be found instrument makers and specialist material suppliers, manufacturers and retailers of CDs, music and books on music, specialist courses and specialist societies, and there is a variety of maker's demonstrations, concerts and other events depending on location. The principal fairs are:

- June: Boston Early Music Festival (Cambridge, MA)
- June: The Berkeley Festival & Exhibition (U of California)
- June: Early Music Day, Sopron, Hungary
- June: Tage Alter Musik, Regensburg
- July-Aug: Innsbruck Festival of Early Music
- July: York Early Music Festival
- July: London Lufthansa Festival of Baroque Music
- August: Flanders Early Music Festival
- August: Amherst Early Music Festival, New York
- August: Glasgow International Early Music Festival
- October: London (Royal College of Music)
- October: Berliner Tage für Alte Musik
- November: Bach Festival of Lausanne

▶ SPECIALIST RETAILERS

Instrument builders and specialist suppliers may be contacted from directories, advertisements in the specialist press and at early music fairs. However, one notable feature of the early music movement has been the emergence of specialist retailers in both Europe and the USA. A good example is the Early Music Shop, which claims (on its website, <http://www.e-m-s.com>) to be 'the largest single source of early musical instruments worldwide.'[8]

▶ WEBSITES

For extensive listings and links to Early Music websites see *Early Music FAQ* (<www.medieval.org/emfaq/concerts/other.htm>)

▶ REFERENCES

Andrews, H. (1948) *Westminster Retrospect: A Memoir of Sir Richard Terry*. Oxford: OUP

Brown, H.M. and Sadie, S. (1989) *Performance Practice*. London: Macmillan

Campbell, M. (1975) *Dolmetsch: The Man and his Work*. London: Paul Elek

Cohen, J. and Snitzer, H. (1985) *Reprise: the Extraordinary Revival of Early Music*. Boston, MA: Little, Brown & Co.

Croucher, T. (1981) *Early Music Discography*. London: Library Association

Donington, R. (1973) *A Performer's Guide to Baroque Music*. London: Faber

Donington, R. (1974) *The Interpretation of Early Music* (2nd edn.). London: Faber

Douglas-Home, J. (1997) *Violet*. London: Harvill Press

Duckles, V.H. and Reed, I. (1997) *Music Reference and Research Materials – an Annotated Bibliography* (5th edn.). New York: Schirmer

Fellowes, E.H. (1946) *Memoirs of an Amateur Musician*. London: Methuen

Hardwick, M. and Hardwick, M. (1980) *A Singularity of Voice* (rev. edn.). London & NY: Proteus Pub. Co.

Haskell, H. (1988) *The Early Music Revival: a History*. London: Thames & Hudson

Henry, D. (1983) *The Listener's Guide to Medieval & Renaissance Music*. London: Facts on File

International Directory of Current Early-music Periodicals (1994). Cleveland, OH: Early Music American

Jackson, R. (1988) *Performance Practice, Medieval to Contemporary: a Bibliographic Guide*. New York: Garland [Music Research & Information Guide 9]

McGee, T.J. (1985) *Medieval and Renaissance Music: a Performer's Guide*. Toronto: University of Toronto Press

Restout, D. (ed.) (1965) *Landowska on Music*. London: Secker & Warburg

Sabin, R. (1959) And so I am Going On . . . *American Record Guide*, xxvi, 239

Sherman, B.D. (1997) *Inside Early Music: Conversations with Performers*. NY: OUP

Robinson, S. (ed.) (2002) *Michael Tippett: Music and Literature*. Aldershot: Ashgate

Turbet, R. (1999) Peter Warlock and Early Music: an assessment. *Brio*, Autumn/Winter, 105–110

▶ NOTES

1. The Planets/St Paul's Suite New Queen's Hall Orch/Roy Goodman IMP 30366 00432.
2. A dim echo of these gargantuan occasions may be heard on Sir Henry Wood's recording for Colombia of extracts recorded live at the 1926, and last, Handel Festival at the Crystal Palace (reissued on CD on Symposium 1251).
3. For Terry, see Andrews (1948).

4.   For Dolmetsch, see Campbell (1975).
5.   For Deller, see Hardwick and Hardwick (1980).
6.   Robinson (2002) includes a chapter by Suzanne Cole ' "Musical Trail-Blazing and General Daring": Michael Tippett, Morley College and early music'.
7.   Walter Goehr's recording of a 'concert version' of Monteverdi's *The Coronation of Poppea* was issued by the Concert Hall Record Club on CM 2028.
8.   Manningham Lane, Bradford BD1 3EA. Also at: London Early Music Shop, 34 Chiltern Street, London W1 1PH (check <http://www.e-m-s.com> for up-to-date information).

10 Standard reference sources and collected editions

Ian Ledsham

What is a reference source? In practice, almost anything can be a reference work. A major composer biography may well provide the nugget of essential information you have been searching for for weeks. Or a periodical article may provide an invaluable reference in its bibliography. In general, however, the term 'reference works' is taken to mean works not intended to be read 'cover-to-cover' but to be consulted for specific points of information. The following chart shown in Figure 10.1 defines five main types of reference source.

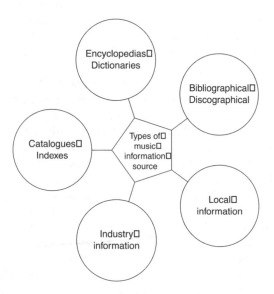

Fig. 10.1: Types of music reference source.

(Source: Ledsham, Ian. 'IL34710 Advanced Music Information', University of Wales Aberystwyth: Open Learning Unit, 1998.)

The one area listed above that we shall not cover in this chapter is local information. By its very nature, local information is unique to each library or information centre. This might include indexes to local newspapers; collections of material relevant to local composers, artists or venues; directories of local teachers; or calendars of local events. In many public libraries, this information may be found in the 'local studies' section as well as the music department.

▶ ENCYCLOPAEDIAS AND DICTIONARIES

There are two major music encyclopaedias, *The New Grove Dictionary of Music and Musicians* (Sadie, 1980), and *Die Musik in Geschichte und Gegenwart* (Blume, 1949) (MGG). Both these are substantial, multi-volume works of scholarship. They include work-lists and bibliographies which provide the starting-point for much research. As with most major reference works, it is important to understand the structure of the information to get the best out of these works. MGG uses very small print for certain areas of information – especially work-lists and bibliographies. New editions of both works are currently being prepared. The second edition of MGG is being published volume by volume. The 'Sachteil' subject section is now complete. The biographical section (*Personenteil*) is being published separately. This division of subject and biographical information is becoming seen more often. A similar division will be seen in *Dizionario Enciclopedico della Musica e dei Musicisti* (1983) – the main Italian music dictionary. The second edition of *The New Grove* was published in February 2001.[1]

The New Grove format has spawned several offshoots covering musical instruments (NG), jazz (Kernfeld, 1988), American music (Hitchcock and Sadie, 1986) and opera (Sadie, 1992). There is also a single volume *New Grove Dictionary of Women Composers* (Sadie and Samuel, 1994). Most of these dictionaries so far considered have a classical music bias, but serious study of popular music has led to a number of excellent dictionaries in this area. The most substantial of these is *The Encyclopaedia of popular music* (Larkin, 1995). An older, but still excellent, study of popular music in the first half of the twentieth century is Kinkle (1974). This provides a year-by-year survey of 1900–50, biographies of composers, performers, lyricists, and an enormous song index, which is especially valuable.

Many of these encyclopaedias are multi-volume works with a multi-zero price tag. Perhaps more affordable for the individual user are the excellent single-volume *New Harvard Dictionary of Music* (Randel, 1986), which contains only subject entries (no biographies) and its biographical companion, *The Harvard Biographical Dictionary of Music* (Randel 1996). *Baker's Biographical Dictionary of Musicians* (Slonimsky and Kuhn, 2001), remains readable, substantial and scholarly, but is increasingly beyond the financial reach of the individual researcher.

Biographical dictionaries include the useful *Contemporary Composers* (Morton and Collins, 1997), which though not comprehensive includes some in-depth information about practising composers. Another area of hard-to-find biographical information – in this case of singers – is well served by *Grosses Sängerlexikon* (Kutsch and Riemens, 1997). In German, this covers singers of all periods, though principally art music singers.

Dance and drama are regular bedfellows of music. In ballet and in musical theatre – that particularly 20th-century art form – research may involve study in all three areas. Musical theatre is well served by *The Encyclopedia of the Musical Theatre* (Gänzl, 1994). Ballet is covered by many dictionaries, including *The International Dictionary of Ballet* (Bremser, 1993), *Tanzlexikon* (Schneider, 1985). The *International Encyclopedia of Dance* (Cohen, 1998) looks likely to become a major resource in this discipline.

Finally, mention must be made of dictionaries of musical theory and musical terms. Many general musical dictionaries will cover both these areas. One single-volume work that experience has proved useful in this area is *The New Everyman's Dictionary of Music* (Blom, 1988). A very useful multi-lingual dictionary of musical terms has been produced by the Incorporated Society of Musicians and the International Association of Music Libraries, Archives and Documentation Centres. *Terminorum Musicae Index Septem Linguis Redactus* (1978) covers musical terms in English, French, German, Spanish, Italian, Russian, and Hungarian. Study of the instructions for use will be amply repaid.

▶ BIBLIOGRAPHICAL SOURCES

The bibliography of printed music is approached on a national basis. Many national bibliographies include a music section. This may be included with the main bibliographical information week by week, or month by month; or it may be a supplement to the national bibliography published on a quarterly or annual basis; or it may be a separate bibliography. There is a clear distinction between a national bibliography and the catalogue of a major library collection which, because of its size, may fulfil a bibliographical function. A national bibliography has as its main aim the listing of bibliographical information on published material emanating from a particular country. A major library catalogue lists publications it acquires from any country. Given the international nature of music – whose language does not know the national boundaries that text publications have – some of these major music library catalogues serve better as music bibliographies than the national bibliographies. In the UK, the two functions have been fused in *The British Catalogue of Music* (1957–) which, since 1981, has listed not only UK music publications, but all music publications received by the British Library Music Library.

National bibliographies provide evidence of the existence of an item, but not of its availability. In-print guides to monograph material are common in many countries. There are few equivalents for printed music. The best – if imperfect – source is Musicdata's *Music-in-Print* (1973–) series. This is not updated on a frequent basis, and lacks sections for piano and chamber music. There is also a range of bibliographies covering repertoire for musical instruments. A useful guide to these is Bernhard Bruchle's *Music Bibliographies for all Instruments* (Bruchle, 1976).

Mention must be made of two bibliographies of a rather specialised nature, covering material not always listed in other music bibliographies. Stubblebine (1996) provides a guide to published music from Broadway musicals. Much music from stage and film is not published, and it is therefore useful to have a comprehensive guide to what has been published. *Katzmarek's Encyclopedia of Public Domain Music* (1993) is a listing of music in the public domain – especially useful for designers of websites, amongst other things.

The Music Library Association (US) has produced two useful guides under the title *A Basic Music Library*. Fling (1983) covers music books and printed music; Davis *et al.* (1997) covers printed and recorded music. These provide a good basic coverage of library stock of all types. A good recent guide to popular music reference material is Haggerty (1995). Dance literature is well covered in *Research in Dance: a Guide to Resources* (Bopp, 1994). Finally in this section, mention must be made of Fuld (1995), which provides valuable bibliographical information about a range of well-known classics. Apart from the individual entries, the preface provides an excellent guide to aspects of music bibliography to be considered in this kind of research.

► CATALOGUES AND INDEXES

As has been mentioned, the line between catalogues and bibliographies is sometimes difficult to draw. Because music is international in scope and publication, the catalogues of a number of major libraries have come to be regarded as international bibliographies of music. These include the catalogues of the British Library (1979–1987) and of the Library of Congress (1953 and 1981–). In addition to these, the catalogues of four other major music library collections are invaluable reference sources: those of the Music Department of the Bibliothèque Nationale (1990); of the Bavarian State Library (Bayerische Staatsbibliothek, 1988, now on CD-ROM, 1999); and of the Music Division of the New York Public Library (1982). Lastly

– and differing from the other catalogues mentioned – the BBC Music Library catalogue (BBC 1965–1982). This catalogue of the oldest broadcasting library in the world, with one of the largest music library collections, is especially valuable for its extensive title index to choral and vocal works and for its complicated but extremely effective index to any and every chamber music combination imaginable. Designed as a finding aid for the BBC Music Library staff and music producers, it does not concern itself too much with the niceties of bibliographical description. Popular music was regarded as a separate species in the rarefied atmosphere of the BBC, and a separate, microfiche catalogue of the Popular Music Library was published in 198?.

Many other libraries have published catalogues of their holdings – especially their research holdings. These are as many and varied in their style and approach as the libraries that produce them. Besides the academic and public sector libraries, mention must be made of ecclesiastical and other private libraries, which often have important collections. Examples of these are the catalogues of various parts of the Vatican Library (Llorens, 1960 and 1971); the catalogue of the Library of Westminster Abbey (Squire, 1903); and various handlists of parts of the collection of the Paul Sacher Stiftung (1988–). These catalogues provide a rich resource for exploring the wealth of printed and manuscript music in libraries and private collections around the world.

Recorded sound collections have been less well served by published catalogues, perhaps reflecting the attitude of an earlier generation of librarians and scholars that recordings were not a serious part of musical study and research – a view long since discredited. As recording moves into its second century – and earlier recordings assume greater research value – we shall undoubtedly see the growth of archival recordings collections and the publication of appropriate catalogues. At present, the best approach is through the various guides to archival recordings collections that have been published in the last 20 or 30 years, such as Foreman (1974), Weerasinghe (1989) and Klaue (1993) (see also CHAPTER 21).

Some more specialised types of catalogue deserve mention here:

- publishers' catalogues
- musical instruments collection catalogues
- dance and theatre catalogues
- union catalogues
- thematic catalogues.

Publishers' catalogues

Publishers' catalogues will be familiar as sources of information and publicity about the current availability of music. Such catalogues are ephemeral, and often thrown away when new editions are received. Older catalogues, however, can be a useful source of musicological and bibliographical information. A number of publishers' catalogues have been published, either in facsimile or as historical studies. Examples of these are the Breitkopf thematic catalogues for 1762–1787 (1966) and the Ricordi numerical catalogue of 1857 (Laterza, 1984).

Musical instruments collections catalogues

Musical instruments are not always found in the same place as printed and recorded music collections. Museums are more likely venues for such collections than libraries. The *International Directory of Musical Instrument Collections* (Jenkins, 1977) is the starting point for finding out where collections can be found. For keyboard instruments also note Edward L Kottick and George Luckenberg's *Early Keyboard Instruments in European Museums* (1997). Many collections have published catalogues, and Coover (1981) provides the most substantial guide to this literature.

Dance and theatre catalogues

It has already been noted that drama and dance studies are frequently allied to music research. Mention must be made here of the catalogues of the excellent research collections in these subjects held at the New York Public Library, the *Catalog of the Theatre and Drama Collections* (1967) and the *Dictionary Catalog of the Dance Collection* (1974). These catalogues complement the catalogue of the music collection already mentioned. Besides these catalogues, mention should also be made of the Derra de Moroda dance archives (Derra de Moroda, 1982). For a guide to performing arts resources – especially those in the United States, see Slide *et al.* (1988).

Union catalogues

The most important of the various published union catalogues is the series on worldwide holdings of early printed and manuscript music and books on music entitled *Répertoire International des Sources Musicales* (1972–). *RISM* is divided into three series:

- Series A – General alphabetical series
- Series B – Classified series
- Series C – Directory of music research libraries.

The coverage of early printed music and music theory is generally good. Early printed music is divided into two basic types – individual works or collections by a single composer (*Einzeldrucke*) in Series A; and anthologies (*Recueils imprimés*) in Series B. The individual works are treated in a series of volumes covering the period from the invention of music printing in the last quarter of the fifteenth century to 1800 with supplementary volumes to 1830, occasionally even later. Each entry in these volumes is given a reference number consisting of the initial letter of the composer's name followed by a running number within that letter. Thus, H3379 refers to the Imbault edition of Haydn's Opus 50 string quartets.

The anthologies are treated in two separate sections, one covering the sixteenth and seventeenth centuries and one covering the eighteenth century. The sixteenth and seventeenth-century volumes are arranged chronologically, and the reference numbers for these items consist of the year of publication followed by a superscript running number within each year. Thus, 1601^{16} refers to *The Triumphes of Oriana*. These reference numbers are frequently used in publications such as *The New Grove* as a convenient shorthand. The eighteenth-century volume is arranged alphabetically by title, and has no reference numbers, possibly because music published in the eighteenth century is difficult to date accurately.

Manuscript material is covered in separate volumes covering the eleventh to fourteenth centuries and the fifteenth and sixteenth centuries. Manuscripts post-1600 have proved much more difficult to catalogue in traditional printed form, simply because of the volume and diversity of the material. An interim microfiche index was published in the 1980s (1983–6), but the most satisfactory and economic solution has been to publish this material electronically. From mid-2002 the RISM database 'Music Manuscripts after 1600' is available via a commercial subscription from NISC Biblioline (<www.nisc.com>).

Mention must be made here of the *National Union Catalog*, which lists the holdings of the Library of Congress, supplemented by the holdings of other major research collections in the United States. The mammoth *National Union Catalog Pre-1956 Imprints* (1968), which runs to almost 800 volumes, is the nearest we shall ever get to a universal bibliography. Sadly, its cataloguing of printed music leaves much to be desired. Various union catalogues now exist in electronic form, often hosted by the library cataloguing utilities whose members can make use of such shared data. These catalogues are often not available to non-members, or available only by subscription. Detailed coverage of these catalogues is outside the remit of this chapter.

Thematic catalogues

Thematic catalogues provide an example of the overlap between indexes and catalogues. A genuine thematic catalogue should, as the name suggests, contain themes from the works being catalogued. If it does not, it is really a work-list; but, in practice, the term 'thematic catalogue' is sometimes used to cover both these items. Most thematic catalogues cover the work of a single composer, as for example with Schmieder's catalogue of the works of J.S. Bach (1990). However, some cover the works of more than one composer (such as the Strauss, Lanner, Ziehrer catalogue – Schönherr, 1982).

The best thematic catalogues are substantial works of scholarship, not only identifying the themes but including information about the location of manuscripts, details of early printed editions of each work, and sometimes a bibliography of literature pertaining to each work. At the opposite end of the scale, some of the nineteenth-century thematic catalogues are little more than publishers' selling aids. Brook and Viano (1997) provides a guide to thematic indexes – both monographic publications and thematic catalogues published in journals.

There are also some related thematic *indexes* which can help to identity themes of which you do not know the composer. Barlow and Morgenstern (1976 and 1983) and Parsons (1975) are the best-known examples. In addition to these, there have been thematic indexes compiled to the works of some of the best-known composers. These can be helpful when you know the composer of a theme but cannot identity the specific work it is taken from.

► INDEXES

The indexes most frequently used by music researchers are

- periodical article indexes
- song indexes
- indexes to contents of music anthologies (recorded or printed).

Periodical article indexes will be discussed in CHAPTER 11, and the indexing of recordings in CHAPTER 21. Indexes to collected editions and anthologies will be considered at the end of this section. This leaves song indexes. Despite the value of such indexes, and the long-accepted view that an index to all published song collections would be highly desirable, there is no sign of such an ideal solution. As a result, a number of approaches have to be used. For classical material, Sears (1966) remains a valuable tool – though now of retirement age. Not strictly song indexes are the *Singer's Repertoire* series (Coffin 1960), and the *Repertoire for Solo Voice* (Espina 1977). The popular repertoire has been covered in various ways by Kinkle (1974), and by Havlice (1975) (with later supplements). In the UK, POPSI provided a regular indexing service for a few years before its untimely demise. For a useful popular song index on the Web see Plymouth Public Library's Song Index (<http://www.webopac.plymouth.gov.uk/>). Incidentally, you can find any British public library on the Web from the alphabetical list at

<dspace.dialpipex.com/town/square/ac940/ukpublib.html>. A similar list of UK higher education and research libraries is at <www.ex.ac.uk/library/uklibs.html>.

▶ COMMERCIAL INFORMATION AND DIRECTORIES

This covers material relating to the industries – recordings, publishing, broadcasting, performing – that are involved in music.

The industry (*aka* The Music Business – as if that were the only aspect of music!) has generated a vast amount of print – on topics ranging from sales statistics to how to make a career as a pop star. Amongst these many offerings, Granow and Saunio (1998) provide a history of the recording industry, as does Steffens (1992). The US market – an important player in this aspect of music – is handsomely dealt with in *The Encyclopedia of Recorded Sound in the United States* (Marco, 1993). There are plenty of 'A-Z' guides to particular aspects of the industry, such as Schreiber (1992). This market is currently fragmenting, and independent production is becoming more common, with a consequent rise in DIY guides such as Stanfield (1997). For the performing artist, the *Back Stage Handbook* (Eaker, 1995) is invaluable. The UK equivalent is the *Stage and Variety Artiste's Guide and Handbook*.

Record charts are best accessed these days through the World Wide Web, where regular updating is available. In the US, this service is provided on the *Billboard* site (<http://www.billboard-online.com>), and in the UK *Music Week* provides a web chart index (<http://www.dotmusic.com/charts/MWcharts.html>).

The *British Music Yearbook* (BMY) is a model of the kind of directory needed in the music world. Now known officially as the *British and International Music Yearbook*, this annual publication provides information on performing artists and ensembles, UK music and record retailers, music publishers, instrument manufacturers, major libraries – including hire libraries – music journalists, and so on. The format has been copied in some other directories. BMY includes details of music festivals. There is also an *International Guide to Music Festivals* (Smith and Barton, 1980), though now somewhat out of date. The *BBC Music Magazine* regularly provides information on festivals with a supplement in the summer.

▶ COLLECTED EDITIONS

Collected editions are not strictly speaking reference works. In most cases the editions contain full scores which could be used as authoritative performing scores. In practice, the considerable expense – and, in some cases, rarity – of collected editions means that many libraries regard them as reference items for 'in library' use only. This trend is acknowledged by some publishers who now make available cheaper copies of the editions contained in collected works as 'performing editions'. These editions will often be paper bound – as opposed to the hardback scholarly editions – and will probably not include the extensive critical apparatus to be found in the subscription copy. It is not my intention to enter the debate on whether or not collected editions should be regarded as reference works or not. Their inclusion in this chapter simply reflects the reality in most libraries.

- Composers' complete editions.
- Historical sets and anthologies.

The first category covers items such as the *Neue Bach-Ausgabe*, for example, whilst the second covers works that have been selected on a national basis, such as *Musica Britannica* or *Denkmäler der Tonkunst in Österreich*, a chronological basis, such as *Polyphonic Music of the Fourteenth Century* (1956–91), or a repertoire basis, such as *Tudor Church Music* or *The Sixteenth-century Motet* (1987), as well as general collections with no thematic basis.

The earliest collected editions date from the eighteenth century. Boyce's *Cathedral Music* (Boyce 1760–73) is the first collection that can conceivably be regarded as a collected edition. The first composer collected edition – at least, the first attempt – is the Arnold edition of Handel's works, (Arnold 17 –) which was never completed. There is then something of a gap until the mid-nineteenth century when the Bach-Gesellschaft began its pioneering edition of *Johann Sebastian Bach's Werke*. The scholarly approach brought to this edition, and the high standard of publication, was to provide a model for successive complete editions which came in the latter half of the nineteenth century, many of them, like *Bach's Werke*, published by the Leipzig firm of Breitkopf & Härtel. Today, many of these are published by Bärenreiter.

This publishing activity was brought to a halt by the First World War, and though some editions were issued in the inter-war years, the next phase of publishing came immediately after the Second World War and in the 1950s, when the advances in musical scholarship during the previous century had rendered the pioneering efforts of the nineteenth century ripe for replacement. The *Neue Bach-Ausgabe* and *Neue Mozart-Ausgabe* both date from this post-war period.

The expansion in the academic study of music which took place from the 1960s onwards, and the development of music libraries that accompanied that expansion, encouraged the publication of more composers' collected editions, and brought twentieth-century composers into the list of those honoured in this way (this is developed in CHAPTER 17).

The 'historical set' type of collected edition also had its first flowering in the second half of the nineteenth century, with the development of major collections such as *Denkmäler deutscher Tonkunst*. The inter-war years of this century saw the continuing development of major anthologies such as *Tudor Church Music*. The last two decades have seen a substantial expansion of this type of collected edition. One factor in this expansion has been the increasing publication of facsimile collections as a result of technological developments making such publication much easier.

Articles on 'Editions' can be found in the *New Grove* and in the *New Harvard Dictionary of Music* (Randel, 1986). Both these sources provide lists of collected and historical editions. The German bookseller, Harrassowitz[2] also provides useful guides to composers' collected editions and to historical sets that are currently available. (Harrassowitz is, of course, a commercial company and these guides are generally available only to those intending to buy, but you may find a library that has subscriptions with Harrassowitz that has copies of these guides). These sources only provide information on the complete collection.

More difficult is identifying individual items within a collected edition. With composer collected editions, this is not too difficult. At least if you know the composer of the piece you are seeking, you know which collected edition to look in. With many major composers, *New Grove* provides a useful guide to the volume and page numbers for individual works. This information is buried in the work-lists at the end of articles on composers such as Beethoven, Mozart, Mendelssohn and so on.

Historical sets are more of a problem. There are many rare editions of pieces otherwise unobtainable elsewhere buried in historical sets. Two useful, but inevitably incomplete, guides are available. Heyer (1980) provides a two volume guide. The first volume lists the collected editions (both composer collected editions and historical sets) in alphabetical order with, in many cases, a volume by volume analysis. The second volume contains a selective index to individual works with pointers to the relevant collections containing each work. Valuable though it is, the index is far from complete. Hill and Stephens (1997) supplements Heyer, including many sets issued in the past 20 years, and is intended to have a more comprehensive indexing system, though the recent demise of its publisher leads one to wonder whether the index volume, or CD-ROM versions, will ever appear.

References will be found to many historical sets in standard histories and textbooks also, but sometimes the only approach will be to peruse the indexes of individual volumes to find a desired work.

▶ REFERENCES

Barlow, H. and Morgenstern, S. (1976) *A Dictionary of Opera and Song Themes including Cantatas, Oratorios, Lieder, and Art Songs* (rev. edn.). London: Benn

Barlow, H. and Morgenstern, S. (1983) *A Dictionary of Musical Themes* (rev. edn.). London: Faber

BBC Music Magazine (BBC, 1992–)

Bayerische Staatsbibliothek (1988–1990) *Katalog der Musikdrucke* (17 vols). München: Saur. [CD-ROM (1999)]

Bibliothèque nationale: Departement de la musique (1990) *Catalogues du Departement de la musique*. [Paris]: Chadwyck-Healey. 1836 microfiches

Blom, E. (1988) *The New Everyman's Dictionary of Music* (6th edn.), ed. Cummings, D. London: Dent

Blume, F. (1949–1986) (ed.) *Die Musik in Geschichte und Gegenwart* (17 vols). Kassel: Bärenreiter. [New edn. ed. Ludwig Finscher 1996–]

Bopp, M.S. (1994) *Research in Dance: a Guide to Resources*. New York: G.K. Hall

The Breitkopf Thematic Catalogue 1762–1787 (1966). New York: Dover Publications [c 1966]

Bremser, M. (1993) (ed.) *International Dictionary of Ballet*. Detroit; London: St. James Press

British Broadcasting Corporation (1965–1982) *BBC Music Library Catalogues*. London: BBC Music Library

    Piano and Organ Music (1965) (2 vols)

    Chamber Music (1965) (1 vol.)

    Choral and Opera Catalogue (1966) (2 vols)

    Song Catalogue (1966) (4 vols)

    Orchestral Catalogue (1982) (4 vols)

The British Catalogue of Music (1957–). London: Published on behalf of The British Library National Bibliographic Service by Bowker-Saur [Annual with two cumulating interim issues during the year]

British Library (1979–1987) *Catalogue of printed music in the British Library to 1980* (62 vols). London: Saur

The British and International Music Yearbook. London: Rhinegold Publishing. Annual

Brook, B.S. and Viano, R.J. (1997). *Thematic Catalogues in Music: an Annotated Bibliography*. Stuyvesant, NY: Pendragon Press

Bruchle, B. (1976) *Musik-Bibliographien fur alle Instrumente = Music bibliographies for all instruments* [English by Colleen Gruban]. München: Bemhard-Bruchle-Edition

The Classical Catalogue. London: Retail Entertainment Data. Master edition issued twice yearly. Monthly cumulative supplements issued between master editions

Clough, F. and 6.J. Cuming (1952) *The World's Encyclopaedia of Recorded Music*. Sidgwick & Jackson
    1st supplement: 1950–51. 1952 (bound in with main volume)
    2nd supplement: 1951–52. 1953
    3rd supplement: 1953–55. 1956
    [All re-issued: Westport, Conn.: Greenwood Press, 1970.]

Cohen, S.J. (1998) (ed.) *International Encyclopedia of Dance*. Oxford: OUP [Founding editor, Selma Jeanne Cohen; area editors, George Dorris *et al.*; consultants, Thomas F. Kelly *et al.*]

Coover, J. (1981) *Musical Instrument Collections. Catalogues and Cognate Literature*. Detroit: Information Coordinators

Davis, E. *et al.* (1997) *A Basic Music Library: Essential Scores and Sound Recordings/Compiled by the Music Library Association*. Chicago: American Library Association

Derra de Moroda, F. (1982) *The Dance Library: a Catalogue/ Derra de Moroda Dance Archives*. Edited from the manuscript left by the author by Sybille Dahms and Lotte Roth-Wölfle. München: Robert Wölfle

Deutsch, O.E. (1946) 'Music publishers' numbers'. In: *Journal of Documentation*, 1, 206–16 & 2, 80–91. Published the same year London: Aslib as a separate booklet. A 2nd revised edition, in German, was published Berlin: Merseburger, 1961

Devriès, A. and Lesure, F. *Dictionnaire des éditeurs de musique français* (2 vols). Genève: Minkoff
    Vol. 1: Des origines a environ 1820 (1979)
    Vol.2: De 1820 à 1914 (1988)

Dizionario enciclopedico universale musica e della musicisti (13 vols). (1983–1990) Torino: UTET

Duckles, V. (1997) *Music Reference and Research Materials: an Annotated Bibliography*. New York: Schirmer Books

Eaker, S. (1995) (ed). *The Back Stage Handbook for Performing Artists: the How-to and Who-to-Contact Reference for Actors, Singers, and Dancers* New York: Back Stage Books

Fling, R.M. (1983) *A Basic Music Library: Essential Scores and Books* (2nd edn.). Chicago: American Library Association

Foreman, L. (1974) *Archive Sound Collections; an Interim Directory of Institutional Collections of Sound Recordings in Great Britain Holding Material other than that Currently Commercially Available*. Aberystwyth: College of Librarianship, Wales

Fuld, J.J. (1995) *The Book of World-Famous Music: Classical, Popular and Folk* (4th edn.) (revd. and enlarged). New York: Dover

Gänzl, K. (1994) *The Encyclopaedia of the Musical Theatre* (2 vols). New York: Schirmer Books

Gray, M.H. (1989) *Classical Music Discographies, 1976–1988: a Bibliography*. New York: Greenwood Press

Gray, M.H. (1977) and Gerald D. Gibson. *Bibliography of Discographies* (3 vols). New York: Bowker, 1977–1983

Gronow, P. and Saunjo, I. (1998) *An International History of the Recording Industry*, trans. Christopher Moseley. London; Washington: Cassell

Haggerty, G. (1995) *A Guide to Popular Music Reference Books: an Annotated Bibliography*. Westport, Conn.: Greenwood Press

Havlice, P.P. (1975) *Popular Song Index*. Metuchen, NJ: Scarecrow Press, 1975. [Suppls. 1979, 1984 & 1989]

Heyer, A.H. (1980) *Historical Sets, Collected Editions, and Monuments of Music: a Guide to their Contents* (3rd edn.). Chicago: American Library Association

Hill, G.R. and Stephens, N.L. (1997) *Collected Editions Historical Series & Sets & Monuments of Music: a Bibliography*. Berkeley, CA: Fallen Leaf Press

Hitchcock, H.W. and Sadie, S. (1986) (ed.) *The New Grove Dictionary of American Music*. London: Macmillan

Jenkins, J. (1977) (ed). *International Directory of Musical Instrument Collections*. Buren (Gld.), Netherlands: Frits Knuf for International Council of Museums (ICOM)

Katzmarek's Encyclopedia of Public Domain Music (1993). Monticello, MN: Katzmarek Pub.

Kernfeld, B. (1988) (ed.) *The New Grove Dictionary of Jazz*. London: Macmillan

Kinkle, R.D. (1974) *The Complete Encyclopedia of Popular Music and Jazz, 1900–1950*. New Rochelle, N.Y.: Arlington House, [1974]

Klaue, W. (1993) (ed.) *World Directory of Moving Image and Sound Archives*. München: K.G. Saur

Kottick, E.L. and Luckenberg, G. (1997) *Early Keyboard Instruments in European Museums*. Bloomington: Indiana UP

Kutsch, K.J. and Riemens, L. (1997) *Grosses Sängerlexikon* [Biographical Dictionary of Singers.] (3rd edn.) (5 vols). Bern: K.G. Saur. vol. 6: supplement, 1999; vol. 7 supplement 2002

Larkin, C. (1995) (ed.) *The Guinness Encyclopaedia of Popular Music* (3rd edn.) (8 vols). London; New York: Muze

Laterza, A.Z. (1984) *Il Catalogo numerico Ricordi 1857 con date e indici* Prefazione di Philip Gossett. Roma: Nuovo Istituto Editoriale Italiano

Library of Congress (1953) *National Union Catalog: Music, Books on Music and Sound Recordings*. Totowa, NJ: Rowman & Littlefield [Five-year cumulation from 1953 to 1977. Three-year cumulation from 1978–1980.]

Library of Congress (1981–) *The Music Catalog*. Washington, DC: Library of Congress, 1981–. Microfiche (1981–1990 (a single ten-year cumulation); 1991– (cumulative quarterly supplements))
   [Also available online or on CD-ROM from 1960 – from NISC Biblioline.]
   (<www.nisc.com>)

Llorens, J.M. (1960) *Capellae sixtinae codices musicis notis instructi sive manuscripti sive praelo excussi.* Città del Vaticano: Biblioteca Apostolica Vaticana

Llorens, J.M. (1971) *Le opere musicali della Capella Giulia.* Città del Vaticano: Biblioteca Apostolica Vaticana

Marco, G.A. (1993) (ed). *Encyclopedia of Recorded Sound in the United States.* New York: Garland Publishing

Morton, B. and Collins, P. (1997) (ed.) *Contemporary Composers* (2nd edn.) (2 vols) (revd. and enlarged). Detroit, MI: Gale Research, 1997

Music-in-Print (1973–). Philadelphia: Musicdata, Inc.
       1. Daugherty, F.M. and Simon, S.H. (comps.) *Sacred Choral Music in Print* (1985) (2nd edn.). (Suppls. 1988, 1992, 1996. Master Index 1996)
       2. Eislinger, G.S. and Daugherty, F.M. (comps.) *Secular Choral Music in Print* (1987) (2nd edn.). (Suppls. 1991, 1993, 1996. Master Index 1996)
       3. *Organ Music in Print* (1984) (2nd edn.). (Suppls. 1990, 1997)
       4. *Classical Vocal Music in Print* (1976). [Out of print] (Suppls. 1985, 1998. Master Index 1998)
       5. Jape, M. (comp.) *Orchestral Music in Print* (1979). (Suppls. 1983, 1994, 1999 Master Index 1999)
       6. *String Music in Print* (1973) (2nd edn.). (Suppl. 1984, 1999)
       7. Farish, M.K. (comp.) *Classical Guitar Music in Print* (1989) (Suppl. 1998)
       8. *Woodwind Music in Print* (1997)
       Xc *Master Composer Index* (1999)
       Xt *Master Title Index* (1999)

Music Master. London: Retail Entertainment Data. Printed version issued annually, with monthly updates

The National Union Catalog, pre-1956 Imprints; a cumulative author list representing Library of Congress printed cards and titles reported by other American libraries (754 vols) (1968). Compiled and edited with the co-operation of the Library of Congress and the National Union Catalog Subcommittee of the Resources Committee of the Resources and Technical Services Division, American Library Association. London, Mansell, 1968–1981

Neighbour, O.W. and Tyson, A. (1965) *English Music Publishers' Plate Numbers in the First Half of the Nineteenth Century.* London: Faber & Faber

New York Public Library (1967–76) *Catalog of the Theatre and Drama Collections* (51 vols). Boston: G. K. Hall

New York Public Library (1974) *Dictionary Catalog of the Dance Collection: a list of authors, titles, and subjects of multi-media materials in the Dance Collection of the Performing Arts Research Center of the New York Public Library* (10 vols). [New York]: New York Public Library, Astor, Lenox, and Tilden Foundations; Boston: distributed by G.K. Hall

New York Public Library (1982) *Dictionary Catalog of the Music Collection.* Boston, MA: G.K. Hall

Parsons, D. (1975) *The Directory of Tunes and Musical Themes.* Cambridge: Spencer Brown

Polyphonic Music of the Fourteenth Century (1956–91). Monaco: L'Oiseau-lyre

Preston, M. (1995) *Tele-tunes: the Reference Book of Music for Television Commercials, Programmes, Films and Shows.* Morecambe: Mike Preston Music

Randel, D.M. (1986) *The New Harvard Dictionary of Music.* Cambridge, Mass.; London: Belknap Press of Harvard University Press

Randel, D.M. (1996) *The Harvard Biographical Dictionary of Music.* Cambridge, Mass: Belknap Press of Harvard University Press

Répertoire International des Sources Musicales (1972–)
    A/I *Einzeldrucke vor 1800* (1972–). Kassel: Bärenreiter
    A/II *Musikhandschriften 1600–1800* (1983–6). Kassel: Bärenreiter [microfiche index only] Now available online from NISC Biblioline (<www.nisc.com>)
    B/I–B/II *Recueils imprimés* (1960–4). München-Duisburg: Henle [Suppl. for 18th cent. vol. In *Notes* 28 (1972)]
    B/III *The Theory of Music from the Carolingian Era up to 1400* (1961–) [later vols to ca. 1500]. München-Duisburg: Henle
    B/IV *Manuscripts of Polyphonic Music* (1966–). München-Duisburg: Henle
    B/V *Tropen- und Sequenzenhandschriften* (1964). München-Duisburg: Henle
    B/VI *Écrits imprimés concernant la musique* (1971). München-Duisburg: Henle
    B/VII *Lauten- und Gitarrentablaturen des 15 bis 18 Jhs* (1978). München-Duisburg: Henle
    B/VIII *Das deutsche Kirchenlied* (1978). Kassel: Bärenreiter
    B/IX[1] *Hebrew Notated Manuscript Sources* (1989). München-Duisburg: Henle
    B/IX[2] *Hebrew Writings Concerning Music* (1975). München-Duisburg: Henle
    B/X *The Theory of Music in Arabic Writing (c.900–1900)* (1979). München-Duisburg: Henle
    B/XI *Ancient Greek Music Theory* (1988). München-Duisburg: Henle
    B/XII *Manuscrits persans concernant la musique* (1996). München-Duisburg: Henle
    C *Directory of Music Research Libraries* (5 vols) (1971). Kassel: Bärenreiter
    Music Manuscripts After 1600: Thematic Catalogue on CD-ROM. 9th cumulated edition, 2001 (7th CD-ROM) München: K.G. Saur Verlag

Paul Sacher Stiftung (1988–) *Inventare der Paul Sacher Stiftung.* Winterthur: Amadeus

Sadie, J.A. and Samuel, R. (1994) *The New Grove Dictionary of Women Composers.* London: Macmillan

Sadie, S. (1980) (ed.) *The New Grove Dictionary of Music and Musicians* (20 vols). London: Macmillan

Sadie, S. (1992) (ed.) *The New Grove Dictionary of Opera.* London: Macmillan

Sadie, S. and Tyrréll, J. (2001) *The New Grove Dictionary of Music and Musicians* 2nd ed (29 vols). London: Grove/Macmillan

Schmeider, W. (1990) *Thematisch-systematisches Verzeichnis der musikalischen Werke von Johann Sebastian Bach Bach-Werke-Verzeichnis (BWV)*. Hrsg. von Wolfgang Schmieder. Wiesbaden: Breitkopf & Härtel

Schneider, O. (1985) *Tanzlexikon: Volkstanz, Kulttanz, Gesellschaftstanz, Kunsttanz, Ballett: Tänzer, Tänzerinnen, Choreographen, Tanz- und Ballettkomponisten: von den Anfangen bis zur Gegenwart*. Hrsg. unter Mitarbeit von Riki Raab. Mainz; New York: Schott

Schönherr, M. (1982) *Lanner, Strauss, Ziehrer: synoptisches Handbuch der Tänze und Märsche*. Wien: Doblinger

Schreiber, N. (1992) *The Ultimate Guide to Independent Record Labels and Artists: an A-to-Z Source of Great Music*. New York: Pharos Books

Sears, M.E. (1966) *Song Index; an index to more than 12,000 songs in 177 song collections comprising 262 volumes and supplement, 1934* (2 vols in 1) (assisted by Phyllis Crawford) [n.p.]: Shoe String Press

The Sixteenth-century Motet (1987). New York; London: Garland Publishing

Slide, A., Hanson, P.K. and Hanson, S.L. (1988) *Sourcebook for the Performing Arts: a directory of collections, resources, scholars, and critics in theatre, film, and television*. New York: Greenwood Press

Slonimsky, N. and Kuhn, L. (2001) *Baker's Biographical Dictionary of Musicians* (10th edn.). Revised by Nicolas Slonimsky. New York: Schirmer Books

Smith, D. and Barton, N. (1980) (eds). *International Guide to Music Festivals*. New York: Quick Fox

Squire, W.B. (1903) *Musik-katalog der Bibliothek der Westminster-abbei in London*. Leipzig: Breitkopf & Härtel

The Stage & Variety Artiste's Handbook. Annual

Stanfield, J. (1997) *The Musician's Guide to Making & Selling your own CDs & Cassettes* Cincinnati: Writer's Digest Books

Steffens, B. (1992) *Phonograph: Sound on Disk*. San Diego, CA: Lucent Books

Stubblebine, D.J. (1996) *Broadway Sheet Music: a Comprehensive Listing of Published Music from Broadway and other Stage Shows, 1918–1993*. Jefferson, NC: McFarland

Terminorum musicae index septem linguis redactus = Polyglot dictionary of musical terms: English, German, French, Italian, Spanish, Hungarian, Russian (1978). Budapest: Akadémiai Kiadó

Wadhams, W. (1990) *Sound Advice: the Musician's Guide to the Record Industry*. New York: Schirmer Books; London: Collier Macmillan

Weerasinghe, L. (1989) *Directory of Recorded Sound Resources in the United Kingdom*. Compiled and edited by Lali Weerasinghe; Research by Jeremy Silver. London: British Library National Sound Archive

▶ NOTES

1. Published in 29 volumes. Volumes 24 and 26 were reissued in June 2001 owing to the omission of catalogues in the Stravinsky and Wagner articles. The corrected volumes have pages 560A/B and 970 A/D inserted, respectively.
2. D-65174 Wiesbaden, Germany. Tel: + 49 611 5300. Fax: + 49 611 530560. Internet <http://www.harrassowitz.de>.

11 Musical periodicals

Ian Ledsham

▶ HISTORY

A brief inspection of the 'Periodicals' article in *The New Grove Dictionary of Music and Musicians* reveals a comprehensive list of almost 6000 classical music periodicals covering a wide range of topics, though omitting many jazz titles, and emanating from countries from Argentina to Zimbabwe. This is a vast repertory of material, all of which, in the definition of *The New Grove*, displays 'an intention of continuance, an approach determined by publisher or editor, an objective variety of content and to some extent contemporary relevance.'[1]

The earliest type of music periodical consisted of regular or irregular publication of musical items, and it was not until the end of the eighteenth century that the music periodical as we now conceive it – a collection of more or less literary articles, reviews and events listings on a broad or specific range of musical topics – came into being. The first music periodical of this type was the *Allgemeine musikalische Zeitung*, first published in Leipzig in 1798 and enjoying a lifespan of 50 years. As its name suggests, it was general in nature and was soon to be followed by similar, influential French (*Le Ménéstrel*, Paris, 1833–1940) and English (*The Musical Times*, London, 1844–) periodicals.

The study of the history of musical periodicals owes much to the author of *The New Grove* article, Imogen Fellinger.[2] *The New Grove* article is itself an expansion of Dr Fellinger's article 'Zeitschriften' in *Die Musik in Geschichte und Gegenwart* (Blume, 1949, vol. 14). She considers the nineteenth-century music periodical in her *Verzeichnis der Musikschriften des 19Jhs.* (Fellinger, 1968), which spawned several supplements in *Fontes Artis Musicae* (Fellinger, 1970–76). This work presents a chronological union catalogue of what we might call the 'literary' periodical titles, with locations, published from 1898 to around 1920 – the kind we understand by the term today. In a more recent work, *Periodica musicalia 1789–1830*

(Fellinger, 1986), Dr Fellinger has also considered those music periodicals consisting largely of music items rather than writings about music. These two studies represent the major historical survey of the early history of the music periodical.

The German contribution to this literature, however, is a long-standing one. One of the earliest such reviews is Mendel's article 'Zeitschriften' in his *Musikalisches Conversations-Lexikon* – still interesting for its contemporary views.[3] François Vincent has considered the development of the French music periodical from 1750 to the present day in 'Le parcours historique des revues musicales' (Vincent, 1986). The nineteenth-century English music periodical is similarly reviewed in Langley (1994). Krummel (1990) looks at the 'music item' periodical from the same period. An interesting study of the 'music item' periodical in eighteenth century Poland is given by Szwedowska (1984). Deaville 1986 has produced a useful study of early inventories of European music journals.

The study of music periodicals has developed considerably in the last 20 years, and the Center for Studies in Nineteenth-Century Music at the University of Maryland has produced a journal devoted to the subject – *Periodica Musica* – since 1983 which ceased with issue 10/11 (1995). This has a wide range of historical articles on this subject.

► TYPES OF PERIODICAL

Within the broad spectrum of 'literary' music periodicals a number of specific types can be identified:

- general
- academic, institutions, society
- composer- or artist-related
- commercial
- ephemeral
- national, regional
- newspapers.

General

The majority of music periodicals inevitably fall into this category. The range of information carried can be enormous: scholarly articles; editorial comment; publication and performance reviews; concert and events lists; biographies; advertisements.

Academic, institutions, societies

These emanate from academic or other non-commercial institutions. There was a substantial growth in this kind of journal in the inter-war years – especially as national musicological societies began to proliferate. These periodicals may reflect the proceedings of academic meetings – such as the *Proceedings of the Royal Musical Association*; or they may invite scholarly contribution from society members or the scholarly community at large – as in the case of the *Journal of the American Musicological Society*. In this category come also the journals of specialist organisations, such as those devoted to music librarianship – such as *Notes* (the journal of the Music Library Association); to music teaching – such as the journal of the National Association of Teachers of Singing; to instrument-making or study – such as the *Galpin Society Journal* or the *BIOS Journal* (from the British Institute of Organ Studies); to various musical enthusiasms – such as *Record Collector*. These journals may carry scholarly articles, but will also carry news of society events, letters, reviews and ephemeral information.

Composer- or artist-related

This is really a specialised sub-section of the previous category. These periodicals may be produced by a society or institution – as is the case with the *Journal of the Arnold Schönberg Institute*; by official agents or promoters; or by enthusiasts. Many journals devoted to popular music performers – so-called 'fanzines' – fall into this category. The target audience for many of these latter products is very specific and not in the least academic. These periodicals may include photographs or line drawings; biographical information; or simply journalistic gossip. Such contemporary material may assume greater significance for study and research as time passes. But in many cases, such immediately popular material may be extremely difficult to locate after it has passed out of fashion. Many fanzines are now, effectively, produced on the Web.

Commercial

Commercial organisations have a long history of producing periodical material. This may be essentially scholarly and unbiased in its presentation – as with *The Chesterian*, for example, particularly active in the 1920s, produced by the publishing firm J. & W. Chester, which continued publication to 1961, or *Hinrichsen's Musical Year Book*, which also closed in 1961. On the other hand, such periodicals may have an avowedly promotional function, as is the case with many newsletters emanating from music publishers or instrument and equipment manufacturers. Here again, such apparently short-lived material acquires an increasing research value just as it becomes increasingly difficult to obtain.

Ephemeral

Many of the periodicals already considered are ephemeral in nature. Specialist journals, with limited circulation, or mass-market throw-away publications, it makes little difference. The distinguishing feature of most of this type of material is usually its apparent lack of academic respectability and the difficulty of acquiring it – especially acquisition by the institutions that form the major repositories for periodical material. By its nature, such material is often unindexed, and sometimes uncatalogued.

National/regional

There is a broad range of periodicals covering national and regional music. Some of these, such as *American Music*, are predominantly scholarly in nature. Others are produced by the various national Music Information Centres under their brief to promote the music of their country or region.

Newspapers

There is a long and honourable history of music material in newspapers and, more recently, of music newspapers. The popular music scene – live performance and recording – is well covered by newspapers such as *Billboard* in the USA or *New Musical Express* in the UK. The references to music in newspapers pre-date the appearance of the music periodical, and these earlier references are of considerable value not only for musicological research but also as a source of bibliographical information for dating and tracing contemporary music publications. Newspapers are discussed at length in CHAPTER 12.

▶ PERIODICAL CONTENTS

This brief survey of periodical types has revealed a range of information types.

- Articles and news reports
- Editorial comment
- Correspondence

- Reviews, previews and calendars of events
- Advertisements

Each of these types has its own value and pitfalls.

Articles and news reports

Articles may be of a scholarly or 'newsy' character. Knowledge of the approach or reputation of the periodical and of the author can help in assessing the accuracy of an article. But the reader must bear in mind that attitudes and approaches to scholarship and news reporting have changed over the years. Articles in nineteenth-century periodicals may well be unsigned, and identifying reviewers and feature writers in newspapers was still not universal 30 years ago. Even now, British newspaper editorials and obituaries are often published unsigned.

Users of scientific literature may be surprised at the longevity of some music periodical literature. Articles written 50 or more years ago may still be of academic relevance and importance in their own right, not simply as evidence of historic approaches to the subject, but because they help trace the development of a scholarly argument.

Editorial comment

This is not intended to be factual. It provides the opportunity for polemic and rhetoric. It can throw fascinating light on the musical attitudes and opinions of an era; and where the writer is also a composer – as in the case of Schumann's editorship of the Allgemeine Musikalische Zeitung – can provide an insight into the composer's mind and milieu.

Correspondence

This provides a similar window onto the thoughts and concerns of contemporary musicians, audiences, promoters, etc. It might incidentally provide factual information, but this is not usually its main purpose.

Reviews, previews and calendars of events

These provide some of the most valuable and most difficult to find information in periodicals. Frequently unindexed, they provide evidence of performance dates and histories; contemporary reception of pieces; and later listening fashions. Newspapers are a particularly valuable source of this type of information.

Advertisements

Like reviews, these are often unindexed, but can provide important performance history and bibliographical information. They can be fascinating for the student of music technology.

▶ ACCESSING PERIODICALS

In order to gain access to periodical literature the reader needs to know:

- what periodicals exist
- where those periodicals can be found
- what is contained in individual periodicals

What exists?

The New Grove list (Sadie, 1980; Sadie and Tyrell, 2001) remains the most comprehensive listing of periodicals to date. It is arranged by country of publication, and within each country titles are listed chronologically by initial date of publication. An alphabetical list of titles is provided to help in finding a specific periodical. This list will not tell the reader whether titles are still published, nor where they can be found. Nor is there any attempt to categorise the periodicals. A classified list can be obtained in *Performing Arts Books* (1981). Similarly, the Library of Congress Catalog (1980–) provides subject access to the range of current periodicals, as well as title access. Entries for periodicals will only appear in such a catalogue at the time of first publication (or, more accurately, the time of acquisition by the library.) It will be necessary, therefore, to consult earlier versions of the Library of Congress Catalogue to obtain the broadest coverage. This can be avoided by using the web-based catalogue of the Library of Congress (<http://catalog.loc.gov>).

Title access to the periodical holdings of the British Library can be obtained via the web-based British Library Public Catalogue (<http://blpc.bl.uk>). The division of materials in the British Library catalogue means that the general reference catalogue must be searched for 'literary' music periodicals, whilst periodicals consisting of music items (rather than text) will be found in the music catalogue.

The printed versions of the British Library book catalogue (1976) and printed music catalogue (1979–1987) may also be used to locate the British Library's periodical holdings. However, in the printed version of the catalogues the entries for periodicals will be found under the heading 'Periodical Publications'. The arrangement of material is by place of first publication, and then chronologically by date of first issue. An alphabetical list of titles provides additional access to the full entries.

Access to other National or other Library catalogues on the World Wide Web can be obtained by using lists available on both the British Library and Library of Congress sites. In addition, the University of Saskatchewan maintains an excellent list of links to library catalogues worldwide (<http://library.usask.ca/catalogs/world.html>).

A more unusual approach to music periodicals is that taken in Basart (1989). She lists some 400 periodicals giving their editorial policies and requirements. There are subject, title and organisation indexes. Reference must also be made to Ulrich (1994), the principal source for publication information on periodicals of all types. This is also available on CD-ROM from Bowker-Saur.

In addition to these general guides, there are a number of specific bibliographies listing journals of a particular subject coverage or country. Meggett (1978) provides a useful guide to all kinds of bibliographical material related to periodicals. Typical examples of this type of listing are Coover (1956–1962) and Seaman (1986) with their listings of music periodicals in Eastern Europe; and Mekkawi (1978), which looks at record reviews and indexes in music periodicals.

Where can it be found?

Some of the resources already listed – notably the various library catalogues – will obviously provide details of potential locations. But it would be tedious work to search every library catalogue for specific titles. Union lists of music periodicals have been produced in a number of countries. Fellinger (1981) gives 54 such lists from 30 countries. There are a number of more recent union catalogues, listed in Section B(i) of the bibliography in Fellinger's 'Periodicals' article in *The New Grove* (Sadie and Tyrell, 2001). Amongst countries not covered in that list is the UK, which has substantial music periodical holdings. The UK Branch of the International Association of Music Libraries (IAML(UK)) was instrumental in producing such a list, giving library locations of permanent files of musical journals (Hodges 1984). A second, revised edition of this list was published in 1998, including the holdings of six libraries in the Republic of Ireland, edited by John Wagstaff.

What do they contain?

Finding out what information is contained in particular periodicals is what concerns most users. Library catalogues list the titles of the periodicals to which they subscribe; they do not list the contents. Indexing of music periodicals, in either printed or electronic form is not ideal.

Current periodical material has been indexed by a number of indexing services over the last 60 years or so. *Bibliographie des Musikschriftums*

Table 11.1 Comparison between printed version of *RILM* and *Music Index*.

RILM	Music Index
Includes periodicals, articles, books, dissertations	Includes periodicals only
Indexes reviews, articles, book chapter, comment	Includes reviews, articles, comment and performance
Includes abstracts	No abstracts
Abstracts provided either by the author or by volunteer musicologist or music librarian contributors in many countries	Indexed by staff indexers
Classified catalogue in print form	Dictionary catalogue in print form
Cumulative five year-year index	No cumulative indexes
Some delay in publication - sometimes 2–3 years behind	More current than RILM

began in 1936, and is published irregularly. In 1949, *Music Index* began regular annual publication, subsequently also appearing monthly. While the journals indexed may show something of an American bias, it covers a substantial range and includes some more popular titles. However, reviews, correspondence and news articles are all indexed in *Music Index*. The lack of academic coverage and a perceived need for abstracts and coverage of other music literature, such as dissertations, led to the musicological community establishing the *Répertoire International de Littérature Musicale* (1967). This began life in 1967, and is now published annually. Unlike *Music Index*, which has no cumulative index, *RILM* has produced a number of five-year indexes. TABLE 11.1 highlights the main differences between these two publications.

Turning music indexes into electronic form has proved to be far more difficult than might be imagined. *Music Index* was released on CD-ROM by Chadwyck-Healey in 1992 (Music Index 1992). This contained material from 1981–1992. As one reviewer has stated: 'the product received poor reviews, and Chadwyck-Healey ultimately decided to abandon it ...' (Abromeit, 1997). *Music Index* has since been re-launched both in a Web version and on CD-ROM. *RILM* has also been available on CD-ROM and via the Web, but at high cost.

In 1996, Chadwyck-Healey, having had little success with its *Music Index* CD-ROM, launched its own, online music periodical index, *The International Index of Music Periodicals* (IIMP, 1996–). With its ambition to include the full text of the journals indexed this will eventually be a superb source, but at present this feature is far from comprehensive, making it a complementary rather than a first choice source. This is available both as a CD-ROM and via the World Wide Web, though at a high subscription price and with no access for casual users. *RILM* is also available now via the World Wide Web, either through OCLC's FirstSearch service, or through NISC's Biblioline. *Music Index* is also available online again, through Harmonie Park Press (<http://www.harmonieparkpress.com/musicindex.html>).

The cost of all these electronic versions is substantial, putting them beyond the reach of most individual researchers. Unfortunately, they are also beyond the means of many smaller music libraries, whose total annual budget for periodicals may well be less than the cost of one of these indexes. As yet, there is no 'pay-as-you-go' option for any of the electronic services, – though this would seem an obvious way forward in such a disparate market.

There are, as yet, few independent reviews of all three indexes. One of the best reviews, which considers only *Music Index* and *IIMP*, is Abromeit (1997). Her review concludes, rather damningly, 'For the time being, it would be judicious for music librarians to continue directing scholars and students to the print versions of *Music Index* and *RILM*.'

Alongside these general indexes, there have been attempts at providing limited subject indexes. One of the more recent of these is *POMPI: Popular Music Periodicals Index* (Clark and Linehan, 1988). As the name suggests, this index concentrates solely on material devoted to popular music and jazz. Unfortunately it ceased after five years.

It will have been obvious that the indexes referred to so far post-date, in the main, the Second World War. Indexes to earlier material are more diverse. The major music dictionaries and encyclopaedias, such as *The New Grove*, and *Die Musik in der Geschichte und Gegenwart* (Blume, 1949), include substantial bibliographies that provide access to earlier material. Bibliographies in major monographs on individual subjects and people should also provide access to earlier material.

Jahrbuch der Musikbibliothek (Peters) was a good source for periodical indexing.

Aware of this lacuna in indexing coverage, the International Musicological Society and the International Association of Music Libraries established a programme in the 1980s to index major music periodicals of the nineteenth century. The project is known as *Répertoire International de la Presse Musicale du dix-neuvième siècle* (Center for Studies in Nineteenth-Century Music, 1988–). The genesis and methodology of this project is described in Cohen (1983). Each periodical is described in calendar form, issue by issue. An index is then provided to this calendar. RIPM subsequently plans to issue, on microfilm, copies of the periodicals indexed.

In addition to these printed and electronic indexes, many libraries have maintained card indexes of periodical articles over many years. The

Subject Catalogue of the Music Section of the New York Public Library includes such index entries. It is always worth enquiring whether a library maintains such an index. Many periodicals publish an annual index. This will, hopefully, be bound in with the library issues of the periodical – though this does not always happen. In some cases, cumulative indexes may be available.

▶ NON-MUSIC PERIODICALS AND INDEXES

Music articles do not appear exclusively in music periodicals. There can be extremely interesting and useful material in periodicals of all types. The *MLA Newsletter* includes a list of music-related articles in non-music journals, usually in one issue each year. In the 1960s, the periodical *Analecta Musicologica* carried a series of lists of music articles in non-music Italian periodicals (1963– , vols 1–5, 7).

Many libraries subscribe to general electronic indexes of periodical literature, such as *Faxon Finder* or *British Humanities Index*. Music librarians have long felt that these are inadequate for music materials, though, as already mentioned, there may be no money to buy the specific music indexes. An article by Michael Colby (1997) rather confirms this view. 'What may be surprising is just how badly lacking the music coverage in some of these indexes can be. The paucity of music titles in [a certain title] effectively disqualifies it as a research tool for music.'

▶ ELECTRONIC JOURNALS

The latest chapter in the periodicals tale is the development of electronic journals, available via the World Wide Web. In practice, there are difficulties with this kind of journal, not least how they are to be paid for. There is user resistance to paying subscriptions electronically, yet publishers can scarcely be expected to produce journals free of charge. At present, there seem to be three basic approaches being used in such sites:

- use the site simply as a means of advertising a title, perhaps including a list of contents or index
- add abstracts to the previous type of site
- a full-scale journal, with the full text of articles

This last type of site is predominantly hosted by university or other academic sites, where there is not an imperative to return a profit on the site. Since this article was first completed, there have been substantial developments in electronic journals, both subscribed for and free. The University of California at San Diego maintains a list of e-journals in all disciplines (http://govt.ucsd.edu/newjour/). Unfortunately this list is arranged by title only. There is also a listing of music journals on Indiana University's website (<http://www.music.indiana.edu>).

▶ REFERENCES

Abromeit, K.A. (1997) Interactive multimedia and software reviews: "Music Index on CD-ROM: a subject guide to music periodical literature" Harmonie Park Press; "International Index to Music Periodicals" Chadwyck-Healey'. In *Notes*, 53, 1215–20

Analecta Musicologica (1963–) Köln; Graz: Böhlau Verlag

Basart, A.P. (1989) *Writing about Music: a Guide to Publishing Opportunities for Authors and Reviewers*. Berkeley, CA: Fallen Leaf Press

Blume, F. (1949–1986) (ed.) *Die Musik in Geschichte und Gegenwart* (17 vols). Kassel: Bärenreiter

British Library (1975) *Catalogue of the Newspaper Library, Colindale* (8 vols). London: British Museum Publications Ltd for the British Library Board

British Library (1976) *The British Library General Catalogue of Printed Books to 1975*. London: C. Bingley: K.G. Saur 1979–87

British Library (1979–1987) *Catalogue of Printed Music in the British Library to 1980* (62 vols). London: K.G. Saur

Center for Studies in Nineteenth-Century Music, University of Maryland (1988–) *Répertoire International de la Presse Musicale*. Ann Arbor, MI: UMI

Clark, C. and Linehan, A. (1988) *POMPI: Popular Music Periodicals Index*. [London:] The British Library Board

Cohen, H.R. (1983) An introduction to the fourth 'R': Le rèpertoire international de la presse musicale du dix-neuvième siècle. *Periodica Musica*, 1, 1–5

Colby, M. (1997) Music periodical indexing in general databases. *Notes* 54 (1997–88), 27–34

Coover, J. (1956–62) A bibliography of East European Music periodicals. *Fontes Artis Musicae*, 3, 219–26; 4, 97–102; 5, 44–5, 93–9; 6, 27–8; 7, 16–21, 69–70; 8, 75–90; 9, 78–80

Deaville, J.A. (1986) Earliest known inventories of European music journals. *Periodica Musica*, 4, 14–17

Fellinger, I. (1968) *Verzeichnis der Musikzeitschriften des 19Jhs*. Regensburg: Bossel. (Studien zur Musik des 19.Jhs.; Bd.10)

Fellinger, I. (1970–76) Supplements to Fellinger 1968 in *Fontes Artis Musicae*, 17–21 and 23

Fellinger, I. (1981) List of union catalogues of (music) periodicals. *Fontes Artis Musicae*, 28, 323–7

Fellinger, I. (1986) *Periodica Musicalia (1789–1830)*. Regensburg: Bosse. (Studien zur Musik des 19. Jhs.; Bd.55)

Fidler, L., James, L.M. and James, R.S. (1990) (ed.) *International Music Journals*. New York: Greenwood Press

Hodges, A. (1984) *The British Union Catalogue of Music Periodicals*. London: Library Association Pub. [Updated as Wagstaff, 1998]

IIMP (1996–) *International Index to Music Periodicals* (CD-ROM). Alexandria, VA: Chadwyck-Healey, Inc. Also available to subscribers in a World Wide Web version

Langley, L. (1994) Music. In: Vann, J.D. and van Arsdel, R.T. (eds.) *Victorian Periodicals and Victorian Society*. Toronto: University of Toronto, pp. 99–126

Library of Congress (1980) *The Music Catalog* Washington, DC:

Library of Congress (1980–)
        1981–1990: Ten-year cumulation
        1991– : Quarterly, cumulating issues

Meggett, J.M. (1978) *Music Periodical Literature: an Annotated Bibliography of Indexes and Bibliographies*. Metuchen: Scarecrow

Mekkawi, C.L. (1978) 'Music periodicals: popular and classical record reviews and indexes'. In: *Notes*, 34, 92–107

Mendel, A. (1879) *Musikalisches Conversations-Lexikon*. Berlin: Heimann

Music Index (1950–) Detroit:

Performing Arts Book: 1876–1981 including an international index of current serial publications (1981). New York; London: Bowker

RILM Abstracts of Music Literature. (1967–) New York: RILM

Sadie, S. (1980) (ed.) *The New Grove Dictionary of Music and Musicians* (20 vols). London: Macmillan

Sadie, S. and Tyrell, J. (2001) (eds.) *The New Grove Dictionary of Music and Musicians* (2nd edn.) (29 vols). London: Grove/Macmillan. [also available by online subscription at: <http://www.grovemusic.com>]

Seaman, G.R. (1986) Nineteenth-century Russian music periodicals: an annotated checklist. *Periodica Musica*, 4, 6–i 1

Szwedowska, J. (1984) *Muzyka czasopismach polskich XVIII wieku: Okres Stanislawowski (1764–1800). Bibliografia i antologia*. Krakow: Polskie Wydawnictwo Muzycne

Tilmouth, M. (1961) A calendar of references to music in newspapers published in London and the provinces (1660–1719). *RMA Research Chronicle*, 1, 1–107

ULRICH's (1994) *International Periodicals Directory*. New York: Bowker

Vincent, F. (1986) Le parcours historique des revues musicales. *Revue des Revues*, 2, 44–51

Wagstaff, J. (1998) (ed.) *The British Union catalogue of Music Periodicals*. Aldershot: Ashgate

▶ APPENDIX: SELECTIVE LIST OF ELECTRONIC JOURNALS

General guide

New-Jour
- http://gort.ucsd.edu/newjour/

This site provides details of new electronic journals in all disciplines as they appear.

Individual titles

Addicted to Noise
- <http://www.addict.com>

Amazing Sounds – the alternative Music E-Magazine
- <http://www.amazings.com/>

Billboard
- <http://www.billboard-online.com>

Computer Music Journal
- <http://www,mitpress.mit.edu/e-journals/ Computer-Music-Journal/>

Critical Musicology Journal
- <http://www.leeds.ac.uk/music/info/CMJ/cmj.html>

Current Musicology
- <http://roar.music.columbia.edu/~curmus/>

Electronic Musicological Review (EMR)
- <http://www.cce.ufpr.br/~rem/remi.html>

Finnish Music Quarterly (Archive)
- <http://www.siba.fi/FMQ/articles85-96.htm>

Gramophone
- <http://www.gramophone.co.uk/gfgbsi.html>

Journal du Conservatoire National Superiéur de Musique et de Danse
- <http://www-old.ircam.fr/CNSMP/journal-22 .html>

Journal of Music Theory
- <http://www.yale.edu/jmt/>

▶ NOTES

1. Sadie and Tyrell (2001) vol. 14, p. 407.
2. This article was completed before the publication of the second edition of The *New Grove Dictionary of Music and Musicians* (Sadie and Tyrell, 2001). Dr Fellinger's article, further revised, appears in the second edition in vol. 19, pp. 404–36. The list of periodical titles, which in Sadie (1980) follows the article, is transferred to the new Appendix volume (vol. 29) in Sadie and Tyrell (2001), pp. 339–573.
3. Mendel (1879) vol. 11, pp. 443–62.

12 Music in newspapers and non-musical periodicals

Diana Dixon

Newspapers and periodicals, particularly weeklies, are important sources for all interested in music, not least because they formally establish when all the most important (and many of the minor) works were first performed and when particular artists and performing organisations appeared. They also often incorporated the writings and criticism of leading composers, ranging from Schumann and Berlioz in the nineteenth century to Philip Heseltine[1] (the alter-ego of the composer Peter Warlock) and Constant Lambert[2] in the twentieth.

Newspapers are particularly known as a source of reviews of concerts, opera and ballet, and in the heyday of newspapers, say between 1880 and the Second World War, concerts and opera were often reviewed nationally. Even comparatively local newspapers printed reports of events in the major centres. If one is searching, say, for an Elgar performance or for an opera tour, once a date has been identified a range of newspapers need to be scanned to obtain a good feeling for critical and public reaction.[3]

Newspapers, of course, are valuable not only for criticism of recent performances, but for news and comment about buildings, finance, public policy – even for disasters. Regular musical columns were a feature of a wide range of newspapers until very recently, and although some of these were collected, many need to be trawled for through the bound volumes and microfilms of the various publications. Also the correspondence columns of the various papers can be valuable, though here there is little guidance to what appeared over the years, and press cuttings collections (see CHAPTER 26) may well be the best way of tracing them, other than serendipity!

From time to time editorials have been written about musical topics and these, too, are worth reviewing in the context of a span of dates relating to any particular topic. Finally, the obituary columns of the press can be unique sources for the biographical details of personalities now relegated to the historical shadows, but possibly important figures in their day.

Periodicals in Britain can be traced back to the seventeenth century, and were originally the medium for reporting the results of scientific and scholarly investigations. By the eighteenth century they had extended their influence and were often a forum for political comment. Famous titles of the era are *The Gentleman's Magazine* (1731–1907) and the *Spectator* (1711–12) Periodicals as we know them did not really flourish until the nineteenth century, when a series of weighty and influential titles such as the *Edinburgh Review* (1802–1929) and the *Westminster Review* (1824–1836) became essential reading matter for all educated people. Periodicals of all kinds came into being, reflecting all tastes and interests, and many such as the *Economist* (1843–) and *The Illustrated London News* (1841–) have celebrated their sesqui-centenaries. The learned or political journal has flourished at the expense of many reputable literary or general weeklies, and titles such as *Blackwood's Edinburgh Magazine* (1817–1980) no longer exist. In 1895, in their Victorian heyday, the *Newspaper Press Directory* estimated that there were at least 2081 magazines of all kinds in circulation.

Many of these periodicals were vital sources of information for musical activity of all kinds. Titles such as *The Illustrated London News* (1841–) carried a regular column musical news as well as advertisements for new music and supplies. Other magazines carried biographical accounts of composers and performers, living and dead, as well as reviews of new works and performances. Sometimes unexpected sources prove treasure troves of information. *The Builder* (1843–) was a rich source of illustrations and architectural details of new opera houses and music halls. For instance, in 1859 it carried illustrations of the new Royal Italian opera house in Covent Garden. Access to the illustrations in *The Builder* is facilitated by the excellent index by Ruth Richardson and Robert Thorne, *The Builder Illustrations Index 1843–1888* (1994). *The Girl's Own Paper* (1880–1956) regularly printed short pieces of contemporary music, including Grieg and Walter MacFarren,[4] as well as informative features on composers and continental music academies.

Newspapers also originated in the seventeenth century, as pamphlets, in the form of newsletters and news sheets. By the eighteenth century a number were published daily, with a fair coverage of advertisements and news. The lifting of restrictions on provincial printing saw the rise of the weekly newspaper in provincial towns such as Worcester, Norwich, Bristol and Nottingham. Although the news was derived almost entirely from London, the advertisements in particular showed a local flavour and are important for tracing information on forthcoming concerts and visits of performers from all over Europe. Studies by Paul Sturges (1978) and Rosy Evans (1984) on musical activity in Derby and Nottingham in the eighteenth century relied heavily on provincial newspapers.

Restrictive taxation on newspapers and advertisements gravely hampered the development and spread of newspapers in Britain until the middle of the nineteenth century. Once these taxes on knowledge were removed, progress was rapid and newspapers of all kinds flourished. Notable was the rise of the daily press, both in London and large provincial cities such as Liverpool and Manchester, and also the proliferation of weekly local newspapers. Most sizeable provincial centres could boast five or six competing titles at any one time, and with the advent of the provincial evening newspaper in the 1880s this number increased, so that towns the size of Kettering boasted two evening papers. To give some idea of the magnitude of the newspaper press, in 1884 the *Newspaper Press Directory* advertised 275 new newspaper and magazine titles. In 1895 it claimed there were some 2304 newspapers flourishing in the British Isles. The problem was that newspaper publishing in the nineteenth century was extremely volatile and many newspapers had extremely short lives. In recent years, a number of long-established newspapers have ceased publication,[5] but these have been replaced by free newspapers, dependent on advertising. Initially the free newspapers were disregarded as having little information content, but increasingly they are recognised as information sources in their own right, and in many cases they are the only source of local news and carry advertisements of many kinds of musical activity.

In Britain by far the largest and most comprehensive collection of British and foreign newspapers is held at the British Library Newspaper Library at Colindale. Although its holdings are impressive, there are some serious gaps in coverage, especially of British provincial newspapers before the middle of the nineteenth century and also for the years 1895, 1896, 1897, 1911 and 1912, which suffered serious bomb damage in World War II. A printed catalogue, *Catalogue of the Newspaper Library, Colindale*, appeared in 1975 but is now seriously out of date as it only covers holdings of British newspapers up to 1970 and foreign ones up to 1971. However, the current catalogue is on the British Library Online Public Access Catalogue (OPAC), and can be accessed via the British Library website.

Besides Colindale, impressive holdings of newspapers are held in the British copyright libraries of Oxford and Cambridge universities, major academic libraries and the national libraries of Wales and Scotland. Their OPACs are available via the internet. Many eighteenth-century newspapers are included in the Burney collection at the British Library at St Pancras (not Colindale); the collection is also available on microform there. Additionally, many of the major local studies collections in public libraries hold significant runs of local titles and these are often much more comprehensive than those held in the British Library's Newspaper Library. Thus, collections in Liverpool, Birmingham, Bristol and Nottingham will yield many more titles than a glance at the Colindale catalogue reveals. For instance, if a researcher is interested in the 1846 Birmingham Festival at which Mendelssohn's *Elijah* received its first performance, it is advisable to search national and local Birmingham newspapers for information.

Similarly, the local newspaper should be the first port of call for information on the opening or closing of the local concert hall or opera house.

As all researchers using nineteenth-century newspapers are aware, tracing a title in a bibliography is no guarantee that the newspaper is in a state to permit browsing of its pages. Indeed, the condition of many is so precarious that it is no longer possible to read them at all. The British Library's NEWSPLAN project is an ambitious programme intended to audit the physical state of all British provincial newspapers and to priorotise their microfilming for posterity. NEWSPLAN covers the British Isles, including the Republic of Ireland, and assesses the extent and standard of newspaper microfilming. For administrative reasons, the project is based on ten regions, all of which have now published a separate NEWSPLAN report. Researchers can now trace holdings of newspapers in local libraries, record offices and newspaper offices throughout the British Isles and also be aware of their physical condition.

Before publication of the ten NEWSPLAN volumes, bibliographic control of the provincial British press was both incomplete and patchy. By no means all provincial titles, especially short-lived nineteenth-century titles, found their way into the British Library Newspaper Library at Colindale. Local libraries do not always hold all titles published in a region, and in some cases the only files of a particular title can be found in provincial newspaper offices, to which access is by no means certain.

The *Bibliography of British Newspapers* currently covers eight English counties but it is still woefully incomplete, with many parts of the country still awaiting investigation. Although the first volume covering Wiltshire was published in 1975, the project lacks funding and is dependent on the labours of hard-pressed local studies librarians and bibliographers in individual counties. Consequently few volumes have appeared, although others are in preparation. Counties that have been covered include: Wiltshire; Derbyshire; Nottinghamshire; Northumberland and Durham; Kent; and Devon and Cornwall. These list all known locations, in the UK and abroad, of any title published in the relevant county, with full bibliographic details of all title changes. The result is impressive and thorough, but there is a long way to go before England achieves anything approaching national coverage. The position in Scotland, Ireland and Wales is better because of the active involvement of the respective national libraries in listing their newspapers in a different, but effective manner. Because the initial NEWS-PLAN project in the South West was less detailed than its successors, efforts have been concentrated on these counties, and a number of volumes, covering Hampshire, Gloucestershire, Dorset and Somerset, and the Channel Isles, are being prepared for publication. A lot, however, still remains to be done. No other single listing goes far enough in providing researchers with reliable information on all newspapers that ever existed in a locality, and, more importantly, with information on locations, gaps in holdings, and whether files are hard copy or microfilm.

Neither the *Bibliography of British Newspapers* nor NEWSPLAN covers periodicals or national newspapers, and these have to be traced either by using the catalogues of major libraries, including the British Library, or alternatively via bibliographies of serials. If a title of an older periodical is known it is still helpful to turn to the *British Union Catalogue of Periodicals (BUCOP)*, which appeared in 4 volumes between 1955 and 1958 with subsequent supplements. Besides identifying titles, it gives locations in academic and major public libraries, as well as the British Library. It should be remembered that it only covers newspapers that started publication after 1799. Some localities have their own regional holdings lists, such as *Hosnill* (1973–) covering public libraries in London, and are concerned with retrospective material as well. Because so much nineteenth-century material is held in the United States, it would be a mistake to ignore the vast *Union List of Serials* (1965), which locates serial titles in major American libraries. For the nineteenth-century *The Waterloo Directory of Victorian Periodicals 1824–1900 Phase 1* (1976) is a useful starting point for tracing and locating titles. The first stage of the project listed some 24 000 titles, including newspapers, but it was estimated that the actual total was probably nearer 50 000 titles. The second stage involved a shelf check of titles on library shelves and separate volumes have been already been published for England, Scotland, and Ireland. It is intended to publish the directory on a CD-ROM.

Just because a title is listed as available in a particular library or record office, this is no guarantee that it will be possible to read it. Even the existence of microfilm is no surety that it is legible. Sadly, in many cases the microfilming has not been carried out to acceptable international standards, and creased (illegible) pages, poor lighting, and cut margins all make many microfilms of newspapers impossible to read. The NEWSPLAN project revealed just how urgent the problem was. In all the regions implementation committees have been established to identify 'at risk' files and to microfilm them. The success of this can be seen in the publication of NEWSPLAN updates in several regions: Yorkshire and Humberside region has already published two updates, one in 1991 and the other in 1992, while the National Library of Ireland has produced a second edition *NEWSPLAN Ireland* in 1998. A number of regions, including London and the South East, are putting material on the internet. What we now have is an accurate, state-of-the-art listing of the condition and availability of all British provincial newspapers, giving historians and researchers reliable information on whether a particular title is worth making the effort to consult or not.

Many current newspapers are now available electronically, either on CD-ROM or on the internet, or both, and the number is increasing all the time. Well established titles on CD-ROM include *The Times* (1990–), *Guardian* (1990–), *Northern Echo* (1988–) and *The Independent* (1988–) and these are generally networked in academic libraries. Illustrations are rarely included, and advertisements, letters and even reviews may be excluded. The disadvantage is that few offer more than a decade retrospectively, with the exception of Chadwyck-Healey's ambitious plan for *The Electronic Times* (1998–2000). The project was initially intended to cover 1815–1905 to link in with the electronic *Palmer's Index to the Times* but it now seems to have been cut back to 1870. The advantage to searchers is seemingly enormous but there are limitations. The magnitude of the project means that it is likely to be available only in the largest libraries. *The Electronic Times* is available on the internet as well as on CD-ROM.

Indeed, an ever-increasing number of titles, in all languages, now are available on the internet. Once initial registration (the requirements vary for individual titles) has taken place, searchers may have several years of a newspaper at their fingertips. However, few newspapers offer much retrospective coverage and readers may have to pay to search an archive if it exists.[6] Again, coverage is rarely complete and, as with CD-ROMs, peripheral information and illustrations may not be provided. The amount of information available differs from newspaper to newspaper. Thus while *Moscow News*, *Washington Post* and *El Pais* have virtually full coverage, others may be restricted. Newspapers such as the *Electronic Telegraph*, *the Times*, *USA Today*, *Le Monde* and the *South China Morning Post* are currently available.

In some cases when internet services prove inadequate, it will be necessary to turn to online full text retrieval systems which scan current newspapers and periodicals, and may enable researchers to access their archives. Two of the leading services are *FT Profile* and *Lexis–Nexis*, which carry the full text of a number of leading newspapers and journals including the *Financial Times*, *Washington Post*, *Guardian* and the *Economist*. Access to these services will normally incur charges.

In order to exploit the contents of newspapers efficiently, adequate indexing services are needed. The forerunner of the modern newspaper index was the extensive series of indexes covering the *Times*. *Palmer's Index to the Times 1790–1922*,[7] is continued by the quarterly *Official Index to the Times*, which is now published monthly as the *Times Index* (1973–). It now also includes the *Sunday Times*, and the supplements; the *Times Educational Supplement* (TES); *Times Literary Supplement* (TLS) and *Times Higher Educational Supplement* (THES). *Palmer's Index to the Times* is also available on CD-ROM and on the internet and access to its contents is greatly improved as the contents of 297 volumes can be searched simultaneously. However, the idiosyncrasies of the original index still remain. Printed indexes also exist for the *Financial Times* (1990–) and the *Guardian* and *Observer* (1995–). The most recent addition is *Daily Telegraph* and *Sunday Telegraph* indexes which appeared in 1997. The CD-ROM *British Newspaper Index* (1991–) offers a useful comprehensive indexing service to a number of British newspapers. Commendable as all the indexing services are, they are expensive and will only be available in large libraries. For this reason, the inexpensive *Clover Newspaper Index* (1986–), now entitled *The Newspaper Index* (1998–), is particularly welcome, as it is a modestly priced, general index to the contents of the leading British daily and Sunday newspapers. A relative newcomer is the internet *News Index* (<http://www.newsindex.com>), which is a keyword index to newspapers appearing on the internet. It offers no retrospective archival searching and is purely a current index.

The situation for periodicals, especially of the nineteenth and early twentieth centuries, is less straightforward. Poole's *Index to Periodical Literature* covers some 479 periodicals including 190 British titles but it is not easy to use.[8] The five volume *Wellesley Index to Victorian Periodicals 1824–1900* (1966–1989) edited by Walter Houghton and Jean Slingerland is a masterly and detailed analysis of the contents of some 43 major British periodicals including *The Quarterly Review* and the *Cornhill Magazine*. *Victorian Periodicals Review* (1969–) provides an annual update to the *Wellesley Index*, listing corrections and the results of new scholarship. Unfortunately, a project of this nature only covers a few titles and cannot assist those whose interests lie in the twentieth century. However, publication of the *Subject Index to Periodicals* (1915–1961) and its successor, the *British Humanities Index* (1962–), has greatly facilitated access to the contents of British popular magazines and also newspaper colour supplements. Since its appearance on CD-ROM as *BHI Plus* (1986–), searching has become simpler, although there is a substantial time lag before material is indexed. For American titles, the *Humanities Index* (1974–) developed out of the *Reader's Guide to Periodical Literature* which began in 1907. The service, like *BHI Plus*, has expanded to include abstracts and now appears online as *Humanities Abstracts* (1996–) as well as on CD-ROM.

Indexing of files of local newspapers is much more haphazard. In a few public libraries, for instance Poole, Huntingdon and Dumfries, work is under way on indexing local titles, but retrospective indexing is a fearsome task and, without voluntary labour, difficult to accomplish. The ambitious project to index the complete run of the *Glasgow Herald* is an all too rare example of an indexing project receiving government funding. The British Library Newspaper Library compiled a location list of provincial newspaper indexes in 1987, but this is no longer accessible.

Traditionally, large collections of press cuttings were amassed by public libraries, and these provided easy access to news items of the past. Those in Sheffield Public Library are a good example. In many cases files have become too expensive to maintain, and many important collections, such as that of the *Evening Standard*, have been destroyed. Sometimes collections have been dispersed and may appear piecemeal in academic libraries. Libraries are looking now to storage on video or optical disks instead, and digitisation of local studies collections, including illustrations and press cuttings, is becoming a viable option.

Obituaries are a vital source of biographical information. Newspapers and professional journals regularly carry obituaries, and where a title has its own index it may be a simple task to trace them. For this reason *Palmer's Index to the Times* is a useful starting point, as once a person has been located, the date may enable searchers to access files of other newspapers. However, the problems of searching the original index remain. For instance, it is necessary to realise that obituaries are indexed not under the name of the deceased but under the general heading 'deaths'.

Collected editions of obituaries from the *Times* are reprinted in various series: originally as *Eminent Persons: Biographies Reprinted from the Times* (The Times Office, 1880–1897). From 1991 they have been entitled *Times Obituaries* with different sub-titles. Personalities are classified under subject headings: thus Sir Geraint Evans appeared under the heading 'media/musicians' in 1992. The long-running *Annual Register* (1758–) contained an important and often substantial obituary section throughout the nineteenth century but this is greatly reduced now. *The Annual Obituary* (1990–), as its title indicates, gives obituaries of eminent personalities from all walks of life. A number of headings will be useful, including Musical performers and conductors, Composers, arrangers, librettists and songwriters, Theatrical, musical impresarios. Obituaries in leading English language newspapers such as *The Times*, *The New York Times*, *The Los Angeles Times*, *The Washington Post*, *Chicago Tribune*, *The Boston Globe* and *The Atlanta Constitution* can be traced via the *Obituary Index* from 1988.

Fortunately, the British Library Newspaper Library at Colindale receives not only British but also copies of leading foreign newspapers, and it deals zealously with the problems associated with newspaper storage and helps other libraries with theirs. Besides co-ordinating the microfilming of local British newspapers, through its NEWSPLAN programme, it also publishes an informative *Newsletter* keeping readers up to date with new developments in the newspaper world. It has also taken responsibility for publication of the *Bibliography of British Newspapers*, county by county.

The importance of older newspapers and periodicals as an area of study in its own right was recognised in 1969 with the formation of the Research Society for Victorian Periodicals in the United States. Tracing information about the wealth of Britain's vast periodical literature became a high priority and the result was the appearance a number of bibliographies. Lionel Madden and Diana Dixon's *The Nineteenth Century Periodical Press in Britain: a Bibliography of Modern Studies 1901–1971* traced over 2600 books and articles on all aspects of the Victorian periodical press including provincial newspapers. This was updated by Larry Uffelmann's *The Nineteenth Century Periodical Press in Britain; a Bibliography of Modern Studies 1971–1991* (1995) but a gap still remains for contemporary literature from the nineteenth century and earlier. For newspapers this has been partially filled by David Linton and Ray Boston's *The*

Newspaper Press in Britain: an Annotated Bibliography. (1987) and David Linton's *The Twentieth Century Newspaper Press in Britain* (Mansell 1994). University departments in a number of British universities including Cardiff, Westminster and the City University offer courses in journalism, encouraging interest on media history and to this end a new journal *Media History* began publication in 1997. This developed out of the *Journal of Newspaper and Periodical History* (1984–1992) and its successor, *Studies in Newspaper and Periodical History* (1993–1995) under the editorship of Michael Harris. Both of these titles carried an annual bibliography of works on newspaper and periodical history compiled by Diana Dixon. The bibliography now appears annually in the journal *Media History*. A useful overview of current press information sources is *Information Sources for the Press and Broadcast Media* (2nd edn.), edited by Sarah Adair (1999). This needs to be read in conjunction with the remarkably different first edition by Selwyn Eagle (1991),[9] underlining the amazing rate of change in the face of new electronic media. For information on electronic developments *News Information: Online, CD-ROM and Internet Sources* (British Library 1997) is a welcome update. Similarly, the chapter by Christine Reid in *The Reference Sources Handbook* (1996) is a clear and helpful introduction to a rapidly changing scene.

The fragility and storage problems posed by hard copy newspaper and periodical runs has meant that many retrospective files are available for purchase on microfilm. University Microfilms International is one of the leading providers of serials in microform. Its two annual catalogues *Serials in Microform* and *Newspapers in Microform* cover over 21 000 and 7000 titles respectively. They are available in hard copy and online via the internet.

▶ REFERENCES

Adair, S. (ed.) (1999) *Information Sources for the Press and Broadcast Media* (2nd edn.). London: Bowker Saur

The Annual Register: a Review of Public Events at Home and Abroad. (1758–) Edinburgh: Longman

The Annual Obituary. (1990–) Detroit & London: St James Press

Bennett, S. (1978) *Victorian Periodicals: a Guide to Research.* New York: Modern Languages Association [of America]

British Humanities Index. (1962–) London: Bowker Saur. [Also *BHI Plus* CD-ROM (1986–) East Grinstead: Bowker Saur]

British Newspaper Index. (1991–) Reading: Primary Source Media (CD-ROM). Internet version 1998–

British Union Catalogue of Periodicals: a Record of Periodicals of the World from the Seventeenth to the Present Day in British Libraries (4 vols). (1955–1958) London: Butterworths (with supplements)

Catalogue of the Newspaper Library, Colindale (8 vols). (1975) London: British Library Board

Clover Newspaper Index. (1986–1998) (weekly), *The Newspaper Index* (1998–) (fortnightly). Biggleswade: Publications. Latest issues available on the Clover Publications web-site. CD-ROM version 1986–1991; 1992–

Dubon, L. (1998) Enhancing a newspaper collection using the World Wide Web. *International Reference Services Quarterly*, 3

Eagle, S. (ed.) (1991) *Information Sources for the Press and Broadcast Media*. London: Bowker Saur

Electronic Edition of the Times 1785–1905. (1998–). Cambridge: Chadwyck-Healey

Evans, R. (1984) Theatre music in Nottingham 1760–1800. *Transactions of the Thoroton Society*, 88, 47–53

Hosnill: a Handlist of Selected Newspaper Holdings, National, Regional and Foreign in London Public Libraries. (1973–). Croydon: Croydon Libraries

Houghton, W. and Slingerland, J. (eds) (1966–1989) *The Wellesley Index to Victorian Periodicals* (5 vols). Toronto & London: Toronto University Press and Routledge. CD-ROM (1998)

Humanities Abstracts (1996–). New York: Wilson. Available online, on Wilson Web and on CD-ROM

Humanities Index (1974–) formerly *Reader's Guide to Periodical Literature* (1907–1915); *International Index* (1916–1965) and *Social Sciences and Humanities Index* (1966–73). New York: H.W. Wilson. Available on CD-ROM and online

Journal of Newspaper and Periodical History. (1984–1992) continued as *Studies in Newspaper and Periodical History*. (1993–1995). (Annual). New York: Greenwood

Linton, D. (comp.) (1994). *The Twentieth Century Newspaper Press in Britain*. London: Mansell

Linton, D. and Boston, R. (comps.) *The Newspaper Press in Britain: an Annotated Bibliography*. (1987). London: Mansell

Lives Remembered. Times Obituaries. (1991–) (Annual) Pangbourne: Blewbury Press [Issues up to 1990 entitled *Obituaries from The Times*]

Madden, L. and Dixon, D. (comps.) (1976). *The Nineteenth Century Periodical Press in Britain: a Bibliography of Modem Studies 1901–1971*. New York: Garland

Media History. (1997–) 2pa Oxford: Carfax Publishing

The Newspaper Press Directory. (1846–) (Annual) now the *Media Directory*. (Annual) London: Benn

Newspapers in Microform. Ann Arbor, MI: UMI. (annual) <http://www.UMI.com>

NEWSPLAN (10 vols). London: The British Library
> Report of the pilot project in the South West (1986)
> East Midlands (1989)
> Northern (1989)
> North West (1990)
> West Midlands (1990)
> Yorkshire and Humberside (1990)
> Wales (1994)
> Scotland (1994)
> South East (1996)
> Ireland (1998) (2nd edn.)

Nicholas, D. (1996) (Really) getting to grips with the Internet: what it has to offer in the way of newspapers. *Vine*, 104, 29–34

Obituaries from the Times 1951–1960: including an index to all obituaries. (1979); 1961–70 (1975); 1971–1975 (1978); Reading: Newspaper Archive Developments

Palmer's Index of the Times Newspaper 1790–1922 (1868–1905), continued as *The Official Index to the Times* (1906–1980) (quarterly) now *The Times Index* (1980–) monthly. Available from Chadwyck-Healey on CD-ROM (1994–) and *The Official Index* (1998–1999). Also available on the internet at <http://www.historyonline.chadwyck.co.uk/>

Poole's Index to Periodical Literature 1802–1906. (1882–1908). Boston, Mass: Osgood; London: Turner

Reid, C.D. (1996) News and current affairs. In: Lea, P.W. & Day, A. (eds) *The Reference Sources Handbook.* London: Library Association, pp.251–271

Richardson, R. and Thorne, R. (eds) (1994). *The Builder Illustrations Index 1843–1888* London: Builder Group and Hilton and Rostron

Serials in the British Library. British Library (1981–)

Serials in Microform. Ann Arbor, MI: UMI. (annual) <http://www.UMI.com>

Spencer, N. (ed.) (1997) *News Information: Online, CD-ROM and Internet.* London: British Library SRIS

Sturges, R.P. (1978) Harmony and good company. the emergence of musical performance in eighteenth century Derby. *Music Review*, 39, 178–95

Subject Index to Periodicals. The Library Association (1915–1961)

The Times Office (1880–1897) *Eminent Persons: Biographies Reprinted from the Times* (6 vols). London, New York: Macmillan
> *(1870–1879)*
> *(1876–1881)*
> *(1882–1886)*
> *(1887–1890)*
> *(1890–1892)*
> *(1893–1894)*

Titus, E.B. (ed.) (1965) *Union List of Serials in the Libraries of the United States and Canada* (3rd edn.) (5 vols). New York: Wilson. Updated by *New Serial Titles* (1953–). Monthly with annual and quinquennial cumulations

Toase, C.A. (ed.) *Bibliography of British Newspapers*. London: British Library
Bergess, W. *et al.* (eds) (1982) *Kent*
Bluhm, R. (ed.) (1975) *Wiltshire*
Brook, M. (ed.) (1987) *Nottinghamshire*
Manders, F.W.D. *et al.* (eds) (1982) *Northumberland and Durham*
Mellors, A. and Radford, J. (eds) (1987) *Derbyshire*
Rowles, J. and Maxted, I. (eds) (1991) *Cornwall and Devon*

Uffelmann, L. (comp.) *The Nineteenth Century Periodical Press in Britain: a bibliography of modern studies 1971–1991*. (1995) Edwardsville, Il: *Victorian Periodicals Review*

Walford's Guide to Current British Periodicals in the Humanities and Social Sciences (1985). London: Library Association

The Waterloo Directory of Victorian Periodicals 1824–1900 [Phase 1]. Wolff, M. *et al.* (ed.):
The Waterloo Directory of Victorian Periodicals 1824–1900 (1976) Waterloo, Ont.: Wilfred Laurier University Press

The Waterloo Directory of Victorian Periodicals 1824–1900 [Phase 2]. North, J.S. (ed.):
The Waterloo Directory of Irish Newspapers and Periodicals. (1987) Waterloo, Ont.: Waterloo Academic Press
The Waterloo Directory of Scottish Newspapers and Periodicals (2 vols). (1989) Waterloo, Ont.: Waterloo Academic Press
The Waterloo Directory of English Newspapers and Periodicals 1800–1900. (1997) Waterloo, Ont: Waterloo Academic Press

► NOTES

1. Heseltine's newspaper criticism in the *Daily Mail* and elsewhere, and his various occasional writings, have been collected and edited by Barry Smith (4 vols, Thames Publishing, 1997–9).
2. In the 1930s Lambert wrote, particularly in the *Sunday Referee*, criticism which has yet to be collected.
3. In 1935 Sir Thomas Beecham produced Frederick Delius's opera *Koanga* for the first time in the UK, at first at Covent Garden, but subsequently touring it to cities in the Midlands and the North. Press coverage was very wide; see Lewis Foreman's account of the production in *Delius Society Journal*, 113, Winter 1994, 1–64 and 116, Spring 1995, 1–44.
4. The volume of *Girl's Own Paper* for 6 December 1884, p. 149 contained *A Norwegian Melody* by Grieg, and on 7 February 1885, p. 296, Walter MacFarren's *Tendresse*.

5. Nicholas (1996) estimated that in 1945 in France there were 26 daily news-papers and in 1994 there were only 11.
6. Nicholas (1996) and Dubon (1998) discuss the situation for accessing archives of newspapers.
7. Chadwyck-Healey announces new releases. (1999) *Advanced Technology Libraries*, 28(7), 8 advertises the initial launch of *Palmer's Full Image Online* and *Historical Newspapers Online*.
8. Bennett (1978, pp. 37–41) discusses the problems associated with using *Poole's Index to Periodical Literature*.
9. The reader will find it useful to keep the two editions to cover the field fully.

13 Theses

Jeremy Dibble

The large number of academic theses, monographs and dissertations written for higher degrees is undoubtedly one of the most important research tools for any student engaged in serious research. It is often the case that theses contain much detailed work of an analytical, historical or statistical nature that does not find its way into books, and yet theses are neglected because their more 'localised' orientation (i.e. their association with and retention by universities or colleges) invariably either deters students from consulting them or at least creates an ethos of inaccessability in the student's mind. Additionally, the task of searching out academic theses is still one of the most haphazard to be faced by a researcher, and this frequently acts as a psychological obstacle to students and scholars who foresee much time being wasted in the hunt for wanted material.

This article will attempt to present some important means of establishing some of the important reference sources of theses and how one could set about tracking them down within a number of countries around the world, namely the United Kingdom, Ireland, the United States, Canada, Australia, New Zealand, South Africa, France, Germany, Denmark, Poland and the Czech Republic. In the United States the importance of theses and dissertations as a major untapped resource for musicological research was highlighted by Guy A. Marco (1975). In chapter 4 ('Guides to other sources of information in general categories'), he discusses registers of theses and dissertations in various countries at some length (see pp. 87–91), and this makes a valuable introductory guide for students and scholars.

It was the very question of inaccessability that led to the first register of British theses in the *R.M.A. Research Chronicle* in 1963 by Paul Doe.[1] This was an attempt to list as comprehensively as possible all British theses and dissertations for higher degrees 'within the last twenty-five years or so' which either had been submitted or were still in progress.[2] The register, replete with useful subject divisions, included theses for both M.A., the Oxford B.Litt. and Ph.D (or D.Phil.), a few theses from Departments and

Faculties other than music as well as a few bibliographical exercises undertaken for the Diploma in Librarianship of London University.

Theses in Ireland were first registered in the *R.M.A. Research Chronicle* No. 13,[3] after which British and Irish theses and dissertations were listed together, as is the case in *R.M.A. Research Chronicle* No. 15 (1979).[4] With the advent of computer databases more sophisticated indexing became possible. The *R.M.A. Research Chronicle* No. 21 (1989), compiled by Ian Bartlett, contains separate author and subject-matter indexes, while that in *R.M.A. Research Chronicle* No. 23 (1990), compiled by Ian Bartlett and Benedict Sarnaker,[5] contains an index of universities and colleges of origin. The subsequent history of theses (i.e. from 'in progress' to 'completion') can also be traced through a section entitled 'Changes and Corrections'.

All British and Irish universities and colleges require at least one copy of every thesis and dissertation accepted for higher degrees to be deposited in their University's Library; all theses and dissertations can be borrowed on inter-library loan except those of Cambridge University. Photocopying is permissible but is subject to the author's consent. Anyone wishing to make photocopies should enquire to the Librarian of the university concerned. It is also perhaps worth mentioning that various British and Irish theses and dissertations, albeit revised and sometimes even reworked, have appeared later as publications in book form with Garland Press (New York) in their series 'Outstanding Dissertations in Music from British Universities' edited by John Caldwell, though this has now ceased.

As a register of British and Irish theses and dissertations, the *R.M.A. Research Chronicle* has been the most comprehensive source of listings, though many British and Irish works are also listed in American publications such as UMI (University Microfilms International), RILM (*Répertoire Internationale de Littérature Musicale*), *Dissertation Abstracts International* (DAI) and, in the sixth cumulation of 1977, *Doctoral Dissertations in Musicology*. In 1988 the task of listing British and Irish theses was undertaken by the MRIN (Music Research Information Network) in an annual publication called the *Register of Music Research Students in Great Britain and the Republic of Ireland*. The last publication of this register (ISSN 0956–263X – compiled and edited by Gerald Gifford, Royal College of Music) took place in 2000, at which time invitations were extended to all institutions and individuals to register their dissertation topics and completed dissertations with *Doctoral Dissertations in Musicology* at Indiana University, U.S.A. Indiana gives internet access to *Doctoral Dissertations in Musicology* at <http://www.musicindiana.edu/ddm>. A comprehensive listing of theses with abstracts accepted for higher degrees by universities in Great Britain and Ireland can also be obtained from Expert Information (Staple Hall, Stone House Court, 87–90 Houndsditch, London EC3A 7PB), and can be accessed at the website: <http://www.theses.com>.

There are various sources of reference for theses and dissertations in the United States which can be referred to in the hunt for research material. For theses and dissertations written in the earlier part of this century, a resource particularly useful and pertinent to scholars interested in the development and history of musicology, there is the *List of American Doctoral Dissertations* printed in 1912–38 published in Washington by the U.S. Library of Congress Catalog Division. In addition there is the publication *Doctoral Dissertations Accepted by American Universities 1933/34– 1954/55*, which was compiled for the Association of Research Libraries (New York). This ceased publication with No. 22 but continued with the *Index to American Doctoral Dissertations 1955/56–* , compiled for the Association of Research Libraries (Ann Arbor).

Almost all American theses are deposited with Bell and Howell Learned Information (formerly University Microfilms International (UMI)), from which they can be purchased on 35mm microfilm or hard copy,[6] with titles published after 1976 also available on microfiche. The theses used to be listed in the monthly publication *Dissertation Abstracts International* (DAI), which may still be available as a reference source in all good libraries.[7] One of the most comprehensive printed listings for music was published by UMI in December 1983, which listed doctoral dissertations from 1861 until 1983. Since then further supplementary music catalogues have been issued. In these subject listings there is a wide variety of categories under which a thesis or dissertation could be listed. Some are listed under several different headings. Take the following example:

> Boethius' "The Principles of Music", An Introduction, Translation, and Commentary. *Bower, Calvin Martin (Ph.D. 1967 George Peabody College for Teachers of Vanderbilt University) 518p. 28/06A, p. 2279. RSD67–15005*

This appears under 'Aesthetics', 'Manuscript Studies' and 'Theory'. Each dissertation is given a reference number so that the corresponding abstract in DAI can be found. The prefix to the order number also indicates the year of publication. For example:

> Charles Avison: An Eighteenth-Century English Composer, Musician and Writer. *Stephens, Norris Lynn (Ph.D. 1968 University of Pittsburgh) 360p. 29/09A, p. 3175. RSD69–04106*

29/09A p. 3175 indicates that the abstract is in DAI volume 29, issue 9, section A, on page 3175. The prefix to the order number, RSD69–04106, shows that the dissertation was published in 1969.

Many clients of UMI subscribe to a printed *Quarterly Update* for which they specify specialist research areas. However, consultation of the UMI lists (as part of Bell & Howell) and ordering of theses can now be accomplished quickly on the World Wide Web (<http://www.umi.com/ hp/products/dissertations.html>) – this takes you through to 'ProQuest',

UMI's digital library of dissertations and theses[8]), which is now the simplest and quickest form of search mechanism. Indeed, this method provides quickest access to new titles which are available well before they appear in printed listings. Furthermore, you will be able to search, read and print out abstracts, a service not available through the printed sources. And there is also the possibility of customising the search, specifying key words or subject combinations. Besides UMI there is also the service DissertationsOnline.com (<http://www.dissertationsonline.com>), which is another valuable search engine for both finding and ordering theses.

Perhaps the most important register on the North American continent is *Doctoral Dissertations in Musicology*, published by the American Musicological Society and the International Musicological Society.[9] Only American-Canadian dissertations were covered through 1972. However, the sixth cumulation of 1977 was the first international edition which included musicological dissertations from all over the world and also non-student work in progress. For the seventh cumulation of 1984, *Doctoral Dissertations in Musicology* (ed. Cecil Adkins and Alis Dickinson) reverted to dissertations only but with the broadest international coverage. This edition contained 6520 titles, 63 per cent of which were American-Canadian and 37 per cent from 30 other countries. *Doctoral Dissertations in Musicology* maintains listings of incomplete dissertations for five years after which time they must be recertified by the sponsoring university.[10] Supplementary publications of *Doctoral Dissertations in Musicology* by the American Musicological Society and the International Musicological Society have been published since 1984 with the intention of publishing further cumulations every five years.[11] A comprehensive list can now be consulted on the World Wide Web (<http://www.music.indiana.edu/ddm/>). A general search on the World Wide Web (under 'dissertations') will also reveal that many individual American universities keep their own online databases of theses, and though these can be found through UMI or Doctoral Dissertations, more detailed listings can often be found by contacting the individual universities.

Three other major sources of English-speaking theses and dissertations are Australia, New Zealand and South Africa. The first register of theses and dissertations in Australia and New Zealand was Frank Callaway's 'Register of Theses on Musical Subjects Accepted for Higher Degrees and Research Projects of Musical Subjects in Progress for Higher Degrees at Australian and New Zealand Universities'. This was published in *Studies in Music* I in 1967 pp. 102–7 and covered a period from 1927 to 1967. Further issues of *Studies in Music* included registers of theses from Australia and New Zealand until the last issue in 1992. *Musicology Australia* have been publishing the register as from their 1995 issue, incorporating the backlog from 1992, and the volumes can be ordered easily through their website (<http://www.msa.org.au/ma.htm>).[12]

Suzanne Robinson's looseleaf *Register of Theses in Australian Music* lists 450 theses from a range of Universities (Robinson, 1996).

In South Africa the Human Sciences Research Council (which grants postgraduate scholarships) maintains a database. 'A list of Masters and Doctoral Theses Completed since 1985' was compiled from the database by Sarita Hauptfleisch which appeared in vol. 12 of the *South African Journal of Musicology* in 1992. A more recent list (1932–1996) appeared in vol. 17 of the *SAJM*, which can be ordered through the SAMUS (Musicological Society of Southern Africa) website (<http://www.und.ac.za/und/samus>); a supplement to this catalogue appeared in *SAJM* vol. 19 (published in 2000). Another source is the SABINET listing which is also available on the Web on a paying basis. South African theses can be borrowed through the inter-library loan service. More recently theses from all three countries have been included in *UMI* and *Doctoral Dissertations in Musicology*.

In Germany there are various types of dissertation. The *Magisterarbeit* (Master's degree dissertation) is effectively the first qualification in German universities.[13] Its publication is however forbidden by law. The *Doktorarbeit* or *Promotionsarbeit* is the equivalent of the British doctorate. Finally there is the larger *Habilitationsschrift*, which is an extensive piece of work resulting from many years of research. Normally this type of thesis is written by those intending to become professors. Since higher education in Germany is entirely the responsibility of the Länder, not the federal government, the rules governing the publication of dissertations vary. In Bavaria the *Doktorarbeit* and *Habilitationsschrift* must be published in some form, yet in Baden-Württemburg publication is not mandatory, though for some careers such as university teaching it is hard to avoid. To obtain or find out details about individual theses it is advisable to contact the institutions in question.

There are a number of important published lists of German-language theses in musicology which cover German, Swiss and Austrian universities. Perhaps the most significant is Richard Schaal's *Verzeichnis deutschsprachiger musikwissenschaftlicher Dissertationen 1861–1960*, Musikwissenschaftliche Arbeiten, 19 (Kassel, Bärenreiter, 1963). A supplement, *Verzeichnis deutschsprachiger musikwissenschaftlicher Dissertationen 1961–1970* mit Ergänzungen zum Verzeichnis 1861–1960, Musikwissenschaftliche Arbeiten, 25 (Kassel, Bärenreiter, 1974) followed 11 years later. More recent German, Swiss and Austrian dissertations are listed annually in *Die Musikforschung*.[14] Unpublished dissertations are also listed in series H. (Hochschulschriften) of the *Deutsche Nationalbibliographie* since 1990. Moreover, since 1992, dissertations on musicology are also listed in series M. (Musik). Unpublished dissertations are generally easily available through inter-library loan either directly or as microfilms or photocopies. Some German universities (like some British universities) have also allowed their students to list their dissertations with *UMI*. Published theses are best acquired by obtaining catalogues from the relatively small number of German academic publishing houses (e.g. Bosse at Regensburg, Wilhelm Fink at Munich).

There are two types of doctoral research degree in Denmark. The first closely resembles the German *Habilitationsschrift* in which the thesis, a lengthy piece of work, must be published by law as a printed book. The Ph.D. degree, for postgraduates, which normally takes three years as in the United Kingdom, has been recently introduced to the Danish curriculum. Theses for this degree are not published. A complete bibliography of all musicological theses and dissertations written in Denmark from 1892 can be found in *Danske Doktordisputater i musikvidenskab* by Thomas Holme Hansen (in: Ccilia, rbog 1992–3, rhus Universitet 1993, 233–64). Another source of valuable reference for Danish theses of this kind is the *Dansk Bogfortegnelse* (the Danish national bibliography). Ph.D. theses are not registered in any special publication. They are however listed in the annual reports of the different music departments (e.g. the Department of Musicology in the University of Copenhagen lists its Ph.D. theses in its annual publication, *Musik & Forskning*). The published theses for the *Habilitationsschrift* can be borrowed through inter-library loan. Copies of Ph.D. theses are kept by the relevant department of musicology (Copenhagen, Arhus or Alborg), from whom photocopies may be ordered.

The most comprehensive listing of French theses and dissertations is contained in Jean Gribenski's *French Language Dissertations in Music: An Annotated Bibliography 1883–1976*. This appeared in the series of RILM Retrospectives in 1979, published by Pendragon Press, and covers French-language theses and dissertations written in Belgium, Canada, France and Switzerland. For works after 1976 *Doctoral Dissertations in Musicology* is again useful. There is also Daniele Piston's *Répertoire des Travaux Universitaires, Relatifs à la Musique Françaix du Moyen Âge à Nos Jours (Theses and Memoires)* published in 1992 by Librairie Honoré Champion (7, quai Malaquais, Paris).

With the opening up of Eastern and Central Europe and the opportunities for exchange programmes and inter-university co-operation, the resource of theses and dissertations from countries such as the Czech Republic, Slovakia and Poland will become increasingly important. Listings are however rather haphazard and more comprehensive up-to-date registers are yet to be compiled. For Czech and Slovak theses and dissertations there is only one list which appeared for the period 1945–1973 published in the journal *Hudebni Veda* (1976, No. 3, 257–286). In Poland there are a number of listings, though these also need to be updated. Musicological theses and dissertations for the period 1911–1986 from the Jagiellonian University in Krakow appeared in *Uniwersytet Jagiellonski: Muzykologia krakowska 1911–86* edited by Elzbieta Dziebowska (Krakow: Uniw. Jag. 1987). Two other sources, written in English, could also be useful. In 1977 the first volume of Polish Musicological Studies was published in Krakow (*Polskie Wydawnictwo Muzyczne*) edited by Zofia Chechlinska and Jan Steszewski. One chapter is entirely devoted to Polish theses and dissertations in musicology for the period 1947–74 compiled by Kornel

Michalowski (see pp. 261–270). A second volume was published in 1986 with listings for the period of 1973–77 (see pp. 341–345).

This article has dealt primarily with theses and dissertations for higher research degrees at M.A. and Ph.D. level. Such degrees have in the past been considered almost exclusively in the field of musicology and its subdivisions (e.g. history, analysis, ethnomusicology, aesthetics, theory), but the scope of higher degrees is now rapidly widening to include areas such as composition and performance. Although the Master's degree in research is set to continue, most universities have now developed a range of taught one-year 'training' M.A. courses which can be an advantage to students contemplating a three-year doctoral study. This system, recognised first by the British Academy and later by the Arts and Humanities Research Board, allows a student to take a one-year Master's degree without placing in jeopardy his or her chance of securing a further three-year grant required for doctoral work.[15] Dissertations for these taught degrees are naturally much smaller in scope and are not necessarily retained in the same way as those for exclusively research degrees.

▶ REFERENCES

Dawney, M. (compiler) *A Register of Theses on Music at Universities in the Republic of Ireland.* Cork: University College

Marco, G.A. (1975) *Information on Music: A Handbook of Reference Sources in European Languages.* Basic and Universal Sources, vol. I. Littleton, Colorado: Libraries Unlimited Inc.

Marshall, K. (1995) Home and Away. *Musical Times,* January, 56–9

Register of Theses on Music in Britain and Ireland (compiled by Nick Sandon), 38–116

Robinson, S. (1996) *Register of Theses in Australian Music.* Melbourne: Centre for Studies in Australian Music

Rushton, J. (1994) Scylla and Charybdis. *Musical Times,* March, 179–80

▶ NOTES

1.   Noble, J. (1963) (ed.) *R.M.A. Research Chronicle* No. 3, pp. 1–25.
2.   The register did not include degrees awarded in respect of published work nor those awarded in Departments of Education or Psychology. The latter subject areas were included in later R.M.A. registers.
3.   Dawney (1977), *R.M.A. Research Chronicle* No. 13 pp. 64–6.
4.   *Register of Theses on Music in Britain and Ireland* (compiled by Nick Sandon), 38–116.
5.   pp. 149–63.

6.   Theses before 1969 may not be borrowed on Inter-Library Loan; after 1969 theses can be borrowed on microfilm.

7.   All universities in the U.S.A. keep copies of Masters and Doctoral Dissertations, but given the UMI system, these are not normally sent out on loan. For dissertations not available from UMI, particularly older theses, it often means a visit in person to the university in question. A direct enquiry is also strongly advised. UMI can be contacted in the United Kingdom at The Quorum, Barnwell Road, Cambridge CB5 8SW. Abstracts are now available on CD-ROM. In the U.S.A. UMI can be contacted at 300, North Zeeb Street, Ann Arbor, Michigan, 48106.

8.   Dissertation Abstracts Online (DAO) can be accessed through the OCLC FirstSearch online reference service.

9.   For further information the American Musicological Society can be contacted at 201, South 34th Street, Philadelphia PA19104–6313, USA.

10. Doctoral Dissertations in Musicology also indicates within its listings whether the dissertations are located in RILM and Dissertations Abstracts International.

11. In 1990 the Second Series, First Cumulative Edition of Doctoral Dissertations in Musicology was published.

12. The business address for Musicology Australia is GPO Box 2404, Canberra ACT 2601, Australia.

13. There is also a category known as the Diplomarbeit which is a dissertation written for professional purposes. This is the first 'degree' in some technical and scientific subjects and the Diplomarbeit is usually associated with final projects in professional schools other than universities. This would apply particularly to projects and dissertations in music education.

14. Some German dissertations also begin to appear in UMI and Doctoral Dissertations in Musicology.

15. For more discussion on this subject see Rushton (1994); also Marshall (1995) provides an interesting perspective of the influence of American curricular models on music courses in British universities both at undergraduate and postgraduate levels.

14 Foreign language material: a general overview with particular reference to publications in German

Jürgen Schaarwächter

This is a chapter to encourage those who do not have a close command of languages other than English to try to get to grips with literature in other languages, particularly German. The field of music and musicology has been blessed with literature in many languages and the student who can take account of the full breadth of the literature has a natural advantage. Nevertheless one notes a certain insularity in many English writers on music.

Many English-speaking readers regularly ignore the fact that if they deal with a special area of research they have to consult sources that are not necessarily written in or translated into English. For example, one of the leading experts on Franz Schubert, in his book on Schubert and the Symphony, never refers to Peter Gülke's German language publications on Schubert, an important counterpart, not even quoted by him in the bibliography. (On the other hand, other musicologists are very wide ranging in their use of sources, such as Julian Budden in his Verdi and David Brown in his Russian music research.)

On the other side one has to stress that this situation is not at all restricted to British musicology, but can be found in nearly all countries. True, one cannot expect anyone to speak seven languages fluently, but there are even British composers who were extremely interested in foreign languages to the extent that they either wrote on these composers (Norman Demuth wrote several books on a number of French composers) or composed music in different languages (Hölderlin Fragments, *Les Illuminations* or *Michelangelo Sonnets* by Britten, German songs by Bernard van Dieren, and Goethe's Faust (I) or *Schiller's Turandot* by Havergal Brian).

Every country is naturally particularly interested in its own music, and for this reason it cannot be doubted that the best insights into French music come from French authors, or the best ones into Italian music from Italians. Who is better placed to study Italian academic life than Nestore Morini or Giuseppe Turrini, who will know Strauss better than a German-language author such as Willi Schuh, Roland Tenschert or Franz Trenner? It is not only that the primary sources are mostly rather more simply available – it is also that the necessity for translation, that has provoked many misunderstandings, is obviated. However, exceptions can be found to this in any country, e.g. Walton's research on Othmar Schoeck or Fifield's book on Hans Richter.

Completeness is neither intended nor possible in this chapter, but I will attempt to give an extensive overview of many important fields of research on music, which can naturally be done best by referring to the books themselves.

Numerous biographies or monographical studies on composers were published only in their own country, none of them being translated into English. This happened to Spanish as well as French, Estonian, Italian, Russian, Dutch or German composers. Did you know, for example, that Vincent d'Indy, himself a distinguished composer, has written not only a book on César Franck (which has been translated into English), but also books on Paul Dukas, Emmanuel Chabrier and the French reception of Richard Wagner? And still Wagner's autobiography *Mein Leben* is not available in an English translation proper (Newman's edition of the autobiography has to be revised carefully). Peter Petersen produced two studies on Hans Werner Henze, Constantin Floros a highly important three-volume study on Gustav Mahler, a point of special interest in German musicology (compare the books by Sponheuer, Adler, Adorno, Danuser or Eggebrecht). Richard Specht and Paul Bekker published several first-class reference works just after World War I, e.g. on Beethoven, Brahms, Liszt, Richard Strauss, Mahler, and the Symphony from Beethoven to Mahler, and there are important analytical studies on Beethoven by Schenker (which have nearly all been translated into English) and Riemann.

However, there are uncountable details that can never be translated. For this reason, German musicology has always tried to maintain the original text as widely as possible, with lots of quotations in the original language – or has not dealt with other countries at all.

With any kind of source it is often difficult to realise how rich they can be, how useful to the needs of the researcher. For this reason it is advisable to consult large bibliography one or other (such as the National Union Catalogue, the *Répertoire Internationale de Littérature Musicale* or a catalogue, e.g. of the British Library or of the Bavarian State Library) to find out how voluminous a book is and what exactly the title tells. Often books dating from before 1935 are not real musicological books – certainly with lots of exceptions – so one cannot really know what to expect when actually consulting the books. Consulting one of the above-mentioned catalogues beforehand can, however, help you to concentrate on the most important titles first.

Numerous general introductions to important fields of music have never been issued in English, say, on Rumanian, Spanish, Netherlands, middle-American, Norwegian and also German music. A highly important work in its time was Guido Adler's *Handbuch der Musikgeschichte* (1924), controversely discussed in UK due to its critical notes on Elgar (by Edward J. Dent). The introduction to Romantic music by Wolfgang Boetticher (1983), who also wrote an important biography on Schumann, is really a desideratum for anyone who is interested in the period. In the field of medieval music lots of the standard reference literature of past decades, by, say, Jammers, Wagner and Ferretti (1934), have to be consulted in the original language, though at least Wagner has in part been published in English. Any period of music requires reference to foreign language studies on single composers as well as to special studies on highly specialised areas such as the motet or the frottola, or general surveys of the period (such as the ones by de La Borde or Ambros, or, in later times, Saint-Saëns, Hanslick or Bie).

Many sources for Robert Schumann, including the complete diaries and one volume of letters, are still unavailable in English. Several volumes of Bach documents, documentation on Bartók, Berlioz, Tchaikovsky, Mozart, Strauss, Debussy, Verdi, Bruckner and the Second Viennese School, self-documentation by Pousseur, Henze, Berio or Schaeffer or the Beethoven Konversationshefte – all of these are available in the original language only. A new edition of the Beethoven letters has just been published, edited by the Beethoven-Archiv Bonn, and also just recently published has been a new edition of the correspondence between Cosima Wagner and King Ludwig II. of Bavaria.

There are books on music printing and business in Paris or Vienna, and Peter Cahn has written on the Hoch'sches Konservatorium in Frankfurt am Main where, among others, studied Percy Grainger, Cyril Scott, Paul Hindemith, Otto Klemperer, Hans Pfitzner and Hans Rosbaud – and where the teaching staff included Clara Schumann, Joachim Raff, Julius Stockhausen and Engelbert Humperdinck.

A general overview and introductory bibliography on music in Nazi Germany was published in an exhibition catalogue which has since reached its third edition. It can be seen that a number of well-known German musicologists who intended to continue their career in Nazi Germany behaved accordingly, but one has to be careful in immediately calling them fascist or Nazi authors (e.g. Heinrich Besseler, Josef Müller-Blattau, Ernst Kirsch, Walther Vetter, Ernst Bücken, Rudolf Gerber or Wilibald Gurlitt). Many musicologists (e.g. Alfred Einstein and Egon Wellesz) had to emigrate, not necessarily due to their non-Nazi ideas but due to their descendence. Dümling/Girth and others give a rough survey of those who happened to be Nazi and who rejected conformity, such as Friedrich Blume, editor of the important German encyclopaedia *Die Musik in Geschichte und Gegenwart* (1949–1986), Fritz Jöde and Hans Joachim Moser, all of whom did run through the times and the difficulties of musical ethics.

Certainly the *New Grove Dictionary of Music and Musicians*, with all its following special volumes on musical instruments, jazz, opera, etc., is one of the best musical encyclopaedias ever, though there have, in former times, been others that were of great importance in their own time. The most important in Germany is *Die Musik in Geschichte und Gegenwart*, of which an entirely new edition is in progress (Finscher, 1994–), though some reservations about it have been expressed. There are certainly further, mainly national, encyclopaedias, but those are largely out of date and of interest only if one is looking for a topic particularly concerned with this country. The Riemann encyclopaedia was the antecedent to *Die Musik in Geschichte und Gegenwart*, but has meanwhile lost its importance in the musicological field, an importance Marc Honegger's and Alberto Basso's encyclopaedias still can claim in their language area. One real major achievement, not yet completed, is Hans Heinrich Eggebrecht's *Handwörterbuch der musikalischen Terminologie*, a loose-leaf collection that contains detailed, carefully researched information on any musical term; two collections of musical terms have since been published separately. A last encyclopaedia to be mentioned is Pipers *Enzyklopädie des Musiktheaters*, the first 7-volume treatment of all aspects of music theatre ever.

Almost every German university has published a series of books, most of them Ph.D. dissertations, many of them dealing with important topics (dissertations can be traced via the appropriate catalogues). Other series include Musik-Konzepte, each volume of which deals with a different composer from Monteverdi to Stockhausen and collects important articles either from the past or especially written for the volume, or Heinrichshofen Verlag's *Taschenbücher zur Musikwissenschaft*, which cover an immensely wide field, from theory of harmony to performance practice, to ethnomusicology, to how a record is produced and an introduction to the so-called *systematische Musikwissenschaft*, which covers sociological or psychological musicology, aesthetics and music theory, modern media and musical acoustics. But the most important series are published by Laaber-Verlag – a series on the history of music theory, a series on composers and their times, sadly in recent times declined in quality (volumes are already available on Palestrina, Monteverdi, Schütz, Bach, Haydn, Beethoven, Schubert, Chopin, Mendelssohn Bartholdy, Berlioz, Schumann, Liszt, Brahms, Verdi, Reger, Debussy, Mahler and Stravinsky), the *Neues Handbuch der Musikwissenschaft*, the *Handbuch der musikalischen Gattungen*, the *Handbuch der Musik im 20. Jahrhundert* and the *Schriften zur musikalischen Hermeneutik*. Generally, it has to be pointed out, German musicology is particularly interested not only in traditional music history, but also in questions of ethnomusicology and the so-called *systematische Musikwissenschaft*. The beginning of this trend can be traced to the late eighteenth century and the interest in musical aesthetics. In the meantime this has grown to become a field of great importance.

The sociological and musical aspects of pop music are dealt with by, for example, Flender and Rauhe, and the aesthetics, psychological aspects and semiotics of music are an important field of interest for Riemann,

Eggebrecht, Dahlhaus, Blaukopf, Karbusicky, Fubini, Adorno and Otto Kolleritsch, who has for several years been editor of *Studien zur Wertungsforschung*.

▶ REFERENCES

Abert, A.A. (1994) *Geschichte der Oper*. Kassel: Bärenreiter

Adler, G. (1924, 2nd ed 1930) (ed.) *Handbuch der Musikgeschichte* (2 vols) (repr. 1961). Frankfurt: Frankfurter Verlags-Anstalt

Adler, G. (1916) *Gustav Mahler*. Wien/Leipzig: Universal

Adorno, T.W. (1968, 2nd ed 1977) *Alban Berg*. Wien: Lafite

Adorno, T.W. (1968) *Einleitung in die Musiksoziologie*. Frankfurt am Main: Suhrkamp

Adorno, T.W. (1960) *Mahler: eine musikalische Physiognomik*. Frankfurt am Main: Suhrkamp

Adrio, A. (1935) *Die Anfänge des geistlichen Konzerts*. Berlin: Junker & Dünnhaupt

Alaleona, D. (1908, 2nd ed 1945) *Studi su la storia dell'oratorio musicale in Italia*. Turin: Bocca

d'Alessi, G. (1954) *La cappella musicale del Duomo di Treviso (1300–1633)*. Treviso: Vedelago

Ambros, A.W. (1862–82, 3rd ed 1887–1911) *Geschichte der Musik* (5 vols) (vols 1–4 repr. 1968). Leipzig: Leuckart

Andersson, O. (1955) *Sibelius i Amerika*. Turku: Bro

de Angelis, P. (1950) *Musica e musicisti nell'arcispedale di S. Spirito in Saxia dal quattrocento all'ottocento*. Rome

Angermüller, R. (1982) *W.A. Mozarts musikalische Umwelt in Paris (1778): Eine Dokumentation*. München/Salzburg: Katzbichler

Anglès, H. (1941) *La música española desde la Edad Media hasta nuestros días*. Barcelona: Biblioteca central

Anglès, H. (1954) *L'opera di Morales e lo sviluppo della polifonia sacra spagnola nel 1500*. Rome

de Azevedo, L.H.C. (1956) *La musique en Amérique latine*. Paris: Centre de Documentation Universitaire

Balakirev, M.A. (1912) (ed.) *Perepiska M.A. Balakireva s. P.I. Cajkovskim*. St. Petersburg

Balan, G. (1962) *George Enescu: mesajul, estetica*. Bucharest: Ed. Muzicala

Ballif, C. (1956) *Introduction à la métatonalité*. Paris: Richard-Masse

Bárdos, L. (1976) *Liszt Ferenc, a jövö zenésze*. Budapest: Akadmiai Kaid

Barraud, H. (1956) *La France et la musique occidentale*. Paris: Gallimard

Basso, A. (1985–88) (ed.) *Dizionario enciclopedico universale della musica e dei musicisti* (8 vols). Turin: UTET

Bauer, A. (1955) *Opern und Operetten in Wien. Verzeichnis ihrer Erstaufführungen in der Zeit von 1629 bis zur Gegenwart*. Graz/Köln: Böhlau

Bekker, P. 1919 *Franz Schreker*. Berlin: Schuster & Loeffler (repr. 1982 and 1983)

Bekker, P. (1921) *Gustav Mahlers Sinfonien*. Berlin: Schuster & Loeffler (repr. 1969)

Bekker, P. (1918) *Die Sinfonie von Beethoven bis Mahler*. Berlin: Schuster & Loeffler

Benoit, M. (1971) *Musiques de cour: chapelle, chambre, écurie, 1661–1733*. Paris: Picard

Berio, L. (1959) *Poesia e musica: un'esperienza*. In: *Incontri musicali* 3, Milan, p. 98–

Bie, O. (1906, 3rd ed 1925) *Die moderne Musik und Richard Strauss*. Berlin: Bard, Marquard & Co

Bie, O. (1931) *Richard Wagner und Bayreuth*. Zürich: Orell Füssli

Blankenburg, W. (1950, 3rd ed 1974) *Einführung in Bachs h-moll-Messe*. Kassel: Bärenreiter

Blaukopf, K. (1982, 21996) *Musik im Wandel der Gesellschaft. Grundzüge der Musiksoziologie*. München: Piper

Blume, F. (1949–1986) (ed.) *Die Musik in Geschichte und Gegenwart* (17 vols). Kassel: Bärenreiter

Boetticher, W. (1983) *Einführung in die musikalische Romantik*. Wilhelmshaven: Heinrichshofen (Taschenbücher zur Musikwissenschaft, 89)

Boetticher, W. (1974) *Die Familienkassette Schumanns in Dresden. Unbekannte Briefe an Robert und Clara Schumann*. Leipzig: Deutscher Verlag für Musik

Boetticher, W. (1989) *Geschichte der Motette*. Darmstadt: Wiss. Buchgesellschaft

Boetticher, W. (1958 and 1998) *Orlando di Lasso und seine Zeit 1532–1594* (2 vols). Kassel: Bärenreiter

Boetticher, W. (1941) *Robert Schumann. Einführung in Persönlichkeit und Werk*. Berlin: Hahnefeld

Boetticher, W. (1942) *Robert Schumann in seinen Schriften und Briefen*. Berlin: Hahnefeld

Boetticher, W. 1976–1984) *Robert Schumanns Klavierwerke: Entstehung, Urtext, Gestalt: Untersuchungen anhand unveröffentlichter Skizzen und biographischer Dokumente* (vols 1–2) (opp. 1–13) (further vols in preparation). Wilhelmshaven: Heinrichshofen

Boutière, J. and Schutz, A.-H. (1950, 2nd ed1964) *Biographies des troubadours*. Toulouse: Privat

Brandenburg, S. (1996–98) (ed.) *Ludwig van Beethoven. Briefwechsel. Gesamtausgabe* (8 vols). München: Henle

Braunbehrens, V. (1986, 2nd ed 1991) *Mozart in Wien*. München: Piper

Brauner, R.F. (1948) *Österreichs neue Musik*. Wien

Brenet, M. (1900) *Les concerts en France sous l'ancien régime*. Paris (repr. 1970)

Brosche, G. (1997) (ed.) *Richard Strauss – Clemens Krauss: Briefwechsel*. Tutzing: Schneider (Publikationen des Instituts für Österreichische Musikdokumentation, 20)

Brosche, G. (1979) (ed.) *Richard Strauss – Franz Schalk. Ein Briefwechsel*. Tutzing: Schneider (Veröffentlichungen der Richard Strauss-Gesellschaft · München, 6)

Bruckner, A. (1924) *Gesammelte Briefe*, ed. F. Gräflinger/M. Auer (2 vols). Regensburg: Bosse

Caffi, F. (1854–55) *Storia della musica sacra nella già cappella ducale di San Marco a Venezia dal 1318 al 1797*. Venice (repr. 1931, 1982 and 1987)

Cahn, P. (1979) *Das Hoch'sche Konservatorium in Frankfurt am Main (1878–1978)*. Frankfurt am Main: Kramer

Cavazzuti, P. (1945) *Bellini a Londra*. Florence: Barbera

Cesari, G. and Luzio, A. (1913) *I copialettere di Giuseppe Verdi*. Milan: Ceretti (repr. 1968 and 1973)

Chion, M. and Reibel, G. (1974) *Les musiques électroacoustiques*. Paris: INA-GRM

Christout, M. (1967) *Le ballet de cour de Louis XIV, 1643–1672*. Paris: Picard

Citron, P. (1972–) (ed.) *Hector Berlioz: Correspondance générale* (8 vols). Paris: Flammarion

Clercx, S. (1960) *Johannes Ciconia: un musicien liégois et son temps*. Brussels: Palais des Acad

Cohen, Y.W. (1976) *Werden und Entwicklungen der Musik in Israel*. Kassel: Bärenreiter

Cosma, V. (1970) *Muzicieni români*. Bucharest: Ed. Muzicalæa

Dahlhaus, C. (1970) *Analyse und Werturteil*. Mainz: Schott

Dahlhaus, C. (1975) (ed.) *Beiträge zur musikalischen Hermeneutik*. Regensburg: Bosse

Dahlhaus, C. (1988) *Klassische und romantische Musikästhetik*. Laaber: Laaber

Dahlhaus, C. and Danuser, H. (1981–95) (eds) *Neues Handbuch der Musikwissenschaft* (13 vols). Laaber: Laaber

Dahlhaus, C. and Döhring, S. (1986–97) (eds) *Pipers Enzyklopädie des Musiktheaters* (7 vols). München: Piper

Danuser, H. (1991) *Gustav Mahler und seine Zeit*. Laaber: Laaber

Danuser, H. (1992) (ed.) *Gustav Mahler*. Darmstadt: Wiss. Buchgesellschaft

Devriès, A. (1976) *Éditions et commerce de la musique gravée à Paris.* Geneva: Minkoff

Dille, D. *et al.* (1964–1981) (ed.) *Documenta bartókiana* (6 vols). Budapest. Bartók
   Archívum

Dömling, W. (2000) *Hector Berlioz und seine Zeit.* Laaber: Laaber

Dragonetti, R. (1960, 2nd ed 1979) *La technique poétique des trouvères dans la chanson
   courtoise.* Bruges: De Tempel

Dufourcq, N. (1941, 2nd ed 1949) *La musique d'orgue française de Jehan Titelouze à Jehan
   Alain.* Paris: Floury

Dümling, A. and Girth, P. (1988, 3rd ed 1993) (eds) *Entartete Musik. Dokumentation und
   Kommentar.* Düsseldorf

Durand, J. (1927) (ed.) *Lettres de Claude Debussy à son éditeur.* Paris: Durand

Dürr, A. (1971) *Die Kantaten von Johann Sebastian Bach.* Kassel: Bärenreiter

Edler, A. (1982) *Robert Schumann und seine Zeit.* Laaber: Laaber

Eggebrecht, H.H. (1996) (ed.) *Handwörterbuch der musikalischen Terminologie.* Stuttgart:
   Steiner 1972-. Loose leaf collection. From this edited: *Terminologie der Musik im
   20. Jahrhundert.* Stuttgart 1995. *Terminologie der musikalischen Komposition.*
   Stuttgart

Eggebrecht, H.H. (1982, 2nd ed 1986) *Die Musik Gustav Mahlers.* München: Piper

Eggebrecht, H.H. (1959, 3rd ed 1998) *Heinrich Schütz. Musicus poeticus.* Göttingen:
   Vandenhoeck & Ruprecht

Eggebrecht, H.H. (1979, 2nd ed 1985) *Sinn und Gehalt. Aufsätze zur musikalischen Analyse.*
   Wilhelmshaven: Heinrichshofen (Taschenbücher zur Musikwissenschaft, 58)

Erler, H. (ed.) 1887) *Robert Schumanns Leben. Aus seinen Briefen geschildert* (2 vols).
   Berlin: Ries & Erler

Ertelt, T.F. (1995–) (ed.) *Briefwechsel der Wiener Schule* (9 vols) (vols 2–9 in
   preparation). Darmstadt: Wiss. Buchgesellschaft

Fellerer, K.G. (1972 and 1976) (ed.) *Geschichte der katholischen Kirchenmusik* (2 vols).
   Kassel: Bärenreiter

Fellerer, K.G. (1929) *Der Palestrinastil und seine Bedeutung in der vokalen Kirchenmusik des
   18. Jahrhunderts.* Augsburg: Filser

Ferretti, P. (1934) *Estetica gregoriana.* Rome: Pontificio Istituto di Musica Sacra

Fifield, C. (1993) *True artist and true friend. A biography of Hans Richter.* Oxford: OUP

Finscher, L. (1983) (ed.) *Ludwig van Beethoven.* Darmstadt: Wiss. Buchgesellschaft

Finscher, L. (1994–) (ed.) *Die Musik in Geschichte und Gegenwart* (2nd edn.) (ca. 20 vols)

Flender, R. and Rauhe, H. (1989) *Popmusik. Aspekte ihrer Geschichte. Funktionen, Wirkung,
   Ästhetik.* Darmstadt: Wiss. Buchgesellschaft

Floros, C. (1980) *Einführung in die Neumenkunde.* Wilhelmshaven: Heinrichshofen (Taschenbücher zur Musikwissenschaft, 60)

Floros, C. (1977–85) *Gustav Mahler* (3 vols). Wiesbaden: Breitkopf & Härtel

Flotzinger, R. and Gruber, G. (1977–79) (eds) *Musikgeschichte Österreichs.* Graz: Böhlau

Forchert, A. (2000) *Johann Sebastian Bach und seine Zeit.* Laaber: Laaber

Fubini, E. (1964, 10th ed 1987) *L'estetica musicale dal settecento a oggi.* Turin: Einaudi

Geck, M. (1967) *Die Wiederentdeckung der Matthäuspassion im 19. Jahrhundert.* Regensburg: Bosse

Gericke, H. (1960) *Der Wiener Musikalienhandel von 1700 bis 1778.* Graz: Böhlau

Goléa, A. (1958) *Georges Auric.* Paris: Ventadour

Gülke, P. (1979) *Neue Beiträge zur Kenntnis des Sinfonikers Schubert. Die Fragmente D 615, D 708A und D 936A.* In: Metzger, H.-K. and Riehn, R. (eds) *Musik-Konzepte, Sonderband Schubert.* München, pp. 187–

Gülke, P. (1985) *Zwischen Angriff und Zurücknahme, Wagnis und Taktik. Die Fragmente D 615 und D 708A.* In Aderhold, W. et al. (eds) *Franz Schubert – Jahre der Krise 1818–1823. Bericht über das Symposium Kassel 30. September bis 1. Oktober 1982.* Arnold Feil zum 60. Geburtstag am 2. Oktober 1985. Kassel: Bärenreiter, pp. 48–

Hanslick, E. (1869–70) *Geschichte des Concertwesens in Wien.* Wien: Braumüller (repr. 1971)

Henze, H.W. (1996) *Reiselieder und böhmische Quinten. Autobiographische Mitteilungen 1926–1993.* Frankfurt am Main: Fischer

Hesbert, R.-J. (1957) *Structures grégoriennes.* Paris

Honegger, M. (1970–77) (ed.) *Dictionnaire de la musique* (4 vols). Paris: Bordas

Huglo, M. (1956) *Fonti e paleografia del canto ambrosiano.* Milan

d'Indy, V. (1920) *Emmanuel Chabrier et Paul Dukas.* Paris

d'Indy, V. (1930) *Richard Wagner et son influence sur l'art musical français.* Paris: Delagrave

Jammers, E. (1955) *Die Anfänge der abendländischen Musik.* Strasbourg: Heitz

Jammers, E. (1962) *Musik in Byzanz, im päpstlichen Rom und im Frankenreich.* Heidelberg: Winter

Jeppesen, K. (1968–70) *La frottola.* Copenhagen: Munksgaard

Karbusicky, V. (1986) *Grundriß der musikalischen Semantik.* Darmstadt: Wissenschaftliche Buchgesellschaft

Karbusicky, V. (1990) (ed.) *Sinn und Bedeutung in der Musik. Texte zur Entwicklung des musiksemiotischen Denkens.* Darmstadt: Wissenschaftliche Buchgesellschaft

Klusen, E.A. (1975) *Johann Wilhelm Wilms und das Amsterdamer Musikleben (1772–1847)*. Buren: Knuf

Köhler, K.-H. *et al.* (1968–2001) (eds) *Ludwig van Beethovens Konversationshefte* (11 vols) (further vols in preparation). Leipzig: Deutscher Verlag für Musik

Kolleritsch, O. *et al.* (1968–) (eds) *Studien zur Wertungsforschung* (43 vols) (further vols in preparation). Graz: Universal

Konold, W. (1986) *Bernd Alois Zimmermann: Der Komponist und sein Werk*. Köln: DuMont

Konrad, U. (1992) *Mozarts Schaffensweise. Studien zu den Werkautographen, Skizzen und Entwürfen*. Göttingen: Vandenhoeck & Ruprecht (Abhandlungen der Akademie der Wissenschaften in Göttingen, 3/201)

Kross, S. (1989) *Geschichte des deutschen Liedes*. Darmstadt: Wissenschaftliche Buchgesellschaft

Kunze, S. (1984) *Mozarts Opern*. Stuttgart: Reclam

de La Borde, J.-B. (1780) *Essai sur la musique ancienne et moderne* (4 vols) (repr. 1972). Paris: Onfroy

de Laborde, L.E. S.J. (1965) *Musiciens de Paris 1535–1792*. Paris: Picard

de La Laurencie, L. (1922–24) *L'école française de violon de Lully à Viotti* (3 vols) (repr. 1971). Paris: Delagrave

Lockspeiser, E. (1957) (ed.) *Lettres inédits de Claude Debussy à André Caplet (1908–1914)*. Monaco: Rocher

Luzio, A. (1935 and 1947) *Carteggi verdiani* (4 vols). Rome

Mahnkopf, C.-S. (1998) *Kritik der neuen Musik. Entwurf einer Musik des 21. Jahrhunderts*. Kassel: Bärenreiter

Mauser, S. (1993–) (ed.) *Handbuch der musikalischen Gattungen*. Laaber: Laaber

Mauser, S. (1992–) (ed.) *Schriften zur musikalischen Hermeneutik*. Laaber: Laaber

McGowen, M.M. (1963, 2nd ed 1978) *L'art du ballet de cour en France, 1581–1643*. Paris: Centre national de la recherche scientifique

Mertens, C. (1967) *Hedendaagse muziek in Belgie*. Brussels

Messager, J.-A. (ed.) (1938) *L'enfance de Pelléas. Lettres de Claude Debussy à André Messager*. Paris

Mompellio, F. (1956) *Sigismondi d'India, musicista palermitano*. Milan: Ricordi

Mooser, R.-A. (1948–51) *Annales de la musique et des musiciens en Russie au 18e siècle* (3 vols). Geneva: Mont-Blanc

Morini, N. La R. (1930) *Accademia filarmonica di Bologna*. Bologna: Cappelli

Moser, H.J. (1935, 2nd ed 1943) *J.S. Bach*. Berlin: Hesse

Müller von Asow, H. and Müller von Asow, E.H. (1935, 2nd ed 1950) (ed.) *J.S. Bach Gesammelte Briefe* Regensburg: Bosse

Müller-Blattau, J. (1950) *Johann Sebastian Bach: Leben und Schaffen.* Stuttgart: Reclam

Neumann, W. *et al.* (1963–79) (eds) *Bach-Dokumente* (4 vols). Kassel: Bärenreiter

Newbould, B. (1992) *Schubert and the Symphony.* London: Toccata

Nowak, L. (1964, 3rd ed 1995) *Anton Bruckner. Musik und Leben.* Wien: Österreichischer Bundesverlag

Osthoff, W. (1969) *Theatergesang und darstellende Musik in der italienischen Renaissance.* Tutzing: Schneider

Pereira Salas, E. (1941) *Los orígenes del arte musical en Chile.* Santiago de Chile: Santiago UP

Petersen, P. (1995) *Hans Werner Henze. Werke der Jahre 1984–1993.* Mainz: Schott (Kölner Schriften zur Neuen Musik, 4)

Petersen, P. (1988) *Hans Werner Henze. Ein politischer Musiker.* Hamburg: Argument

Pierre, C. (1975) *Histoire du Concert spirituel, 1725–1790.* Paris: Société Française de Musicologie

Pousseur, H. (1970) *Fragments théoriques sur la musique expérimentale.* Brussels: Institut de Sociologie

Pütz, W. (1968) *Studien zum Streichquartettschaffen bei Hindemith, Bartók, Schönberg und Webern.* Regensburg: Bosse

Racek, J. (1965) *Stilprobleme der italienischen Monodie.* Prague: Státní pedagogické nakl

Rathert, W. (1989, 2nd ed 1996) *Charles Ives.* Darmstadt: Wissenschaftliche Buchgesellschaft

Rauhe, H. (1974) *Popularität in der Musik. Interdisziplinäre Aspekte musikalischer Kommunikation.* Karlsruhe: Braun

Reeser, E. (1950) *Een eeuw Nederlandse muziek: 1815–1915.* Amsterdam: Querido

Riemann, H. (1900) *Die Elemente der musikalischen Ästhetik.* Berlin/Stuttgart: Spemann

Riemann, H. (2nd ed 1920) *Geschichte der Musiktheorie im neunten bis neunzehnten Jahrhundert.* Berlin: Hesse (repr. 1961) (in English published only in part)

Riemann, H. (1918–19, 4th ed 1920) *L. van Beethovens sämtliche Klavier-Solosonaten.* Berlin: Hesse

Riemann, H. (1882, 12th ed 1959–75) (ed.) *Musik-Lexikon* (5 vols). Leipzig: Bibliographisches Institut

Saint-Saëns, C. (1913) *École buissonière.* Paris: Lafitte

Salazar, A. (1930) *La música contemporánea en España.* Madrid: La Nave (repr. 1982)

Saldívar, G. (1934, 2nd ed 1941) *Historia de la música en México.* Mexico City: Cultura

Schad, M. (1996) (ed.) *Cosima Wagner und Ludwig II. Briefe. Eine erstaunliche Korrespondenz.* Bergisch Gladbach: Lübbe

Schaeffer, P. (1967, 2nd ed 1973) *La musique concrète.* Paris: UP de France

Schnebel, D. (1970) *Mauricio Kagel. Musik, Theater, Film.* Köln: DuMont

Schollum, R. (1977) *Das oesterreichische Lied des 20. Jahrhunderts.* Tutzing: Schneider

Schuh, W. (1976) *Richard Strauss – Jugend und frühe Meisterjahre. Lebenschronik 1864–1898.* Zürich: Atlantis

Schuh, W. (1954) (ed.) *Richard Strauss. Briefe an die Eltern 1882–1906.* Zürich: Atlantis

Schuh, W. (1969) (ed.) *Richard Strauss. Briefwechsel mit Willi Schuh.* Zürich: Atlantis

Schumann, R. (1971–1987) *Tagebücher (incl. Haushaltsbücher)* (4 vols), ed. Eismann, G. and Nauhaus, G. Leipzig: Deutscher Verlag für Musik

Sikorski, A. (1997) *Musikwirtschaft und Neue Musik. Das unternehmerische Entscheidungsverhalten zwischen Ästhetik und Ökonomie.* Frankfurt am Main: Lang (Europäische Hochschulschriften, 5/2163)

Solerti, A. (1905) *Musica, ballo e drammatica alla corte Medicea dal 1600 al 1637.* Florence: Bemporad (repr. 1968 and 1969)

Specht, R. (1913, 4th ed 1925) *Gustav Mahler.* Berlin: Schuster & Loeffler

Specht, R. (1909) *Johann Strauß.* Berlin: Marquardt

Specht, R. (1921) *Richard Strauß und sein Werk* (2 vols). Leipzig: Tal

Sponheuer, B. (1978) *Logik des Zerfalls. Untersuchungen zum Finalproblem in den Symphonien Gustav Mahlers.* Tutzing: Schneider

Stahl, W. (1937) *Die Lübecker Abendmusiken im 17. und 18. Jahrhundert.* Lübeck

Stephan, R. (1958) *Neue Musik. Versuch einer kritischen Einführung.* Göttingen: Vandenhoeck & Ruprecht

Stephan, R. (1989) (ed.) *Die Wiener Schule.* Darmstadt: Wissenschaftliche Buchgesellschaft

Stephan, R. (1994) (ed.) *A. Berg: Musikalische Schriften und Dichtungen. Analysen musikalischer Werke Arnold Schönbergs.* Wien: Universal

Stockhausen, K. (1963–1989) *Texte zur Musik* (6 vols). Köln: DuMont

vander Straeten, E. (1867–88) *La musique aux Pays-Bas avant le XIXe siècle* (8 vols). Brussels: van Trigt (repr. 1969)

Stuart, E.M. (1925) *Kurt Atterberg.* Stockholm

Subirá, J. (1953) *Historia de la música española e hispano-americana.* Barcelona: Salvat

Szabolcsi, B. (1956, 2nd ed 1968) (ed.) *Bartók: sa vie et son œuvre.* Budapest: Corvina

Szöllösy, A. (1966) (ed.) *Bartók Béla összegyüjtott irásai* (vol. I). Budapest: Zenemukiad

Tenschert, R. (1949) *Richard Strauss und Wien. Eine Wahlverwandtschaft.* Wien: Hollinek

Tenschert, R. (1944) *3 x 7 Variationen über das Thema Richard Strauss.* Wien: Frick

Tenschert, R. (1955) (ed.) *Richard Strauss und Joseph Gregor. Briefwechsel 1934–1949.* Salzburg: Müller

Thijsse, W.H. (1949) *Zeven eeuwen Nederlandse muziek.* Rijswijk: Kramers

Tiersot, J. (1904) *Hector Berlioz et la société de son temps.* Paris: Hachette

Torchi, L. (1901) *La musica istrumentale in Italia nei secoli XVI, XVII e XVIII.* Turin: Bocca (repr. 1969)

Tosi, G. (1948) (ed.) *Debussy et d'Annunzio: correspondance inédite.* Paris: Denoël

Trenner, F. (1977) *Die Skizzenbücher von Richard Strauss aus dem Richard-Strauss-Archiv in Garmisch.* Tutzing: Schneider (Veröffentlichungen der Richard-Strauss-Gesellschaft · München, I)

Trenner, F. (1978) (ed.) *Cosima Wagner – Richard Strauss. Ein Briefwechsel.* Tutzing: Schneider (Veröffentlichungen der Richard-Strauss-Gesellschaft · München, 2)

Trenner, F. (1954) (ed.) *Richard Strauss. Dokumente seines Lebens und Schaffens.* München: Beck

Trenner, F. (1980) (ed.) *Richard Strauss – Ludwig Thuille. Ein Briefwechsel.* Tutzing: Schneider (Veröffentlichungen der Richard-Strauss-Gesellschaft · München, 4)

Turrini, G. (1941) *L'Accademia Filarmonica di Verona dalla Fondazione (Maggio 1543) al 1600 e il suo patrimonio musicale.* Verona: Tipografica Veronese

Vallery-Radot, P. (1957) (ed.) *Lettres de Claude Debussy à sa femme Emma.* Paris: Flammarion

Valls, M. (1962) *La música española depués de Manuel de Falla.* Madrid: Revista de Occidente

Vlad, R. (1958) *Storia della musica dodecafonica.* Milan

Vogel, M. (1984 and 1997) *Schönberg und die Folgen: Die Irrwege der neuen Musik.* Bonn: Verlag für Systematische Musikwissenschaft

Wagner, P. (1913) *Geschichte der Messe, I: bis 1600.* Leipzig: Breitkopf & Härtel (repr. 1963 and 1972)

Wagner, P. (1895–1921) *Einführung in die gregorianischen Melodien* (3 vols) (repr. 1962 and 1970) (only Vol. I translated into English). Fribourg: Fribourg UB

Wagner, R. (1976) *Mein Leben*, ed. M. Gregor-Dellin. München: dtv

Wagner, R. 1970–) *Sämtliche Briefe* (11 vols) (further vols in preparation) ed. Strobel, G. and Wolf, W. Leipzig: Deutscher Verlag für Musik and Wiesbaden: Breitkopf & Härtel

Walton, C. (1994) *Othmar Schoeck. Eine Biographie*, trans. from the English by K.W. Bartlett. Zürich: Atlantis

Wellesz, E. (1919) *Die Opern und Oratorien in Wien von 1660 bis 1708*. Leipzig: Breitkopf & Härtel

Wiora, W. (1969) (ed.) *Die Ausbreitung des Historismus über die Musik*. Regensburg: Bosse

Wolff, H.C. (1937) *Die venezianische Oper in der zweiten Hälfte des 17. Jahrhunderts: eine historisch-soziologische Untersuchung*. Berlin: Elsner (repr. 1975)

Wolff, H.C. (1981) *Geschichte der komischen Oper: Einführung*. Wilhelmshaven: Heinrichshofen (Taschenbücher zur Musikwissenschaft, 73)

Wouters, J. (1971) *Henk Badings*. Amsterdam

Zaminer, F. and Ertelt, T.F. (1985–) (eds) *Geschichte der Musiktheorie* (16 vols) (vols 2, 8/1 and 12–16 in preparation). Darmstadt: Wissenschaftliche Buchgesellschaft

15 Musical sources in government publications in Great Britain

Lewis Foreman

▶ BRITISH GOVERNMENT PUBLICATIONS

British government publications do not become a widely useful source for research in music until after the Second World War, and indeed the recent interest of government in musical and artistic matters is unprecedented. This has resulted in a rapidly growing bibliography of reports and evidence, of considerable potential value to future scholarly investigation, which otherwise would not have been available. From the nineteenth century there are a few items of interest (see below) but between the wars almost nothing if we exclude reports and material relating to the BBC and its charter. Since the war the number of relevant publications increases considerably, particularly after the 1970s.

British government publications may best be considered in four main groups:

1   Parliamentary publications including select committee reports;
2   The record of Parliament (*Hansard* and the *Journals*);
3   Legislation (Acts, Statutory Instruments, etc.);
4   Non-parliamentary publishing.

Most government publishing in the UK was once centralised through Her Majesty's Stationery Office, HMSO, (now privatised as The Stationery Office, TSO) but from the 1970s onward there was an enormous growth in departmental (i.e. local) publishing of all kinds, not issued through HMSO, which enormously complicated the complexities and difficulties of tracing and obtaining government publications, especially when out of print, until Chadwyck-Healey launched their *Catalogue of British Official Publications Not Published by The Stationery Office*,[1] and its incorporation into their UKOP CD-ROM.[2]

▶ CATALOGUES AND LISTS

The tradition of HMSO catalogues extends back to the nineteenth century, and the current series of annual catalogues with five-yearly indexes stretch back to the First World War. HMSO/TSO must be the only publisher in the world to issue a *Daily List* of new publications, cumulated monthly and annually. These days details of current government publications are also available via the internet. (<http://www.official-documents.co.uk/menu/byhmso.htm>) For the main run of the twentieth-century publications from HMSO, the Carrollton Press's cumulative index covers the half-century from 1922 to 1972 (Blackmore, 1976).

For the nineteenth century Peter Cockton's *Subject Catalogue* (1988) is probably the most convenient source when searching for music and related topics, though there is little material (but see below).

Compared to the huge volume of government publications, music does not make a frequent appearance in HMSO catalogues, yet over the years it has been the subject of a significant number of publications which can be discussed as follows:

1 legislation, primarily copyright and performing rights, but also impinging on public assembly, broadcasting, education and employment;
2 Parliament – debates on musical matters have largely been on legislative aspects, but written answers have been given from time to time on contentious musical matters of the moment, and they can be traced in the indexes to *Hansard*;
3 reviews and discussion papers on specific matters, which over the years have included the provision of concert halls, subsidies (e.g. the Royal Opera House), and orchestras;
4 non-parliamentary publications including exhibition and museum catalogues, and museum publications generally.

Departmental publications relating to music tend to focus on the Department of Culture, Media and Sport (formerly the Department of National Heritage) in its various incarnations over the years. Not a government department, but an agency, the Arts Council (now the Arts Council of England) is also a significant focus of activity. Any extensive research relating to Arts Council of England or DCMS matters might usefully start with their libraries, both available for reference use by appointment.

Press notices are issued by these organisations and by the Select Committee for CMS are available in hard copy from the issuing body or via the internet (<http://www.parliament.uk/commons/selcom/cmshome.htm>) for current announcements. Although by their very nature press releases are ephemeral documents, back issues of press notices are also listed in the Chadwyck-Healey *Catalogue of British Official Publications Not*

Published by HMSO/TSO and subsequently cumulated in the *UKOP* CD-ROM and are permanently available from them on microfiche. From time to time individual press releases acquire a documentary value, particularly when they contain statistics, or document the formal starting date of an administrative or quasi-legal initiative.

The Arts Council of England issue a useful free catalogue of their publications, and their library[3] has a series of excellent free bibliographies available to callers. Titles relevant to this article include:

- *Arts Attenders* bibliography (April 1999);
- *Arts Council of England/Arts Council of Great Britain* bibliography (third rev ed, November 1997);
- *The Arts, Planning and Regeneration* bibliography (April 1998);
- *Copyright* bibliography (September 1997);
- *Cultural Policy: UK* bibliography (October 1997);
- *Cultural Policy: International* bibliography (July 1998);
- *Economics of the Arts* bibliography (June 1997);
- *Fundraising* (May 1996);
- *Grants for Education and Training* (January 1999);
- *Marketing the Arts* bibliography (June 1997).

▶ PARLIAMENTARY PAPERS: COMMAND PAPERS

Parliamentary government publications are published effectively in two series, House of Commons (or Lords) papers and Command Papers (that is 'Printed by Command of . . .'. White papers and green (i.e. consultative) papers appear as Command Papers, and appear in a numerical series prefaced by varying abbreviations of the word 'command'. When the numbering had advanced into the 9000s in each series, a new abbreviation was chosen, the sequences being: C; Cd; Cmd; Cmnd. The current series is designated Cm. The numbers used and the dates they represent are

- C 1 to C 9550: 1870 to 1899;
- Cd 1 to Cd 9239: 1900 to 1918;
- Cmd 1 to Cmd 9889: 1919 to 1956;
- Cmnd 1 to Cmnd 9927: 1956 to 7 November 1986;
- Cm 1 . . . : 12 November 1986 to date.

A select list of Command Papers on music and related subjects

Home Office (1904) *Report of the Committee Appointed by the Home Secretary to Inquire into the Piracy of Music Publications, with Evidence and Appendix.* Cd 1960 London: HMSO

Report of the Committee (Chairman Professor L C Robbins) to Consider a new Queen's Hall (1955) (with corrigenda). Cmd 9467. London: HMSO

Department of Trade and Industry (1977) Public Inquiry into Music Royalties Payable under Section 8 of the Copyright Act 1956. Report by Mr Hugh Francis, QC. Cmnd 6903. London: HMSO

Office of Arts and Libraries (1984) Public and Private Funding of the Arts: Observations by the Government on the 8th Report from the Education, Science and Arts Committee. Cmnd 9127 London: HMSO

Monopolies & Mergers Commission (1994) The Supply of Recorded Music – Monopolies and Merger Commission Report on Supply in the UK of Pre-recorded Compact Discs, Vinyl Discs and Tapes Containing Music. Cm 2599 London: HMSO

Monopolies & Mergers Commission (1996) Performing Right – a Report on the Supply in the UK of the Services of Administering Performing Rights and Film Synchronisation Right. Cm 3147 London: HMSO

▶ PARLIAMENTARY PAPERS: HOUSE OF COMMONS PAPERS

House of Commons Papers are published in sessional series (e.g. 1993/94). These include annual reports and accounts of a multitude of organisations that have to report regularly to the House of Commons. A similar series appears for the Lords. Since the establishment of Select Committees the most interesting material in the music field appears in the reports of the Department of Culture, Media and Sport Select Committee (formerly the Department of National Heritage, and before that the Office of Arts and Libraries, and before that other designations) in its various incarnations over the years. Topics they have covered that have achieved wide publicity in the press have included the Royal Opera House, the provision and funding of orchestras, and the ending by the PRS of the Classical Music Subsidy.

These are all of value, not only for their ostensible subject matter but for the light the detailed evidence submitted throws on the petitioners as well as their overall subject. Similarly, the line of questioning and apparent assumptions of members of the Select Committee in itself constitutes a vivid snapshot of the time. In this, while the hearings on the Royal Opera House were wide-ranging and extensively reported in the press, the much less high profile report on the PRS and the Classical Music Subsidy generated extensive thoughtful and well-considered statements on music publishing the working of composer and music trusts and the business of twentieth-century British music from a remarkable range of composers, publishers and managers of trusts unavailable from any other source. As an example, Giles Easterbrook's four-page statement, based on a wide first-hand experience, is likely to become a prime source for future historians.[4]

A select list of House of Commons Papers on music and related subjects

1979/80 HC 722, 722-I. Education, Science and Arts Committee. Third report (sess 1979–80) *The Future of the Promenade Concerts*, together with minutes of evidence (1980). London: HMSO

81/82: HC 49-I, II, III Education, Science, and Arts Committee. Eighth Report. Sess 1981–2. *Public and Private Funding of the Arts* (1982). London: HMSO

83/84: HC 264-vii and viii Education, Science and Arts Committee. *The Effect of the Abolition of the GLC and Metropolitan Counties Upon Support for the Arts*. Minutes of evidence. London: HMSO, 1984

95/96: HC 23 National Heritage Committee: *Funding of the Performing and Visual Arts*. Minutes of evidence. London: HMSO, 8/2/96

95/96: HC 23-ii *Funding of the Performing and Visual Arts*. [Evidence by Association of County Councils; Association of Metropolitan Authorities; South Bank Centre]

95/96: HC 23-iii *Funding of the Performing and Visual Arts*. [Evidence by Arts and Entertainment Training Council; Equity; NFMS

95/96: HC 23-iv *Funding of the Performing and Visual Arts*. [Evidence by Arts Council of England]

95/96: HC 23-v *Funding of the Performing and Visual Arts*. [Evidence by ENO; Glyndebourne Festival Opera; Opera North; Royal Opera; Scottish Opera; Welsh National Opera; Association of British Orchestras]

95/96: HC 23-vi *Funding of the Performing and Visual Arts*. [Evidence by the Tate Gallery; Visual Arts ad Galleries Association; National Arts Association Public Art Forum and British Tourist Authority.]

95/96: HC 23-vii *Funding of the Performing and Visual Arts*. [Evidence by the BBC and other non-musical organisations the Tate Gallery; Visual Arts and Galleries Association; National Arts Association; Public Art Forum and British Tourist Authority.]

95/96: HC 23-viii *Funding of the Performing and Visual Arts*. [Evidence by non-musical organisations]

95/96: HC 23-ix *Funding of the Performing and Visual Arts*. [Evidence by DNH]

97/98: HC 199-I: *The Royal Opera House* (1997). Vol I: report and proceedings of the committee. London: HMSO

97/98: HC 199-I: *The Royal Opera House* (1997). Vol II: minutes of evidence and appendices. London: HMSO

97/98: HC 493: *The Royal Opera House* (1998). Responses by the Government and the Arts Council of England to the First Report from the Culture, Media and Sport Committee. London: HMSO

97/98: HC 994: *The Eyre Review of the Royal Opera House* (1998). Report together with proceedings of the Committee and Minutes of Evidence, London: HMSO

98/99: HC 468-I: *PRS and the Abolition of the Classical Music Subsidy* (1999). Report and proceedings of the committee. London: HMSO

98/99: HC 468-II: *PRS and the Abolition of the Classical Music Subsidy* (1999). Minutes of evidence and appendices. London: HMSO

▶ THE RECORD OF PARLIAMENT

The day-to-day verbatim transcript of the proceedings of Parliament is published in the daily *Hansard* (cumulated weekly and annually) with its own indexing arrangements. *Hansard* is published in two series, Commons and Lords, providing the proceedings of the two Houses. Long after the end of each session a *Journal* for each House, in a single volume, is also published, constituting a formal record of the activities of the House. It is much more of an overview, providing an authoritative record on procedure but of little interest to musical researchers.

▶ LEGISLATION

The British legislative framework falls into four areas: Bills, Public Acts, Statutory Instruments, and departmentally issued rules and orders. Legislative and regulatory issues in music largely relate to copyright, licensing of premises, employment, education, grants and award of qualifications and concerning the BBC. For Acts see the *Index to the Statutes*;[5] for Statutory Instruments, the *Index to Government Orders*.[6] For general access to legislation see *Halsbury's Laws of England*,[7] the index to which[8] gives nearly a column of terms relating to music, or specialist legal textbooks.

▶ DEPARTMENT OR AGENCY BY DEPARTMENT

The following constitutes a high-level overview, department by department, with selected examples, summarising likely interest in musical matters.

Audit Commission

Detailed examinations of the function of government agencies, departments and activities. A useful example would be *Local Authorities, Entertainment and the Arts* (1991). London: HMSO.

Department for Culture, Media and Sport

Since July 1997, formerly Office of Arts and Libraries (see below). See the department's website for a wide range of publications (<www.culture.gov.

uk>). The 'glossy' departmental report *Consumers Call the Tune* (2000) highlights the impact of new technologies, especially MP3, on the music industry. A similar 'glossy' executive summary of a discussion of the funding issues, *Banking on a Hit* (2001) highlights a report by Kingston University's Small Business Research Centre, also available free of charge and from the web at the address given above, and from <www.kingston.ac.uk.sbrc>.

Department of Trade and Industry

Copyright and intellectual rights is the principal DTI interest impinging on the music industry. IT issues also have a musical interest and a guide to DTI involvement appeared jointly with an Information Society Initiative in 1996 (Communications and Information Industries Directorate, 1996). Exports and trade issues will also provide a small amount of material of interest. Unpublished company and bankruptcy records are a major source for historical research into musical organisations, see page 207.

Education and Science (now Education and Skills)

Reports and rules and orders relating to curriculum, grants and schools inspection issues, and music in the National Curriculum which has generated a range of documentation.

English Tourist Board

Promotional publicity, notably the leaflet *Singing in Cathedrals*.

Foreign and Commonwealth Office

Music is more likely to find a place in the activities of British missions round the world than in the mainstream of the Office in the UK. A typical example would be *British Fashion and Music Industries*, a promotional publication last issued in 1995.

General Synod (of the Church of England)

Issues to do with church music, published by Church House Publishing. The principal recent report is *In Tune With Heaven*, the report of the Archbishop's Commission on Church Music, which also produced a financial comment and a report from a follow-up group.[9]

Health and Safety Executive

Public safety issues, topically surveys of sound levels at pop concerts, and resulting hearing loss.

Health and Social Security

Pay and conditions of service, particularly relating to music therapists.

Home Office

Generally little to do with music, other than in relation to anti-drugs initiatives. There was some comment on a prison rock band cutting a charity disc in 1981.

Monopolies and Mergers Commission

Reviews of perceived monopolies referred to it, which in the music field have largely been focused on the supply and pricing of recorded music. The reports are published as Command Papers (*qv*).

Office for Standards in Education

OFSTED Publications may all be downloaded from the internet (<www.ofsted.gov.uk>). They are presented in age ranges 3–11 and 11–16. A search on 'music' gets an amazing 20,985 matches, ranked in order of relevance.

Office of Arts and Libraries

Now Department for Culture, Media and Sport, and discussed above. Has had various changes of name and responsibility. The first report on the Royal Opera House has tended to be overlooked in the high profile criticism of the mid-1990s. However, the earlier study was published by HMSO as a Departmental report, though outside the usual Parliamentary series. It is a historically valuable source.

Financial Scrutiny of the Royal Opera House Covent Garden and the Royal Shakespeare Company (1983). Report to the Minister for the Arts by Clive Priestley. London: HMSO

Financial Scrutiny of the Royal Opera House Covent Garden Ltd (1984). Report by Clive Priestley. Vols I and II. London: HMSO

▶ HISTORICAL PUBLICATIONS: THE NINETEENTH CENTURY

Generally there are few musical items in the Parliamentary papers for the nineteenth century. However, a search of the Chadwyck-Healey *Index to House of Commons Papers on CD-ROM* under the search term 'music' gets 64 hits for the period from 1835 to the First World War. The earliest of these include:

1835 *(349)* Bill to repeal pal4 of Act as restrains Amusement of Music and Dancing

1837 *(380)* Bill to consolidate and amend Laws relating to Copyright in Printed Books, Music, Plays and Engravings

1856 *(251)* Correspondence on Suppression of Music in Kensington Gardens on Sundays

1864 *(90)* Bill for better Regulation of Street Music in Metropolitan Police District

1864 *(186)* Bill for better Regulation of Street Music in Metropolitan Police District (as amended in Cttee.)

1864 *(319)* Instructions to Police Constables of Metropolitan District defining their Duties with regard to Removal of Street Musicians

1871 *(214)* Memorials to Govt. on behalf of Irish Academy of Music for Grant-in-Aid of Institution, and Correspondence

1872 *(185)* Return of Number of Students in Training Colleges who obtained Mark for Papers in Music, 1871

1875 *(178)* Bill intituled, Act for amending Law relating to Houses of Public Dancing, Music or other Public Entertainment in Cities of London and Westminster

1878 *(264)* Memorials to Education Dept. on Musical Instruction in Public Elementary Schools

1878–79 *(142)* Return of Amounts paid in respect of Shilling Grant for Singing, 1877–78

1880 *(81)* Return of Amounts paid in respect of Shilling Grant for Singing, 1878–79

1880 *(82)* Mr. Hullah's Rep. on Musical Education Abroad

1880 *(258)* Petition of Prince of Wales, praying for Grant of Charter of Incorporation to Royal College of Music

1881 *(143)* Return of Amounts paid in respect of Shilling Grant for Singing, 1 879–80

1883 *(100)* Petition of Prince of Wales and others for Charter of Incorporation to College of Music

1884 *(61)* Bill for better Regulation of Theatres and Music-Halls in Metropolitan Area

1884–85 *(67)* Bill for better Regulation of Theatres and Music-Halls in Metropolitan Area

1886 *(44)* Bill to confer further Powers on Metropolitan Bd. of Works for inspecting Theatres and Music-Halls and granting Certificates

1886 *(69)* Bill for better Regulation of Theatres and Music-Halls in Metropolitan Area

1887 *(15)* Bill for better Regulation of Theatres and Music-Halls in Metropolitan Area

1887 *(117)* Bill to confer further Powers on Metropolitan Bd of Works for inspecting Theatres and Music-Halls and granting Certificates

1888 *(37)* Bill for better Regulation of Theatres and Music-Halls in Metropolitan Area 1889 (8) Bill for better Regulation of Theatres and Music-Halls in County of London

1889 *(298A)* Bill to confer Powers on London County Council for inspecting Theatres Music-Halls and other Places of Entertainment and granting Certificates (Memo.)

1889 *(298)* Bill to confer Powers on London County Council for inspecting Theatres Music-Halls and other Places of Entertainment and granting Certificates

1890–91 *(63)* Bill to limit Hours of Street Organs and other Street Music in Metropolis

1890–91 *(106)* Bill to provide for Control and Regulation of Theatres Music-Halls and Places of Public Entertainment in Administrative County of London

1890–91 C 6426 Rep. from HM Ambassadors in Europe and HM Minister in United States on Regulations for Control of Itinerant Street Musicians

The nineteenth-century parliamentary papers, generally known as 'blue books', were selectively reprinted in the 1970s by Irish University Press in co-operation with the University of Southampton, in a subject arrangement. Three volumes of this series were categorised as 'Stage and Theatre'.[10]

▶ NON-DEPARTMENTAL PUBLICATIONS

Many publications relating to music have been issued by government agencies, principally but not exclusively the Arts Council, in the face of increasingly exacting financial strictures from government. The following is a select list of the principal titles relating to music, listed chronologically.

Goodman, A. (Chairman) (1965) *Committee on the London Orchestras – report.* London: Arts Council of Great Britain

Opera and Ballet Enquiry – 1966 including Outline Index to Minutes and Papers (1967). London: Arts Council of Great Britain

Report on Opera and Ballet in the United Kingdom 1966–69 (1969). London: Arts Council of Great Britain

Peacock, A. (Chairman) (1970) *A Report on Orchestral Resources in Great Britain, 1970.* London: Arts Council of Great Britain

Shaw, R. (Chairman) (1971) *Training Arts Administrators.* Report of the Committee of Enquiry. London: Arts Council of Great Britain

Opera in England, Scotland and Wales: Report by a Working Party (1972). London: Arts Council of Great Britain

Scottish National Orchestra (1974) *Scottish National Orchestra – Aberdeen Audience Research Analysis 1974.* Edinburgh: Scottish Arts Council

Opera Tours in England by the Major Companies 1970–1975 (1975). London: Arts Council of Great Britain

Rump, A. (1977) *Money for Composers.* London: Arts Council of Great Britain

Rump, A. (1979) *How We Treat Our Composers*. [Arts Council] (This report was commissioned by the Department of Education and Science as the British contribution to the Council of Europe's symposium on aid to musical creation, held in October 1979.)

Peggie, A. (1981) *New Approaches to New Music – a Report on the Contemporary Music Network Educational Activities 1980–81*. London: Arts Council of Great Britain

South East Arts (1981) *Pricing and Marketing for Grant-Aided Orchestral Concerts – Report to the South East Arts Association*. London: Arts Council of Great Britain

Light Opera Enquiry: Report of the Enquiry set up by the Music Panel and the Touring Committee (1981). London: Arts Council of Great Britain

Lawrence, R. (1984) *The Arts Council and the Four Independent London Orchestras*. London: Arts Council of Great Britain

Neil, D. (1985) *Promoting Regional Orchestral Music: a Discussion Paper*. London: Arts Council of Great Britain

Mitchell, P. (1989) *Enlarging the Domain of the Playable Music of the Moment – Improvised Music Touring Scheme 1988/89*. Part I a report. London: Arts Council of Great Britain

Mitchell, P. (1989) *Enlarging the Domain of the Playable Music of the Moment – Improvised Music Touring Scheme 1988/89*. Part II some advice. London: Arts Council of Great Britain

Millward Brown Market Research Ltd (1992) *Research Digest for the Arts: Classical Music*. London: Arts Council of Great Britain

Millward Brown Market Research Ltd (1992) *Research Digest for the Arts: Opera*. London: Arts Council of Great Britain

Millward Brown Market Research Ltd (1993) *Research Digest for the Arts: Jazz*. London: Arts Council of Great Britain

Hoffmann, Sir L. (Chairman) (1993) *The Advisory Committee on the London Orchestras: Report*. London: Arts Council of Great Britain

Harris Research Centre (1993) *Orchestral Concerts Research – Qualitative Finding Report*. London: Arts Council of Great Britain

Appraisal Team (1994) *Appraisal Report – Halle Concerts Society*. Summary. London: Arts Council of England

Research Surveys of Great Britain Ltd (1994) *Classic Orchestral Concerts Research*. London: Arts Council of England

Research Surveys of Great Britain Ltd (1994) *Orchestral Concerts Quantitative Research*. London: Arts Council of England

Shakspeare, A. (1994) *Contemporary Dance Audience Survey 1993/4 – Report for the Art Council of England*. London: Arts Council of Great Britain

Report of the Arts Council Orchestral Working Group (1994). London: Arts Council of Great Britain

BBC/Arts Council (1994) *Review of National Orchestral Provision.* Consultation Document. London: Arts Council of England

Stevenson, D. *et al.* (1995) *Lyric Theatre Review: a report . . .* London: Arts Council of England

Ritterman, J. [for] BBC/Arts Council of England (1995) *National Review of Orchestral Provision.* Report of the consultation. London: Arts Council of England

Review of Jazz in England (1995): consultative green paper. London: Arts Council of England, October 1995

The Arts Council of England Strategy for the Support and Development of Orchestras and their Audiences (1995). London: Arts Council

Appraisal Team (1995) *Appraisal Report – City of Birmingham Touring Opera.* Summary. London: Arts Council of England

The Arts Funding System: an Introduction to the Components of the UK Arts Funding System (2nd edn.) (1996). London: Arts Council of England

Striking A New Note: Consultative Green Paper on Publicly Funded New Music in England (1996). London: Arts Council of England

Creating New Notes: a Policy for the Support of New Music in England (1996). London: Arts Council of England

Jazz: a Policy for the Support of Jazz in England (1996). London: Arts Council of England

Year of Opera & Musical Theatre in the East of England 1997 (1997). London: Arts Council of England (A colour illustrated promotional pamphlet)

Appraisal Team (1997) *Appraisal Report – Philharmonia Orchestra* Summary. London: Arts Council of England

South Asian Music: a Policy for the Support of South Asian Music in England (1997). London: Arts Council of England

Hacon, D., Dwinfour, P. & Greig, P. (1997) *A Statistical Survey of Regularly Funded Organisations Based on Performance Indicators for 1996/97.* London: Arts Council of England

Arts for Everyone: Music Policy Summary (1997). London: Arts Council of England

Hacon, D., Dwinfour, P. & Jermyn, H. (1998) *A Statistical Survey of Regularly Funded Organisations Based on Performance Indicators for 1997/98.* London: Arts Council of England

Arts Council/National Lottery Department (1998) *Brass Bands – Additional Guidance.* London: Arts Council of England

Donagh, H. and O'Brien, J. (1998) *An Analysis of the ACGB and ACE Grant to the Royal Opera House 1946/47 to 1996/97.* London: Arts Council of England.

Touring Department (1998). *Review of Large-Scale Touring: the provision of lyric work in England.* London: Arts Council of England.

Reeves, M. (2002) *Measuring Social and Economic Impact of the Arts: a review* (Research Report No 24). (Available on the web at <www.Artscouncil.org.uk>)

Occasionally one comes across a publication of some apparent importance which has been issued without imprint; for example, Richard Wilding's report *Supporting the Arts: a Review of the Structure of Arts Funding*, which states it was 'presented to the Minister for the Arts, September 1989'. Another example is *The Submission to Government for the Royal Opera House Covent Garden Project*, June 1990. Such items can best be traced through the libraries of the departments or agencies concerned, or through the Library of the House of Commons, where any paper presented to a minister would have to be deposited.

▶ QUASI-OFFICIAL PUBLICATIONS

A variety of reports on various aspects of music have been published since the war by independent institutions or publishers, which had an official or formal status at the time of their publication and represented informed thinking at the time. The following is a select list of the most important.

The Dartington Hall Trustees (1949): *The Arts Enquiry – Music: a report on musical life in England.* London: Political and Economic Planning

Robbins, Lord (1964) *Chairman: London Opera Centre – Report of the Committee Appointed by the Governing Body to Investigate Recent Criticisms of the Centre.* London: London Opera Centre for Advanced Training and Development Ltd

Hutchison, R. (1982) *A Hard Fact to Swallow. The Division of Arts Council Expenditure between London and the English Regions.* London: Policy Studies Institute

Sweeting, E. (1982) *Patron or Paymaster? The Arts Council Dilemma: a Conference Report.* London: Calouste Gulbenkian Foundation

Allen, K. & Shaw, P. (1993) *A Fair Hearing – a Review of Music Commissioning in the UK and the Republic of Ireland.* London: Calouste Gulbenkian Foundation

Howson, J. (1995) *Folk Arts Archive Research Project.* Final report by John Howson. London: Arts Council/National Folk Music Fund

The Value of Music (1996). A National Music Council Report into the Value of the UK Music Industry. London: National Music Council

Hurley, R. and English, S. (1998) *Women and Jazz: Research Project Report.* Gandy Street, Exeter: South West Jazz ('Women and Jazz is a national research project into women's participation in jazz, as audience and as musicians. The project is organised by South West Jazz in partnership with Chard Festival of Women in Music, and is funded by the Arts Council of England (Music and Touring Dept) and South West Arts.')

All Our Futures, Culture and Education (1999). London: National Advisory Council on Creativity and Cultural Education

Levitt, R. and Rennie, R. (1999) *Classical Music and Social Result*. London: Office for Public Management

On the fringe of such material comes an increasing variety of market research reports. A useful guide to these is the Arts Council's *Market Research Index for the Arts* (Arts Council Library, 1992), which at the time it was published was promoted as a 'a new resource developed by the Arts Council of Great Britain. It is a computerised index of market research reports . . .'.

Note that Chris Smith's book of essays, *Creative Britain*, topical while he was Minister for the Arts, was actually published by Faber & Faber (1998). Nicholas Kenyon's *Where's Music Gone?* (1998) was the inaugural Belle Shenkman Memorial Lecture at the Royal College of Music.

▶ EXHIBITIONS AND MUSEUM PUBLICATIONS

Over the years HMSO has been responsible for the publication of a variety of musical materials from the main London museums and the British Library (when it was part of the British Museum). These have appeared in its catalogues. However, there are anomalies, and even when they otherwise published for them, exhibition catalogues might not bear their imprint. A typical, and important, example of the latter case is the catalogue of the Victoria and Albert Museum (V&A) exhibition *Berlioz and the Romantic Imagination*,[11] which was published by the Arts Council. The catalogue of the equivalent exhibition held in Paris, which in no way duplicates it, was published by the Bibliothèque Nationale.[12] Otherwise, publications from museums have tended to be catalogues of the holdings of the specific institution such as the V&A's *Catalogue of Musical Instruments*,[13] or popular guides to them, such as Patey (1979). Sometimes they are confused in a popular illustrated introduction such as Catherine Haill's booklet on *Victorian Illustrated Music Sheets* (1981).

▶ BBC REGULATORY

The BBC has been a constant subject of government publishing, and for many years was a responsibility of the Postmaster General. Each renewal of the BBC's charter has been preceded by much debate, a government report and legislation. Each volume of Briggs's official history of the BBC (1995), widely available in libraries, contains a listing of government publications for the period in question, and the interested reader should refer to them there.

► SOUND RECORDINGS

From 1942 the British Council subsidised the recording of selected contemporary music by British composers, starting with E.J. Moeran's *Symphony in G minor*, and, soon after, Walton's *Belshazzar's Feast*. A notable early British Council recording was Sir Malcolm Sargent's celebrated first recording of Elgar's *The Dream of Gerontius*, which first appeared in 1945. Carl Newton's study (1999) of the story behind the making of this recording is not only the documentation of a remarkable bureaucratic jungle but also an elegant demonstration of using British Council files in the writing of musical history.[14] However, these recordings were all issued by commercial record companies; in the days of 78s it was HMV, later other companies were involved. A large percentage of the recordings dating from the days of LP were acquired in the 1980s by the Lyrita label, of which at the time of writing only Michael Tippett's opera *A Midsummer Marriage*[15] has been reissued on CD. Later this promotional function moved to the Arts Council, and parallel initiatives were started by the Welsh and Scottish Arts Councils, the former also later acquired by Lyrita.

However, only very few recordings have actually been issued and sold by HMSO, and all are on cassette. One such recording from the Buildings Research Establishment does not contain music, but two issued for the Victoria and Albert Museum are worth noting, including *Musical Instruments at the Victoria and Albert Museum*, a tape/slide presentation,[16] and an audio cassette: *Solemn and Sweet Airs: a Recital of Historic Music for Strings*.[17]

► INTERNATIONAL ORGANISATION PUBLICATIONS

A wide survey of international publications is outside the scope of this chapter. However, musical publications have appeared from various international organisations, particularly Unesco. In the UK, these titles were distributed through the agency of HMSO, and thus appear in their catalogues. Although the UK withdrew from membership of Unesco between 1985 and 1997, it is their publications which are of most musical interest in the early period of its existence.

Archives of Recorded Music. Series B. Oriental Music. *A Catalogue of Recorded Classical and Traditional Indian Music* (1952). General discography and introduction by Alain Danielou. Unesco

Archives of Recorded Music. Series C. Ethnographical and Folk Music. Vol. I. *Collection Phonotheque Nationale (Paris)* (1952). Catalogue prepared by the International Commission on Folk Arts and Folklore. Unesco

Archives of Recorded Music. Series C. Ethnographical and Folk Music. Vol. 2. *Collection Musée De L'Homme (Paris)* (1952). Catalogue prepared by the International Commission on Folk Arts and Folklore. Unesco

But note later items in these series were issued by commercial publishers:

Archives of Recorded Music. Series C: Ethnographical and Folk Music. Vol. 3. *Katalog*
   der europäischen Volksmusik in Schallarchiv des Instituts für Musikforschung
   Regensburg (1952). Bearbeitet von Felix Hoerburger. Regensburg, Gustav Bosse

Archives of Recorded Music. Series C. Ethnographical and Folk Music. Vol. 4.
   International Catalogue of Recorded Folk Music (1954). Edited by Norman Fraser,
   with a preface by R. Vaughan Williams and introduction by Maud Karpeles.
   Prepared and published for Unesco by the International Folk Music Council in
   association with the Oxford University Press. Oxford: OUP

▶ LIBRARIES AND ARCHIVES

Very often the best way to access government publications is to approach
a specialist library. The government publications section of public and
university libraries will be a good starting point for the more mainstream
publications. Otherwise, the libraries of government departments and agencies are usually available by appointment, though it should be noted that
the British Council, the agency responsible for the provision of libraries
overseas, has closed down its libraries in the UK, and the best contact is
now the Archives and Records Unit.

For policy papers and archives one usually needs to contact the
Departmental Records Officer (these days sometimes called Manager) who
will be responsible for current archives. After 30 years the policy papers
and files of government departments, after weeding, which in some cases
can be heavy, pass to the Public Record Office (PRO).

In the case of music, the most useful archives will probably be those
of the British Council, which are at the Public Record Office (PRO), details
of whose holdings may be viewed on the internet (<http://www.pro.gov.
uk>)[18]. At the PRO different letter abbreviations, known as 'classes', are
used to designate each department. The British Council material may be
found at class BW. Within BW, general administration is at 1, 2, 3. The
Music Advisory Committee will be found in BW80, but listings of music
promoted in BW 2.[19] Class BW83 ('Tours by specialists') contains details of
overseas tours by British musicians, some of them very celebrated. A brief
administrative history of the British Council will be found on its website.

More recent files are held by the British Council in a country store
and are available by appointment either at the British Council's offices in
London or Manchester. For advice and to make an appointment contact
the British Council's Archives and Records Unit (0207-389-4016).

The British Council operates under the aegis of the Foreign and
Commonwealth Office and the *Index to the Correspondence of the Foreign
Office 1920–51*[20] covers the early period after the Council was established
in 1935. Although the index refers to some files that have now been
destroyed it can still be a useful source for indicating official involvement
in subjects of interest (such as, for example, proposals to promote a
recording of *Peter Grimes* soon after the war).

▶ REFERENCES

Arts Council Library (1992). *Market Research Index for the Arts.* London: Arts Council

Baines, A. (1976) *Non-Keyboard Instruments* (2nd edn.) (Catalogue . . . vol. 2). London: HMSO

Banking on a Hit: the Funding Dilemma for Britain's Music Business (2001) [Executive summary]. London: Department for Culture, Media and Sport. (The full report available free of charge from DCMS and Kingston University's Small Business Research Centre.)

Blackmore, R.M. (1976) *Cumulative Index to the Annual Catalogues of her Majesty's Stationery Office Publications 1922–1972.* Washington & Inverness, Carrollton Press

Briggs, A. (1995) *The History of Broadcasting in the United Kingdom* (rev. edn.) (5 vols). Oxford: OUP

Cockton, P. (1988) *Subject Catalogue of the House of Commons Parliamentary Papers 1801–1900* (5 vols). Cambridge: Chadwyck-Healey

Communications and Information Industries Directorate (1996) *Multimedia in Music – Promotion, Guidance, Support.* London: DTI

Haill, C. (1981) *Victorian Illustrated Music Sheets.* London: HMSO

Kenyon, N. (1998) *Where's Music Gone?* London: RCM, 22 Oct

Music Industry Forum (New Technology group) (2000) *Consumers Call the Tune: The Impact of New Technologies on the Music Industry.* London: Department for Culture, Media and Sport.

Newton, C. (1999) The Nightmare of Gerontius – the story behind a famous recording. In: Hodgkins, G. (ed.) *The Best of Me: a Gerontius Centenary Companion.* Rickmansworth: Elgar Editions, pp. 306–27

Patey, C. (1979) *Music Instruments at the Victoria and Albert Museum – an Introduction.* London: HMSO

Patey, C., Hulse, M. & Cogan, R. (1979) (Education Department (Victoria and Albert Museum)) *Musical Instruments at the Victoria and Albert Museum.* London: HMSO

Russell, R. (1968) *Keyboard Instruments.* (Catalogue . . . vol. 1). London: HMSO

Smith, C. (1998) *Creative Britain.* London: Faber

▶ NOTES

1. *Catalogue of British Official Publications Not Published by The Stationery Office.* Cambridge: Chadwyck-Healey Ltd. (annual with quarterly supplements).
2. UKOP – CD-ROM database of government publications issued by TSO and not by TSO. Published jointly by Chadwyck-Healey and TSO. Chadwyck-Healey has now been taken over by ProQuest Information & Learning.

3. Great Peter Street, London SW1P 3NQ; tel: 0171 333 0100; e-mail: information.acc@artsfc.org.uk.

4. Culture, Media and Sport Committee (1999) *The Performing Right Society and the Abolition of the Classical Music Subsidy*. Vol II: Minutes of Evidence and Appendices. HC 468-II TSO, Appendix 29 pp. 93–97.

5. *Index to the Statutes covering the Legislation in force on 31 Dec 1990* (1992) (2 vols). London: HMSO.

6. *Index to Government Orders in force on 31 December 1991*. Subordinate Legislation, The Powers and their Exercise (1995) (2 vols). London: HMSO.

7. (1989) *Halsbury's Laws of England* (5th edn.). London: Butterworth.

8. Op. cit. Butterworth, 1998 vol. 56.

9. *In Tune With Heaven: the Report of the Archbishops' Commission on Church Music* (1992). Report by the Standing Committee. London: Church House Publishing; Financial Comment by the Central Board of Finance Under Standing Order 109 (1992). London: Church House Publishing; *Report of the In Tune Follow-Up Group* (1995). London: Church House Publishing.

10. See "Irish University Press Series of British Parliamentary Papers" ed Professor P Ford. *Catalogue of British Parliamentary Papers*. Irish University Press, 1977.

11. *Berlioz and the Romantic Imagination* (1969). An exhibition organised by the Arts Council and the Victoria and Albert Museum on behalf of the Berlioz Centenary Committee in co-operation with the French Government 17 October to 14 December. London: The Arts Council.

12. *Hector Berlioz* (1969). Paris: Bibliothèque Nationale.

13. Russell, 1968 and Baines, 1976.

14. A listing of the British Council files at the Public Record Office (PRO) may be seen on the PROwebsite (<www.PRO.gov.uk>). The files on the choice of music to record are BW2; for example the Bliss Piano Concerto is at BW2/173, Walton's *Belshazzar's Feast* is at BW 2/174 and Elgar's *The Dream of Gerontius* at BW 2/178. The series long continued and later, for example, we find Robert Simpson's First Symphony at BW 2/618, a file interesting for its long chronologival coverage, from 1955 to 1962 and for the inclusion of press cuttings on it.

15. Lyrita SRCD 2217.

16. Patey et al. (1979) Consists of introductory booklet, leaflet, cue sheet, 53 slides and cassette tape.

17. *Solemn and Sweet Airs: a recital of historic music for strings* (1982). Cassette ISBN 0 11 290363 0 London: HMSO. It is very unusual for a sound recording to be given an ISBN number rather than a numbering in a record company series, in this case responding to the demands of HMSO order processing.

18. One can search the PRO catalogue, PROCAT, on the PRO website, either by class or across all 8.5 million records. A search on 'orchestra' gets 153 hits, on 'symphony' 47 hits and 'opera' 319 hits. The most promising Departmental records for 19th and 20th century histories of musical life will be the Board of Trade (later the DTI) classes for companies (BT 31) and bankruptcy information. Bankruptcies in the London Bankruptcy Court are at BT 38 and BT 40 for County Courts. Of course one needs to visit the Pro to read the files.

19. Administrative surveys of the recordings made were maintained by British Council staff, for example BW 2/172 covers 1942–1946, BW 2/170 1943–1945 and BW2/171 1945–1947.

20. *Index to the Correspondence of the Foreign Office 1920–1951* (1969–1982) (131 vols). Nendelm, Liechtenstein: Kraus-Thomson Organisation.

16 From J. S. Bach to John Dillinger: music in American government documents

*Elizabeth Baur**

▶ INTRODUCTION

Exploring government publication resources has never been a traditional part of research on the arts. Most music and art scholars never consult government publications collections for important primary resource material. However, the arts are funded by most governments not only in direct grants to researchers, performers or composers but as budget appropriations to national museums and libraries, thus providing the opportunity for publications. Fine arts publications are produced by all governmental entities, including foreign and state; however, nothing approaches the level of activity of the US federal government. Joe Morehead in the introduction to the *Cumulative Subject Guide to US Government Bibliographies* wrote, 'No theme, however fey, antic, arcane or ostensibly inapposite, remains far from the omnivorous curiosity of the federal establishment' (Kanely, 1976). One can always find examples of the fey and antic in any subject area, but the fine arts publications of the federal government certainly do not fit this category. Music publications, in particular, are often major reference resources written by leading international experts.

▶ LIBRARY OF CONGRESS

This article will concentrate on several departments that have contributed some of the most important music publications; the first of these is the Music Division of the Library of Congress. The Library of Congress received its first scores and books about music from the original Thomas Jefferson purchase.[1] However, it was not until the late 1890s that much headway was made in the development of a separate collection for music.

The Librarian of Congress wrote in his *Annual Report* of 1897 that, 'the Department of Music has 187,178 compositions. This department is yet an experiment, but there is reason to believe that with proper care ... it may become one of the most important.' In the following year it did indeed become a distinct department. However, it was not until 1902, when Librarian of Congress Herbert Putnam named Oscar Sonneck, American musicologist, librarian, editor and composer, as the head of the department, that the department began to take shape. Sonneck provided the original impetus behind the systematic development of the collection, an approach that continues even today. He also developed the M classification schedule in 1904, which, with certain modifications, is still in use. He resigned in 1917 after being harassed by the government because of his German education and antiwar attitudes. He later served as director at G. Schirmer, Inc., a major music publisher and was a significant influence in the promotion of American new music.[2]

During Sonneck's tenure at the Library of Congress, he personally wrote and/or oversaw the publishing of several comprehensive catalogs that have proven to be invaluable reference resources. Among these are *Dramatic Music: A Catalogue of Full Scores* (LC 12.1: D 79), a catalog of full scores of operas, ballets, and incidental music; *Catalog of Opera Librettos Before 1800* (LC 12.1: Op. 2/v.1 & 2; 1914); and the *Catalogue of Early Books of Music (Before 1800)* (LC 12.1: M 9).[3]

Sonneck was also responsible for several other notable works such as the *Catalogue of First Editions of Edward MacDowell (1861–1908)* (LC 12.1: M 14), *Catalogue of First Editions of Stephen C. Foster (1826–1864)* (LC 12.1: F 81), and the *Report on the Star Spangled Banner, Hail Columbia, America and Yankee Doodle* (LC 12.1: St 2). The latter is an absolutely exhaustive report on the history of both the musical and literary derivations of these tunes. It is not only scholarly in nature, including many quotes, newspaper accounts, excellent musical illustrations and an extensive bibliography, but contains entertaining anecdotes as well. Sonneck writes that the author of 'Hail Columbia' found it his misfortune to have written it because 'his friends and admirers became so numerous that his health, and accordingly his career, were ruined by the excessive demands of conviviality.'[4] An additional interesting note about this report can be found in the April 1910 *Monthly Catalog*. Apparently, a private publisher reprinted it and sold it for $1.25, 50% more than the Government Printing Office price. Herbert Putnam, the Librarian of Congress, wrote that the reprint is a 'handsome illustrated report ... and is a cheap book at $1.25, but that is no reason why a purchaser should pay 40 cents more than the price at which it is sold by the Superintendent of Documents.'[5]

In 1945, the Library of Congress received a bequest honouring Louis Charles Elson, a teacher at the New England Conservatory of Music and music editor of the *Boston Courier* and the *Boston Daily Advertiser*, to provide lectures on music and music literature. These lectures were delivered by some of the leading experts in their fields and were published and widely distributed. Some of the lectures in this series were *Symbolism in the Music of Bach* (LC 12.8: G 27) by Karl Geiringer, *Some Aspects of the Use of Flutes in the Sacred Choral and Vocal Works of Johann Sebastian Bach* (LC 12.2: F 67) by Albert Riemenschneider, and *Music, Its Past and Its Present* (LC 12.8: W 52) by Sir Jack Westrup.

The Music Division has continued its publishing record with works such as a detailed bibliography on Paderewski (*Ignacy Jan Paderewski, 1860–1941: a Biographical Sketch* and a *Selective List of Reading Materials* LC 1.2/2: P 13) and even reprints of autograph scores by Mendelssohn (*Octet for Strings, opus 20*) (LC 1.2: Oc 7) and Mozart (*Gran Partita, K. 361*) (LC 1.2: G 76/2).

Another music division at the Library of Congress is the Library Service for the Blind and Physically Handicapped Music Division. This section began in 1962 and contains many books on music and musicians, music manuscripts, and scores in braille. It publishes an excellent monthly magazine entitled *The Musical Mainstream* (LC 19.12:), which contains large-print reprints of important music articles from scholarly journals as well as up-to-date information on the services of the National Library Service. In 1979, the division published a unique work entitled *Dictionary of Braille Music Signs* (LC 19.2: B 73/10) and has continued to produce numerous catalogs and circulars that are distributed free to the blind.

Another section at the Library of Congress that deserves discussion here is the American Folklife Center. This section began in 1928 under. the name of the Archive of Folk Song and has assembled a voluminous collection of folk music and folklore. Its archival policy has been to collect music in otherwise neglected areas outside the realm of Western art music and to encourage its study and preservation.[6] It has published numerous books, such as *Ethnic Recordings in America: A Neglected Heritage* (LC 39.11: 1), but, perhaps most importantly, it has produced many bibliographies and short lists, often on unusual topics of folklife, many of which feature music. These bibliographies contain references to newspapers, journal articles, monographs, songbooks, and music collections. A representative sample of these titles include *Bibliography on the Ballad* (LC 1.12/2: B 21/2), A *Brief List of Material Relating to American Railroad Songs* (LC l. 12/1: Am 3/4), *Bela Bartok on Folk Music* (LC 1.12/2: B 12/2),[7] and *List of Songs Concerning John Dillinger* (LC 1.12/2: D 58), which includes such songs as 'Death of John Dillinger', 'Dillinger's Doom', 'John Dillinger's Fate' and a short discography. The Center also produces a monthly periodical entitled *Folklife Center News* (LC 19.10:), which often features articles on diverse music topics such as soldier songs from the Vietnam War and the history of the guitar.[8]

▶ PAN AMERICAN UNION

The Pan American Union is not widely recognised for producing federal documents. Prior to 1948, however, it carried out an extensive publishing program through the Government Printing Office. The Pan American Union (PAU) was originally founded in 1890 as the International Bureau of American Republics and was organised under the Secretary of State even though it was never a division of the Department of State. It was actually an international organisation supported by its 21 members. In 1907 it was reorganised and changed its name to the Pan American Bureau. Renamed the Pan American Union in 1910, it was reorganised once again in 1948 and became the Organization of American States.

The arts publications from this department, while not exhaustive, do provide a rich source of documents on music of the Americas, in particular Central and South America. Latin American music is not widely studied in this country and is seldom covered in college curricula except as an upper level specialty course. The publications from the PAU, which are mostly in English, contain many interesting details that complement commercial resources. Its major contributions are a periodical called the *Monthly Bulletin*, which often contained articles on music, and three specialised series: the Fine Art Series (PA 1.36: nos.);[9] the Club and Study Series (PA 1.54: nos.); and the Music Series (PA 1.51: nos.).

The Music Series consisted of 16 publications that were printed between 1941 and 1948. These are substantial works focusing on many diverse subject areas. Several titles from this series are *Catalog of His Works* (Carlos Chavez) (PA 1.5 1: 10); *Bio-Bibliographical Index of Musicians in the United States of America from Colonial Times* (PA 1.51: 2), a particularly useful book because it lists not only widely known performing musicians and composers but publishers, instrument makers, and local musicians from a variety of cities: and *Partial List of Latin American Music Obtainable in the United States* (PA 1.51:1). This latter monograph was written by Gilbert Chase, noted expert in the music of the Americas. While the Music Series was scholarly in nature, articles in the *Monthly Bulletin* were much shorter, with less detail. Still, they provide considerable insight. In one particular article on Uruguay, the author discusses ancient instruments and gives a brief musical history of Uruguay and Montevideo covering its folk songs, music societies, and its composers and local musicians. The article is nicely illustrated with both photographs and musical examples.[10]

▶ SMITHSONIAN INSTITUTION

Moving back to the more mainstream federal establishment, the Smithsonian Institution is another publisher in the field of music. While a significant portion of its publications have been of a scientific nature, it has also published in the humanities and, more specifically, about music. One source of these publications is the appendices of the *Annual Reports*, which from 1849 to 1963 contained scholarly articles.[11] Two examples of articles pertaining to music are 'Music of Primitive Peoples and the Beginnings of European Music' (US Smithsonian Institution, 1913) and 'The Science of Musical Instruments' (US Smithsonian Institution, 1954). When the practice of appending articles ended in 1963, several new series were begun that included a wide variety of musical titles such as *The Orchestra at San Petronio in the Baroque Era* (SI 1.28: 35), *The Organs of Mexico City Cathedral* (SI 1.28: 47), and *The Musical Instruments of Joseph Haydn* (SI 1.28: 47).[12] In addition, two new series are currently being introduced that are devoted specifically to music: The Smithsonian Library of American Music will consist of collected works of American composers,[13] and the Smithsonian Studies of American Musicians will provide biographical and critical studies of musicians from all areas of American music.

Another office within the Smithsonian that has also published significant musical research, is the Bureau of American Ethnology, now the Office of Anthropology. Since 1879, it has produced a distinguished record of research on North American Indians. Many authors produced musicological works for the Bureau, but Frances Densmore, ethnomusicologist and one of the earliest researchers on Native American music, was particularly productive. During her 50 years as a collaborator, she produced 13 monographs, five anthropological studies and one paper, which appeared in the Annual Report Series (Rhodes, 1986). Works by Densmore and her colleagues on the music of the Chippewa, Pawnee and many other Native American tribes constitute exhaustive studies containing many pictures, illustrations and musical examples.[14]

► DEPARTMENTS OF WAR AND TREASURY

The Departments of War and Treasury surprisingly have produced the greatest amount of original musical scores. One of the earliest examples is a catalog of trumpet calls that first appeared in *Cavalry Tactics* (W 3.16: C 31) during the 1860s. This catalog contains calls for virtually every movement of the company, from mess to retreat, from right turn to left. This was an important form of communication because oral commands issued at the head of the company could not be heard over the noise of horses. Commands were first given by a trumpet at the head of the column and then relayed orally to the troops by unit commanders.[15]

Music played an important part in the war efforts of both World War I and World War II. During World War I, documents such as *Music in the Camps* (W 85.2: M 97) and *Army Band: Vital Necessity to Military*

Establishment in Peace and War (W 3.2: B 22) were published, as well as a songbook entitled *Songs of Soldiers and Sailors, U.S.* (W 85:2: So 5). World War II produced an even greater variety of music publications. There are field and instructor manuals, Army/Navy hymnals, and even *A Pocket Guide for Army Song Leaders* (W 109. 102: So 5/1–2). There was also a monthly publication containing piano score music of popular tunes. This publication was produced throughout the war and into the 1950s and was variously titled *Army Hit Kit of Popular Songs, Army, Navy Hit Kit of Popular Songs*, and *Army, Air Force, Navy, Hit Kit of Popular Songs* (W 109. 109:nos.).[16]

The War Department also produced at least two full-blown musicals: *Hi Yank!* (W 109. 114: 2) and *PFC Mary Brown* (W 109.102: P 93). Both are co-authored by Frank Loesser, who wrote *Guys & Dolls* and *How to Succeed in Business Without Really Trying*. Loesser was an experienced writer of song lyrics before the war but his work on these army shows marked the first time he began to write music on his own. The shows were a part of a series called Blue Print Specials and are complete with orchestrations, scenic and costume designs, and dance routines. Both shows contain over 300 pages of music and cleverly drawn illustrations.

The Department of the Treasury also entered into music publishing with a series of songbooks for World War II war bond rallies. Some of these publications are *Songs for Schools at War* (T 1.102: So 5), *Songs for the Home Front* (F 66.2: So 5/3), and *Songs for War Bond Rallies* (T 66.2: So 5/2). Treasury also produced a musical revue, *Figure It Out* and published the music separately as *Songs from 'Figure it Out'* (T 66.2: F 46/songs). This show is far less detailed than *PFC Mary Brown* and contains only several very simple songs. However, the instructions tell the director that the style should be modelled after Broadway shows like *No, No, Nannette* and *Hit the Deck* and urge him/her to use his/her own ingenuity in fully producing the show.

▶ CONCLUSION

The term 'wealth of information' has been used to describe government publications so often it is a cliché. However, no better description exists. The same can be said to describe the federal government's contribution to musical scholarship. Represented are not only major reference resources such as the catalogs produced by the Library of Congress but sources of sociological minutiae such as songs about John Dillinger. The authorship of these documents by such noted music experts as Oscar Sonneck, Sir Jack Westrup and Gilbert Chase lend a scholarly respectability not often offered by federal bureaucrats.

This article offered only an overview of the many musical examples available and seeks to present an enticing glimpse of the possibilities. Many more publications remain that expand the depth of the material available. The enterprising music researcher will uncover a satisfying collection worthy of serious consideration.

▶ REFERENCES

Kanely, E.A. (comp.) (1976) *Cumulative Subject Guide to U.S. Government Bibliographies 1924–1973.* Arlington, VA: Carrollton Press

Rhodes, W. (1986) Densmore, Frances. In H.W. Hitchcock and S. Sadie (eds.) *The "New" Grove Dictionary of American Music.* New York: Grove's Dictionaries of Music

Schorr, A.E. (1987) *Guide to Smithsonian Serial Publications.* Juneau, AK: Denali Press

US Smithsonian Institution (1913) *Annual Report of the Board of Regents of the Smithsonian Institution for the Year Ending June 30, 1912.* Washington: Government Printing Office, pp. 679–700

US Smithsonian Institution (1954) *Annual Report of the Board of Regents of the Smithsonian Institution for the Year Ended June 30, 1953.* Washington: Government Printing Office, pp. 253–61

▶ NOTES

* Reprinted from *Journal of Government Information* formerly *Government Publications Review*, Vol. 20, pp. 485–493, Baur, "From J. S. Bach to . . .", 1993, with permission from Elsevier Science.

1. Thomas Jefferson sold his personal library to the Library of Congress in 1815 for the sum of $23,950. These volumes were to serve as the basis of a new collection to replace the ones destroyed by fire in the War of 1812. Among the 6,700 volumes in the collection were nine volumes on music, the most notable of which are two works by Charles Burney, an early musicologist-critic, and Geminiani's *Art of Playing the Violin: Rules for Playing in Taste.* U.S. Library of Congress, *Thomas Jefferson's Library: A Catalog with Entries in His Own Hand*, ed. James Gilreath and Douglas L. Wilson (Washington: Government Printing Office, 1989) 1, 110–11.
2. A new professional organisation has recently grown up around Sonneck's ideals. In 1973–4, a critic at the Washington Star founded the Sonneck Society, which is dedicated to promoting all aspects of America music, including history and all musical genres from film scores to classical. Today the society has about 1,000 members representing all areas of musical interest, including one from the Country Music Foundation.(Source: Telephone interview with Dr John Baron, Department of Music, Newcomb College, Tulane University, 12 June 1991.) Sonneck was also editor of the Musical Quarterly.
3. It has been estimated that the Music Department owns over two-thirds of all those listed in original editions. US Library of Congress (1972) *The Music Division: A Guide to its Collections and Services* (Washington: Government Printing Office, 1972), 11.

4. US Library of Congress. Music Division. *Report on the Star-Spangled Banner, Hail Colombia, America, Yankee Doodle* by Oscar G. T. Sonneck (1909: reprint. New York; Dover. 1972), 44.

5. US Government Printing Office (1910) *Monthly Catalogue.* United States Public Documents. 184, April, 572.

6. US Library of Congress, *The Music Division in the Library of Congress* (Washington: Government Printing Office, 1960). 22.

7. Bartók was not only a composer but a pioneering ethnomusicologist.

8. 'Instrument of Blind Men and Kings: A Mini-History of the Guitar,' (Spring 1990) and 'Vietnam War-American Songs: The General Edward G. Lansdale Collection,' (Summer, 1989).

9. This series consists of reprints from the *Monthly Bulletin.*

10. It is important to note that the *Monthly Bulletins* are available in the Serial Set and are indexed by the *Readers' Guide to Periodical Literature.*

11. Music material in these appended reports are accessible by using two specialised indexes: U.S. Smithsonian Institution, *Author-Subject Index to Articles in Smithsonian Annual Reports 1849–1961* compiled by Ruth M. Stemple (1963: reprint, Arlington, VA: Carrollton Press. 1967) and Mamie Tanquist Miller, comp. *An Author, Title, and Subject Check List of Smithsonian Institute Publications Relating to Anthropology* (University of New Mexico Bulletin 450. Bibliographical Series. vol. 1 no 2) (Albuquerque: The University of New Mexico Press, 1946). The Annual Reports are also available in the Serial Set.

12. Schorr (1987) indexes 750 titles from 14 important series published since 1964. Publications with brief annotations are arranged by series. Authors, titles, and subjects are indexed. SuDoc numbers are not included.

13. The Music of Stephen C. Foster, a complete critical edition, is the first title in this series.

14. Many of these reports have been reprinted, but not all. Once again all were entered into the Serial Set. There are two excellent bibliographies that help to identify these important works: US Smithsonian Institution. Bureau of American Ethnology, Bulletin 178: *Index to Bulletins 1–100 of the Bureau of American Ethnology, with Index to Contributions to North American Ethnology, Introduction and Miscellaneous Publications* by Biren Bonnerjea (Washington: Government Printing Office, 1963) and U.S. Smithsonian Institution, Bureau of American Ethnology, Bulletin 200: *List of Publications of the Bureau of American Ethnology with Index to Authors and Titles.* (Washington: Government Printing Office. 1971).

15. It is interesting to note that the trumpet call heard at race tracks was originally the call to assemble the trumpeters themselves.

16. A March 1949 edition included such tunes as 'Cruisin' Down the River', 'No Orchids for My Lady', 'Powder Your Face with Sunshine' and 'I Love You So Much It Hurts'.

17 Composer catalogues, thematic catalogues and bibliographies

Lewis Foreman

All music-lovers are familiar with the catalogue numbers by which some composer's music is identified: Köchel[1] for Mozart; BWV (Bach Werke Verzeichnis) or Schmieder (1950) for J.S. Bach; Kirkpatrick (1953) or Longo (1913) for Domenico Scarlatti keyboard sonatas. If one walks into any music library there will usually be a sequence on the reference shelves – short in smaller libraries, longer in others – of such publications. If they are not immediately apparent, ask the librarian, for they are almost certainly kept behind the scenes as an aid to cataloguing.

One needs a catalogue to frame the study of any composer; to identify a piece of music, to choose and source music for performance; to time a programme. The only essential difference between thematic catalogues and other very detailed catalogues is the absence of music incipits (brief music-type extracts) in the latter, to aid identification. From time to time both composers (most notably Mozart) and publishers have made catalogues of their own works, and these have documentary evidence for us today, especially when they list works which have not come down to us. Catalogues have been published, sometimes in great detail, of the works of many but not all individual composers. Other catalogues list music by genre (e.g. eighteenth-century symphonies);[2] or by type (e.g. Fuld's incredibly useful *The Book of World Famous Music* (1971), a thematic catalogue of famous tunes, alphabetically arranged by title with their compositional and bibliographical history). The celebrated catalogue of the publisher Breitkopf und Härtel[3] appeared between 1760 and 1787 and listed all then available works including music then supplied in manuscript, with a thematic index, which now makes its modern facsimile reprint a prime source, ranked by *New Grove* as 'the most useful single bibliographic aid to 18th-century research ... and the incipits may be the sole means of identifying anonymous and doubtful works.'[4]

The *New Grove* article on thematic catalogues categorises them in nine groups according to function:

1   mnemonic aid;
2   table of contents;
3   guide to a composer's output;
4   inventory of a library's holdings;
5   copying firm advertisement;
6   publishing firm advertisement;
7   legal document;
8   index of themes;
9   musicological documentation.

The standard bibliography of such catalogues is the late Barry S Brook's *Thematic Catalogues in Music: an Annotated Bibliography* (1972, rev. edn. 1997).

The form of catalogue that most general users require will be (3) and (9) of these. In the mid-nineteenth century, catalogues began to appear prepared with an exacting scientific rigour and documentary accuracy that was new. The case in point was Köchel's famous catalogue of Mozart's music (*Chronologisch-thematisches Verzeichnis*), compiled with reference to the manuscripts of the music catalogued, and arranged in chronological order of composition as far as it could be deduced. The Köchel number thereafter suggested the approximate date and order of composition. Work on this started in 1850 and the first edition appeared in 1862 (Köchel, 1862).

This is where the tradition developed in later twentieth-century non-thematic catalogues of being all-inclusive. Not only was there full listing and dating of the work, and the location of the manuscript, but the context was also documented, with the listing of early editions and performances, a bibliography of references and reviews and even the quotation of contemporary sources and letters referring to the music.

The second half of the nineteenth century saw this tradition expand, with catalogues of many of the leading names of the German tradition, plus Saint-Saëns[5] and Tchaikovsky (Jürgenson, 1897), both of these started while their subjects were still alive. Of these, the Beethoven (Nottebohm, 1868) and Schubert (Nottebohm, 1868) catalogues by Nottebohm were both ultimately superseded in the twentieth century. Many of these catalogues were spin-offs of ambitious plans to publish collected editions of the composers in question. Later in the 1930s there was a resurgence of this activity including one for Reger[6] who had only died during the First World War.

In the 1950s there was a re-birth of the scholarly development of thematic catalogues in the work of Schmieder (1950 – J.S Bach), Deutsch (Schubert)[7] or Kinsky and Halm (Beethoven).[8] Also, one or two independent scholars completed valuable pioneering work, of which Cecil Hopkinson's thematic catalogue of John Field is a fine example (1961).

For most purposes major studies of individual composers will usually include a catalogue or list of works which may be adequate for many practical day-to-day purposes. Lists of works have long appeared appended to studies of individual composers, and also follow composer entries in major musical reference books; generally authors of these have contented themselves with simple lists. However, some have been very detailed, for example, Moldenhauer's *Anton von Webern* (1978), and long constituted a significant reference source in their own right; similarly with many of the catalogues in the *New Grove*, though enthusiasts for the music of lesser-known British composers are more likely to find them adequately represented in the Fifth edition than in its revision. All the editions of *Grove* have a continuing place in the library for similar reasons.

In the nineteenth century many publishers issued detailed catalogues of the leading composers they published, and this tradition continues today in the very varied and extensive series of free promotional booklets issued by most musical publishers, most of which are devoted to substantial and detailed catalogues often including discographical and performance infor-mation. These catalogues often include the most up-to-date published summary of younger composers' careers and the listing of their works with the important information necessary for performance including duration and orchestration. Novello's of Edward Gregson (1998), J & W Chester's of Michael Nyman (1992), and OUP's 16-page catalogue of the music of Michael Finnisey (OUP, 1963), are typical examples of such catalogues of composers active today, and are usually free on request.

The pioneering work catalogue which in its day filled an enormous gap and demonstrated to scholars that there was an urgent need for published catalogues of twentieth-century composers was Kenneth Thompson's magnificent *A Dictionary of Twentieth Century Composers 1911–1971*, which appeared in 1973. Although not a champion of them-atic catalogues, Thompson was influential in evolving formats for listing the fullest details about a given work by the use of abbreviations and typographical shorthand. It consisted of a full listing of the work of 32 composers. It was some time before it was challenged as the prime source for many of the composers included, and despite the extensive corrigenda that the author must have accumulated, it is still an invaluable source for most of the names covered, particularly for such information as first perfor-mances in different cities or on the air.

The concept of a collection of catalogue data for a range of composers under a particular umbrella reached its zenith in Alan Poulton's ency-clopaedic three-volume dictionary catalogue (2000) of 54 twentieth-century British composers born between 1891 and 1923, modelled, as Poulton acknowledges in his introduction, on Thompson's *Dictionary*. The com-posers included by Poulton include several not included in *New Grove*. The canon of 'great' names covered are Britten, Tippett and Walton. Vaughan Williams, Bax, Ireland and their contemporaries are excluded as belonging to an earlier generation. The particular value of this massive compilation is its coverage of the 'middle' generation of British twentieth-century composers. Women composers covered include Ruth Gipps, Phyllis Tate, Grace Williams, Rainier, Maconchy and Lutyens. Poulton gives special treatment to film music, whose composers include Arnold, Alwyn, Frankel, Rawsthorne, Lutyens, Bliss, Benjamin and Addison.

Although covering a relatively specialised area, Alan Poulton's *A Dictionary-Catalog of Modern British Composers* needs to be noted for its pioneering format as a collection of catalogues of most of the significant serious British composers born between 1891 and 1923. This is almost a life's work, and in covering 54 significant composers of the period provides a notable reference work not only for each composer included, but also for all students of the period and, indeed, those planning concerts and recordings and wanting to explore new repertoire. One hopes that it might be emulated by enthusiasts elsewhere in the world. The complete list of composers covered is:

- John Addison (1920–1998)
- William Alwyn (1905–1985)
- Denis Aplvor (1916–)
- Richard Arnell (1917–)
- Sir Malcolm Arnold (1921–)
- Don Banks (1923–1980)
- Stanley Bate (1911–1959)
- Arthur Benjamin (1893–1960)
- Sir Lennox Berkeley (1903–1989)
- Sir Arthur Bliss (1891–1975)
- Benjamin Britten (1913–1976)
- Alan Bush (1900–1995)
- Geoffrey Bush (1920–1998)
- Francis Chagrin (1905–1972)
- Arnold Cooke (1906–)
- Christian Darnton (1905–1981)
- Howard Ferguson (1908–1999)
- Gerald Finzi (1901–1956)
- Benjamin Frankel (1906–1973)
- Peter Racine Fricker (1920–1990)
- John Gardner (1917–)
- Roberto Gerhard (1896–1970)
- Ruth Gipps (1921–1999)
- Sir Eugene Goossens (1893–1962)
- Patrick Hadley (1899–1973)
- Iain Hamilton (1922–2000)
- Herbert Howells (1892–1983)
- Gordon Jacob (1895–1984)

- Daniel Jones (1912–1993)
- Constant Lambert (1905–1951)
- Walter Leigh (1905–1942)
- George Lloyd (1913–1998)
- Elisabeth Lutyens (1906–1983)
- Elizabeth Maconchy (1907–1994)
- E.J. Moeran (1894–1950)
- Herbert Murrill (1909–1952)
- Andrzej Panufnik (1914–1991)
- Ian Parrott (1916–)
- Priaulx Rainer (1903–1986)
- Alan Rawsthorne (1905–1971)
- Franz Reizenstein (1911–1968)
- Edmund Rubbra (1901–1986)
- Humphrey Searle (1915–1982)
- Matyas Seiber (1905–1960)
- Robert Simpson (1921–1998)
- Bernard Stevens (1916–1983)
- Phyllis Tate (1911–1987)
- Sir Michael Tippett (1905–1998)
- Sir William Walton (1902–1983)
- Peter Warlock [Philip Heseltine] (1894–1930)
- Grace Williams (1906–1977)
- Peter Wishart (1921–1984)
- William Wordsworth (1908–1988)
- David Wynne (1900–1983)

A number of pioneering catalogues were published in the 1960s and 1970s which became models for the cataloguers who followed. The two most notable were both published by the Oxford University Press: Michael Kennedy's 'List of Works Arranged in Chronological Order' in his *The Works of Ralph Vaughan Williams*,[9] and Stewart Craggs's *William Walton: a thematic catalogue of his musical works*.[10] Kennedy's catalogue impressed by its sheer thoroughness and extent, including the composer's own programme notes reprinted *in extenso*, and was later issued separately as *A Catalogue of the Works of Ralph Vaughan Williams*.[11] Although the Oxford University Press has not published an extended systematic series of composer catalogues, three further examples documenting music by British composers are significant contributions to the literatures of their subjects – Stewart Craggs's catalogue of John Ireland,[12] Graham Parlett's of Bax[13] and Rosemary Williamson's pioneering thematic catalogue of the Victorian composer Sir William Sterndale Bennett (1993). Parlett's *Bax* in particular, the outcome of a 25-year enthusiasm and study and previously accepted as the major component of a doctoral thesis at King's College London (1994), is fully exhaustive in all respects, and makes an excellent model for future compilers of catalogues, and is as typographically correct as it is possible for such a catalogue to be. Unfortunately the OUP's regrettable decision to close down their music book operation in the UK and transfer editorial responsibility to New York probably means that such scholarly catalogues of British music will no longer find a welcome with them; we must hope that a sympathetic American editor emerges and that suitable subjects present themselves.

It quickly became apparent in the 1970s that there was a market for detailed bibliographical reference books presenting bibliographies of composers and their works, and an early series was issued by White Lion Publishers Ltd. These were more bibliographies of writing about their subject than rigorous catalogue, and of these Michael Short's *Gustav Holst (1874–1934): a centenary documentation*[14] is still a useful sourcebook. Also from White Lion, David Moldon's *Bibliography of Russian Composers*[15] lists articles, largely in English, about 113 Russian composers, but does not list the composers' music.

Holst was the subject of a pioneering thematic catalogue by his daughter[16] published in the year of the centenary of his birth, undoubtedly a key tool in the widespread revival of his earlier music that has taken place since. Holst, too, was the ostensible subject of a unique and little-known reference book which I would recommend as one of the cornerstone reference sources for anyone working on twentieth-century British music. This is Sheila Lumby and Vera Hounsfield's enormously detailed *Catalogue of Holst's Programmes and Press Cuttings in the Central Library Cheltenham*,[17] another outcome of the Holst birth centenary celebrations in 1974. working from an existing collection of programmes and cuttings, all Holst's works are listed in alphabetical order, and under each work their performances up to Holst's death appear in chronological order with details of where reviews (often in a huge number of newspapers and journals) appeared. It is invaluable not only for reception studies of Holst's music and its performers but for the other works which were in the programmes when Holst was played, covering the years up to his death in 1934. This was an example of inspired local authority publishing. Another, perhaps of more local interest, is Colin Bayliss's *The Music of Anthony Hedges* published by Hedges' local authority, Humberside Central Library in Hull.[18] Such initiatives are, however, rare.

These various compilers of reference books have all been seeking a format which would elegantly present the composer of their choice and economically incorporate a mass of varied detail. Another notable pioneer in the development of such catalogues is Robert Threlfall, whose narrative style encompassing a mass of detail and documentation finds suitable subjects in his *A Catalogue of the Compositions of Frederick Delius: Sources and References*,[19] and (with Geoffrey Norris) in *A Catalogue of the Compositions of S Rachmaninoff*.[20]

Threlfall's two significant catalogues remind us of those monuments of the cataloguing of twentieth-century composers which are indissolubly linked with specific musicologists. As we have already seen, as catalogue has succeeded catalogue, the concept of the inclusiveness of such compilations has become more and more all-embracing. Two particularly valuable works, both now in their second editions, and so without the inevitable minor errors, literals and updating inevitable in the first edition of any major reference source, are Eric Walter White's *Stravinsky: the Composer and his Works* (1979) and Derek C. Hulme's *Dmitri Shostakovich: a Catalogue, Bibliography and Discography* (1991). These are both remarkable achievements and set standards that deserve to be emulated by others contemplating such studies. No library that has any substantial musical coverage can be without, at the very least, these two. White's *Stravinsky* is essentially an analysis and discussion of all Stravinsky's works in chronological order, each entry preceded by catalogue data including details of first performances. This is preceded by a 150-page biography. Librarians and those concerned with the published editions of Stravinsky's music will also want to refer to Dominique-René de Lerma's *Igor Fedorovitch Stravinsky, 1882–1971; A Practical Guide to Publications of His Music* (1974), particularly for his indexes of publishers (listing every work issued by each publisher) and of proper names. It needs to be used with slight care as Professor de Lerma does not necessarily transcribe the full title page legend in each case. Scholarly catalogues of printed editions have an significant rôle in our understanding of the developing career and performing tradition of certain composers, a study pioneered by Cecil Hopkinson with his catalogues of Berlioz (1980), Gluck (1959), Puccini (1968) and Verdi (1973). As Alec Hyatt King remarked in his introduction to the second edition of Hopkinson's *Berlioz*, 'it was quickly recognised as a pioneering work – the first detailed catalogue of the first and early editions of any single composer . . . it remained for Hopkinson to record all the details of the complete published works of a composer, in both their original form and in arrangements, and to supply locations of copies in a score of libraries throughout the United Kingdom, France and Belgium.' Hopkinson's annotated copies of his catalogues were offered for sale by Lisa Cox in 2002.[21]

On the other hand, Hulme's *Shostakovich* presents a 330-page catalogue in chronological order with an amazing level of detail, including varied lists of premières, very extended discographies, and considerable data about scores both manuscript and printed. Not the least of the importance of this catalogue is that it provides access in English to a vast array of material in Russian. The list of BBC broadcasts about Shostakovich even includes Radio 3 record reviews and summarises the recommendations.

It is only in the last decade or so that the systematic development of series of scholarly catalogues of a wide range of twentieth-century composers, not necessarily of the first rank, have been published. The most vigorous activity is taking place at the present time, and is particularly confined to three series: the Ashgate (previously Scolar Press) 'Resource guides' and two American series. In fact the principal publishers of composer catalogues in the 1990s are American, and both surprisingly little known in the UK. The series are: 'Bio-bibliographies' and 'Discographies' published by Greenwood Press, and 'Composer Resource Manuals' (sub-titled 'Guides to research') and 'Research and information guides' from Garland Press. These series are now substantial and despite their functional layout and typography and high price have established themselves as important sources of which librarians, academics and music lovers need to be aware. Greenwood's 'Bio-bibliographies' have reached volume 54 (their associated 'Discographies' series is discussed in CHAPTER 20); Garland's 'Composer resource manuals' volume 37.

Composer catalogues need to be compiled from primary sources – the music both published and manuscript, actual performances for timings, programmes and press cuttings for performances. It is amazing how much incorrect data is constantly recycled from secondary sources. (In Anthony Payne's article on Bax in *New Grove* he inadvertently refers to Arnold Bax's novels. Bax did not write novels, he wrote short stories; but it is notable how many reference books and catalogues since have assured us that he did write novels.) Often catalogues that appear at the end of biographies and studies of composers tend, I fear, to be compiled from secondary sources. If they are merely repeating other people's errors they are suspect. Knowing a work exists, the forces it is written for and its chronology, is only the starting point. Any useful catalogue must give:

- title (with translation where appropriate);
- form and forces required, including compass of solo voices;
- date of composition, with supporting evidence if necessary;
- dedicatee;
- duration (preferably based on actual timings in performance);
- recordings (commercially or extant performances privately recorded conducted/played by the composer surviving);
- manuscript and publication history;
- source of performing materials;
- details of first and important performances;
- author of words set and source of text;
- non-musical sources/programme;
- history;
- documentation, including the composer's own programme notes and related;
- annotated bibliography, including criticisms of first and important performances.

Areas that are frequently neglected are the provision of a detailed catalogue of literary sources, words set, etc., a note of material sold at auction and in dealer's catalogues (when, where, and to whom); 'filmography' (including videos of the films the composer wrote music for, and videos or laser-discs if it is a stage work). All would be practical features in a resource guide. From the perspective of this author, the main rule in generating any catalogue is that there can never be too much detail. The series under discussion succeed to a varying extent in achieving these aims, but generally they manage to achieve a good core of these requirements, mostly adequately indexed. What users need is as much detail as possible. Thus Christopher Kent in his generally admirable and pioneering *Edward Elgar: a Guide to Research* does not spell out the voices required in individual movements of vocal works, nor does he index them. This is actually a very practical problem and makes the list difficult to use when looking for Elgar vocal pieces for a programme.

While discussing Elgar, we have a useful example of how the provision of catalogue information developed over time. The first reasonable Elgar catalogue, because it tried to give locations and first performance details, was that in Diana McVeagh's *Edward Elgar: his Life and Music* (1955). It was superseded by Kenneth L. Thompson's catalogue of Elgar (Thompson, 1983). In fact, Thompson in turn is not completely entirely superseded by Kent (and indeed, as far as one can see, is not listed by him) for the citation of performance dates other than the first. Scolar Press (now Ashgate) had announced competition in *An Elgar Source Book* 'intended as a vade mecum of facts' by Paul Wilson, but this was a victim of the compiler's tragic death in a road accident. The hurried subsequent issue of a substitute volume compiled by Stewart Craggs was ill-advised, with an unacceptable level of error and the lack of its compiler's customary detail (see the review in *Musical Times*).[22] This is an unreliable source which is not recommended.

Experts often develop as a result of early interest in their subjects, and it is truly said that where composers are concerned an interest expressed in a PhD thesis may well result in a *de facto* lifelong recognition as the expert or guardian of that name. Certainly, for example, Peter Dodgson's 1970 thesis *The Music of Herbert Howells* (1970) contains a Howells catalogue compiled in correspondence with the composer that was only superseded in 1999 by Paul Andrews's Aberystwyth PhD on Howells.

Elliott Antokoletz's contribution to the Garland Press series, the Bela Bartók volume, is a valuable and distinguished guide by any measure and sets standards for compilers of all such works. Its coverage however, is different to that for other volumes seen, and underlines the uneven and subjective nature of this series.

A list of the composers covered in these various series appears at the end of this article, and one should also note that such publishers include important compilations on related composers outside these series for no apparent reason, the most notable example being that on Michael Tippett (in Greenwood Press's 'Music Reference Collection' series.) A wide range of living or recently dead composers includes such well-known figures as John McCabe, Elliott Carter, Peter Sculthorpe, but also, with the series' American bias, a number of lesser-known names to a British audience such as the Canadian Violet Archer or the American Radie Britain. Some of these compilations, which are expensive, may be difficult to find in British libraries. (Incidentally, readers wishing to purchase these and similar titles will find it worth accessing Abebooks, the internet world database of second-hand books (<www.abebooks.com>). 'Bio-bibliography' in the title field is all that is required to locate that series,. Many of them will often thus be found at second-hand or remainder prices.)

There is duplication of a few subjects between these series, but in fact it is more apparent than real. Garland have focused on living and twentieth-century composers, often those considered of the second rank and otherwise difficult to document, while Greenwood have tended to prefer publishing resource guides to the biggest names from the repertoire. If we take as an example Paul Hindmarsh's *Frank Bridge: a Thematic Catalogue 1900–1941* (Faber Music, 1983; transferred to Thames Publishing; new edition in preparation, 2002) and compare it with Karen R Little's *Frank Bridge: a Bio-bibliography* (1991), we find that both have a role to play, though ostensibly there should be no need for the Little. Hindmarsh is not only a thematic catalogue but is also the most extensive published source for Bridge's letters and source material, reproduced after each entry. Also Hindmarsh gives the orchestrations, a crippling omission in Little's compilation. However, Little gives a run of performances as well as the first – always a valuable feature, and often neglected by compilers of catalogues. Little also annotates her much longer bibliography and attempts a full discography of commercially issued discs. But overall, if only one catalogue of Bridge is needed then Hindmarsh is to be preferred.

Mention of correspondence raises one final issue: composers' unpublished or uncollected letters. In his *Elgar Source Book* Kent states that over 8,000 letters from or to Elgar are preserved at the Hereford and Worcester Record Office alone. Sotheby's catalogue for the Novello Sale[23] lists and summarises many Elgar letters. I am not aware of any catalogue of a twentieth-century composer that has yet attempted to calendar all the surviving letters of that composer, though Craggs makes a good start in his Ashgate Bliss and Walton 'Source Books', yet one has only to use Mary Lago's invaluable calendar of 11,814 E.M. Forster letters[24] to realise how important such a procedure is. Lago lists as a separate sequence letters sold through dealers' catalogues which have subsequently disappeared, highlighting yet another key issue for compilers of catalogues.

The following list summarises the catalogues, bibliographies or resource guides – call them what you will – that have been issued in the series published by Ashgate/Scolar, Faber/Thames Publishing, Garland Press, Greenwood Press and Oxford University Press.

▶ LIST OF PUBLISHED CATALOGUES

(ASSB = Ashgate/Scolar Press Source Books; FM = Faber Music; GCRM = Garland Composer Resource manuals or Guides to Research; GBB = Greenwood Press Bio-bibliographies in Music; OUP = Oxford University Press; TP = Thames Publishing, London.)

Adam, A. [and Delibes] (William E Studwell; GCRM No. 5, 1987)
Archer, V. (Linda Hartig; GBB No. 41, 1992)
Arnold, Sir M. (Alan Poulton; FM, 1986)
    (Stewart R. Craggs; GBB No. 69, 1998)
Ballou, E.W. (James E. Heintze; GBB No. 5, 1987)
Barber, S. (Don A. Hennessee; GBB No. 3, 1985)
Bartók, B. (Elliott Antokoletz; GCRM No. 11, 1988)
Bassett, L. (Ellen S. Johnson; GBB No. 52, 1994)
Bax, Sir A. (Graham Parlett; OUP, 1999)
Beethoven, L. van (Theodore Albrecht; GCRM, No. 30, 1990)
Bennett, Sir R. Rodney (Stewart R. Craggs; GBB No. 24, 1990)
Bennett, R. Russell (George J. Ferencz; GBB No. 29, 1990)
Bennett, Sir W. Sterndale (Rosemary Williamson, OUP, 1996)
Berkeley, Sir L. (Stewart R. Craggs; ASSB, 2000)
Berlioz, H. (Jeffrey A. Langford & Jane Denker Graves; GCRM 22,
    1989)
Bliss, Sir A. (Stewart R. Craggs; GBB No. 13, 1988)
    (Lewis Foreman; Novello 1980)
    (Stewart R. Craggs; ASSB, 1996)
Bloch, E. (David Z. Kushner; GCRM 14, 1988)
Bridge, F. (Paul Hindmarsh; FM/TP, 1983)
    (Karen Little; GBB No. 36, 1991)
Britain, R. (Walter B. & Nancy Gisbrecht Bailey; GBB No. 25, 1990)
Britten, B. (Stewart R. Craggs, GBB No. 87, 2001)
Busoni, F. (Marc-Andre Roberge; GBB No. 34, 1991)
Byrd, W. (Richard Turbet; GCRM 7, 1987)
Carpenter, J.A. (Joan O'Connor; GBB No. 54, 1994)
Carter, E. (William T. Doering; GBB No. 51, 1994)
Chaminade, C. (Marcia J. Citron; GBB No. 15, 1988)
Chopin, F. (William Smialek; GCRM No. 50, 2000)
Copland, A. (JoAnn Skowronski; GBB No. 2, 1985)

De Falla see Falla

Debussy, C. (James Briscoe; GCRM 27, 1990)

Delibes, L. [and A Adam](William E Studwell; GCRM No. 5, 1987)

des Prez, J. (Sydney Robinson Charles; GCRM 2, 1983)

di Lasso, O. (James Erb; GCRM 25, 1990)

Elgar, Sir E. (Christopher Kent; GCRM 37, 1993)

Falla, M. de (Gilbert Chase and Andrew Budwig; GCRM 4, 1986)

Fauré, G. (Edward R. Phillips; GCRM No. 49, 2000)

Finzi, G. (John C. Dressler; GBB No. 64, 1997)

Foss, L. (Karen L. Perone; GBB No. 37, 1991)

Foster, S.C. (Calvin Elliker; GCRM 10, 1988)

Frescobaldi, G. (Frederick Hammond; GCRM 9, 1988)

Gluck, C.W. (Patricia Howard; GCRM 8, 1987)

Gershwin, G. (Norbert Carnovale; GBB No. 76, 2000)

Granados, E. (Carol A. Hess; GBB No. 42, 1992)

Handel, G.F. (Mary Ann Parker-Hale; GCRM 19, 1988)

Hanson, H. (James E. Perone; GBB No. 47, 1993)

Harris, R. (Dan Stehman; GBB No. 40, 1991)

Haydn, F.J. (Floyd K. and Margaret G. Grave; GCRM 31, 1990)

Hicks, P.G. (Deborah Hayes; GBB No. 27, 1990)

Hill, E.B. (Linda L. Tyler; GBB No. 21, 1989)

Hoddinott, A. (Stewart R. Craggs; GBB No. 44, 1993)

Husa, K. (Susan Hayes Hitchens; GBB No. 31, 1991)

Ireland, J. (Stewart R. Craggs; OUP, 1993)

Isaac, H. (Martin Picker; GCRM 35, 1991)

Ives, C. (Geoffrey Block; GBB No. 14, 1988)

Josquin des Prez see des Prez, J

Kay, U. (Constance Tibbs Hobson & Deborra A. Richardson; GBB
      No. 53, 1994)

Krenek, E. (Garrett H. Bowles; GBB No. 22, 1989)

Langlais, J. (Kathleen Thomerson; GBB No. 10, 1988)

Lasso, O. di see di Lasso, O

Ligeti, G. (Robert W. Richart; GBB No. 30, 1991)

Liszt, F. (Michael Saffle; GCRM 29, 1991)

Luening, O. (Ralph Hartsock; GBB No. 35, 1991)

Machaut, G. de (Lawrence Earp; GCRM 36, 1995)

Mahler, G. and A. (Susan M Filler; GCRM 28, 1989)

Martin, F. (Charles W. King; GBB No. 26, 1990)

Mascagni, P. (Roger Flewy; GBB No. 82, 2000)

Mason, L. (Carole A. Pemberton; GBB No. 11, 1988)

Maxwell Davies, P. (Carolyn J. Smith; GBB No. 57, 1995)

McCabe, J. (Stewart R. Craggs; GBB No. 32, 1991)

Menotti, G.C. (Donald L. Hixon; GBB No. 77, 2000)

Messager, A. (John Wagstaff; GBB No. 33, 1991)

Milner, A. (James Siddons; GBB No. 20, 1989)

Monteverdi, C. (K. Gary Adams and Dyke Kiel; GCRM 23, 1989))
Mozart, W.A. (Baird Hastings; GCRM 16, 1989)
Musgrave, T. (Donald L. Hixon; GBB No. 1, 1984)
Nielsen, C. (Mina F. Miller; GCRM 6, 1987)
Obrecht, J. [and Ockeghem] (Martin Picker; GCRM 13, 1988)
Ockeghem [and Obrecht] (Martin Picker; GCRM 13, 1988)
Pergolesi, G.B. (Marvin E. Paymer and Hermine W. Williams; GCRM
        26, 1989)
Persichetti, V. (Donald L. and Janet Patterson; GBB No. 16, 1988)
Pinkham, D. (Kee Deboer and John B. Ahouse; GBB 1988)
Poulenc, F. (George R. Keck; GBB No. 28, 1990)
Prez or Pres see des Prez
Purcell, H. (Franklin B. Zimmermann; GCRM 18, 1989)
Rachmaninov, S. (Robert Threlfall & Geoffrey Norris; ASSB, 1982)
        (Robert Palmieri; GCRM 3, 1985)
Rameau, J.-P. (Donald Foster; GCRM 20, 1989)
Reger, M. (William E. Grim; GBB No. 7, 1988)
Reich, S. (D.J. Hoeck; GBB No. 89, 2002)
Rimsky-Korsakov, N. (Gerald Seaman; GCRM 17; 1988)
Rorem, N. (Arlys L. McDonald; GBB No. 23, 1989)
Rosbaud, H. (Joan Evans; GBB No. 43, 1992)
Roussel, A. (Robert Follet; GBB No. 19, 1988)
Ruggles, C. (Jonathan D. Green; GBB No. 59, 1995)
Sauger, H. (David L. Austin; GBB No. 39, 1991)
Scarlatti, A. and D. (Carole F. Vidali; GCRM 34, 1993)
Schuller, G. (Norbert Carnavale; GBB No. 6, 1987)
Schutz, H. (Allen B. Skei; GCRM 1, 1981)
Scott, C. (Laurie J. Sampsel; GBB No. 79, 2000)
Sculthorpe, P. (Deborah Hayes; GBB No. 50, 1993)
Sterndale Bennett see Bennett, Sir W. Sterndale
Tailleferre, G. (Robert Shapiro; GBB No. 48, 1994)
Takemitsu, T. (James Siddons; GBB No. 85, 2001)
Tcherepnin, A. (Enrique Alberto Arias; GBB No. 8, 1989)
Thompson, R. (Carolin Cepin Benser & David Francis Urrows;
        GBB No. 38, 1991)
Thomson, V. (Michael Meckna; GBB No. 4, 1986)
Tippett, Sir M. (Gordon Theil; Greenwood Music Ref Collection
        21A, 1989)
Vaughan Williams (Neil Butterworth; GCRM 21, 1989)
        (Michael Kennedy; OUP, 1964)
Villa Lobos, H. (David P Appleby; GBB No. 9, 1988)
Vivaldi, A. (Michael Talbot; GCRM 12, 1988)
Walton, Sir W. (Carolyn J Smith; GBB No. 18, 1988)
        (Craggs, Stewart R; OUP, 1977)
Ward, R. (Kenneth Kreitner; GBB No. 17, 1988)

Warren, E. Remick (Virginia Bortin; GBB No. 46, 1993)
Weber, C.M. von (Donald G & Alice H Henderson; GCRM 24, 1989)
Wilder, A. (David Demsey; GBB No. 45, 1993)
Wolf, H. (David Ossenkop; GCRM 15, 1989)
Wuorinen, C. (Richard D. Burbank; GBB No. 49, 1994)

▶ REFERENCES

Andrews, P. (1999) *Herbert Howells – a Bibliographical and Documentary Study.* Aberystwyth: University of Wales (PhD thesis)

Brook, B.S. (1972) *Thematic Catalogues in Music – an Annotated Bibliography.* (rev ed 1997)

Craggs, S.R. (1993) *John Ireland – a Catalogue, Discography and Bibliography.* Oxford, Clarendon Press

de Lerma, D.-R. (1974) *Igor Fedeorovitch Stravinsky, 1882–1971.* Kent, Ohio: Kent State University Press

Dodgson, P. (1970) *The Music of Herbert Howells.* University of Colorado (PhD thesis – available on demand from University Microfilms 71-21,593)

Fuld, J.J. (1971) *The Book of World-Famous Music – Classical, Popular and Folk* (rev. and enlarged edn.). New York: Crown

Hopkinson, C. (1959) *A Bibliography of the Printed Works of C W von Gluck 1714–1787.* London: (rev. ed. 1967)

Hopkinson, C. (1961) *A Bibliographical Thematic Catalogue of the Works of John Field 1782–1937* The Author

Hopkinson, C. (1968) *A Bibliography of the Works of Giacomo Puccini 1858–1924.* New York:

Hopkinson, C. (1973) *A Bibliography of the Works of Giuseppi Verdi, 1813–1901* (vol. 1 1973; vol. 2 rev 1978). New York:

Hopkinson, C. (1980) *A Bibliography of the Musical and Literary Works of Hector Berlioz 1803–1869, with Histories of the French Music Publishers Concerned* (2nd edn.), ed. Richard MacNutt. Tunbridge Wells: Richard Macnutt Ltd. [First published in 1951 by the Edinburgh Bibliographical Society]

Hulme, D.C. (1991) *Dmitri Shostakovich – a Catalogue, Bibliography, and Discography* (2nd edn.). Oxford: Clarendon Press (First edition published by Kyle and Glen Music, Muir of Ord, Ross-shire, 1982)

Jürgenson, B (ed.) (1897) *Catalogue Thématique des Oeuvres de P Tschaikowsky.* Moscow (reprint 1965)

Kirkpatrick, R. (1953) *Domenico Scarlatti* (rev edn. 1968). Princeton: Princeton University Press

Köchel, L. von (1862) *Chronologisch-thematisches Verzeichnis sämtlicher Tonwerke Wolfgang Amadeus Mozarts.* Leipzig

Lago, M. (1985) *Calendar of the Letters of E M Forster.* Mansell

Little, K.R. (1991) *Frank Bridge: a Bio-bibliography.* Greenwood Press

Longo, A. (1913) *Domenico Scarlatti e la sua figura nella storia della musica.* Naples

McVeagh, D. (1955) *Edward Elgar: His Life and Music.* London: Dent

Moldenhauer, H. (1978) *Anton von Webern – a Chronicle of his Life and Work.* London: Gollancz

Nottebohm, M.G. (1868) *Thematisches Verzeichniss der im Druck erscheinenen Werke von Ludwig van Beethoven.* Leipzig

Nottebohm, M.G. (1874) *Thematisches Verzeichniss der im Druck erscheinenen Werke von Franz Schubert.* Wein

Parlett, G.F. (1994) *The Music of Arnold Bax – Documentation and Analysis.* London: University of London, Kings College (PhD thesis). The catalogue published as *A Catalogue of the Works of Sir Arnold Bax.* Oxford: The Clarendon Press, 1999.

Poulton, A. (2000) *A Dictionary-Catalog of Modern British Composers* (3 vols) (vol. 1: A–C; vol. 2: D–L; vol. 3 M–Z). Connecticut: Greenwood Press

Schmieder, W (1966) *Thematisch-systematisches Verzeichnis der musikalischen Werke von Johann Sebastian Bach: Bach-Werke-Verzeichnis* (3rd edn.). Leipzig

Thompson, K.L. (1973) *A Dictionary of Twentieth Century Composers 1911–1971.* London: Faber

White, E.W. (1979) *Stravinsky – the Composer and his Works* (2nd edn.). London: Faber [first published in 1966]

Williamson, R (1996) *William Sterndale Bennett: a Descriptive Thematic Catalogue.* Oxford, Clarendon Press

▶ NOTES

1. Köchel, L. von (1964) *Chronologisch-thematisches Verzeichnis sämtlicher Tonwerke Wolfgang Amadeus Mozarts.* (6th edn.) F. Giegling, A. Weinmann and G. Sievers, Leipzig
2. Brook, B.S. and Heyman, B.B.(1986) *The Symphony 1720–1840 – a comprehensive collection in full score in sixty volumes: Reference Volume.* New York: Garland Publishing
3. Brook, B.S.(1966) *The Breitkopf Thematic Catalogue.* New York: Dover
4. Vol. 18, p 734

5. *Catalogue Générale et Thématique des Oeuvres de Saint-Saens.* (1897) Paris: Durand & Cie, rev ed 1908

6. Stein, Fritz Wilhelm. (1936) *Thematische Verzeichnis der im Druck erschienen Werke von Max Reger.* Leipzig: Breitkopf & Härtel, rev ed 1953.

7. Deutsch, O. E. (1951). *Schubert. Thematic Catalogue of all his works in chronological order,* by O.E.Deutsch in collaboration with Donald R. Wakeling. London, Dent

8. Kinsky, G. and Halm, H. (1955) *Das werke Beethovens. Thematische-Bibliographisches Verzeichnis seiner samtlichen vollendeten Komponistionen von Georg Kinsky. Nach den Todedes verfassers abgeschlossen und heraus-gegeben von Hans Halm.* München-Duisburg: G. Henle Verlag

9. Kennedy, M. (1964) *The Works of Ralph Vaughan Williams.* Oxford: Oxford University Press, rev ed 1971, 1980.

10. Craggs, S. R. (1977) *William Walton: a thematic catalogue of his musical works.* London: Oxford University Press

11. Kennedy, M. (1982) *A Catalogue of the Works of Ralph Vaughan Williams.* Oxford: Oxford University Press, rev ed 1996.

12. Craggs, S. R. (1993). A list of 'selected errata and addenda' is issued by the John Ireland Trust.

13. Graham Parlett's Bax catalogue first appeared as part of his Doctoral thesis.

14. Short, M. (1974) *Gustav Holst (1874–1934).* London: White Lion Publishers Ltd

15. Moldon, D. (1976) *Bibliography of Russian Composers.* London: White Lion Publishers Ltd

16. Holst, I. (1974) *Thematic Catalogue of Gustav Holst's Music.* London: Faber Music

17. Lumby, S. and Hounsfield, V. (1974) *Catalogue of Holst's Programmes and Press Cuttings in the Central Library Cheltenham.* Cheltenham: [Cheltenham Public Library]

18. Bayliss, C. (1990) *The Music of Anthony Hedges: a catalogue of the works of the composer, with an autobiographical essay.* Hull: Humberside Leisure Services.

19. Threlfall, R. (1977) *A Catalogue of the Compositions of Frederick Delius: sources and references.* London: The Delius Trust. This was updated by Threlfall's *Frederick Delius Supplementary Catalogue.* London: Delius Trust, 1986.

20. Threlfall, R. and Norris, G. (1982) A Catalogue of the Compositions of S. Rachmaninoff. London: Scolar Press. (Threlfall, the pianist in the first London concert performance of the final version of the Fourth Piano Concerto, adopts his spelling of Rachmaninov's name, on the grounds that the composer himself did the same.)

21. Hopkinson (1980) p vii. Lisa Cox Music's catalogue 'Cox's Gallimaufrey 9' (Summer 2002) offered Hopkinson's file copies (items 124–160), the most important of which were purchased by the National Library of Scotland.

22. Review by Robert Anderson. *Musical Times* May 1995 vol 136, no. 1827 246

23. *The Novello Sale: Autograph Letters, Music Manuscripts and Books from the Novello Collection.* Sotheby's, 15 May 1996

24. Lago, M. (1985). For his letters to Benjamin Britten see pp. 28–31

18 Music publishing and publishers

John Wagstaff[1]

▶ **DEVELOPMENT OF MUSIC PRINTING AND PUBLISHING**

Four principal methods of producing printed music have developed since its beginnings in the sixteenth century. In chronological order these are: printing from type, engraving, lithography, and production by means of specifically-designed computer software.[2] Different techniques have had their own advantages and disadvantages: printers producing music set from type required fonts with an enormous number of different type characters that were expensive to make, store and maintain.

Engraving had at least two factors in its favour. From an aesthetic point of view it could produce beautiful results unavailable to the printing press, such as extravagantly ornate lettering and borders; and it was a very flexible medium that enabled the quick mass production of single-sheet items. An extravagantly engraved title page would attract a potential purchaser in the same way as today's book dust-jacket: good engravers were artists as well as craftsmen. But a disadvantage was that the metal plates (in copper or pewter), once created, had to be stored for possible re-use, requiring strong floors at publishers' premises, or payment for storage facilities elsewhere.[3] (Lithography, in which images were created by the application of a special ink onto a chemically-prepared stone, and whose main advantage was that the image could be created and corrected more quickly than on an engraved plate, raised the same problem.)[4] On the other hand, of course, the existence in perpetuo of an engraved plate or lithographed stone did mean that a publisher could risk making a smaller print run of a new publication, whereas in the case of type, overproduction would, one assumes, have been preferable to having completely to re-assemble a publication using thousands of pieces of type metal.[5]

The market for printed music developed massively during the nineteenth century, and by the second half of that century cheap popular music publishing for a mass market was built, particularly in England, on music setting from type. But engraving retained a place in this market, and at the opposite end of the spectrum was used for production of complex or high-class scores, Breitkopf & Härtel's complete edition of the works of J.S. Bach in the Bach-Gesellschaft edition from 1850 onwards being a notable example of the latter.[6] (Breitkopf & Härtel's premises in Leipzig were the training ground for many music engravers, who then took their skills to other parts of the world, including Britain.) Engraved music made possible the published full scores of the extravagant orchestral music of such composers as Richard Strauss and early Stravinsky, and continued to be produced until the 1960s, though towards the end of this time in increasingly limited quantities.[7]

Much scholarly work on music printing and publishing has confined itself to the bibliographic description of editions issuing from particular publishers, especially of the sixteenth to eighteenth centuries.[8] Studies and listings of nineteenth- and twentieth-century music publishers are few, but include Parkinson (1990); the second volume of Anik Devriès and François Lesure's *Dictionnaire des Éditeurs de Musique Francais* (1988), which covers the period 1820–1914 (the first volume covers the period from the rise of music printing to 1820); and Cecil Hopkinson's celebrated *A Dictionary of Parisian Music Publishers 1700–1950*, which appeared in London under its author's imprint in 1954 (reprinted 1979). A selective list of Spanish music publishers and printers of the nineteenth and early twentieth centuries in included in Lara 1995. Publishers of the United Kingdom have been further dealt with by Charles Humphries and William C. Smith (1970), and by Frank Kidson (1900). Krummel and Sadie (1990) include a dictionary of music printers and publishers of all periods, with useful bibliographies (p. 135–486). Histories of modern publishing houses are also few and far between, the most recent being that of Oxford University Press's Music Department, a comparatively young imprint that first appeared in the early 1920s.[9] The other significant 'new' British imprint, established in 1965, is Faber Music, set up to publish Benjamin Britten's music after he left his previous publisher, Boosey & Hawkes.[10] There is a history of the house of Novello, by Michael Hurd (1981); and Stainer & Bell, known today for its publications of church music and for the Early English Church Music and Musica Britannica series, but originally established to promote young British composers, produced a short history in 1997 which, while primarily promotional in nature, includes much useful historical information.[11] For those who read French, Durand (1969) should be noted; while those with a knowledge of German will wish to take account of Oskar von Hase's study of Breitkopf & Härtel, one of the most important background studies of music printing and publishing ever produced (1968). The book covers not only the eighteenth century, when Breitkopf and its catalogues were enormously important,[12] but also the high points of the decade preceding World War I, and the split after World War II between the residual company in East Germany (Leipzig) and the West German arm in Wiesbaden, now reunited. Other German-language histories of houses include those by Karl Vötterle (1963 and 1981). One hundred years of the Viennese publishing house of Doblinger was celebrated by two publications, these being volume 11 (1976) of the *Österreichische Musikzeitschrift* and Herbert Vogg's extensive monograph (1976). Those with an interest in Italian music, particularly opera, will find the history of the Sonzogno publishing house of interest (Morini *et al.*, 1995).

Finally in this section, some account should be taken of a sub-genre of the literature on music printing and publishing: that is, the memoirs of particular publishers themselves. Chief among these are Jacques Durand's *Quelques Souvenirs d'un Éditeur de Musique* (1924), and William Boosey's *Fifty Years of Music* (1931), which includes material on Chappell's publishing house as well as that of Boosey. Maurice Senart's *Editions Maurice Senart, ou L'injuste Conclusion de Toute une Vie de Travail* (1942) is of a lugubrious cast as befits its title. *Le Monde de la Musique* by Paul Bertrand (1947), a long-time director of the French firm of Heugel, is chatty and opinionated, and thus typical of a genre that tends to dwell more on anecdotes of the good and great than on the minutiae of business practices, and is fun rather than scholarly in nature. A 'rags-to-riches' tale appears in Witmark and Goldberg (1939) and is a rare, if not unique, account of a publisher of popular and light music.[13] Günter Henle's account of the development of his business is an honourable exception to this general rule (1973), as is that of Ernst Roth, who in the course of a long career worked for both Universal Edition and Boosey & Hawkes (1969). Correspondence between publishers and the composers they represent is a sub-branch of this type of literature, and its presentation is rather more scholarly in nature. Examples include *Ludwig van Beethoven: der Briefwechsel mit dem Verlag Schott* (Beethoven-Haus, 1985); Pistone (1984) and Moore (1987).

Beginners who wish to increase their knowledge of music printing and publishing should start with the article on 'Printing and Publishing of Music' in *The New Grove*, 2nd edn. and with King (1964). Krummel (1992) will then provide the 'next step': it includes an exhaustive bibliography of work in the field. Much work on music printing and publishing appears in bibliographical and scholarly journals, and the searcher for material published post-Krummel (i.e. post-1990, which was Krummel's cut-off date) will need to consult bibliographies such as *RILM* Abstracts, the *International Index of Music Periodicals* and such like to discover further useful essays and reports. Few books on the topic have been published since Krummel's text, but three are worth noting: Lenneberg (1994); Hunter (1994); and van Orden (2000).

▶ TAKEOVERS AND MERGERS

Thousands of music publishers have come and gone over the centuries, and the history of music publishing is a history of moves, takeovers, and mergers. The most notable recent example of takeover for the purpose of consolidation of market share has been the increased presence in the UK of the Music Sales group, which, having operated in Britain at a fairly low level since establishing a UK branch in 1970, rose to prominence from the 1980s onwards through its absorption, first, of Chester Music and its agencies, including Edition Wilhelm Hansen, and second, through its acquisition of the Novello group and its agencies, including Ricordi (more information on the use of agencies by publishers appears below).

A more recent phenomenon has been that of an increasingly fragmented and segmented market, with new publishers producing small numbers of titles for a niche sector. A further notable development during the (fairly) recent past has been the necessity for those Eastern European and Soviet publishers that were previously state-funded, or otherwise heavily state-supported, to find new markets in the West, and to find Western partners to distribute and promote their publications. Undoubtedly the Russian Federation has been one of the main losers in this process: while the work of some Russian composers is published in Hamburg by Sikorski, and while Boosey & Hawkes has long had a connection with Russia through its ownership of many copyrights of the former Anglo-Soviet Music Press, the *European Music Directory 2001* lists only 12 music publishers currently active in Russia.[14] Among those companies that have been successful in penetrating Western markets, Supraphon, of the Czech Republic, has amalgamated with Bärenreiter, giving its products access to Western markets; Polskie Wydawnictwo Muzyczne (PWM), the Polish publishing house that among other things publishes the collected works of Karol Szymanowski, and the Polish music encyclopaedia (*Encyklopedia Muzyczna PWM*: 5 volumes published at the time of writing), has its own site on the World Wide Web (<http://www.pwm.com.pl>) and distributes its products in the UK via Kalmus. Editio Musica of Budapest (EMB) likewise has a website (<http://www.emb.hu>), and has established a good distribution network in Europe and the USA. Since 1970 EMB has in any case had a profile in the West through its joint publication, with Bärenreiter, of the collected works of Franz Liszt, and via a relationship with Doblinger of Vienna that has led to joint production and marketing of some items in Doblinger's 'Diletto Musicale' series.

▶ SERVICES PROVIDED BY MUSIC PUBLISHERS

Supply of music

It is an almost laughable truism to say that music publishers exist to publish music: but in fact this rather obvious statement is worth examination, not least because of the differences between music and book publishing. For as well as printing music and selling it via the usual commercial outlets, some publishers also provide 'archive' or 'on demand' services, by means of which they will supply on request a copy of a piece of music that is in their archive, even where that piece may, technically, have been out of print for many years.[15] An example of such services is Music Sales' 'Special Order' edition. Universal Edition's London branch and United Music Publishers will also make to special order copies of works by the living composers they represent where they consider that commercial publication of those works is not viable, an example also followed by Faber with its Faberprint series. The enquirer typically receives a photocopy of the composer's manuscript fair copy, softbound and often in a wire binding, or stapled. From a library's point of view 'archival' and 'on demand' works can present problems, not only because the availability of such works is not widely advertised, meaning that library staff must contact publishers on a speculative basis to find out if they will supply a work or not (not necessarily a large problem if the publisher is based in one's home country or has an agent there, though rather more complicated in other cases); but also because such works do not fall under copyright deposit legislation and will not, therefore, find their way into the legal deposit libraries unless 'chased' and purchased.

Additional to 'on demand' publishing is the designation of some scores and parts as 'hire only'. This means that the material required is not formally published, but can only be used if hired direct from the publisher, who will have printed a very small number of copies to cope with anticipated demand. Some music later designated as 'hire only' may at a former time have been available for normal purchase; or it may never have been on commercial sale, and may, indeed, exist only in manuscript. In the first case an enquirer may be able to borrow the material from a library that has a collection of orchestral or vocal scores;[16] in the second, the publisher is likely to be the only option, a state of affairs that can lead to works being lost for good, for example where a publisher has not kept an archive copy, or where an archive has been destroyed (this situation may also arise with 'on demand' material too, of course). Much music for the theatre, including musical shows and operas, is very closely controlled by publishers, and is usually available on hire only. Occasionally a score will be available but the orchestral and vocal parts (see 'TYPES OF MUSIC: SOME BASIC DEFINITIONS' below) will be on hire only, enabling publishers to keep track of performances using their material, with a fee charged accordingly. Finally, a vocal score may be commercially available, but not the full score or parts. Since hire charges for material obtained direct from publishers can be quite high (fees are normally charged on a monthly rental), the material earns its keep that way. Many publishers have separate premises for storage of hire material. This is more fully discussed in the next chapter.

Few UK publishers now run their own showrooms, though a number still exist in London. Many rely on distributing their products via displays in retail music shops (see 'RETAIL OUTLETS' below) or from their warehouses to customers via a complex web of agents (see 'AGENTS AND AGENCIES' below). Some operate online services by which customers can purchase items via a website: for example, Music Sales runs the 'Internet Music Shop' (<http://www.musicsales.co.uk>). The attractive front page of this site, targeted at the popular music market, claims 'the world's largest source of sheet music, tutor methods, MIDI files, videos and new media', while the classical page offers over 2000 titles. It thus provides an online order system for currently available music, without making it altogether clear that it is the site of a specific group promoting only its own material. Boosey & Hawkes also has an online music shop for its own products (<http://www.boosey.com/shop/>). French publishers with an online presence include Editions Jobert at <http://www.jobert.fr>, Lemoine at <http://www.editions-lemoine.fr> and Alphonse Leduc at <http://www.alphonseleduc.com>.

Whereas in the world of book publishing some authors (especially those with established names) will regularly change publisher, relationships between composers and their publishers may be of much longer duration, a situation brought about either through a sense of friendship or loyalty or, more prosaically, because first refusal on future works will have been written into the composer's contract. A publisher will therefore, over time, build up a list of composers whom he/she represents.[17]

Disputes or other circumstances occasionally arise that lead to a composer moving from one publisher to another: the case of Britten has already been cited, and, more recently, Sir Harrison Birtwistle has left Universal Edition for Boosey & Hawkes, and Robert Saxton transferred from Chester Music to University of York Press, a niche publisher specialising in contemporary music and based, unusually, in the academic sector. Some knowledge of which works have been issued by which publisher is important to the music librarian, because he/she needs to have an idea of whom to contact to obtain a particular composition. Who would guess that Gabriel Fauré's first violin sonata was published, not in France, but by Breitkopf & Härtel of Leipzig? Or that several works of Parry and Delius were also first published in German editions? The librarian also needs to be able to track down publishers that no longer exist, as their stock and, more lucratively, their copyrights will almost certainly have been bought by another company: it is very unusual indeed for a music publisher simply to 'disappear'. A useful, international, albeit outdated list of music publishers, their agents and successors, appeared in the second edition of John Davies's *Musicalia* (1969). Since then there have been considerable other changes, and the major publishers of today are listed at the APPENDIX to this book. Further lists of current UK publishers appear in the *British (now British and International) Music Yearbook*; the annual *Musical America International Directory of the Performing Arts* lists American agents for publishers worldwide; and for the European scene the newly-published *European Music Directory 2001*, already referred to, has useful lists arranged by country, and there is also the *Music Publishers' International ISMN Directory* (International ISMN Agency, 2001). The US Music Publishers' Association website at <http://www.mpa.org> contains details of its members, including addresses and contact details. Italian music publishers are partially covered in the *Dizionario degli Editori Musicali Italiani 1750–1930* (Antolini, 2000).

Publishers can range from the very large, such as Music Sales and the US publisher Theodore Presser, to small companies operating in small markets. Karlheinz Stockhausen's compositions, and recordings of his works, are available from Stockhausen-Verlag, a company set up specifically for that purpose; Terry Riley also has his own company, at <http://www.terryriley.com>; while societies such as the Frank Bridge Trust subsidise publications of that composer's music, which have been re-issued under the imprint of Thames Publishing (a situation which may change following the death of its founder John Bishop). Stainer & Bell's work in church music publishing has already been mentioned, and Oxford University Press issues several publications jointly with the Church Music Society. Other publishers may specialise in publication of, say, flute music, lute music, or in the composers of a particular country: the Donemus Foundation of the Netherlands, which has a strong publishing programme, is a shining example of this last category.

Agents and agencies

Music is a product that is arguably less sensible of national boundaries than the printed word, which means that music publishers can, in theory, set up in business wherever they choose. But in order to sell their products, a good system of advertising and distribution is needed. There are at least two possible solutions: either publishers may choose to establish branches in as many countries as they intend to market goods in; or they may make arrangements with other publishers in those countries for the mutual marketing of each others' goods. Examples of each method are easy to find. Peters Edition has several European arms, and a branch in New York. Universal Edition, established in Vienna, opened premises in London in the 1930s, with that part of the company becoming an independent branch in 1949; and Boosey & Hawkes has both UK and US branches. Conversely,

Novello's London publications for many years also included the imprint of H.W. Gray of New York; and other examples may easily be discovered.[18] Agencies developed rapidly in the nineteenth century, though some recent research has suggested that a rudimentary agency network was already established by the end of the eighteenth.[19]

The activities of agents vary widely. Some will carry a broad range of the stock of publishers whom they represent, while others may simply act as ordering agents, forwarding any requests for publications back to the original publisher. Agents also distribute, in their own country, catalogues of the publishers they represent. The advantage to purchasers is that they can be billed by the agent in their own currency, and are dealing with an agent who speaks their native language. The disadvantage for the non-specialist is that both the act of finding out who publishes a particular title, and then trying to discover how best to obtain that title, can be time-consuming and frustrating. A good retailer can be a great help in such circumstances (see 'RETAIL OUTLETS' below).

Dissemination of information

Most music publishers issue free printed catalogues, some of them very substantial.[20] Many also now have their own website, of which some examples have already been given above. Printed catalogues may take the form of complete inventories of publications arranged by composer, but more likely will be categorised by instrument or voice, or printed format, as for example flute or piano music, miniature scores, or parts for hire (see 'TYPES OF MUSIC: SOME BASIC DEFINITIONS' below for further information on formats and types of score). Catalogues are broadly of two sorts: either comprehensive listings of material currently available, or lists of new material only, supplementing an earlier comprehensive list. Many libraries maintain a collection of such catalogues (though they are often kept in library staff areas, and therefore have to be asked for), which, in the absence of a worldwide 'Music in Print' catalogue, are a valuable resource. Some catalogues may even have historical value, particularly in the case of publishers that no longer exist, or whose catalogues have suffered a drastic reduction in size. Examples are the Breitkopf & Härtel catalogue of 1914, or that of the British publisher Goodwin & Tabb from 1939; of Novello's catalogue of 1964, before the dissolution of their old London showroom, or Chappell's catalogue from the same year, before their disastrous fire.[21]

In addition to catalogues, some publishers issue free newsletters highlighting their new publications, or promoting the work of their house composers – *Contemporary Music News* from Peters Edition, and Music Sales' *High Notes* are just two current examples. There is also a long tradition of music publishers publishing music journals, notable examples being the *Musical Times* (published for over a century by Novello), *The Chesterian*

(J. & W. Chester, 1915–61), *Ricordiana* (Ricordi, 1954–67) and the *Monthly Musical Record*, published by Augener between 1871 and 1960. Continental examples include *Der Bär*, the yearbook of Breitkopf & Härtel; and the *Jahrbuch der Musikbibliothek Peters* (1894–1941). Of this type of journal, only one – *Tempo*, published by Boosey & Hawkes – survives.

Finally, publishers advertise extensively in specialist journals read by musicians – *Musical Times*, *Classical Music*, *Music and Letters*, and so forth – and/or by music librarians – *Brio*, *Fontes Artis Musicae*, *Notes*. Such journals frequently also include reviews of new publications; research suggests that a bad review generates a broadly similar amount of sales to a good one, so placing materials for review in appropriate journals is important to publishers. They are also able to promote their products outside their own country through journals produced by the worldwide network of Music Information Centres. These titles are normally provided to libraries free of charge, and are specifically designed to promote a country's composers, musical heritage, and publications. Examples include the *Finnish Music Quarterly*, *Hungarian Music Quarterly* (published in part by Editio Musica Budapest, which guarantees good coverage of its products), *Listen to Norway* (recently ceased publication) and *Nordic Sounds*, the last of which contains data from the Danish, Finnish, Icelandic, Norwegian and Swedish MICs.

► MUSIC IN PRINT

There has long been a need for a music trade bibliography similar to those published by Whitaker for books. Various services have been developed over the years, but vary in their usefulness. The UK Music Publishers' Association catalogue of music in print, formerly published twice a year on microfiche but now available on CD-ROM only, has good coverage of titles that can be supplied by MPA members, including material available only on hire (items that have gone out of print are also often listed). The Musicdata Company of Philadelphia has produced 'Music in print' guides to different repertories, including *Secular Choral Music in Print* (2nd ed. 1987, supplements to 1996); *Sacred Choral Music in Print* (2nd ed. 1985, supplements to 1996); *Classical Guitar Music in Print* (1989, supplement 1998); and *Orchestral Music in Print* (1979, supplements to 1999). As will be seen from their dates of publication, these guides are no longer current: but they can still be useful in tracking older material, and the recent launch of the guides in electronic form looks very promising. Many guides to special types of printed music material exist, such as DeVenney (1988) or Maxwell (1993). Those seeking to build up a good-quality collection of scores and sound recordings should consider the latest (3rd) edition of *A Basic Music Library* (Davis, 1997). Earlier editions of this guide, published in 1978 and 1983, also covered books on music, but omitted recordings.

For those with large budgets, approval plans between libraries and suppliers are another excellent way of building a collection while leaving the headaches of actually finding suitable material to the supplier. The larger library suppliers will undertake approval plans, and some, such as Theodore Front Music Literature in the United States, will supply libraries with details of new publications of potential interest by means of printed cards. The firm of Otto Harrassowitz, based in Wiesbaden, is also a major player in the operation of music approval plans and in the supply of music from European publishing houses (for further details see Harrassowitz's web page at <http://www.harrassowitz.de/mus_approval_plan.html>).

Because of the rather haphazard and diffuse nature of the field of music publishing, experience, either on the part of the librarian or music dealer, counts for a lot. It is productive to think laterally when dealing with enquiries for more obscure material, and this ability tends to develop with experience. A good network of contacts among musically-literate people – players, musicologists, retailers, publishers – is invaluable.

The role of music publishers today

In recent decades publishers have become much more aggressive about exploiting the performing and recording rights that come as part of their publishing a piece, rather than relying solely on money generated from sales of copies. Money from the royalties flowing from these rights is collected in the UK on composers' behalf by the Performing Right Society (PRS), and in the field of recordings by the Mechanical Copyright Protection Society (MCPS). The Music Publishers' Association (MPA) represents the corporate interests of UK music publishers in matters of general policy. Similar groups exist in other countries. A modern phenomenon in the non-classical field is the setting-up of companies that, although claiming to be music publishers, undertake publicity rather than publishing, and concentrate their efforts towards product launches and merchandising of accessories that have no connection with the printing of music. Some music publishers are owned by media interests such as EMI and Warner Chappell, enabling co-ordinated printed music and sound/video recordings releases.

Types of music: some basic definitions

A number of terms used by musicians to describe the formats in which music is published have already been used in this chapter. The basic formats are summarised here: those familiar with them may wish to skip this section. Because music is a performance art, the way in which it is published reflects this. Orchestral music, and large-scale pieces for orchestra and voices, will be made available in a full score for the use of the conductor, whose job it is to keep all the parts under control, while the individual performers will have separate parts. In a work for chamber ensemble (that is, a work, primarily instrumental, in which there is usually only one player to a part, and for forces smaller than those required for a full orchestra), players will again have their own part, but a full score will not necessarily form part of the set except where a piano is included in the instrumentation, in which case the pianist will perform from a score that enables him/her to see what is happening in all the other parts too.

The following definitions are by no means exhaustive, but are included here in the hope of helping the musical novice to understand the different formats in which music may be published:

- Full score: A large-format score (usually of a height of some 30 cm upwards) primarily for the use of the conductor (and, where a piece is being recorded, for use by a record producer too). Where an orchestral work is abbreviated onto a few staves, or reduced for piano only, it is termed a short score.[22] Before the days of recording, new orchestral works were often published in reductions for piano solo, for piano duet (two players at one piano) or for two pianos: this is now very rare.
- Study score: A smaller format score than a conductor's full score, often containing textual matter analysing the piece and/or providing a short history of it. A study score (German *Studienpartitur*) is normally of a size between full score and miniature score.
- Miniature score: A pocket-sized score, useful for following at a concert or when listening to a recording. The terminology used by publishers to designate a miniature score is somewhat hazy: the products of Ernst Eulenburg, one of the major publishers of miniature scores, are all around 19 cm in height. In the nineteenth century, Ewer and Co. imported and marketed scores that were much smaller than this, while today items of 23 cm and more are still occasionally referred to as 'miniature'. In the manner of study scores, miniature scores will occasionally carry prefatory textual matter that provides a historical or analytical context for the work.
- Piano conductor: In light music arrangements and some band music no full score is provided, and a piano part annotated with orchestral cues is supplied instead. The conductor uses this, rather than a full score, to direct the performance.
- Vocal score: Used by choirs for rehearsal purposes, a vocal score gives voice parts on separate lines (staves), and also carries a reduction of the orchestral parts for the work arranged for piano. This enables choirs to rehearse a work without having to go to the expense of hiring a full orchestra

for each session, since they can 'make do' with a rehearsal pianist instead. Older vocal scores will sometimes include tonic sol-fa notation above the conventional staves, and for some works a separate tonic sol-fa version may exist. Some choral works, especially from French publishers, will also exist as choral parts, meaning that the music for each voice part (soprano, alto, tenor, bass and so on) is printed discretely in a separate book, more in the fashion of an orchestral player's part. A variation on this theme is the Chorus score, which comprises all the voice parts in score, but without the piano accompaniment that one would find in a vocal score. Most choirs prefer vocal score format, because they can see what is going on in all the voice and orchestral parts simultaneously, and fit their own part around it.

- Orchestral parts: For an orchestral performance to take place, each member of the orchestra requires his/her own part; and this part, either in printed or manuscript form, will have been extracted from the full score. Parts are usually acquired and made available as complete sets. Orchestras frequently employ a specialist librarian to manage the provision of scores and parts needed for performances, though amateur ensembles will often press a player into service in this role. The orchestral librarians of the United States have their own association, MOLA (Major Orchestra Librarians' Association), and produce a newsletter, *Marcato*; while UK orchestral librarians operate informally under the aegis of the Association of British Orchestras, and through the Broadcasting and Orchestra Libraries section of the International Association of Music Libraries, Archives and Documentation Centres (IAML).

- Urtext: When performing the music of the classical masters one will occasionally hear reference to an 'Urtext'. This simply means that the text as printed represents the score as the composer left it or published it, without editorial additions by another hand. While such editions are of interest to the musicologist, they are sometimes inadequate for the performer. Perhaps because of this, over time the meaning of an 'Urtext' score has shifted from the basic definition to be applied more generally to a scholarly edition that might also include some editorial intervention.

- Sheet music: While all music is printed on sheets, the term 'sheet music' has a special definition, usually referring to publications of four or fewer pages containing songs, popular ballads or, occasionally, light instrumental works. For 150 years sheet music, often with decorative covers to entice purchasers, has been the principal mechanism for the dissemination of popular music. Thus the popular ballads and piano solos of pre-World War I are as attractive today for their artwork as for their contents – and sometime more so.[23] Songs from films were for many years distributed in this form. Such music, once thought of as ephemeral by musicologists (and by some librarians and archivists) is now viewed as having potential for sociological, as well as musicological, research. Thus the Harding Collection of American popular music in the Bodleian Library in Oxford is arranged by subject – 'Christmas'; 'Snow'; 'Transport', etc. – which enables sociological research to be carried on alongside musicological investigation.[24]

With the rise of recordings, and especially the invention of sophisticated studio recording techniques, pieces of sheet music have increasingly come to represent only the 'skeleton' of a work, bearing little significant similarity to the work as recorded. Conversely, in some cases publishers will print scores that reproduce exactly what is on a particular recording, making the recording the definitive artefact. Scores described as an 'authentic recorded version' of, for example, a Beatles song are examples of this practice.

▶ RETAIL OUTLETS

Although music shops can still be found in many towns and cities in the UK, the number that carry anything like a broad range of printed stock is now very small, this side of the business having diminished in favour of sales of instruments and instrumental accessories. Typical of the survivors are Cramer Music in London, Banks Music of York, Allegro Music and James Pass in Birmingham, the Cambridge Music Shop, and Blackwells Music Shop in Oxford. Blackwells has a separate 'Music Library Services' department staffed by specialists in the field, and supplies music to customers all over the world. In France, the 'FNAC' chain carries good stocks of books on music, and recordings. A useful list of UK retailers, arranged by region, may be found in the British and International Music Yearbook.

▶ REFERENCES

Adams, S. (1994) "International Dissemination of Printed Music during the Second Half of the Eighteenth Century." In Lenneberg, H. (ed.) *The Dissemination of Music: Studies in the History of Music Publishing.* Lausanne: Gordon and Breach, p. 21–42

Antolini, B.M. (ed.) (2000) *Dizionario degli Editori Musicali Italiani 1750–1930.* Pisa: Edizioni ETS/Società Italiana di Musicologia

Beethoven-Haus, Bonn (1985) *Ludwig van Beethoven: der Briefwechsel mit dem Verlag Schott*. München: Henle

Bernstein, J.A. (1998) *Music Printing in Renaissance Venice: the Scotto Press (1539–1572)*. New York, Oxford: Oxford University Press

Bertrand, P. (1947) *Le Monde de la Musique*. Geneva: La Palatine

Boosey, W. (1931) *Fifty Years of Music*. London: Ernest Benn

British and International Music Yearbook. London: Rhinegold Publishing

Davies, J. (1969) *Musicalia*. London: Pergamon

Davis, E. (ed.) (1997) *A Basic Music Library* (3rd edn.). Chicago and London: American Library Association

DeVenney, D. (1988) *Early American Choral Music: an Annotated Guide*. Berkeley, CA: Fallen Leaf Press

Devriès, A. and Lesure, F. (1979–88) *Dictionnaire des Éditeurs de Musique Francais* (2 vols). Geneva: Minkoff

Dichter, H. and Shapiro, E. (1941) *Handbook of Early American Sheet Music, 1768–1889*. New York: Dover Publications. (Reprinted 1977)

Durand, J. (1924) *Quelques Souvenirs d'un Éditeur de Musique*. Paris: Durand & Co

Durand (1969) *1869–1969: Livre du Centenaire*. Paris: Durand & Co

European Music Directory 2001 (2001) (2 vols). München: K.G. Saur

Geil, J. (1978) American Sheet Music in the Walter N.H. Harding Collection at the Bodleian Library, Oxford University. *Notes* 34, 805–13

Hase, O. von (1968) *Breitkopf & Härtel: Gedenkschrift und Arbeitsbericht*, 5th ed. Wiesbaden: Breitkopf & Härtel

Henle, G. (1973) Anfänge als Musikverleger. In: *25 Jahre G. Henle Musikverlag, 1948–1973*. München: Henle, p. 9–15

Hinnells, D. (1998) *An Extraordinary Performance: Hubert Foss, Music Publishing and the Oxford University Press*. Oxford: Oxford University Press

Hodges, A. (1995) *North West Union Catalogue of Vocal Scores*. Manchester: North West Regional Library System

Hopkinson, C. (1954) *A Dictionary of Parisian Music Publishers 1700–1950*. Reprinted New York: Da Capo Press, 1979

Humphries, C. and Smith, W.C. (1970) *Music Publishing in the British Isles from the Earliest Times to the Middle of the Nineteenth Century* (2nd edn.). Oxford: Blackwell

Hunter, D. (ed.) (1994) *Music Publishing & Collecting: Essays in Honor of Donald W. Krummel*. Urbana-Champaign, IL: University of Illinois

Hunter, D. (1997) *Opera and Song Books Published in England, 1703–1726: a Descriptive Bibliography*. London: Bibliographical Society

Hurd, M. (1981) *Vincent Novello and Company*. London: Granada

International ISMN Agency (2001) *Music Publishers' International ISMN Directory* (3rd edn.). München: K.G. Saur

Jones, M. (1997) *Vocal Sets in West Midlands Libraries*. Birmingham: West Midlands Regional Library Service

Kidson, F. (1900) *British Music Publishers and Engravers, London, Provincial, Scottish, and Irish, from Queen Elizabeth's Reign to George the Fourth's*. London: W. E. Hill. (Reprinted New York: B. Blom, 1967)

King, A.H. (1964, 2nd ed. 1979) *Four Hundred Years of Music Printing*. London: British Museum

Krummel, D.W. *et al.* (1981) *Resources of American Music History*. Urbana, IL; London: University of Illinois Press

Krummel, D.W. and Sadie, S. (1990) *Music Printing and Publishing*. Basingstoke and London: Macmillan Press

Krummel, D. (1992) *The Literature of Music Bibliography: an Account of the Writings on the History of Music Printing & Publishing*. Berkeley, CA: Fallen Leaf Press

Lara, C.J.G. (1995) *La edicion musical española hasta 1936*. Madrid: AEDOM

Lenneberg, H. (ed.) (1994) *The Dissemination of Music: Studies in the History of Music Publishing*. Lausanne: Gordon and Breach

Lewis, M.S. (1988–97) *Antonio Gardano, Venetian Music Printer*. New York, London: Garland

Mason, H (comp.) (1997) *Music for Choirs* (2nd edn.) (1st edn. comp. K. Anderson (1984)). East Midlands Regional Library System

Maxwell, G.L. (1993) *Music for Three or More Pianists: a Historical Survey and Catalogue*. Metuchen, NJ and London: Scarecrow Press

Moore, J.N. (ed.) (1987) *Elgar and his Publishers: Letters of a Creative Life*. Oxford: Clarendon

Morini, M., Ostali, N. and Ostali, P. (eds.) (1995) *Casa Musicale Sonzogno: Cronologie, Saggi, Testimonianze*. Milan: Sonzogno

Musical America International Directory of the Performing Arts. Primedia NJ: Hightstown

Music-in-Print (1973–). Philadelphia: Musicdata, Inc.
   1. Daugherty, F.M. and Simon, S.H. (comps.) *Sacred Choral Music in Print* (1985) (2nd edn.). (Suppls. 1988, 1992, 1996. Master Index 1996)
   2. Eislinger, G.S. and Daugherty, F.M. (comps.) *Secular Choral Music in Print* (1987) (2nd edn.). (Suppls. 1991, 1993, 1996. Master Index 1996)
   5. Jape, M. (comp.) *Orchestral Music in Print* (1979). (Suppls. 1983, 1994. Master Index 1994)
   7. Farish, M.K. (comp.) *Classical Guitar Music in Print* (1989) (Suppl. 1998)

90 Glorious Years: the Continuing Story of Stainer & Bell, Great British Publisher (1997). London: Stainer & Bell

Oxford Music: the First Fifty Years, '23–'73 (1973). London: Oxford University Press

Parkinson, J. (1990) *Victorian Music Publishers: an Annotated List.* Michigan: Harmonie Park Press

Pearsall, R. (1972) *Victorian Sheet Music Covers.* Detroit, Mich.: Gale

Pistone, D. (ed.) (1984) *Heugel et ses Musiciens: Lettres à un Éditeur Parisien.* Paris: Presses Universitaires de France

Reed, T. (comp.) (1982) *The British Union Catalogue of Orchestral Sets* [BUCOS] (1st edn.) London: Polytechnic of North London/IAML(UK); (1989) (2nd edn.) Boston Spa: British Library Document Supply Centre/IAML(UK); Dye, P. and Reed, T. (eds.) (1995) (2nd edn. supplement). Boston Spa: British Library Document Supply Centre/IAML(UK)

Roth, E. (1969) *The Business of Music: Reflections of a Music Publisher.* London: Cassell

Senart, M. (1942) *Editions Maurice Senart, ou L'injuste Conclusion de Toute une Vie de Travail.* Paris: Senart

Twyman, M. (1996) *Early Lithographed Music: a Study Based on the H. Baron Collection.* London: Farrand Press

van Orden, K. (2000) *Music and the Cultures of Print.* New York and; London: Garland

Vogg, H. (1976) *1876–1976: 100 Jahre Musikverlag Doblinger.* Wien: Doblinger

Vogg, H. et al. (1976) *Österreichische Musikzeitschrift* (vol. 11). Wien: H. Bauer Verlag

von Hase, O. (1968) *Breitkopf und Härtel: Gedenkschrift und Arbeitsbericht.* (5th edn.). Wiesbaden: Breitkopf und Härtel

Vötterle, K. (1963) *Haus unterm Stern: über Entstehen, Zerstörung und Wiederaufbau des Bärenreiter-Werkes.* Kassel, London: Bärenreiter

Vötterle, K. (1981) *An Stelle einer Festschrift: 70 Jahre Gustav Bosse Verlag.* Regensburg: Bosse

Witmark, I. and Goldberg, I. (1939) *From Ragtime to Swingtime: the Story of the House of Witmark.* New York: Furman

Wright, D. (1990) *Faber Music: The First 25 Years, 1965–1990.* London: Faber Music

▶ NOTES

1. I am extremely grateful to Lewis Foreman, and to Peter Ward-Jones of the Bodleian Library, for assistance in the preparation of this chapter.
2. Useful surveys of music printing may be found in King (1964, 1979) and in the long, illustrated article on 'Printing and Publishing of Music' by Stanley

Boorman, Eleanor Selfridge-Field and Donald W. Krummel in The New Grove, 2nd edn. (vol. 20, pp. 326–81). Pages 66–81 of Krummel and Sadie (1990) introduce the topic of computer-based music notation software. Some of this software can reproduce very sophisticated and specialised types of notation, such as chant notation or lute tablature. Reviews of new notation software are often carried in the Directory of Computer Assisted Research in Musicology (now entitled Computing in Musicology), published by the Center for Computer Assisted Research in the Humanities at Menlo Park, California (ISSN 1057–9478).

3. For further information on the rise of engraving see, for example, Hunter (1997).

4. The standard authority on all aspects of music lithography is Twyman (1996), which is unlikely to be superseded for some time.

5. The invention of 'stereotyping', by which an impression in plaster or in a compound of papier mâché and clay was taken from a page of type, and in turn used to make an impression in metal, very largely solved this problem. See 'Stereotype' in Krummel and Sadie (1990), p. 540. It is important to note, too, that repeated print runs taken from an engraved or lithographed plate would eventually lead to that plate wearing out, and requiring recasting or 'refreshment'. Plates and stones did not, therefore, last forever.

6. The caption 'Stich und Druck von [i.e. engraving and printing by] Breitkopf & Härtel in Leipzig' appears in each volume of the Bach edition.

7. [Editor's note: When a student I was fortunate to catch the end of this process when I visited the Augener factory at Park Royal, probably in January 1963. At that time the whole operation was dedicated to engraving on pewter plates, though within a very few years the factory and the skills involved were a thing of the past.]

8. Examples include Bernstein (1998) and Lewis (1988–97).

9. See Hinnells (1998). The press also produced a celebratory booklet for its golden jubilee – Oxford Music: the First Fifty Years, '23–'73 (1973).

10. See Wright (1990) for a short history of the company. Faber Music's catalogue has expanded considerably since its inception, and now takes in the work of such composers as Nicholas Maw, Oliver Knussen and George Benjamin.

11. 90 Glorious Years: the Continuing Story of Stainer & Bell, Great British Publisher (1997).

12. Krummel and Sadie (1990), p. 184: 'Virtually all notable composers of the second half of the 18th century attempted to have at least a few works printed or published by the Breitkopf firm.' A facsimile edition of Breitkopf's thematic catalogues for the period 1762–1787, edited under the supervision of Barry S. Brook, was published in New York by Dover in 1966.

13. The Tams-Witmark catalogue, which came into being following the amalgamation of the Witmark firm with that of Arthur Tams in 1925, was huge. From 1971 onwards material from the Tams-Witmark library of light, popular and choral music found its way to such American libraries as the Library of Congress in Washington, Princeton University Library and the library of Westminster Choir College. See Krummel et al. (1981).

14. European Music Directory 2001. Publishers appear in vol. 2, p. 249–80. One wonders how many of the 12 publishers listed have anything like a sizeable output, and how much their catalogues rely on reprints and translations.

15. It is important for the enquirer to know of these services when talking to publishers, as they are not always offered unless specifically asked for.

16. The British Union Catalogue of Orchestral Sets (Reed, 1982) is an excellent guide to the location of orchestral material, some of it long out of print. There

is currently no similar single-volume tool for the location of vocal sets, though regional catalogues, such as Hodges (1995), Jones (1997) and Mason (1984) have been produced. In 2001, IAML (UK) launched *Encore!*, an online union catalogue of performance sets (both vocal and orchestral) in the UK. Its site is accessible via URL <http://www.music.ox.ac.uk/iaml/encore.html>, or at <http://www.peri.nildram.co.uk/encore.htm>.

17. However, recent years have seen even leading composers having their retainers withdrawn, and consequently sometimes seeing their printed works remaindered or wasted.

18. The Gray example is especially interesting, since Gray in fact originally was sent to New York to be head of a Novello branch office there. He later bought the office, and set up under his own name in 1906. A glance at the list of 'Subsidiary music publishers' in the British and International Music Yearbook will give a clear idea of how the agency system works in the UK today. A noteworthy example is that of United Music Publishers in London, which distributes the products of a large number of French publishers, including Heugel and Durand.

19. See Adams (1994) for a discussion of this topic.

20. The outstanding example of this practice is the Parisian publisher Alphonse Leduc, which in 1993 reissued book-format catalogues for a number of instruments. These reproduce the first pages of music of each publication listed.

21. In connection with Novello one should also note the extensive catalogues of works for chorus and orchestra that before World War I were bound into all Novello's major vocal scores, and can still be found in copies from that period. Many of the works listed there are now completely, or in large part, unavailable from Novello, a phenomenon true of many choral works of the period from various publishers, owing to the loss of orchestral full scores and performing materials, which, unless the music was printed, probably only ever existed in a single copy, only the vocal score being printed. Revivals of one or two of these lost works are beginning to be attempted by specialist groups by commissioning re-orchestrations.

22. In a conventional full score each instrument or group of instruments (flutes, clarinets, first or second violins, etc.) has its own stave: a short score squeezes more than one group of instruments onto a stave, and therefore condenses the amount of space needed.

23. Pearsall (1972) is the best starting point for the study of sheet music artwork of nineteenth century Britain; while Dichter and Shapiro (1941, reprinted 1977) serves a similar function for the American market.

24. Given some libraries' lack of interest in popular ballads, it is perhaps no surprise that the Harding Collection was built up by a private collector, not by a library. For some information on the collection and its organisation see Geil (1978).

19 Performance (orchestral, opera and ballet)

Simon Wright

The successful management of the printed music requirements for orchestral and choral performance is perhaps the most complex operation in the music service industry. Its practitioners (orchestral librarians, publishers' hire librarians and many institutional music library staff) require very special skills and attributes which include, particularly, a broad (yet in-depth) grasp of the repertoire, a thorough knowledge of music theory, history and orchestration, and, above all, an understanding of players' and conductors' needs. On the podium for the first rehearsal must be a full score; the orchestral pads will contain individual parts, bowed and marked as appropriate for each instrument; and each chorus member will be holding a vocal score. It will have been the job of the orchestra's librarian (often via the services of a hire librarian) to source, assemble and check each piece of music present at that and subsequent rehearsals, and then to return or re-house it after the performance. Such a task (often multiplied over the hundreds of works played at a major music festival such as the BBC Promenade Concerts, or complicated by the large-scale music materials of opera and ballet) requires many hours of labour, a deep knowledge of music publishers' catalogues, contact with other music libraries, and, very often, negotiation with conductors and opera producers to ensure that the music obtained is exactly as required.

Little attempt has been made to codify or record the practices of orchestral or music hire librarianship: there is no formal written handbook on either subject. Rather, the librarians rely on a collective wisdom, shared industry practices, personal experience, and on valued and often home-made databases, catalogues and card indexes – which may in their own right indeed constitute invaluable snapshot archives of the music publisher or orchestra concerned. A unique record of the role of the orchestral librarian, *A Voice from the Pit* (1988), was written by Richard Temple Savage, who served as librarian of the London Philharmonic Orchestra from 1939 to 1946, and of the Royal Opera House between 1946 and

1982, as well as playing Bass Clarinet for both. From its pages tumble anecdotes of the great and the not-so-great, at their best, and sometimes their worst, moments. With humility and humour Savage tells of near-disasters when parts were lost and had to be copied at short (or no) notice; and he gives an honest picture of the daily grind of part bowing, marking vocal scores, and tracking down obscure opera materials. In his entire career, Savage notes, only once was the special work of the Music Library publicly acknowledged in a printed programme. Yet, in the end, disgruntled soloists, upset composers, temperamental conductors, and of course the ever-faithful players themselves, all come to line before the person on whom they all depend: the music librarian.

▶ PERFORMANCE MATERIAL

The performance material is defined as the total music requirements necessary for the execution of the work. In simplest form this would comprise: one full score, one string part per two players, and one part for each other player. In addition, vocal material is required for choral and operatic works.

The full score is used by the conductor and shows the complete musical work. Further copies may be required for recording purposes in studio work, etc. While the provision of a full score is the norm in most orchestral music, and opera and ballet scores, much light music and many operettas and shows exist only in 'piano reduction', 'short', or 'condensed score' format: the music librarian may mark or enhance these as appropriate.

All non-string orchestral parts are grouped into a 'windset' which is arranged in full score order, starting with flutes and ending with harps and keyboards. Parts are generally allocated a number from '1' (for example, Flute I) to 'end' (for example, Organ): an automatic check as to the completeness of the set is thus provided. A simple example of a windset and its numbering may be taken from Ravel's *Le tombeau de Couperin* (1919):

1	Flute I
2	Flute II
3	Oboe
4	Cor anglais
5	Clarinet I
6	Clarinet II
7	Bassoon I
8	Bassoon II
9	Horn I
10	Horn II
11	Trumpet
12	Harp

Nineteenth- and early twentieth-century notation commonly placed 'first' and 'second' instruments on the same part, with either two copies provided in the set, or both players sharing one part. However, modern practice is to prepare different and separate parts for each player. If Flute II doubles Piccolo, the music for Piccolo will be printed in Flute II; if a separate Piccolo is scored, it will have its own part. These principles run through all groups in the wind and brass families, and can accommodate all the permutations of doubling.

In symphonic music involving four horns, larger orchestras will commonly field five players, the fifth assisting Horn I after long or taxing passages, or doubling in robust music. This is termed a 'bumper', and a duplicate copy of Horn I is required in the set for this player.

The ramifications of percussion parts are many and complex. In a work with simple percussion involving one player only, there will be one part in the set, with all music notated on one or two staves. For larger requirements there are two options: either to show all the percussion work on a multi-stave 'score', and to provide as many copies as necessary, or to provide separate parts for each instrument or group of instruments. A large multi-percussion work (for example, Alberto Ginastera's *Cantata para américa mágica* (1961)) may demonstrate a mixture of both.

Off-stage, on-stage or other parts to be played outside the orchestra itself are commonly placed at the end of the windset. Additionally, their music may also be cued in the appropriate main orchestral part. Keyboard continuo parts and non-notated items such as tapes are normally also included at the end of the windset.

In rare cases, chorus material may be cued into the orchestral parts, for performance only in the absence of the chorus. Examples of this may be found in Ravel's *Daphnis et Chloé*, (1913) where the unaccompanied choral passage between figures 83 and 92 appears in an orchestrated version as an appendix to the score, with appropriate cues in the parts.

The number of string parts in an orchestral set is variable, and is generally determined by the playing strength of the orchestra in question. Modern symphony orchestras commonly play at 16.14.12.10.8, or 18.16.14.12.10, and thus the string constitution of a set would be 8.7.6.5.4 or 9.8.7.6.5, respectively. However, complications may arise in works requiring combined, divided, split or multiple string parts. The Requiem, op. 48, by Gabriel Fauré, for example,[1] merges Violin I and II into a single part, splits both the Violas and Cellos into I and II parts, and has unison Double basses. The string disposition in a typical set would therefore be 15 Violins, 3 Viola I, 3 Viola II, 3 Cello I, 2 Cello II, 4 Double bass. The division of string parts has occasionally been taken to extreme lengths, so that each desk, or even each player, receives a unique part, resulting in 30 or more individual and different copies.

The amount of vocal scores in a performance material is determined by the number of singers involved. Vocal scores, in opera, are also used for a variety of other purposes. A complete vocal set for an opera production may comprise the following.

- Vocal scores: These show all sung material, and all orchestral work in piano reduction; used by soloists, chorus master, répétiteur, music staff.
- Role parts: Cut-and-pasted vocal scores showing only the music for secondary and minor roles.
- Interleaved vocal scores: Vocal scores adapted so that each music page faces a blank sheet, on which lighting, design and choreographic staff can make notes and diagrams.
- Chorus parts: These show only chorus work, with or without piano reduction.

In addition, an opera's material may also include libretti and synopsis booklets.

In summary, it can be seen that one musical work may generate 50 or 60 different 'elements', and for many of these multiple copies may be required.

▶ THE ORCHESTRAL LIBRARY

Most professional orchestras and opera/ballet companies will accrue a basic, or large, collection of orchestral and vocal sets for works frequently performed: the larger orchestras will employ a librarian, or librarians, to administer this collection, and to serve all the music provision needs of the organisation. In smaller companies it is common for a playing member of the orchestra to act as 'librarian'. In the unique case of the BBC, with its various house orchestras, choirs and performing groups, centralised collections are made available, as well as collections maintained by the BBC's individual and regional performing bodies: throughout the BBC specialist music library staff are employed as part of the umbrella 'Information & Archives' business centre, or as employees of the orchestras. The relationship of music provision to other BBC services is described in the BBC's internally issued guide, *Information & Archives*.[2]

The core of a standard orchestral library will be the 'classical' western repertoire; the opera/ballet library will carry materials that are, or have been, in the particular company's repertoire. While standard repertoire is generally available to purchase in modern editions, both critical and non-critical, some orchestras may possess and still play from parts of earlier vintage, particularly if 'great' conductors of the past were associated with the orchestra, and bequeathed (or simply abandoned) working sets with special, personalised markings. The library of the Hallé Orchestra, for example, contains material from the working collections of Charles Hallé and John Barbirolli. The libraries of major orchestras may therefore become, de facto, archival collections and research resources in their own right (together with associated collections of concert programmes, posters, handbills, sound recordings, and correspondence), alongside their prime functions as playing collections. The orchestral librarian should always be approached in the first instance for access to such collections.

As well as administering the orchestra's own collections, and adding to them by selecting and purchasing as materials become available for sale, the librarian will be responsible for: obtaining music from hire libraries; borrowing music from other orchestras, and public or national collections; creating unique sets of parts; bowing and marking materials; repairing and binding music; liaising with composers over newly commissioned works; and assisting the orchestral administration in programme planning and research. In new works, particularly, the librarian is often required to make on-the-spot changes and corrections in orchestral parts at rehearsals.

A small brochure prepared in 1992 by the Major Orchestra Librarians' Association (USA), *The Orchestra Librarian: A Career Introduction*, is a well-written and succinct guide to the role (including the specialist areas of opera and ballet). In its coverage of training, the brochure laments the almost complete lack of formal qualifications available for orchestral librarianship, but concludes that 'there is no substitute for on-the-job training and experience.'

▶ THE HIRE LIBRARY

Composers and publishers have always expected to earn money from musical performance, but before the establishment of collecting societies for 'performing rights', the rationale behind the 'fees' charged by music publishers for the provision of music (beyond its straightforward sale) was, to say the least, hazy. Terminology was confused, and practice varied between publishers and between countries. Elgar's correspondence with his publishers, for example, makes frequent mention of 'terms', 'fees' and 'arrangements' without specifying exactly to which income streams these refer (Moore, 1987). Although the supply of orchestral material was usually implicit, the monies mentioned sometimes covered not only a 'hire fee', but also a 'performing right', and even a 'conducting fee' in cases where the publisher acted simultaneously as Elgar's agent. A 1914 correspondence between Elgar and Novello concerning the orchestral material of the Violin Concerto, through which it was decided to place parts both on sale and on hire, as well as abolishing a performing fee without rescinding the performing right, makes for an excellent illustration of the confusion surrounding payment for orchestral performance after the passing of the 1911 United Kingdom Copyright Act, but prior to the foundation of the Performing Right Society in March 1914.[3]

Statutory collecting societies such as the PRS (in the United Kingdom), the American Society of Composers, Authors and Publishers (ASCAP) (in the USA) and various international affiliates and sister societies now almost exclusively manage the collection of performing and broadcast right income for publishers (except in dramatic works, which are normally licensed direct by publishers). Equivalent societies collect from mechanical (recorded) performance: in Britain this is the responsibility of the Mechanical-Copyright Protection Society (MCPS), and in the USA the Harry Fox Agency. The PRS publishes its summarised accounts and a statistical survey in the annual *PRS Yearbook and Report & Accounts*. An excellent official history of the PRS is Cyril Ehrlich's comprehensive *Harmonious Alliance: a History of the Performing Right Society* (1989), written to commemorate the Society's 75th anniversary, and which gives a detailed picture of music rights collection in Britain during the course of the twentieth century.

The publisher is left, therefore, to control the income generated specifically by the provision of music, both by sale and hire, and through certain other intellectual property rights. And today, the majority of copyright orchestral works, much choral music, and some public domain music, is commonly placed on hire only, and supplied through a hire library (American usage: rental library), run usually (but not always) as part of a music publishing operation. Placing a work 'on hire' means that the publisher can be economical in producing material, rather than risking the big and often speculative print runs required for sale items. Performances of hire works are easily controlled, logged and tracked. Works by living (or even dead) composers are easily revised and/or corrected when their material is lodged in a hire library. And specially marked or bowed sets are routinely kept intact, and can be provided for specific conductors and orchestras as required. For the performer, the cost of hiring music is inevitably less than the nominal purchase price would be. Hire also means that once a work has been performed, organisations can immediately divest themselves of material, rather than being encumbered with large amounts of unwanted materials.

Hire fees are calculated in a variety of ways, and practice varies enormously. Some or all of the following elements are normally present in the calculations: number of performances, duration of work, length of hire, status of performing body, amount of music supplied, and nature of usage (live, broadcast or recorded performance). In some territories, industry agreed hire tariffs are in place; in others, to engage in such collusion would be illegal. In practice, hire fees are pitched through a system of tariffs, but are often negotiable.

It is common for music publishers to operate their hire services internationally through a network of affiliates, sub-publishers and agents. Many of these arrangements are reciprocal, but they are not necessarily so.

In Great Britain, the Music Publishers Association liaises regularly with various music hire user groups on behalf of its members, and from these discussions have arisen various 'guidelines' on music hire, designed to codify industry practice, and to give advice to those hiring music. The *Aide Memoire for Music Hire* (1980) was designed primarily for schools, colleges and amateur users, while *Guidelines for Practice in Music Hire* (1999) was drawn up in conjunction with the Association of British Orchestras, for professional users.

While the needs of publishers' hire libraries were a prime candidate for computerisation, competitive development of specialised systems has been limited. The most advanced system, and one which has carefully taken account of all user requirements, is the Hire Library Management System (HLMS), now in place in 13 major music libraries around the world. HLMS was developed from a simple programme designed by the hire library of Boosey & Hawkes (Australia) in 1986. The system is now managed, marketed and developed by BTM Innovation, Australia, and has become an advanced and powerful tool, capable of successfully managing the varied tasks involved in a music hire operation. HLMS is currently available as a DOS-based system only, but a Windows NT version is planned for release in 2002.

A full overview of HLMS is given at the BTMI website (<http://www.btmi.com.au>), but its functions may be summarised as follows. The system, via its four main databases (composer, composition, set and client) is able to plan and record the movement of stock to and from clients. Its management of material is designed to accommodate both dedicated professionally marked sets, and general, more fluid pools of stock, as well as vocal scores, chorus parts and libretti. Sets may be reserved; missing parts are dealt with; and overdue materials are automatically recalled. Full performance details are recorded, which may be fed to a variety of statementing functions. An invoicing and hire fee calculation system is driven by the standard fee building components. Finished transactions are archived (but easily retrieved), and the system is also designed to account royalties, both to the composers, and to other publishers. Many HLMS features can be adapted for local usage: all systems are in English, although the menus are completely configurable to the language of choice. The invoicing system functions in any decimal currency.

The title/orchestration information on HLMS (which in itself is unique to each user) may be exported to a further BTMI programme, Repertoire 2000. This programme is a cataloguing system specifically designed for orchestral and choral music, and opera, but it can also be used to list recordings, or other printed music. Repertoire 2000 is particularly useful in programme planning and publicity work, as titles may be searched by genre, duration, instrumentation and anniversary (for example, of composers' birth). Details may be found on the BTMI website.

▶ BIBLIOGRAPHIC TOOLS

The bibliographic tools of both hire and orchestral librarians are broadly similar. Their principal works of reference will be the whole range of catalogues specific to individual music publishers, a range too vast to describe here, and in any case one that changes almost daily. Almost all major music publishers now place their hire catalogue, or portions of it, on their individual websites. However, it is essential to point out that the annually renewed Edwin F. Kalmus & Company Inc. catalogue is the largest source for reprints of public domain (in the USA) repertoire. It lists the orchestrations and durations of almost all standard classical orchestral works. Beyond this, the various composite or union catalogues published by national institutions or libraries provide invaluable guides to specific repertoire and collections.

The availability of orchestral and vocal performing materials held by public and institutional libraries in the U.K. is now made much easier for the general user by the launch on the Internet of *Encore!,* the IAML(UK) database of such material (<www.music.ox.ac.uk/IAML/encore.html>).

In the UK, a vast and comprehensive listing is provided by the various catalogues produced by the erstwhile BBC Music Library and its successors. Although intended primarily as a directory of the Corporation's own holdings, and designed for 'internal use', these holding are, in reality, comprehensive enough to result in almost complete repertoire listings, containing much unique detail not available elsewhere. The BBC Music Library Orchestral Catalogue (Compton, 1982) gives the complete orchestral holdings of the BBC at the time of publication, including purchased material, scores and parts resulting from BBC commissions and programme making, and hire material held on permanent loan. The catalogue lists vast amounts of works in main versions, and also in alternative arrangements, transpositions and orchestrations. For each item duration, orchestration, key, publisher and BBC location are listed. A parallel catalogue for choral music and opera was published in 1967, but is now seriously out of date:[4] although the catalogue lacks orchestration details there is a useful list of hymnbooks. A comprehensive listing of hymns and congregational songs in collections used in Great Britain and Ireland is *HymnQuest: A Dictionary of Hymnody* (1997), which lists the first lines of hymns alphabetically, followed by the numbers in the collections in which they appear, together with a list of hymn publishers.

James J. Fuld's *The Book of World Famous Music (Classical, Popular, and Folk)* (1995) gives a generous selection of entries with music incipits, and describes compositional, publishing and printing histories of well-known works. The information on first editions (including parts) is detailed and comprehensive. Neil Butterworth's *Neglected Music* (1991) lists selected 'second rank' repertoire (for example, Schoenberg's orchestration of Brahms's Piano Quartet in G minor, op. 25), with orchestration/choral details, duration and publisher, together with discographies.

Succinct information on all aspects of the operatic repertoire is given in *The Viking Opera Guide* (Holden, 1993). This thoroughly researched one-volume encyclopaedia gives career resumés of all composers known to have written operas (including major 'shows'), followed by short articles on each opera, giving information on compositional chronology, performance history, editions, casts/voices, orchestration summary, plot synopsis and commentary. For ballet, similar information is contained in the *International Encyclopedia of Dance* (Cohen, 1998). This is a comprehensive and detailed work of high quality and informed research, and in addition to straightforward information on composers and their ballets, there is a wealth of detail on related matters: choreographers, different versions of scores and productions, ballet companies and bibliography.

The orchestral librarian may occasionally be required to prepare parts in transposed versions, or even to provide a customised scoring of an item, in which cases queries on the technical specifications, range and capabilities of instruments may arise. The standard sources of reference are Alfred Blatter's *Instrumentation and Orchestration* (1997) and Walter Piston's classic and still indispensable *Orchestration* (1955). A broad reference book on the history, science, and manufacture of instruments is Sibyl Marcuse's *Musical Instruments: a Comprehensive Dictionary* (1966). Norman Del Mar's *Anatomy of the Orchestra* (1981) is a comprehensive guide to all aspects of orchestration, instrumentation, orchestral layout, and other connected issues.

Individual players might request from the librarian specific parts required for audition purposes, or for advance rehearsal. A large number of orchestral parts from the standard repertoire, including potentially difficult or exposed passages of the type often required at audition, are published in anthology form. A guide to this repertoire, listed by composer, and cross-referenced by instrument, is Carolyn Robson's *Orchestral Excerpts: a Comprehensive Index* (1985). This book will, for example, point to sources in which the principal Flute part of Beethoven's Pastoral Symphony is included. The most extensive series of such excerpts is the *Kalmus Orchestra Albums* (various dates) which provide the Violin I, Viola, Cello, Bass, Flute I, Oboe I, Clarinet I, Horn I, Trumpet I and Trombone I parts for well over 300 music titles.

The information presented to an orchestral librarian in the hope that a particular piece of music is swiftly located may often be far from clear or complete. A nickname, sobriquet or 'foreign translation' title of a work (and, in particular, of an operatic excerpt) may not be sufficient to enable the identification of the music in question. *Music Titles in Translation: a Checklist of Musical Compositions*, by Julian Hodgson, (1976) gives in one alphabetical sequence original title and English translations, or the reverse, as appropriate. Typical entries read:

> *Abendlied – Evening Song: Mendelssohn*
> *How calm is my spirit – Ridante la calma: Mozart*

A similar function is supplied by *Popular Titles and Subtitles of Musical Compositions* (Berkowitz, 1975) which lists works by nicknames, cross-referenced to a composer list; brief explanations of nicknames are given. Harold Barlow and Sam Morgenstern's *A Dictionary of Opera and Song Themes* (1976) lists incipits of operatic arias, stage musical songs, etc., and has an index from which all the entries may be located by an ingenious 'C major' code system.

Historic information on music publishers, and technical matters to do with printing and publishing are well covered in the 'New Grove Handbook' *Music Printing and Publishing* (1990). This work deals particularly well with terms such as 'plate number', impression', and 'edition', which although commonly used by music publishers have enjoyed changing definitions over the years, and which thereby may present difficulties to music librarians seeking, particularly, editions of 'early' music. As the current details of music publishers' addresses, international offices, representation, distribution, and agency arrangements are complex, and vary tremendously for each territory, it is not possible to indicate one single source giving comprehensive coverage and listings. For the UK, an annually updated list appears in the *British and International Music Yearbook* (annual). This work lists the UK offices of main publishers, and details of representation arrangements in Britain for other catalogues.

Both hire and orchestral librarians will be required to create, edit or amend parts and scores: a full grasp of music notation and graphics is essential. The standard works on the subject are Alan Boustead's *Writing Down Music* (1975) and the thoroughly comprehensive handbook by Gardner Read, *Music Notation* (1969). Boustead's book is primarily concerned with hand-copied (manuscript) material, while Read's looks at aspects of engraved and printed music, and also covers topics such as proofreading, and the whole history of music notation. Also useful is *The Essentials of Music Copying*, by Susan Homewood and Colin Matthews (1990). Although various computerised systems of music engraving are now on the market, a comprehensive manual on the subject has yet to appear. Information on the widely used notation software Sibelius can be found at the company's website, <http://www.sibelius.com>.

▶ REFERENCES

Aide Memoire for Music Hire (1980). London: Music Publishers Association

Barlow, H. and Morgenstern, S. (1976) *A Dictionary of Opera and Song Themes*. London: Ernest Benn

BBC Music Library Choral and Opera Catalogue (1967). London: British Broadcasting Corporation

Berkowitz, F.P (1975) Popular Titles and Subtitles of Musical Compositions (2nd edn.). Metuchen, NJ: Scarecrow Press

Blatter, A. (1997) Instrumentation and Orchestration (2nd edn.). New York: Schirmer Books

Boustead, A. (1975) Writing Down Music. London: Oxford University Press

British and International Music Yearbook (annual). London: Rhinegold Publishing

Butterworth, N. (1991) Neglected Music: A Repertoire Handbook for Choirs and Orchestras. London: Robert Hale

Cohen, S.J. (ed.) (1998) International Encyclopedia of Dance. New York: Oxford University Press

Compton, S. (ed.) (1982) BBC Music Library Orchestral Catalogue. London: British Broadcasting Corporation

Del Mar, N. (1981) Anatomy of the Orchestra. London: Faber & Faber

Deutsches Musikarchiv, ed: Bonner Katalog. Verzeichnis reversgebundener musikalischer Aufführungsmateriale. (Index of rental material for musical performance.) München: K.G. Saur Verlag (CD-ROM ed, 4th ed 2002).

Edwin F. Kalmus Orchestra Catalog (annual). Florida: Edwin F. Kalmus & Co., Inc.

Ehrlich, C. (1989) Harmonious Alliance: a History of the Performing Right Society. Oxford: Oxford University Press

Fuld, J.J. (1985) The Book of World Famous Music (Classical, Popular, and Folk). New York: Dover Publications Inc.

Ginastera, A. (1961) Cantata para américa mágica. Buenos Aires: Barry

Guidelines for Practice in Music Hire (1999) (2nd edn.). London: Music Publishers Association/Association of British Orchestras

Hodgson, J. (1976) Music Titles in Translation: a checklist of musical compositions. London: Clive Bingley

Holden, A. (ed.) (1993) The Viking Opera Guide. London: Viking

Homewood, S. and Matthews, C. (1990) The Essentials of Music Copying. London: Music Publishers' Association

HymnQuest: A Dictionary of Hymnody (1997). London: Stainer & Bell, for the Pratt Green Trust

Kalmus Orchestra Albums (various dates). Florida: Edwin F. Kalmus & Co., Inc.

Krummel, D.W. and Sadie, S. (eds.) (1990) Music Printing and Publishing. Basingstoke: Macmillan Press

Marcuse, S. (1966) *Musical Instruments: a Comprehensive Dictionary*. London: Country Life

Moore, G.N. (1987) *Elgar and His Publishers: Letters of a Creative Life*. Oxford: Clarendon Press

Piston, W. (1955) *Orchestration*. New York: Norton

PRS Yearbook and Reports & Accounts 99/00. London: Performing Right Society

Rabson, C (1995) *Orchestral Excerpts: a comprehensive index*. Berkeley, CA: Fallen Leaf Press

Ravel, M. (1913) *Daphnis et Chloé*. Paris: Editions Durand

Ravel, M. (1919) *Le tombeau de Couperin*. Paris: Editions Durand

Read, G. (1969, reissued 1985) *Music Notation: A Manual of Modern Practice*. London: Victor Gollancz Ltd

Savage, R. Temple (1988) *A Voice from the Pit*. Newton Abbot: David & Charles

The Orchestra Librarian: A Career Introduction. (1992) USA: Major Orchestra Librarians' Association

▶ NOTES

1. In its fully orchestrated version published by Hamelle et Cie., Paris (study score is undated).
2. *Information & Archives* (updated approximately annually) London: British Broadcasting Corporation.
3. Moore (1987), pp. 783–87.
4. BBC Music Library *Choral and Opera Catalogue* (1967).

20 New music: its publication and dissemination

Matthew Greenall

The role of the composer has changed considerably in the last 20 years or so. Very few composers today are the sort of people who solely write music, composing only to a commission, producing a piece, seeing it performed and then going on to the next piece. Even if you were to look at a prolific and well-known composer, such as Peter Maxwell Davies, you would find a much wider portfolio of activity: conducting, for example, or work with the community, educational work of various kinds, and in Maxwell Davies's case (as with Britten before him) running a local international festival. This has become, to a growing extent, the pattern of a composer's life.

With the introduction of music as part of the curriculum of GCSE, for many composers things changed further. There was suddenly a lot of work in burgeoning education departments, or ensembles, orchestras which demanded somebody with a creative flair to work alongside performers in involving people in new music in a new way. Courses have been developed at places like London's Guildhall School of Music and Drama, where the Professional Development programme initiated by Peter Renshaw trains a different kind of composer. The composer may be a skilled improviser and 'world music' practitioner as well as being able to work with conventionally notated music.

Residencies by various composers with orchestras and ensembles have been another agent of change and coming together. Typically they have led to a much more direct connection between a composer and a university or performing group, resulting in a formal arrangement that might last for several years. Under these circumstances those involved can get to know each other very well, and how the creator applies him or herself to various areas of the ensemble. So the composer is a much more integrated figure now than might have been the case 15 or 20 years ago. This is often reflected in the music that composers write. There is much more music which might be described as 'accessible' now than was the case 20 years ago, and this is due not only to changes in the aesthetic climate, but also in working pattern.

The number of active composers relentlessly grows, prompting the question of how one decides how many composers there are or, indeed, how one defines what a composer is. There are perhaps some 80 composers in the UK who are under contract to a major publisher and therefore have the imprimatur and confidence of the music business, which is in effect saying: we believe this music is good and we can sell it to orchestras, ensembles and, of course, to the wider audience, and one day this music may make money for us. Those composers are only a small percentage of the people who are out there actually writing. In terms of the British Music Information Centre and what it has on its database, there are more than 2500 British composers represented, of whom at least half are still living and writing. Those composers are at all sorts of levels but they are all getting performances from professional musicians.

The criteria applied when the BMIC takes music are themselves some indication of whether the composers concerned have the imprimatur of others as to their validity and standing. They might have been commissioned by the Arts Council or Regional Arts Boards, be published by a significant publisher (Boosey and Hawkes, Faber Music, etc.), performed or workshopped by the spnm (SEE BELOW); they might belong to major composer organisation, such as the Composer's Guild of Great Britain, which is now subsumed in the British Academy of Composers and Songwriters (The British Academy), or meet none of the above criteria but be a member of the Performing Rights Society (PRS) and receiving professional performances. This does not embrace all those who might just be writing for the fun of it – so-called 'Sunday afternoon' music – who may well be composers of some significance. The PRS has something like 29 000 writer-members, although that embraces quite a lot of librettists and writers as well as composers.

To become a composer is a long and arduous task. It is like beginning any craft: there is an apprenticeship period which might go on for some composers into their thirties and even forties, while others assimilate their influences very quickly and come out with personal voices or as immensely skilled craftsmen in their early twenties. There are very few composers in their teens who would be likely to interest, say, a publisher, although some composers do receive major performances at a very young age: George Benjamin's orchestral work *Ringed by the Flat Horizon* was performed at the Proms when the composer was just 20, and still a student.

Most of the major universities that have music departments have courses that feature composition as a significant component. These include York University, which has a very active composition programme, Kings College London, Royal Holloway, and most of the conservatoires, including Guildhall, Royal Academy of Music, Royal College of Music, and Royal Northern College. A lot of composers would not specialise in composition at undergraduate level, although they might well be composing at that point. The tradition of evening classes fostering composers, so active with Michael Tippett at Morley College after the war, has tended to fade, though Morley College and the City Lit itself are still active.

There are of course residential courses at summer schools of music, such as Dartington where composers such as Birtwistle and John Woolrich have been associated with the teaching, as have a variety of international figures. Canford Summer School of Music has a course which provides a focus for aspiring composers of all ages.

▶ PUBLICATION

It is getting more and more difficult to be published today, particularly for young composers. Ten years ago one could easily count a dozen British composers under 35 on publishers' lists. Today there is probably half that number. Because of the economics of music publishing, and perhaps because of some lack of dynamism by the publishers themselves, there are some significant publishers' lists that have disappeared in recent years. For example, the British composers list that Universal Edition used to run has more or less vanished as a significant force, leaving some quite major composers, such as David Bedford, without a publisher. Novello also has drastically reduced the number of composers on its books. So it is not easy to be published today. Also, a different kind of composer is starting to get a publisher. One is seeing less the kind of composer who might have come through the traditional route of conservatoire, spnm, specialist performing groups like the London Sinfonietta and the BBC; more composers are coming through routes like TV music or establishing their own band, or are performers who are also composers. Composers like John Harle, for example, are being taken on, which might not have happened ten years ago. The pre-eminent example, of course, is Michael Nyman, a composer who was outside the former, accepted route but because of the success of his band – whose concerts frequently sold out – and of his films and commercial music, has now become part of the accepted publishing world with Music Sales.

This shift is starting to alter the role of publishers themselves, who are becoming more involved in a promotion or agency role and less and less in publication of the music as traditionally defined. The amount of music by you will see in a music shop that is by contemporary composers is now not very high at all. Most music is available only on special order, or on hire only, and it is the rare composer who has it written into a contract that his music shall be published in conventional formats. The music may exist in batches of 50, down to a handful of copies often distributed to promoters rather than being sold to the generality of music libraries and individually to music lovers. Instrumental music is a special case, where repertoire is still published in conventional format, though less and less will you be able to go into your local shop and look through a cross-section of new pieces.

Computer setting of music through notation programmes, such as Sibelius 7, Finale or Score, has dramatically improved presentation standards and has meant that we are looking at fewer handwritten scores, so prevalent from the 1960s to the 1980s. At the same time, very little material produced by unpublished composers in this way will find its way into the world other than by mail order or direct contact with the composer.

A composer's income will only be partly be made up from writing and performing his own work. If they are published, the publisher will take a significant percentage of the income, as much as 50%. So some composers choose to stay out of that whole system and actually publish themselves, an activity made easier with the modern score notation programmes mentioned above, copying equipment and communications, particularly over the internet.

There are significant threats to composers' income from performances of their works, particularly with the reduction of what has been called the Classical Music Subsidy whereby the Performing Right Society gave 'classical' composers an enhanced payment in recognition of the slow payback on such music. Thus the restructuring of payments may have a knock-on effect throughout the music industry, reducing the income of publishers, composer trusts and composer estates as well as composers themselves. Commissioning rates are quite low, and many commissioning bodies do not pay the full amount – the Association of Professional Composers (now part of The British Academy – SEE BELOW) have traditionally set the boundaries of rates.

People's perception of new music is perhaps influenced by a prevailing ideology, particularly dominant in the 1960s, which incorporated an evolutionary view of new music from an essentially modernist perspective. In particular, the aesthetic associated with Pierre Boulez and his immediate contemporaries, whilst responsible for music that continues to have resonance and significance, led to a (mis)perception of new music as elitist and difficult to listen to. The whole shift of music in the last 30 years has been away from that aesthetic which, while it still has its passionate adherents, has never been the totality of new music, even less so in the 1980s and 90s. Nor indeed does it have primacy in today's more eclectic climate. Ultimately this acceptance of stylistic diversity can only be good for new music. And of course there are still people writing traditional genre music for traditional audiences, and this work has its validity as well. Church music is still being written, brass band music is still being written.

► ORGANISATIONS

The Society for the Promotion of New Music (spnm) (<http://www.
spnm.org.uk>) was set up in 1943 and it has a lot of loyalty from
composers, many of whom had their start as composers in concerts organised by the spnm. It exists to give professional performances of works by
composers who are starting out. It tends to be younger composers, of
course, but composers can be of any age, as testified by the success of Minna
Keal at the age of 75, who had works first performed by the spnm before
her recent wider exposure at the Proms and elsewhere.

The structure works like this. The society issues a call for new scores,
which are read by a reading panel of established composers and performers,
people with a background in new music. They make a recommendation
that a work should be short-listed for possible performance or workshop-
ping by a professional ensemble within a period of three years. In a typical
year the spnm will receive 400–500 works, of which they will short-list 70
or 80. Each work is looked at by at least three readers and composers can
receive (anonymously) the comments by those readers on their works. The
spnm then sets up a series of performance opportunities, either their own
concerts or the placing of a few spnm works in the concerts or concert
series of a professional ensemble or orchestra. Those works will then be
performed, there will be discussion and comment about them, and a
recording will be provided for the composer. So it is a remarkable organisation and fairly unique in world terms. The list of composers first
performed by the spnm who later became well-known is very considerable
and includes many of the most significant British composers to emerge since
the Second World War.

Sonic Arts (<http://www.sonicartsnetwork.org>) represents electro-
acoustic and computer music in this country. It is a minority music, but an
important one. Essentially, they act as a performance and promotion body
for that music. They have a big educational arm as well, and they have a
lot of connections with international events such as the Bourges Festival in
France. They have their own collection of tapes which you can go and listen
to at their premises in Southwark.

In 1998 a new organisation was formed, the British Academy of
Composers and Song Writers (The British Academy <www.britishacademy.
com>). It is a merger of the Composers Guild of Great Britain, the
Association of Professional Composers (APC) and the British Academy of
Songwriters Composers and Authors (BASCA), which was the basically the
pop song writers. It has a collective membership of about 3000, representing a conglomeration of composers across genre, and a journal, *The Works*,
incorporating the newsletters or magazines of the three organisations.

Making Music <www.makingmusic.org.uk>, formerly known as The
National Federation of Music Societies (NFMS) is this country's major

representative body for amateur performing groups. A recent Making Music initiative is to create a database of their catalogues of music suitable for amateur performance, which will in part be an updating of their existing catalogues (which end in 1985). Another organisation is COMA <www.coma.org.uk> (Contemporary Music Making for Amateurs). This is a national organisation and, like Making Music, now has Arts Council funding. COMA is organised in Regional Chapters throughout the UK, and exists to promote contemporary music-making by amateur performers and composers. Quite a number of significant composers have written works for COMA performers.

▶ SPECIALIST INSTRUMENTAL COMMUNITIES

The National Federation of Brass Bands serves as an umbrella organisation which also has a library of scores and a journal. The wind band community has BASBWE – the British Association of Symphonic Bands and Wind Ensembles – and they have an annual conference and a magazine.

There are several organisations for Asian music in this country, of which the most prominent is the Asian Music Circuit. AMC <www.amc.org.uk> is funded by the Arts Council and is basically a touring agency, though it also offers advice for people wanting to know how to find areas of specialist expertise, from all parts of Asia not just India. For example someone wanting to know more about the Javanese gamelan might be assisted in locating the various gamelan groups across the UK. There is also an Afro-Caribbean Music Circuit, again funded by the Arts Council. Then there are organisations like Folkworks <www.folkworks.co.uk> in Newcastle and WOMAD <www.womad.org/reading/> which deal with folk music (and world music, in WOMAD's case), in addition to the EFDSS <www.efdss.org> (English Folksong and Dance Society), which traditionally handled this area. The principal representative organisation for jazz is Jazz Services <www.jazzservices.org.uk>, which combines a touring and publicity function with an essential information service.

In terms of popular music, there have been several abortive developments. A Lottery-funded Centre for Popular Music, opened in Sheffield, closed within two years amid much adverse publicity after failing to make visitor targets and running out of cash. Plans for a London-based British Music Centre, a record industry-driven resource for pop music have not borne fruit. However, an argument over what music should receive public funds continues to spark debate inside arts funders and outside. The Arts Council of England's most recent new music strategy, set out in the policy document *Creating New Notes* (Arts Council of England, 1996), seeks a re-definition of a new music that cannot solely be defined in terms of western 'classical music'. It argues that music receiving money from the public purse should rather embrace a whole range of new vernaculars, including jazz and improvised music, the less commercial end of rock, pop and dance, folk and traditional music, multi-cultural and world music. So the Arts Council and other public funders have set themselves the ambition of providing funds across the whole range of new music, much more broadly defined, although how this will work out in the long term, given their well established, budget-consuming client base (in particular, orchestras and opera companies) remains to be seen

► SELF-PUBLISHING AND GROUP PUBLISHING

Self publishing as an accepted and legitimate activity for a reputable composer really dates from the wide dissemination of photocopying machines in the mid-1960s, though it came to maturity with the availability of easy-to-use score notation software for running on domestic personal computers. The advent of the internet has also provided a way for such composers to keep in touch and to promote their works, and doubtless will increasingly become a medium for delivering it. The book *Publishing for Composers*, produced by the APC (Gunning, 1994), is well worth reading as background to this whole issue.

Many individual publishers now publish their music in this way, while occasionally it has come about as a group activity. For example, the North West Composers Alliance put out a promotional brochure of their works, and have even issued a promotional CD. Another group is the Portsmouth District Composers Alliance (PDCA): they put on joint performances where they hire a group in, give them all the works they have for those particular forces, and the group then chooses the works to perform. There are a lot of groupings like that working at various levels. The best way to access such groups is through the internet, where either the BMIC (<http://bmic.co.uk>) or The British Academy (<http://www.britishacademy.com>) websites will provide links on to them.

► PROMOTIONAL MATERIAL

A major part of a publisher's promotional work is to issue free leaflets and booklets devoted to the composers they publish. These not only provide a short biography and career history, but also a catalogue of works with the essential details of duration and forces required, and often also a discography and even a bibliography. Thus for composers who have not yet received coverage in the literature by a monograph, articles or up-to-date entry in major reference books these are a major source, effectively providing free monographs on each composer, and are an essential feature in any musical reference library. Publishers also issue press releases, list of works in their catalogue announced for performance, and increasingly they run their own free magazines (*QuarterNotes* from Boosey & Hawkes; *The Full Score* from Music Sales – covering Novello, Chester Music, Schirmer Music, William Hansen and others).

Publishers quite often produce specialist lists, such as much for specific instruments and of course the hire library catalogue (see CHAPTER 19) will be a prime source for new music which is not otherwise available.

Publishers will give out promotional material under appropriate circumstances and this does include cassettes of music in their catalogue when they are not otherwise available. They tend to be for study purposes only or where they could lead to a performance of the piece concerned or promotion in the national press. Thus if you are genuinely considering a work for performance its publisher will provide a tape to listen to, as they will if you are writing about their composer in the national press.

▶ NOTATION

There was a time in the 1960s and 70s when graphic notation of one sort or another was a big issue, particularly in the works of Stockhausen, Ligeti, Penderecki, Xenakis and others. At a tangent to these developments were notational practises based on the work of Cage, and typified by the work of the English 'experimental' composers in the 1970s, where scores might exist entirely in terms of instructions, pictures or fanciful titles (*Drinking and Hooting Music* or *The Balkan Sobranie Smoking Mixture*).

Today notation has largely stabilised in the traditional appearance on page but with perhaps some refinements developed over this time. Also the appearance of musical notation programmes has made producing beautifully laid out score massively easier than ever before. The whole movement of experimental graphic score notation seems to have receded, whilst leaving its mark on contemporary practise. Those not using such conventional notation tend to be composers whose music exhibits extreme complexity, where they tend to use an enhanced notation – irrational rhythms, extreme density of note on page – which some score notation systems would struggle to cope with. Compositions such as those which Cage, Ligeti or Xenakis were creating 25 years ago, or those which just use pictures or games, are quite unusual now.

▶ SPECIALIST NEW MUSIC RECORDING LABELS

The most important specialist recording label in the UK is NMC Recordings <www.nmcrec.co.uk>, which was set up in the early 1990s with funding from the Holst Foundation, and administration from SPNM (although subsequently it has set up its own independent office). The intention was to create a label which was representing solely new music that has been written recently, to provide a kind of picture of the range of new music which no other specialist record label was doing. It has produced well over 50 releases including some major recordings such as Birtwistle's opera *The Mask of Orpheus*. It has become an established and very significant label, and it has diversified into issuing historical and individual performer recordings. It was the label which issued Anthony Payne's reconstruction of Elgar's Third Symphony, one of the best selling classical records of the late 1990s.

There are also smaller companies, such as Metier, while some established labels have tended to represent individual composers. Unfortunately this has meant than when a company of the standing of Collins Classics stopped issuing classical recordings, their entire Maxwell Davies programme was put at risk and with it his representation in the catalogue. Among the youngest composers, EMI has a relationship with Thomas Adès, whilst labels such as Argo (a subsidiary of Decca, itself owned by Polygram) have recorded quantities of Nyman, Fitkin and Turnage.

One very interesting idea is Unknown Public <www.unknown public.com>, a subscription organisation that provides CDs in a brown box format with an enclosed booklet. promoting a sample recording of a great range of new music, often at the experimental edge – contemporary classical, improvised, various forms of independent pop, a thorough cross-section of new music activity. There are quite a number of organisations that produce CDs. The British Music Society does, though rarely featuring music of the present day. Quite a lot of composers or local organisations have issued privately made CDs, and information about them can often be found via the internet, the BMIC, the SPNM listings publication *New Notes*, or reviews in the *British Music Society Newsletter*.

▶ LOOKING TO THE FUTURE

With publishing opportunities for emerging composers so restricted, it is likely that alternative schemes will have a key role to play in ensuring distribution of composers' work. The New Voices scheme, focused on the British Music Information Centre <www.bmic.co.uk/newvoices>, was established in 1999 for younger generation composers, providing them with a website, publicity leaflets, and a central point for copying and distribution of their scores. There is also an annual promotional pack including all the information and leaflets for each individual composer, which is be mailed round to promoters New Voices now has 30 composer members. Another important development is the establishment by London Sinfonietta, in collaboration with spnm, BMIC, COMA, Sonic Arts and others, of a high-profile initiative called 'State of the Nation'. This consists of an annual weekend of performances specifically profiling music by emergent composers, with an accompanying mixture of workshops and events.

The internet is a growing resource and it may well develop into the resource for the dissemination of composer's works. As a source for information it already offers some formidable examples of what can be achieved (such as the Peter Maxwell Davies site, <http://www.maxopus.com>). As regards delivery of music online, there are a variety of copyright issues which preclude it developing in quite the way we might hope. Composers are reluctant to put works or complete recordings onto the Web if there is no mechanism for collecting payment for them. But doubtless as the problems of security codes, plug-ins, add-ons and payment systems are resolved by other users, there will be a major benefit for new music. There is also the possibility of internet and satellite broadcasting, already a reality in the US, so that a concert held anywhere could be received by a specialist audience worldwide. Unknown Public's initiation of a new music radio station online, for one month only in November 2001, is an example of what may be ahead.

▶ REFERENCES

Creating New Notes: a Policy for the Support of New Music in England (1996). London: Arts Council of England

Gunning, A. (1994) *The Composer's Guide to Music Publishing* (2nd edn.). Lonodn: The Association of Professional Composers

21 | Recordings as a research source

Lewis Foreman

In the past almost all sources of scholarship have been written. Even when recourse was made, in the pursuit, say, of biography, to the memories of the still living, the outcome would be a written statement. In the field of music what is now possible has no precedent: a viable comparative criticism of performance styles in various periods based on repeated actual hearing of the performances in question. Equally, it becomes increasingly possible to hear a wider and wider repertoire of music, though a knowledge of sources and a feeling for the specialised research methodology involved is necessary in tracing material not currently commercially available.

Sound recordings have a vast potential in many fields of interest, but the importance of audiovisual media is not fully acknowledged by archivists and librarians even now. The relative importance we place on these materials may be seen reflected in the comparative smallness of the funding of libraries for their preservation as compared to the major libraries and archives of the printed and written word (or increasingly for computer and internet access). The outcome is that scholars still have difficulty in obtaining the sound recordings they require for their work through channels similar to those that they would use for the written word. Different strategies are necessary, including becoming a collector, joining the 'invisible college' of experts and enthusiasts in the same field and tapping the antiquarian market.

▶ HISTORY AND TECHNICAL EVOLUTION

The history of sound recording is the chronicle of the establishment of successive technical norms, and their development over 10 or 20 years, only to be replaced in turn by better methods, each technical upgrade being accompanied by a massive re-recording and a further expansion of the recorded repertoire. All this with the necessity to document the recordings made by a notoriously unregulated industry, and until recently little back-up by national and regional libraries.

The very earliest recordings were on cylinders. It was the develop-ment of acoustic flat disc recording around 1900 which enabled mass production and saw the gradual development of a wider market, until superseded by electrical recording late in 1925. Electrical 78s stimulated a dramatic growth in the number of recording labels and of recordings made, dramatically reduced by the 'crash' in 1929 (which saw the end of inde-pendent labels such as Vocalion and Edison Bell), and later reduced again by the war in 1939–45. 78s were followed by microgroove long-playing records (LPs) in the late 1940s and early 1950s, followed by stereo in the 1960s, the abortive attempt to establish quad in the 1970s, and then the rapid migration from LP to compact disc (CD) in the 1980s. Each format was accompanied by the trade catalogues of the individual companies, in themselves valuable documentary sources, and each has generated its own discography, largely covering those recordings made with each process. For the history of the record industry in the UK see Anthony Pollard's sump-tuous illustrated history of *Gramophone* magazine (1998), Peter Martland's history marking the centenary of EMI (1997), and Timothy Day's thoughtful over-view of recordings and musical history (Day, 2000). Probably the most useful general history of the gramophone or phonograph is Roland Gelatt's *The Fabulous Phonograph* (1997), while those wanting to investigate the social and economic ramifications might well find Ross Laird's history of the early recording industry in Australia (1999) to be revealing about the British industry as well as the Australian.

The problem facing any potential user of sound recordings is tracing what was at one time available and has survived, and then obtaining it in a format for which one has replay equipment. Formats (reviewed in reverse order of currency) might include mini disc, DAT, compact disc, microgroove record (LP, EP, single '45') in mono or stereo, quarter-inch tape (in a variety of reel sizes, track formats and speeds), video (u-matic) tape for digital or analogue recordings, electrical course-groove recordings (78s or related speeds and different groove pitches and equalisations); acoustic course-groove 78s (or 80rpm as most of them were rated) and cylinders. From each period a large and growing, but still by no means exhaustive, library of reissued earlier material has reappeared and is now on CD, and hence finds its way into current catalogues.

Most recordings have always been a short-lived commodity, and new titles come and go and are sometimes reissued and again deleted with fright-ening rapidity. If one is developing a specialised interest one is forced to become a collector in one's research field to ensure that all relevant material remains available for continued listening and analysis.

▶ DISCOGRAPHY

Discographies have divided themselves into three main areas: classical, jazz and pop, and other than in label discographies, these different categories tend not to be mixed in the major discographies. This reflects how the market segmented, and the tastes of collectors in each area, which was served from the 1930s onwards by specialist dealers. This discussion is confined to 'classical' in the widest sense.

The two major general discographies of 78rpm records are R.D. Darrell's *Gramophone Shop Encyclopedia* (1936) and Clough and Cuming's *The World's Encyclopaedia of Recorded Music* (always referred to as '*WERM*') first published in 1952 (with supplements, largely of early LPs, in 1953 and 1957). These are invaluable sources, reflecting respectively the American and British perspectives at their publication dates. All research in which recordings feature needs to refer to these two. No library covering recordings can be authoritative without them.

Darrell was the real pioneer, with his helpful 'thumbnail' composer summaries before each entry, especially valuable in the case of unfamiliar names. It should be on all music reference shelves, and can help with a wider range of reference queries than merely the looking up of pre-war recordings. Wider in scope, and chronology, *WERM* aspired to document the electrical era on 78s. It dominates British reference collections in its field, but for some users at least it has a crippling self-imposed limitation: the omission of little-recorded composers at the time thought minor or obscure (some examples might include Cowen, B.J. Dale, Dunhill, Dyson, Armstrong Gibbs, Montague Phillips, Schreker, von Schillings, Haydn Wood), excluded to keep it within manageable bounds. Of these Gibbs, Schreker and von Schillings do appear in Darrell (1936). Yet for most purposes *WERM* is still the cornerstone of all discographical reference.

▶ ACOUSTIC RECORDINGS

The very earliest acoustic recordings, starting around 1900, were largely vocal and have been the domain of specialist collectors of vocals and opera.

The earliest period is usefully though not comprehensively covered by Roberto Bauer's *Historical Records 1898–1908/9* (1947). This invaluable source book is arranged by singer and the recordings by dated recording session. Bauer aimed to include 'all internationally famous opera and concert singers to have made lateral cut discs during the years, roughly, from 1898 to 1908–09, as well as recordings of other important vocalists whose reputations never travelled … beyond the confines of their own countries'.[1] An earlier edition, which appeared in 1937, included some names dropped from the later issue, but this is rarely seen today.

Bauer is best supplemented by Rodolfo Celletti's *Le Grandi Voci* (1964), a dictionary of singers with extensive discographies, including not only 78s and LP reissues of them, but all manner of limited availability and 'pirate' material. Since it was published, activity in researching and reissuing historical recordings has grown enormously. It nevertheless provides a useful guide, much of which has not been superseded.

Any researcher looking for early recordings of singers will want to know if a discography has ever been compiled (see Gray and Gibson, 1977) and the most likely source for a thorough detailed discographical history is the journal *The Record Collector* (not to be confused with a similarly named journal devoted to second-hand pop recordings and memorabilia), each issue of which is devoted to a single singer.[2]

Recently compiled discographies of historical recordings will also document their reissue on LP and CD, as in Arnold's discography of acoustic 78s (1997); and indeed by consulting the artists' index of the current *Classical Catalogue* one will find many historical figures who are available and reissued on CD.

As far as orchestral recordings are concerned, a surprisingly large number, considering the primitive technical quality then possible, were made in the acoustic era. These have now been documented by Claude Graveley Arnold in a massive compilation (1997) which provides a unique additional source to be placed alongside Bauer (1947), *WERM* and Darrell (1936) as a cornerstone discography of western music. Arnold demonstrates that the extent of orchestral recording using the acoustic medium is much larger than hitherto suspected, and as one knows from items that have been reissued, the quality could vary from remarkably good considering the conditions under which recordings were made, to, at their primitive worst, dreadful. But as Arnold shows, it preserved the art and styles of many artists of its period and also enshrines the music of a range of composers not performed since. This is an eye-opening compilation; it fills a long-felt need for a proper systematic documentation of the pre-electrical era of recording; the only pity is that it restricts itself to orchestral music, and does not cover the voice with orchestral accompaniment or opera, unless there is a purely orchestral interlude or overture involved. Although both *WERM* and Darrell (1936) listed a few acoustic recordings, it is now clear that they were very selective. Arnold is so much more useful, because the numbers of LP and CD reissues are given, thus providing a tool for acquiring at least some of the material for current sound collections.

Arnold is also valuable for its indexes, including two of conductors, distinguishing between those whose discography is included in its entirety, and those (such as theatre conductors) who are only selectively presented. A third index lists orchestras (invaluable, this) and a fourth instrumental soloists. These indexes have a reference value in their own right, citing discographies of the conductors, orchestras, etc. where they exist. (For a more general guide to conductors who recorded see J.L. Holmes's

Conductors on Record (1982), valuable for the extent of its coverage, though not providing details of its subjects' record numbers.)

As can be seen, any discography which takes one name or one medium and attempts to document it over the full history of recording will have a wider value to all interested in recorded music. Perhaps the best example is Creighton's monumental *Discopaedia of the Violin 1889–1971* (2nd ed 1994). A massive and exhaustive listing of violinists and the music they have recorded, it immediately becomes of value to those also researching specific composers, conductors and orchestras.

Another similarly useful guide is Brian Rust's *London Musical Shows on Record 1897–1976* (1977), which takes a very wide definition of 'musical shows' including theatre music and light music. The shows are arranged by title, and this provides another excellent window on the earliest recorded repertoires. This is an interest where Arnold's light shines brightly. To see the composers concerned listed by Arnold, with invariably longer lists than one might have compiled from other sources – Howard Carr, Percy Fletcher, Victor Herbert, Norman O'Neill, Arthur Wood, even the original production of *Hassan* (music by Delius) – is to be reminded of a repertoire now forgotten on the stage and remarkably hard to document in any other way; music today almost impossible to hear without these old recordings, and Arnold's assistance in identifying them.

▶ CURRENT RECORDINGS ON CD

In most developed countries with a significant record industry there is published a major printed catalogue of all available CDs, used equally by the trade and by collectors. These are the *RED Classical Catalogue*[3] in the UK, and the *Schwann Opus* in the USA. A comparison with the *Classical Catalogue*'s predecessor, the *Gramophone Classical Catalogue*[4] makes one realise how the number of companies and the available repertoire has grown. One only needs to glance at the current issues and then at those from 20 or 30 years ago to realise the unprecedented repertoire of recorded performances that are available on CD.

▶ REPERTOIRE SURVEYS AND 'BEST BUYS'

The Stereo Record Guide by Edward Greenfield, Robert Layton and Ivan March started publication in 1960 and developed over a dozen years, together with the *Penguin Guide to Bargain Records*.[5] The format of a continuous comparative discussion of all the 'classical' recordings available in the UK, by three of the best informed and most readable record critics, makes a long run of these valuable. After 1973 the main series was taken over by Penguin Books and became the *Penguin Guide to Compact Discs*, appearing almost every year in a variant updated edition. If a recording is deleted or not reissued it is dropped from the current issue, which maintains the distinction between less expensive CDs and full price ones.

There have been other one volume guides to recorded music. The Rough Guide series includes a useful though far from comprehensive volume on classical music (Buckley, 1994). Worth having for its independent views and younger reviewers, for this writer it is not a first choice source. In the 1990s the *Gramophone Classical Good CD Guide* (Taylor, 1998) developed as a direct competitor, drawing on the authority and style of its parent magazine, and has considerable authority.

▶ NARRATIVE GUIDES

There have been a variety of narrative guides to the recorded repertoire, some aspiring to cover all available issues, others discussing specific topics, the latter notably published by *Gramophone*. From the LP era the one all-embracing guide which retains its documentary value is Arthur Cohn's massive *Recorded Classical Music* (1981). This covers the American market and is particularly valuable for the American composers included. Apart from the Penguin and *Gramophone* guides already mentioned there has been no other widely circulated general guides to compact discs published in English.

However, there have been a number of more specific guides. Perhaps the most distinguished series is that edited by Alan Blyth (1986–), each with a distinguished panel of contributors. It started as a three volume guide to opera on record, and later included two volumes of *Song on Record* and a volume on choral music. There have been several guides to recorded opera, of value depending on the coverage required. Paul Gruber's *The Metropolitan Opera Guide to Recorded Opera* (1993) covers all the well-known operas by the leading composers but also includes a number of works by lesser figures such as Zandonai's *Francesca da Rimini*, American operas such as Douglas Moore's *The Ballad of Baby Doe* and Barber's *Vanessa*, and modern operas such as Thea Musgrave's *Mary, Queen of Scots*. These are extended discussions making a substantial hardback book, with useful and detailed index.

Singing is, however, one of the major areas in which exhaustive narrative guides and histories have almost exclusively discussed recorded performances, many of them from the earliest days of recording. John Steane's wide-ranging history (1974), based on a massive first-hand knowledge of recordings, is very helpful, as is *The Record of Singing* (Scott, 1977,

1979), a three volume illustrated survey of singers first published as the printed companions to EMI's multi-LP boxed surveys of 78rpm recordings of singers. The LPs have since appeared on CD.

Discography was long a peripheral activity in the eyes of most musicologists, developed by a host of collectors who published their work in obscure specialist journals, often in typescript. However, it was these collectors who developed the basic tools and carried out the research through co-operation between individuals and their collections. Probably the most important of these was J.R. Bennett, whose series of typescript, casebound 'Voices of the Past' label discographies (1955–77) documented the main 78rpm series principally issued by the Gramophone Company (HMV). Bennett's discography *Smetana on 3000 Records* (1994), is notable as a unique example of thematic discography (the recorded extracts from Smetana's operas being identified by music incipits). This is a wide-ranging reference book, easily overlooked, valuable also for its first-hand history of the development of recording, particularly in Germany, between the wars, and for discographical essays on the singers, data difficult to find elsewhere, and not indexed in the cumulative indexes of discographies.

Guides to specific areas were a feature of the LP era, and because of the extensive reissue of such recordings they can still be read profitably. Notable among these was Arthur Cohn's pre-stereo guide to American music on LP, *The Collector's 20th-century Music in the Western Hemisphere* (1961). Later, another distinguished treatment of the same approach was John H. Yoell's *The Nordic Sound* (1974), in which he discusses the music of 43 composers from Denmark, Norway and Sweden, with extensive reference to recordings and with an extended discography. In the CD era Dr Yoell has turned his attention to Dvorak, with *Antonin Dvorak on Records* (1991).

Such detailed discussions of recordings of specific works or groups of works are now a characteristic feature of modern musicology, a development that has involved a wide spectrum of musical amateurs and record collectors.

Lewis M. Smoley's *The Symphonies of Gustav Mahler: a critical discography* (1986) documents the critical reception of recordings of Mahler's symphonies, and underlining the continuing activity in recording Mahler since his discography first appeared, Smoley has produced a substantial supplementary volume, *Gustav Mahler's Symphonies: Critical Commentary on Recordings since 1986* (1996).

Gramophone magazine has been active in this field, and as well as the monthly magazine, with reviews also available on CD-ROM and the internet, it has published a series of magazine format guides including *Explorations* (which has appeared in three editions) a guide to avant-garde composers; the *Gramophone Film Music Good CD Guide* (1998) and the *Gramophone Opera Good CD Guide* (1997).

▶ INDEXING SERVICES

Gramophone and *Fanfare* publish annual indexes to their own magazines, the latter also available on floppy disc. The journal of the [American] Music Library Association, *Notes*, publishes a regular list of reviews of selected new recordings, indicating whether assessed pro or contra, presumably as an aid for library stock selection. Record reviews are also indexed in the musical indexing services, notably *Music Index* (see CHAPTER 11). Widely available in the USA but little known in the UK is the annual guide to CD reviews, *Index to Record and Tape Reviews* (1971–), an invaluable permanent record of CDs issues as well as to reviews.

▶ REVIEWING MAGAZINES

Where they survive, the once celebrated mass-market American record reviewing magazines (e.g. *Stereo Review*) have largely lost their role as authoritative reviewers of the full range of new recordings, and *Fanfare* and the *American Record Guide* remain as specialist journals which jointly carry an enormous international coverage and in-depth (if opinionated) reviewing. It is difficult to understand why they have little currency in music libraries in the UK, but they are available through such outlets as Tower Records, and anyone who wishes to keep abreast of the more obscure issues on an international range of labels needs to see them.

▶ RECORDINGS NOT ISSUED COMMERCIALLY

During the period of shellac records it was very difficult for individuals to make a recording without the intervention of one of the main record companies, dependent as the activity was on trained staff and an industrial facility to produce the finished product. The development of home recording, and the demands of radio for an instantaneous recording medium of high quality resulted in the development of a variety of direct cut disc machines during the 1930s and 1940s and ultimately the tape recorder, which appeared in Germany during the war and was disseminated as a home recording medium from the 1950s onwards, at much the same time as VHF radio appeared. Consequently, individuals were able to develop private collections of off-air and non-commercial material. Well-known musicologists, critics and performers in particular, often own substantial collections of material unparalleled even by official archives. These remain almost completely undocumented, unless they are deposited in an archive or library. A prime example is the Leech Collection, now in the National Sound Archive, British Library. This consists of some 1,200 78rpm acetates[6] of BBC broadcasts recorded domestically off-air between 1934 and 1954. Little is complete owing to the necessity to turn over every four minutes or so, but it includes some remarkable items, including the first performance of Vaughan Williams's Fifth Symphony conducted by the composer in 1943, and also his 1946 Promenade Concert performance of his *London Symphony*.

With the emergence of LPs, the 1950s was also the time when it became easy to have custom-pressings made, and this resulted in the proliferation of unauthorised issues of off-air and private material, loosely referred to as 'pirate'. A typical example, important in retrospect, is the 'Golden Age of Opera' series of LPs. They are documented in Greenwood Press's 'Discographies' series in *EJS: Discography of the Edward J Smith Recordings: "The Golden Age of Opera" 1956–1971* (Shaman *et al.*, 1994). ostensibly an analysis of the catalogue of none too carefully prepared pirate opera recordings issued in the 'Golden Age of Opera' series between 1956 and 1971. To any collector that has any of the LPs issued in the series, this book is a must. Yet because of the vast range of operatic performances covered, and the authors' detailed scholarly investigation of these performances and Smith's recordings of them, encompassing material going back to the turn of the century and before, this is an essential reference book for anyone interested in opera in the first half of the twentieth century, and its composers and performers. Because of the amazing detail and authority of the research it is, unlike most catalogues and discographies, an excellent and stimulating read in its own right.

There have been comparatively few studies of composers from the viewpoint of their recorded repertoire, but Alan Poulton's volume-length illustrated discography of Walton (1980) is still valuable.

▶ THE MEANING OF DISCOGRAPHY

The term 'discography' originated in the 1930s to describe a catalogue of sound recordings. At that time the only medium used for making such recordings was the disc; cylinder records were outmoded and no longer manufactured, and tape and other forms of recording had not been brought to practical realisation. Thus the fact that the physical format of a disc became synonymous with sound recordings made logical a term such as 'discography' to describe a catalogue of recordings on disc, and by extension any catalogue of sound recordings and associated material. The earliest published use of the word discography appears to be in *Melody Maker* in December 1935. However, it may well be that the term was in use verbally before it appeared in print, for T.W. Southam claimed first use in 1933.[7]

The first use of 'discography' in a scholarly tool is probably Charles Delaunay's *Hot Discographie*, first published in France in 1936.[8] While amateur discographers in the jazz field pioneered the art of discography – as indeed they had to do in a field where the tradition was predominantly an aural one, the influence of Darrell (1936) was probably more considerable in the long run. It was the establishment of Darrell's encyclopaedia in America in the 1930s, and the *World Encyclopedia of Recorded Music* in the UK in 1952, that put the seal of respectability on what had been previously regarded as an amateur art. At the same time these two initiatives became a model for, and provided the basic working tools for, all future workers in this field.

Clough and Cuming wrote in their introduction that 'The principles and procedures of discography were laid down by R.D. Darrell in his *Gramophone Shop Encyclopedia of Recorded Music* ... and have been followed by subsequent compilers; the present work is planned on similar lines, and we must acknowledge what is indeed obvious, the inspiration and instruction we have derived from Darrell's work.'[9]

R.D. Darrell (in a letter to the present author)[10] briefly sketched the circumstances of the publication of the first edition of his work as follows: 'In the mid '30s (I started formal work on *GSERM* in the spring of 1934) we didn't even have the word discography, much less the art/science itself. What I had in mind was the first *catalogue raisonné* of all (I hoped) serious music on records, and my approach was largely intuitive (lacking any models that I knew of). I spent a great deal of time, thought and experiment on the typographical arrangement of my materials, seeking to get the maximum information in a minimum space. You might be interested to learn about a couple of influential factors: I made use of two different types of preparatory exercise as it were: 1 – a series of pseudonymous letters in the *Phonograph Monthly Review* (1926–1932) outlining the principal recorded works of various mostly contemporary composers; 2 – more formal surveys, recorded symphonies, recorded chamber music, etc. in the *Music Lovers' Guide* (1932–1934) (precursor of the present day *American Record Guide*).'

▶ BIBLIOGRAPHY OF DISCOGRAPHIES

There have been several attempts to compile a bibliography of discographies, but the established source is now Gray and Gibson's bibliography (1977), which by treating separate musical topics in five volumes, has presented specific experts with an appropriate single volume source:

1   Classical Music, 1925–1975
2   Jazz
3   Popular Music

4   Ethnic and Folk Music
5   Label Lists, Speech and Animal Sounds.

The appearance of Michael H. Gray and Gerald Gibson's *Bibliography of Discographies* (1977) and its monster supplement (Gray, 1989) gave the activity academic 'respectability' as well as allowing the widespread existing discographical literature to be retrieved and cited. This has been updated by annual bibliographies in the *Journal of the Association of Recorded Sound Collections*, but the enormous growth of the 'Classical Music' volume between the first and second editions underlines what an active field this is.

► DISCOGRAPHIES IN SERIES

Greenwood Press's 'Discographies' series is the major series, notable for its variety, and already numbering over 70 titles. Its early preoccupation with label histories, pop music and jazz, may have caused those interested in classical repertoire and opera not to investigate the series, which includes valuable additions to the research library. The series has been particularly influential in publishing discographical histories of major orchestras in the USA and the UK. Possibly the most substantial of these is Philip Stuart's *The London Philharmonic Discography* (1997), which by its chronological arrangement of sessions and massive assembly of detail constitutes a major documentary history of the British orchestral scene from 1932 to 1996 valuable to all future historians. This documentary importance as a general reference tool is reinforced by the indexes of repertoire, conductors and the annotated index of recording locations.

Emphasising the importance of detailed documentation of a complex field, we might also note from the Greenwood Press series *Parsifal on Record: a Discography of Complete Recordings. Selections and Excerpts ...* by Jonathan Brown (1992). Among performers Glenn Gould was a particularly interesting figure in the history of recording, in view of his opinion that recording had now superseded live performances for most people. Nancy Canning's *A Glenn Gould Catalogue* (1992) documents Gould's recordings, repertoire and bibliography against the chronology of his career.

There is also a strong discographical component in the Greenwood Press parallel series 'Bio-bibliographies in the performing arts' though here the emphasis is on a much more popular repertoire. William McKeen's *Bob Dylan: a Bio-bibliography*, William McKeen's *The Beatles: a Bio-bibliography* and Patsy Guy Hammontree's *Elvis Presley: a Bio-bibliography* are probably self-recommending for many collections. James Fisher's *Al Jolson: a Bio-bibliography* is interesting for the inclusion of both 'filmography' and discography.

▶ DISCOGRAPHIES IN MONOGRAPHS

Should monographs on composers, performing artists and musical topics contain a discography? It has certainly been said that some publishers' editors are not sympathetic, because it is a feature that quickly goes out of date. This is short-sighted, for discographies have a documentary importance central to any permanent musical study, because of the difficulty of obtaining such information. Composer and performer biographies are to be censured if they fail to provide a discography.

Thus Carole Rosen's *The Goossens: a Musical Century* (1993) has wide-ranging performer discographies of the Goossens family by Raymond E. Cooke, though regrettably omitting a discography of the music Eugene Goossens composed. This documents Sir Eugene Goossens' recording career between the wars for the first time, starting in the acoustic era and lasting until LP. Similarly pioneering is the discography in Arthur Jacobs' *Henry J Wood: Maker of the Proms* (1994), listing all his orchestral 78rpm recordings. Yet another conductor similarly treated is Stephen Lloyd's detailed study of Sir Dan Godfrey (1995) with a detailed discography of the Bournemouth Municipal Orchestra.

▶ RECORD REVIEWING AND GUIDES TO RECORDINGS

As we have seen, the record industry is characterised by a well-developed infrastructure of reviewing, with published guides and 'best buys'. Depending on the subject, any researcher may find it rewarding to explore American or European reviewing journals or guides.

Reviewing takes place widely, in newspapers and the weekly and monthly press, though tracing some of them retrospectively may well not always be easy. Probably all in the record business would still agree that the principal British reviewing journal is *Gramophone*, which has been published monthly since 1923. With its annual index and using the *Classical Catalogue* as an index to reviews of current material, and with the availability of reviews from 1983 free of charge on the internet, it retains its position as a *the* British reviewing journal of record.

Generally, the reviewing scene has changed dramatically over the last 20 years, with the demise of a range of reviewing journals and the rise of new ones. Probably the second most important British reviewing journal is now the *BBC Music Magazine* (1992–), together with three other active journals: *CD Review* (1985–), *Classic CD* (1990–) and *Classic FM* (1995–). A number of CD retailers have started their own (usually free) reviewing magazines, of which the Music Discount Centre's *Classical Express* in newspaper format reached its 113th issue in August 1999, and is probably the most useful. With the appearance of MusicWeb (see p. 88) as a major reviewing journal on the internet the printed journals may well find themselves faced with a new competitor able to cover many reviews per issue in a timely way.

► SOUND ARCHIVES

Existing sound recording libraries are not as well developed as book libraries, nor are their facilities and practices. In the UK the principal collection is the National Sound Archive (NSA) at the British Library, where listening carrels are available without charge, by appointment. The NSA catalogue, CADENSA is available via the internet (Gordon, 2001) but although a powerful tool when searching for specific items, when compiling a discography its front-end is somewhat cumbersome in terms of layout, discographical elements and the generation of lists.

The Barbican Music Library of the City of London Public Libraries hosts the Music Performance Research Centre collection, founded by John Tolanski (<www.musicpreserved.org>), and consists of DAT recordings of 'live' material, including not only off-air but also items recorded live in the hall and in London opera houses, which MPRC has permission to make in London halls. Historical material includes such items as 1940s performances of Mahler symphonies conducted by Sir Adrian Boult. Recordings are available for listening in the library. There is no published catalogue, but a printed handlist is held in the library, and a printed occasional *Journal of MPRC* promotes the collection and the concept.[11]

The first attempt at a directory of sound recordings collections had appeared in the USA in 1967 (Association for Recorded Sound Collections, 1967) and consisted largely of private collections of individuals. That is probably almost entirely superseded. The most recent directory in the UK was issued by the British Library in 1989 (Weerasinghe, 1989).

► REFERENCES

American Record Guide: the Record Connoisseur's Magazine (1976–) (bi-monthly). Previously *The Music Lover's Guide, Listener's Record Guide* (1935–72). Record Guide Productions, 4412 Braddock Street, Cincinnati, Ohio 45204

Arnold, C.G. (1997) *The Orchestra on Record 1896–1926 – an Encyclopedia of Orchestral Recordings made by the Acoustical Process.* Westport, Connecticut: Greenwood Press [Discographies, Number 73]

Association for Recorded Sound Collections (1967) *A Preliminary Directory of Sound recordings Collections in the United States and Canada.* New York: New York Public Library

Bauer, R. (1947) *Historical Records 1898–1908/9.* London: Sidgwick & Jackson

Bennett, J.R. (1955–77) *Voices of the Past.* Tarrant Hinton: The Oakwood Press
    Vol. 1: *HMV English Catalogue*
    Vol. 2: *HMV Italian Catalogue*
    Vol. 3: *Dischi Fonotipia*
    Vol. 4 *The International 'Red Label' Catalogue HMV DB 12-inch series*
    Vol. 5: *HMV Black Label Catalogue (D & E Series)*
    Vol. 6: *The International 'Red Label' Catalogue HMV DA series*
    Vol. 7: *HMV German Catalogue*
    Vol. 8 *The Columbia Catalogue*
    Vol. 9: *HMV French Catalogue*

Bennett, J.R. (1974) *Smetana on 3000 Records.* Tarrant Hinton, Dorset: The Oakwood Press

Blyth, A. (ed.) (1986–) *Song on Record.* Cambridge: Cambridge University Press
    Vol. 1: *Lieder* (1986)
    Vol. 2: (1988)

Brown, J. (1992) *Parsifal on Record: a Discography of Complete Recordings. Selections And Excerpts . . .* Westport, Conn.: Greenwood Press

Buckley, J. (1994) *Classical Music on CD The Rough Guide.* The Rough Guides

Canning, N. (1992) *A Glen Gould Catalogue.* Westport, Conn.: Greenwood Press

Celletti, R. (ed.) (1964) *Le Grandi Voci – dizionario critico-biografico dei cantanti con discografia operistica.* Rome: Istituto per la Collaborazione Culturale

Clough, F.F. and Cuming, G.J. (1952) *The World's Encyclopaedia of Recorded Music* (supplements 1953, 1957). London, Sidgwick & Jackson

Cohn, A. (1961) *The Collector's 20th-Century Music in the Western Hemisphere.* Philadelphia & New York: J.B. Lippincott (Keystone Books)

Cohn, A. (1981) *Recorded Classical Music – a Critical Guide to Compositions and Performances.* New York: Schirmer Books

Creighton, J. (1994) *Discopaedia of the Violin 1889–1971* (1st edn. Toronto, 1971). Burling, Ontario: Records Past Publishing

Darrell, R.D. (1936) *Gramophone Shop Encyclopedia* (new editions in 1942 and 1948) New York City: The Gramophone Shop Inc.

Day, T. (2000) *A century of Recorded Music: listening to musical history.* New Haven and London: Yale University Press

Delaunay, C. (1936) *Hot Discographie.* Paris

Fanfare: the Magazine for Serious Record Collectors (1977–) (bi-monthly). PO Box 17, Tenafly, NJ 07670 (<fanfaremag@aol.com>)

Foreman, L. (1974) *Systematic Discography.* Hawdon, Conn: Linnet Books and London: Clive Bingley

Gelatt, R. (1997) *The Fabulous Phonograph 1877–1977* (2nd rev. edn.). London: Cassell

Gordon, A. (2001) 'Cadensa on the web' *Brio* Autumn/Winter 2001 vol 38 no 2 pp. 24–30

Gramophone Classical Catalogue (quarterly 1953–) (later *RED Classical Catalogue*)

Gramophone Explorations: Counter-currents in Modern Music (1996–8) (Issues 1–3). Harrow: Gramophone

Gramophone Opera Good CD Guide (1997) (2nd edn.). Harrow: Gramophone

Gray, M.H. and Gibson, G. (1977) *Bibliography of Discographies: Vol. 1 Classical Music 1925–1975.* New York: Bowker

Gray, M.H. (1989) *Classical Music Discographies 1976–1988: a bibliography.* Westport, Conn.: Greenwood Press

Green, A. (1999) Sound Stage. *Classical Music,* 7 (August), 22

Gruber, P. (1993) *The Metropolitan Opera Guide to Recorded Opera.* London: Thames & Hudson

Holmes, J.L. (1982) *Conductors on Record.* London: Gollancz

Jacobs, A. (1994) *Henry J Wood: Maker of the Proms.* London: Methuen

Laird, R. (1999) *Sound Beginnings – the Early Record Industry in Australia.* Sydney: Currency Press

Lloyd, S. (1995) *Sir Dan Godfrey Champion of British Composers – a Chronology of Forty Years' Music-making with the Bournemouth Municipal Orchestra.* London: Thames Publishing

Martland, P. (1997) *Since Records Began – EMI the First 100 years.* London: B.T. Batsford

Pollard, A. (1998) *Gramophone – the First 75 years.* Harrow: Gramophone Publications Ltd

Poulton, A. (1980) *The Recorded Works of Sir William Walton – a Discography Celebrating 50 years of Recording History 1929–79.* Kidderminster: Bravura Publications

Record and Tape Reviews Index (1971–) (annual) (later *Index to Record and Tape Reviews*). Metuchen, NJ: Scarecrow Press

R E D Classical 1997 Catalogue (1997) (master edition). London: Retail Entertainment Data

Rosen, C. (1993) *The Goossens: a Musical Century.* London: Andre Deutsch

Rust, B. (1977) *London Musical Shows on Record 1897–1976.* Harrow: Gramophone

Schwann Opus (Reference Guide to Classical Music) (quarterly). Woodland, California

Scott, M. (1977) *The Record of Singing to 1914.* London: Duckworth

Scott, M. (1979) *The Record of Singing Volume Two: 1914 to 1925.* London: Duckworth

Shaap, W.E. and Avakian, G. (1948) *New Hot Discography.* New York: Criterion

Shaman, W., Collins, W.J. and Goodwin, C.M. (1994) *EJS: Discography of the Edward J Smith Recordings: "The Golden Age of Opera" 1956–1971.* Westport, Conn.: Greenwood Press [Discographies Series vol. 54]

Smoley, L.M. (1986) *The Symphonies of Gustav Mahler: a Critical Discography*. Westport, Conn.: Greenwood Press

Smoley, L.M. (1996) *Gustav Mahler's Symphonies: Critical Commentary on Recordings since 1986*. Westport, Conn.: Greenwood Press

Steane, J. (1974) *The Grand Tradition — Seventy Years of Singing on Record*. London: Duckworth

Stuart, P. (1997) *The London Philharmonic Discography*. Westport, Conn.: Greenwood Press [Discographies, Number 69]

Taylor, M. (ed.) (1998) *Gramophone Classical Good CD Guide 1999* (12th edn.). Harrow: Gramophone

Walker, M (ed.) (1998) *Gramophone Film Music Good CD Guide* (3rd edn.). Harrow: Gramophone

Weerasinghe, L. (1989) *Directory of Recorded Sound Resources in the United Kingdom* (research by Jeremy Silver). London: British Library

Yoell, J.H. (1974) *The Nordic Sound*. Boston, Crescendo Publishing Co.

Yoell, J.H. (1991) *Antonín Dvořák on Records*. Westport, Conn.: Greenwood Press (Discographies, Number 46.)

▶ NOTES

1. 'Foreword' in Bauer (1947), p. 7.
2. The Record Collector, 111 Longshots Close, Broomfield, Chelmsford, Essex CM1 7DU. (See <www.Therecordcollector.org>)
3. *R E D Classical 1997 Catalogue*. The master edition appears in June and December and is updated by monthly supplements available on subscription.
4. *Gramophone Classical Catalogue* became *RED Classical Catalogue*. The change to large format came in 1990.
5. *The Stereo Record Guide* first appeared from the Long Playing Record Library Ltd in 1960. In parallel came *A Guide to the Bargain Records*, starting in 1962. Later the project was taken over by Penguin who developed it into the era of compact discs.
6. Direct disc recording was developed in the 1930s, the discs being of glass or aluminium, and the recording medium a thin layer of cellulose acetate, hence 'acetates'.
7. T.W. Southam (1974) Discography [letter to the editor]. *Gramophone*, Jan, 1974, p. 1503. 'In 1933 some friends and I brought out a rather high-brow quarterly in Hong-Kong ... in the second of which I wrote "which also contains an up to date discography". (I should like to think that I am the first in the field with this ugly, though now necessary word.)'
8. Delaunay, C. (1936) *Hot Discographie*. Paris. (For an enthusiastic discussion of discography see Jerry Atkins' essay 'Magnificent Obsession: the discographers' <www.16.brinkster.com.fitzgera/discog/obsess.htm>).
9. Clough and Cuming (1952), p. v.
10. Foreman (1974), p. 136.
11. Various articles have appeared describing it, most recently at the time of writing, Green (1999).

22 Film and its music

David Whittle

Film music, as an area for musicological research, has grown enormously in recent years. The wealth of material, by both specialist composers for film and by those who made their name in the concert hall, has been discovered and much research is now in progress.

The scores (or at least themes) from major recent films are frequently published in one form or another, and the soundtracks are issued, but the person whose interest is in older work will find that it has not been preserved to anything like the same degree. Indeed, it is fair to say that film scores have been treated disgracefully by many studios and production companies, and as a result of their (in some cases systematic) destruction, much has been lost. Acclaimed scores have fared no better. For the 70th birthday concert of the English composer Malcolm Arnold in 1991, it was decided that some of the Oscar-winning score he had written for *The Bridge on the River Kwai* should be included. Investigations revealed that the manuscript no longer existed, and the music had to be rescored from the soundtrack.

The music score has always suffered from being the last part of the film to be completed. It could not be composed until the film had been shot, and there was a consequent pressure from the production team for it to be written and recorded within as short a period as possible. As a result, there was little chance to make copies of a score, and the manuscript was held either by the studio or mislaid after recording.

Any work on film music is also hampered by the lack of a central register of the genre. Attempts are being made to correct this (see below), but for the moment most work has to be done piecemeal. The archives of production companies are often sadly incomplete, if indeed they exist at all. Many companies have, over the years, been taken over, merged or gone out of existence, and their archives have gone with them.

▶ BOOKS ABOUT FILM MUSIC

There has been a rich literature about film music, characterised by the fact that the earliest published accounts of the music written in the first 10 or 15 years after the introduction of the sound film retain their importance. Possibly the earliest of these is Kurt London's *Film Music*, published with a foreword by Constant Lambert in 1936. For its coverage, for its detail and for its illustrations, this is a valuable source.

During the war there was an enormous burgeoning of the British film industry, and particularly of film music written by leading composers. This was the time of Walton's music for Shakespeare's *Henry V* and Vaughan Williams's *Forty Ninth Parallel*, *Coastal Command* and *The Story of a Flemish Farm*. Many scores soon to be regarded as classics were about to appear. John Huntley's wide-ranging guide of the time, *British Film Music* (1947), with its composer and artist biographies, accounts of films and general over-view of the time has never been superseded and it remains a valuable source. This is also true of Roger Manvell and John Huntley's later book *The Technique of Film Music* (1957), particularly in its later enlarged edition by Richard Arnell and Peter Day (1975). The early success of British film music resulted in the fifth edition of *Grove* including a long and detailed entry with a valuable bibliography to which early reference should be made by all exploring this subject for the first time.

In the *New Grove*, which appeared in 1980, a new film music article by Christopher Palmer reflected the more established character of film music a further quarter-century on. Palmer, the author of one of the cornerstone books on film music, *The Composer in Hollywood* (1990) was one of the key figures in pioneering the rescue of film scores whose score was lost, and recording them for issue on CD. His many CD booklet notes are themselves important contributions to the literature.

There have been various other general guides to film music, and any good music library will probably have a selection. A typical example is Tony Thomas's *Music for the Movies* (1973), written very much from an American perspective. Its list of recordings and extended list of scores by a limited repertoire of composers reflects its early-1970s perspective, though it is still very useful for figures such as George Antheil and Laurence Rosenthal.

▶ SOURCES

My own work on the English composer Bruce Montgomery (Whittle, 1998), who was active as a composer of film music in the 1950s and 1960s, has highlighted many of the problems with which one is faced when attempting to catalogue film music. There are five possible sources for an accurate description of the music for any film. In order of completion these are: music measurement sheets, score, soundtrack, music cue sheets and, sometimes, correspondence. The music measurement sheets are compiled by the director and composer after the film has been shot and list with detailed timings the music which is to be composed and which action it accompanies. If these survive, they are likely to be found in the composer's own archive. The manuscript scores do not always survive, particularly from earlier films. In the UK in the 1950s and 1960s, for example, it was common for composers to work with contracts that made their scores the copyright property of the film company. Short deadlines and lack of copying facilities led to the original autograph score being the sole copy.[1]

After the recording, a score remained in the studio archives until such time as it was deemed surplus to requirements, at which point it was often destroyed. The soundtrack should always be available, but there are instances of films of which even the British Film Institute (BFI) has neither record nor copy. The music cue sheets were compiled after the film was completed and detail each section of music, its location within the film, the action it accompanies, its duration and composer. These were produced for reasons of copyright and royalties, and were lodged with the Performing Right Society (PRS). The production company also retained a copy. Correspondence between the composer and the production team can throw light on certain difficulties, as can personal papers.

With five such sources, it should be possible to give an accurate description and provenance of all music within any film. But my experiences with the music of Bruce Montgomery have proved this is not always the case. The music measurement sheets rarely survive. If they do, they do not always represent the music which actually finds its way on to the soundtrack. Subsequent conversations between composer and director occasionally altered a decision made in the original discussion. The same is true of that rarity, a surviving score. The existence of a section in manuscript does not always mean that it found its way on to the soundtrack. There are many examples of sections which were either not recorded at all, or were recorded but subsequently not used. If a section was found to conflict too much with dialogue or action, for instance, the volume might be taken down, or the section might be left out completely. This happened at the dubbing stage. There are examples in Montgomery's work where sections are faded out on the soundtrack before their conclusion in the original score. When sections do not survive in manuscript, even within an apparently quite complete score, this does not necessarily mean that the section was never composed or used.

The soundtrack provides concrete evidence of music but, for the reasons given above, it is not always possible to hear it. The music cue sheet, produced for legal reasons, ought to be the most accurate document.

It was the last document to be produced, and contains details which had important legal and financial implications for the composer and publisher. The production company would produce a detailed sheet which the PRS usually abbreviated to the bare essentials. However, there are, in my experience, instances of cue sheets not being accurate. They may give the wrong composer, or an inaccurate duration of a section or fail to list a section which is heard on the soundtrack or, in some cases, list a section which does not appear on the soundtrack. One composer might have written a theme which another orchestrated or arranged. Composers under pressure of time (and Montgomery frequently was) sometimes called for help from a colleague, and for contractual reasons the name of this composer did not appear on the film credits, nor, on occasions, did it feature on the cue sheet. In 1955 Montgomery wrote the score for *Cartouche*, and he engaged Douglas Gamley to write one lengthy section for him. Gamley's name does not appear on the cue sheet, and a letter through Montgomery's agents notes that all the rights in the music by Gamley for the film pass to Montgomery. The situation is made worse by the fact that, despite their important status, there are films for which the PRS does not hold a copy of the cue sheet, and those retained by the production companies have often been lost. Correspondence can occasionally throw light on the possible involvement of other composers. In the case of Montgomery, the production company paid him his total fee, and any helpers received their fee directly from Montgomery.

And there are further anomalies. One example will suffice to illustrate the problems. In 1958 Montgomery wrote the score for an Irish film *Sins of the Father* (also known as *Home is the Hero*). The cue sheet compiled by the production company has not survived, and the sheet held by the PRS lists sections only by time and not by action. The music measurement sheets, however, do survive. From these it has been possible to make up a more detailed cue sheet, along the lines of the one that should have been compiled by the production company. The timings asked for on the measurement sheets match exactly the timings given on the PRS sheet. The strange thing here, though, is that the timings on Montgomery's surviving autograph score do not always agree with these documents. It is possible that Montgomery might have needed to alter certain timings, but if he did why does the cue sheet show the timings which were originally agreed? Something is wrong here if we believe that the progression was measurement sheets, score, recording, cue sheet. Could it be that the production company failed to check the completed film properly and merely assumed the timings were the same as originally measured? This possibility raises doubts about cue sheets for other films for which we do not have so much detail. In this particular instance the question cannot be answered conclusively, as neither the BFI nor the Irish Film Institute has a copy of *Sins of the Father*.

► ARCHIVES

As far as the British scene is concerned, a good starting point for the researcher is the British Universities Film and Video Council's *Researcher's Guide to British Film and Television Collections* (1989), which as well as accounts of a wide selection of archives, many of which are not going to be of musical interest, also includes a wide-ranging bibliography, a useful section of the 1988 Copyright Act and a list of British legislation.

Now somewhat out of date, Richard A. Nelson's 1978 list of media archives in the then West Germany also touches on the rest of Europe and American media archives. Also out of date, but still a valuable source, with a strong American bias, is Martin Marks's extended 40-page-article 'Film Music: the material, literature, and present state of research' which appeared in the journal *Notes* of the Music Library Association (December 1979).

In the UK the first port of call for researchers into film music should be the British Film Institute (BFI) (21 Stephen Street, London W1P 1PL; Tel: 020 7255 1444; Fax: 020 7436 7950). The BFI is the world's largest collection of information on films and is a member of the International Federation of Film Archives (FIAF). Although its holdings of actual scores are negligible, its central catalogue will often be the start of any search into particular films. The BFI contains the National Film Archive, and it is possible to view films although, as previously noted, there are films which are not in the Archive. The Performing Right Society (PRS) (29–33 Berners Street, London W1P 4AA; Tel: 020 7580 5544; Fax: 020 7631 4138) holds music cue sheets to most films and, in the case of deceased composers, can direct communications to the present copyright holder.

The tracing of surviving scores is a more difficult business, as they are scattered throughout private and public collections. As the study of film music grows in universities, so departments are attempting to build up their own libraries of material. As is the case for the actual films, there is no central register, but the National Register of Archives (<http//www.hmc. gov.uk/nra>) may yield information, as may the *ASLIB Directory of Information Sources*.

For recordings of film music, the National Sound Archive (now at the British Library, 96 Euston Road, London NW1 2DB) has growing holdings of material of both commercial and private natures.

In the USA, much archival material relating to the major studios concerning film music has been discarded. Columbia and Universal destroyed portions of their archives because of a lack of space, but it was MGM discarding almost everything of value that led, in 1974, to the founding of what is now known as the Film Music Society (P.O. Box 93536, Hollywood, CA 90093–0536). This society is increasingly building up a collection of film scores (including the Louise Schnauber Silent Film Music

Collection and scores by Ray Heindorf). It is also developing a systematic plan for undertaking the long-term goal of creating a catalogue of film music. *The Union Catalog of Film Music* (described in a brief note in the *Music Library Association Newsletter*[2]) will be a comprehensive list of all film music holdings, archives and collections currently housed in various repositories throughout the United States, including film studio archives and music libraries, university libraries, government facilities and private collections. Until this work is completed, a more than adequate substitute is the accurately titled *Film Music Collections in the United States: A Guide*, a lengthy and comprehensive account of the locations of preserved film scores in the USA, which can be found on the internet at <http://www.film-musicsociety.org/guide>.

The prime focus of the interest of most film music buffs is to hear the music and to see the films for which it was written. The general guides to films, such as *Halliwell's Film Guide* (Walker, 1999), while mentioning the composer of many of the entries, tend not to provide full information and certainly do not provide an index of composers. Nevertheless these guides now indicate the commercial availability of films on video (or, increasingly, laser disk) and many enthusiasts will want to purchase the video in order to hear the music, from where the authentic statement of the performers and musical direction can be obtained.

Complete lists of composer's films can be hard to come by, and although they will usually be included in complete catalogues of a composer's music (see CHAPTER 17), film guides can be supplemented by reference works listing film music comprehensively. An early attempt to address this need, and valuable for that, is Clifford McCarty's *Film Composers in America: a Check List of their work*, which covered 163 names and added an index of orchestrators. But for all practical purposes James L. Limbacher is the first place to consult with the two basic queries: 'what else did that composer write?', and (the question of all film music buffs looking through TV listing magazines such as *Radio Times*) 'who wrote the music for that film?' It is curious but, even now, it does not seem to have dawned on those scheduling films on television, that some viewers are there for the music! Limbacher's basic volume, *Film Music: from Violins to Video*, appeared in 1974 and covered film titles and dates, listing films with their composer and composers and their films, with an extended discography. That made an enormously large volume at 835 pages, but such was the rate of development that by 1981 a supplementary volume was necessary, which provided corrections and addenda to the first and continued the story with various new lists such as a list of Academy Awards for best film music and a list of composers who had died. A later attempt to provide access to the film music written by a large number of composers, *Soundings* by Stewart R. Craggs, while useful and much more up-to-date, is compromised by a variety of errors (usefully discussed by Erik Levi in his review in *Brio* Spring/Summer 1999 p. 79–80).

Most interest in film music tends to be centred on recordings, but a wide representation of short numbers, title music and songs also appeared (and still does) as sheet music, and Donald J. Stubblebine's *British Cinema Sheet Music* (1997) covers 80 years and includes Australia and Canada in its scope.

Film music is an area where all manner of composer-societies are active, usually producing a journal or newsletter. William Alwyn, Malcolm Arnold, Jerry Goldsmith, Bernard Herrmann, Erich Korngold, Ennio Morricone, Alan Rawsthorne, Max Steiner and John Williams are examples of composers who have a society dedicated to their work. Taking just one of these at random, *Pro Musica Sana*, the quarterly publication of the Miklós Rózsa Society, in the issue for Summer 1980 included an invaluable article on the film music of William Alwyn with a comprehensive filmography and discography of recorded film music, both surprisingly long. Such a citation tends to evade the standard bibliographical sources, and yet is of prime importance to anyone researching Alwyn. Periodicals such as *Film Score Monthly* (5455 Wilshire Blvd., Suite 1500 Los Angeles, CA 90036–4201 or <www.filmscoremonthly.com>) are other sources of information. Film scripts in printed form are also of value to the researcher, particularly when (as with the series *Classic Film Scripts* published by Lorrimer Publishing, one of which is Laurence Olivier's *Henry V*[3]) they signal music cues.

► ACADEMIC RECOGNITION OF FILM MUSIC

Universities are beginning formally to recognise the importance of film music with the establishment of film music resource centres and programmes of study. In the UK a leading example is the Film Music Resource Centre in the Department of Music at the University of York, established primarily to preserve British film scores in manuscript, and the development of a library of books and periodicals as the tools of research. In the 1970s and 1980s, major projects were 'mounted in reconstructing silent film scores. Erik Satie's music for René Clair's *Entr'acte* was performed to the film in staged productions of Satie's dada ballet *Relâche* in 1975 and in 1979 York heard the first modern synchronised performances (with full orchestra) of Edmund Meisel's powerful music to Sergei Eisenstein's epic *October.*'[4] Inventories such as the *Index to Theses* (<www.theses.com>) list current research. (See Jeremy Dibble's account of tracing theses in CHAPTER 13.)

David Kershaw, the founder-director of the Film Music Resource Centre at York, underlines how our current interest in film music was not reflected in the early days, composers in particular regarding their film music as of little importance. He tells how the British composer 'Elizabeth

Lutyens came to talk at York some time ago when she was a lecturer. She had no regard whatsoever for her film music, and was really quite irritated by our interest in it. If you knew Elizabeth Lutyens you will know just how irritated she could be; really *quite* irritated . . .'[5]

Anecdotal evidence suggests that when Denham Studios was bull-dozed, its archive of music manuscripts was burned. It is known that destroyed scores included music by William Alwyn and Clifton Parker. However, other scores and sketches were held by the composers themselves and survive.

Various recording companies have specialised lists which include film music. In the UK, Silvascreen specialises in soundtracks, whilst Marco Polo, Chandos and ASV (amongst others) follow to a lesser extent. In the USA, Varèse Sarabande is one of the leading companies in this field. *The Gramophone Film Music Good CD Guide*[6] (1998) (presently in its third edition) is a comprehensive mine of information to current releases.

▶ REFERENCES

ASLIB Directory of Information Sources (10th edn.). (1999)

British Universities Film and Video Council (1989) *Researcher's Guide to British Film and Television Collections*

Craggs, S.R. (1998) *Soundtracks – an International Directory of Composers for Film.* Aldershot: Ashgate

Huntley, J. (1947) *British Film Music.* Skelton Robinson

Kershaw, D. (1992) 'Film Music' In: L. Foreman (ed.) *Lost and Only Sometimes Found – a Seminar on Music Publishing and Archives,* pp. 40–3. Upminster, Essex: British Music Society

Limbacher, J. (1974) *Film Music: from Violins to Video.* Metuchen, NJ: Scarecrow Press

Limbacher, J. (1981) *Keeping Score: Film Music 1972–79.* Metuchen, NJ: Scarecrow Press

London, K. (1936) *Film Music,* trans. E.S. Bensinger. London: Faber

Manvell, R. and Huntley, J. (1957) *The Technique of Film Music.* Communications Arts Books. New York, Hastings House (revised and enlarged by R. Arnell and P. Day – 1975)

Marks, M. (1979) Film Music: the material, literature, and present state of research. *Notes: The Quarterly Journal of the Music Library Association,* 36, No. 2 (December), 282–325 [This article appears updated in the same author's (1997) *Music and the Silent Film,* OUP]

McCarthy, C. *Film Composers in America: a Check List of their Work*

Nelson, R.A. (1978) Germany and the German Film, 1939–1945: an annotated research bibliography, Part 3: Research libraries, archives and other sources. *Journal of the University Film Association*, 30, No. 1 (Winter), 53–72

Oliver, E. (ed.) (1989) *Researcher's Guide to British Film & Television Collections*. London: British Universities Film & Video Council (new revised edition)

Palmer, C. (1990) *The Composer in Hollywood*. London: Marion Boyars

Stubblebine, D.J. (1997) *British Cinema Sheet Music – a Comprehensive Listing of Film Music Published in the United Kingdom, Canada and Australia, 1916 through 1994*. Jefferson, North Carolina: McFarland & Co.

Thomas, T. (1973) *Music for the Movies*. South Brunswick & New York: A S Barnes & Co; London: Tantivy Press

Walker, J. (ed.) (1999) *Halliwell's Film & Video Guide 2000*. London: Harper Collins

Whittle, D.M.T. (1998) *Bruce Montgomery (1921–1978): a Biography with a Catalogue of the Musical Works* (unpublished PhD thesis, University of Nottingham)

Wright, S. and Fry, S.M. (eds) *Film Collections in the United States: a Guide*. (Society for the Preservation of Film Music) http://www.film-musicsociety.org/guide or access from the University of Virginia Library's Online Resources guide to Film Music (http://www.lib.virginia.edu/MusicLib/resources/film.html).

▶ NOTES

1. In conversation with the editor, the distinguished British film composer John Veale, probably best known for his music to *The Purple Plain*, described how, years ago, his film company requested the return of his unique personal copies of the scores for his feature films, and subsequently destroyed them. Revival of Veale's film music on CD has been rendered virtually impossible by this loss of the scores. – Ed.
2. *Music Library Association Newsletter* (1988), 75, Nov–Dec, p. 8.
3. *Henry V by William Shakespeare* Produced and directed by Laurence Olivier (1984). Classic Film Scripts, No. 2. Lorrimer Publishing.
4. Source: Kershaw (1992).
5. ibid.
6. Gramophone *Film Music Good CD Guide* (3rd edn.) (1998). Harrow, Middlesex: Gramophone Publications Ltd.

23 Composer trusts as sources of information, documentation and funding

Helen Faulkner

This chapter covers the resources available from British Trusts. Similar bodies function in other countries, under different legal systems, and are often called 'foundations'.

Composer Trusts are legally constituted bodies set up receive, administer and distribute income which originates from copyrights, performing rights, music hire fees and other similar payments. The terms under which Trusts operate are strictly controlled in law because they receive large tax exemption advantages. All Trusts have trustees, individuals or corporate bodies who are charged with the obligation to ensure that the Trust is legally and efficiently run. Composer Trusts are distinct from composer societies, which are generally formed by enthusiasts for the works of a particular composer, though increasingly they too are registered charities. Some societies may receive funding from Trusts but are otherwise entirely separate and should not be confused.

As a rule, Composer Trusts are set up to administer the *post mortem* estate of a composer but the individual composer is often involved initially in establishing the precise terms (the 'objects') of a Trust as, for example, in the case of the RVW [Ralph Vaughan Williams] Trust. Alternatively, a Trust may be established by a widow, as was the case with the Delius Trust, or other family member to administer income which they themselves have been receiving from a composer's works. Trusts are essentially business organisations and they must be clearly non-profit making. Of course, Trusts have income, but this income must be assigned for purposes which are clearly charitable and accepted as such by the Charity Commission. In some circumstances a Trust will run alongside a commercial company, as is the case with the RVW Trust and RVW Limited, where income from certain works, or works of a certain type, goes into a company from which the monies can be used for non-charitable purposes (such as payments to dependants) and is subject to taxation in the same way that profits in any commercial company are taxable, but other income goes into a charitable trust where, as long as it is used 'charitably', it is currently largely protected from significant areas of taxation, though not from VAT. Whilst Composer Trusts might not automatically spring to mind as sources of information and documentation, some can prove very valuable. However, there is no discernible consistency and the only documents which Trusts are uniformly required to hold are those which have a legal or fiscal consequence. To determine the value of a Trust's holdings from a bibliographic point of view it is necessary to know the following:

- how and why the Trust was established;
- what the objects of the Trust are; and
- whether the Trust has archives and access policies.

► HOW AND WHY?

Documentation surrounding the establishment of a Trust will almost always provide materials of biographical importance, particularly relating to the end of a composer's life and often, most specifically, surrounding the contents of a composer's will. Trusts tend to accumulate quantities of material, letters, photographs and ephemera, which are sent to the Trust in the absence of any other obvious home for it. This is particularly the case when a composer has few or no descendants. Over the years material may continue to trickle in from a variety of sources including former friends and acquaintances of the composer and their heirs who come across the odd letter, postcard or photo. Some Trusts, such as the John Ireland Trust, will actively try to acquire materials by donation or purchase (if their objects allow this), often to stop items becoming too diffusely spread across other collections. They may subsequently lodge these items elsewhere, or indeed may help other bodies or institutions to acquire them. Whatever the case, the Trust is likely to be a useful source of information on the location of biographically related materials.

Because Trusts are concerned with the protection and legal exploitation of rights they can prove to be rich sources of information on the publishing and performance history of a composer. This can be particularly useful when a composer has had a variety of publishers in a number of countries and when musical works exist in a number of different versions. All Trusts will keep correspondence relating to the granting of permission for such things as performances and arrangements of a composer's music.

► OBJECTS

This, the fundamental activity of a Trust, is probably the least useful from a bibliographical or musicological point of view. The objects of any legally constituted registered charity are a matter of public record and are obtainable from the Charity Commission. Trust objects vary enormously from one Trust to another and though the objects may well appear to be very broad there is no obligation on Trusts to fulfil all their allowable objects at any one time. As long as a Trust only does that which is within the objects and uses an acceptable proportion of the income it receives, the Trustees may establish a policy of priorities for the Trust and policy can change from time to.

Some Trusts are able to support performances, recordings, etc. of the subject's music (e.g. the Delius Trust, Bax Trust, Finzi Trust). Other Trust's deeds (their individual governing documents) expressly exclude this area of activity (e.g. The RVW Trust). Some Trusts support the performance of music by a specific class of composer (e.g. the Holst Trust) or of a specific musical genre (e.g. The Ouseley Trust). Some will combine aspects of some or all of these areas of activity.

Trusts will keep documentation relating to all aspects of the administration of the income and the grants they make, but in order to assess whether there is anything to which you would be likely to want access, you will need to know about the policy in place at any particular time. However, one area which might be of particular interest is where a Trust has been responsible for the preparation and publication of a scholarly edition of the founder's works. A Trust may own autograph scores, retaining preliminary editorial material and even performing materials where these have a bearing on the editorial work, as was the case with Beecham's materials for the works of Delius.

▶ ARCHIVES AND ACCESS POLICIES

It is rare for a Composer Trust to have an explicit archives policy, though as archives get larger, either by accident or design, decisions will undoubtedly have been taken on what to keep and what to discard. Unfortunately, availability of space is as likely to be a criterion for these decisions as is bibliographic consideration. Some Trusts, however, have as an object the maintenance of a collection or library. If this is neither an object nor a priority, access is likely to be very restricted. In any case, few Trusts have the luxury of full-time staff or Trustees who can make items available without a good deal of prior warning and unless they are obliged to do so under their Deed of Trust there is no automatic right of access to papers held.

Increasingly, Trusts which originally held autograph scores and other significant, valuable and physically vulnerable items have taken the decision to give these, either as outright gifts or on permanent loan, to libraries where access will be much easier and where the works will be located with other items of similar genres. The British Library already has significant holdings of the music of twentieth-century British composers in its manuscript department which have been given to them by enlightened trustees. Another significant collection of such material is at the Royal College of Music, which is itself the Administrator of the Frank Bridge Trust.

Even when a Trust holds little that is itself significant or helpful to a researcher it may prove to be a useful source of information on the location of source materials, both primary and secondary, and may keep files of photocopied or microfilmed materials, particularly relating to copyright and publication issues. It is, therefore, always worth contacting a Trust if a particular item or piece of information is proving hard to locate. A Composer Trust is certainly not the obvious, or sensible, first port of call for a extensive research project but is more appropriately treated as a last resort when other more obvious sources have been fully trawled.

Most Trusts produce written guidelines on their grant-making policies and some will have other publications of a more general nature. A few now have websites and this is bound to grow in the near future. The British Music Yearbook lists some but not all Composer Trusts in the 'Associations' section, where a brief description of their activities is included. The *Directory of Grant-making Trusts* which is published annually by the Charities Aid Foundation also lists some, though they are hard to find in this substantial publication. Publishers of a particular composer's music will also be able to advise on the existence of a particular Trust.

▶ SELECTED LIST OF BRITISH COMPOSER TRUSTS

Sir Arnold Bax Trust
22 Pheasants Way
Rickmansworth
Hertfordshire
WD3 7ES

Sir Arthur Bliss Trust
PO Box 21
Hereford
HR1 3YQ

The Rutland Boughton Music Trust
25 Bearton Green
Hitchin
Herts
SG5 1UN

Frank Bridge Trust
Royal College of Music
Prince Consort Road
London
SW7 2BS

Britten-Pears Foundation
The Red House
Aldeburgh
Suffolk
IP15 5PZ

Delius Trust
16 Ogle Street
London
W1W 6OA

Sir George Dyson Trust
22 Pheasants Way
Rickmansworth
Hertfordshire
WD3 7ES

Finzi Trust
Hillcroft
Shucknall Hill
Hereford
HR1 3SL

Holst Foundation
179 Great Portland Street
London
W1N 6LS

John Ireland Trust
35 St Mary's Mansions
St Mary's Terrace
London
W2 1SQ

Kenneth Leighton Trust
38 McLaren Road
Edinburgh
EH9 2BN

Ralph Vaughan Williams Trust
16 Ogle Street
London
W1W 6JA

William Walton Trust
9 Central Chambers
Wood Street
Stratford-upon-Avon
CV37 6JQ

Percy Whitlock Trust
32 Butcher Close
Staplehurst
Kent
TN12 0TJ

24 The music publisher as research source

Chris Banks

The last 200 years have seen a massive growth in the music publishing industry. To take the whole of the nineteenth century for example, for UK publishing John A. Parkinson lists numbers of items registered at Stationers' Hall, London as follows:[1]

- 1800:   159
- 1857: 2581
- 1874: 6077
- 1901: 8063

This publishing activity was also reflected throughout Europe, and from Hofmeister[2] the numbers of new music publications cited for a similar period are:

- 1829:   1748
- 1857:   3164
- 1874:   6125
- 1900: 13 140

To put that last figure in context, the number of publications listed in Hofmeister for the single year 1900 represents about 10% of the total number of citations in *RISM* series Ai.

Music publishers have become recognised increasingly as a major source of information for the researcher in topics ranging from source studies to sociological and economic studies, but at the same time their collections and archives are among some of the more difficult repositories to describe and document because of the very manner in which they have been assembled. Publishers, in their role of making available works of music for performance, and in producing multiple copies for onward sale, generate their own in-house records in order to manage these tasks. The nature of the records generated by each publishing house will depend on the nature of the music they are making available, the purpose for which they are making it available, the period in which they are working and their own in-house administrative and production processes. This chapter aims to provide information on the types of information that may be found in the records of a publishing firm. It does not necessarily reflect in totality what actually might be found in the archives of any one publisher, but is aimed more at providing the researcher with some idea of the records that might be assembled by publishers, in order to enable them to ask questions appropriate to their own research interests.

In dealing with publishers' archives it should be recognised that it is quite likely that the information will be in a form that will make the archive difficult to use from some perspectives and whatever the circumstances of their creation, the archives will not necessarily be constituted or arranged to directly answer musicologists' questions. Archives of long-established publishing houses may not be accessible to private researchers if the publisher considers that the information they hold is still commercially sensitive. Moreover, with the advent of new technologies publishers are increasingly storing their information on computers, sometimes in a form that, because not incremental, gives no feeling for the history but reflects only the current state of play.

Publishers' archives survive in a great variety of forms: some remain as part of the active business records of existing firms, some are passed in whole or in part to libraries or local records offices, some pass, with the sale of a business, to the new owner of that business, some are split up for sale if it is thought that individual 'treasures' might realise useful capital for re-investing within the firm while others end up in a skip following the transfer of the publisher's interests to another firm, or following their closure as a business and are consequently lost forever. It is not the intention here to begin to list those archives that survive, nor those active publishers who are willing and able to provide access for the researcher to their records; rather the purpose is to illustrate the nature of the information that might be held, which in turn should aid in the devising of research strategies.

In building up a shopping list of information that might be retrievable from publishers, the information could be grouped, for the purposes of the researcher, into the following broad categories

- musical materials;
- correspondence;
- production records;
- performance-related records;
- copyright records;
- retail records; and
- business records.

It should be stressed that publishers are unlikely to make such clear-cut distinctions in the way in which they assemble their records, and that all these categories are interrelated.

► MUSICAL MATERIALS

- Autograph or manuscript scores: The object that a composer or editor submits to the publishing house may be an autograph or copyist's manuscript, an annotated printed document or (today) a floppy disk or some other electronic storage medium. Such scores or copies of them will probably be annotated by editors to reflect a house style, and may also be annotated by the music setter during the process of casting off the pages for publication. Sometimes such scores remain with the publishers but they may be returned to the composer/editor (in which case they may find their way into public collections with the composer's archive). Robert Anderson's work on Elgar (1990) demonstrates the potential richness of such sources.

- Proof(s): Surviving proofs may be annotated, revised and corrected by in-house editors and/or by the composer/or outside editor. Annotations by the composer may also include 'second thoughts'. Proofs sometimes remain with the composer.

- Printed scores: Publishers frequently keep file copies of works they publish. Scores may have been printed for sale, or may have been produced for hire only. Where more than one edition has been produced, the archive may include a printed score annotated with changes to be made in a subsequent edition. Publishers do not always retain file copies of works they produce and sometimes it is necessary to trace these elsewhere (e.g. in libraries benefiting from legal deposit legislation). Sometimes ex-file copies (i.e. copies bearing the stamp or label of the publisher) are offered for sale through second-hand dealers.

- Hire library scores: This material might be manuscript copies (and/or copies duplicated from manuscript), printed copies, or a mixture of the two (e.g. orchestral part sets with printed or dyeline string parts and manuscript wind parts), and may contain markings by conductors and performers. In the late nineteenth and early to mid-twentieth centuries it would not have been uncommon for the composer's own autograph score to have been lent as part of a hire set. This practice has largely ceased over the past 20 years. Some publishers keep sets of parts aside for particular conductors or performing organisations that may reveal much about what was performed and the duration(s) of performance(s). Orchestral players – and in particular the wind and brass players who often have periods of 'bar counting' – have been known to annotate orchestral parts with wide varieties of comments ranging from timings of movements, or scenes in operas (the latter sometimes to indicate how long they have in the local pub before they next have to play!), to personal comments on the conductor or the music. Sometimes it is possible to pin such comments down to a particular performance but more often it is not.

▶ CORRESPONDENCE

In addition to correspondence with composers and editors, a publisher may retain copies of incoming and outgoing correspondence with others involved in any aspects of their printing and publishing activities. These might be broadly grouped as follows.

- Correspondence with the composer relating to works or performances of works: Where a composer remains with a publishing house for a substantial part of his/her career a large body of correspondence may be built up (particularly in the pre-telephone era). Elgar's own correspondence with his publishers is a particularly rich example of this category of material (Northrop Moore, 1987).
- Correspondence with editors/translators, etc.: This category of material will document the commissioning and production of editions and translations.
- Correspondence with performing bodies: The publisher may retain correspondence relating to first and subsequent performances of new works in their catalogue, particularly for those works subject to performing or grand rights.
- Correspondence with reviewers: This may include anything from details of information sent to reviewers to more extensive discussions of publications that have been reviewed.
- Correspondence with retailers and with printers and suppliers of equipment.

▶ PRODUCTION RECORDS

The nature and extent of material surviving in a publisher's own archive relating to the production of scores will, to a large extent, depend on whether the publisher also has its own in-house music-setters and printers or whether this work is consigned to an external printer. In order to correctly interpret such records one must have a good understanding of the firm's working practices and specifically the printing processes involved. Assuming that all work is done in-house there may be the following records.

Print runs: Where a publisher is printing for retail they will not want to tie up capital in stock that remains unsold for a substantial period of time and they will therefore attempt to judge the market and print enough copies both to make the unit cost of the publication a viable figure, and to avoid having to house surplus stock. Comparative studies of publishers' printing records can often be very revealing in determining whether a publisher is being cautious with a particular genre. Depending on the method of printing, a publisher may (e.g. for works produced using photolithography) or may not (e.g. typeset music before stereotyping) be able to re-print scores where they have underestimated the original volume of sales. Where a publisher uses a method that does allow for reprinting, records can reveal where there have been substantial underestimates of a work's popularity (e.g. where a small print run is followed very quickly by a much larger print run).

Storage records: Such records are needed in order to manage stock and will give details of its location, and when stock of a particular score is added to, or whether it is diminishing through sales. Again, such records can be a very good indicator of the relative popularity of works, and of peaks and troughs in interest in a work. Sometimes it is possible to link such peaks and troughs to performances or reviews, or the use of a composition for an examination.

Records of storage or destruction of plates/stock: In addition to the records of the unsold stock for a work, a publisher might also keep records of plates being retained for further use, and whether or not those plates are destroyed (after which some of the materials can be re-used to create new plates). Many publishers will assign edition numbers and/or plate numbers to a particular publication format, and such numbers are often used as the basis of their own stock and ordering control systems. Plate numbers have long been recognised as being a potentially useful dating tool for printed music (particularly where a date of publication does not appear on a work) and the existence of records for plates can further aid in building up a picture of a publisher's activities.

Extent and costs of raw materials: If a publisher deals with all aspects of the production process in-house it is likely that a substantial proportion of their capital will be tied up in equipment (including presses and tools), and in paper stocks. Such equipment is not small and may take up the equivalent of a smallish warehouse, and thus have implications for the type of building in which the printing operation is housed (is it in the same building as the main editorial departments, or located elsewhere; was it a specially-built building; does the printing arm of the publishing firm undertake work for other publishers as part of its business activities?) and consequently on the sort of lease a publisher holds. The archive may contain inventories of equipment, designs for layout of the equipment or proposals for expanding the equipment base, details of the number of staff/apprentices employed, etc.

▶ PERFORMANCE-RELATED RECORDS

For some works, particularly for those in copyright, a publisher will not issue performing materials for sale, but will keep a limited number of sets in a hire library for hire to specific performance groups for a fee. In administering the issuing and recall of performance materials a publisher will *inter alia* build up some of the following information.

Numbers of performances of a work: The performance history of a work can usually be reconstructed from the hire records for the orchestral materials (both for performance and broadcast use) and from the returns sent in by opera companies for works in which grand rights subsist.[3]

Performers of a work: In particular, conductors, soloists and orchestras (for concert works) and other performing organisations for stage works. As has already been mentioned above, it is occasionally possible to link specific performing materials with specific performers.

Returns showing income from hire fees/grand rights/performing rights/recording or broadcasting fees: Whereas hire fees will only indicate the number of performances, those works which are subject to 'grand rights' (i.e. where the publisher's income is determined by box office takings) will spawn records that will indicate takings (and hence will be an indication of audience size) for specific performances, since the performing bodies will be required to submit box office returns. Clearly such information needs to be treated with caution: a small company with a small capacity venue and low seat prices will, on the basis of the figures, not generate as much income for the publisher as a larger company with more substantial ticket prices in a larger venue.

Promotional tapes: For new works, publishing houses are increasingly offering to make available one-off tapes of works for promotional purposes. These can be particularly valuable to scholars where no commercial recording exists.

Secondary sources such as programmes, handbills, press cuttings, etc. (all discussed elsewhere) may add further information to that held by the publisher.

▶ CONTRACTS, ASSIGNMENTS, PRIVILEGES, COPYRIGHT AND LEGAL RECORDS

A composer's income is derived from various sources: commission fees, publishing fees, and performance and broadcast fees. Publishers will usually negotiate with the composer either a fixed fee payable on the sale of copies (i.e. fee payments which do not take into account any inflationary pressures) or, more recently, a percentage payable on the sale of copies of the work, and will undertake negotiations with performing and broadcasting bodies for the fees due for performance, some of which will also be passed back to the composer. The publisher may negotiate a one-off payment for the publication of a work, an edition or a translation and in such cases the publisher will have a larger initial outlay but will be gambling on the success of a work for which they will have nothing further to pay to the composer, editor or translator (contracts on such terms are particularly common in the nineteenth and early twentieth centuries, and for relatively unknown composers).

Details of fees payable on the basis of sales/performances/recordings to composer/editor/author of text/translator of text: A number of different copyrights may subsist in a work depending on the death dates of the composer, librettist, editor, translator and the original date of publication (see CHAPTER 5). In addition to the correspondence relating to the negotiation of the payments due (see above), publishers will also normally be obliged to keep financial records of payments made to any of the interested parties. These records will interrelate with those kept for the number of copies sold, the numbers of performances, etc.

Copyrights secured: Depending on the copyright regulations in force at the time a work is created, and any additional international agreements in force between countries, publishers may need to secure their copyright interests by, for instance, sending a copy of the publication to a recognised institution in a particular country (e.g. to secure copyright in the USA for certain periods it was necessary to deposit a copy of a published work at the Library of Congress). In securing such interests a publisher may keep very detailed records of exactly what was sent, when and where it was sent, and the method of transport (e.g. shipping records).

► RETAIL RECORDS

Number of copies sold: In order to maintain accurate stock records in addition to the need to be able to calculate any royalties due, a publisher may also record the dates and numbers of sales.

Price at which copies sold: In order to maintain accurate financial records, a publisher will need to keep records of the unit costs of their publications. Such records will also form the basis for the calculations of royalty payments due, and might also reveal information on the publishing costs of particular works over a period of time (e.g. a rise and fall in the cost of paper).

Details of purchasers/those receiving complimentary copies: In addition to keeping records of the numbers of copies sold, publishers will often retain details of purchasers, be they members of the public, or shops retailing music. Records will also be kept of those who have received complimentary copies, which may include national libraries (as part of

Legal Deposit legislation), potential reviewers and potential performers as well as, of course, any free copies due to the composers, etc. For those items sold on subscription, there will also be subscription lists.

▶ BUSINESS RECORDS

This is perhaps the most varied category and in part covers records not easily categorised above.

Directors' minutes: These may include details of a publishing company's policy and might illuminate decisions taken to accept or reject composers or individual works for publication. They might also record details surrounding the acquisition of other companies, or the flotation or winding up of their own company.

Commissioned artwork: Publishers may commission typographic artwork for their own letterheads as well as for their publications. In some instances, special artwork will be commissioned for covers or title-pages. Accepted and rejected designs might form part of a publisher's archive.

Ownership or alteration of premises: Premises occupied by a publisher, particularly when they house printing operations as well as the editorial offices, may, over the years, need to be altered either because of the effects of economy (expansion or contraction) or because of the intro- duction of new technologies. Leases and planning agreements may survive that reflect such changes.

Press cuttings, etc./photographs/biographical information/promo- tional materials: During the process of advertising and promoting publications, a publisher will tend to build up a collection of miscellaneous documents relating to their activities as a whole, and to specific composers and publications.

Published catalogues: These may be annual publications listing mate- rials for sale/hire, or occasional publications listing the materials available by a particular composer, or for a particular genre (e.g. choral music, orchestral music, etc.). Such catalogues may be made available in the publisher's own archive, but may also have been retained by libraries.

Sale catalogues: If, on the winding-up of a publisher's activities, the assets (both material and intellectual) are sold, an auction catalogue might exist giving details of what was to be sold. Occasionally it is possible to trace such catalogues marked with the names of purchasers of particular lots.

▶ ILLUSTRATION

As mentioned at the beginning of this chapter, many publishers' archives are maintained in a way which will reflect the firm's operational requirements, and this may sometimes make such archives difficult to use from the researcher's perspective. Moreover, the situation may become more complicated where a publisher deems some of its materials either of no further business use or, a more recent trend, of monetary value and therefore a realisable capital asset. Despite the fact that they are still in business, long-standing publishers dispose of some of their archives and in doing so much of the archival integrity of a collection may be lost, requiring the researcher to piece together information from dispersed and frequently re-organised sources. The following example is given in order to put some flesh on the theoretical bones outlined above, and serves to highlight some of the issues that the researcher might have to face.

The music publishing firm of Novello and Company originated in the late 1820s with Vincent Novello.[4] Novello himself prepared many of the editions for the early publications, and portions of his own working library were evidently transferred back to the firm.[5] In the 1960s the then owners of the publishing firm decided to dispose of parts of the musical archive. Some items were presented to the British Library[6] and further materials, including part of Vincent Novello's own library, were acquired by the Royal College of Music.[7] At about the same time further music manuscripts were placed on loan at the British Library by the company.[8] Some items from this loan collection have subsequently been withdrawn. During the 1980s, further musical materials from the library of Vincent Novello and from the publishing firm were presented to the British Library,[9] along with a substantial portion of the surviving business archive.[10] At this time a second collection of music manuscripts was placed on loan.[11] Items from this second loan were subsequently withdrawn by the publishers and offered for auction,[12] although before the sale some autographs were withdrawn from the publishers by composers' heirs, to whom they belonged.[13] In 1996 more materials, including correspondence, music manuscripts and parts of the business archives, were offered for sale.[14] It is evident that in order to construct viable 'lots' in this sale, the archival integrity of some of the correspondence was destroyed. Again, some manuscripts described in the catalogue were withdrawn from sale by the heirs of composers. A not inconsiderable proportion of the correspondence offered for sale at this time was unsold and has subsequently been re-lotted and offered for sale through the same auction house.

Today, the situation is that while proportions of the musical and business archive survive intact in the British Library, in the Royal College of Music, and with the current owners of the firm, much has been dispersed, and no public record of its original archival organisation (and hence function) has been preserved. A summary of the collection at the British Library can be found in the appendix to this chapter.

▶ CONCLUSION

Music publishers are generally very interested in their own history and are often willing to co-operate with researchers. When approaching a publisher for information it is worthwhile to remember that providing information to researchers is not part of their core activity. It is therefore important that essential background work has been done before making direct contact. As new generations of staff take over it is not unusual for the 'corporate memory' to fade a little. However, retired members of staff are sometimes able to help, indeed some continue to take active interest in the work of their former employers.

▶ BIBLIOGRAPHY

The bibliography on publishing and on individual publishers is very extensive indeed and it is not possible to begin to list all relevant sources here. The following, therefore, is provided to guide the researcher to resources which themselves will provide further bibliographical information:

For information in the UK of archives which are now in institutional hands: National Register of Archives, Quality House, Quality Court, Chancery Lane, London WC2A 1HP (database: <http://www.hmc.gov.uk/nra/nra2.htm>).

Foster, J. and Sheppard, J. (2002) British Archives: a guide to archive resources in the United Kingdom. Basingstoke: Palgrave

Krummel, D.W. [for the] International Association of Music Libraries Commission for Bibliographic Research (1974) Guide for Dating Early Published Music: a Manual of Bibliographical Practices. Hackensack, NJ: Boonin

Krummel, D.W. and Sadie, S. (1990) Music Printing and Publishing. London: Macmillan [New Grove Handbooks in Music]

Répertoire International de Littérature Musicale (1961–) [under the following headings:]
● Catalogues – publishers'
● Copyright
● Dating aids
● Publishers and printers
● Publishing and printing

▶ REFERENCES

Anderson, R. (1990) *Elgar in Manuscript*. London: The British Library

Banks, C. (1995) From Purcell to Wardour Street: a brief account of music manuscripts from the library of Vincent Novello now in the British Library. *The British Library Journal*, 21, 240–58

Dibble, J. (1983) The RCM Novello Library. *Musical Times*, cxxiv, no. 1680, 99–101

Elvers, R. and Hopkinson, C. (1972) A Survey of the Music Catalogues of Whistling and Hofmeister. *Fontes Artis Musicae*, 19 [1]-7

Foreman, L (1991) Britten's *Ballad [of Heroes]*: Lewis Foreman traces a performance history. *Gramophone*, Nov, 19

Hurd, M. (1981) *Vincent Novello – and Company*. London: Granada

Northrop Moore, J. (1987) (ed.) *Elgar and his Publishers: Letters of a Creative Life* (2 vols). Oxford: Clarendon Press

Parkinson, A.J. (1990) *Victorian Music Publishers: an Annotated List*. Michigan: Harmonie Park Press

Ratliff, N. (1974) The Whistling-Hofmeister Catalogues. In: D.W. Krummell *Guide for Dating Early Published Music: a Manual of Bibliographical Practices*. Hackensack, NJ, pp. 193–5

Whistling, C.F. and Hofmeister, F. (1975) *Whistling & Hofmeister, Handbuch der musikalisches Litteratur: Reprint of the 1817 Edition and the Ten Nachträge (1818–1827)*. New York: Garland

▶ APPENDIX: THE NOVELLO AND COMPANY BUSINESS ARCHIVE – A SUMMARY OF THE MANUSCRIPTS INCORPORATED[15] IN THE BRITISH LIBRARY COLLECTIONS[16]

Add. MSS 69516–69792. Financial and printing records of the music publishers Novello and Co. and associated companies; 1809-c.1976. Music manuscripts from the archives of Novello are Add. 65382–65525 and 69851–69864. Presented by Novello and Company, 14 July 1989.

Paper. Two hundred and seventy-seven volumes. Arranged as follows:

A   Royalty and copyright records: 69516–69553.
B   Printing and stock records: 69554–69594.
C   Directors' records: 69595–69606.
D   Accounts: 69607–69720.
E   Records of shareholdings: 69721–69752.

F   Title deeds, inventories, etc.: 69753–69768.
G   Records of H. C. Dunckley (Wrotham) Ltd.: 69769, 69770.
H   Records of Elkin and Co.: 69771–69774.
I   Records of Goodwin and Tabb Ltd.: 69775–69784.
J   Records of the Hollen Street Press: 69785–69787.
K   Records of Page and Thomas: 69788–69791.
L   Records of William Paxton: 69792.

A   Royalty and copyright records

69516–69532.[17] *Novello And Company Business Archive*. Vols I–XVII. Commission books; 1840–c.1974. Records of royalty payments made to composers, listed by composer and work with, in most volumes, an index of composers and titles. Details include numbers of copies printed, numbers sold or given away, and prices charged. Names of purchasers of copyrights are included where appropriate. Later annotations often indicate where stock has been either returned to the author, sold to another publisher or destroyed. As a result of the system of entry the dates of most volumes overlap, with the entries for some works continued from one volume to another; dates given for each volume are those of the earliest entry, followed by the approximate date of the latest main entries.
    Seventeen volumes.

69533–69545. *Novello And Company Business Archive*. Vols XVIII–XXX. Registers of works sent to New York for copyright; 1891–1947. Entered by title on *printed* forms giving composer, date of publication and number of copies sent. Index of composers from Add. 69537. With related *typewritten* correspondence inserted.
    Thirteen volumes.

69546–69550. *Novello And Company Business Archive*. Vols XXXI–XXXV. Registers of works sent to New York for copyright: 'Authors works' [i.e. those works where composers retain ownership of copyright]; 1891–1934. Entered by title on *printed* forms, with name of composer, etc., as Add. 69533–69545 above. With related correspondence.
    Five volumes.

69551. *Novello And Company Business Archive*. Vol. XXXVI. New York royalty accounts; 1901–1952. Sums debited to New York agents, entered under title of work. With an index of titles.

69552. *Novello And Company Business Archive*. Vol. XXXVII. Permissions book; 1947–1954. Payments received for reproduction and performance of works.

69553. *Novello And Company Business Archive*. Vol. XXXVIII. Debits, Authors and Royalties No. 8; 1957–1962. Records of works sent mainly to performing organisations in England and abroad, listed by date, giving composer, title, number of copies sent and recipient.

B   Printing and stock records

69554–69564. *Novello And Company Business Archive*. Vols XXXIX–XLIX. Stock books and index; 1870–1949. Listed by title, giving number of copies of a work printed, type of binding and the dates on which stock was sent from the warehouse, or destroyed. In some instances the name of the printer is also given. The system of entry is similar to that in Add. 69516–69532, with the same continuation of entries from one volume to another and overlapping dates. For a stock book immediately preceding this series see Victoria Cooper-Deathridge (1987) The Novello stockbook of 1858–1869: a chronicle of publishing activity. *Notes [of the Music Libraries Association]* 43i, 240.[18]
    Eleven volumes.

69565–69567. *Novello And Company Business Archive*. Vols L–LII. Litho printing books and index; 1895–1951. Listed by title, recording date and number of copies printed. Entries continued, and dates overlapping, between the two volumes as in Add. 69516–69532 above.
    Three volumes.
- 69565. *Novello And Company Business Archive*. Vol. L. Litho printing book [1]; 1895–c.1950. Begun 1895, but including retrospective information from 1869 taken from old stock labels.
- 69566. *Novello And Company Business Archive*. Vol. LI. Litho printing book 2; 1913–1951. Later annotations record renewal of copyright, destruction of stock or plates, etc., to c.1976.
- 69567. *Novello And Company Business Archive*. Vol. LII. Composer index. Contains numerous notes, particularly on destruction of plates, to c.1937.

69568–69576. *Novello And Company Business Archive*. Vols LIII–LXI. Printing stock books and index; 1876-c.1950. Arranged by title (or series title), with date and number of copies. System of entry and dating similar to Add 69516–69532. Some volumes are devoted to specific series, as indicated.
    Nine volumes.
- 69568. Vol. LIII. Printing stock book 1; 1876–after 1911.
- 69569. Vol. LIV. Printing stock book 2; 1889–c.1950.
- 69570. Vol. LV. Printing stock book 3; 1879–c.1950.

- 69571. Vol. LVI. Printing stock book 4; 1879–c.1950. *Parish Choirbook*, 'Short Anthems', Bishop's Glees, *Orpheus* series, 'Octavo Choruses', *Choral Songs for Schools*.
- 69572. Vol. LVII. Printing stock book 5; 1889–c.1950.
- 69573. Vol. LVIII. Printing stock book 6; 1891–c.1950. Stainer's Carols, 'Novello's Carols', 'Novello's Duets' and 'Two Part Songs', *School Songs*.
- 69574. Vol. LIX. Printing stock book 7; 1902–c.1950. 'Octavo Anthems'.
- 69575. Vol. LX. Printing stock book 8; 1909–c.1950. *The Musical Times*.
- 69576. Vol. LXI. Index by composer or series title; begun c.1900.

69577–69579. *Novello And Company Business Archive*. Vols LXII–LXIV. Plate books; begun 1911. Arranged alphabetically by composer, giving title, stock number of work, and number of plates. With some details of subsequent melting or transfer of plates.

Three volumes.
- 69577. Vol. LXII. A–F.
- 69578. Vol. LXIII. G–N.
- 69579. Vol. LXIV. O–Z.

69580. *Novello And Company Business Archive*. Vol. LXV. Plate book No. 2;[19] begun c.1900, annotated to 1961. Lists plates nos. 10001–17750 in numerical order, giving composer and title. With a separate list of plates to be melted, 1961.

69581, 69582. *Novello And Company Business Archive*. Vols LXVI, LXVII. Printing accounts; 1904–1975. Lists costs of printing, binding, etc., by customer; apparently concerned only with work for outside bodies or individuals.

Two volumes.
- 69581. *Novello And Company Business Archive*. Vol. LXVI. Printing accounts No. 8; 1904–1907, 1916–1942. The entries for 1904–1907 on an inserted gathering, apparently from an earlier volume.
- 69582. *Novello And Company Business Archive*. Vol. LXVII. Printing accounts No. 9; 1941–1975.

69583. *Novello And Company Business Archive*. Vol. LXVIII. Odd work book; 1925–1964. Chronological entries, giving title, quantity and work done, for small binding and lettering jobs of hire library material, for shop sales, and for private customers. The front of the volume stamped 'Novello & Company Limited. Odd Sales No. [5]. A to F'.

69584–69586. *Novello And Company Business Archive*. Vols LXIX–LXXI. Orchestral printing books and index; 1890–1970. Orchestral parts listed by title of work, giving date and quantity printed. System of entry similar to Add. 69516–69532; dates given are ascertainable period of use.

Three volumes.

- 69584. Vol. LXIX. Orchestral printing book 1; 1890–1938.
- 69585. Vol. LXX. Orchestral printing book 2; 1909–1970.
- 69586. Vol. LXXI. Index by composer.

69587–69592. *Novello And Company Business Archive*. Vols LXXII–LXVII. Bound stock books and indexes; 1929–1962.

Six volumes.

- 69587–69589. *Novello And Company Business Archive*. Vols LXXII–LXXIV. Bound stock books; 1927–1962. Arranged alphabetically by composer, giving numbers and type of binding of bound copies of works in stock; with dates and quantities taken from stock.

Three volumes

- 69590. *Novello And Company Business Archive*. Vol. LXXV. Bound stock book, A–W; 1941–1962. A separate sequence from Add. 69587–69589 above, but with similar content and arrangement.

Bound (loose-leaf).

- 69591. *Novello And Company Business Archive*. Vol. LXXVI. Index to 'Bound Stock Reserve'; compiled 1929–1933. Index by composer or title to bound stock books earlier in date than Add. 69587–69590.
- 69592. *Novello And Company Business Archive*. Vol. LXXVII. Stock Book; 1949–1962. Lists stocks of 'Novello Primers' and *School Songs* only.

69593. *Novello And Company Business Archive*. Vol. LXXVIII. *Alphabetical catalogue of vocal compositions published by Novello and Company Ltd*; 1932, revised 1965. *Photocopy* of an annotated printed catalogue. Gives details of the collections in which individual songs are published.

69594. *Novello And Company Business Archive*. Vol. LXXIX. Miscellaneous papers relating to music publishing; 1850–1950, n.d.

Various sizes.

1 Correspondence relating to publication of tonic sol-fa edition of Mendelssohn's 'Elijah'; 1866–1869.

2 Account for legal costs incurred by J.A. Novello in case concerning infringement of his copyright by the Philharmonic Society of Liverpool, 1850–1852; – correspondence, etc., concerning alleged infringement of copyright by Max Griebsch of Wisconsin, 1901.

3   Memorandum of Agreement with the Society for the Promotion of Christian Knowledge concerning publication of *Church Hymns*; 1903. *Typewritten.* With related papers.

4   Miscellaneous correspondence and papers, including an undated libretto for a proposed two-part oratorio, 'Abraham'; 1887–1950.

C   Directors' records

69595. *Novello And Company Business Archive.* Vol. LXXX. Company papers; 1886–1908.

1   Articles of Partnership; 1886, 1889. *Copies.*

2   Agreement and *printed* prospectus for flotation as a public limited company; 1898. With two *copies* of the Agreement.

3   Certificate of Incorporation in 1898 as a limited company; issued 1908.

4   Correspondence concerning printing prospectus and advertising the share issue; 1897–1898.

69596–69599. *Novello And Company Business Archive.* Vol. LXXXI–LXXXIV. Minutes of directors' meetings; 1898–1961.

Four volumes.

69600. *Novello And Company Business Archive.* Vol. LXXXV. Lists of directors; 1901, 1905. Entered on *printed* forms.

69601, 69602. *Novello And Company Business Archive.* Vols LXXXVI, LXXXVII. Directors' attendance books; 1949–1965. With signatures of those present at meetings.

Two volumes.

•   69601. Vol. LXXXVI. 1949–1958.

•   69602. Vol. LXXXVII. 1958–1965. With attendances at directors' and general meetings of the Hollen Street Press, 1958–1965, at the end (vol. rev.).

69603. *Novello And Company Business Archive.* Vol. LXXXVIII. Minutes of ordinary general meetings; 1898–1948. With *printed* copies of the *Annual Reports* pasted in, together with some *typewritten* letters from the accountants.

69604. *Novello And Company Business Archive.* Vol. LXXXIX. Annual reports and balance sheets nos. 1–42; 1899–1940. *Printed. Imperfect*, wanting 1906, 1908, 1917 and 1939.

69605. *Novello And Company Business Archive*. Vol. XC. Annual Reports and Balance Sheets nos. 40–47, with detailed balance sheets; 1938–1945. Partly *printed*.

69606. *Novello And Company Business Archive*. Vol. XCI. *Printed* notices of shareholders' meetings, blank dividend warrants, copies of Annual Reports; 1898–1919. With signed statements of posting of dividend warrants, notices, etc.

D   Accounts

69607–69609. *Novello And Company Business Archive*. Vols XCII–XCIV. Trading ledgers; 1903–1962. Include costs of plates and engraving, postage, singers' royalties, salaries, composers' royalties, cash sales, fittings and furniture, and broadcasting fees.
    Three volumes.

69610–69613. *Novello And Company Business Archive*. Vols XCV–XCVIII. Capital account and general ledgers; 1898–1963. Include payments to the Inland Revenue, dividends, mortgages, advertising and payments to directors.
    Four volumes.

69614. *Novello And Company Business Archive*. Vol. XCIX. Works bought ledger; 1948–1959. Lists purchases from other publishers and printers, arranged alphabetically by company.
69615–69617. *Novello And Company Business Archive*. Vols C–CII. Journals; 1898–1971. *Incomplete*.
    Three volumes.

69618. *Novello And Company Business Archive*. Vol. CIII. Petty cash book; 1962–1965.

69619–69675. *Novello And Company Business Archive*. Vols CIV–CLX. Detailed trading accounts, profit & loss accounts, and balance sheets; 1899–1955. Partly *typewritten*. From 1921, in addition to the general company accounts, separate accounts for the Publishing Department are given. Similarly, separate accounts for the Manufacturing Department are given 1921–1937; from 1938 these give way to separate accounts for the Hollen Street Works and for the Hollen Street Press. Summary balance sheets 1899–1945 are to be found in Add. 69604, 69605; the latter also includes detailed balance sheets 1938–1945.
    Fifty-seven volumes.

69676–69720. *Novello And Company Business Archive.* Vol. CLXI–CCV. Annual list [of shareholders] and summary of capital and shares; 1898–1947. List of directors included from 1901. With separate returns for the Hollen Street Press from 1937. The returns for Novello & Co. Ltd. 1942–1947 contain the summary and list of directors only, omitting list of shareholders.

Forty-five volumes.

E   Records of shareholdings

69721. *Novello And Company Business Archive.* Vol. CCVI. Share allotment book; 1898. Lists allocations of shares, giving applicant's profession and the number of shares applied for.

69722. *Novello And Company Business Archive.* Vol. CCVII. Register of members and share ledger [preference shares]; 1898–1928. With index of members' names.

69723. *Novello And Company Business Archive.* Vol. CCVIII. Register of members and share ledger [ordinary shares]; 1898–1928. With index of members' names.

69724. *Novello And Company Business Archive.* Vol. CCIX. Register of members and share ledger; to c.1945. Preference and ordinary shares; includes details transferred from older registers. Arranged alphabetically by members' names.

69725. *Novello And Company Business Archive.* Vol. CCX. Share register; gives details for 1911–1970. Preference and ordinary shares. Arranged alphabetically by name of shareholder.

69726–69733. *Novello And Company Business Archive.* Vols CCXI–CCXVIII. Preference share certificates; 1898–1969.

Eight volumes.

69734. *Novello And Company Business Archive.* Vol. CCXIX. Preference share dividend ledger; 1961–1970.

69735–69738. *Novello And Company Business Archive.* Vols CCXX–CCXXIII. Ordinary share certificates; 1898–1963.

Four volumes.

69739. *Novello And Company Business Archive.* Vol. CCXXIV. Transfer deed receipts; 1952–1956.

69740. *Novello And Company Business Archive*. Vol. CCXXV. Register of transfers; 1898–1948.

69741–69752. *Novello And Company Business Archive*. Vols CCXXVI–CCXXXVII. Share transfer certificates; 1898–1966.
   Twelve volumes.

F   Title deeds, inventories, etc.

69753–69759. *Novello And Company Business Archive*. Vols CCXXXVIII–CCXLIV. Leases, etc., of properties occupied by Novello and Company; 1809–1927.
   Seven items.
   - 69753. *Novello And Company Business Archive*. Vol. CCXXXVIII. 1 Berners Street; 1841–1906. Includes consent to carry on the business of music printing, 1867.
   - 69754. *Novello And Company Business Archive*. Vol. CCXXXIX. 69a Dean Street; 1853–1859.
   - 69755. *Novello And Company Business Archive*. Vol. CCXL. 87 Regent Street; 1859–1870.
   - 69756. *Novello And Company Business Archive*. Vol. CCXLI. 111 Southwark Street; 1877, 1884. With related correspondence, 1890–1897.
   - 69757. *Novello And Company Business Archive*. Vol. CCXLII. Miscellaneous properties; 1844–1892.
     1 Land in Isleworth, co. Midd.; 1844.
     2 First floor room at 35 Poultry; 1855.
     3 80–81 Queen Street; 1876–1898.
     4 112, 114 Oxford Street; 1809–1892.

69758, 69759. *Novello And Company Business Archive*. Vols CCXLIII, CCXLIV. Wardour Street (and fronting on Little Chapel and Hollen Streets), Soho; 1896–1934.
   Two volumes.

69758. *Novello And Company Business Archive*. Vol. CCXLIII. Title deeds, etc.; 1896–1934.
     1 Agreements to demolish, leases; 1896–1908. With undated drawing of elevations of new building, and correspondence, 1923–1927, relating to sub-letting.
     2 Mortgage deeds and related correspondence; 1904–1934.

69759. *Novello And Company Business Archive*. Vol. CCXLIV. Register of mortgages and bonds; 1905–1920.

69760–69768. *Novello And Company Business Archive*. Vols CCXLV–CCLIII. Inventories, valuations, etc., Wardour Street premises; 1897–1957.[20]

Nine volumes.

- 69760. *Novello And Company Business Archive*. Vol. CCXLV. Miscellaneous papers; 1897–1947.
  1 Detailed statements of account, with receipts, etc., for fitting out Wardour Street premises and for setting up Novello & Co. as a limited company; 1897–1899.
  2 Rating valuations; 1919–1920.
  3 Miscellaneous financial papers, Novello & Co.; 1849–1947.

- 69761. *Novello And Company Business Archive*. Vol. CCXLVI. Correspondence, etc.; 1897–1944.
  1 Correspondence and papers relating to insurance and valuation of premises, plant and stock; 1897–1944.
  2 Correspondence and papers relating to local rating valuations; 1919–1935.

- 69762. *Novello And Company Business Archive*. Vol. CCXLVII. Summary valuation of furniture and fittings, and inventory and valuation of furniture, etc.; 1907. Partly *typewritten*.

- 69763. *Novello And Company Business Archive*. Vol. CCXLVIII. Valuation of fittings; 1907.

- 69764. *Novello And Company Business Archive*. Vol. CCXLIX. Register of insurance policies; [1906]-1957. Also includes some details of rates and taxes paid, a list of subscriptions to charities to 1926, and schedules of rents received, 1908–1926. With related correspondence and plans inserted.

- 69765. *Novello And Company Business Archive*. Vol. CCL. Inventory and summary valuation of plant, machinery and fittings; 1920.

- 69766. *Novello And Company Business Archive*. Vol. CCLI. Register of plant and machinery purchased and disposed of; 1920–1950.

- 69767. *Novello And Company Business Archive*. Vol. CCLII. Valuation of plant and machinery for war damage insurance; 1939–1943. Lists items acquired from 1898.

- 69768. *Novello And Company Business Archive*. Vol. CCLIII. Inventory and valuation of plant and machinery at Wardour Street premises and at Germain Street, Chesham, co. Bucks.; 1944. *Typewritten*.

G   Records of H.C. Dunckley (Wrotham) Ltd.

69769, 69770. *Novello And Company Business Archive.* Vols CCLIV,
CCLV. Records for H. C. Dunckley (Wrotham) Ltd.; 1952–1972.
>   Two volumes.
>   - 69769. *Novello And Company Business Archive.* Vol. CCLIV.
>   Minutes of directors' and general meetings; 1952–1972.
>   *Typewritten.*
>   - 69770. *Novello And Company Business Archive.* Vol. CCLV.
>   Register of members and share ledger; 1952–1972.

H   Records of Elkin and Co.

69771–69774. *Novello And Company Business Archive.* Vols
CCLVI–CCLIX. Records of Elkin and Co.; 1903–1962.[21]
>   Four volumes.
>   - 69771. *Novello And Company Business Archive.* Vol. CCLVI.
>   Minutes of general and directors' meetings; 1903–1960.
>   - 69772. *Novello And Company Business Archive.* Vol. CCLVII.
>   Stock ledger; 1918–1961. Gives numbers of copies of a work,
>   listed by title, and arranged by printer, paper size, etc. With
>   papers inserted concerning paper stocks, 1959–1962.
>   - 69773. *Novello And Company Business Archive.* Vol. CCLVIII.
>   Preference share certificates; 1903–1950.
>   - 69774. *Novello And Company Business Archive.* Vol. CCLIX.
>   Ordinary share certificates; 1903–1959.

I   Records of Goodwin and Tabb Ltd.

69775–69784. *Novello And Company Business Archive.* Vols
CCLX–CCLXIX. Records of Goodwin and Tabb Ltd.; 1914–1971.
>   Ten volumes in eleven parts.

69775, 69776. *Novello And Company Business Archive.* Vols CCLX,
CCLXI. Minutes of directors' and general meetings; 1914–1958. Partly
typewritten.
>   Two volumes.

69777. *Novello And Company Business Archive.* Vol. CCLXII. Directors'
attendance book; 1957–1971.
69778–69780. *Novello And Company Business Archive.* Vols CCLXIII–
CCLXV. Register of members and share ledger; 1914–1923, 1928.
>   Three volumes.

69781, 69782 A, B. *Novello And Company Business Archive.* Vols CCLXVI, CCLXVII A, B. Annual list and summary; 1920–1944. See Add. 69778 for 1915–1919.

Two volumes in three parts.

69783. *Novello And Company Business Archive.* Vol. CCLXVIII. Register of transfers of ordinary shares; 1920–1923.

69784. *Novello And Company Business Archive.* Vol. CCLXIX. Ordinary share certificates; 1914–1953.

J   Records of the Hollen Street Press

69785–69787. *Novello And Company Business Archive.* Vols CCLXX–CCLXXII. Records of the Hollen Street Press; 1936–1963. For inventories, etc. of premises and plant see Add. 69760–69768.

Three volumes.

- 69785. *Novello And Company Business Archive.* Vol. CCLXX. Costs and general ledger; 1936–1963. See also Add. 69658–69675.
- 69786, 69787. *Novello And Company Business Archive.* Vols CCLXXI, CCLXXII. Annual summary of capital and shares and list [of shareholders]; 1949–1961. See also Add. 69715–69720.

K   Records of Page and Thomas

69788–69791. *Novello And Company Business Archive.* Vols CCLXXIII–CCLXXVI. Records of Page and Thomas Limited; 1940–1961.

Four volumes.

- 69788. *Novello And Company Business Archive.* Vol. CCLXXIII. Private ledger; 1940–1955.
- 69789. *Novello And Company Business Archive.* Vol. CCLXXIV. Private ledger; 1955–1961.
- 69790. *Novello And Company Business Archive.* Vol. CCLXXV. Agreement for use of land in Red Lion Street, Chesham; 1960.
- 69791. *Novello And Company Business Archive.* Vol. CCLXXVI. Inventory and valuation of plant, machinery, fixtures and fittings; 1957. *Typewritten.* With related correspondence, 1958–1961. See also Add. 69768.

L   Records of William Paxton.

69792. *Novello And Company Business Archive*. Vol. CCLXXVII. Assignments of copyrights, etc., to Paxtons; 1880–1914. Mostly entered on *printed* forms, *signed* by the composers. With some related correspondence.

► NOTES

1.   Parkinson (1990), p. x.
2.   Hofmeister here refers to the *Hofmeister Monatsberichte* (and their predecessors, the *Whistling Handbuch* and *Nächtrage*). For details of the history of these publications see Elvers and Hopkinson (1972), Ratliff (1974) and Neil Ratliff's introduction to Whistling and Hofmeister (1975) p. iii-xxv.
3.   For an example, see Foreman (1991).
4.   For a history of the firm, see Hurd (1981).
5.   For details, see Banks (1995).
6.   Now Add. MSS 57056–57087.
7.   See Dibble (1983).
8.   As Loan 69.
9.   Add. MSS 65382–65525, and 69851–69864.
10.   Add. MSS 69516–69792.
11.   Loan 93.
12.   Phillips auction, Wednesday 14 June 1989: Highly important musical manuscripts formerly in the archives of Novello & Co [lot numbers 1–24].
13.   Including Elgar manuscripts which were subsequently presented to the British Library under the terms of the bequest of Mrs Carice Elgar (Mrs Samuel Blake), daughter of the composer, as Add. MSS 69827–69840.
14.   Sotheby's (London) auction, Wednesday 15 May 1996: Autograph Letters, Music Manuscripts and Books from the Novello Collection [lot numbers 1–148].
15.   In addition to this collection, the Library purchased further items from the Novello Business Archive at the 1996 Sotheby Sale (117). This collection has been assigned the temporary deposit number Deposit 1996/09 (parts A–Z, AA–GG).
16.   Fuller details can be obtained from the Curator of Music Manuscripts at the British Library.
17.   Indexes to these Commission Books are now Deposit 1996/09 parts F–G.
18.   This stockbook is now Deposit 1996/09 part E.
19.   Deposit 1996/09 (Part H) is 'Pewter plate Register no. 1'.
20.   Deposit 1996/09 (Part I) is an 1898 inventory.
21.   Further records relating to Elkin & Company are now Deposit 1996/09 (Parts AA and BB).

25 The BBC's written archives

Jacqueline Kavanagh

The role of the BBC during the 80 years of its existence in promoting and broadcasting music is well known. Much of the music from all genres composed in this century, and most performances of music of previous centuries, have been heard at some time and in some form on BBC programmes – either on the domestic or worldwide radio services or on television. Most significant performers of this century have appeared in BBC programmes, and the programmes reflect, and in some cases have instigated or influenced, musical trends that have characterised twentieth-century music of all types. The BBC has commissioned music to accompany programmes of all kinds as well as specific pieces for particular occasions. Music for broadcasting has by no means been confined to art music repertoires – all kinds of lighter and popular music, dance, pipe music, choral and religious works, brass and military bands, jazz, rock and ethnic music both from Britain and other parts of the world, are all featured.

The BBC's Written Archives, held at Caversham Park, Reading, constitute the working papers of the organisation from 1922 to the 1970s. They show in great detail how the BBC went about the task of making programmes, first for radio and later also for television. They detail the planning, production and content of these programmes, encompassing internal memoranda and minutes of meetings, financial records, correspondence with contributors, programme records of various types, extensive press cuttings, audience reaction, concert programmes, publicity and publications. These detailed internal records are available for research from the beginning up to 1979.[1] They provide an excellent source for the study of all areas of the BBC's music output.

From the very beginning, in a new aural medium, music was an obvious choice to capture and entertain a new audience. The British Broadcasting Company was founded in 1922 by a consortium of British radio manufacturers keen to promote their products after the First World War. The Company's potential market was wide. At one end were enthusiastic

BBC Internal Circulating Memo

Subject: COPYRIGHT MUSIC BY ENEMY COMPOSERS

From:

Mr.L.Isaacs

To:

M.O.

28th November, 1940

1. There has been little actual inconvenience caused to chamber-music and recital programmes by the banning of certain composers. Of course, one misses a few works which were formerly part of the standard repertoire and also several others which would have been of interest for more recherché programmes: but the number of large-scale German and Italian copyright works which might have been used for broadcasting with only one wavelength available is in any case not great, and consequently it is not possible to say that British composers have profited by their exclusion. There has been no tendency to fill a gap with a second-rate British work just because it is British.

There have, on the other hand, been more recitals than formerly intentionally devoted to British music. That many of these were song recitals is largely due to the ban on the German language, since almost all Lieder are now impossible.

2. With the possible entry into the War of more countries the implications of removing copyright enemy works from our programmes would assume large proportions and I would like to use this opportunity to question, with the greatest respect, the principles underlying this ban. I admit from the start that in war-time we should allow our own composers and performers to benefit as much as possible from our programmes. We are, however, fighting a war to restore the moral and artistic freedom of the individual as well as his national and economic freedom. I feel very deeply that by withholding performances of music by men who themselves are anti-Nazi or who have been persecuted by the Nazis or who even died before 1933, we are using the enemy's own technique to our own moral disadvantage. To me it seems an indefensible state of affairs when we perform Wagner - himself a 'proto-Nazi', and will not play a note of Schönberg who was driven out of his country by these very Nazis. The matter embraces both money and ethics and I submit that the economic aspect of the question should be subservient to the ethical one.

Imagine the position if, (to take the worst possibility), we found ourselves at war with Hungary, Spain, Russia or the Vichy Government of France . The composers affected would include Dohnanyi, Kodaly, Bartok; Falla, Turina, Albeniz; Prokofiev, Stravinsky, Medtner; Debussy, Ravel, Poulenc, Délibes, Fauré, Franck, Massenet,etc., We have little to offer to take the place of these. I believe we should include music in our programmes on its merit, nor can I see the value of any compromise which might be suggested on the grounds of expediency - for no such compromise could stand up to an accusation of inconsistency or intellectual dishonesty

(1)

Fig. 25.1: A typical page of minuting from BBC files - here showing part of the debate on banning certain enemy composers during the Second World War.
(Copyright BBC Written Archives Centre)

amateurs interested in building their own sets, many of whom were already fans of the highly entertaining experimental broadcasts put out from the Marconi Company's headquarters in Chelmsford. These frequently included broadcasts of live music – if only by the Marconi engineers – and most notably the once famous recital in June 1920 by Dame Nellie Melba, which gave wide publicity to the exciting new medium. At the other end of the market was the potentially more lucrative middle class audience, who might buy the more expensive official valve sets. It was towards this latter group that the Company's efforts were principally aimed. Although some of that audience appreciated art music, others were more likely to be wooed by more popular fare, and schedules were accordingly planned to tempt both.

The story of how the British Broadcasting Company established its credentials, became the British Broadcasting Corporation in 1927, and went on to promote to the full its famous objects – to educate, inform and entertain – is to be found in the organisation's own records. Relatively few of the Company papers survive – it was indeed only in existence for just over four years, but from the time the Corporation was founded, the archives are remarkably detailed and have survived in quantity. They reveal not merely the content of the programmes but the whole process that went into their creation. Music figured prominently and the records relating to every aspect of music programme making are particularly rich.

Because music is used as part of many different programmes, not only those which might be described as music programmes, documents giving information which is of importance to researchers occur among the papers generated by many different parts of the BBC. Programme making takes place in radio, television and the BBC's overseas services in London and its regional centres throughout Britain. It involves producers, choirs, orchestras, contracts booking managers, broadcasting engineers and accountants. Discussions of what should be broadcast and how best to carry it out, are conducted at all levels. The archives of any organisation are to some extent interconnected, but the BBC's are particularly so. For anyone intending to use the files for an extensive project, it is essential to undertake some preliminary research for the relevant period before tackling the files themselves, if their full significance is to be appreciated. The archives are the basis of Asa Briggs' history of the BBC, which is the first source for anyone needing to use them (Briggs, 1996).

The central and most important series of documents relating to programmes is the programmes-as-broadcast ('P-as-B'). This is a daily log of the content of each broadcast, made after transmission. It accurately records what went out each day on each service, radio and television, national or regional, domestic or overseas, giving details of the item – opera, recital, talk, dance band programme, radio feature, television documentary, interview – those who took part, the music used including gramophone discs, with numbers and the exact timings. These details were – and still are – needed principally for copyright reasons and for payments to those who had taken part. The sequences start with the experimental broadcasts during 1922 and carry on unbroken through the Company and Corporation's programmes.

The daily logs of national domestic radio programmes were regarded as of such importance that an edited version, entitled *BBC Programme Records*, was printed throughout the 1920s and 30s, together with index volumes, but the outbreak of war prevented any after the 1938 volume, which is unindexed. These volumes provide the only index to pre-war BBC programmes, but because the printed records have been condensed, these indexes, while useful, cannot be relied upon to identify all performances by specific performers or works by specific composers. From 1946, indexing of the daily logs was resumed but merely as an internal card index. This is available at the Centre on microfilm.

From 1923 the BBC published *Radio Times*, its official popular weekly magazine giving full details of forthcoming programmes together with articles and other information. The programmes-as-broadcast, however, provide a far more accurate record of programme content, since *Radio Times* was printed up to two weeks before the broadcasts went out. In the days of live broadcasting all kinds of last minute alterations might mean that what was published beforehand may have borne little resemblance to the final broadcast – a classic example being the first week of September 1939, as Britain declared war with Germany and scheduled programmes were abandoned.[2]

The Written Archives Centre holds a complete bound set of *Radio Times*, including all its regional variations.[3] The articles and shorter items are of great interest, particularly up to the 1960s, covering composers, conductors, orchestras, performers and incidental music for plays. A selection from the 1950s, for example, shows a regular music diary in 1951 with a piece on Kathleen Ferrier, an interview with Michael Tippett on *A Midsummer Marriage* in 1955, and items on ballads, jazz, the Llangollen International Eisteddfod and the Cheltenham Festival. There is, however, no index to *Radio Times*. From 1929 the BBC also published *The Listener*, a weekly magazine intended to support the broadcast programmes by publishing some of the talks, together with regular reviews and other articles on music, literature and science. This initially caused immense opposition from other publishers, who saw it as unfair competition, but it established itself as the BBC's serious journal and continued until 1990. The Centre has a complete set in bound volumes, with an index at the front of each volume. The talks published in *The Listener* from the previous week's programmes include many of the wide range the BBC produced on different aspects of music by both musicians and critics. However, these represent only a small proportion of the talks that were broadcast.

'As broadcast' radio talk scripts were filed for reference and survive in quantity from the 1930s onwards. The technique of sound recording for broadcasting before the Second World War was expensive and could be of uncertain quality – in effect it involved cutting a gramophone record – so that not much was undertaken, especially before c.1935.[4] Since nearly all programmes until after the war were scripted, far more scripts exist than recordings, although by no means all scripts have survived. The bulk have been transferred to microform, and are available at the Centre approximately three to four years after transmission. Some originals have been retained where they have handwritten alterations or other intrinsic value. A comprehensive personal and subject index to the national radio talks scripts, including overseas broadcasts, was maintained up to 1969, but there is no comparable index to the television scripts and few regional indexes exist.

Almost from its inception, the BBC saw its role specifically as a public service and as educational, both in the range and content of programmes. 'The policy of the BBC being to bring the best of everything into the greatest number of homes, it follows that if this policy be carried out, that many educative influences must have been stirred.'[5] There were no previous patterns to follow, no distinct guidelines, and there was a great willingness to experiment, to try all kinds of new methods in building the programmes. This applied in the field of music as much as in drama or talks, including talks about music. While many in the musical establishment were suspicious of the new medium, others embraced its opportunities enthusiastically. 'While admitting the desirability or even necessity of catering for extreme tastes, the endeavour has been to transmit as much music as possible . . . It is an accepted fact that broadcasting has been the means of educating musically large numbers of people.'[6]

Educational broadcasts included on the one hand programmes specifically for schools and on the other those aimed at an adult audience. Sir Henry Walford Davies was popular with both groups. He began experimental broadcasts for schools with a talk on music in April 1924. The Centre has copies of many scripts of the programmes designed specially for schools, together with correspondence files and the published pamphlets issued both for pupils and teachers. These provide examples over many years of how music was presented to all ages of schoolchildren, from *Adventures in Music* for the youngest to programmes for senior schools. The BBC Schools Broadcasting Council had special committees discussing music education, whose minutes are also available.

One of the earliest series for adults was *Music and the Ordinary Listener* in 1926. The *Foundations of Music* series begun in 1927, included many first broadcast performances of early English music and served as an introduction to the Western art music canon.[7] A report on the series in the *BBC Handbook* for 1930[8] speaks of 13 weeks devoted to Schubert as well as performances of Beethoven, Wolf, Handel's harpsichord pieces and English madrigals. This was in addition to other regular broadcasts of 'most of the standard works by the great masters at least once from every station . . . the cream of nearly four centuries' orchestral music'. In this same year listeners heard new British chamber music from Bax, Ireland, Goossens, Bliss, Alan Bush and Gordon Jacob, and 50 first performances in Britain of works by contemporary composers from Britain and the continent, many taking place in the remarkable series *BBC Concerts of Contemporary Music* (see Doctor, 1999)

'Until now the public has never had the opportunity broadcasting gives in keeping *au fait* with what is happening in the world of modern music.'[9] Later during the 1930s and 40s series such as *Music and Dance*, *The Musician Speaks* and *Writers and Music* brought composers, performers and critics to the microphone to talk about their work and share their knowledge and enthusiasm.

The producers in both radio and television are the key to programme making. Production staff were employed for their knowledge of their subject and wide range of contacts, so that they could introduce new and exciting broadcasters and work with them on an equal footing. In the main it is the producers who put up ideas for new programmes, whether single broadcasts or series. At first the process was very informal but as the BBC became larger, it was organised into departments with a division between Programmes and Administration and the process became more formalised, partly as the result of the demands of wartime broadcasting. Suggestions for programmes were submitted to the head of the department. If approved, the programme would be 'offered' to the Controller in charge of a particular channel or service.

Once accepted, the producer would put the programme together, contacting the people he wanted to take part, discussing the best approach, arranging rehearsals, mounting the final broadcast and thanking the participants. In radio particularly, each step of this process was very largely in the producer's own hands and was normally set down on paper until the telephone gradually took over, although some producers were naturally better organised than others.[10] The resulting files document the growth of the idea, the influence of different people, the changes made on the way and the success or failure of the finished broadcast. The correspondence is of great value both to the biographer and the bibliographer. A variety of material may survive, ranging from quite personal letters to trivial or ephemeral items. Any enclosures are likely to have been filed with the original covering letter and may include concert handbills, a list of composers' works or a press cutting. Television programmes require a much more complex team of people, so the programme files have a less personal feel and tend to contain more forms and fewer letters.

The coming of television in 1936, even though it was available only to very few people in the London area, allowed programme makers to tackle a new range of musical subjects. In spite of enormous technical limitations imposed by the cumbersome cameras and hot lights, producers like Christian Simpson and Paddy Foy put on ballet, including *Façade* from Sadler's Wells with Margot Fonteyn in 1937, and opera, including *Amahl and the Night Visitors*, an opera by Gian Carlo Menotti written for television in America. Television closed down for the duration of the war in 1939 and did not reopen until 1946, but following the reopening there were wide-ranging productions such as the *Workshop* series with subjects from Pierre Boulez to The Beatles. The advent of a second BBC television channel in 1964 also extended the opportunities, and many files are available up to the 1970s for programmes about music such as the *Monitor* series and Ken Russell's imaginative feature *Isadora*.

For those who were asked to take part in radio programmes, the BBC issued different contracts depending on the capacity in which they were being asked to contribute. Each type of contract was negotiated by a different contractual office and generated a separate file. Someone like Benjamin Britten, therefore, might have a number of different files: *Artist* for programmes where he performed; *Composer* if he was asked to compose music – as he did, for example, for Louis MacNeice's radio 'feature' *The Dark Tower*; *Talks* if he spoke about music; *Copyright* for permission to use his compositions. Contracts for television appearances after 1946 are to be found in a separate sequence of *Television Artists* files. Appearances booked in the regions would result in correspondence and contracts in the regional registry at, say, Glasgow or Birmingham. Known collectively as contributors' files, these are the main source for music biographers and bibliographers. Far from being dry and formal or solely concerned with the negotiation of fees, in many ways they complement the programme files and are often full of original letters discussing the musicians' contributions.[11] The relationships with BBC staff were often friendly and open, since many personal contacts were established over the years. The exchanges are certainly very revealing. There is a handwritten letter from Paul Hindemith addressed in heartfelt gratitude to Adrian Boult, who helped him leave Switzerland for America early in 1940, by sending an official letter to the British Consul in Geneva in support of Hindemith and describing him as 'a friendly Alien who is devoting his life not only to his own, but to all music.' As a German passport holder, Hindemith had feared detention by the British in Gibraltar. It is also delightful to read, in neat green ink, Havergal Brian's unassuming pleasure at the prospect of hearing his music played for the first time. Others, not necessarily so modest, made shrill demands or complained of neglect.

While the producers got on with the work of making programmes, slightly broader discussions would be going on at departmental level – Should there be more avant-garde or well-known music? Fewer operas and more dance bands? What emphasis should be given to special interests such as folk song or madrigals? At what time were certain types of music most suitable for broadcasting and what new initiatives should be considered? Many of these discussions appear in the Music Department's papers, recorded both in the minutes of meetings and in memoranda. Discussions between more senior managers across departments tend to be found in the files in the Radio and Television Policy sections and address the thorny issues of standards and matters of taste which affected all programme areas. These might range from applause in programmes to crooning, from opera subsidy to programme presentation. The debate of these issues makes the BBC's files an excellent source for the study of popular culture and changing taste in all areas of music.

Regular research into audience reaction to both radio and television[12] programmes was undertaken from 1937 onwards. This covered both broad surveys of the number of listeners to particular programmes or services and reports on specific topics such as Chamber Music and Studio Orchestral Concerts (1937); *Music While You Work* (1940); Ballet (1956); Age, Sex and Social Class Viewing (1963). Copies of the reports were sometimes placed on programme files but the Centre also has a comprehensive set available up to 1982. The Centre's extensive collection of press cuttings on broadcasting from the 1920s to the 1960s is also a major source of additional details of performances and contemporary criticism.

All major initiatives, such as the initiation of the Music Programme in 1964,[13] regional development or the centralisation of certain functions, for example during the war, would be referred first to the BBC's executive Board of Management and then perhaps to its highest authority, the Board of Governors, and would appear in the series of minutes and papers that exist for both. Board Papers often give an excellent summary of the history of a particular issue to that point.

From the days of the Company, the BBC also enlisted the help of advisory councils or committees, both nationally and in the regions. A Music Advisory Committee was set up as early as 1925, which included Walford Davies, Hugh Allen and Donald Tovey. It was consulted regularly, although it tended to be far more conservative than the Music Department staff. There was an Opera Advisory Committee (1927–36) and the Music Programme Advisory Panel helped with detailed programming decisions from 1934. The minutes of these advisory bodies, including regional music advisory committees, are available together with the music reports – assessments of recently composed works to be considered for inclusion in BBC programmes – which in the 1930s and 40s were prepared by members of the Music Advisory Panel.

Percy Pitt, the BBC's first Director of Music, and his successors, Adrian Boult, William Glock and others, saw broadcasting as a tremendous opportunity to bring all kinds of music from all over Europe to their audience in a way that had never been possible before. In the earlier years, concert managers, like their theatrical counterparts and newspaper proprietors, regarded broadcasting as a tremendous threat to their livelihoods, and it took some time before it was realised that the new medium in fact fed the older ones. Broadcasting, far from killing concert attendance, created opportunities and interest among those who had never previously had the opportunity to hear performances of such a high standard.[14]

That these archives are available for research today is largely the result of good record-keeping practices at the time. During the late 1920s the BBC formalised its record-keeping systems in London along lines similar to those used in most British government departments at that time. This involved the introduction of centralised filing registries whose function was to create and keep track of files by 'registering' them, i.e. keeping a record of the existence and whereabouts of each file and the papers it contained. The registries created their own filing systems and issued the files as necessary to those staff who required them. The registry services were used by all staff from the Director General down and the regional centres based in Scotland, Wales, Northern Ireland and throughout England followed suit by setting up registries in the early 1930s. Although there were major disruptions during the Second World War, this system of records management carried on in substantially the same way in most areas until the late 1960s or mid-1970s. From that time the London registries began to introduce numerical classification schemes for the files and there was a gradual tendency to move away from large centralised registries towards smaller filing units situated nearer to and tailored to their users. This has resulted in a greater fragmentation of the sources from that time.

Although the documents were brought together in the original large registries, they were not placed in one huge sequence of files. The registry systems largely arranged the files firstly according to the department from which the papers originated, and only then according to subject of the documents, since each department calling for the files would want to refer to its own papers rather than those of another. Files within each section were stored alphabetically by title, although there were often subsections grouping topics together. The Written Archives Centre has followed standard archival practice in preserving the original arrangement as far as possible. As far as the Music Department's papers are concerned, registry practice resulted in a large sequence of files entitled Music General, which gives an excellent overview of the department's work and concerns. These covered topics as disparate as the Aldeburgh Festival, the Broadcasting House Organ, Commissioned Works, Folk Music, the International Society for Contemporary Music, Song Plugging and Swing, among many others. This sequence can be supplemented by reference to others generated by other departments and dealing with the BBC's orchestras and singers, with advisory committees, television music, schools broadcasts, outside broadcasts and foreign relays, and by files from some of the regions, where similar topics arose – there are papers about the Aldeburgh Festival, for example, among the Midland Region files – in addition to those with a local flavour, such as pipe music in Scotland.

The sheer quantity and range of music the BBC wished to broadcast, particularly symphony concerts, led the BBC to establish its own orchestras. On the one hand they faced opposition from the concert organisers and gramophone record manufacturers, and on the other, lack of co-operation and poor standards among many of the orchestras of the time. Initially, London and the main regional stations had instrumental ensembles of about 18 players, combinations of which provided orchestral, chamber and light music for early programmes. The 2LO[15] Wireless Orchestra, formed on an *ad hoc* basis in 1924, was eventually succeeded by the permanent BBC Symphony Orchestra[16] in 1930, after the BBC failed to reach agreement with Sir Thomas Beecham over the foundation of a new national orchestra. It became one of the finest orchestras of the world. A parallel development of singers began equally early.[17] Apart from the files covering these topics, complete bound volume sets of printed concert programmes exist in the archives for the BBC Symphony Concerts as well as those for the Promenade Concerts, which the BBC rescued from the threat of closure in 1927[18] after the death of Robert Newman, the Proms founder.

The BBC's involvement with the Proms led to the inclusion of a far wider repertoire, since it was no longer imperative to consider the box office before all else. The files show that broadcasting, however, also brought its own difficulties, as programme makers tried to persuade the Proms organisers to consider the radio listeners as well as the audience in the hall. New works were commissioned for the Proms and for many other programmes from both established and comparatively unknown composers. It is possible to read the letter from George Bernard Shaw suggesting to Reith in 1932 that he should commission Sir Edward Elgar to write a new symphony, and Elgar's delighted reply accepting it. The 'Commissioned Works' files contain the background to a whole catalogue of exciting new music over the years from composers as different as Walton (*Belshazzar's Feast* and *Crown Imperial*), Bliss (violin concerto), Rubbra (piano concerto) and Vaughan Williams (*Thanksgiving for Victory*, later called *A Song of Thanksgiving*), as well as pieces for the BBC Light Programme Music Festival from Coates, Farnon, Phillips and Haydn Wood, military band works from Alan Bush, and religious pieces from Finzi and Jacob. Benjamin Britten's television opera *Owen Wingrave* was a commission from the European Broadcasting Union, in which the BBC was closely involved, but Britten also wrote incidental music for a number of radio programmes before he became so well known.

The inauguration of the Third Programme[19] in 1946 greatly increased the scope for experimental broadcasting. It was from the outset conceived as a place where full rein could be given to broadcasting the unusual and the exciting in both speech and music, unrestricted by the need to observe fixed points for broadcasts such as news bulletins. This allowed much greater flexibility for example in broadcasting concerts and opera. The BBC also experimented with new forms of music and the Written Archives Centre has examples of music composed by the BBC Radiophonic Workshop to accompany radio features with titles such as *The Wall Walks Slowly* or *The Snail Has Jammed Again*.

In 1948 an ambitious project was begun in co-operation with the New

Oxford History of Music for a *History of Music in Sound*, which involved weekly concert programmes with accompanying notes. It was intended to cover European music from the Middle Ages to the present day, with accompanying gramophone records produced by the HMV company, but the series ran into difficulties and was never completed.

In addition to the music broadcast on the Third Programme, much standard repertory and lighter music was performed during these years on the Home Service and the Light Programme. Many British composers were keen for their work to be represented on the Home because it meant they had been accepted as part of the mainstream of British music. The Centre also has much to offer the student of these strands of music.

The whole range of popular music has featured in the BBC's programmes from dance bands in the days of Harry Roy and Geraldo's Gaucho Tango Orchestra through hot jazz and swing, to big bands and the birth of skiffle, rock and 'pop' music. The files at the Written Archives Centre can be used to trace the early appearances of major figures on Radio 1, *The Old Grey Whistle Test* or *Top of the Pops*,[20] as well as those featured in more classical areas. They record attempts to ban song plugging and the fierce debates which raged around whether particular kinds of music should be broadcast at all, particularly those which were regarded by some as 'degenerate' or 'barbarous' – terms which have been applied to most kinds of popular music at different times.

All these sources are available to researchers at the Centre, but they should be aware that for copyright reasons it is often not possible to supply copies of documents without the written permission of the copyright holder. Anyone wishing to use the BBC's written archives should contact the Written Archivist, BBC Written Archives Centre, Caversham Park, Reading RG4 7ER well in advance, giving as much information about the nature of their research as possible. Because of pressure on resources, the reading room is open only on certain days and access is restricted. Available places may be booked up for many weeks ahead, particularly during busy periods. The Written Archives Centre now has a website (<www.bbc.co.uk/thenandnow>) and may be contacted by e-mail (<wac.enquiries@bbc.co.uk>). Otherwise by phone or fax (tel: 0118-948-6281; fax: 0118-946-1145).

▶ REFERENCES

Briggs, A. (1996) *History of Broadcasting in the United Kingdom* (vols I–V). London: OUP

Carpenter, H. (1996) *The Envy of the World: Fifty Years of the BBC Third Programme and Radio 3*. London: Weidenfeld & Nicolson

Cox, D. (1980) *The Henry Wood Proms* London: BBC

Doctor, J.R. (1993) *The BBC and the Ultra-modern Problem: A Documentary Study of the British Broadcasting Corporation's Dissemination of the Second Viennese School Repertory, 1922–36* (Dissertation for Doctor of Philosophy of the Northwestern University, Evanston, Illinois, USA)

Doctor, J.R. (1999) *The BBC and Ultra-Modern Music, 1922–1936: shaping a nation's taste,* Cambridge, Cambridge University Press

Foreman, L. (1981) Grainger at the BBC. In: *The Percy Grainger Companion.* London: Thames

Garner, K. (1993) *In Session Tonight* London: BBC

Hibberd, S. (1950) *This Is London . . .* London: Macdonald & Evans

Kenyon, N. (1981) *The BBC Symphony Orchestra: The First Fifty Years 1930–1980.* London: BBC

Reith, J.C.W. (1924) *Broadcast Over Britain* London: Hodder and Stoughton

Scannell, P. and Cardiff, D. (1991) *A Social History of British Broadcasting Vol. 1: 1922–39.* Oxford: Basil Blackwell

Silvey, R. (1974) *Who's Listening?* London: George Allen & Unwin

▶ NOTES

1.   This date is revised regularly.
2.   Hibberd (1950) gives a good idea of the nature of broadcasting in the 1920s and 30s.
3.   A number of libraries hold extensive sets, including Westminster Central Reference Library.
4.   Facilities for listening to BBC recordings can be provided at National Sound Archive at The British Library.
5.   Reith (1924).
6.   ibid.
7.   See Doctor (1993), pp. 128–30. This thesis gives an extensive account of the BBC's music policy and output during this period. It is now published as Doctor (1999).
8.   *BBC Handbooks* (also called *Yearbooks*) were published for each year except 1953 and 1954. A complete set is held at the Centre. The articles they contain provide an excellent overview of the previous year's broadcasting.
9.   *BBC Yearbook* 1930, p. 67.
10. Some also tended to regard letters received on BBC business as their own, Letters addressed to Edward Clark, for example, are now to be found in The British Library's Additional MSS 52256–7. Clark's own papers are now at Northwestern University Music Library.
11. For examples of items to be found on Percy Grainger's files see Foreman (1981).
12. For the setting up and work of the BBC Audience Research Department see Silvey (1974).
13. See Carpenter (1996), pp. 227–8.

14. See Carpenter (1996) and Briggs (1996).
15. In the early years each station had to have its own call sign. 2L0 was the call sign of the BBC's London station.
16. See Kenyon (1981).
17. 'By the mid-thirties the BBC was easily the largest single employer of professional musicians and the most powerful patron of music in the country' (Scannell, 1991). This book provides an excellent account of the pre-war BBC music policies and output.
18. For an account of the history of the Promenade Concerts, see Cox (1980).
19. For a detailed history of the Third Programme see Carpenter (1996).
20. For an account of bands recorded live on Radio 1 see Garner (1993).

26 Ephemera of concert life: programmes and press cuttings

Stephen Lloyd

Music researchers, music historians, musicologists – call them what you like – are more often than not, like the criminal detective, in search of one thing: the truth. And if they are concerned with past performances of a work – often the first performance – that truth is often only reached after sifting through what one might term musical ephemera: old programmes, press cuttings, letters, diaries, etc. The Royal Academy of Music's acquisition in 1999 of a very extensive collection of programmes, photographs, cuttings and miscellaneous recordings from the music agent Norman McCann[1] conveniently focuses our attention on the unique archival value of ephemera in musical research.

The changing habits, patterns and customs of concert-giving over the past 200 years, the make-up of the programmes, the popularity or otherwise of certain composers (the one-time absence of much Mozart, the remarkable 'boom years' of Sibelius and Mahler), are all aspects for which the researcher is dependent on such ephemera that can often be difficult to locate, in some cases non-existent or lost. Even material relating to more recent years can sometimes be beyond the researcher's grasp: war-time bombing, fires and wholesale clearances have resulted in much being lost. Much which the researcher is seeking is by its very nature essentially transitory as far as most of its original users were concerned: concert programmes that may have consisted of only a single sheet or two being an obvious example. Although there have been studies of the rise of concert-giving,[2] so far as it is known, no one has thought to review systematically the availability of such fugitive material, or assess its importance, though there are signs of activity in the British research community as this chapter closes for press. This chapter can only touch on certain aspects but it is nevertheless hoped that it will offer suggestions for the new researcher.

The chief items of documentation that one may be seeking are:

- programmes;
- handbills, posters and press advertisements; and
- press coverage, reviews, press cuttings,

together with pictures, publishers' catalogues and auction catalogues (discussed by other contributors). Sound recordings also constitute a related but separate category of material and are dealt with in CHAPTER 21.

From the researcher's viewpoint such material is unique and is only reassembled retrospectively with great difficulty. This is especially true of collections of press cuttings which, particularly when they are loose and unmounted, may not be properly valued by those finding them among collections of miscellaneous papers. It is probably fair to say that many libraries, particularly public libraries, when in receipt of such material from bequests and house clearances, are not always aware of its value. Neither do they always have the necessary funds to have such collections bound or conserved for safer handling. Newsprint is not a permanent medium, but cuttings once mounted can be remarkably durable. However, they need to be treated with care, because the paper of some turn-of-the-century scrapbooks – as also some photograph albums – has deteriorated much more quickly and dramatically than the cuttings mounted on it. A spectacular example is the scrapbook of the Apollo Musical Club of Chicago, now held at the Chicago Historical Society, where the extreme fragility of the album pages threatens the survival of the cuttings themselves. A similar case are the 13 volumes of scrapbooks of press cuttings, programmes, articles, letters, photographs and other memorabilia that once belonged to Sir Dan Godfrey (founder conductor of the Bournemouth Municipal Orchestra, 1893–1934). Deteriorating through constant use and with many letters from such figures as Elgar and Dame Ethel Smyth lying loose within these scrapbooks, the urgent need for binding and cataloguing was, at the time of enquiry, beyond the means of the Bournemouth Reference Library, in whose care they reside. It is arguable too that material belonging to less well-known or local composers and musicians such as Godfrey may be of greater historical significance, though less monetary value, in that it is unlikely to be replicated elsewhere in any way. An indicator of how we regard such ephemera may be deduced from time to time when it appears in dealers' catalogues, but rarely commands significant prices. (See also Nigel Simeone's remarks on dealers and ephemera in CHAPTER 4.)

▶ PROGRAMMES

Concert programmes are often a vital source of information. A copy of a programme may help to establish such details as a place and date of performance, the actual performers involved, sometimes which version of the

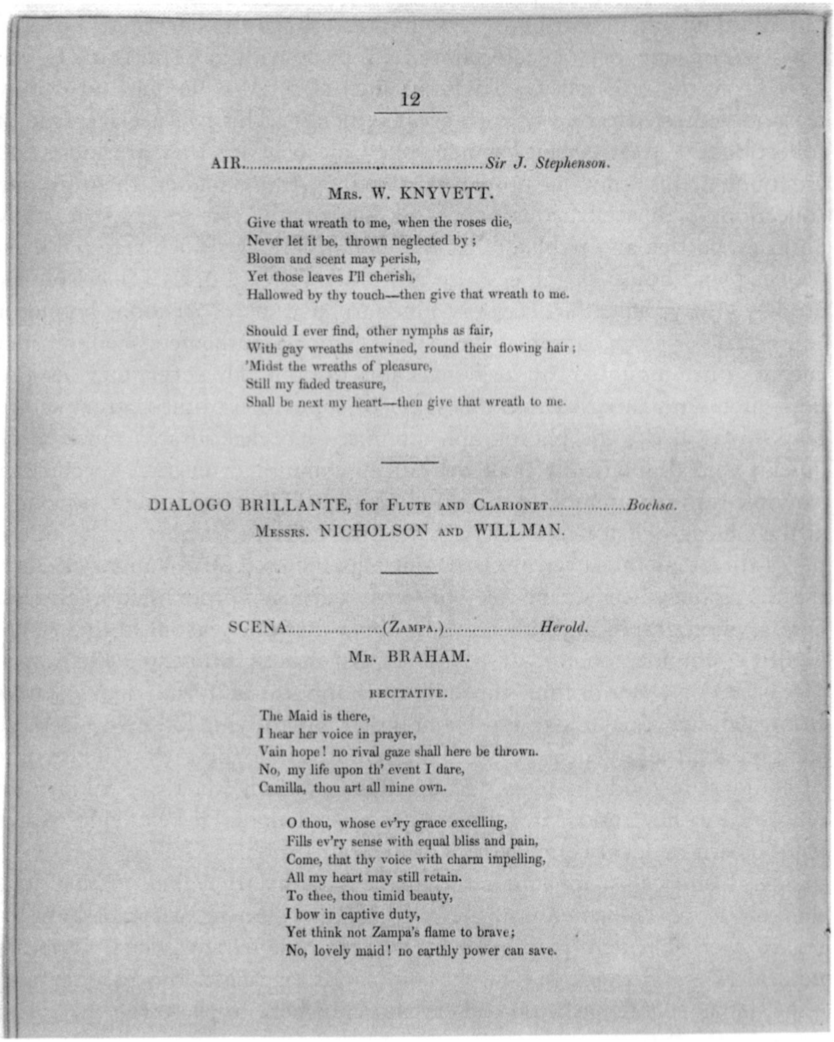

12

AIR...Sir J. Stephenson.

MRS. W. KNYVETT.

Give that wreath to me, when the roses die,
Never let it be, thrown neglected by ;
Bloom and scent may perish,
Yet those leaves I'll cherish,
Hallowed by thy touch—then give that wreath to me.

Should I ever find, other nymphs as fair,
With gay wreaths entwined, round their flowing hair ;
'Midst the wreaths of pleasure,
Still my faded treasure,
Shall be next my heart—then give that wreath to me.

DIALOGO BRILLANTE, for FLUTE AND CLARIONET...............Bochsa.

MESSRS. NICHOLSON AND WILLMAN.

SCENA..............(ZAMPA.).................Herold.

MR. BRAHAM.

RECITATIVE.

The Maid is there,
I hear her voice in prayer,
Vain hope ! no rival gaze shall here be thrown.
No, my life upon th' event I dare,
Camilla, thou art all mine own.

O thou, whose ev'ry grace excelling,
Fills ev'ry sense with equal bliss and pain,
Come, that thy voice with charm impelling,
All my heart may still retain.
To thee, thou timid beauty,
I bow in captive duty,
Yet think not Zampa's flame to brave ;
No, lovely maid ! no earthly power can save.

Fig. 26.1: A page from the Grand Miscellaneous Concert of the 1836 Manchester Festival, on 13 September, showing the typical layout of the time without discussion of the works performed.

work was used – whether complete or in part – and can offer other important details. Even the context of the performance – the remainder of the
programme and the other performers – may be of particular interest.
Equally helpfully, the programme may contain an authoritative note, even
one by the composer, and in certain cases it may contain music examples.

This chapter is largely written from a British, indeed a London,
perspective, but the sheer variety of music in London provides a useful
parallel for those studying musical life in any great city. The article on
'Concert' in the third edition of *Grove's Dictionary* lists the following
London-based institutions as then being of primary importance from the
historical point of view (1927):

- Orchestral:
    - Royal Philharmonic Society (originally Philharmonic
      Society, 1813)[3]
    - New Philharmonic Society (1852–79)
    - Crystal Palace Symphony Concerts (1855–1901)
    - British Orchestral Society (1872–75)
    - Richter (Symphony Concerts begun 1879)
    - Henschel (London Symphony Concerts begun 1886)
    - Promenade Concerts (1895)
    - New Queen's Hall Orchestra (originally Queen's Hall
      Orchestra, 1897)
    - London Symphony Orchestra (1902)
    - Royal Albert Hall Orchestra (originally New Symphony
      Orchestra, 1906).

- Choral:
    - Sacred Harmonic Society (1832–82)
    - Royal Choral Society (1872)
    - Bach Choir (1875)
    - London Choral Society (1903)
    - Philharmonic Choir (1920).

- Chamber music:
    - Popular Concerts
    - People's Concert Society (1878)
    - Classical Concert Society.

To these one can add the triennial festivals of Leeds, Sheffield, York,
Norwich, Cardiff, Bristol, Birmingham,[4] Newcastle-upon-Tyne and other
less celebrated centres, together with the Three (Cathedral) Choirs of Worcester, Gloucester and Hereford; the Bournemouth Municipal Orchestra
concerts (from 1895);[5] Granville Bantock's New Brighton concerts
(1897–1900); the pre-World War One chamber concerts run by the piano-
making firm of Broadwood; the Josef Holbrooke chamber concerts (from

Fig. 26.2: Queen's Hall programme for Debussy's appearance to conduct the first English performance of his *Three Nocturnes*, Queen's Hall, 27 February 1909.

1902) held in different towns and cities; the Royal College of Music and the Patron's Fund Concerts (begun in 1903 and becoming after the First War public rehearsals instead of formal concerts);[6] the Oriana Madrigal Society concerts (1905–1922); the Thomas Dunhill chamber concerts (from 1907); the Edward Mason Choral and Orchestral Concerts of British music (1908–1914); the two series of Balfour Gardiner Choral and Orchestral Concerts of British music (1912 and 1913);[7] the F.B. Ellis Chamber and Orchestral Concerts (1914); the London Musical Festivals; the Courtauld-Sargent Concerts (1930–1940);[8] and many others. The Ellis Orchestral Concerts programmes (copies in the British Library) provide an example of the worth of such documentation, containing as they do not only George Butterworth's note for the first performance of Vaughan Williams's *A London Symphony* but also 27 extensive music examples of that work in short score, some of them illustrating passages that the composer cut when revising the symphony.

The same edition of *Grove* carries an important article on 'Analytical Notes' by H.C. Colles[9] that is worth consulting. In British concert life it was Sir George Grove who consolidated the format of the analytical programme. This provided a brief biography followed by a detailed description of the music to be played, with extensive music-type examples. However, the first coherent series of such programmes came with John Ella's Musical Union in the 1840s, when he published a 'record of the Musical Union' from 1845,[10] including what he called a 'Synopsis Analytique'. After a few years this publication increased its value to us as a research tool when it included a listing of the works (including operas) performed in London.[11]

As far as London was concerned, 1859 saw the establishment of the Monday Popular Concerts and 'the programmes contained notices of the pieces.'[12] In 1869 the Philharmonic Society (later Royal Philharmonic – RPS) started publishing analytical programmes, at first written by Sir George Macfarren, and subsequently continued by a wide variety of leading commentators and historians, including such significant names as Edward J. Dent. The bound run of their programmes still held by the RPS constitutes one of the major research tools on concert life in London over more than 100 years.

However, perhaps the most influential series of London concerts was the Crystal Palace Saturday Concerts, conducted by Sir August Manns, which ran from the mid-1850s until their gradual demise between 1900 and 1902. In the preface to his history of the Crystal Palace, Michael Musgrave underlines the value of such material:

> *I first became interested in the music of the Crystal Palace whilst researching the first performance of Brahms orchestral music in England: I had no idea of the true extent of its importance. I soon discovered that Brahms formed only a very small part of*

its musical story: that a considerable slice of what was soon to be regarded as the standard orchestral repertoire had first been heard in Britain at the Crystal Palace.[13]

The Crystal Palace was destroyed by fire in 1936, with its archives, and, as Musgrave has pointed out 'Crystal Palace programmes are never to be found in complete runs of more than a few years without significant omissions, and the programmes for the early years are very rare indeed.'[14] Programmes for these concerts are most informative, with extensive notes on the works performed and music examples. The support that Manns gave to British music through these concerts makes these programmes all the more important. The Crystal Palace is a prime example of the need of a union catalogue or finding list of such material, for in spite of the considerable collections of programmes at the Royal College of Music, in the British Library, and Bromley and West Norwood public libraries, the most consistent collection of these programmes is actually held at the Henry Watson Music Library in Manchester,[15] but there is no systematic method save creative use of published directories such as the *ASLIB Directory* and specialist directories of music libraries and a wide acquaintance with music archives to know that they are there.

Generally, until well after the Second World War it was the practice to print programmes in a standard format, often paged successively, and thus suitable for binding into volumes. (Of course there were special occasions – such as the Henry Wood Jubilee Concert at Queen's Hall in October 1938, whose large format programme is of particular value for the many photographs of those taking part.) Sets were made up both by individuals and organisations, significantly increasing the likelihood of their survival. This is a practice still continued by the major American orchestras. One concert series had programme notes of such quality that they demanded wider dissemination. These were those written by Donald Francis Tovey for the Reid Orchestra of Edinburgh throughout the inter-war period. In 1937 a broad selection of Tovey's programme notes were issued in six volumes by Oxford University Press as *Essays in Musical Analysis*.[16] However, a large number of Tovey's notes were not collected and these make a set of the Reid Concert programmes of some importance, particularly for the cumulative index of works performed in previous seasons.

OUP clearly saw such notes as a source of continuing revenue, for the following year they published Rosa Newmarch's notes for Queen's Hall concerts and for the Proms, which were selectively reprinted in hardback pocket book format in six volumes as 'The Concert-Goer's Library of Descriptive Notes'.

▶ TRACING PROGRAMMES

Where do we find collections of concert programmes? To answer this question we need to consider who would have collected programmes and why. In fact, the following are all likely collectors of programmes at the time they were current, and a good guide to where collections may be held today:

- local libraries or archives (e.g.: Manchester, Birmingham, Leeds, Torquay, especially those towns that had their own municipal orchestra or held festivals);
- conservatoire libraries;
- performing artists;
- individual composers or their families;
- societies promoting concerts (including the orchestras themselves);
- halls where concerts were presented;
- artists' agents;
- critics;
- individual concert goers; and
- legal deposit in national libraries.

If we consider concert halls in London, we find that the Wigmore Hall has a fairly comprehensive collections of its programmes dating from the founding of the hall as the Bechstein Hall before the First World War, and kept on deposit at the Royal College of Music. In the case of the more recently established Royal Festival Hall, a comprehensive archive has been maintained by the hall since it was opened in 1951. However, the more recently founded Barbican Hall does not appear to be maintaining an archive of such material, though its resident orchestra, the London Symphony Orchestra, does. A complete set of its programmes is maintained by the orchestra, though access to them is usually at one remove, through a member of the office staff. Similarly in the case of opera houses; certainly the Royal Opera's archives include programmes, cuttings (mounted in large guard books), photographs and a wide variety of stage ephemera.

Many libraries have a variety of miscellaneous programmes, but finding them in catalogues can present a problem. In the UK, the largest collection of miscellaneous programmes is probably that at the Royal College of Music, though for most researchers the extent of its holdings is an unknown quantity.[17] These are usefully indexed on cards for first performances. But there are others collections, notably at the Henry Watson Music Library in Manchester, in Birmingham Central Library, Glasgow Public Library, Edinburgh City Libraries and the Central Music Library at Westminster Music Library. There are constant anomalies; for example, despite the large holdings at the RCM, we should not forget the 40-year run of Queen's Hall programmes at the Royal Academy of Music Library,

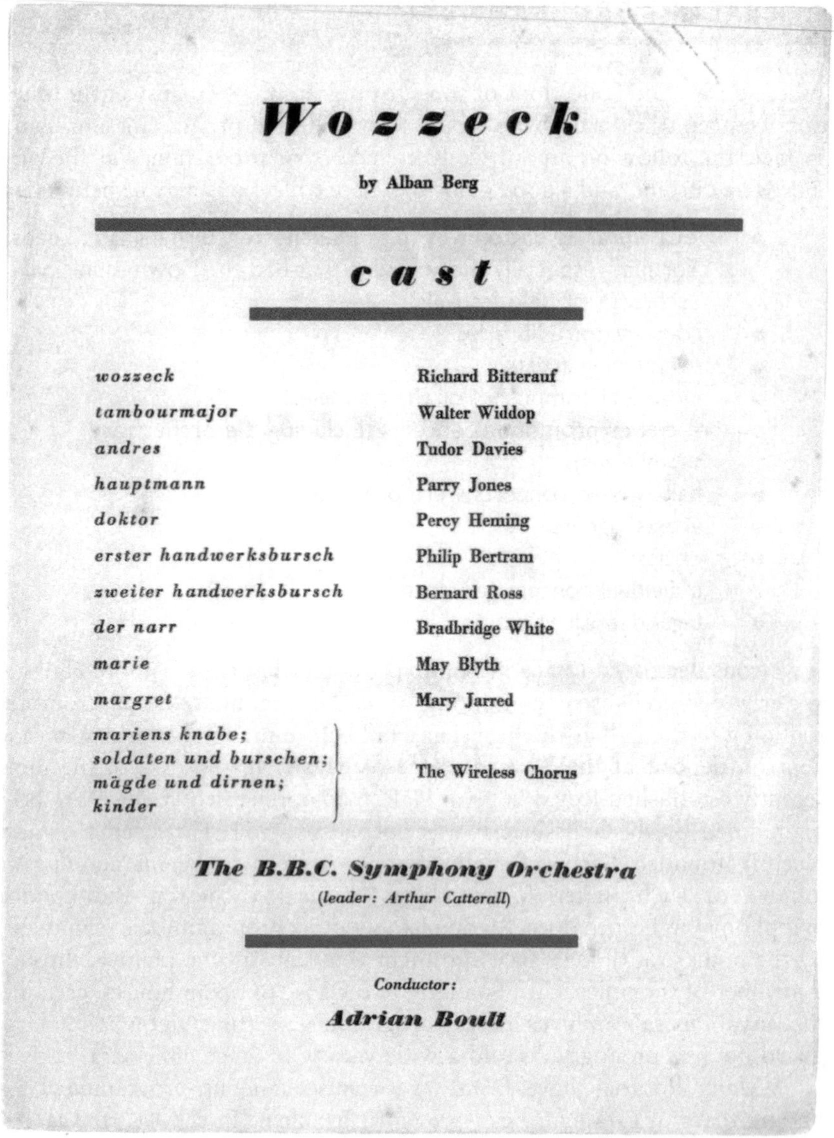

Wozzeck

by Alban Berg

cast

wozzeck	Richard Bitterauf
tambourmajor	Walter Widdop
andres	Tudor Davies
hauptmann	Parry Jones
doktor	Percy Heming
erster handwerksbursch	Philip Bertram
zweiter handwerksbursch	Bernard Ross
der narr	Bradbridge White
marie	May Blyth
margret	Mary Jarred
mariens knabe; *soldaten und burschen;* *mägde und dirnen;* *kinder*	The Wireless Chorus

The B.B.C. Symphony Orchestra

(*leader: Arthur Catterall*)

Conductor:

Adrian Boult

Fig. 26.3: BBC promotional literature, particularly from the 1930s, can be a useful documentary source. Here the two sides of the one page flier (printed in red and black) for the first British performance of Berg's *Wozzeck* on 14 March 1934.

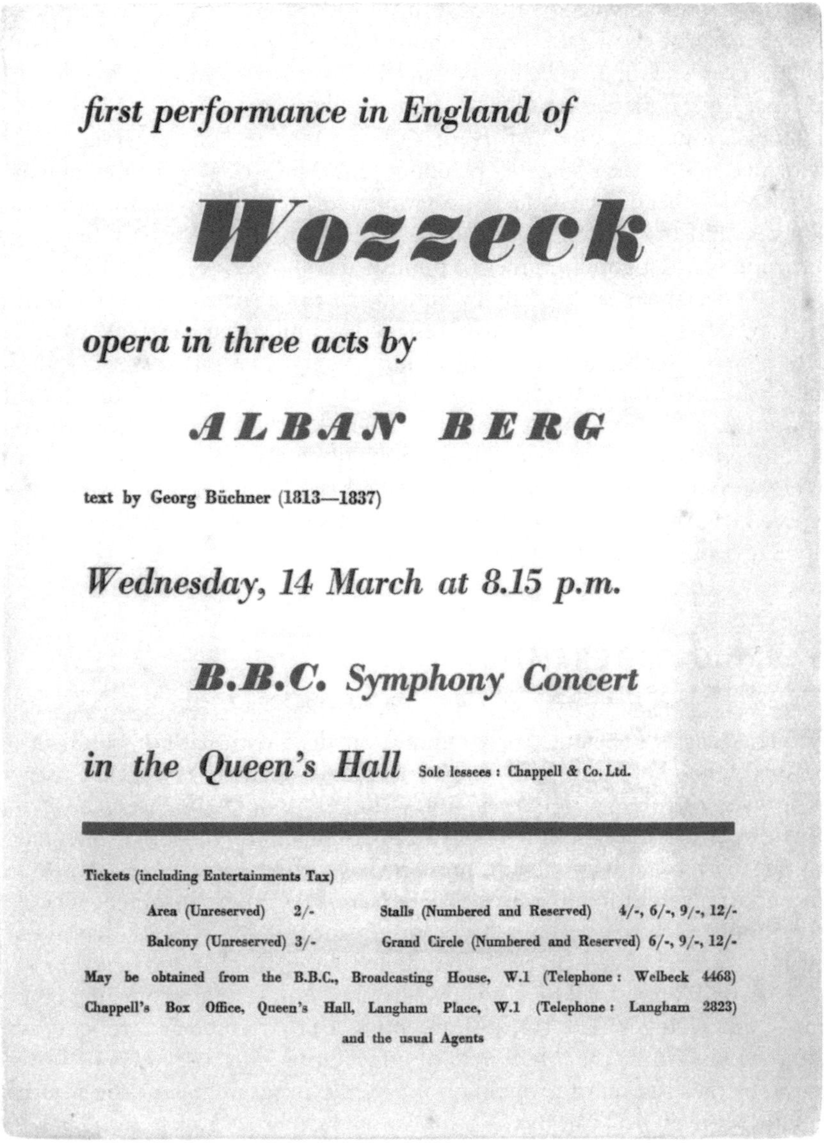

first performance in England of

Wozzeck

opera in three acts by

ALBAN BERG

text by Georg Büchner (1813—1837)

Wednesday, 14 March at 8.15 p.m.

B.B.C. *Symphony Concert*

in the Queen's Hall Sole lessees : Chappell & Co. Ltd.

Tickets (including Entertainments Tax)

Area (Unreserved) 2/-	Stalls (Numbered and Reserved)	4/-, 6/-, 9/-, 12/-
Balcony (Unreserved) 3/-	Grand Circle (Numbered and Reserved)	6/-, 9/-, 12/-

May be obtained from the B.B.C., Broadcasting House, W.1 (Telephone : Welbeck 4468)

Chappell's Box Office, Queen's Hall, Langham Place, W.1 (Telephone : Langham 2823)

and the usual Agents

Fig. 26.3: (continued)

the RCM only having a broken and miscellaneous set, though including material not at the RAM. And although most British music publishers no longer keep such material, Boosey and Hawkes still hold, and can provide access to, a complete run of Boosey Ballad Concert programmes 1864–1939, a unique source in any history of British song, and the emergence of a wide range of leading singers, including John McCormack. There are many published collections of such programmes, particularly from American sources, and researchers should note that Westminster Music Library has a card index to a good number of published collections of such notes.

A special case is the BBC, where at the BBC Written Archives Centre at Caversham, Reading[18] are preserved complete collections of BBC programmes with related cuttings and papers (see CHAPTER 25 for a detailed discussion of the BBC Written Archives.) The programmes are cut up and mounted on sheets filed in sequence in box files and interleaved with press reviews. However, those looking for programmes of the Henry Wood Promenade Concerts may well find the bound sets in the Central Music Library collection at Westminster Music Library, or at the RCM or the RAM more convenient sources.

▶ USING PROGRAMMES

Though generally reliable, programmes on their own cannot be taken as 'gospel', and there are many traps to lead the unwary researcher astray. Whenever possible programme notes (unless annotated/corrected at the time of performance) need to be read in conjunction with other documentation, the most obvious being press reviews. Where available, diaries are an important additional source. There have been many instances where a programme, printed perhaps a day in advance of the concert, has subsequently been changed or even abandoned altogether. If a correction slip was inserted it may well by now have dropped out, leaving the reader ignorant of any changes. The traps of accepting a programme at face value are too obvious. An invaluable source of information on the byways of British music of the first quarter of this century, the programmes of the Bournemouth Municipal Orchestra,[19] offer an interesting case in point. That for 13 December 1906 clearly states that Bax's *An Irish Overture* was performed for 'the first time at these concerts'. This was not, as one might hurriedly suppose, its première, but a work that had had its first hearing elsewhere and was being given its first Bournemouth Municipal Orchestra performance – and it was 'conducted by the composer'. This would seem to be indisputable (unless, of course, the composer was taken ill on the day). Yet it is known that Bax did not conduct: the orchestra's founder-conductor Dan Godfrey took the composer's place, Bax having vowed never to conduct again after a traumatic experience over a year earlier. The only

two reviews of the concert are in this instance confusing. One, written probably by the writer of the programme note, emphatically states that Bax *did*
conduct, although as Graham Parlett suggests in *A Catalogue of the Works
of Sir Arnold Bax*,[20] 'it seems likely that the review was written before the
concert' – a snare we shall come across again. The other review would seem
to imply that Godfrey was the conductor. While memories are not always
reliable, it is fortunate that the soloist at the concert in question (Frank
Merrick) was approached while still alive to confirm that Bax did not
conduct. With the work now lost, the programme note itself is of considerable importance. From it one can deduce that the Overture was the same
work in all but name as the earlier *A Connemara Revel* (also lost) – or a
slightly revised version. We also learn that in it Bax used two traditional
Irish tunes, something that he was hardly ever to do again. Such is the value
of an original programme.

Another example of the importance of the programme is supplied by
the discovery in 1999 in a dealer's catalogue of a copy of the previously
untraced programme for the first public performance of the Walton-Sitwell
Façade on 12 June 1923. For many years after its private première the
content of Walton's 'entertainment' was to vary from performance to
performance until a definitive version was arrived at and published; poems
would be taken out and new ones tried, the order and the groupings of the
poems would change from performance to performance, and even the
number of poems set to music would vary. The newly-found 1923
programme (which lists only the performers and poems) is of especial
importance, for it reveals two settings hitherto unknown that were down
for performance: *Gone Dry* and *Dark Song*. One must, of course, hold
open the possibility that there could have been last minute changes to the
programme. Press reviews here are of little help: reviewers were by and
large too taken aback by the originality and the uniqueness of the proceedings to make more than the occasional comment on the individual poem
settings. (Hence the fireman's often misinterpreted comment that he had
'never known anything like it'.) Staying with *Façade* a moment longer,
programme and reviews cannot assist in establishing beyond doubt that
Constant Lambert was the co-reciter at the first of the New Chenil Galleries
performances on 27 April 1926 before becoming the sole reciter two
months later at the same venue. A letter he wrote to his mother makes it
clear that he did take part in the earlier of the two presentations, but
whether he replaced the actor Neil Porter (who was photographed outside
the Chenil Galleries with the Sitwells and Walton but without Lambert) or
shared the reciting with him has yet to be established. Existing copies of
the programme mention Edith Sitwell alone.

Some years ago at a music society talk the speaker related with an air
of authority an amusing instance when during the interval at an operatic
first night he was joined by an established critic. 'The performance of *xxx*
is going well?' he was asked. 'Well, actually it is not *xxx* tonight. Because

the principal singer is ill they have decided to perform *yyy* instead.' 'O my god!' muttered the critic. 'I must see if I can pull my review!' Such tales are often apocryphal, but there have been occasions of a review giving misinformation and an instance can be cited from May 1981. At the end of his period as chief conductor of the BBC Symphony Orchestra, Gennadi Rozhdestvensky had to withdraw from a concert of British music because of illness. The programme was taken over by Nicholas Cleobury with some changes. Nevertheless, one press report told of the original programme with the original conductor! One must add that to his credit the reviewer commented on the works only and not on their performance!

On rare occasions even multiple reviews need to be treated with circumspection. For the first performance of Delius's *A Mass of Life* under Sir Thomas Beecham on 8 June 1909, reviews in *The Times*, the *Monthly Musical Record*, *The Daily Telegraph*, *Daily News*, *The Standard* and the *Musical News* name five soloists compared with the four given by *The Morning Post* and *The Sunday Times*. Yet the score specifies only four soloists, and four are named by the conductor of that première in his biography of the composer.[21] In the absence of an extant programme, one cannot be sure whether the fifth soloist was the result of a last-minute change or incorrect publicity (three days before the concert his name was added to the advanced announcement in *The Daily Telegraph*), or – perhaps unlikely – Beecham giving a few bars normally sung by chorus voices to a solo singer instead. Whatever the case, his subsequent performances all had four soloists and the mystery remains. This work provides an excellent example of the sort of information that only the programmes themselves are likely to offer. Since his 1929 Delius Festival performance of *A Mass of Life*, Beecham seems never to have given the work with the movements in the published order or with the interval positioned as in the score. Only programmes (or perhaps markings on his score and the orchestral parts) can show how he changed the order of some of the movements.

Prospectuses for concert series should of course be approached with similar caution. A good example is that for the Henry Wood Promenade Concerts as announced for the 1914 season. Five concerts were to have included music by Mahler, these constituting a significant event in the performance history of Mahler in England: 'Six new songs for soprano and orchestra' on 2 September, *Kindertotenlieder* on 14 October, *Lieder eines fahrenden Gesellen* on 17 October, and *Lieder aus Des Knaben Wunderhorn* on the 7 and 21 October. There is printed evidence that would seem to support this, and these performances are all dutifully listed by the excellent card index in the Royal College of Music library. But they were all cancelled because of the outbreak of war, a fact only recorded on corrected programmes, such as those in the BBC's possession at Broadcasting House. The prospectus for the 1967 season contains similar inaccuracies because of changes resulting from Sir Malcolm Sargent's withdrawal from the series because of his final illness, and the 1980 season was thrown into even greater chaos by the cancellation of many concerts through the Musicians' Union strike. Even in 1999, Norman Lebrecht commented, in his regular weekly column in *The Daily Telegraph*, on how many changes of artists there had been during the Promenade Concerts season (Lebrecht, 1999).

One must also be wary of summary concert listings, however helpful they may be as a short-cut to data of the original programmes. Robert Elkin, in an appendix to his history of the Royal Philharmonic Society (1946), most usefully lists all the RPS concerts from 1912 to 1945 (the programmes from 1813 to 1911 having been documented by Myles Birket Foster (1912)). But not all the concerts can be taken literally as printed. For example, for that on November 27 1916 Landon Ronald was indisposed and his place taken by Beecham and Elgar. The concert information for March 16 1914 and January 24 1924 would seem to suggest respectively that Willem Mengelberg conducted the first performance of Frank Bridge's *Dance Poem* and Wilhelm Fürtwangler conducted the first performance of the orchestral version of Vaughan Williams's *On Wenlock Edge* song-cycle. But in both instances the composer conducted. These two examples have on occasion been taken as fact, the latter even appearing thus in Cyril Ehrlich's otherwise excellent history of the Philharmonic Society (1985), which otherwise corrects many such errors. And to cite an example of the programme book being inaccurate, on 28 February 1916 a full programme note by Bax himself appears in the programme for his *Spring Fire*, conducted by Beecham, though an inserted correction slip admits the work was not performed because it proved too difficult to produce on one rehearsal, and another work by Bax was performed instead.

Diaries and other autobiographical writings can often provide corroboration or additional information that the programmes themselves may not include. How interesting it is, for example, to read from Granville Bantock's diary of a concert of the Birmingham Festival on 1 October 1912: 'Elgar conducted first performance of *The Music Makers* & Sibelius his new symphony in A minor which was very well received. Delius was also at concert and *we three sat together during Elgar's work*.' Diaries can contain unexpected gems. The critic Herbert Thompson habitually noted timings of works he heard over nearly 50 years. Thus, attending the second performance of Vaughan Williams's *A London Symphony* in its original version at Harrogate in 1914, Herbert Thompson noted the timings of each movement, giving us the only reliable source for this information.

Hearsay should be treated with caution. With the Three Choirs Festival première of Delius's *Dance Rhapsody No. 1* (the composer conducting), Beecham, writing in his autobiographical *A Mingled Chime* (p. 79), relates that 'I was unable to be present . . . but I was afterwards told by several who were there that the performance . . . sent shivers of excitement running down the backs of everyone sitting in the massive nave of the Norman cathedral.' We may well be amazed – since the performance took place in the Hereford Shire Hall.

► CATALOGUING OF PROGRAMMES

Some concert series have been documented by extensive published indexes, of which those for the Aldeburgh Festival (Strode, 1987) and the Three Choirs Festival (Boden, 1992) are particularly useful and are currently available. One might add here that festival programmes such as those of Aldeburgh, the Three Choirs and Cheltenham, that in one, often bulky, annual volume cover the whole of the festival, will often contain articles of great interest that add to their value, but these are rarely indexed by formal indexing services and so are easily missed. Less immediately useful but still of value is the summary of *The Cheltenham International Festival of Music 1945–1994*, which lists by year first performances only without supplying any further information, such as the date of the concert, performers, etc. Thomas Batley's extensive compilation of the Hallé programmes from 1858 to 1895 is very hard to find but an invaluable documentary source to the development of concert-giving in the nineteenth century (Batley, 1896).

Because, as we have seen, programmes may be filed for a number of reasons, and often as individual items rather than sets or bound volumes, there are no clear consistently applied rules for cataloguing them, assuming they are catalogued at all.

It is unclear whether programmes have been covered by legal deposit laws in the UK. The British Library have indicated that there is nothing to exclude programmes, and they normally retain all such items sent in, their receipt appears to have been, and continues to be, very haphazard in the UK. Indeed the British Library normally buy collections or outstanding individual programmes when they are available and also accept donations, and there are some useful holdings. These are not catalogued consistently. The most convenient first place to look is under 'Programmes' in the printed version of the *British Library Catalogue of Printed Music* (vol. 46 POT-RAGO pp. 133–151). In fact in the *General Catalogue of Books* the entry will be under the place of the concert, and then either under the subheading of the hall, or under the name of the organisers. Some online searches will retrieve a programme by the name of the writer of the notes. However, a quantity of rarer material will be found in the Hirsch Library, typical material in this collection being the programmes of early ISCM festivals.

The Music Libraries Trust initiative to commission a scoping study for a future union catalogue of concert programmes is a welcome initiative as we close for press.[22]

► HANDBILLS AND POSTERS

Fliers of one sort or another have long been used to promote recitals, and they still are. However, the fact that these are single sheets of paper, often only one-sided, has meant that their potential historical value has not been recognised, and it is doubtful if anyone is maintaining a systematic collection even at the halls concerned. They acquire historical value later when the artists concerned have developed their reputation, and are usually to be retrieved from scrapbooks and the loose papers of the artists concerned. Often these handbills feature portraits of those involved, and for the period up to the Second World War may well be the only source for a likeness of the artist, or a likeness at the early date in question. During the 1930s the BBC promoted many of the major European works of the period, producing valuable fliers announcing casts and other details (see Fig. 26.3).

▶ PRESS CUTTINGS

Newspapers as a research source are considered fully in CHAPTER 12, but when reviewing the ephemera of concert life that might be found among a musician's papers, press cuttings constitute an invaluable resource and are worth separate mention here. Before the Second World War coverage of the arts in the national press was considerably more extensive than it is today. More newspapers carried concert reviews – and in many instances allowed them more column inches. Alongside – or even in the absence of – the concert programme, newspapers and journals are an essential source for programme information. Nearly all national newspapers and many local papers can be consulted at the British Library Newspaper Library, Colindale, London, where they are held either in hard copy or on microfilm. A reader's pass is obtainable on the day. Up to four requests for a newspaper or journal may be submitted at one time, and the researcher should allow a waiting period of up to an hour. Photocopying services are available with either postal delivery or later personal collection. If a visit to Colindale is not always convenient for the researcher, the reference sections of many local libraries have back copies of *The Times* – and in some instances their local newspaper – either on microfilm or hard copy, with the additional facility of an index, either in book form or on microfilm.

For concert information, by and large the most widely useful music journal is *The Musical Times*, a complete bound sequence of which is held, in London, at the Barbican Library and the Westminster Music Library. While indexes were published to all volumes, some, but not all, of these annual volumes have indexes, and the Barbican Library provides a more convenient service by having the volumes on the open shelves, allowing the researcher to browse at leisure without having to request a particular volume for perhaps one small reference. (Nineteenth-century volumes of *The Musical Times* are listed in the RIPM series.) BUCOMP2 lists[23] extensive holdings in the UK, and this is a journal fairly widely available in the USA, and it should be possible to consult to locate the most convenient set.

Other journals, such as *Musical Opinion*, while often of interest, are less helpful in their lay-out, and lack an index. The centralisation of collections of concert programmes is an aspect of resources for music research that needs to be more widely adopted.

As in the case of programmes, cuttings collections might well have been assembled by:

- the composer;
- by a performing artist;
- by a critic;
- by an agent;
- by a concert hall or opera house as a record of activity; and
- by an enthusiast.

Cuttings collections usually start systematically and often later degenerate into accumulations of loose cuttings. Sometimes they are systematically annotated as to source and date, but it is not unknown for such information to be absent, presenting the researcher with a further problem of identification. For example, in the wide-ranging and superb *Daily Express* press cuttings collection at the British Library at Colindale, a general collection, but valuable for music in the 1920s–1940s in particular, the source of cuttings is usually attributed but there are instances where they are unidentified.

The value of accumulations of press cuttings is difficult to over-estimate; and published lives of musicians have been based on such collections. In the late nineteenth century and the first half of the twentieth the range and variety of the press was remarkable, and the coverage accorded to concerts and opera very considerable. Perhaps the prime example of an almost comprehensive collection of cuttings is that of Elgar, maintained by the composer's wife and mounted in 32 large volumes, now in the Elgar birthplace at Broadheath. The value of such a collection, which encompasses overseas cuttings as well as those from the UK, is not only to those researching the life and music of Elgar, but also for the commentary it contains on the musical life of the times. If one is researching a composer who shared a programme with Elgar, one will find all the cuttings for that performance at Broadheath, together with copies of the programmes.

Until recently all newspapers maintained large cuttings collections that were considered the raw material of subsequent journalism. When writing a story the journalist would be loaned a box or folder of cuttings that would show them the journalistic history of a topic, and very often provide much of the information for a new article. Over the last 20 years these collections, expensive and space-consuming to maintain, have gradually faded away in the face of new technology. Yet, in fact, digital sources cannot replace so convenient a source for anything except the most recent stories. In this respect really large collections may be just as rich for the specialist musical researcher as much smaller, more specific, collections.

Many institutions may file cuttings as incidental material in more general files. Thus at the BBC Written Archives Centre at Caversham, newspaper cuttings appear on general files as well in collections of cuttings. Their documentation of concerts in the 1930s had the individual pages of concert programmes mounted on larger sheets together with the cuttings stored in chronological order in box files.

Personal cuttings collections include examples still in private hands, such as those of the late Edmund Rubbra, and of the critic Felix Aprahamian. The critic Edwin Evans's library became the foundation stock of the Central Music Library, administered as part of Westminster Music Library, and his extensive library of cuttings remains with that collection. The Evans collection consists of a wide range of cuttings, assembled in the first place to support his work as a musical journalist over many years, as well as his own writings. It is worth noting the example of the collection of the late Ernest Bradbury, for many years the music critic of the *Yorkshire Post*, whose collection of his own writings has been systematically checked, organised and completed retrospectively by his widow Susan Bradbury, partly funded by a grant from the Music Libraries Trust, for deposit in the Brotherton Library of the University of Leeds, where with the extensive archives of Bradbury's predecessor Herbert Thompson it now provides an almost unbroken documentation of a century of musical commentary.

Collections of cuttings exploring one particular event or theme have been published. Particularly useful is the 'Dossier de Presse' series published in Geneva by Editions Minkoff, which reproduces the cuttings in facsimile. The first two volumes, on *The Rite of Spring* and *Pierrot Lunaire*, set the tone for a valuable source, including cuttings from English, French, German and Italian newspapers.

Very few indexes or catalogues to such material have appeared, though Christopher Kent's summary of the contents of the Elgar scrapbooks[24] shows what can be done in small space. The splendidly painstaking catalogue of Holst press cuttings published by Cheltenham Public Library[25] remains the benchmark of quality as far as such collections are concerned, for not only does it guide one to what is available but also provides a guide of much wider application for anyone researching the period. The catalogue is arranged by Holst's works in alphabetical order, and performances of each work are then listed chronologically. Again, once one knows that there was a Holst work in any programme one is researching, it is possible to use the Holst work as an index to trace relevant cuttings.

Collections of published press cuttings (as opposed to writings on music) are comparatively rare, but one invaluable source not to be overlooked is *Shaw's Music: The Complete Musical Criticism of Bernard Shaw (1876–1950)* available in three paperback volumes (Lawrence, 1981). Of a different nature is *Sir Thomas Beecham: Fifty Years in 'New York Times'* compiled and edited by J.D. Gilmour (1988) which, as one might suppose, offers some amusing reading as well as offering a good documentation of

Beecham's music-making in New York (and a little of elsewhere as well). Also worthy of investigation is the collected musical criticism of Philip Heseltine, part of a four-volume series of Heseltine's writings on music (Smith 1998–9).

▶ OTHER SOURCES

Composer catalogues increasingly list major reviews of first performances and these may well be a mechanism for tracing press reviews in newspapers when a cuttings collection is not available. The listing may be rather more extensive, as in Lewis Foreman's *Havergal Brian and the Performance of his Orchestral Music* (1976), which lists chronologically all known performances of the composer's works. Broadcasting, like sound recordings, is almost a separate category, but Ronald Taylor's fascinating compilation (1996) of the live broadcasts of Elgar's music during the composer's lifetime is worthy of mention. Thorough-going catalogues such as Stewart Craggs's superb one on William Walton (1990) may have bibliographies for each work, providing the researcher with a very welcome short-cut to reviews and articles (for more detail see CHAPTER 17). Orchestral histories (e.g. those of the Hallé (Kennedy, 1960), London Symphony (Foss and Goodwin, 1954; Pearton, 1974), City of Birmingham Symphony Orchestra (King-Smith, 1995) and the BBC Symphony Orchestra (Kenyon, 1981)[26]), will give a helpful lead to performances, although not always providing full details of the date and complete programme. David Cox's *The Henry Wood Proms* (1980) provides very useful year-by-year lists of the works introduced, together with a good number of sample programmes. Stephen Lloyd's *Sir Dan Godfrey: Champion of British Composers* (1995), in being a performance history of the Bournemouth Municipal Orchestra, opens a vista of 40 years of municipal music-making. Elkin's *Queen's Hall* (1944) and *Royal Philharmonic* (1946) are other helpful starting points. Neither should the bound volumes of the *Royal College of Music Magazine* be overlooked when researching the London musical scene.

Biographies or studies of conductors will often include appendices of performances (as distinct from commercial recordings), such as the list of first performances in Arthur Jacobs's excellent biography of Sir Henry Wood (1994), and that of Constant Lambert's concerts for the BBC's Third Programme in Richard Shead's biography of Lambert (1973). The traps and difficulties open to the researcher of programmes are no better exemplified than in the calendar of Sir Thomas Beecham's concerts by Maurice Parker (1985) and the meticulously researched volume of additions and corrections by Tony Benson (1990). These are models of their kind, particularly the additional volume, in which nothing has been taken at face value, programmes have been tested against reviews, one review has been judged against another, even when it comes to establishing not just which works were played in a concert but the order in which they were performed. (Beecham was notorious for not always keeping to the printed programme, so that on at least one occasion he is known to have announced: 'We are now going to play the work that you think you have just heard!') Where possible Tony Benson also includes information that no programme will include – any encores or 'lollipops' as Beecham termed them.

▶ CRITICS IN BRITISH NEWSPAPERS

Until the 1960s it was customary for many music critics in British newspapers not to sign their criticism or, at least use initials. The following list is to aid identification of the authorship of the main critical writing in the British press from the late nineteenth century. For a nineteenth century list in selected newspapers, see Hughes (2002).

- Joseph Bennett: *Daily Telegraph* 1870–1908
- Ernest Bradbury: *Yorkshire Post* 1947–84 but he actually wrote 1943–93
- Richard Capell: *Daily Mail* 1911–31; *Daily Telegraph* 1931–54
- Neville Cardus: *Manchester Guardian* 1917–39; 1951–75 (*Sydney Morning Herald* 1939–47)
- Henry Cope Colles: *The Times* 1905–43 (chief from 1911)
- James William Davison: *The Times* 1846–79
- Edward J Dent[27] a critic from 1918–26; *The Athenaeum/Nation* and *Athenaeum* 1919–24; Truth 1920–22; *The London Mercury* 1919–20
- Edwin Evans: *Pall Mall Gazette* 1912–23; *Daily Mail* 1931–45
- Arthur Henry Fox-Strangways: *The Times* 1911–25; *Observer* 1925–39
- J.A. FullerMaitland: *The Times* 1889–1911
- Cecil Gray: *Daily Telegraph* and *Manchester Guardian* c. 1930–1950
- Arthur Hervey *The Morning Post* 1892–1911
- Frank Howes: *The Times* 1925–60 (chief 1943–60)
- Dyneley Hussey: *The Spectator* c.1923; *The Times* 1923–46
- Alfred Kalisch: *The World* 1899–1915; *Daily News* c.1912–1930
- Constant Lambert: *Sunday Referee* mid and late 1930s
- Samuel Langford: *Manchester Guardian* 1905–27
- Robin Legge: *The Times* 1891–1906; *Daily Telegraph* 1906–31
- Basil Maine: *Daily Telegraph* 1921–6; *Morning Post* 1926–37
- Ernest Newman: *Manchester Guardian* 1905–6; *Birmingham Post* 1906–19; *Observer* 1919–1920; *Sunday Times* 1920–58
- Steven S. Stratton: *Birmingham Post* 1877–1906

- Herbert Thompson *Yorkshire Post* 1886–1945
- Francis Toye: *Morning Post* 1925–37
- Walter J Turner: *New Statesman* 1916–40

Fortunately, the study of the history of concert life is beginning to attract the active interest of the wider academic community, notably in the UK with the 'Concert Life in the Nineteenth-century' project focussed at Oxford Brookes University, which will see the development of a substantial database. This is an inter-university research project, which brings together academic staff in the music departments of Oxford Brookes University, the University of Leeds and Goldsmiths' College, University of London. The first phase of research began in January 1999 and involves studying in depth selected years from the nineteenth century, and entering the resultant data into a web-based, fully-relational database. The years chosen were 1815, 1855 and 1895. Phase Two, involving an investigation of the 1830s and 1870s, started in 2001. See the website, <http://www.brookes.ac.uk/schools/apm/music/19thc.htm>.

▶ REFERENCES

Bashford, C. Introducing the Concert Life in 19th-Century London Database. *Brio*, 36, No. 2, 111–16

Batley, T. (comp & ed.) *Sir Charles Hallé's Concerts in Manchester – a List of . . . the Whole of the Programmes of Concerts from Jan. 30th 1858 to March 7th 1895*. Long Millgate, Manchester: Chas Sever, printer [1896]

Beecham, Sir T. (1959) *Frederick Delius*. London: Hutchinson

Benson, T. (comp.) (1990) *Sir Thomas Beecham Bart, C.H. – Supplement to the Calendar of his Concert and Theatrical Performances*. Privately circulated

Myles Birket Foster (1912) *History of the Philharmonic Society of London*. London: John Lane

Boden, A. (1992) *Three Choirs: a History of the Festival*. London: Allan Sutton

Cox, D. (1980) *The Henry Wood Proms*. London: BBC

Craggs, S. (1990) *William Walton: A Catalogue* (2nd edn.). Oxford: Clarendon Press

Ehrlich, C. (1995) *First Philharmonic: A History of The Royal Philharmonic Society*. Oxford:

Elkin, R. (1944) *Queen's Hall 1893–1941*. London: Rider & Co

Elkin, R. (1946) *Royal Philharmonic*. London: Rider & Co

Foreman, L. (1976) *Havergal Brian and the Performance of his Orchestral Music*. London: Thames Publishing

Foss, H. and Goodwin, N. (1954) *London Symphony: Portrait of an Orchestra*. London: Naldrett Press

Gilmour, J.D. (comp. and ed.) (1988) *Sir Thomas Beecham: Fifty Years in 'New York Times'*. London: Thames Publishing

Haward, L. (1956) *Edward J Dent – a Bibliography*. Cambridge: King's College

Hughes, M. (2002) *The English Musical Renaissance and the Press 1850–1914: Watchmen of Music*. Aldershot: Ashgate

Jacobs, A. (1994) *Henry J Wood: Maker of the Proms*. London: Methuen

Kennedy, M. (1960) *The Hallé Tradition: A Century of Music*. Manchester: Manchester University Press

Kent, C. (1993) *Edward Elgar: a Guide to Research*. New York & London: Garland Publishing

Kenyon, N. (1981) *The BBC Symphony Orchestra 1930–1980*. London: BBC

King-Smith, B. (1995) *Crescendo! 75 Years of Birmingham Symphony Orchestra*. London: Methuen

Laurence, D.H. (ed.) (1981) *Shaw's Music: The Complete Musical Criticism of Bernard Shaw (1876–1950)* (2nd rev. edn.). London: Max Reinhardt (The Bodley Head)

Lebrecht, N. (1999) How About an Audience Charter? *The Daily Telegraph*, 25 August, 14

Lloyd, S. (1984) *H Balfour Gardiner*. Cambridge: Cambridge University Press

Lloyd, S. (1995) *Sir Dan Godfrey: Champion of British Composers*. London: Thames Publishing

Musgrave, M. (1995) *The Musical Life of the Crystal Palace*. Cambridge: Cambridge University Press

Parlett, G. (1999) *A Catalogue of the Works of Sir Arnold Bax*. Oxford: Clarendon Press

Parker, M. (comp.) (1985) *Sir Thomas Beecham Bart, C.H. – A Calendar of his Concert and Theatrical Performances*. Privately printed

Pearton, M. (1974) *The LSO at 70: A History of the Orchestra*. London: Gollancz

Shead, R. (1973) *Constant Lambert: his Life, his Music and his Friends*. London: Simon Publications

Smith, B. (ed.) (1998–9) *Musical Criticism: The Occasional Writings (Complete) of Philip Heseltine (Peter Warlock)* (vols 1–2: 1998; vols 3–4: 1999) London: Thames Publishing

Strode, R. (1987) *Music of Forty Festivals – A List of Works Performed at Aldeburgh Festivals from 1948 to 1987*. Aldeburgh: The Aldeburgh Foundation

Taylor, R. (1996) *A Chronological List of Live Broadcasts of Elgar's Music by the BBC November 1922 to February 1934*. Privately printed

Tovey, D.F. (1935–1939) *Essays in Musical Analysis* (6 vols). Oxford: Oxford University Press

Tovey, D.F. (1941) *Some English Symphonists: a Selection from Essays in Musical Analysis*. Oxford: Oxford University Press

Wagstaff, J. (ed.) (1998) *The British Union Catalogue of Music Periodicals: Second Edition Including the Holdings of Six Libraries from the Republic of Ireland*. Aldershot: Ashgate

Weber, W. (1975) *Music and the Middle Class – the Social Structure of Concert Life in London Paris & Wien*. London: Croom Helm

▶ NOTES

1. Access to the McCann Collection for the general public is dependent on completion of building work at the RAM.
2. For example: Weber (1975).
3. The 1912–1945 concerts are listed in an appendix to Elkin (1946), the programmes from 1813 to 1911 having been documented in Myles Birket Foster's *History of the Philharmonic Society of London*, John Lane 1912.
4. For a list of 'First Performances as Part of the Birmingham Triennial Festivals', 1837–1912 see IAML(UK) Newsletter, 37 (Aug 1999), 25–28.
5. An almost complete sequence of bound programmes of the Orchestra's concerts is held at the Camm Music Library, Bournemouth, some at the Bournemouth Pavilion, and those of the Bournemouth Symphony Orchestra at the orchestra's home at Poole. Programmes of other municipal orchestras would seem to be much less well preserved, some towns, such as Harrogate and Hastings, having only a small file containing a few programmes.
6. Their programmes can be found in the bound volumes of the *Royal College of Music Magazine* held both at the RCM and at the Barbican Library.
7. Listed in Lloyd (1984).
8. Robert Elkin's *Queen's Hall 1893–1941* (1944) is a useful starting point for information on these and many other series held in that hall.
9. Vol. 1, pp. 84–5.
10. The programmes were collected as slim paper-bound annual volumes. Thus in No II for Tuesday April 1, 1845 we have 'Synopsis Analytique [for] Quartet No. 4 Mozart'. *Record of the Musical Union*. Cramer, Beale & Co., [1847] pp. 8–9.
11. Also of value is the account of 'Promises Now Fulfilled'. *Record of the Musical Union 1847*. Cramer, Beale & Co., 1848, pp. 40–1.
12. Colles op. cit.
13. Musgrave (1995), p. xiii.
14. ibid., p. xiii.
15. Holdings include 1867–1894 in bound volumes, plus various loose programmes. Apart from the extent of the run, the advantage of using this set is personal access to a photocopying machine by researchers.
16. Tovey (1935–1939). Selected notes on works by British composers were published separately as *Some English Symphonists: a Selection from Essays in Musical Analysis* (Tovey, 1941).
17. In the Department of Portraits rather than in the Library.
18. BBC Written Archives Centre, Caversham Park, Caversham, Reading RG4 7ER. See CHAPTER 25.
19. See note 3.
20. Parlett (1999), p. 55.
21. Beecham (1959), p. 155.
22. Ridgewell, Rupert: 'The Concert Programmes Project' *Making Music News* [Journal of the NFMS] no. 5 April 2002 p. 10
23. Wagstaff (1998), pp. 264–6.
24. Kent (1993), pp. 442–7.
25. *Catalogue of Holst's Programmes and Press Cuttings in the Central Library, Cheltenham* compiled by Sheila Lumby and Vera Hounsfield, Gloucester 1974.
26. The appendix of first performances is of special interest.
27. See Haward (1956).

27 Pictures and picture research

Elisabeth Agate

▶ **INTRODUCTION**

Picture research is the identifying of images (in this context, those relating to the history of music) and the acquisition of copies of those images, normally in photographic form, either in support of a research project, or for publication in a printed or electronic medium (images can now often be scanned electronically, and this method is likely to increase dramatically in the near future). Such images may be found in almost every visual medium (both representational and concrete), and may illuminate and enhance subject matter is diverse as Cheironomy (the ancient form of conducting by hand signs), Acoustics, Stage Design, Dance and Notation, as well as the life and times of composers and music of non-Western cultures. For the study of the social history of music, and performance practice, illustrations are an invaluable source of documentation, while for certain areas of enquiry (for example the early history of instruments) they may be the only available evidence.

Illustrations supporting musical history are most often to be found in the visual arts (from the figurative to the abstract), but may equally well be found in the decorative arts, and in the concrete form of autograph manuscript and letters, instruments, printed music, photographs, programmes, advertisements and other ephemera – the possibilities are almost limitless.

While picture research is essentially a practical matter requiring a good deal of persistence and lateral thinking, it will often cross paths with the associated discipline of musical iconography (see 'ICONOGRAPHY' below). The challenge of picture research is to find the most appropriate (and usually authentic) illustration for a particular context, and to obtain a good photograph by a given deadline, within a limited budget. The purpose of this chapter is to suggest the scope of the subject, and to provide information on how, and from where, to obtain photographs.

▶ SCOPE

To give an idea of the visual material available, historical periods can be divided approximately as listed below. There is obviously a gradual accumulation of visual resources, but certain categories of material come to the fore at different times.

- Ancient Civilisations (including music of the Greeks, Romans, Egyptians, Hittites, Etruscans, the early Christian Church, the Byzantine era, Jewish music and – outside Western cultural traditions – the music of China, Japan, India, the Inca, Maya, etc.):
  - sculpture and relief
  - fresco
  - vase paintings
  - coins and medals
  - mosaic
  - architecture
  - carving.

- Medieval and Renaissance (to the end of the sixteenth century; in addition to the above):
  - manuscript illumination
  - stained glass
  - tapestry
  - intarsia
  - woodcut
  - engraving
  - printed/manuscipt music
  - archival documents
  - painting in fresco and tempera
  - oil painting
  - portraiture
  - instruments.

- Baroque and Classical (seventeenth and eighteenth centuries; in addition to much of the above):
  - instruction manuals for instruments
  - trade cards
  - playbills
  - concert tickets
  - stage and costume designs
  - caricature
  - title pages
  - architectural drawings

- concert programmes
- silhouettes.

The seventeenth century sees a great increase in engravings, published singly, in sets, or incorporated into opera libretti and festival books (see Bowles, 1989). Musical scenes abound in paintings of courtly subjects, and also in studies of everyday life, especially in the low countries, but portraits of musicians are still comparatively rare due to their low social status.

- Nineteenth century: the increasing popularisation of music is reflected in the wide diversity of printed materials and ephemera: sheet music covers, advertisements, posters, lithograph and engraved portraits of singers and composers, photographs (one of the earliest is the daguerreotype of Chopin, 1849) and other memorabilia.

   The incidence of portraits (and monuments) becomes more frequent, reflecting the higher status accorded creative artists in the Romantic era, and the increasing mass appeal of music; later in the century photographic portraits become widely available and collected.

   Illustrated and satirical periodicals appear from the early 1840s, for instance *L'illustration* (see Cohen, 1983), *Musica* and *Le théâtre*, in France; *L'illustrazione italiana* and *Il teatro illustrato* in Italy; the *Leipzig Illustrirte Zeitung* in Germany, and the *Illustrated London News*, *The Graphic*, etc. in England.

- Twentieth century: the explosion of visual material that gathered pace during the twentieth century, broadening to include more sophisticated photography, film, television and now electronic imaging, reflects the changing taste of audiences, globalisation, and the politicisation of all the arts. In our culture of museum opera, stage design is often no longer the preserve of the opera composer and designer working together, but of a new breed of designer and director who looks for ever new ways of interpreting and presenting masterpieces from the past. Ironically, while on the one hand we reach out for the new, we are busy, as never before, researching and recording every shred of evidence to reveal how performances of the past were presented; visual materials form a crucial part of this quest. Film and television, while affording new techniques and horizons, have also brought into play new issues of interpretation, usually supported by still and moving photographic documentation. Communication in the form of books newspapers, magazines, concert programmes, packaging of recorded music, websites, television and film, have combined with the cult of the superstar, to stimulate an ever-increasing number of photographers. Photographs can bear witness to encounters between musicians, record performances (even become a player in them), convey a sense of place and of character, and be transported round the world instantly. Concert halls can now be adapted acoustically to suit almost any kind of performance. There will, however, always be room for debate over the extent to which the visual images all around us can be relevant to an essentially aural medium.

► ICONOGRAPHY

The terms 'iconography' and 'iconology' were first used by sixteenth-century humanists in the study of visual evidence from ancient archaeology (see Panofsky, 1939). Today iconography is considered by some to be one aspect of research in the pictorial documentation of musical instruments and performance practice; for others it is research in the visualisation of music, in which an image with musical subject matter is considered as a work of art in its own right. For an illuminating and wide-ranging discussion of the term (with extensive bibliography), that includes reference to non-Western cultures, see the article 'Iconography' by Tilman Seebass in the *New Grove Dictionary of Music and Musicians* (2/2001); see also 'Iconography of Music' by H.M. Brown in *New Grove* (1980). There is a temptation to take depictions of music-making at face value, but it must be remembered that every culture and period produces its own visual sources, and has its own traditions and conventions, so that the musical iconographer must be aware not only of the history of instruments and performance practice, but of art historical method and interpretation. This is especially true with illustrations depicting the non-visual, ephemeral world of sound; because of its transitory nature, music has often been used in art as a symbol for the frailty of human life.

The interpretation of visual sources with musical content must therefore take into account the cultural and artistic conventions of the time, as well as the intentions of their creators; of decisive influence in this context is the audience for which a work of art is created. In depicting a scene of music-making an artist may wrongly position players in his painting for the sake of spatial balance, or include an additional figure, perhaps to flatter a patron. The artist may be a witness of a particular musical performance, but not be part of the culture that he sees. He may or may not have reason to depict an instrument accurately: it may be copied from an earlier visual source, or he may have changed its construction for allegorical or symbolic reasons. For further discussion of these themes see E. Winternitz, *Musical Instruments and their Symbolism in Western Art* (1967, 2/1979), and R. Leppert, *Music and Image* (1988).

The most concrete visual evidence for the role of music in a given society tends to be found in works of art that record contemporary events such as courtly entertainments, religious festivals and military activities.

If approached with caution, works of art are often the best source of information on the early history of instruments, and can reveal details that are difficult to discover in any other way. They can also tell us which groupings of instruments and voices were used for various kinds of music at a given time and place, and about the social context of performance, the role of the conductor, seating arrangements, etc.

In the study of operatic history knowledge of the conventions of production and stage design are essential; for example until the end of the eighteenth century it was customary for stock designs for 'a shady grove', 'gloomy dungeon', 'seascape', 'ballroom', 'terrace of a palace', 'temple', etc. to be interchangeable between operas at a given theatre (the style of course dependent on the resident designer) – a situation unthinkable today! The method of musical iconography is to develop systems for collecting, cataloguing and interpreting the widest possible range of visual material relating to music, in order to be able to formulate theories about the role of music in our past. In this the role of RIdIM (*Répertoire International d'Iconographie Musicale*), founded in 1971, has been of great significance (see 'RESEARCH TOOLS' below, p. 384).

▶ IDENTIFYING IMAGES AND OBTAINING PHOTOGRAPHS

The best starting point is to look at published material concerning the subject of interest in order to familiarise yourself with the range of illustrative material previously used by other authors, and the most likely sources (see 'SELECT BIBLIOGRAPHY' below); original sources for illustrations are normally given in the form of 'acknowledgements', or as part of the List of Illustrations, at the beginning or end of a book (but they may also be appended to the captions); crucial information can also sometimes be gleaned from the author's own prefatory remarks, where a particularly helpful archive, foundation or individual may be thanked.

If you are hoping to illustrate a relatively narrow subject in some depth it can be rewarding and productive to visit the most specialised sources available; this is the best path towards finding new, or less well-known illustrative material, and will usually give you personal contact with a curator or archivist who will be able to impart further insight and information. Often, however, there is neither the time nor the financial resources available to do this, especially if the source is abroad.

It is important at this stage to bear in mind the suitability of an illustration to the purpose for which it is required, whether or not a portrait is considered to be authentic, and how well it brings out the personality of a composer or performer, or fits the period under discussion. (The biography articles in *Grove* often have a sub-section devoted to the authenticity of portraits, while iconographic studies are cited in bibliographies.)

Having identified an image it is normally necessary to obtain a photograph from an original source (although photocopies may suffice for private research). Unless there is no other source, photographs should not be made from printed secondary sources for two main reasons:

There will normally be considerable loss of quality due to the screen of dots superimposed during the printing process;

A publisher does not have the authority to give permission to a third party to reproduce images from its books when the copyright of the photograph belongs with the original source (and there may be more than one copyright-holder involved) The exception to this can be in the use of line illustrations (maps or diagrams) where the publisher may own the copyright, having commissioned the artwork; if not their copyright, the publisher should be able to direct you to the artist, or perhaps the publisher of an earlier edition of the book.

Having identified the desired image, it is necessary to obtain a photograph, either from an original source or from another source empowered to act on the original source's behalf. This is the case with unique works of art, but for engravings or photographs, being non-unique, you may well be able to find a source nearer to home than the source cited in a book. Engravings are most commonly found in print collections closest to their place of origin, or in the main national or specialist collections, most of which have good subject catalogues. For unique works the most common procedure is to order a photograph from the relevant museum, gallery or library, but in some countries the supply of photographs is centralised. For example, in France, the Réunion des Musées Nationaux supplies photographs of works in the state museums, while the Photothèque des Musées de la Ville de Paris acts on behalf of the museums of the city of Paris; in Germany, Berlin has a centralised source of supply in the Bildarchiv Preussischer Kulturbesitz. Another situation pertains in Italy, where until recently the private organisations Alinari and Scala have had a virtual monopoly on the supply of photographs from Italian museums (many of which therefore neglect to respond to letters requesting photographs). For a description of some of the most useful sources see 'SOURCES' below. The choice of source from which a photograph is to be requested is likely to be dictated by matters of cost and expediency: if you need a photograph of a specific painting or engraving it may well be cheaper to order it from a museum, but this may take longer than obtaining the same or a similar image from a commercial picture library which, although it may be more expensive, will be able to send the photograph out almost immediately – and will probably also be able to send alternative choices. This is ultimately a matter of experience, and of asking around.

It should be mentioned at the outset that reproducing illustrations can be an expensive business, involving not only the cost of the photograph itself but also a 'reproduction' or 'permission' fee for the use of the illustration, and possibly also a fee to an artist or other additional copyright holder. It is important to minimise these costs (being fair to everyone concerned); you can also build up your own collection of originals relatively cheaply if you have the time and the determination. I will return to both these points.

Apart from the internet there are a number of essential reference works providing addresses of museums, galleries, libraries, and archives, as well as other types of picture source (further useful reference works are given under 'Select bibliography' below):

- *The World of Learning* (annual). London: Europa Publications
- *International Directory of Arts* (annual). München: K.G. Saur
- Evans, H. and Evans, M. (7/2001) *The Picture Researcher's Handbook*. Pira International

When requesting a photograph from any source it is wise to telephone first to check the address and fax number, and also to ascertain the department that would deal with the request (if possible, also the name of the person in charge, and their e-mail address.). This is especially important if your request is urgent. Delivery times can vary enormously, from a day to three months – I have waited five years for photographs from a Russian library (fortunately when working on a lengthy project where such a time-scale could be accommodated!). Larger museums and libraries will have a 'photographic service', or 'department of rights and reproductions' (in some cases the registrar handles photographic requests); when dealing with smaller institutions you can write to the director, who will pass your letter to the appropriate person (sometimes a photographer with whom you will have to make your own arrangements). Some sources require payment in advance for the photograph itself, but will not normally insist on the reproduction fee until just before publication.

Requesting photographs from sources

When requesting a photograph you should clearly state the following information:

- The *title and author* of your publication/programme.
- An *exact description of the work you want*, giving the title, artist/engraver, date, inventory or negative number (if you have them), manuscript and folio number, book title and author (plus edition, date, page/plate number) – anything you can to help the source locate the work (send a photocopy whenever possible).

- The *type of photograph* you want: glossy black and white photograph, or colour transparency (the larger the photograph – within reason – the better the quality of reproduction). 35mm colour transparencies can be good enough, provided they have not been degraded by duplication, but most museums will supply these only for private study or lecture purposes. Sources will generally respond first by sending you a price list giving relative sizes and costs, and will increasingly ask if you would like the image to be sent electronically, either by e-mail or on CD-ROM (if a scan is required for reproduction, check on the optimum dpi resolution to ask for, especially if the original is likely to be smaller than the output size).

- A *realistic date* by when the photograph is needed: it is better to state a definite time limit than to say 'as soon as possible'. You may have to wait between one to eight weeks for photographs from museums or libraries; give yourself a buffer zone, and ask if a 'rush service' is available if the request is urgent (this service can double the cost of the photograph).

- Ask for *up-to-date caption/catalogue information* relating to the work concerned (verify the facts; these may change in the light of new research, and what you have read in a secondary source may not be accurate)

- Ask for the preferred *form of acknowledgement*: citation of a source (which can involve a detailed description) is normally a required condition of permission to reproduce the work.

- Ask the likely *reproduction fee*: advisable if the photograph is to be published. To determine this the source will normally need to know the type of publication, the rights required (languages and countries of distribution), and often the print-run, the price of the book, the ISBN number, and the size of the reproduction on the page (and whether the illustration is to appear on the jacket or in the text). You are unlikely to have all this information at this stage, so can request a list giving the scale of fees, but you will have to write again nearer the time of publication to supply any missing details that are required.

- Ask for any information on *further copyright holders*: a representative of the artist (or artist's estate if deceased), or of a photographer, if the work is likely to be in copyright (see 'COPYRIGHT' below)

Costs

As mentioned above, the costs involved in purchasing and reproducing photographs can be high, and it is advisable to ensure that it is clear at the outset who is going to bear these costs (author or publisher). It would be as well to be aware of the following points:

- *The photograph itself* (from museums or libraries): black and white photographs are normally purchased outright from museums, while colour transparencies are hired for a set length of time (usually one, three or six months). Libraries more often sell both black and white and colour photographs outright. Each source will inform you of its own procedure, and you are likely to be asked to pay both hire and purchase costs in advance.
- *Service fee* is often charged by commercial picture libraries for lending you a selection of photographs (sometimes this is refunded if one or more photographs are reproduced) for a set period of time
- *Overdue/holding fees* are charged by museums and commercial picture libraries (usually by the week or month) for pictures not returned within the loan period. However, many picture libraries are willing to extend the loan period, without charge, by arrangement, and rarely charge holding fees if a picture is used. Museums, though willing to extend loan periods, are more likely to charge accordingly.
- *Reproduction fees* are charged for the use ('reproduction') of an illustration in a publication or programme. The charges are usually based on the following criteria.

  - *The rights required* (one or more languages, number of countries of distribution). If several language translations are expected, it can be more economical to request 'world all language rights'.
  - *The print-run*: charges are often bracketed 'under 1000', 'up to 5000', '5000–10 000', etc.
  - *The size of the image* as reproduced on the page: commercial picture libraries in particular charge according to the size of the illustration, whether a quarter, half or whole page.
  - *Jacket or within the text*: higher charges are made by most sources for illustrations used on covers or books, CDs, etc. (and some have special restrictions regarding jackets; see 'COPYRIGHT' below).
  - *Reductions* may be made for publications with a very low print-run, for educational textbooks, charitable

> publications, or if a large number of pictures are used from any one source. Each source will have its own policy; some museums may waive the fee altogether.

- *Loss fees* are charged by most sources for the loss (or damage) of photographs, particularly colour transparencies, that are out on loan. These vary greatly, but may range from £25 to £400 (for a unique colour transparency loaned by a professional photographer or commercial picture library). For this reason it is well worth checking all photographs on arrival, and asking any third party to sign for them when handed over, for instance to a designer or production department.

Captions

An illustration is of little worth without a caption identifying at least the title, artist, date and medium, and it is normally the responsibility of the picture researcher to provide and check this information, taking notes from any primary or secondary sources. If you are unsure of the medium a useful book is *How to Identify Prints* (Gascoigne, 1986); this is a complete guide to manual and mechanical processes, from woodcut to inkjet. The period of the costumes (and any typography) can be an indication of the approximate date of the illustration if no further exact information is available. There are many books on costume history, but a good comprehensive general introduction is *A History of Costume in the West* (Boucher, 1966). Captions in secondary sources should always be regarded with caution – mistakes are often made! While captions should at the least give basic factual information about an illustration, they can also provide an opportunity to draw the reader in with comments on details and interpretation that might otherwise be missed (and can give additional commentary that runs parallel with the accompanying text without interfering with the line of argument).

Acknowledgements

Most sources insist that they receive acknowledgement, either as part of the caption, or in a List of Illustrations, or on a page devoted to this purpose (at the front or back of a publication). It is generally helpful to give as much source information as there is space for (publication titles, manuscript and folio numbers, inventory numbers, etc.). Some museums are very strict about the exact form of the acknowledgement (which may include reference to a donor). If the work is in copyright, acknowledgement of the copyright holder should be included at this point.

Points to be aware of

It is always advisable to read the small print in the conditions sent by the source as part of the delivery note or invoice, and to take careful note of the stated requirements. The supply of a photograph does not necessarily confer permission to reproduce it (although some sources prefer to deal with this as part of the initial transaction). You may need to write to the source again before publication to ask official permission to reproduce the illustration, and to ascertain any information that was unavailable at the time of requesting the photograph. Many museums will not allow a detail of a work to be reproduced without prior agreement (and usually request that the full work is also reproduced; or at least that the word 'detail' is included in the caption). Commercial picture libraries are much more flexible.

Jackets/covers can be a problem: many museums will not allow 'over-printing' of, for instance, a book title, and can refuse permission for cropped details to be used on jackets. It is always as well to seek permission as early as possible, especially if the work is the copyright of a living artist or photographer (or their estate, if deceased – estates can be a great deal more troublesome than artists).

Colour proofs are required by many museums in order to check the colour balance, and truth to the original. Allow time for this, since a second proof can sometimes be requested.

Free books: many sources ask for a complimentary or 'voucher' copy of the book as part of (or sometimes in lieu of) the reproduction fee. If the book is in more than one volume (or otherwise very costly), the source will often accept an offprint of the page or article concerned.

Future editions: permission is normally granted for 'one-time use'. It is necessary to contact the source again for permission for new editions (including foreign language translations, unless negotiated at the outset); re-use fees are normally only a percentage of the original fee. If you expect many translations it can be more economical to ask for 'world all language rights' to start with, but some sources will not allow this approach. If the photograph is used again in a different book, permission should be sought again.

I have mentioned above the importance of being aware of loan periods, additional hire, and loss fees. Try to ensure that the pictures are returned to sources as quickly as possible after the production process (using some form of recorded/registered post if the package contains colour transparencies, or rare material).

▶ SOURCES

There is an almost bewildering variety of potential picture sources from the broadly general to the minutely specific. To complicate matters, the same picture can often be obtained from more than one.

The division of picture sources into 'commercial' and 'non-commercial' is no longer really possible since virtually every source makes charges of one kind or another, except those that consider the use of their photographs to be advertisements for their products or activities. It is still possible, if you have the time and energy, to build up your own collection of images (see 'Building up your own collection of musical images' p. 382 below), depending on your field of interest.

I will outline the types of source from the broadest to most particular. The internet is increasingly providing the quickest access to available images.

National museums and libraries are generally the largest, most comprehensive sources, but finding what you want can be difficult unless you have the precise reference for the work concerned (page or folio number, as well as shelf-mark, inventory or manuscript number). It may be necessary to go there in person. Increasing numbers of national collections have departments dedicated to providing photographic access to their collections (and sometimes other associated collections), for example Bildarchiv der Österreichisches Nationalbibliothek, Vienna, and the British Library Picture Library, London, and these will maintain subject indices, at least of portraits in their collections. Individual departments usually maintain relevant photographic files, supported by extensive reference libraries, and may have websites. A personal visit will always yield fresh insights into the holdings of a collection, and can often speed up the ordering of photographs. Many libraries have departments of 'special collections' that may relate either to the history and culture of the area, or to some other particular sphere of interest developed by that institution (these can often be in the form of legacies donated by private collectors); for instance, New York Public Library has a special Library for the Performing Arts. Few museums have a reference tool as useful to the musical researcher as Alec Hyatt King's *A Wealth of Music* (King, 1983), a cross-departmental listing, with descriptions, of musical images and objects in the British Museum and Library. The National Portrait Gallery, London (for example), maintains an index of portraits of British subjects, not only in its own collection, but in a wide variety of other sources throughout the country. Other countries have their own equivalents; the scope and subject of indices will often depend on the particular interests of the departmental curator. In the USA, every state has a historical society with collections relating to the cultural life of its region.

Wherever your field of interest is centred, the relevant national museum of library should be able to assist in aspects of your research. A word of warning, however: while these collections used to be a relatively cheap source of illustration, the centralisation of picture access has often been accompanied by a steep rise in reproduction fees. Certain national sources are very slow; others have taken steps to speed up their photographic services, and may also offer a 'rush' service. *The World of Learning* lists all national museums and libraries (more geographically widespread in Germany and Italy, due to those countries' histories); *The Picture Researcher's Handbook* (Evans, 7/2001) lists organisations supplying pictures for the institutions concerned.

Such national institutions are supplemented by a wide variety of other more or less specialist museums and libraries with both international and regional scope. A local public library may well be the best place to start if your subject of enquiry can be pinpointed to a precise geographical area.

Some centralised photographic services

Belgium

Institut Royal du Patrimoine Artistique (Service Photographique)
Parc du Cinquantenaire 1
B-1000 Brussels
Belgium
Tel: +32 (0)2 739 67 11
Fax: +32 (0)2 732 01 05

France

Réunion des Musées Nationaux (Agence Photographique)
10 rue de l'abbaye
75006 Paris
France
Tel: +33 (0)1 40 03 46 07
Fax: +33 (0)1 40 13 46 01
Email: jean-paul.bessieres@rmn.fr
URL: www.photo.rmn.fr
●   Represents 33 national collections in France.

Photothèque des Musées de la Ville de Paris
18 rue du Petit Musc
75004 Paris
France
Tel: +33 (0)1 44 78 81 50
Fax: +33 (0)1 42 72 69 15

Germany

Bildarchiv Preussischer Kulturbesitz (Berlin Museums and Libraries)
Märkisches Ufer 16–18
10179 Berlin
Germany

Tel: +49 (0)30 278 792 0
Fax: +49 (0)30 278 792 39
Email: bildarchiv@bpk.spk-berlin.de
URL: www.bildarchiv-bpk.de

SLUB Dresden: Deutsche Fotothek (Dresden Collections)
Sächsische Landesbibliothek
D-01054 Dresden
Germany
Tel: +49 (0)351 81668-31/81668-0
Fax: +49 (0)351 81668-32
Email: fotothek@slub-dresden.de

Spain

Institut Amatller d'Art Hispànic (Arxiu Fotogràfic)
Passeig de Gràcia 41
08007 Barcelona
Spain
Tel: +34 (0)93 216 0175
Fax: +34 (0)93 467 0194
Email: Arxiu.mas@amatller.com

Picture libraries and historical photograph collections exist for the sole purpose of supplying the demand for images which, in turn, is their only source of income. While many of them have an international scope, most have a national bias; their collections often number many millions. Although the same images may sometimes be also be found in public libraries and archives, the added advantage of going to a picture library is that there will be access by a wider variety of indices, and you may be offered a selection of relevant pictures, usually delivered within only a matter of days.

Examples of important historical photographic collections are Roger-Viollet (Paris), Mary Evans Picture Library, and Getty Images (London), Ullstein Bilderdienst (Berlin), Archiv für Kunst und Geschichte (AKG – London and Berlin), Foto Marburg (Marburg), Culver Pictures (New York), The Bettmann Archive (New York), Alinari (Florence) and Institut Amatller d'Art Hispànic (Barcelona) – most of these specialise in cultural history, and even if they cannot help over a particular request, they may be willing to offer advice on how to obtain the image concerned. Certain picture libraries carry colour transparencies of works of art from a variety of museums and galleries; again these are international in scope, with national bias. Examples include Scala (Florence and London), Bridgeman Art Library (London, Paris and New York), Giraudon (Paris) and Art Resource (New York). A number of individuals and institutions, listed below, have specialised in music.

Picture agencies represent living photographers who are actively practising their art and need someone to handle the day-to-day practicalities of supplying their work.

Specialist archives relating to music can be a treasure trove to a picture researcher. These collections have been formed as adjuncts to larger organisations, for instance the archives of opera houses, record companies, universities, and schools of music. Of special note is the Department of Portraits and Performance History at the Royal College of Music in London which, in addition to archival material relating to its own activities, has a vast, well documented iconographic collection of portraits, photographs, posters, title pages, opera and ballet programmes, albums, scrapbooks, concert tickets, newspaper cuttings and memorabilia. The department also maintains an index of musical engravings from the *Illustrated London News* and other periodicals and, as British headquarters for RIdIM (see 'RESEARCH TOOLS' BELOW), an accumulating index to musical subjects in British galleries, museums, cathedrals, etc. Others include the Raymond Mander and Joe Mitchenson Theatre Collection, now rehoused at Trinity College, London, the Royal Opera House Archives, Covent Garden, the Museo Teatrale alla Scala, Milan, the Harvard Theater Collection, and the Library of Performing Arts at the Lincoln Center, New York.

Music publishers (and to a lesser degree concert agents) are assiduous in keeping iconographic records of the activities their composers and performers; if they do not have a particular image, they will invariably be able to suggest who can help. Photographs supplied by these sources are not normally free of charge, unless used directly as promotion for a particular work (for instance to accompany a review). These sources may not have complete records regarding copyright holders of specific images.

Foundations, institutes, archives have been established to further the reputation and influence of a number of composers. They are often to be found in a composer's country of birth, and can be traced through national music information services (see *British and International Music Yearbook*). Such institutions can be counted on to have iconographic files, and may supply material cheaply, though there can often be a photographer's copyright involved – and also, in some instances, the composer's. Examples include the Britten-Pears Foundation (Aldeburgh), Stravinsky (Basel), Bartók Archive (Budapest), Paul Hindemith Institut (Frankfurt-am-Main), Stiftung Alban Berg (Vienna) and the Internationale Stiftung Mozarteum (Salzburg)

Composer houses are closely related to the above, but except for the major composers are less well endowed, and so may find it difficult to respond to requests for photographs. Few will have illustrated catalogues, though some may have postcards and printed lists of their holdings. Where they are unable to supply photographs, they may be able to answer limited written enquiries, or suggest the best person or institution to contact for assistance. A personal visit may be the most rewarding approach. There

Fig. 27.1: 'The Handel Festival at the Crystal Palace: the Royal Box.' This engraving appeared in the *Illustrated London News* for 20 June 1868 (p 613). As well as providing a vivid contemporary record, nineteenth century illustrated journals constitute an inexpensive source of out-of-copyright images. This example was purchased from a London dealer for £2.

are over 200 composer houses in Europe alone (see Julie Anne and Stanley Sadie, *Calling on Composers* (due 2002, Yale University Press)).

Societies/Journals: There are large numbers of periodicals and societies of enthusiasts for almost every aspect of musical history; many maintain collections of original iconographic material or related cuttings, or will know who knows. Such organisations can be traced, for example, through the internet, or the *British and International Music Yearbook*.

Private collections of iconographical material have been formed by a number of individual enthusiasts who are sometimes willing to share their passion, and may use fees earned in this way to increase their collections. These collections can be discovered by looking at the picture credits in books and programmes. Approaches should be tactful and considerate.

Picture libraries/photographers specialising in music (selection only): In most Western countries there are photographers (and umbrella organisations) specialising in music and the performing arts. Some examples are: Arena (London), Dominic Photography (London), Guy Gravett Collection (Hurstpierpoint; Glyndebourne productions to 1996), Mike Hoban Photography (Glyndebourne productions from 1994), Lebrecht Music Collection (London), Performing Arts Library (London), Photostage (Milton Keynes), Redferns and Val Wilmer (London; mainly popular music and jazz).

Some useful addresses

Austria

Österreichische Nationalbibliothek
  (Porträt-Sammlung
  und Bild-Archiv)
Josefplatz 1
Postbox 308
A-1015 Wien
Austria
Tel: +43 (0)1 53410 329
Fax: +43 (0)1 53410 331
Email: <bildarchiv@onb.ac.at>
URL: <http//www.onb.ac.at>

France

Bibliothèque Nationale de France
  (Service Photographique)
Quai François Mauriac
75706 Paris Cedex 13
France

Tel: +33 (0)1 53 79 82 22
Fax: +33 (0)1 53 79 42 60
Email: <reproduction@bnf.fr>
URL: <http//www.bnf.fr>

Caisse Nationale des Monuments
  Historiques et des Sites
  (Agence Photographique)
4 rue de Turenne
75004 Paris
France
Tel: +33 (0)1 44 61 21 00
Fax: +33 (0)1 44 61 21 81
Email: <degand@monuments-france.fr>
URL: <http//www.monuments-france.fr>

Giraudon
152 Avenue Malakoff
75782 Paris Cedex 16

France
Tel: +33 (0)1 53 64 60 97
Fax: +33 (0)1 53 64 60 97
Email: <contact@pix.fr>
URL: <http//www.
    stock-directory.fr>

Roger-Viollet
6 rue de Seine
75006 Paris
France
Tel: +33 (0)1 43 54 81 10
Fax: +33 (0)1 43 29 72 88
Email: <roger-viollet@
    roger-viollet.fr>
URL: <http//www.roger-viollet.fr>

Germany

*Archiv fur Kunst und Geschichte
    (AKG), Berlin [see under
    Great Britain: AKG London]*
Bayerische Staatsbibliothek
    (Bildarchiv)
Ludwigstrasse 16
D-80539 München
Germany
Tel: +49 (0)89 28 638 22 79
Fax: +49 (0)89 28 638 266
Email: <bildarchiv@bsb.badw-
    muenchen.de>
URL: <http//www.bsb.badw-
    muenchen.de>

Foto Marburg (Bildarchiv)
Postbox 1460
D-35004 Marburg
Germany
Tel: +49 (0)6421 282 3600
Fax: +49 (0)6421 282 8931
Email: <bildarchiv@fotomr.uni-
    marburg.de>
URL: <http//www.fotomr.uni-
    marburg.de>

*Germanisches Nationalmuseum
    (Fotostelle)*
Postfach 9580
D-90105 Nûrnberg
Tel: +49 (0)911 1331-0
Fax: +49 (0)911 1331-200

Great Britain

AKG London
5 Melbray Mews
158 Hurlingham Road
London SW6 3NS
Tel: +44 (0)20 7610 6103
Fax: +44 (0)20 7610 6125
Email: <enquiries@akg-
    london.co.uk>
URL: <http://www.akg-
    london.co.uk>

Arena
1st Floor
55 Southwark Street
London SE1 1RU
Tel: +44 (0)20 403 8542
Fax: +44 (0)20 403 8561
Email: <enquiries@arenaimages.
    com>
URL: <http://www.arenaimages.
    com>

Bridgeman Art Library
17-19 Garway Road
London W2 4PH
Tel: +44 (0)20 7727 4065
Fax: +44 (0)20 7792 8509
Email: <info@bridgeman.co.uk>
URL: <http://www.bridgeman.co.uk>

British Library Picture Library
96 Euston Road
London NW1 2DB
Tel: +44 (0)20 7412 7614
Fax: +44 (0)20 7412 7771
Email: <bl-repro@bl.uk>
URL: <http://www.bl.uk/services/
    repro/picture-library>

British Museum Department of Prints and Drawings
Great Russell Street
London WC1B 3DG
Tel: +44 (0)20 7323 8408
Fax: +44 (0)20 7323 8999
Email: <photolibrary@british-museum.ac.uk>
URL: <http://www.tbm.ac.uk>

Dominic Photography
4b Moore Park Road
London SW6 2JT
Tel: +44 (0)20 7381 0007
Fax: +44 (0)20 7381 0008

Mary Evans Picture Library
59 Tranquil Vale
Blackheath
London SE3 0BS
Tel: +44 (0)20 8318 0034
Fax: +44 (0)20 8852 7211
Email: <lib@mepl.co.uk>
URL: <http://www.mepl.co.uk>

Getty Images (Hulton Archive)
Unique House
21-31 Woodfield Road
London W9 2BA
Tel: +44 (0)20 7266 2662
Fax: +44 (0)20 7266 3154
Email: <hulton.marketing@getty-images.com>
URL: <http://www.marketing@getty-images-com>

Glyndebourne Festival Opera
Lewes
East Sussex BN8 5UU
Tel: +44 (0)1273 812321
Fax: +44 (0)1273 812783
URL: <http://www.glyndebourne.com>

Guy Gravett Collection
Hope Lodge
Hassocks Road
Hurstpierpoint
Sussex BN6 9QL
Tel: +44 (0)1273 834817
Fax: +44 (0)1273 834817

Mike Hoban Photography
New House
Church Lane
Ripe
East Sussex BN8 6AS
Tel: +44 (0)1323 811568
Email: <mike@mikehoban.com>

Lebrecht Music Collection
58B Carlton Hill
London NW8 0ES
Tel: +44 (0)20 7625 5341
Fax: +44 (0)20 7625 5341
Email: <pictures@lebrecht.co.uk>
URL: <http://www.lebrecht.co.uk>

Mander and Mitchenson Theatre Collection
Jerwood Library of the Performing Arts
Trinity College of Music
King Charles Court
Old Royal Naval College
London SE10 9JF
Tel: +44 (0)208 305 4426
Fax: +44 (0)208 305 3993
Email: <rmangan@tcm.uk>
URL: <http://www.mander-and-mitchenson.co.uk>

Performing Arts Library
Production House (1st floor)
25 Hackney Road
London E2 7NX
Tel: +44 (0)20 7749 4850
Fax: +44 (0)20 7749 4858
Email: <performingartspics@pobox.com>
URL: <http://www.performingartslibrary.co.uk>

Photostage
Postbox 65
Shenley Lodge
Milton Keynes
Buckinghamshire MK5 7YT
Tel: +44 (0)1908 262 324
Fax: +44 (0)1908 262 082
Email: <donaldmcooper@aol.
com>

Redferns
7 Bramley Road
London W10 6SZ
Tel: +44 (0)20 7792 9914
Fax: +44 (0)20 7792 0921
Email: <info@redferns.com>
URL: <http://www.redferns.com>

*Royal College of Music
(Department of Portraits
and Performance History)*
Prince Consort Road
London SW7 2BS
Tel: +44 (0)20 7591 4340
Fax: +44 (0)20 7589 7740

*Scala Art Resource
[see also under Scala Group
SpA, Italy]*
1 Willow Court (1st floor)
Off Willow Street
London EC2A 4QB
Tel: +44 (0)20 7782 0044
Fax: +44 (0)20 7782 0011
Email: <infor@scala-art.demon.
co.uk>
URL: <http://www.scala.firenze.it>

*Theatre Museum (Victoria &
Albert Museum)*
1E Tavistock Street
London WC2E 7PA
Tel: +44 (0)20 7836 7891
Fax: +44 (0)20 7836 5148
URL: <http://www.theatremuseum.
vam.ac.uk>

Val Wilmer
10 Sydner Road
London N16 7UG
Tel: +44 (0)20 7249 1205

Reg Wilson
Celadon
Westbrook Close
Bosham
West Sussex PO18 8ND
Tel: +44 (0)1243 574 852
Fax: +44 (0)1243 574 852

Greece

*Hellenic Republic Ministry of
Culture (Archaeological
Receipts Fund – TAP)*
57 Panepistimiou Street
GR-10564 Athens
Greece
Tel: +30 21 03253 901-6
Fax: +30 21 03242 684/3242254
Email: <protocol@tapa.culture.gr>

Italy

Alinari
Largo Fratelli Alinari 15
50123 Florence
Italy
Tel: +39 055 2395 237
Fax: +39 055 2395 234
Email: <info-more@alinari.it>
URL: <http://www.alinari.it>

Giancarlo Costa
Via Valparaiso 18
20144 Milan
Italy
Tel: +39 02 481 3181
Fax: +39 02 481 94562

*Istituto Archeologico Germanico
  (Deutsches Archäologisches
  Institut)*
Via Sardegna 79
00187 Rome
Italy
Tel: +39 06 488814-70/71
Fax: +39 06 4884-973

*Istituto Centrale per il Catalogo e
  la Documentazione [ICCD]
  (Archivio Fotografico)*
Ministero per i Beni Culturali e
  Ambientali
Via di S. Michele 18
00153 Rome
Italy
Tel: +39 06 5880960/58552244
Fax: +39 06 58367123/58332313

*Scala Group SpA [see also under
  Scala Art Resource, GB]*
Via Chiantigiana 62
50011 Antella (Florence)
Italy
Tel: +39 055 623320
Fax: +39 055 641124
Email: <archivio@scalagroup.
  com>
URL: <http://www.scalagroup.
  com>

USA

*Art Resource: represents Pierpont
  Morgan Library, NY;
  Smithsonian Institution,
  Washington;*
New York Public Library (Rare
  Books, Manuscripts, Maps,
  Schomburg Center for
  Research in Black Culture)
536 Broadway (5th floor)
New York

NY 10012
USA
Tel: +1 (212) 505 8700
Fax: +1 (212) 505 2053
Email: <requests@artes.com>
URL: <http://www.artres.com>

Culver Pictures
150 West 22nd Street (Suite 300)
New York
NY 10011
USA
Tel: +1 (212) 645 1672
Fax: +1 (212) 627 9112
Email: <info@culverpictures.com>

*New York Public Library
  (Central Research Library) –
  see also above under Art
  Resource*
Fifth Avenue at 42nd Street
New York
NY 10018
USA
Tel: +1 (212) 930 0834 (Art);
  +1 (212) 930 0817 (Prints);
  +1 (212) 930 0837
  (Photography)
Fax: +1 (212) 930 0530
URL: <http://www.nypl.org>

*New York Public Library for the
  Performing Arts*
40 Lincoln Center Plaza
New York
NY 10023-7498
Tel: +1 (212) 870 1657 (Dance
  Collection)
Tel: +1 (212) 870 1650 (Music
  Division)
URL: <http://www.nypl.org/
  research/lpa/lpa>

Building up your own collection of musical images[1]

If you have time (especially), and the interest and determination, this is a distinct possibility. Many musical images suitable for reproduction, which would cost many tens of pounds each in reproduction fees if obtained from institutional or library sources can still be purchased from dealers and junk shops for very small sums. All writers about music who have publication in view should assemble their own collection. This is something which can only be done effectively over time and so it is never too early to start. Having acquired a collection and the first-hand expertise that goes with it, it will also be possible for the resulting collection to become a source for other picture researchers. Generally the material to be acquired in this way will date from the period 1850–1950 or earlier and as such it will be largely out of copyright (though beware being caught out by rights owners who were very long-lived and produced any given illustration early in their career).

The likely sources that most collectors can aspire to are:

- cartes de visite;
- cabinet photographs;
- picture postcards; and
- engravings and drawing from illustrated magazines, especially the *Illustrated London News, The Graphic, Black & White, The Musical Times, Musica* and *Comoedia Illustré*.

These constitute a valuable and easily accessible source for musical research (Foreman, 1986). Certainly if one is trying to illustrate musicians and events from their heyday they are a valuable source, and while individually they are of small cash value, they can be historically significant, and picture post-cards when postally used and thus date-stamped provide certain evidence of their date and non-copyright status.

As far as postcards are concerned, it is important to realise that many from the pre-First World War period are real photographs, rather than printed reproductions, and from a picture research viewpoint these are preferable to images that have been screened (i.e. the picture is revealed as a mass of small dots when viewed under a magnifying glass). These can be collected by visiting the monthly London Postcard Fair (at prices usually in the range £1–£10) at the time of writing long established at London's Royal National Hotel, or similar fairs held from time to time throughout the UK and in many countries of the world. The specialist collecting maga-zines, or in the USA the collector's newspapers *Barr's News*[2] will provide further contacts to those researchers wanting to develop this specialism. A number of websites have appeared and these can best been traced by typing 'post cards' in a general search engine such as Alta Vista and browsing the results.

Fig. 27.2: A pre-revolutionary Russian picture postcard of the conductor Arthur Nikisch. Nikisch was an example of an artist whose image appears on many postcards immediately before the First World War.

A number of anthologies of musical postcards have been published, good examples being Charles Osborne's *The Opera House Album: a Collection of Turn-of-the-century Postcards* and Richard Bonynge's *A Collector's Guide to Theatrical Postcards*. The photographs of composers in Foreman's *British Music 1885–1920* (1994) are all from postcards.

One only has to look at the various pictorial biographies of great composers, such as Mahler,[3] Wagner[4] and Strauss[5] to have a feeling for the rich variety of illustrations available. When searching for colour portraits of earlier composers (and indeed twentieth-century ones) one normally has to look for paintings, and some of the leading examples can usefully be reviewed in Buettner and Pauly's *Great Composers Great Artists Portraits* (1992). However, a more systematic and extensive collection, not so easily found in British libraries, was published in Munich in 1982–3 (Salmen, 1982–3).

Collections of pictures thematically presented have also appeared, often as exhibition catalogues. Two good examples are the Bibliothèque Nationale and the Théâtre National de l'Opéra de Paris's *Wagner et la France* (Kahane and Wild, 1983) and Helmet Loos's collection of vivid

Fig. 27.3: Production photographs of new operas were widely used in Europe as promotional tools. This example by Zander and Labisch is printed as a 'real photographic' postcard of the first production of Richard Strauss's Salome with Marie Wittsich in the title rôle. 1905

musical caricatures (1982), the latter a convenient source for further reproduction, though copyright, as anthologised. If copies of the publications in which the originals appeared could be found they would be out of copyright (depending on the death date of the artist).

► RESEARCH TOOLS

The pursuit of fresh and appropriate images can greatly be assisted by a number of organisations that exist to further research in iconography, occasionally even in musical iconography. By far the most important tool to have developed in recent years is, of course, the internet. Organisations, societies, libraries, publishers, photographers, auctioneers, individual musicians (alive or dead) – sources of every kind can readily be traced with some persistence, ingenuity and lateral thinking. Most picture libraries now have subject lists accessible, and many display actual photographs. Increasingly images are being supplied electronically, either by e-mail, or on CD-ROM. Here are a few examples that may be useful.

● RIdIM *(Répertoire International d'Iconographie Musicale)* was founded in 1972 on the initiation of Geneviève Thibault-de Chambure, Barry S. Brook and Harald Heckmann, with the aim of developing methods of classification, cataloguing and study of iconographical material worldwide to assist scholars, historians, performers, instrument makers, etc. It seeks to establish musical iconography as a discipline in its own right. With headquarters at the City University of New York Graduate School, the organisation (now called the Research Center for Music Iconography) has established cataloguing centres in various countries (England, France, Italy, Germany, Sweden), with associated conferences, and publishes a bibliography, a newsletter (Since 1997 called *Music in Art: International Journal for Music Iconography*) Zdravko Blažeković (Director) Research Center for Music Iconography, Barry S. Brook Center for Music Research and Documentation, The Graduate Center, The City University of New York, 365 Fifth Avenue, New York, NY 10016–4309 USA (Tel: 001 212 817 1992; fax: 001 212 817 1569; E-mail: <mailto:zblazekovic@gc.cuny.edu>; web: <www.gc.cuny.edu>), catalogues and a yearbook (*Imago Musicae*). Certain centres have developed software for the computerised cataloguing of pictures with musical subject matter.

Address: Research Center for Music Iconography, 33 West 42nd Street, New York, NY 10036; Tel: +1 (212) 642 2709; Fax: +1 (212) 642 1973; E-mail: <zblazeko@email.gc.cuny.edu>.

● *Witt Library, The Courtauld Institute, University of London* holds thousands of images of paintings, engravings, etchings, drawings and designs (some original works, mostly photographs and cuttings from saleroom and exhibition catalogues, monographs, etc.), arranged by national school, and by artist. This is a wonderfully fertile research aid: if you know the names of likely artists, trawling through the boxes rarely fails to bring up new and interesting musical subject matter. There are often several versions of records of the same image, and the extensive caption and commentaries attached can chart not only varying critical opinion, but the movement of a painting, with, if not the name of the present owner, at least the saleroom last known to have handled it. Copies of photographs can only be purchased when the Courtauld holds the original work, or the copyright of the photograph.

Address: Witt Library, Courtauld Institute of Art, Somerset House, Strand, London WC2R 0RN; Tel: 020 7872 0220; Fax: 020 7873 2772; E-mail: <cath.gordon@courtauld.ac.uk>; URL: <www.courtauld.ac.uk>.

● *Conway Library, The Courtauld Institute, University of London* is the architectural equivalent of the Witt Library, holding vast quantities of photographs of buildings arranged by country, city, building. Photographs can be ordered where the CIA owns the copyright, or addresses given of photographers when known. The Conway also holds extensive photographic files on sculpture, metalwork, ivories and manuscripts.

Address: Courtauld Institute of Art (as above, under Witt Library)

● *The Warburg Institute (University of London) Photographic Collection* has continued to be built on the original iconographic collection of Aby Warburg. Most of the photographs are of works of Western art from the Middle Ages to the end of the eighteenth century, but they include works up to the present day when these fall within the categories of special interest to the Institute. The main categories of the collection are as follows (within these there are innumerable subdivisions): Antiquities, Gestures, Ritual, Gods and Myths, Religious Iconography, Secular Iconography, Medieval and Later Literature, Magic and Science, Portraits, History, Social Life, Artists, Architecture, Ornament, Manuscripts, etc. This is a private collection for the serious art historian; visitors are welcomed on daily research basis, but may be asked to contribute a fee for the use of the facility (it is advisable to telephone in advance to arrange a visit).

Address: Warburg Institute, University of London, Woburn Square, London WC1H 0AB; Tel: 020 7580 9663 or 020 7862 8917

● *Fondazione Giorgio Cini, Venice: Istituto per le Lettere, il Teatro e il Melodramma* houses a very large collection of opera libretti (often with engravings), and a large collection of photographs of stage and costume designs from public and private collections in Europe, filed by designer. The collection includes photographs of theatres.

Address: Fondazione Giorgio Cini, Isolo San Giorgio Maggiore, Venice, Italy. Tel: +39 (041) 52 89 900; Fax: +39 (041) 52 38 540

● *Centre National de la Recherche Scientifique (CNRS)* has a team researching organology and musical iconography, and has established a scientific review, *Musique-Images-Instruments*, dedicated to research in these fields.

Address: Centre National de la Recherche Scientifique, Laboratoire d'organologie et d'Iconographie Musicale, Musée des Arts et Traditions Populaires, 6 Avenue du Mahatma Gandhi, 75116 Paris, France; Tel: +33 (01) 44 17 60 96; Fax: +33 (01) 44 17 60 60; E-mail: <getreau@atp.culture.fr>.

● BAPLA (British Association of Picture Libraries) publishes a regularly updated handbook with list of members, and subject index. Helpful over many related professional matters, technical and copyright.

Address: BAPLA, 18 Vine Hill, London EC1R 5DZ; Tel: 0207 713 1780; Fax: 0207 713 1211; E-mail: <enquiries@bapla.co.uk> URL: <http://www.bapla.org>.

● The *Picture Research Association* is a professional organisation for picture researchers, managers, picture editors and all those specifically involved in the research, management and supply of visual material to all forms of the media, worldwide. It aims, among other things, to provide a forum for information exchange and interaction for anyone involved in the picture profession. It also maintains a register of freelance picture researchers.

Address (head office): 455 Finchley Road, London NW3 6HN; Tel: 020 7431 9886; Fax: 020 7431 9887; E-mail: <pra@pictures.demon.co.uk>).

▶ COPYRIGHT

In the realm of picture research, copyright (the ownership of rights in a created work) exists in two distinct categories that are often confused.

The copyright in any photograph commissioned by a museum, library or archive of a work in its collection (whether or not the work is itself in copyright) belongs to that institution, unless assigned elsewhere. Therefore the purchase of a photograph never (unless specifically stated otherwise at the time of purchase) carries with it the automatic right to reproduce it in any form. Permission should be requested (and a fee normally paid; see 'Costs' above) for every edition (including foreign translations) or transmission. (Separate permission is required for reproduction in any electronic medium.) This copyright is often known as the 'reproduction', or 'publication' right. The potential loss of revenue from this source leads many institutions to forbid photography by visitors, except by permit.

The copyright in an 'artistic work', whether it be a painting, drawing, musical composition, sculpture, photograph, film, map or diagram (called hereafter a 'work of art'), regardless of merit. It is important to note that copyright remains with the creator of the work of art and does not pass to the owner of the work (even when it is sold or destroyed), unless directly assigned to the owner by the artist in writing. The owner, however, may have limited control over any secondary copyright (reproduction right) created in new photographs of the work. The author/artist (or his estate) may grant a licence to reproduce a work of art on direct written application, or through a copyright agency such as DACS (Design and Artists Copyright Society Ltd; see p. 391 below) empowered to act on his behalf. Sometimes, when purchasing a work that is in copyright, a museum may also purchase the copyright outright from the artist, but this must be agreed in writing.

The first copyright act was passed in 1709, since when further acts have been passed and repealed, culminating in the Copyright, Designs and Patents Act 1988, which came into force on 1 August 1989, and was amended by the 1995–96 Regulations under the EC Copyright Directive aimed at harmonising copyright laws in the European Community. Since 1996 the duration of copyright protection is, generally, the duration of the life of the author/creator plus 70 years (or 40 in the USA and Japan).

Copyright is a very complicated matter, and I would recommend readers to the relevant sections in *Practical Picture Research* (Evans, 1992) and *A User's Guide to Copyright* (Flint, 1997), to which I am indebted in the preparation of these brief notes. Further complication lies in the fact that copyright is not standardised through the world.

Firstly it should be stressed that it is the picture researcher's responsibility to clear all copyright relevant to an illustration; if you are unable to trace the copyrightholder(s), you must be able to demonstrate that you have made every reasonable effort. If you obtain a photograph from a recognised source, that source should normally be able to advise you, but the addresses they provide can often be out of date.

Many artists and photographers are represented by one or more private galleries that exhibit their works on a regular basis. These galleries usually have information on whom should be contacted regarding copyright, and may be more up-to-date than larger, public institutions. Living photographers are more difficult to trace (unless you know the city in which they live), and you may have to ring round many professional associations, internationally, in search of them, or try the internet (some are represented by DACS).

Publishers (via their Rights & Permissions Departments) may sometimes be willing to provide addresses for photographers whose work appears in their books – but don't count on it! In the search for major art photographers, bodies such as the Royal Photographic Society can provide helpful pointers. A number of useful directories are listed at the end of this chapter, as are names of photographers who have specialised in music; these may operate individually, or be grouped into a syndicate. If you obtain a photograph from a general or specialised commercial syndication, that organisation will clear the necessary copyright with the photographers concerned. In these instances 'copyright' and 'reproduction right' can be cleared as one and the same thing. However, if you obtain a photograph from a historical source of any kind, the onus is on you to trace the copyright-holder.

A picture (original photograph, work of art, or photograph of a work of art) is either 'in copyright', or 'out of copyright'. If the picture is out of copyright you may reproduce it freely as long as you are the owner (or you have the permission of the owner) of the work, and are not infringing the copyright of any secondary source (for example an engraving reproduced in a book), or a museum's photograph of the picture (or photograph). Permission should generally be sought, as a courtesy, from private owners before reproducing works in their possession, whether they are in or out of copyright.

Auction houses will often forward letters to new owners, but since the copyright of auction house photographs belongs with the auction house concerned (taken, as they were, before the new owner took possession of the work) this is only a problem if, say, the provenance of a work is in dispute, or if there are 'political' considerations. Private owners often wish to remain anonymous (especially in credit lines) for security reasons.

Between the 1989 Act and 1996 Regulation, copyright in artistic works (excluding photographs and engravings) in Britain lasted for the artist's life plus 50 years. Even when a work is commissioned from an artist (on or after 1 August 1989), the artist retains the copyright (unless otherwise assigned); before 1 August 1989 the commissioner of a work of art was deemed to own the copyright in that work (unless otherwise agreed). The situation regarding photographs and engravings is more complicated.

- Photographs taken before 1 June 1957 are in copyright until 50 years after the end of the year in which they were taken, or 70 years after the photographer's death if longer. Photographs published between 1 June 1957 and 1 August 1989 are protected for 50 years from the end of the calendar year of publication, or 70 years after the photographer's death if longer. Photographs taken after 1 June 1957, and unpublished at 1 August 1989are protected for 50 years from the end of 1989, or 70 years after the photographer's death, if longer. All other photographs are now protected for 70 years after the death of the photographer.

- Engravings with a known artist:
    - published after the death of the artist, but before 1 August 1989, are protected for 50 years from the end of the calendar year of publication, or 70 years after the death of the artist if longer;
    - published before the death of the artist are protected for 70 years from the death of the artist;
    - if still unpublished are protected for 70 years after the death of the artist if longer than 50 years from the end of 1989.

There are further regulations concerning anonymous engravings. If you fail to obtain the necessary permission from a copyright holder, but go ahead and reproduce a picture, that person may subsequently demand a fee in retrospect (and in Britain has the legal right to do so for up to six years after publication). If the creator of a work of art is unknown, copyright in that work expires 70 years from the end of the year in which it was made; if during that period the work of art is made available to the public, then copyright expires 70 years from the end of the year in which it was first made available.

Particular caution must be observed when reproducing a painting or photograph in a prominent place such as the jacket of a book; restrictions may be imposed by copyright holders on cropping and over-printing, and higher fees usually apply since the use of the picture in such a position is normally expected to 'sell' the publication. Copyright can apply even when an in-copyright work of art is not reproduced directly, but used for reference (say for a diagram or drawing), as long as the original can be recognised

Dr. O. Böhler: Siegfried Wagner.

Fig. 27.4: Silhouettes, particularly of conductors and soloists, were widely used in the early 1900s. This example, which was published as a postcard by Emil Muller, Stuttgart in 1913, shows Richard Wagner's son Siegfried Wagner, conductor and composer.

in the newly created work; but this is a matter of degree. If a picture library or agency photograph is used for reference, normally only half the reproduction fee would be charged. Using, say, a snapshot as a reference would not be an infringement of copyright; in other words, the original must be considered a work of art in its own right. If a work of art in copyright is used a the basis of a parody of that work, then copyright may be infringed.

There is no infringement of copyright in a work of art if it is included incidentally in other copyright work: for instance, a piece of public sculpture appearing in a photograph of a building (where the photographer is the primary copyright holder), or works of art appearing incidentally as part of a film set.

A photographed portrait should not be reproduced without the consent of the subject when that person has been asked to pose for the photograph. Unposed snapshots are not subject to this restriction, but any reproduction of a photograph can be considered defamatory if the subject is shown in a compromising situation.

The Design and Artists Copyright Society Ltd (DACS; address p. 391) is an international copyright agency representing many artists, designers, photographers and their estates. It also represents sister organisations in other countries (for instance VAGA and the ARS in the USA and Bild-Kunst in Germany), and will advise on similar organisations elsewhere. DACS normally grants a three-year licence for a maximum print-run in single language, world English language, or world all-language, rights (whichever is applicable).

The question of reproduction from published books often comes up. There is copyright in the 'typographical arrangement' of a published work, regardlesss of whether material within that work is itself in copyright or not; this copyright protection lasts for 25 years from the end of the calendar year in which the edition was first published. If you wish to reproduce a diagram from a published source you should seek permission from the publisher (normally Rights & Reproductions Department). The publisher may or may not hold the copyright for the diagram: they may in turn have sought permission to reproduce it from an earlier published source, and there may be an artist's copyright involved. A publisher is not in a posi-tion to grant permission to reproduce a work of art from one of its books since there is the additional copyright in the photograph of that work supplied by the museum or library to the publisher; the publisher will have been granted a 'one time only' right to reproduce the work. Facsimiles of earlier published out of copyright works are not protected by copyright since their production involves no new 'typographical arrangement'; however, any new commentary or prefatory material would be protected.

Occasionally a museum or library will grant permission to reproduce one of its works from a book if the original has, for instance, been destroyed, or if for some reason it is quite impossible to have the work re-photographed. An artist may give permission in the same way. Then it is up to the publisher. Reproducing from books is possible when not only the book itself is out of copyright, but also the photographs within it. A late nineteenth/early twentieth-century book may be the only known source for certain historical photographs, portraits and other illustrations. The loss of quality when reproducing 'screened' images from books means that it is always preferable to use an original photograph whenever possible, though computer processing has made this less of a problem than it once was. This is not a problem when reproducing from books with engravings, litho-graphs or woodcuts and, to a certain extent, photogravure.

●   Design and Artists Copyright Society: DACS, Parchment House, 13 Northburgh Street, London EC1V 0JP; Tel: 020 7336 8811; Fax: 020 7336 8822; E-mail: <info@dacs.org.uk>.

Fig. 27.5: Positive organ player in a domestic setting: engraving by Israhel van Meckenem (d. 1503).

▶ PICTURES[6]

In the United Kingdom, the tax on newspapers was cut from 4 pence to 1 penny in 1836 and abolished in 1855, advertisement tax was abolished in 1853, and the first of W.H. Smith's railway bookstalls opened in 1848. This signalled a rapid growth of journalism, and with it came a rise in the status of musical criticism and an appetite for illustrations. Among many new titles launched in the 1840s was *The Illustrated London News*. This reflected a time of major technical developments in printing. During the

Fig. 27.6: Engraving (1698) by Christoph Weigel showing a bassoon maker (possibly Denner) at work on a two-key dulcian, with a three-key 'basson' to his right.

second half of the nineteenth century the development of the press exactly paralleled the emergence of a substantial public appetite for photography as exemplified by the rise of the *carte de visite*[7] and later the cabinet photograph, both precursors of popular illustrated journalism, and succeeded by the craze for photographic picture postcards before the First World War, and the success of popular illustrated musical journals such as the monthly *Musica*, and the Paris journal *Comoedia Illustré*.

One does not necessarily have to search for the more exotic titles, for example the London *Musical Times*, while not heavily illustrated, can be a useful source of out-of-copyright portraits of performing artists and composers from the late nineteenth century onward. A feature of the musical times for many years was an inserted photographic plate, which are often seen in ephemera trays of dealers for nominal sums. Providing we can locate convenient sources for such materials (often inexpensively to be found as cuttings on market stalls and from dealers in ephemera) these provide us with an excellent source of vivid and out-of-copyright material.

Nineteenth century engravings from *Illustrated London News* are also available from the Illustrated London News, and also from other picture libraries, but at reproduction fees set at picture library price levels. It is always cheaper to buy an original if one can be found. However, the Illustrated London News maintain their index to the journal in-house and it is only accessible to researchers taking pictures from them. Another (incomplete) index is freely available in the Department of Portraits at the Royal College of Music. If pictures are reproduced from copies in major public archives, such as the British Library, reproduction fees will be charged by the institution.[8]

All these provide us with a vivid, albeit sometimes idealised, window on nineteenth-century music, the composers and performers, halls and great events, theatrical productions and festivals, not forgetting the occasional fire or disaster. The richness of Victorian and Edwardian musical iconography means that many libraries may well have a resource the value of which they and their users do not themselves altogether recognise.

Before photographs began to appear in the press towards the end of the nineteenth century, they were disseminated and collected in the form of *cartes de visite*, which first appeared in 1859. These generally used the collodian process and can still be found today from specialist dealers – and in junk shops – often for a few pounds. Examples of musicians of the mid-Victorian era are fairly common, though they are rare in superb and unfaded condition. Examples of how good they can be was seen at the National Portrait Gallery's 'Variation on a Theme' exhibition of portraits of British composers in the spring of 1997.[9]

The National Portrait Gallery's exhibition included a wonderful selection of *cartes de visite* of Victorian figures such as an albumen print of Sir George Smart, who died in 1867, a Woodburytype *carte de visite* of Sir Michael Costa taken around 1868, of Sterndale Bennett also taken by the London Stereoscopic Company in the 1860s, and perhaps most interesting of all, J. Bleibel's image of Henry Hugo Pierson of 1865. Although one occasionally sees such items on dealers tables, such as Elliott & Fry's Sir John Stainer, it is rare to find them in truly unblemished condition. These are all part of the NPG's permanent collection and hence are available to researchers on payment of the appropriate fees.

The varied photographic processes – difficult to illustrate in reproduction – were fascinating, imparting to the earlier pictures, in particular, a unique quality all their own. Once photographs came to be generally

Fig. 27.7: Francesco Maria Veracini playing the violin: engraving from his *Sonate accademiche* (1744).

available they were widely collected, at first as *cartes de visite*, though later on, larger, more impressive, cabinet photographs of the good and the great were also popular. Both lead on to the craze for postcard collecting after the turn of the century. These were sometime published in part works such as *Men and Women of the Day* (1889),[10] which included a splendid carbon print of Maude Valérie White by Herbert Barraud, and *Our Celebrities*,[11] which included a portrait of the forty-year-old composer Sir Alexander Mackenzie by Walery. Turn of the century photographic journals such as *Black & White* can also be a valuable source of illustrative material.

Some music libraries may have small collections of highly interesting items, though, like much of this material, knowing they exist can prove problematic. An example may be found in Birmingham Public Library, where, although they have a large and well-respected photographic collection, the Music Library is the repository for a remarkable albumen print by H.J. Whitlock consisting of a photographic montage of the 16 principal artists taking part in the 1867 Birmingham Triennial Festival.

► SELECT BIBLIOGRAPHY

General reference

Anyone interested in a serious study of musical iconography would do well to begin with the important and comprehensive article 'Iconography' (with extensive bibliography) by Tilman Seebass in *The New Grove Dictionary of Music and Musicians* (London: Macmillan, 2/2001).

Sadie, S. (ed.) (1984) *The New Grove Dictionary of Musical Instruments*. London: Macmillan

Sadie, S. (ed.) (1992) *The New Grove Dictionary of Opera*. London: Macmillan

Evans, H and Evans, M. (2001) *Picture Researcher's Handbook: An International Guide to Picture Sources and How to Use Them* (7th edn.). Pira International

Evans, H. (1979) *Practical Picture Research (A Guide to Current Practice, Procedure, Techniques and Resources)* (revised edn. 1992). London: Blueprint/Chapman & Hall

The World of Learning (annual). London: Europa Publications: details of over 26 000 universities, colleges, schools of art and music, libraries, archives, learned societies, research institutes, museums and art galleries

International Directory of Arts (annual). München: K.G. Saur (includes addresses of museums, galleries, universities, associations, dealers, auctioneers, publishers, periodicals and booksellers)

British and International Music Yearbook (annual). London: Rhinegold Publishing Ltd

BAPLA Directory [British Association of Picture Libraries and Agencies] (2002; updated at regular intervals) London

Flint, M.F. (1997) *A User's Guide to Copyright*. London: Butterworths/Reed Elsevier

Turner, J. (ed.) (1996) *The Dictionary of Art* (34 vols). London: Macmillan

House, S. (comp.) (1981) *Dictionary of British Book Illustrators and Caricaturists 1800–1914*. Woodbridge: Antique Collectors Club

Lewis, J. (1990) *Printed Ephemera* (2nd edn.). Woodbridge: Antique Collectors Club

Gascoigne, B. (1986) *How to Identify Prints*. London: Thames & Hudson

Boucher, F. (1966) *A History of Costume in the West* (expanded 1987). London: Thames & Hudson

King, A.H. (1983) *A Wealth of Music in the Collections of the British Library (Reference Division) and the British Museum*. London: Clive Bingley Ltd

Crane, F. (1971) *A Bibliography of the Iconography of Music*. Iowa City

Seebass, T. and Tilden, R. (ed.) (1984–) *Imago musicae* (yearbook). New York [published under auspices of RidIM]

Early Music (1973–) Oxford University Press (quarterly journal, ed. Tess Knighton)

Musica Kalender (1954–) Kassel: Bärenreiter

Kinsky, G., Haas, R. and Schnoor, H. (1929) *Geschichte der Musik in Bildern* (eng. trans. 1930). Leipzig

Musikgeschichte in Bildern (1961–89) Leipzig (eds. H. Besseler, M. Schneider and W. Bachmann)

Henning, R. and Henning, U. (1975) *Zeugnisse alter Musik: Graphik aus fünf Jahrhunderten.* Herrsching

Winternitz, E. (1979) *Musical Instruments and their Symbolism in Western Art* (2nd edn.).

Leppert, R.D. (1988) *Music and Image: Domesticity, Ideology and Socio-Cultural Formation in Eighteenth-Century England.* Cambridge: Cambridge University Press

Bowles, E.A. (1983) *La Pratique Musicale au Moyen Age.* Geneva: Minkoff & Lattes [Iconographie Musicale]

Volek, T. and Jares, S. (1977) *The History of Czech Music in Pictures.* Prague: Supraphon [in Czech, German and English]

Lesure, F. (1972) *L'Opera Classique Français.* Geneva: Minkoff & Lattes [Iconographie Musicale]

Salmen, W. (1979) *Bilder zur Geschichte der Musik in Osterreich.* Innsbruck

RIdIM/RCMI Inventory of Music Iconography (1986–) New York (ed. T. Ford)

Fischer, P. (1975) *Music in Paintings of the Low Countries in the 16th and 17th Centuries.* Amsterdam

de Mirimonde, A.P. (1975–7) *L'iconographie Musicale sous les Rois Bourbons: la Musique dans les Arts Plastiques (XVIIe-XVIIIe siècles).* Paris

Leppert, R.D. (1977) *The Theme of Music in Flemish Paintings of the Seventeenth Century.* München

Wangermée, R. (1968) *La Musique Flamande.* Brussels: Editions Arcade

Cohen, H.R. (ed.) (1983) *Les Gravures Musicales dans 'L'illustration'* (3 vols). Quebec: Les Presses de l'Université Laval

Wild, N. (1987) *Décors et Costumes du XIXe Siècle.* Paris: Bibliothèque Nationale

Join-Diéterle, C. (1988) *Les Décors de Scène de l'Opéra de Paris a l'époque Romantique.* Paris: Picard

Canmer, J. (1981) *Great Composers in Historic Photographs (1860s to 1960s).* New York: Dover

Camner, J. (1978) *The Great Opera Stars in Historic Photographs (1840s to 1950s).* New York: Dover

Fraenkel, G.S. (ed.) (1968) *Decorative Music Title Pages.* New York: Dover

Bowles, E.A. (1989) *Musical Ensembles in Festival Books 1500–1800: an Iconographical & Documentary Survey.* Ann Arbor/London: UMI Research Press

Musikgeschichte in Bildern [History of Music in Pictures], a series founded by Heinrich Besseler and Max Schneider, edited by Werner Bachmann, and published by VEB Deutscher Verlag für Musik under the sponsorship of UNESCO. Forty volumes were planned, but just over half were published [commentary in German]:

Series I: Ethnomusicology
Volume 1: Collaer, P. (1965) *Oceania*
Volume 2: Collaer, P. (1967) *America: Eskimo and American Indian Peoples*
Volume 3: Collaer, P. (1979) *South-East Asia*
Volume 4: Danielou, A. (1978) *South Asia*
Volume 8: Collaer, P. and Elsner, J. (1983) *North Africa*
Volume 9: Gansemans, J. and Schmidt-Wrenger, B. (1986) *Central Africa*
Volume 10: Kubik, G. (1982) *East Africa*

Series II: Music of Ancient Times
Volume 1: Hickmann, H. (1961) *Egypt*
Volume 2: Rashid, S.A. (1984) *Mesopotamia*
Volume 4: Wegner, M. (1963) *Greece*
Volume 5: Fleischhauer, G. (1964) *Etruria and Rome*
Volume 7: Martí, S. (1970) *Ancient America*
Volume 8: Kaufmann, W. (1981) *Ancient India*
Volume 9: Karomatov, F.M., Meskeris, V. and Vyzgo, T. (1987) *Ancient Middle Asia*

Series III: Music of the Middle Ages and the Renaissance
Volume 2: Farmer, H.G. (1966) *Islam*
Volume 3: van Waesberghe, J.S. (1969) *Musical Education*
Volume 4: Stäblein, B. (1975) *Notation of Monophonic Music*
Volume 5: Besseler, H. and Gülke, P. (1973) *Notation of Polyphonic Music*
Volume 8: Bowles, E.A. (1977) *Fifteenth-Century Musical Life*
Volume 9: Salmen, W. (1976) *Sixteenth-Century Musical Life*

Series IV: Music from 1600 to the Present
Volume 1: Wolff, H.C. (1968) *Opera*
Volume 2: Schwab. H.W. (1971) *Concert*
Volume 3: Salmen, W. (1969) *'Hausmusik' and Chamber Music*

Composers

Neumann W. (1979) *Bilddokumente zur Lebensgeschichte Johann Sebastian Bach*. Kassel: Bärenreiter

Schwendowius, B. and Dömling, W. (ed.) (1977) *Johann Sebastian Bach: Life, Times and Influence*. Kassel: Bärenreiter, with Polydor International

Bónis, F. (1981) *Béla Bartók: His Life in Pictures and Documents*. Budapest: Corvina Kiadó

Robbins Landon, H.C. (1970) *Beethoven, A Documentary Study*. London: Thames Hudson

Vincenzo Bellini: mostra di oggetti e documenti provenienti da Collezione pubbliche e private italiana (1988). Catania: Giuseppe Maimone

Jullien, A. (1888) *Hector Berlioz: sa vie et ses oeuvres*. Paris: à la Librairie de L'Art

Berlioz and the Romantic Imagination (1969) (exhibition catalogue, Victoria & Albert Museum). London: Arts Council

Braam, G. (ed) (due 2003) *Hector Berlioz: Iconography*. Kassel: Bärenreiter [New Berlioz Editor, vol 26]

Jacobsen, C. (ed.) (1983) *Johannes Brahms: Leben und Werk*. Wiesbaden: Breitkopf & Hartel, with Polydor International, Hamburg

Mitchell, D. (comp.) (1978) *Benjamin Britten: Pictures from a Life 1913–1976*. London: Faber and Faber

Herbert, D. (ed.) (1979) *The Operas of Benjamin Britten*. London: Herbert Press

Bory, R. (1951) *La Vie de Frédéric Chopin par L'Image*. Geneva: Editions Alexandre Jullien

Burger, E. (1990) *Frédéric Chopin: Eine Lebenschronik in Bildern und Documenten*. München: Hirmer Verlag

Lesure, F. (1975) *Claude Debussy*. Geneva: Minkoff [*Iconographie Musicale*]

Carley, L. and Threlfall, R. (1977) *Delius: A Life in Pictures*. Oxford: Oxford University Press

Northrop Moore, J. (1972) *Elgar: A Life in Photographs*. Oxford: Oxford University Press

Kimball, R. and Simon, A. (1974) *The Gershwins*. London: Jonathan Cape

Benestad, F. and Schjelderup-Ebbe, D. (1988) *Edvard Grieg: the Man and The Artist*. Gloucester: Alan Sutton

Simon, J. (ed.) (1985) *Handel: A Celebration of his Life and Times 1685–1759* (exhibition catalogue). London: National Portrait Gallery

Robbins Landon, H.C. (1984) *Handel and his World*. London: Weidenfeld and Nicolson

Somfai, L. (1969) *Joseph Haydn: His Life in Contemporary Pictures* (eng. trans. Faber and Faber 1969). Budapest: Corvina Press

Robbins Landon, H.C. (1981) *Haydn, A Documentary Study*. London: Thames & Hudson

Svt Janáckovch Oper [The World of Janácek's Operas] (1998) (exhibition catalogue). Brno: Moravské Zemské Muzeum

Zsigmond L. and Mátéka, B. (1967) *Franz Liszt: Sein Leben in Bildern* (eng. trans. 1967). Budapest: Corvina

Burger, E. (1989) *Franz Liszt: a Chronicle of his Life in Pictures and Documents*. Princeton University Press

Blaukopf, K. (comp.) (1976) *Mahler, a Documentary Study* (eng. trans. Thames & Hudson 1976). Wien: Universal Edition

The Mahler Album (1995) London: Thames & Hudson, with the Kaplan Foundation, New York

Wiesmann, S. (ed.) (1977) *Gustav Mahler in Wien*. London: Thames & Hudson

Giacomo Meyerbeer: Weltbürger der Musik eine Ausstellung der Musikabteilung der Staatsbibliothek Preussischer Kulturbesitz (1991) (exhibition catalogue). Wiesbaden: Dr Ludwig Reichart Verlag

Blunt, W. (1974) *On Wings of Song: Felix Mendelssohn*. London: Hamish Hamilton

Deutsch, O.E. (1961) *Mozart und seine Welt in zeitgenössischen Bildern* (in English and German). Kassel: Barenreiter

Mozart's Operas (1988). Freibourg: Office du Livre/New York: Rizzoli

Bianchi, L. and Rostirolla, G. (1994) *Giovanni Pierluigi Palestrina: immagini e documenti del suo tempo*. Lucca: Libreria Musicale Italiana Editrice

Marchetti, L. (1949) *Puccini nelle immagini*. Milan: Garzanti

Lesure, F. (1975) *Maurice Ravel* (exhibition catalogue). Paris: Bibliothèque Nationale

Radiciotti, G. (1927–9) *Gioacchino Rossini: vita, documentata, opera, ed influenza su l'arte* (3 vols). Tivoli: Arti Grafiche Majella di Aldo Chicca

Gioacchino Rossini 1792–1992: mostra storico-documentaria a cura Mauro Bucarelli (1992) (exhibition catalogue). Milan: Electa

Kallir, J. (1984) *Arnold Schoenberg's Wien* (exhibition catalogue). New York: Galerie St Etienne and Rizzoli

Hilmar, E. (1989) *Franz Schubert*. Graz: Akademische Druck- u. Verlagsanstalt

Burger, E. (1999) *Robert Schumann: eine Lebenschronik in Bildern und Dokumenten*.

Heinrich Schütz, His Time in Pictures (1972). Kassel: Bärenreiter

Hartmann, R. (1980) *Richard Strauss: the Staging of his Operas and Ballets* (eng. trans. 1981). Fribourg: Office du Livre

Wilhelm, K. (1984) *Richard Strauss, an Intimate Portrait* (eng. trans. 1989). München: Kindler Verlag

Craft, R. (comp.) (1982) *Igor and Vera Stravinsky: A Photograph Album 1921 to 1971*. London: Thames & Hudson

Schouvaloff, A. and Borovsky, V. (1982) *Stravinsky on Stage*. London: Stainer & Bell

Strawinsky. Sein Nachlass. Sein Bild (1984) (exhibition catalogue). Basel: Kunstmuseum, with the Paul Sacher Stiftung Basel

Northrop Moore, J. (1992) *Vaughan Williams. A Life in Photographs*. Oxford: Oxford University Press

Gatti, C. (1941) *Verdi nelle imagini*. Milan: Garzanti

Weaver, W. (comp.) *Verdi. A Documentary Study*. London: Thames & Hudson

Bory, R. (1938) *Le vie et l'oeuvre de Richard Wagner par l'image*. Lausanne

Kreowski, E. and Fuchs, E. (comps.) (1907) *Richard Wagner in der Karikatur*. Berlin: B. Behr Verlag

Barth, H., Mack, D. and Voss, E. (comps. and eds.) (1975) *Wagner. A Documentary Study* (eng. trans. Thames & Hudson, 1975). Wien: Universal

Mander, R. and Mitchenson, J. (1977) *The Wagner Companion.* London: W.H. Allen

Geck, M. (1970) *Die Bildnisse Richard Wagners.* München

Bauer, O.G. (1982) *Richard Wagner. The Stage Designs and Productions from the Premières to the Present.* New York: Rizzoli

▶ REFERENCES

Barth, H., Mack, D. and Voss, E. (comps. and eds.) (1975) *Wagner. A Documentary Study* (eng. trans. Thames & Hudson, 1975). Wien: Universal

Blaukopf, K. (ed.) (1976) *Mahler: A Documentary Study.* Thames & Hudson

Bonynge, R. (1988) *A Collector's Guide to Theatrical Postcards.* B.T. Batsford

Boucher, F. (1966) *A History of Costume in the West* (expanded 1987). London: Thames & Hudson

Bowles, E.A. (1989) *Musical Ensembles in Festival Books 1500–1800: an Iconographical & Documentary Survey.* Ann Arbor/London: UMI Research Press

British and International Music Yearbook (annual). London: Rhinegold Publishing Ltd

Buettner, S. and Pauly, R.G. (1992) *Great Composers Great Artists Portraits.* Duckworth

Cohen, H.R. (ed.) (1983) *Les Gravures Musicales dans 'L'illustration'.* Quebec: Les Presses de l'Université Laval, 3 vols

Evans, H. (1992) *Practical Picture Research.* Blueprint

Evans, H. and Evans, M. (2001) *The Picture Researcher's Handbook* (7th edn.). Routledge

Flint, M.F. (1997) *A User's Guide to Copyright.* London: Butterworths/Reed Elsevier

Foreman, L. (1986) Picture postcards and the picture researcher: a personal case study. *Audiovisual Librarian,* Nov, 198–204

Foreman, L. (1994) *Music in England 1885–1920 as recounted in Hazell's Annual.* Thames Publishing

Foreman, L. (1997) Variations on a Theme. *BMS News,* 74 (June), 51–2

Gascoigne, B. (1986) *How to Identify Prints.* London: Thames & Hudson

Hartmann, R. (1980) *Richard Strauss – The Staging of His Operas and Ballets.* Oxford: Phaidon

Heck, T.F. (1999) *Picturing Performance – The Icongraphy of the Performing Arts in Concept and Practice.* Rochester, N.Y.: University of Rochester Press

International Directory of Arts (annual). München: K.G. Saur

Kahane, M. and Wild, N. (1983) *Wagner et la France.* Paris, Éditions Herscher

King, A.H. (1983) *A Wealth of Music in the Collections of the British Library (Reference Division) and the British Museum*. London: Clive Bingley Ltd

Lee, D. (1985) Window on 19C News. *BJP: British Journal of Photography*, 16 Aug, 912–5; 23 Aug, 944–50

Loos, H. (1982) *Musik-Karikaturen*. Dortmund, Karenberg

Panofsky, E. (1939/R1962, 1972) *Studies in Iconology: Humanist Themes in the Art of the Renaissance*. New York: Oxford University Press; New York: Harper & Row.

Port, M. (1995) *Imperial London: Civil Government Building in London*. New Haven: Yale University Press

Salmen, W. (1982–3) *Musiker im Portrait* (5 vols). München

The World of Learning (annual). London: Europa Publications

Winternitz, E. (1979) *Musical Instruments and their Symbolism in Western Art* (2nd edn.).

► NOTES

1. 'Building up your own collection of musical images' subsection by Lewis Foreman.
2. *Barr's News*, 70 S Sixth St., Lansing, IA.
3. There have been several collections of pictures relating to Mahler; probably still the best is Blaukopf (1976).
4. There are various Wagner picture books. In uniform with Thames & Hudson's Strauss is Barth et al. (1975).
5. Hartmann (1980).
6. 'Pictures' section by Lewis Foreman.
7. For the rise of the carte de visite, see Lee (1985).
8. For a strongly worded protest against this practice, see Michael Port's introduction to his lavishly illustrated book *Imperial London: Civil Government Building in London* (1995) [Ed.].
9. See Foreman (1997).
10. *Men and Women of the Day: a Picture Gallery of Contemporary Portraiture*. London, Jan 1888–July 1894.
11. *Our Celebrities: a Portrait Gallery*. (1888) Portraits by Walery. Monographs by L.E. (5 vols) London.

Appendix 1: Music publishers – transfer and ownership

During the second half of the twentieth century there were unprecedented changes in British music publishing. This can make considerable difficulties when trying to trace the current source of much music published over the previous 150 years. The following list represents a first attempt to track the most important of these imprints.

The list gives the present owners or source of a variety of imprints active in the UK in the twentieth century, together with the UK representation of major overseas imprints. For British publishers in the nineteenth century who did not survive to modern times, see *Victorian Music Publishers: an annotated list* by John A Parkinson (Michigan: Harmonie Press, 1990). This is not a general listing of active music publishers, with addresses and contact information, for which see the current issue of the *British Music Yearbook*. For current American imprints, see the American MPA website at <http://www.mpa.org>. For established current music publishers, world wide, see the International Standard Music Numbering (ISMN) Agency's listing of 11,600 publishing companies in *Music Publisher's International ISMN Directory*. (München: K. G. Saur Verlag, 3rd ed. 2000). The following listing has been compiled by combining the editor's thirty-year update of John Howard Davies's list originally published in his *Musicalia* with the British Library's rough working list.

Publisher: Publisher/Representative

Accent Music: Boosey & Hawkes
Acuff-Rose Music Ltd: Hal Leonard Corporation
Adjustable Wrench: Boosey & Hawkes
AJM Music: Kassner Ass Pub Ltd
Ambleside Music Ltd: EMI
Andrew, Paul Music Publishers: Amalgamated Music Ltd
Anglo-French Music Co: Oxford University Press

Arcadia Music: Weinberger
Ardmore & Beechwood: EMI
Arnold, E J: Novello [Music Sales]
Ars Viva: Schott
Ascherberg, Hopwood & Crew: divided between Warner Chappell/
    EMI/IMP
Ashdown, Edwin, Ltd: Music Sales
Associated Music Publishers Inc (=AMP): Schirmer [Music Sales]
ATV Music Ltd: SBK
Augener Ltd: became Galliard, now Stainer & Bell
Avison, Charles
Banks & Sons: now Banks Music Publications, The Old Forge, Sand
    Hutton, York YO4 ILB
Belaieff: see: Bieliaev
Belmont Music Publishing: c/o Schoenberg, PO Box 231, Pacific
    Palisade, CA 90272 USA
Belton Books: Stainer & Bell
Belwin-Mills Music Ltd: Concord Partnership (hire from Music
    Sales)
Benjamin, Anton J: Richard Schauer
Bens Music Ltd: Kassner Ass Pub Ltd
Berry Music: Campbell Connelly & Co [Music Sales] and EMI
Bevan Music: Campbell Connelly & Co [Music Sales]
Bieliaev, M P: Peters Edition
Black Swan Music (London) Ltd: EMI
John Blockley, Duncan Davison & Co: Ascherberg
Boca Music: Music Sales
Boethius Press: Mr L. Hewitt, 24 Tefaenor, Comins Coch,
    Aberystwyth, Dyfed SY23 3UB
Editis Mario Bois (Paris): UK agent Weinberger
Bonney Music Ltd: Kassner Ass Pub Ltd
Boston Music Co: Campbell Connelly [Music Sales]
Bosworth & Co: Music Sales
Bratton, J W: Warner Chappell [via Witmark]
Braydeston Press: W. Elkin Ltd
British & Dominions Music Co: Amalgamated Music Ltd
Broadhurst, A V: EMI
Brokaw Music: C Sheard = EMI
Brucknerverlag, Wiesbaden: Alkor Edition, Kassell Gmbh, Heinrich-
    Schutz-Allee 35 34131 Kassel T, Germany
Richard Butler: Laudy & Co
Cameo Music Pub Co: Campbell Connelly [Music Sales]
Campbell Connelly: Music Sales
Carlton Music Service: Amalgamated Music Ltd
Cary & Co: Ascherberg, later Warner Chappell

Chappell: Warner Chappell/EMI/hire library from Maecenas Music;
    recorded music library from Zomba Music
Chappell Archives: IMP set up to sell EMI and Chappell Archives.
    (sheet Music Archive, The Music Vault, IMP, Griffin House,
    161 Hammersmith Road, London W6 8BS)
Chester, J & W: Music Sales
John Church Music Co: c/o T Presser = Kalmus or Universal
City Music Ltd: Kassner Ass Pub Ltd
Musikverlag City: Richard Schauer
R Cocks & Co: [Augener] now Stainer & Bell
Harry Coleman: Carl Fischer
Concord Partnership: EMI
Coslow-Kassner Ltd: Kassner Ass Pub
Alfred Cox: Larway
CPP (Columbia Pictures Publications): Maecenas Music Ltd (Concord
    Hire Library)
Cranz: United Music
Cross Music Ltd: Campbell Connelly [Music Sales]
Cumberland Music Ltd: Kassner Ass Pub Ltd
Editiorie Curci, Milan: Weinberger
Curwen bought by Schirmer: now divided between Music
    Sales/Faber/Roberton
Henri D'Alcorn: Hart & Co
Herman Darewski: EMI
Dash Music: Music Sales
Duncan Davison & Co became Ascherberg, Hopwood & Crew:
    Warner Chappell/EMI/IMP
de Sylva, Brown & Henderson: Music Sales
Deutscher Verlag für Musik, Leipzig: Breitkopf & Hartel
Max Diamond: Music Sales
Oliver Ditson Co: Universal Edition (Kalmus)
Dix Music: EMI
Donajowski: Eulenberg
Donemus: UK agent Music Sales
Donna Music Ltd: EMI
Dorsey Bros Music: Music Sales
Durand & Cie: UMP
Editions Salabert: Salabert [UMP]
Elkan-Vogel [USA]: EMI
William Elkin Music Services: Station Road Industrial Estate,
    Salthouse, Norwich, Norfolk NR136NY
EMI: Archives 10–11 Denmark Street, London WC2H 8LS
Empress Music: Campbell Connelly [Music Sales]
EMS: Sinnott
Enoch & Sons: Ashdown [now Music Sales]

Enoch & Cie [Paris]: UMP
Clifford Essex Co Ltd: Music Sales
Ewer & Co: Novello, Ewer & Co (later Novello, now Music
    Sales)
Leo Feist Inc: EMI
Feldman: EMI
First Music Ltd: Kassner Ass
Carl Fischer NY: Belwin Mills [Warner Chappell]/hire library from
    Maecenas Music
J Fischer & Bro: Belwin Mills [Warner Chappell]
Harold Flammer Inc: Chester Music [Music Sales]
Charles Foley Inc [NY]: Belwin Mills [Warner Chappell]
Sam Fox: Keith Prowse [=EMI]
Francis, Day & Hunter (incorporating Francis & Day): EMI
Furstner: Boosey & Hawkes or Schott
Galaxy [American Publisher]: Stainer & Bell
Gale & Gayles Ltd: Kassner Ass Pub Ltd
Galliard [inc Augener]: Stainer & Bell
GIA Publications (US): Maecenas
Glendale Music Ltd: Campbell Connelly [Music Sales]
GLH Music Ltd: Kassner Ass Pub Ltd
Glocken Verlag Ltd: Joseph Weinberger Ltd
Joseph Goddard & Co: Weekes & Co (later Galliard)
F & B Goodwin = Goodwin & Tabb: Novello [Music Sales]
J Hamelle [Paris]: UMP
A Hammond & Co: William Elkin Music Services
William Hansen: Chester [Music Sales]
Harms Inc [USA] [Chappell]: Warner Chappell
Harrison Music: Campbell Connelly [Music Sales]
Hart & Co: later Pitman, Hart & Co
Hawkes & Co: Boosey & Hawkes
Heinrichshofen: Peters
Hermusic Ltd: EMI
Heugel & Cie/Heugel Ltd: UMP
High-Fye Music: Campbell Connelly [Music Sales]
Hinrichsen Edition: Peters
Musikverlag V Hladky: Heinrichshofen Verlag
J & J Hopkinson: Ashdown now Music Sales
Hopwood & Crew: Ascherberg, Hopwood & Crew, later Warner
    Chappell/EMI/IMP
Howard & Co became Ascherberg, Hopwood & Crew: Warner
    Chappell/EMI/IMP
IMP: EMI
Inter-Art: Weinberger
Ivy Music: Campbell Connelly [Music Sales]

Jurgenson [State Publishers Russia]: Novello [Music Sales] or Boosey
    & Hawkes
F Kahnt Musikverlag [C F Peters]: Peters
Edwin Kalmus: Fentone Music; hire library from Maecenas Music
Kalmus Hire Library [Concord Partnership]: Warner Chappell/EMI
Kalmus: Presser
W Karczag: Josef Weinberger
Edward Kassner Music Pub Ltd: Kassner Ass Pub Ltd., Broadmeadow
    House, 21 Bruton Street, London SW1
Keith, Prowse & Co: EMI
Kennedy Street Music Ltd: EMI
Editio Kunzelmann: Peters
La Fleur & Sons: Boosey & Hawkes
Lareine & Co: Amalgamated Music Pub
J H Larway: Ashdown now Music Sales
Laudy & Co: Bosworth & Co (now Music Sales)
Leeds Music: MCA
Lengnick Alfred: Hire material Chester [Music Sales]
Cecil Lennox Ltd: Kassner Ass Pub Ltd
Leonard & Co: Cramer [Music Sales]
Leonard Gould & Bottler [formerly Montgomery Music]: MSM
Leuchart Verlag: Novello [Music Sales]
F E C Leuckart: Peters
Robert Lienau: Peters
Littolf/Litolff: Peters
Stanley Lucas & Sons in 1907 became Alfred Legnick
Stanley Lucas & Weber: Galliard now Stainer & Bell
Luck's Music Library: Fentone Music
Harold Lyche: Peters
Rae Mackintosh & Co: Chester [Music Sales]
Madrigal Society: Secretary, Monks Cottage, Cullings Hill, Elham, nr
    Canterbury, Kent CT4 6TE
Maecenas Music Ltd: 4 Oakwood Road, Horley, Surrey RH6 7BU
Manchester Music: EMI
Manhatten Music: EMI
E Marks & Co: EMI
Marquis Music Ltd: BOCU Music
Marriott (Marriott & Williams): Swan
Peter Maurice Music: EMI
MCA: Elsinore House, 77 Fulham Palace Road, London W6 8JA
Metzler & Co: Cramer [Music Sales]
Mills Music: Belwin Mills [EMI]
Moeseler Verlag Wolfgenbuttel/Zurich: Novello [Music Sales]
Montclare Music Co: Campbell Connelly [Music Sales]
Monte Carlo Publishing: EMI

Montgomery Music: Leonard Gould & Bottler
Edwin H Morris & Co [Chappell]: Warner Chappell/EMI
Collard Moutrie: Cramer
Murdoch & Murdoch & Co: Chappell now Warner Chappell/EMI
Mutual Music: EMI
New World Music Corp [T Harms US: Warner Bros]: Warner
    Chappell
Norsk Musik: Fentone Music
Northern Songs Ltd: CBS
Orpheus Music Publishing: EMI [via H Freeman & Co]
    (NB There is another Orpheus founded in 1946 but now
    defunct)
Orsborn & Tuckwood: Hopwood & Crew later Ascherberg,
    Hopwood & Crew now Warner Chappell/EMI/IMP
Patey & Willis: Ashdown now Music Sales
Pan Music Ltd: Kassner
W Paxton: Novello now Music Sales
Pepe Music: EMI
Polyphone: Weinberger
Theo Presser/J Church: Kalmus and Universal Edition
Keith Prowse: EMI
PWM: [Polskie Wydownictwo Muzyczne]: Kalmus
D Rahter: Richard Schauer
Reeder & Walsh: EMI [via Feldman]
Billy Reid Publ: Campbell Connelly [Music Sales]
Jerome H Remick & Co: EMI
Renaissance Music, Art & General Publ: EMI
Reynolds & Co: Keith Prowse now EMI
Ricordi (UK): BMG/Music Sales
Sydney Riordan: published individual composers, largely vocal scores,
    without acquiring the rights. Notable works by Walford Davies,
    Bax, Holbrooke and Kessler issued before the First World War
    and later acquired by a variety of publishers.
Roar Music Ltd: EMI
Robbins Music Pub: CBS Songs
Winthrop Rogers: Boosey & Hawkes
Rouart Lerolle et Cie: Editions Salabert [UMP]
Rudall Carte & Co: Boosey & Hawkes
Editions Salabert [Paris]: UMP (US: Schirmer)
Samfindet: Peters
Schaeffers-Kassner Ltd: Kassner Music Pub
Schauer & May: Theodore Presser
Schirmer: Music Sales
Arthur P Schmidt: Summy Birchard/Carl Fischer/Warner
Screen Gems: EMI:

Shapiro, Bernstein Music Pub: Music Sales
Charles Sheard [Darewski/Feldman]: EMI
Shere (Surrey) Music: Campbell Connelly [Music Sales]
Show Music: Campbell Connelly [Music Sales]
Hans Sikorski Ltd: Campbell, Connelly & Co [Music Sales]
Silberman: Campbell Connelly [Music Sales]
N Simrock: Richard Schauer (US: Theodore Presser)
R Smith: Novello [Music Sales]
Southern Music Co: Peer Music
Star Music Pub Co Ltd: Feldman [EMI]
Joseph Stern: EMI
Success Music Ltd: Kassner Ass Pub
Swan & Co: Arcadia Music no Joseph Weinberger
Thames Publishing: William Elkin Music Services
Tischer & Jagenburg: Peters
University of Wales Press now Cwmni Cyhoeddi GWYNN cyf; (John
        Hywel (music editor); Y Gerlan Heoly dwr penygroes,
        Caernarfan, Gwyneth LL54 6LR, Wales (01286 881797)
Varda Music: EMI
Verulam Music: BOCU Music
Christian Vieweg: Peters
Vincent Music: Cramer
Vinco Music Ltd: Campbell Connelly [Music Sales]
Von Tilzer Music Pub. Co.: EMI
Walsh, Holmes: E H Freeman of Brighton
Warner/Chappell: formerly Chappell & Co; hire library now
        Maecenas
Warner Bros: Maecenas
Wawan Press: Schirmer [Music Sales]
A Weekes/Weekes & Co: Galliard later Stainer & Bell
Weintranb Music: Music Sales Corporation
Willcocks & Co: Ashdown now Music Sales
Joseph Williams: Galliard now Stainer & Bell
M Witmark & Sons: Warner Chappell/EMI
The Women's Press: Chester [Music Sales]
C Woolhouse: Warner Chappell
Lawrence Wright: ATV Music
XYZ International, Holland: Fentone
Yearbook Press: Warner Chappell/.EMI
Yukon Music Ltd: Kassner Ass Pub Ltd
Zimmermann: Peters
Zomba Music former Chappell recorded music library

Appendix II: Principal Antiquarian and Second Hand Dealers

The stocks of a large worldwide constituency of dealers in second hand books and music can be searched via the internet at:

<www.abebooks.com>
<www.bibliofind.com>
<www.bookfinder.com>
<www.alibris.com>

To search German dealers (an optional English language search screen is available) use Zentrales Verzeichnis Antiquarischer Bücher (which also includes a growing range of British and American dealers not on abebooks):

<www.zvab.com>

To search French dealers (French only search screen):

<www.chapitre.com>
<www.galaxidion.com>

There is also a books database on the auction and self-styled 'world's active marketplace' (which includes Sotheby's):

<www.ebay.com>

For dealers in LPs and 78s see the classified advertisements in *Classic Record Collector* (<www.classicrecordcollector.com>).

DEALERS

Catalogues have been reported from the following dealers by one or other contributor to this book during the 12 months before publication. Many, but not all, of these can be read via the internet at the web addresses given below.

Australia

DaCapo Music
112A Glebe Point Road
Glebe
New South Wales
Australia 2037
Tel: +61 (0)29 660 1825
Fax: +61 (0)29 660 1268
Email: <Music@dacapo.com.au>
URL: <www.users.bigpond.net.au/
    dacapo/>
    (with a Japanese language
    option)

France

François Roulmann
10 rue le la Grande Chaumière
75006 Paris
France
Tel: +33 (0)1 43 54 46 74
Fax: +33 (0)1 43 54 46 74
Email: <Roulmann@
    club-internet.fr>

*Librarie du Spectacle Garnier
    Arnoul*
5 rue de Montfaucon
75006 Paris
France

Germany

*Musikverlag/Musikantiquariat
    Bernd Katzbichler*
Reichenbachstr 33
D-80467 München
Germany
Tel: +49 (0)89 203 39180
Fax: +49 (089 203 39181
Email: <101700.2410@
    compuserve.com>

URL: <www.katzbichler.de>

Musik Antiquariat Hans Schneider
Mozartstrasse 6
82323 Tutzing
Germany
Email: <musikantiquariat@aol.com>

*Antiquariat für Musik und
    deutsche Literatur
    J. Voerster*
Relenbergstrasse 20
D-70174 Stuttgart
Germany
Tel: +49 (0)711 297186
URL: <www.Stuttgart.de/sde/dept/
    gen/119495.htm>

Heiner Rekeszus
Musik-Antiquariat Rekeszus
Herrngartenstr. 7
D-65185 Wiesbaden
Germany
Tel: +49 (0)611 3082270
Fax: +49 (0)611 308 1262
Email: <Mus-Antik-Rekeszus@
    t-online.de>
URL: <www: musantik.de>

Great Britain

H. Baron
121 Chatsworth Road
London NW2 4BH
England
Tel: +44 (0)208 459 2035
Fax: +44 (0)208 459 2035

Lisa Cox Music
The Coach House
Colleton Crescent
Exeter
Devon EX2 4DG
England

Tel: +44 (0)1392 490290
Fax: +44 (0)1392 277336
Email: <music@lisacoxmusic.co.
    uk>
    <lisa@lisacoxmusic.co.uk>
URL: <www.lisacoxmusic.co.uk>

Decorum Books
24 Cloudesley Square
London N 1 0HN
England
Tel: +44 (0)207 278 1838
Fax: +44 (0)207 837 6424
Email: <decorumbooks@lineone.
    net>

Rosemary M. S. Dooley
Crag House
Witherslack
Grange-over-Sands
Cumbria
LA11 6RW
England
Tel: +44 (0)15395 52286
Fax: +44 (0)15395 52013
Email: <musicbks@rdooley.demon.
    co.uk>
URL: <www.booksonmusic.co.uk>

Travis & Emery
17 Cecil Court
London WC2N 4EZ
England
Tel: +44 (0)207 240 2129
Fax: +44 (0)207 497 0790
Email: <catenq@travis-and-emery.
    com>
(Shop also at this address)

Martin Eastick
42 Craignish Avenue
Norbury
London SW16 4RN
Tel: +44 (0)208 764 3448

Philip Martin Music Books
22 Huntington Road
York
YO31 8RL
England
(Shop: 38 Fossgate, York)
Tel: +44 (0)1904 636111
Fax: +44 (0)1904 658889
Email: <musicbooks@philipmartin.
    demon.co.uk>
URL: <www.ukbookworld.com/
    members/philipmartin>

Austin Sherlaw-Johnson
Secondhand Music & Books on
    Music
Woodland View
Churchfields
Stonesfield
Oxon OX29 8PP
Tel: +44 (0)1993 898223
Fax: +44 (0)1993 898992
Email: <Austin@micro-plus-web.
    net>

Tamarisk Books
80 High Street
Hastings
Sussex TN34 3EL
England
Tel: +44 (0)1424 420591

Holland

Paul van Kuik Muisk Ant
Bram Limburgstraat 70
2251 RR Voorschoten
Netherlands
Tel: +31 (0)71 561 9833
Fax: +31 (0)71 561 7397
Email: <P.Kuik@paulvankuik.nl>
URL: <www.antiqbook.nl/kuik>

Italy

Lim Antiqua SAS
Studio Bibliografico
Via di Aresina 216A
55100 Lucca
Italy
(Post address: PO Box 722 55100
        Lucca)
Tel: +39 0583 490034
Fax: +39 0583 46482
Email: <limantiqua@limantiqua.it>
URL: <www.limantiqua.it>

Index

Guides to
Information Sources

Information Sources in
Art, Art History and Design

Edited by Simon Ford
2001. XX, 220 pages Hardbound € 98.00. ISBN 3-598-24438-X

Like all sectors of the information profession, art librarianship is undergoing a period of major change. Recognition of the economic importance of the creative industries and the expansion of the further and continuing education sector, has meant an increasing number of people are seeking information on art, art history and design. The pressure to connect these people with multiplying fields of knowledge, accessible through an ever increasing variety of formats, has led to innovative new forms of service delivery.

Information Sources in Art, Art History and Design reviews current practice from a variety of perspectives, drawing on the subject knowledge of specialists based in the UK, USA and the Netherlands. Each chapter provides a guide to the best sources of information on a range of subjects, including "General reference sources", "The art book", "Auction catalogues" and "Multicultural art and design".

Information Sources in Art, Art History and Design is a welcome addition to the Guide to Information Sources series. It is edited by Simon Ford, Special Collections Bibliographer at the National Art Library, Victoria and Albert Museum, and written by experts who evaluate the best sources in their field.

Information Sources in
Women's Studies and Feminism

Edited by Hope Olson
2002. xxi, 189 pages. Hardbound € 98.00. ISBN 3-598-24440-1

Women's studies and feminism has been a growing subject area since the 1960s. The increase of sources of information in this area has highlighted the need for an up-to-date guide to sources covering all the recent developments.

Providing you with a guide to information sources in an area that is still unconventional and problematic, the Information Sources in Women's Studies and Feminism will provide you with a way through the maze of sources. This new title is not limited to traditional academic genres. Different use is made in this area of Government and non-governmental organizations (NGO's) publications and more legitimacy is given to grey literature and popular literature than in other areas of the academy. Therefore, a book that treats issues of information as well as specific sources is important to researchers and activists in the area.

The contents include: Archival material, serials, electronic resources, information in/from local and grassroots organizations, Government and non-government organizations documents, Collections and canonicity, Bibliographic control as naming information, Audiences with diverse interests, Lesbian sources, Information for/about women of colour, Indigenous women's information, and the Importance of information to women.

Information Services
Management Series

Guy St. Clair, Series Editor

Guy St. Clair

Beyond Degrees
Professional Learning in the Information Services Environment

2003. xxvi, 315 pages. Hardbound € 88.00. ISBN 3-598-24369-3

Knowledge Services is an enterprise-wide management methodology that enables companies and organizations achieve excel-lence, both in the performance of internal staff and in their interactions with external customers.

Knowledge Services is more than knowledge management. Defined as the convergence of information management, knowledge management, and strategic (performance-centered) learning, Knowledge Services recognizes that the most critical asset in any group or environment is what its people know. This knowledge - this intellectual capital - is the organization's primary asset, and Knowledge Services is the tool the organization uses for managing this corporate asset.

This book provides the Knowledge Services professional with guidelines for conceptualizing, designing, implementing, and measuring successful programs for professional learning, staff development, and professional growth in the organization, all within the knowledge services framework.

Contents include: Knowledge Services as a New Profession - Professionalism, Accreditation, and Certification - KD/KS: Knowledge Development and Knowledge Sharing - Qualification Management in the New Profession - Managing Strategic Learning Within the Organization.

Sue Henczel

The Information Audit
A Practical Guide

2001. xxiv, 272 pages. Hardbound € 68.00. ISBN 3-598-24367-7

The information audit is a process by which a library or information centre reviews and assesses its holdings, services, etc. This topic is one that has generated much interest over the last few years. The Information Audit: A Practical Guide will take the information professional through the stages of conducting an audit, from planning and carrying out to assessing and presenting the results and how to implement findings.

As an aid to understanding, the book contains four international case studies to illustrate the information audit process in action.

The Information Audit is directed at library managers in all sectors, but particularly those in special libraries, students and lecturers in library and information science.

Contents include: The changing role of the corporate information unit; Planning the audit; Data collection; Data analysis; Data evaluation; Communicating recommendations; Implementing recommendations; The information audit as a continuum; Summary and case studies.

Music Publishers' International ISMN Directory

Music Publishers' International ISMN Directory

4th edition 2003
Edited by the International ISMN Agency, Berlin
2003. XXXVIII, 602 pages. Hardbound
€ 178.00. ISBN 3-598-22260-2

This directory includes approximately 15,000 publishing companies, together with their addresses and contact numbers, from 91 countries and territories, i.e. nearly all companies actively publishing music throughout the world. The authors of almost 90% of the music manuscripts produced on an international scale are listed. In addition to large countries with numerous music publishers, small countries are of particular interest, but in the past it was always very difficult to actually follow up what they produced.

As with the ISBN system, each music publisher is assigned an International Standard Music Number. The music industry can therefore use the ISMN number to quickly identify the publisher and familiarize themselves with the specific ordering and delivery procedures. The data contained in this directory is taken both from the results of comprehensive surveys of numerous music publishing associations, music information centers, copyright agencies, music libraries and ISBN agencies, and from information supplied by the ISMN agencies. This guarantees up-to-the-minute, reliable data. A detailed introductory section provides information on the structure and function of the ISMN system.

This unique compendium will simplify research, ordering and sales procedures in all domains of the music trade.